Shooting the Front

Allied Aerial Reconnaissance and

Photographic Interpretation

on the Western Front – World War I

COLONEL TERRENCE J. FINNEGAN

UNITED STATES AIR FORCE RESERVE (RETIRED)

WASHINGTON, DC

OCTOBER 2006

CENTER FOR STRATEGIC INTELLIGENCE RESEARCH

NDIC PRESS

NATIONAL DEFENSE INTELLIGENCE COLLEGE

National Defense Intelligence College Press
National Defense Intelligence College
Bolling Air Force Base
Washington, DC 20340-5100

Library of Congress Cataloging-in-Publication Data

Finnegan, Terrence J.
Shooting the Front: Allied Aerial Reconnaissance and Photographic Interpretation on the Western Front – World War I
        p.   cm.
Includes bibliographical references and index.
ISBN 1-932946-04-7 (paper cover: alk. paper)
ISBN 1-932946-06-3 (hard cover: alk. paper)
Library of Congress Control Number 2005928514
World War, 1914-1918—Reconnaissance operations
Photographic reconnaissance systems—History—20th Century
Aerial Reconnaissance—History—20th Century
World War, 1914-1918—Photography
World War, 1914-1918—Campaigns—Western Front
Photographic interpretation (Military science)—History—20th Century
D600.F56 2006
CIP – 2005928514

Printed in the United States of America
10 9 8 7 6 5 4 3 2 1

∞ The paper used in this publication meets the minimum requirements of the American National Standard for Information Sciences – Permanence of Paper for Printed Library Materials, ANSI Z39.48-1992.

CONTENTS

Part One:

Aerial Reconnaissance and Photographic Interpretation During the War: A Chronological Overview

Part Two:

The Architecture of Allied Aerial Reconnaissance and Photographic Interpretation

Part Three:

Challenges that Shaped Aerial Reconnaissance and Photographic Interpretation

Part Four:

The Enduring Professional Legacy

FOREWORD

World War I marked the beginning of the era of modern warfare. It was a conflict vast in scope, loss of life, and devastation. It was a conflict that forced human adaptation to changing technology, and demanded the incorporation of revolutionary technology. As recorded in this remarkable work, *Shooting the Front*, it was a conflict that saw the development and use of aerial photography, aerial reconnaissance, and the introduction of a vital new dimension of intelligence that has both continued and evolved and is more vital than ever to the operational commander in the 21st century. Terry Finnegan's examination of U.S., British, and French aerial reconnaissance on the Western Front is the result of superb research and makes an extremely valuable contribution to the documented history of the conflict as we approach the centennial of the Great War.

This book focuses on the development of ideas in aerial reconnaissance and photo interpretation, and how some of those ideas came to be accepted during the war. Finnegan identifies the key thinkers and developers, the artists and scientists who, working together, developed fledgling aerial reconnaissance specialties. He shows how they were able to gain acceptance, and how they changed forever the way wars would be fought. Exceptional personalities figure prominently in this study, among them Edward Steichen, one of America's leading photographers in the twentieth century. In Finnegan's work we find the seeds of photographic science and imagery interpretation as they are practiced today. The requirements and challenges have changed little—gather the best information available, analyze it quickly, and get it to units in the field and to headquarters immediately. We learn that even in World War I the observer could shoot a photograph, land, have the crew on the ground develop it, make pictures, quickly assess the situation, and deliver the product to its destination, all in less than half an hour.

Analysts on the Western Front had the challenge of dealing with the other sources of intelligence—the French led in the development of all-source collaboration. They brought together information from radio intercepts, from tapped phone lines, from the sound of artillery, and from visual flashes, and the image of the aerial photograph, which could confirm those sources. Aerial reconnaissance made it possible to put together a battlefield map that could be updated daily, a "plan directeur." From the bits and pieces of intelligence, and from this map, commanders were able, albeit imperfectly, to improve their understanding of the enemy's intent. This book's fresh information on the French contribution to, and leadership in, aerial reconnaissance may be the most surprising aspect of the scholarship.

Shooting the Front will have wide appeal. The volume serves to showcase the incredibly important research on intelligence and intelligence-related issues that is a core part of the mission of the National Defense Intelligence College. The College is to be commended for its publication.

GEORGE A. JOULWAN
General, U.S. Army (Retired)
Former Supreme Allied Commander Europe
Arlington, Virginia
3 January 2006

PREFACE

The origin of aerial combat in the Great War of 1914-1918 has attracted a great deal of popular and scholarly attention over the past 90 years. It remains a marketable subject, capable of fascinating the reader with countless exploits of chivalrous combatants in battle thousands of feet above the trenches. On the other hand, aerial reconnaissance has been sadly neglected in the majority of histories written to date. Aeroplanes committed to that task were, for the most part, impotent in conducting battle, thus generating little excitement for aerial reconnaissance. Further, the roles of the aerial observer and the photographic interpreter have been virtually ignored over the past century, suggesting a subject not worth a moment of the reader's attention. This oversight left a rich vein of documents for my research. I discovered a side of the war that few have known. The real value of aviation, it seems, was the information that was acquired by aerial reconnaissance to better support the combatant on the ground. Everything else, to include the legacy of the fighter pilot, was ancillary.

The Great War represents the most significant catalyst for moving intelligence into a realm familiar to present-day practitioners. Positional warfare—a euphemism for trench warfare—developed a fairly sophisticated intelligence architecture that covered all facets of available and emerging technologies, including the aeroplane and photography, although no new photographic principles were discovered. Combatants, from field command posts to headquarters, quickly came to understand what an aerial photograph provided and to incorporate those findings into their operational plans to shape the campaign. Literally behind every battlefield decision lay an aerial (and other) intelligence source that reinforced or precluded the next step. What was missing was the strategically important ability to transition quickly from prevailing doctrine and strategy, including the intelligence techniques developed for the static battlefield, to find a means to break out of the siege and to bring victory. This finally began to appear in the more mobile battlefield of the final weeks of the war. The strategic application of intelligence was by no means a failure unique to the Great War; it has been a persistent problem for operations and intelligence practitioners through the ages.

Of the three Allies, the French military clearly paid more attention to aerial reconnaissance and photographic interpretation. The present research shows a greater commitment to aerial camera use, backed by French industry, which held the competitive edge in producing critical optics. Their British counterparts made tremendous strides in establishing an important role for aerial reconnaissance despite limited camera production and a disconcerting reliance on airframes lacking maneuverability. In addition to aerial photographic interpretation, which arose out of French emphasis and scholarship, British military seniors discovered early in the war that the French were more committed to the aerial photograph in planning and conducting operations. The sharing of ideas and procedures that resulted from the exchanges benefited both countries' armies and provided the newly arriving Americans with a short course in the realities of warfare in support of a continent-wide siege.

Only recently in academic circles has there been an awareness of the extent of relations between the French and Americans in the final year of the war. My research illuminates the degree of interaction that existed between these two allies in their aviation and aerial photographic interpreter communities. There nevertheless remains an assumption among many observers that the Anglo-American relationship, based on a common language and culture, created a natural conduit for providing the American Expeditionary Force (AEF) with the most current warfighting techniques. However, the archival record clearly proves otherwise. Despite the recommendations of American general officers that intelligence officials model their program after the British, it was French and American pilots, observers, photo interpreters, and technicians who formed their own *entente cordiale* at the working level. This entente was the foundation for meeting AEF wartime requirements and it laid the conceptual framework for aerial reconnaissance and photographic interpretation conducted throughout the 20th century.

Considerable attention to cultural differences significantly influenced my approach to writing this book. Whenever possible, I made a conscious decision to use contemporary terminology, ranging from military ranks and organizational designations to the use of "aeroplane" instead of "aircraft" or "airplane." While the word "aircraft" appears in some reports, it was not common usage. Therefore, I refer to a British or American aircraft as an "aeroplane" and to a French "*aéroplane*" when appropriate to convey their specific identities and to provide readers with a better appreciation of the actual prose. Likewise, various descriptions of the battleground incorporated into this study include French nomenclature to reacquaint the reader with the language that the Allied combatants shared.

This book began simply as I was pursuing part of my duties as a member of the Reserve faculty at the National Defense Intelligence College. I was examining post-war files to substantiate a premise for a journal article: that Allied intelligence services focused on each other during the period leading up to the signing of the Versailles Treaty. I came across a post-war translation of the primary French photographic interpretation manual, *Study and Use of Aerial Photographs*, filed within Record Group 120 at the National Archives and Records Administration in Washington, DC. Serendipity, as all researchers know, smiled at me more than once, in this case leading me away from a narrowly focused post-war topic to a proposal to the College's Center for Strategic Intelligence Research to write a pamphlet-length document highlighting the French manual with an overview essay to put it into its historical context. Original planning for a visit to the British National Archives and the archives of the French Air Force (*Service Historique de l'Armée de Air*) was to add more substance to the planned introductory essay. That trip opened my eyes wider to the nature and extent of the impact of aerial reconnaissance and photographic interpretation. The archives appeared to hold sufficient information for a full-fledged effort to rethink the Allies' entire wartime aerial reconnaissance and photographic intelligence roles. This book became the final result.

Terrence J. Finnegan
February 2006

ACKNOWLEDGMENTS

I might not have recognized the value of diverse material for this book that I uncovered in Washington, London, Paris, Carlisle Barracks, and at the U.S. Air Force Academy library in Colorado without the great good will that I found among a circle of academics, aviation experts, and active and retired intelligence officers. These experts led me to additional pertinent published and archival sources, to obscure texts, and to the rare photographs reproduced here. In turn, I introduced this circle to my unexpected findings about the genealogy of aerial intelligence techniques and procedures. The U.S. interlibrary loan network is a national treasure that gave me access to materials from across the nation, making my two years of research a most pleasurable experience and an invaluable supplement to my visits to archives and libraries. Without doubt, this book would not have been produced without the support from many colleagues and friends.

A. Denis Clift, President of the National Defense Intelligence College (NDIC), enthusiastically shared his vision for this publication on the day he was introduced to my research. He is the strongest advocate in the United States for in-depth research on intelligence. The publishing team at NDIC, Dr. Russell Swenson, Dr. James Lightfoot, and COL (Ret) William Spracher, were instrumental in making *Shooting the Front* a reality. Their long hours of work on my behalf are greatly appreciated.

My research commenced at the United States Air Force Academy's McDermott Library. Direct stack access to a superb selection of secondary sources accelerated my interest and foreshadowed archival research into World War I aerial reconnaissance. Most importantly, the McDermott Library possessed a microfilm copy of the Gorrell Report, one of the most important sources of World War I aviation history. The deeper I dug into the memoranda and reports of the U.S. Air Service the more clearly I realized that a new history of aerial reconnaissance and photographic interpretation must be told. My appreciation extends to the library's entire staff, particularly to Dr. Edward Scott, Sharon Johnson, Shelby Watkins, Robert Cox, and Gail Jenkins.

The Special Collections staff at the McDermott Library also deserves special mention. Dr. Mary Elizabeth Ruwell, John Beardsley, and Trudy Pollok went above and beyond on all requests, from locating rare photographic albums from World War I to sharing every available book on the topic from their rare books section. One of the delights of publishing this book is showing off some of the outstanding artifacts from Special Collections.

At the Air Force Academy I benefited immensely from the assistance of Dr. Michael Neiberg and Lt Col John Abbatiello. Mike made invaluable contacts with colleagues in the United Kingdom and France to launch my efforts overseas. John introduced me to the wonders of digital photography.

When I was still a reserve faculty member, NDIC awarded me a grant to conduct research at the National Archives: Public Records Office (TNA: PRO) in the United Kingdom and at the Château de Vincennes (Service Historique de l'Armée de l'Air [SHAA] and the Service Historique de l'Armée de Terre [SHAT]) in France. The TNA: PRO is a class act. I found its staff superb and always helpful. SHAA and SHAT were equally outstanding in helping me with new research and with follow-up access to rare photographs. Special thanks go to André Rakoto for assistance with accommodations and access to Vincennes. I want to express my greatest appreciation for the assistance provided by Général de division aérienne Roland Le Bourdonnec, and by Daniel Hary and Marcellin Hodier. Marcellin is a world authority on World War I aerial photography. He magnanimously provided his own personal files for review. Thanks to the SHAA, I was able to review the Pépin Papers at Le Centre de Documentation, Aéroport de Paris—Le Bourget and SHAT Division des Archives Iconographiques managed by Jean-Marie Linsolas. Again, thanks to the staffs at those locations for the outstanding support.

I made two trips to the U.S. Army Military History Institute (USAMHI) at Carlisle Barracks, PA. This historical treasure trove made my research more credible as I reviewed an impressive array of memoranda, AEF reports, and diaries. Any research on the U.S. Air Service should include a trip to USAMHI. I want particularly to thank Louise Arnold-Friend, Gary Johnson, and Randy Hackenburg for time spent tracking down rare documents and assisting throughout.

Washington, DC, was my own personal paradise for this research. Materials at the National Archives and Records Administration (NARA), Library of Congress (LOC), and National Air and Space Museum (NASM) could support a serious scholar for a lifetime. I was blessed by superb contacts at all three locations. NARA's Mitch Yockelson and Tim Nenninger made access to Record Group 120 a rewarding endeavor. At the LOC, I accessed the General William Mitchell files, to include rare target folders. The staff was always efficient in tracking down the files requested. Finally, because of Dorothy Cochrane and Von Hardesty at NASM, I was able to review important documents covering aerial photography's role among the Allies.

The photos and maps used in this book are from a variety of archives and private sources, and many people have been quite generous about sharing. All are used with the permission of their owners.

Beyond the archives, special thanks go to a host of family and friends who made this endeavor such a pleasure. The power of the aviation enthusiast network clearly showed itself when I introduced my topic. Starting with Stephen Suddaby, who has authored several award-winning articles on aviation, I was introduced to Jim Streckfuss, former editor of "Over the Front" and Ph.D. candidate at the University of Cincinnati. Jim is a goldmine for important contacts. He linked me to Aaron Weaver, whose outstanding information technology skills brought life to thousands of photographs from this era. Aaron not only helped improve the publishing quality of hundreds of aerial photographs and supporting material; he also introduced me to Alan Toelle and Colin Owers, who provided invaluable insight and rare photographs.

Another key member of the Streckfuss network is Dr. James Davilla. Jim authored the most comprehensive work to date on French aircraft of the Great War. He graciously provided many of the rare photographs on French aviation. Additionally, Jim politely and patiently received my numerous inquiries on French aviation policy and shared his wealth of information.

A long-time family friend, Dr. David Mets, Professor Emeritus at the Air University, Maxwell Air Force Base, Alabama, shared with me several insights on the legacy of aerial reconnaissance throughout the 20th century. Dave's colleagues at the Air University were invaluable in providing documentation on post-war aerial reconnaissance.

Colonel Richard McQuiston, USAF Reserve, a senior member of the NDIC staff, provided an aviator's perspective on the role of intelligence and offered his photographic skills and enthusiastic support for my research.

One of the most important experiences in this project was becoming acquainted with expertise resident in the United Kingdom. Wing Commander Michael Mockford, Honorary Secretary of the Medmenham Society and a former colleague from my years at the 497th Reconnaissance Technical Group, connected me to many world-class experts on aerial photography, including Roy Nesbit and Alf Pyner. Other important contributors were Darren Fagg, RAF Museum, and David Parry, Imperial War Museum.

Leading the support from friends overseas was Nicholas Watkis. Several years ago I came across his seminal book on aerial reconnaissance and photographic interpretation, *The Western Front from the Air*. Thanks to the Imperial War Museum, I was able to track Nicholas down to his address at "Thackers." We enjoyed an extremely close working relationship in examining questions about the range of British aerial photography and debating the extent of the technology's employment throughout the campaigns. Nicholas has been a superb collaborator in all phases of the work. He also introduced me to Dr. Peter Chasseaud, a leading scholar on cartographic developments during the Great War.

Key to my ability to devote the time to this project, despite myriad responsibilities beyond research and writing, was the work accomplished by my brother, Brendan, and his colleague Ric Peltier. Their selfless efforts will be an important source of inspiration into the future.

I remain indebted to those who translated key sources. Yvonne Finnegan and Elisabeth Tornay provided translation assistance while I was at Vincennes. Tom Gudmestad translated rare German accounts to further support estimates on the effectiveness of Allied aerial reconnaissance.

Commandant Marc Rivière, French exchange officer to the Department of Aeronautics, USAFA, as well as an outstanding mountain biker, provided extensive translation of key French documents that opened my eyes to the extent of that nation's accomplishments in aerial reconnaissance. Marc is a superb officer and I wish him the best in his career.

One of the most important relationships from the beginning was with CAPT Steven Maffeo, USNR. Steve helped me with initial research and with important insights on publishing. His acclaimed work on Lord Nelson's intelligence network provided inspiration.

Constructive criticism and insight were provided by a colleague of long standing, Colonel John Hollstein, USAF Reserve. His calls on the approach to intelligence analysis were spot on.

Throughout this endeavor one person remains the cornerstone to getting the project underway and seeing it through to its completion. Colonel John K. Rowland, Ph.D., USAF Reserve, was a visionary and made this book possible. Our friendship goes back over 20 years. His achievements as NDIC Associate Dean and Director of the Postgraduate Intelligence Program for Reserves are legendary. Thanks, John.

Friendships made this effort a blessing of a lifetime. One of my closest friends for almost 50 years, William "Bill" Kelly, consistently helped me throughout the drafting of the book, tracking down rare documents and lending critical advice to succinctly capture the ideas contained within. I hope we remain in touch for the next 50 years.

Thanks are due to other participants working with NDIC. Patricia Chavarria provided typing and editing skills, and printing, layout, and design were done by the Digital Production Branch, Data Services Division of the Defense Intelligence Agency.

Throughout this endeavor, Susan and Willie Lincoln kept me focused every day as I worked the computer trying to piece together a complicated puzzle of data. My greatest love is for their patience and presence.

Finally, I dedicate this book to the greatest influence of my life, my parents.

SELECTED ABBREVIATIONS AND ACRONYMS

AEF	American Expeditionary Force
AIR	Air Ministry Record, Public Records Office
BEF	British Expeditionary Force
BIO	Branch Intelligence Office or Branch Intelligence Officer
CA	*Corps d'Armee*
G-2	Assistant Chief of Staff for Intelligence
GDE	*Group des divisions d'entraînement*
GHQ	General Headquarters
GQC	*Grand Quartier Général*
GPO	Government Printing Office (U.S.)
HQ	Headquarters
IWM	Imperial War Museum (UK)
M&AE	Musée de l'Air et de l'Espace, Le Bourget, France
NARA	National Archives and Records Administration, Washington (U.S.)
NASM	National Air and Space Museum, Washington (U.S.)
OHL	Oberste Heeresleitung
PC	Post Command
RAF	Royal Air Force
RFC	Royal Flying Corps
RG	Records Group
RNAS	Royal Naval Air Service
SHAA	*Service Historique de L'Armée de l'Air*
SHAT	*Service Historique de L'Armée de l'Terre*
SPAé	*Section photo-aérienne*
SRA	*Services des renseignements de l'artillerie*
SROT	*Services des renseignements de l'observation du terrain*
S.S.	British Army Publications and Stationery Service
TNA:PRO	The National Archives: Public Record Office (UK)
TPS	*Télégraphie par le sol*
TSF	*Télégraphie sans fil*
USAMHI	United States Army Military History Institute
WO	War Office Papers (UK)

LEGEND FOR MAPS REPRODUCED
FROM WEST POINT ATLAS

BASIC SYMBOLS:

Regiment	III	Infantry	⊠
Brigade	x	Cavalry	⧄
Division	xx	Cavalry covering force	• • • ⧄ • • •
Corps	xxx	Trains	⊟
Army	xxxx	Artillery	⊡
Army Group	xxxxx		

Examples of Combinations of Basic Symbols:

Small infantry detachment	⊠
Third Reserve Division	⊠3R
Mackensen's XVII Corps	XVII MACKENSEN
Fifth Cavalry Corps with other units attached	⧄ V(+)
French Sixth Army	FR. SIXTH

OTHER SYMBOLS:

	Actual location	Prior location
Troops on the march	➡	⊏==⟩
Troops in position	⟩	⊏=⟩
Troops in bivouac or reserve	◯	◌

	Occupied	Unoccupied
Field works	WWW	⌃⌃⌃⌃

Strong prepared defenses	⊓⊔⊓	⌐⌐⌐
Route of march	– – – → – – – →	
Boundary between units	——xxx—— (Appropriate basic symbol)	
Troops displacing and direction	⇡⇡ or ⬭	
Troops in position under attack	⇩⇩ or ⟩	

Fortified Areas	▨ ▨

PART ONE:
AERIAL RECONNAISSANCE AND PHOTOGRAPHIC INTERPRETATION DURING THE WAR: A CHRONOLOGICAL OVERVIEW

INTRODUCTION

"The aerial photograph is born of trench warfare."[1] Simple and yet profound, this pronouncement expresses an important but frequently overlooked legacy of the Great War. Aerial reconnaissance and photographic interpretation reinvented the way that modern battle was envisioned, planned, and executed. They became the catalytic agents for expanding intelligence acquisition, exploitation, and dissemination in the modern era. The advantages of an elevated platform capable of covering broad areas of enemy territory made photographic images an invaluable commodity for assessing enemy intentions. Acceptance of this new technology and procedure was sometimes challenged. The senior command was initially skeptical of the new intelligence source, but upon comprehending its value became its strongest advocate. Aerial reconnaissance soon became the primary information source behind most battlefield decisions on the Western Front and it provided a permanent photographic record of the results of those decisions. Without it, the First World War would have depended less on artillery, the most destructive of the combat arms, since targeting accuracy would have remained limited to the practices of the previous century. Furthermore, the evolving role of aeroplane aerial bombardment deep behind enemy lines never could have achieved a high degree of sophistication, since validation

FIGURE 1. **"The pride of France was in her aéroplanes." Bleriot Escadrille XI at Belfort prior to the war.** Source: Service Historique de l'Armée de l'Air *(SHAA), B83.932*

of damage inflicted would have been limited to whatever could be acquired through human reporting on the scene. In many ways, trench warfare served as the genesis for what the world knows today as military intelligence. Thanks to an aerial platform and a photographic medium, operational intelligence quickly evolved into a staple of the modern battlefield.

Photography had established itself as a fixture of 19th century society. Its capabilities were well recognized in literary and intellectual circles, not only as a way of capturing and immortalizing a moment in time, but also as a new expression of knowledge and emotion.[2] As the second decade of the 20th century unfolded, photography evolved from being merely a technology of capturing light; it became a recognized art medium alongside canvas and paint. Thanks to a host of commercially produced, mass-market box cameras in Europe and the

---

[1] GHQ, [French] Armies of the North and Northeast, *Study and Use of Aerial Photographs* (trans.), 15 January 1918, sec. I, 10, NARA, RG 120, Box 819.

[2] Jonathan Crary, *Techniques of the Observer: On Vision and Modernity in the Nineteenth Century* (Cambridge, MA: MIT Press, 1991), 13.

Americas, photography was a medium that everyone could recognize and understand. What had been missing was a reasonable aerial platform to create a new view of the world.

Equally intriguing is the legacy of aerial reconnaissance and photographic interpretation. There has been little attention paid to the role of these functions in World War I and their impact on the advancement of intelligence. Shortly after the war ended, however, Theodore Knappen published an account acknowledging that not all aviation in the war was oriented toward a personal tally of victims:

> It is intriguing to reflect upon the numerous post-war reviews of aviation that provided a perspective that was well known at the time, but clearly forgotten today. The thrilling duels and other combats of the air which have marked this war as being conducted in a third element which was not the medium of attack or defense in preceding wars have centered public attention on aerial combat as the end of military aircraft.... While military men admit the great value of airplane offensives on account of their effect on the morale of enemy troops and civilian population, the prevailing view among them seems to be that the chief military use of the airplanes is as a means of securing information — as the modern scout.[3]

Aviation in the Great War provided information to the ground commander and combatants. This was true on both sides of the front lines. Allies and adversaries were trapped in a strategic standoff that extended for hundreds of miles from the Swiss border through northern France, up to the Belgian coast, and over to the Dutch border. Given the frontal standoff, prosecution of the war demanded any information that helped gain the upper hand. In today's military parlance, information and intelligence advantage is a force multiplier. Aviation provided the platform, and

photography served as the ultimate validation source.

Even though aerial reconnaissance and photographic interpretation were important influences on all combatants along the Western Front, this book focuses on three key Allies: France, Great Britain, and the United States. The reason for this is simple: Documentation on the thinking behind the Allied evolution in aerial reconnaissance was accessible and readily translatable. The Germans and their allies went through a parallel evolution. German aeroplanes were superb creations demonstrating the leading edge of flight technology. German cameras were the best in the world. The world's leading optical lens producer was Zeiss, located at Jena, Germany. In spite of German technological superiority, the Allies established their own priorities for aerial reconnaissance and through perseverance created an impressive legacy.

The first five chapters describe the evolution chronologically. The sequence of events shows how aerial observation justified the aeroplane's role in battle in the first months that featured maneuvering armies. The subsequent attrition resulting from the stagnating front lines increased dependency on aerial reconnaissance and the evolving role of photographic interpretation. (Prevailing doctrine and strategy contributed most to the blind application of armies against a well-defended adversary.) Information access improved thanks to aeroplanes capable of flying at higher altitudes fitted with cameras possessing powerful focal arrays. By war's end intelligence derived from aerial reconnaissance and photographic interpretation was as integral to the battle as the artillery itself. Those who disregarded the role of information and intelligence suffered more casualties. Decisions based on intelligence created an air of greater confidence for the front line combatant in what often seemed a fruitless and never-ending endeavor.

The second section describes how Allied intelligence matured along with aerial photography. The pronounced absence of personal reminiscences covering the intelligence experience of this era called for an in-depth study of official writings. Specific entries culled from surviving manuals and written lectures provide a better ap-

---

[3] Theodore M. Knappen, *Wings of War: An Account of the Important Contribution of the United States to Aircraft Invention, Engineering, Development and Production during the World War* (New York: G. P. Putnam's Sons, 1920), 197-198.

preciation for how the intelligence medium transformed itself to serve military objectives through photographic production, cartography, and analysis. There were attempts to publicize the process through the media outlets of the day. The public's knowledge was derived from inflated accounts describing an aerial reconnaissance and photographic interpretation ability to transform basic imagery evidence into a vast storehouse of intimate files describing the adversary's unit and cognitive process. Photography was seen as a major contribution to the enemy's ultimate annihilation. A detailed description of each Ally's intelligence architecture highlights British and French intelligence. When the Americans arrived, they adopted portions of both. For all three, the role of information acquisition, processing, and analysis, refined in the Great War, became the foundation for intelligence for the remainder of the 20th century.

The third section describes the battlefield, the focus of intense Allied scrutiny for four years. Beyond the front line, analysis focused on aerial photographic signatures of rear-echelon activity to confirm German strategic intentions. To understand German military policy, the Allies depended on captured documents. These writings highlighted the German approach to conventional combat, employing an inventory of weapons to include the first use of a weapon of mass destruction (chemical munitions). The affected landscape was transformed into a virtual hell. The evolution of that landscape was captured in the aerial photographic record. This section concludes with an in-depth assessment of the evolving role of modern camouflage and deception.

Art mirrored science in the conflict between military reason and illusion. The combatants fought this war on a battlefield subject to photographs; camouflage and illusion were designed to confuse and contradict reason and undermine analytical procedures.

The final section focuses on mission, technology, training, and the human experience behind aerial reconnaissance and photographic interpretation. All were critical in shaping the ultimate purpose of these specialties. The most intriguing aspect for the author was the absence of any evidence of aerial photographic interpretation reporting on a given target, other than line drawings. The extant reporting consists of summations of daily reports. However, the application of deductive logic is missing in these descriptions. All that exists are dry descriptions of images. The final chapters describe the human experience to the degree possible through memoirs, lectures, and reports. The story rests on the reflections of a group of pioneers who have worked in this new intelligence medium. Each of them brings us some understanding of the way the Allied intelligence process evolved in sophistication and accuracy.

As one of the first French pioneers in the art of photographic interpretation, *Capitaine* Jean de Bissy notes that intelligence in the Great War was originally designed "to follow the destructive work of our Artillery and to register the victorious advance of our Infantry."[4] This early assessment clearly understates the use and value of intelligence derived from aerial reconnaissance as it evolved during the war. From the horrors of trench warfare evolved one of the most important sources of military information in the 20th century.

---

[4] [Capitaine J. de Lennoy de Bissy], *Illustrations to Accompany Captain De Bissy's Notes Regarding the Interpretation of Aeroplane Photographs*, October 1915 (transl., n.p., n.d.). In this instance the title Capitaine, as a French word, is italicized. In this work the first time a non-English word is used it is italicized, but later instances are not, since the use is quite frequent and italicizing all is distracting to the reader.

CHAPTER 1

AUGUST TO LATE 1914:
THE EVOLUTION OF AERIAL RECONNAISSANCE AS A FORCE MULTIPLIER

Aerial Reconnaissance at the Commencement of the War

Aeronautical reconnaissance from the first five months of war clearly demonstrated the acceptance of aerial observation as an integral part of modern warfare. Both sides made significant advances through reconnaissance, thanks to the array of uniquely designed aeroplanes that provided the battlefield commander with a view from the "higher ground." The opening weeks of combat established patterns that became the foundation for one of the most important roles of aviation in the 20th century. Information became an integral part of aeronautics. Observation became both science and art as aeroplanes maneuvered with ground forces, contributing data to commanders that helped reveal enemy intentions. The ability to detect the movement of forces meant that whatever was on the ground was now accessible to reconnaissance. These lessons were quickly learned by aviators and commanders alike. Confidence in the aeronautical arm was established. However, the initial salvos of the first months of combat also demonstrated the need for technology to reinforce aerial observation.

The roots of aerial reconnaissance for military purposes go back to the 18th century. Then the French demonstrated that a balloon was beyond novelty and could support military objectives. With each trial the aerial proponent discovered that an aeronautical advantage correlated to a combat advantage. The powers of Europe had the resources to leverage aeronautics for their standing militaries. Pioneer British aerial historian Sir Walter Raleigh observed in 1922, "The pride of Germany was in her airships, and the pride of France was in her aeroplanes."[1] Britain dabbled with both, albeit not to the extent of being competitive. It was preoccupied with the naval race against Germany. However, it was not blind to the advances achieved through military aviation. British assessments in 1911 concerning French aviation acknowledged it equated to national power projection. As Raleigh stated, "There is no doubt at all but that the Germans have suddenly realized that the French Army since the general employment of aeroplanes with troops has improved its fighting efficiency by at least twenty per cent."[2]

Early aerial reconnaissance introduced a unique technology. Fragile pre-war aerial platforms were incapable of sustaining meaningful sorties of long duration. Yet the opportunity to alert infantry and artillery to the advancing enemy provided the impetus to integrate aviation within the standing forces. The French were keen on this idea: "The aeronautic mission was

---

[1] Sir Walter A. Raleigh and H. A. Jones, *The War in the Air, Being the Story of the Part Played in the Great War by the Royal Air Force* (6 vols., Oxford: The Clarendon Press, 1922-37; reprint, London: The Imperial War Museum, and Nashville, TN: The Battery Press, 1998), I, 75. Raleigh authored the first volume and Jones the others. Hereafter cited as Raleigh for references to vol. 1, and as Jones for vols. 2-6 and Appendices.
[2] Raleigh, I, 177-178.

FIGURE 2. **Capitaine Saconney, the French Aviation Militaire's visionary for aerial observation platforms.** Source: SHAA, photo contained in Charles Christienne and Pierre Lissarague, *A History of French Military Aviation* (Washington, DC: Smithsonian Institution Press, 1986).

ture of the day and was soon recognized as a medium that could contribute to the conduct of a campaign. Advances in aeronautics over the fifty years since the American Civil War had demonstrated observation roles for lighter-than-air balloons and the later-designed dirigibles. In France, the means to capture the aeronautical dimension for military purposes was accomplished through ongoing experimentation with man-carrying kites for observation.

During this vibrant period of experimentation, the roots of aerial photographic reconnaissance took hold. Public awareness of aviation's potential for acquiring information was demonstrated in unique ways prior to powered flight. Innovative aerial platforms for photography went beyond balloon units. In 1896, the public was entertained by the potential of aerial photography through publications describing successful coverage from parakites and pigeons armed with miniature cameras.[4] Throughout the latter half of the 19th century, photography and aerial platforms proved their military usefulness. As early as the late 1860s, the Prussian General Staff organized a corps trained in photographic methods to conduct aerial military surveys, aiding its planning for military operations in the Franco-Prussian War of 1870.[5] Campaigns were employing aerial platforms to commence initial planning. Innovations experienced by balloonists in the U.S. Civil War, the Franco-Prussian War of 1870, and the Spanish-American War confirmed the utility of balloon-hosted aerial observation and photography.

Experimentation blossomed as existing technologies were applied to aviation. In 1906, a British inventor, Samuel Franklin Cody, built a man-carrying kite that was accepted by the British Army. A year later, Cody built the first British-designed aeroplane, which was subsequently identified as Army Aeroplane No. 1.[6] In 1910 Robert Loraine, in a Bristol aeroplane fitted with a transmitting apparatus, succeeded in sending

initially fixed, strategic reconnaissance against a rapidly advancing enemy."[3] Aerial photography at this moment was an experiment, considered by many in the military to be another minor novelty of technology. However, photography was a well-established part of the cul-

[3] "Aeronautics," June 1921, 1, Part XXXVII, sec. 3, in American Mission with the Commanding General, Allied Forces of Occupation, Mainz, Germany, "A Study of the Organization of the French Army Showing its Development as a Result of the Lessons of the World War and Comprising Notes on Equipment and Tactical Doctrine Developed in the French Army, 1914-1921," NARA, RG 120, Box 819.

[4] Gilbert T. Woglom, *Parakites* (New York: G. P. Putnam's Sons, 1896), 41-44.
[5] James W. Bagley, *The Use of the Panoramic Camera in Topographic Surveying* (Washington, DC: GPO, 1917), 12.
[6] Roy C. Nesbit, *Eyes of the RAF: A History of Photo-Reconnaissance* (Phoenix Mill, UK: Alan Sutton Publishing, Ltd., 1996), 9.

radio messages from a distance of a quarter of a mile.[7] The French Aerial Photographic Service conducted research in both aerial photography and restitution (analysis of photographic images applied to developing and enhancing information on a map) under the command of Capitaine Jacques Saconney.[8] French military trials in February 1910 used man-bearing kites to support artillery observation and attempt aerial photography. Saconney developed and employed a man-bearing kite to an altitude of 560 meters. The three-kite configuration allowed various passengers to both observe and photograph the area. Despite the apparent risk, Capitaine Saconney's commander Général Joly went aloft in the kite.[9]

Aéroplane reconnaissance quickly ceased being a concept and became reality. The command staff of the French Armée, the Grand Quartier Général (GQG), supported aviation's role in several instances. They put the idea into practice, demonstrating aerial reconnaissance for military purposes on 18 September 1911. During a military exercise, Capitaine Eteve and Capitaine Pichot-Duclas flew a 42-kilometer track in a Maurice Farman north from Verdun to Étraye and west to Romagne at an altitude of 1,000 meters, providing in-depth observations of activity.[10] The next year, four Blériot Type XI aéroplanes deployed to Morocco, providing aerial reconnaissance for the French Armée. These aircraft were not just a novelty; they were now part of the operational scheme.[11] At the same time, the French reinforced their traditional forces by establishing a Blériot Cavalry (BLC) unit with three Blériot aéroplanes.[12]

FIGURE 3. **Général Joly observes a 1910 French military exercise from a Saconney-designed kite.** Source: SHAA, B76.224.

However, despite the progress through experimentation, aviation's potential was not fully understood. While attending an air race in eastern France in 1910, Général Ferdinand Foch commented, "Flying, you must understand is merely a sport, like any other; from the military point of view it has no value whatever."[13] His attitude was echoed by another future senior commander of the coming conflict, General Sir Douglas Haig. Haig spent his career in the cavalry, and as "the Apostle of Cavalry," he expressed his bias in 1911 on the technology that was being introduced. "Tell Sykes [Colonel F.H. Sykes, soon to become the first British chief of

---

[7] Wireless and radio were interchangeable terms. Radio will be the primary term used in this book. Raleigh, I, 170.

[8] "Lecture on Aerial Photography, Centre d'Etudes de l'Aéronautique," 25 April 1923, NASM A30.2/36.

[9] *Rapport du Capitaine du Génie Saconney, au Sujet des Experiences de Cerfs-Volants Effectuées avec Nacelle Lestrée à bout de Cable*, 21 February 1910, SHAA; Marcellin Hodeir, "La Photographie Aérienne: 'de la Marne à la Somme,' 1914-1916," *Révue Historique des Armées*, No. 2 (1996): 108 (translation by Commandant Marc Rivière, French Air Force).

[10] *Manoeuvres du 6ème Corps d'Armée*, Flight Log, 18 September 1911, SHAA.

[11] James J. Davilla and Arthur M. Soltan, *French Aircraft of the First World War* (Stratford, CT: Flying Machines Press, 1997), 55.

[12] Davilla and Soltan, 1.

[13] Foch, quoted in Georges Blond, *The Marne* (trans., London: Macdonald and Company, 1965), 163.

FIGURE 4. **Prior to the war, French aviation actively exercised aerial reconnaissance in military operations and exercises. Here a Blériot pilot debriefs the reconnaissance to an intelligence officer.** Source: Claude Grahame-White, *The Aeroplane in War* (London: T. Werner Laurie, 1912), 192.

staff for aviation] he is wasting his time, flying can never be of any use to the Army."[14] As the war proceeded, both became recognized advocates of aviation's potential.

Though critics were wary, influential proponents saw potential value, and aviation became more legitimized. On 19 March 1912, Aviation Militaire was recognized by the GQG as an integral part of the French Armée.[15] Ten days later, French Aviation Militaire units were formed under Colonel Hirshauer, comprising an aerial force strength of five escadrilles.[16] The British also commenced structuring their aeronautical force. The Royal Flying Corps (RFC) was constituted by a Royal Warrant on 13 April 1912.[17] In 1913 the French Aviation Militaire was placed under the command of French Corps d'Armée (CA) commanders, or local administrators, to diminish the authority of the permanent inspector for aviation. Military maneuvers that year showed reconnaissance information from Aviation Militaire was extremely useful. On 4 April 1914, Aviation Militaire became a separate department of the Ministry of War, making it an independent French military service.[18] Army sponsorship for aviation also occurred within the U.S. Army Signal Corps. This arrangement existed until the U.S. Air Service was created as a separate entity in 1918.

The French and British militaries both developed coherent aviation organizational structures. The French promoted homogeneity of aircraft types for the various escadrilles to save on maintenance while promoting a diverse collection of craft primarily used in observation and reconnaissance missions. Along with infrastructure came development of a specific air doctrine for observation and reconnaissance missions. By 1913 Aviation Militaire comprised eight companies for aérostat (ballon/dirigeable) work and ten sections for aviation work.[19] British aviation worked with both resources. RFC squadrons comprised a mix of aeroplanes, while the Royal Navy deployed a dirigible fleet for naval missions.[20]

Military staffs also started to refine the routing of information from their aeronautical sources. French officers were encouraged to become familiar with aviation and its reconnaissance potential. Staff officers were expected to make passenger flights, and some were even detached for a period as observers. Absolute familiarity with the maneuvers and formations of all arms was considered essential. The French also realized early on the potential for having aéroplanes observe artillery fire. A British intelligence estimate described the process:

> Two white lines are marked on the ground to show the observer where the battery is in position. The aeroplane ascends behind the battery and rises to a height sufficient to be clear of

---

[14] Maurice Baring, *Flying Corps Headquarters, 1914-1918* (London: William Blackwood & Sons, Ltd., 1968), 306.

[15] "Report on Aeronautical Matters in Foreign Countries for 1913," 16, TNA, PRO: AIR 1/7/6/98/20.

[16] Davilla and Soltan, 1.

[17] Raleigh, I, 199.

[18] Davilla and Soltan, 1-2.

[19] "Report on Aeronautical Matters," 12, TNA, PRO: AIR 1/7/6/98/20.

[20] Charles Christienne and Pierre Lissarague, *A History of French Military Aviation* (Washington, DC: Smithsonian Institution Press), 59.

Chapter 1: The Evolution of Aerial Reconnaissance as a Force Multiplier

the trajectory of the shells. The battery commander then fires his bracket. The observer is provided with a sheet of paper across which two parallel lines are drawn indicating the two extremities of the bracket. Having observed the first rounds he marks on the paper the position of the rounds with reference to the space between the two lines representing the extremities of the bracket. He then drops the paper near the battery commander's position.[21]

In another maneuver, a suitable landing place for the dropped information was selected by marking it with a large white sheet. A party of two noncommissioned officers and eight troopers were permanently on duty so as to be ready to take messages to the proper quarter.[22] Additionally, the French started realigning their command centers to areas where aéroplanes operated. Messengers were stationed at designated landing zones to transfer reports to the various units. Over time the landing zones became the rendezvous point for military commanders to disseminate their own information.[23]

The French proceeded to develop an aerial camera, commencing development under strict conditions of secrecy.[24] An aerial camera was developed by the French Telephotography Laboratory prior to the outbreak of the conflict.[25] By August 1914 the *laboratoire des recherches aéronautique* (Aeronautical Research Center) at Chalais-Meudon had three wood-frame prototype cameras for aérostat observation. They employed 100 cm, 60 cm, and 50 cm focal lengths. However, despite the progress, the laboratory encountered a lack of interest as its cameras were demonstrated to artillery staffs.[26] By the time the French mobilized for war, they had estab-

lished three photographic sections to work with the aérostat units. The Paris section was led by Capitaine Georges Bellenger (chef d'avion VIème Armée). He was an artillery officer whose aviation career had an auspicious beginning. He served as advisor to a leading French parliamentarian, Senator Reymond, on aeronautical matters.[27] Bellenger became the catalyst for creating the aerial observer's role in the upcoming first weeks of the war. The Verdun sector was led by Lieutenant Maurice Marie Eugène Grout, another French artillery officer by training who proved to be the most successful transformer for the French military's adaptation of aerial photography.[28] Lieutenant Grout was a brilliant and extremely hard-working staff officer. Educated at France's elite École Polytechnique, he was a key member of the staff at Chalais Meudon, developing aerial telegraphy and photography before the war started.[29] The third photographic section supported the eastern French region headquarters at Toul.[30]

The British did not strongly emphasize aerial photography prior to the war, although they did experiment with balloons during the Boer War in South Africa at the turn of the century. However, their attempts to combine aerial photography and aeroplanes remained experimental well into the first months of the war. In the first year of its existence, the RFC dabbled with taking photographs from the air (airships, balloons, and kites) at Farnborough using the "Panros" (Pan-Ross) hand-held camera and showing the results at the Annual Exhibition of the Royal Photographic Society. Before the outbreak of the war, an exhibition at Farnborough featured "Photographs from Aeroplanes."[31] The Pan Ross was a press camera with a 6-inch lens using 5-inch and 4-inch glass plates.[32] Interest in aerial photography generated a call for volunteers to join the Military Wing of

[21] "Report on Aeronautical Matters," 16, TNA, PRO: AIR 1/7/6/98/20.

[22] "Report on Aeronautical Matters," 16, TNA, PRO: AIR 1/7/6/98/20.

[23] "Report on Aeronautical Matters," 16, TNA, PRO: AIR 1/7/6/98/20.

[24] Raleigh, I, 177-178.

[25] Raleigh, I, 170.

[26] Gaston Labussière, "La Photographie Aérienne," in Maurice de Brunoff, ed., *1914-1918: L'Aéronautique pendant la Guerre Mondiale* (Paris: M. de Brunoff, 1919), 183 (translation provided by Commandant Marc Rivière).

[27] John H. Morrow, Jr., *The Great War in the Air: Military Aviation from 1909 to 1921* (Washington, DC, and London: Smithsonian Institution Press, 1993), 34.

[28] Hodeir, 108.

[29] *Lieut* Maurice Marie Eugène Grout, Personnel Records, SHAA.

[30] Hodeir, 108.

[31] Original spelling of the Pan Ross was Panros. Lieut Charles W. Gamble, "The Technical Aspects of British Aerial Photography during the War 1914-1918," TNA, PRO: AIR 1/2397/267/7; Raleigh, I, 250.

[32] Nesbit, 11.

the RFC. One volunteer was Frederick Charles Victor Laws. He transferred from the 3rd Battalion of the Coldstream Guards and became a First Class Mechanic Air Photographer. Laws improved the photographic laboratory at the Farnborough test grounds shortly after his arrival. He subsequently was promoted to sergeant and became the RFC's first noncommissioned officer in charge of photography.[33] Laws made RFC history by serving as aerial photographer using the first British-designed aerial camera, the Watson Air Camera. In 1913, Laws flew on a dirigible and took aerial photographs of the Basingstoke Canal. It was an auspicious start. Laws became the leader of many British initiatives in developing aerial photography for the remainder of his military career.[34]

RFC No. 1 Squadron became the initial aeroplane unit to explore aerial photography. In 1913, the British transferred all dirigibles from the RFC to the Royal Naval Air Service (RNAS). No. 1

Squadron served as an "Aircraft Park" to experiment on new aerial capabilities.[35] While assigned to No. 1 Squadron, Laws proved the capability for developing a photograph in-flight. In early 1914, RFC No. 3 Squadron took the lead in developing British aerial photography. The officers purchased their own cameras and commenced to learn the art of photography on their own. They even learned Laws' technique for developing negatives in the air and had them ready for printing upon landing. On their own initiative they

---

[33] Nesbit, 10.
[34] Nesbit, 11.

[35] The Royal Naval Air Service was the naval counterpart of the RFC until the RAF was established in 1918; Nesbit, 11.

photographed the defense of the Isle of Wight and the Solent at an altitude of 5,000 feet.[36]

In June 1914, Sergeant Laws flew as aerial observer in a Henri Farman (HF 7, "Longhorn") with the Watson Air Camera mounted on the nose. The sortie ended when the engine motor cut off and the plane crashed. Not to be dissuaded, two days later Laws took off as observer in a Maurice Farman (MF 11, "Shorthorn") and photographed a military review and parade in progress. What caught Laws' attention as the photographs were developed was the difference in light reflection on the adjoining grass from personnel walking through the area. It gave reason to further explore the potential that aerial photographic interpretation could offer.[37] Despite the amazing effort under way, the prevailing attitude among military circles was mixed: "If that young fool likes to get himself killed, let him do so."[38] With each demonstration of aerial photography, "those who came to scoff remained to pray."[39]

French armées and aviation assets commenced mobilization when the war started. "At the time of mobilization military aeronautics was still in its earliest infancy. We may say it was as the fighting went on that this science was evolved and developed."[40] French aéronautic units were governed under Plan XVII (14 February 1914) comprising both aérostation and aviation.[41] The French aviation section now comprised 21 flights of six aeroplanes. Two BLC flights of four aéroplanes were added at the start of the war. The mainstay Blériot XI was capable of flying for two hours at 1,500 feet, providing a mobile aerial platform that maneuvered over the countryside and acquired vital glimpses of enemy forces. Immediately after mobilization, new flights were created from aéroplanes delivered or salvaged behind the lines. Aviation personnel numbered about 3,500, including 480 officers and non-commissioned officers.[42] Increased awareness of the value of "higher ground" reporting resulted in a support element to convey critical information. Each escadrille had a "fast car" and a motorcyclist assigned to rapidly disseminate airborne-acquired reports to the respective ground commander.[43]

French intelligence, known as the 2ᵉ Bureau, actively monitored the advancing German forces with all the resources at its disposal. The fledgling radio intercept function was effective in view of the capabilities of the time. Established in 1909, the French radio intercept specialists were recognized as experts in this field. 2ᵉ Bureau also conducted cryptological analysis that served the highest levels of the government.[44] The French had committed their intercept service in full, even before the beginning of the war, and were following German Army traffic attentively. After a few days, they had a perfectly clear picture of the operational structure of the German Army in the west as it marched through Belgium in the direction of Paris.[45]

The Commencement of Combat

French aviation was put to the test as battle commenced. Each armée included a flight of aéroplanes. Order of battle for Aviation Militaire comprised Iᵉᵐᵉ Armée (six escadrilles), IIᵉᵐᵉ Armée (four escadrilles), IIIᵉᵐᵉ Armée (four escadrilles), IVᵉᵐᵉ Armée (two escadrilles), Vᵉᵐᵉ Armée (five escadrilles), and two BLC escadrilles.[46] When the war commenced, the French used their aéroplanes for daytime reconnaissance and dirigible fleet for nighttime observation. The first French wartime reconnaissance mission was accomplished by a Maurice Farman (MF) 7 from escadrille MF 2.[47]

Like the French Aviation Militaire, the British Military Wing prior to the commencement of

[36] Raleigh, I, 250.
[37] Nesbit, 13.
[38] Unknown source quoted in Gamble, "Technical Aspects of British Aerial Photography," TNA, PRO: AIR 1/2397/267/7.
[39] Unknown source quoted in Gamble, "Technical Aspects of British Aerial Photography," TNA, PRO: AIR 1/2397/267/7.
[40] "Aeronautics," June 1921, NARA, RG 120, Box 819, 1.
[41] Christienne and Lissarague, 59.

[42] Christienne and Lissarague, 58.
[43] Douglas Porch, *The French Secret Services: From the Dreyfus Affair to the Gulf War* (New York: Farrar, Straus, and Giroux, 1995), 56.
[44] Porch, 56.
[45] Wilhelm F. Flicke, *War Secrets in the Ether*, ed. by Sheila Carlisle (2 vols., Laguna Hills, CA: Aegean Park Press, 1977), I, 23.
[46] Davilla and Soltan, 3.
[47] Davilla and Soltan, 219.

Chapter 1: The Evolution of Aerial Reconnaissance as a Force Multiplier

WESTERN FRONT
September 1914–March 1918

————➤   Schlieffen Plan

••••••••••   Limit of German Advance, Sep 1914

—————   Front Line, Oct 1914

—————   Hindenburg Line

— — — -   Front Line, Mar 1918

0   50
|___|___|___|___|___|
           Miles

FIGURE 6. Overview of the Western Front. This map shows the area encompassed by the Western Front and includes the planned attack of the German Schlieffen Plan, the limit of German Advance in 1914, the Front Line at the close of the Battle on the Marne in 1914, the location of the Hindenburg Line, and the Front Line in March, 1918, coinciding with the first significant American involvement. Source: Center of Military History, United States Army, Washington, DC. Source: *American Military History* (Washington, DC: Army Historical Series, Office of the Chief of Military History, United States Army, 1989), Map 38, 362. Courtesy of the Center of Military History.

the war was designed for aerial reconnaissance, with the squadron assuming the role of the basic British aviation unit.[48] Five squadrons had been established prior to the war. On 31 July 1914, total operational aircraft from RFC Squadrons No. 2, 3, and 4 numbered 22 BE 2a, five Blériot XI monoplanes, and six Henri Farman F.20. An additional 24 aeroplanes were to be added prior to deployment to France.[49] It was indicative of the way aviation evolved between the French and British that a common airframe was used in the first years of the war. Both Blériot XI and

HF 20/F.20 were flown by French and British pilots. Of the two, Blériot XI was a more recognized airframe due to the worldwide publicity gained from the first crossing of the English Channel in 1909. However, as an observation platform, the Blériot design was not ideal. The broad wings were a viewing obstacle to observers.[50] The British had yet to adopt homogeneous airframe types for each squadron. It was not yet practical due to the embryonic condition of the British aircraft industry at the time. However, despite the diversity of aeroplanes that complicated ground maintenance, squadron operations were effectively maintained. Sorties did not include formation flying. The standard procedure called for each aeroplane to act independently.[51]

The German adversary was no stranger to the potential of aerial reconnaissance. This resource had strong advocates within the senior headquarters, the German High Command (Oberste Heeresleitung [OHL]). During the first month of combat, successful aerial reconnaissance gave the German armies an advantage in their initial operations on the Eastern Front. Each active German corps and headquarters (8th Army) was assigned a six-plane Feld Flieger Abteilung, comprised of a composite of monoplanes (Tauben) and biplanes to provide timely information to German battlefield commanders. Priority for the mission and command of the two-seater aeroplane went to the observer, not the pilot. The Germans also employed Zeppelin craft for longer-range strategic reconnaissance.[52] German aerial reconnaissance gained favor in the war's first major battle at Tannenberg in eastern Poland. The OHL was personally briefed by Flieger Abteilung crewmembers as the Russians commenced the attack. German reconnaissance provided locations of maneuvering Russian units and aided planning for appropriate countermoves.[53] Intelligence information proved critical in this first major battle of the

[48] Raleigh, I, 260.

[49] J. M. Bruce, *The Aeroplanes of the Royal Flying Corps (Military Wing)* (London: Putnam, 1982), xvi.

[50] Paul-Louis Weiller, "The French Aviation of Recognition," in de Brunoff, 63 (translation provided by Commandant Marc Rivière).

[51] John Terraine, *Mons: The Retreat to Victory* (New York: The Macmillan Company, 1960), 31.

[52] Dennis E. Showalter, *Tannenberg: Clash of Empires* (Hamden, CT: Archon Books, 1991), 152-153.

[53] W. M. Lamberton, comp., *Reconnaissance & Bomber Aircraft of the 1914-1918 War*, ed. by E. F. Cheesman (Letchworth, UK: Harleyford Publications, Ltd., and Los Angeles, CA: Aero Publishers, Inc., 1962), 9.

war. Success came to the Germans when they intercepted Russian radio transmissions containing exact force disposition and locations. Aerial reconnaissance had reinforced German command decisions, but not as decisively as the radio intercept. Tannenberg became the first battle in history where interception of enemy radio traffic played the decisive role.[54] Intercepts included Russian operational orders and, more significantly, the organization and destination of the Russian Second Army. The Russian maneuvers were successfully countered.[55] Modern intelligence technology had validated itself on the battlefield.

During the first days of combat on the Western Front, the Germans employed dirigibles for aerial reconnaissance and bombardment. Their first aerial bombardment sortie targeted Liège on 6 August 1914. During this sortie, a dirigible was hit by cannon and returned to the German base with damage. Another dirigible was hit over Alsace while on a reconnaissance mission. A third, dirigible ZVIII, was shot down by French artillery.[56]

On 13 August, the RFC under Brigadier-General Sir David Henderson deployed to France. The first unit to make the crossing was No. 2 Squadron, with the first aeroplane departing early that morning and arriving at Amiens approximately two hours later. The transfer of other RFC aeroplanes that day was not so fortunate. Several aircraft of No. 4 Squadron were damaged while following their leader in a forced landing on a plowed field.[57] The following RFC squadrons and aeroplanes that flew to France on 13-15 August 1914 were: No. 2 Squadron, 12 BE 2a's; No. 3 Squadron, 6 Blériot XI's, a Blériot Parasol, 4 F.20s; No. 4 Squadron, 6 Blériot XI's, a Blériot Parasol, 4 F.20s; No. 4 Squadron, 11 BE 2a's; No. 5 Squadron, 4 F.20s, and 3 Avro

FIGURE 7. **The first RFC aerial reconnaissance in wartime was flown by Captain Philip Joubert de la Ferté.** Source: Bleriot No. 260 Netheravon, 1913 (Crown Copyright reserved). Sir Philip Joubert de la Ferté, Air Chief Marshal, *The Fated Sky, An Autobiography* (London: Hutchinson & Co., 1952), 33.

504s.[58] Those were the aeroplanes that arrived; others were lost on the way. Two days later, a British pilot met an unusual welcoming committee while landing near Boulogne-la-Grasse. Lieut. R.M. Vaughan of No. 5 Squadron was arrested by the French and held in prison for nearly a week while local officials tried to determine his true nationality and purpose. Lieut. Vaughan was able to rejoin his squadron on the eve of the Battle of Mons.[59]

British aeroplanes and personnel had limited capabilities. The BE 2a had a maximum speed of 65 mph at 6,500 feet. It took approximately 35 minutes for the aeroplane to reach 7,000 feet.[60] Aerial observation commenced at a speed that fit available airframe and motor technology. Despite Sergeant-Major Laws' successful demonstration of aerial photography, the RFC did not employ his talents when the British Expeditionary Force (BEF) arrived in France. Instead, Laws

[54] Flicke, I, 3.

[55] Flicke, I, 6-7.

[56] Christienne and Lissarague, 61; André-H. Carlier, *La Photographie Aérienne pendant la Guerre* (Paris: Libraire Delagrave, 1921), 16 (translation provided by Commandant Marc Rivière).

[57] Henderson was a career intelligence officer who was a recognized authority on reconnaissance. His work, *The Art of Reconnaissance*, provided vision to the use of aeroplanes in a reconnaissance role; Terraine, 31.

[58] Bruce, *Aeroplanes of the Royal Flying Corps (Military Wing)*, xvi.

[59] Boulogne-la-Grasse is located southeast of Amiens; original text says only Boulogne; Terraine, 31.

[60] Bruce, *Aeroplanes of the Royal Flying Corps (Military Wing)*, 353.

was assigned to an antiaircraft unit as an aeroplane spotter and identifier.[61]

Initial RFC attempts to commence aerial reconnaissance operations against the Germans were precluded by weather. The heat of summer brought thunderstorms, mists, and haze. Flight logs described these conditions as "unsuitable for reconnaissance."[62] Aerial reconnaissance operations got under way on 19 August with the first RFC aerial reconnaissance flight flown by Captain Philip Joubert de la Ferté, No. 3 Squadron, and Lieutenant G.W. Mapplebeck from No. 4 Squadron. Joubert de la Ferté flew a Blériot XI-2 (without observer) while Mapplebeck took off in a BE 2a from Maubeuge (south of Mons) that morning. Mapplebeck flew to the north while Joubert de la Ferté was ordered to inspect the Belgian country west of Brussels and report on any evidence of enemy troops. Shortly after take-off, the pilots struggled with cloudy weather and a general unfamiliarity with the region, resulting in their getting lost. Both considered it "rather bad form to come down and ask people the way," but discretion was soon applied.[63] Joubert de la Ferté recalled:

> I wandered round Western Belgium for some time and then seeing a large town over which the Belgian flag seemed to be flying, I landed on the parade ground. I discovered that this was Tournai, still in Belgian hands, and I was given a most excellent lunch by the commandant of the garrison. Leaving an hour later, I lost myself again very quickly. Finally I recognized the Bruges Ship Canal, flew south from there, and landed near Courtrai. Here my reception was not at all cordial. The local police threatened to put me in jail. I was saved by the kindness of a little North of Ireland linen manufacturer, who was visiting Courtrai, where there are a lot of spinning mills. He placed a Union Jack on my aircraft, and the tone immediately improved. I got what I wanted,

which was petrol, and the directions how to find my way back to Maubeuge, and flew off very thankfully, completed my reconnaissance, and landed back at Maubeuge at 5.30.[64]

As for Lieutenant Mapplebeck in the BE 2a, he flew over Brussels itself without recognizing it. The result of both reconnaissance missions was negative. Joubert de la Ferté and Mapplebeck reported with assurance on where the Germans were not, but had nothing to say about where they were.[65] The time had come for aerial observers to be included on reconnaissance sorties.[66] Mapplebeck's aerial legacy included a narrow escape. While conducting aerial reconnaissance over German lines near Lille, he experienced engine problems, landed, and two German soldiers literally grabbed one of the wings. Mapplebeck escaped into Lille wearing peasant clothing that he found on the way. He found a French businessman who cashed a London cheque that provided him with French notes bearing a German stamp. Mapplebeck proceeded to buy a new suit and walked from Lille through Belgium to the Dutch border. He obtained passage to London and reported in at Farnborough. The Air Ministry provided him with a new aeroplane to fly to France. When he showed up at the squadron in France, Mapplebeck reported for duty "just as though nothing unusual had happened."[67]

That same day, the French committed their dirigeable (dirigible balloon) forces to reconnaissance missions. The French dirigeable Fleurus became the first Allied airship to fly over Germany by successfully flying over the Saar and Trèves while on a night reconnaissance sortie.[68] The irony of early French dirigeable experience was they suffered more from friendly fire than from German antiaircraft artillery. Two dirigeables were damaged. One French dirigeable, the Dupuy de Lome, suffered casualties (the pilot was killed) as well as being shot up fairly

[61] Nesbit, 14.
[62] Lyn Macdonald, *1914: The Days of Hope* (New York: Atheneum, 1987), 74.
[63] Bruce, *Aeroplanes of the Royal Flying Corps (Military Wing)*, 131-132; Terraine, 61-62.
[64] *Capt.* Philip Joubert de la Ferté quoted in Terraine, 61-62.
[65] Terraine, 61-62.
[66] Nesbit, 16.
[67] Account related by J. T. C. Moore-Brabazon to Frederic Coleman, quoted in Frederic Coleman, *With Cavalry in 1915: The British Trooper in the Trench Line* (Toronto: William Briggs, 1916), 130-132.
[68] Christienne and Lissarague, 62.

FIGURE 8. **German Advance on Paris 22-23 August 1914.** Source: *The West Point Atlas of American Wars.* Vol. 2, *1900-1953.* Ed. Vincent J. Esposito (2 vols., New York: Frederick A. Praeger, 1959), map 6. Courtesy, Department of History, U.S. Military Academy.

severely while heading toward the French city of Rheims. Following these mishaps, the French delayed dirigeable operations until April 1915.[69] For the remainder of the war, French dirigeables played a secondary role serving the armée. They were eventually discontinued from serving armée objectives in 1916 and were eventually transferred to the navy.[70]

On 20 August British cavalry were on the move in Belgium. They pushed forward as far as Binche (16 kilometers east of Mons) without encountering the enemy. At the same time, RFC aerial reconnaissance was ordered to find the German Army, pinpoint its position, and estimate its strength. The RFC discovered elements of the German Army heading through Louvain (approximately 25 kilometers southeast of Brus-

sels). Aerial observation estimates of strength proved too difficult since German Army columns went beyond the visual horizon. That day the German Army moved into Brussels. The main echelon was heading toward France.[71] On the morning of 21 August, aerial reconnaissance was incapable of operating due to ground mist. Reconnoitering squadrons and patrols were pushed out toward Soignies and Nivelles in southern Belgium.[72] Once the weather cleared, RFC reconnaissance commenced and quickly acquired significant observations of German cavalry and artillery maneuvering southeast of Nivelles.[73]

Aerial activity assumed a more dynamic role as the armies came in contact. On 22 August British cavalry engaged the Germans for the

---

[69] Christienne and Lissarague, 63.
[70] Christienne and Lissarague, 64.

[71] Macdonald, *1914*, 75; Raleigh, I, 298-300; Constance Babington-Smith, *Air Spy: The Story of Photo Intelligence in World War II* (New York: Ballantine Books, 1957), 9; Brig-Gen Sir J.E. Edmonds (general editor), *Military Operations: France and Belgium, 1914*, 3rd ed. (2 vols., London: Macmillan and Co., Ltd., 1922-25; reprint, London: The Imperial War Museum and Nashville, TN: The Battery Press, 1996), I, 50. Hereafter, titles in this series, 1914-1918, will be referred to as Edmonds, followed by the war year; see bibliography for complete citations for each title.
[72] Field-Marshal Viscount French of Ypres, *1914* (London: Constable and Company, Ltd., and Boston: Houghton Mifflin Company, 1919), 47.
[73] Edmonds, *1914*, I, 52.

Chapter 1: The Evolution of Aerial Reconnaissance as a Force Multiplier

first time near Soignies.[74] That day the RFC flew twelve reconnaissance sorties from Maubeuge, France (on the French-Belgian border, 15 kilometers south of Mons), reporting on extensive German maneuvers and the presence of large masses of troops. One critical RFC reconnaissance revealed a long German column estimated at army corps strength marching along the road from Brussels due west to Ninove. Upon reaching the town, the German forces turned southwest to Grammont. RFC aerial reconnaissance reported that the German infantry was in close support of the advancing German cavalry heading south.[75] Soon the German Army's maneuver brought it outside the British left flank. This critical issue was personally brought to the attention of the British Commander-in-Chief, Field-Marshal Sir John French, by the RFC commander, Brigadier-General Henderson. French was initially skeptical until he received further verification from his French counterparts.[76] The first losses from aerial combat then occurred. An Avro 504 from No. 5 Squadron was shot down while performing aerial observation. The downed aeroplane provided the Germans with their first positive confirmation that British forces were now engaging them.[77] The significance of the occasion was recalled by German commander General Alexander von Kluck, observing that a British reconnaissance aeroplane from Maubeuge was shot down.[78] Aerial combat now commenced in earnest. One RFC pilot, Lieutenant Louis A. Strange, fitted a Lewis gun on his F.20 and took off in pursuit of a German aircraft discovered in the area. However, it was to no avail since the German simply out-climbed the Farman.[79] Additional opportunities for the first aerial combat occurred when two British BE 2a's armed with Lewis guns chased an Albatros biplane for 45 minutes.[80]

---

[74] Terraine, 77-78.

[75] Edmonds, *1914*, I, 63; Baring, 22.

[76] Terraine, 77-78.

[77] Bruce, *Aeroplanes of the Royal Flying Corps (Military Wing)*, 112.

[78] Gen Alexander von Kluck, *The March on Paris and the Battle of the Marne 1914* (trans., London: Edward Arnold, 1920), 40.

[79] Lieut. Strange flew a French-designed, British-built aeroplane called the Henry Farman F.20; Bruce, *Aeroplanes of the Royal Flying Corps (Military Wing)*, 233.

[80] Raleigh, I, 327-328.

The German Advance on Paris

With the campaign now under way, the benefits of aerial observation were beginning to gain appreciation among senior commanders. In his post-war reminiscence, Field-Marshal French described his view of aerial reconnaissance during the German advance on Mons:

The opening phases of the Battle of Mons did not commence until the morning of Saturday, 22 August. The intelligence reports which constantly arrived, with the results of cavalry and aircraft reconnaissance, only confirmed the previous appreciation of the situation, and left no doubt as to the direction of the German advance; but nothing came to hand which led us to foresee the crushing superiority of strength which actually confronted us on Sunday, 23 August. This was our first practical experience in the use of aircraft for reconnaissance purposes. It cannot be said that in these early days of the fighting the cavalry entirely abandoned that role. On the contrary they furnished me with much useful information. The number of our aeroplanes was then limited and their power of observation were not as developed or accurate as they afterward became. Nevertheless, they kept close touch with the enemy, and their reports proved of the greatest value. Whilst at this time, as I have said, aircraft did not altogether replace cavalry as regards the gaining and collection of information, yet, by working together as they did, the two arms gained much more accurate and voluminous knowledge of the situation. It was, indeed, the timely warning they gave which chiefly enabled me to make speedy dispositions to avert danger and disaster. There can be no doubt indeed that, even then, the presence and cooperation of aircraft saved the very frequent use of small cavalry patrols and detached supports. This enabled the latter arm to save horse-flesh and concentrate their power more on actual combat and fighting, and to

FIGURE 9. **Aircraft recognition proved challenging for both sides in the first days of the war, resulting in incidents of friendly fire. A Maurice Farman (MF) 11 is observed flying low over infantry.** Source: SHAA, photo contained in Christienne and Lissarague, *A History of French Military Aviation.*

this is greatly due the marked success which attended the operations of the cavalry during the Battle of Mons and the subsequent retreat.[81]

French was a career cavalryman. However, his follow-on comments reflect the special significance of military intelligence transformation: "At the time I am writing, however, it would appear that the duty of collecting information and maintaining touch with an enemy in the field will in future fall entirely upon the air service, which will set the cavalry free for different but equally important work."[82]

With the Germans pressing in on Mons, the need for more information on their advance became critical. On 23 August 1914 the RFC launched 12 reconnaissance sorties with key sightings of enemy activity and reports of heavy rifle fire. One RFC pilot had been airborne by half past four that morning and was hovering over the German right flank by first light. He was back at the landing ground with his report by breakfast time. It was not a settling experience, for the RFC was on the move, traveling south in a fleet of lorries to set up a new headquarters near Mons (Casteau). Aerial observation did not operate from airfields as understood in today's terms. Aeroplanes and support were totally mobile, operating from any suitable area, known as the "landing ground." It was well past ten a.m. before the day's vital information reached General Fergusson, Commander of the BEF 5th Division. RFC observers were now seeing thousands of Germans moving southwest on the Belgian plain. Some twenty miles to the north

of Casteau, long columns of troops were passing through Lessines and veering westward. To the west another large force snaked over ten miles of road between Ath and Leuze-en Hainaut. The Germans were now a few hours march away from Mons. Over Elouges and Quiévrain on the Belgian-French border, RFC fliers saw signs of more immediate danger. An entire German army corps was there, split into four echelons like the prongs of a fork and massing for an advance. Maneuvering around smoke from burning villages, the observers sighted entire batteries of German guns moving up to cover the immediate attack. German forces were at the same time digging in along the Mons-Valenciennes railway and road, covering the high ground to the north.[83]

The RFC observers drafted their in-flight reports on enemy movements and forwarded information to commanders immediately upon landing. Confusion reigned as the battle heated up. Captain Joubert de la Ferté recalled, "We were rather sorry they [the British soldiers arriving on scene] had come because up till that moment we had only been fired on by the French whenever we flew. Now we were fired on by French and English. To this day I can remember the roar of musketry that greeted two of our machines as they left the aerodrome and crossed the main

---

[81] Field-Marshal French, 43-44.
[82] Field-Marshal French, 44.

[83] Macdonald, *1914*, 118-119.

Maubeuge-Mons road, along which a British column was proceeding."[84]

Aeroplane recognition posed a significant challenge for the early aviator. Infantry on both sides were not accustomed to aeroplanes and their role. The priority for establishing and assigning distinguishing marks of nationality became a necessity to safely operate at lower altitudes. "Union Jacks have been put on the under surfaces of the lower planes. They are not large enough and larger ones are necessary. The French have a blue spot, surrounded at an interval, by a red ring. The Germans have a black cross on some of their machines."[85] Confusion over identity eventually led to the British adopting the French-style roundel with a blue outer circle and red spot.

That afternoon of 23 August, the RFC made further reconnaissance toward Charleroi (about 40 kilometers south of Brussels) and ascertained that at least two German army corps (Guard Corps and the Guard Cavalry Division) were attacking the French Vème Armée on the line of the Sambre. When the observers returned in the evening, they presented grave news that the French center had been driven back.[86] Field-Marshal French learned in the evening when he returned to his headquarters that the French armées on the left flank were pulling back. Since the British Expeditionary Force (BEF) was still advancing, this news, coupled with further ominous reports from the RFC that German movements were putting his forces at risk, made it clear to French that the BEF must fall back as well.[87]

The next day, a German column the size of a corps was observed moving due west on the Brussels-Ninove road. It proved to be General von Kluck's Second Corps. Armed with this critical information, the British senior staff was able to map an accurate picture of the German advance.[88] That evening French met with his staff to discuss the intelligence and determine courses of action.

The battle map showed the British Army's position in relation to the advancing Germans. RFC aerial reconnaissance began to tell the story that the German commander, General von Kluck, was preparing to envelop British forces. The value of aerial observation proved itself to senior staff. The information gleaned enabled the British forces to keep ahead of the German maneuver and avoid a catastrophic situation. Decisions were quickly made. The British now commenced the famous "retreat" from Mons and headed south.[89]

Aerial observation leading up to the retreat from Mons exemplified a dysfunctional reconnaissance routine. Lyn Macdonald described an aerial operation in flux:

> For the past week the Flying Corps, like the Army, had been moving gypsy-like round France sleeping wherever chance had led them, in barns, in châteaux, in lorries, under hedgerows, even occasionally in hotels. Every day they had spent many hours in the air searching for the enemy and half as long again searching to find their own base, for there was no guarantee that the makeshift airfield the patrols had left would still be in the same place when they returned. Standing orders were not much help—Fly approximately twenty miles south and search for aircraft on the ground.[90]

Despite the confusion, the RFC was demonstrating its potential. On 25 August Major Hubert D. Harvey-Kelly and two other pilots from No. 2 Squadron forced a Rumpler Taube to land near Le Cateau.[91] Two RFC pilots from No. 5 Squadron demonstrated aviation's liaison role with the British command in a harrowing confrontation with German forces. In an effort to deliver a critical message to General Haig, they "landed between the firing lines in a field protected by a rise in the ground from the direct fire of the enemy. With the aid of a cavalry patrol

---

[84] Raleigh, I, 288-289; Terraine, 31-32.

[85] W. S. Douglas, "Notes on Equipment of Units of RFC with BEF," 27 September 1914, TNA, PRO: AIR 1/836/204/5/268.

[86] Edmonds, *1914*, I, 66.

[87] Terraine, 124-125.

[88] Raleigh, I, 301-302.

[89] Raleigh, I, 304, 314; Babington-Smith, 9.

[90] Macdonald, *1914*, 244.

[91] M. L. Skelton, "Major H. D. Harvey-Kelly, Commanding Officer, No. 19 Squadron," *The Journal of the Society of World War I Aero Historians* 16, No. 4 (Winter 1975): 365.

FIGURE 10. **Battle of Le Cateau and Battle of Guise, 26-29 August 1914.** Source: *West Point Atlas*, map 8. Courtesy, Department of History, U.S. Military Academy.

they succeeded in delivering their message to General Sir Douglas Haig, after which they returned to their machine, started up the engine, and flew away in the presence of two Uhlans, who had just ridden into the field." The quickening pace of battle created a greater challenge for successful communication within the British Corps. Every possible means of liaison, including the creation of new links with aviation assets, was being put to a critical test.[92]

On Friday, 28 August, du Général Commandant en Chef les Armées, Général Joseph Jacques Césaire Joffre, asked French to undertake air reconnaissance on the western flank of the Allied forces covering French territory.[93] RFC aerial reconnaissance during the day showed German columns sweeping southward over the Somme between Ham and Peronne, coming down on the French VIème Armée and between the Oise

and Somme west of Guise. Aerial observation reported several sightings of devastation as the Germans continued south.[94] Meanwhile, the German commander, General Alexander von Kluck, continued to employ his own aerial reconnaissance near Albert-Doullens-Amiens, but his pilots were unsuccessful in locating the retreating British forces.[95]

While the Germans were advancing on Paris, the most pressing question on the minds of Allied commanders was in what direction the German forces were heading. Unbeknownst to them, General von Kluck deviated from the original strategy of advancing directly on Paris and decided to go after the retreating Allied armies. Von Kluck's solution was to annihilate the French armies in the field without enveloping Paris.[96]

---

[92] Terraine, 150.
[93] Field-Marshal French, 91.

[94] Edmonds, *1914*, I, 241.
[95] Von Kluck, 73.
[96] Barbara Tuchman, *The Guns of August* (New York: Ballantine, 1962), 443-444.

Chapter 1: The Evolution of Aerial Reconnaissance as a Force Multiplier

Von Kluck was convinced that he had crushed the BEF and considered the time opportune to crush the French on the flanks away from Paris.[97] On the evening of 30 August, a message from the overall German commander, General Karl von Bülow, ordered von Kluck's maneuver to help von Bülow "gain the full advantage of victory" over the retreating French Vème Armée. Von Bülow's request complemented von Kluck's perspective and the decision was made to move to the southeast toward Noyon and Compiègne.[98] The next day RFC aerial observation began to see signs of the maneuver. Despite the constant flux of RFC operations as a result of continued mobility, RFC sorties over the Compiègne region managed to detect signs that the Germans were changing direction.[99] On the afternoon of 31 August, RFC pilot Captain E.W. Furse discovered the lead German cavalry corps spearheading the German Army in a new direction. A subsequent sortie from RFC No. 4 Squadron flown by Captain Pitcher and Lieutenant A.H. L. Soames confirmed the maneuver.[100] This, combined with reports from French cavalry, alerted the Allied commanders that something significant was in progress with the German forces. The Germans had reached the limit of their western advance and were now heading southeast.[101] The French Vème Armée commander, Général Charles Louis Marie Lanrezac, and VIème Armée commander, Général de Maunoury, were provided the information at the most critical moment, saving their forces from a decisive German maneuver.[102] The RFC was achieving tremendous credibility at this climactic moment.

Throughout the campaign, the French were equally aggressive in maintaining aerial observation on the advancing German forces. Unfortunately for their aviators, they not only had to find the Germans but also had to convince their seniors of what was observed. The French GQG had a variety of intelligence sources to draw from in determining the location and direction of the German advance. French agents had reported that the German campaign plan called for marching from Brussels toward southwestern Belgium, eventually heading to the Oise River. However, by 1 September the direction of the German advance did not validate that intelligence source. Aerial reconnaissance kept confirming the southeast advance. At this critical moment, French Armée headquarters staff became reticent, not following up on the new information due to apprehension that it contradicted the prevailing opinion of the GQG. With indecision, critical time was lost. French staff began withholding information, afraid to admit possible mistakes. Capitaine Bellenger, commanding the air section of the French VIème Armée, became increasingly alarmed at this state of affairs. He quickly sent one of his observers, Lieutenant André Wateau (a lawyer by training), to the GQG to make the case for their aerial observation sighting of the German maneuver in progress. Wateau successfully explained the case and at the same time took credit for the discovery.[103]

The Allies' aerial observation reporting on the German maneuver received further substantiation from a map retrieved from a German officer.[104] Armed with this more convincing information, the Allies gained an advantage. German forces were now surprised when they came into contact with British forces in unsuspected locations such as Compiègne. With the increase in fighting, the British maneuvered to a more strategic and defendable position.[105] Meanwhile, the RFC demonstrated new roles in the campaign with initial attempts at aerial bombardment. They dropped two bombs on two columns of enemy troops at a crossroad, causing confusion and a stampede.[106]

Allied aerial coverage continued to monitor the enemy's southeastward maneuver. Aviator confirmation of German movement toward

[97] Michael S. Neiberg, *Fighting the Great War: A Global History* (Cambridge, MA: Harvard University Press, 2005), 26.

[98] Tuchman, 443-444.

[99] Macdonald, *1914*, 245.

[100] Michael Occleshaw, *Armour against Fate: British Military Intelligence in the First World War* (London: Columbus Books, 1986), 56.

[101] Robert B. Asprey, *The First Battle of the Marne* (Philadelphia: J.B. Lippincott Company, 1962), 85; Edmonds, *1914*, I, 248.

[102] Occleshaw, 56.

[103] Lt Col Georges Bellenger, letter to François Baban, 6 February 1954, SHAA (translation provided by Commandant Marc Rivière).

[104] Asprey, 86.

[105] Asprey, 86.

[106] Raleigh, I, 327-328.

FIGURE 11. **Western Front Situation, 30 August to 2 September 1914, Battle of the Marne.**
Source: *West Point Atlas*, map 10. Courtesy, Department of History, U.S. Military Academy.

Noyon alerted the headquarters that the enemy was maneuvering toward Soissons on the Aisne. The BEF General Headquarters (GHQ) set up north of Paris at Dammartin-en-Goële, receiving progress reports on several German columns from RFC patrols.[107] The French were equally successful in their observations. On the evening of 2 September, French aerial reconnaissance confirmed the presence of two large German encampments (German First Army) between the Oise and Ourcq Rivers.[108] It was a brief respite for an increasingly fatigued German force. General von Kluck ordered a further march hoping to envelop the BEF. Again, the British were able to escape the trap, crossing the Marne just in time.[109]

Corporal Louis Breguet, an early pioneer in aéroplane design, accomplished one of the key observations of the day. Flying his own prototype Breguet AG 4, Breguet spotted the German Army moving to the east of Paris. The reconnaissance suggested von Kluck was moving southeast to eliminate the British corps and surprise

the French forces moving to the rear. Subsequent aerial observation by escadrilles REP 15 and MF 16 confirmed the information. The French VIème Armée was quickly dispatched to attack the German's flank.[110] Breguet's report further confirmed General von Kluck's intentions were shifting. Capitaine Bellenger complemented the reports by personally flying in the sector. His challenge continued to be with the GQG. This time the intelligence assessment did not confirm the aerial observation. French 2[e] Bureau sources showed von Kluck was working according to the Schlieffen Plan and was maneuvering to encircle Paris.[111] Bellenger was now forced to call on additional aviators to testify to the ongoing observations, while trying to maintain an aggressive aerial observation sortie rate.[112] The Germans under von Kluck also continued their aerial reconnaissance effort. On 2 September, they were ordered to monitor Allied forces across the Marne.[113]

Capitaine Bellenger's luck changed when he made contact with the British Third Army. He

[107] Edmonds, *1914*, I, 270; Macdonald, *1914*, 245.
[108] Bellenger letter, SHAA.
[109] Tuchman, 445.

[110] Davilla and Soltan, 3.
[111] Christienne and Lissarague, 79.
[112] Bellenger letter, SHAA.
[113] Von Kluck, 93.

Chapter 1: The Evolution of Aerial Reconnaissance as a Force Multiplier

FIGURE 12. **Western Front Situation, 5–9 September 1914, Battle of the Marne.** Source: *West Point Atlas*, map 12. Courtesy, Department of History, U.S. Military Academy.

finally gained an audience that listened to what he had acquired from the aerial observations. He subsequently went to Général Joseph Simon Gallieni, commander of French forces within the region of Paris, to emphasize further the meaning of observations from aerial reconnaissance at this critical time. Gallieni proved invaluable in accepting Bellenger's recommendations and taking the time to persuade Général Joffre of their value.[114] Bellenger always retained a high regard for Général Gallieni: "He is one of the rare generals that believe in aviation; he is a man of decision and is not afraid of responsibilities."[115] Général Gallieni's success with Général Joffre helped to direct French maneuvers to counter the Germans at the Marne. This significant event was the final death knell of the German Schlieffen Plan.[116]

RFC aerial reconnaissance of 3 September also substantiated French observations on the German maneuvers. The BEF Intelligence Di-

rector, General Sir George Mark Watson Macdonogh, was profuse in his praise: "A magnificent air report was received disclosing the movements of all the Corps of the 1st German Army diagonally South East across the map toward the Marne." The resultant battle between the French VIème Armée under Général Michel de Maunoury and the German army under General von Kluck helped thwart the Germans' offensive strategy. Key to the battle was the effective position of the BEF, which permitted exploitation of a gap between the German armies in the region, eventually forcing a German retreat.[117]

Despite the positive response to aerial observation, other intelligence sources performed an even more key role. Ironically for the Germans, Allied radio intercepts of German transmissions describing their maneuvers were critical in the overall analysis. Partial credit went to the German "lack of discipline in radio operation." By 4 September French intelligence confirmed "The German First Army, neglecting Paris and our Sixth Army, before which nothing

---

[114] Bellenger letter, SHAA; Hodeir, 108.
[115] Christienne and Lissarague, 78.
[116] Porch, 73.

[117] Occleshaw, 57.

has shown itself, continues its march toward the Marne." German fatigue and logistical shortfalls were also discerned. General von Kluck's order to withdraw, which was being monitored by the French, gave evidence to the French radio intercept analysts that the German retreat had commenced.[118] Finally, Général Joffre personally learned of the Russians' defeat at Tannenberg through a radio intercept of a German transmission that described the destruction of three Russian corps, the capture of two corps commanders and 70,000 other prisoners, while announcing, "The Russian Second Army no longer exists."[119]

The Battle of the Marne

At the Marne, the Germans attempted to swing around the western end of the Allied line and envelop it. Concurrently, they planned to break through the Allied center, forcing the remainder of the western half of the line back to Paris, thereby completing the process of envelopment. The French had a similar plan—flank around the west end of the German line, break through the center, and split the German forces. The two flank attacks began on the plain north of Paris, while the two attempts to break the enemy's center were staged on the low plain of Champagne.[120]

A French aerial observation report reflected extensive activity and a concern for France's future:

> Came down at Tours-sur-Marne to report to Général Foch; then at Heitz-le-Maurupt, to the staff of Langle de Cary. Second reconnaissance on Somme-Suippe and Cuperly; landed at Saint-Dizier. Today's was the maximum speed of retreat attained in one day. How far are we to retreat? To the Loire, some say, to the Central Massif, according to others. It is terrible![121]

Meanwhile, French radio intercept units were providing extensive reporting. In the course of 14 days during the German advance on the Marne, the French radio intercept service picked up approximately 350 radiograms from the cavalry corps under General Johannes Georg von der Marwitz alone. The French radio intercept service did not fail to note the movement of the German First Army toward the north in order to avoid being outflanked by French Général Maunoury's VIème Armée.[122]

RFC aerial observation was also accelerating by keeping track of every German corps of the First Army. Information was forwarded to the GQG and marked on the battle map. The whole of the German right wing had now thrust itself into the arc of a vast circle, with the French VIème Armée on one side of it, the IIIème and IVème Armées on the other, the Vème and IXème Armées and BEF at the base. The time to attack, Joffre decided, had come.[123] The next day French reconnaissance kept seniors informed amid a flurry of activity:

> Saint-Dizier, Reims, Fismes, Bergeres-les-Vertus, where we descended to report to Général Foch, who is in command, it is said, of three army corps, forming the IXème Armée which is from this time to come between us and the army of Franchet d'Esperey on our left. We saw four German army corps today marching in order of battle across the camp of Châlons and the neighborhood of Reims. What feelings it aroused! But what a splendid spectacle it was! I dropped two bombs on a large bivouac and saw dense smoke rising from the very center of it. The bombs had gone home. We then went on to Saint-Remy-en-Bouzemont near Vitry-le-François, where we descended; we lunched off a crust of bread, then went on to Brienne-le-Château. I heard afterwards that my bombs had wounded a captain and three men.[124]

---

[118] Porch, 75.

[119] Tuchman, 429; Porch, 74.

[120] Douglas Wilson Johnson, *Topography and Strategy in the War* (New York: Henry Holt and Company, 1917), 31.

[121] Brindejonc des Moulinais, "Journal de Bord, Guerre Aérienne," in Charles Henri Le Goffic, *Général Foch at the Marne: An Account of the Fighting in and near the Marshes of Saint-Gond* (trans., New York: E. P. Dutton and Company, 1918), 199-200.

[122] Flicke, I, 23-24.

[123] Terraine, 205.

[124] Des Moulinais, 199-200.

FIGURE 13. **Escadrille commander Capitaine Zarapoff in the cockpit of a Blériot XI.** Source: SHAA, B90.2389.

The early escadrilles were often shifted around the battlefield to support the ongoing battle. Among the early Allied aerial inventory, the Blériot XI was a favored airframe because it could be rapidly disassembled, placed in closed containers, and reassembled for transport to a new sector. In a two-month period (September to November 1914) escadrille BL 3 moved to seven locations along the front. It was not without hazard. On 5 September escadrilles supporting Général Foch's IXème Armée were ordered to Mailly-Champagne (near Reims) to support operations in the sector. At seven in the morning, escadrilles BL 3 and BL 10 assigned to the IXème Armée were operating from the aerodrome at Belfort in eastern France. The 12 Blériot XI's at Belfort had a support unit of motor-drawn trailers readied to provide necessary transport should the aéroplanes have maintenance problems. The fragile aéroplanes were wearing down and required delicate handling. Exposure to the cold night air and rain caused structural problems as the airframe wood expanded and canvas stretched.[125] However, the urgency of the moment required that the escadrille reach Mailly (approximately 250 kilometers to the northwest) in the shortest time possible. The Blériot XI escadrille station commander, Capitaine Constantin Zarapoff, set off from Belfort by road with supplies and equipment while his pilots took off with their machines for the aerodrome at Mailly.

Unfortunately, one pilot was killed while taking off. Two other pilots then stayed behind to bury him. Of the twelve aéroplanes in the escadrille, nine eventually landed at Mailly.[126] The stresses on the older airframes were beginning to take their toll. New airframes were ordered to handle the demands of both mobility and endurance. Conversion to more effective aircraft such as Morane-Saulnier Ls, Caudron G.3s, and G.4s would take place in late 1914. For the moment, they had to rely on fragile aéroplanes enduring greater stresses.[127]

On 6 September the British reorganized their aerial reconnaissance resources to reflect the current battle situation. French reallocated three of the RFC aeroplanes directly to the British I and II Corps for tactical reconnaissance—the first time that aircraft were decentralized under Corps authority. The realignment enabled the British commanders to observe the retirement of the German II Cavalry Corps on Coulommiers (due east of Paris) and established that the French Vème and VIème Armées were engaged in battle.[128]

---

[125] The Blériot XI flew at 60 mph and carried enough fuel for a 2½-hour flight. Armament then consisted of one carbine. Blond, 163-164; Davilla and Soltan, 56.

[126] Blond, 164.

[127] Davila and Soltan, 56; Weiller, in de Brunoff, 63; Blond, 164.

[128] Sir John Slesser, "Air Reconnaissance in Open Warfare," TNA, PRO: AIR 75/131; Edmonds, *1914*, I, 299.

Meanwhile, French reconnaissance of the Marne region reported that the Germans were occupying Châlons and the district of Ay due east of Paris.[129] Upon hearing this, Général Gallieni ordered the French 7ème Division to move up to the front line. Rail could only move half of the division. The French had only 250 Army motor vehicles available, resulting in the famous employment of Paris taxis to move the troops of the XIVème Brigade of the 7ème Division that evening to Nanteuil-le-Haudouin.[130] In all, they transported five battalions of 4,000 infantry a distance of thirty miles.[131]

The Germans were now being pressed by Allied maneuvers. Fighting created a gap between the First and Second German Armies, forcing them to stabilize their position. To compensate for this discrepancy, the cavalry corps under General von der Marwitz was ordered to create a screen between the two armies. However, the deception unraveled due to the lack of discipline among the German radio operators who transmitted in the open and provided a clear picture of the situation while being monitored by French radio intercept units. This intelligence breakthrough provided French and British forces the opportunity they needed to counter the German advance at its weakest point.[132] On 7 September aerial reconnaissance confirmed the general impression that the Germans were withdrawing two corps to the north, despite sightings of cavalry and infantry in the same general area of the battleground.[133]

Allied aerial reconnaissance on 8 September monitored the German withdrawal. A large number of infantry were observed waiting their turn to cross the river near La Ferté-sous-Jouarre.[134] French aerial reconnaissance provided a broad overview of the situation. A French pilot recalled:

> Reconnaissance on Vitry and Châlons. We were told to watch the arrival of enemy reinforcements on the Châlons highroads; other machines were to watch the east of Vitry-le-François. The battle was raging below, following a line decidedly east and west. To the right this line seemed to incline toward the northeast of Verdun. To the west, it passed by Sompuis and inclined toward the Marshes of Saint-Gond. A second flight with twenty-three shells: I dropped them on the heavy batteries to the east of Vitry; then I disturbed an artillery brigade (echelons of ravitaillement [resupply]), which scattered in every sense, but reassembled as soon as I had gone. I discovered the positions of twenty-four guns on the line to the west of Vitry. I marked them on the map at 1/80,000 and informed the corps concerned.[135]

The next day's morning reconnaissance (9 September) reported that "large hostile forces" were marching north of Château-Thierry.[136] A noon report placed the Germans about four miles from Château-Thierry with additional small columns on roads to the east all going north. In this moment of high drama, RFC aeroplanes were employed to discover their own BEF positions as well as provide aerial observations of the British flanks. At the same time, RFC aeroplanes were keeping watch on the French units in the area. The nearest troops of the French Vème Armée were seen that morning near Viels-Maisons (24 kilometers south of Château-Thierry) moving northeast away from the BEF.[137] Both French and British aerial reconnaissance remained active with a French liaison to GHQ who passed on the first indications that German movements were under way. The reporting was further substantiated by British aerial reconnaissance. At 1535 hours on 9 September, Captain Grey and Captain Boger of RFC No. 5 Squadron took off in an Avro to reconnoiter the area in front of the II Army Corps. They landed at approximately 1700 hours and reported indications of the withdrawal of von Kluck's left from opposite the French VIème Armée west of the Ourcq River. Additional afternoon aerial reconnaissance discovered an eight-mile-long column marching northward from Lizy (northwest of Soissons on the river Aisne) at the back of the

---

[129] Des Moulinais, 200.
[130] Blond, 170-172.
[131] Blond, 182.
[132] Flicke, I, 23-24.
[133] Edmonds, *1914*, I, 309-311.
[134] Edmonds, *1914*, I, 319.

[135] Des Moulinais, 200-201
[136] Edmonds, *1914*, I, 333.
[137] Edmonds, *1914*, I, 333.

Chapter 1: The Evolution of Aerial Reconnaissance as a Force Multiplier

Ourcq battlefield and then other columns of transport and troops retiring north-northeast on La Ferté-Milon (southwest of Soissons on the river Ourcq). The ground on the left flank of the BEF in the angle between the Marne and the Ourcq was reported clear.[138] With each report greater attention focused on accuracy. Debate arose over aerial reconnaissance's "provisional analysis of how it will be employed tactically, for the benefit of those commanders that have to use it."[139] The lack of headquarters staff and intelligence personnel familiar with the limits of aerial observation was showing strains. Inflated reporting was becoming an issue of concern.[140] German aerial reconnaissance kept General von Kluck apprised of the situation, reporting on the advance of four long Allied columns maneuvering toward the Marne with advance troops on the line at the river Ourcq at Nanteuil-Citry-Pavant.[141]

On 10 September the RFC reported that near Troesnes (on the river Ourcq above La Ferté-Milon) German artillery and cavalry were retreating at a rapid pace:

> Villers-Cotterêts was blocked with trains and all the rail sidings were very full. Later that evening additional reporting observed numerous bivouacs around Soissons, where the troops coming from the south were assembling.[142] French reporting confirmed the fact that the Germans continued to withdraw, on our left [IVème Armée], toward the camp of Mailly, there were no forces opposing us. There was a gap, a space between the two German armies, with only some cavalry a long way behind. Our division of cavalry was in the camp at Mailly. The obvious thing was for us to drive in a division or a corps if possible. Général Dubois was charged with this task. We watched closely for the moment when this movement

could be effected without being noticed by the enemy, and we flew over Sompuis, Mailly, Sommesous, Lenharree, Coole [flight went west-northwest in an area 20 kilometers southwest of Châlons-sur-Marne] in spite of heavy clouds. And we never saw any German reserves. Second reconnaissance with Capitaine Thiron. We alighted beside the XXIst Corps, informing them as to the positions of batteries and troops, telling them that our troops were too far in the rear, that our guns did not carry far enough, and that there were no troops on our left. While we were at Saint-Ouen [Saint-Ouen-en-Brie, approximately 20 kilometers east-southeast of Paris], the général sent us a message that the cavalry had signaled an enemy division in front of him. We told him that that was not the case. But we proposed to make another reconnaissance. We set off, saw a French infantry division which was marching slowly forward, sustained by the artillery. We also saw the French cavalry division in the camp at Mailly. We flew low down, for it was late. No Germans. We returned to carry our information to Saint-Ouen. We had made three reconnaissances. Returned to Brienne [Brienne-le-Château] for the night.[143]

That evening Field-Marshal French estimated that the Battle of the Marne had concluded. Now the Battle of the Aisne was to be fought.[144] The outcome of aerial observation at the Marne was that it had secured for itself an integral role in battle. Daily observation defined the battlefield. Both French and RFC sorties had been successful in reporting the movements of the maneuvering German advance in a timely manner. The observer cadre made the difference, with inputs covering enemy forces sighted, status of bridges and road networks, and other information critical to the command's battlefield awareness. The aerial observation role also had another benefit. British aerial reconnaissance not only covered German positions; it also clarified locations of the

---

[138] Slesser, TNA, PRO: AIR 75/131; Edmonds, *1914*, I, 340.

[139] Unknown source quoted in Slesser, TNA, PRO: AIR 75/131.

[140] Slesser, "Air Reconnaissance," TNA, PRO: AIR 75/131.

[141] Von Kluck, 136.

[142] Edmonds, *1914*, I, 359.

[143] Des Moulinais, 201-202.

[144] Field-Marshal French, 140.

British vanguard. The Allied commanders were impressed. Général Joffre heaped praise on the RFC, saying, "Please express most particularly to Marshal French my thanks for the services rendered to us every day by the English Flying Corps. The precision, exactitude, and regularity of the news brought in by them are evidence of their perfect organization and also of the perfect training of pilots and observers."[145] For the British, the campaign had an additional impact. Those engaged in the early campaign became the strongest proponents of aerial reconnaissance for the remainder of the war.[146]

The Battle of the Aisne

After the conclusion of the Marne campaign, Field-Marshal French and his staff remained optimistic, persisting in their plans to push across the Aisne. French wired Lord Kitchener, the British Secretary of State for War, "Very heavy rain falling to-night, making roads most difficult. Should much hamper enemy's retreat. Pursuit continues at daybreak."[147] The greatest threats to aerial reconnaissance at this critical time, in early September 1914, were torrential rains that made aerial operations impossible. GHQ was desperate to learn where the Germans were digging in. All they could do was hope for an improvement in the weather so that flights could resume. One storm was so violent that British aeroplanes were tossed into the air and wrecked. Unfortunately for RFC squadrons arriving at Saponay (about 20 kilometers north of Château-Thierry) landing ground, the storm wrecked half of the unit. The No. 3 Squadron diary recalled:

> Before anything could be done to make the machines more secure, the wind shifted, and about half of the total number of machines were over on their backs. One Henri Farman went up about thirty feet in the air and crashed on top of another Henri Farman in a hopeless tangle. BEs of No. 2 squadron were blowing across the aerodrome and when daylight arrived and

the storm abated, the aerodrome presented a pitiful sight. The Royal Flying Corps in the field could not have had more than ten machines serviceable that morning.[148]

Aerial reconnaissance now transitioned from recording maneuvers to pinpointing targets for the artillery. At the beginning of the Battle of the Aisne, on the morning of 13 September, the BEF attempted to continue the pursuit of the German forces over the Aisne and succeeded in taking a bridge at Venizel (directly east of Soissons on the river Aisne). However, the Germans had entrenched several hundred yards behind the crest of the ridge north of the Aisne. By mid-morning, it was clear to British commanders that considerable artillery support was required. Additional problems occurred when initial rounds were fratricidal. That night, a British attack could not break through German positions that were being reinforced with more troops. The British were suddenly at a disadvantage since the Germans were staying put in terrain that gave them dominance of the area. Artillery directed at German lines proved ineffectual due to the topography of Aisne valley, which provided excellent cover for German machine guns.[149]

Since the Battle of Mons, the Germans had experimented with aerial observation to increase artillery effectiveness. Now the British realized that they needed any available resource to increase their artillery's effectiveness. At the Aisne, they turned to the aeroplane to meet that urgent need. The British Army had tried aerial spotting for artillery prior to the war, but had not followed up on enhancing the capability.[150] However, there were not enough Allied aeroplanes to meet the immediate demand. The stalemate at the Aisne portended the battle to come. The RFC was still recovering from damage suffered during the recent storm. The critical lack of aerial and cavalry reconnaissance prompted the GHQ to work with mere assumptions about the threat location instead of relying on actual information.[151] That

---

[145] Général Joffre quoted in Raleigh, I, 334-335
[146] Raleigh, I, 324.
[147] Nikolas Gardner, *Trial by Fire: Command and the British Expeditionary Force in 1914* (Westport, CT: Praeger, 2003), 86.

[148] No. 3 Squadron diary, quoted in Macdonald, *1914*, 300.
[149] Gardner, 87.
[150] Gardner, 92-93.
[151] Macdonald, *1914*, 310.

FIGURE 14. **One of the great innovators of the aerial targeting support for artillery was Captain Douglas Swain Lewis. His recommendations revolutionized British artillery operations through the squared map and clock code.** Source: Peter Mead, *The Eye in the Air* (London: Her Majesty's Stationery Office, 1986).

night Field-Marshal French and staff were under the impression that the German Army was retiring. GHQ issued orders the following day directing "the Army will continue the pursuit tomorrow at six a.m. and act vigorously against the retreating enemy."[152] The next morning, the strongly entrenched German forces were successful in holding back the BEF attack and conducting a counterattack.[153]

15 September was frustrating for Field-Marshal French and the BEF. They made no progress on the battlefield and had to endure an intense German barrage. French remained convinced that the German withdrawal was, in fact, over. He wired Lord Kitchener that evening, "We have been opposed not merely by rear-

guards but by considerable forces of the enemy which are making a determined stand in a position splendidly adapted to defense."[154] At 2030 hours Operation Order 26 finally brought the advance to a close, stating "The Commander-in-Chief wishes the line now held by the Army to be strongly entrenched, and it is his intention to assume the general offensive at the first opportunity."[155] The British military historian Brigadier-General James E. Edmonds noted that Operation Order 26 "proved to be the official notification of the commencement of trench warfare." For the rest of September, the BEF endured daily artillery bombardments as well as sporadic artillery infantry attacks.[156]

The demands on aerial observation to locate artillery targets during the Battle of the Aisne now assumed greater prominence. The requirement soon transformed cartography. Artillery targeting required detail that pre-war maps lacked. It took the initiative of several RFC members to meet the challenge. Major Geoff Salmond, Commander of No. 3 Squadron, was approached by Captain Douglas Swain Lewis concerning a role for the radio. Lewis was convinced that radio communication could increase the reconnaissance advantage and better serve the needs of artillery units. Geoff Salmond, an experienced artilleryman prior to his transfer to aviation, understood that artillery fire demanded accuracy. The two set up a radio experiment with the artillery that was an immediate success. They created two maps lined with 400-yard squares. One map was provided to the battery commander involved in the experiment, the other to Lewis. The successful demonstration initiated a cartographic revolution for the British. From then on, maps were reconfigured to serve aerial-field artillery radio coordination.[157] The "squared map," as it was called, revolutionized British maps issued to artillery and aviators. The numbered and lettered squares allowed aerial reconnaissance to effectively identify the target area and relay information to the battery. The process of finding the target was called pinpointing. Soon the

---

[152] Gardner, 88.
[153] Gardner, 88.

[154] Field-Marshal French quoted in Gardner, 88-89.
[155] Gardner, 88-89.
[156] Gardner, 89.
[157] "Papers Collected by Air Vice Marshal Sir W. G. H. Salmond," TNA, PRO: AIR 20/705.

entire battle area was covered by a series of contiguous sheets.[158]

The experiment was then continued with British forces at the front. On 15 September the British III Corps assigned its aeroplanes to the divisional heavy and howitzer batteries. Later that month the British 3rd Division reported to its higher headquarters at II Corps that an RFC radio-equipped aeroplane had successfully supported the artillery in acquiring direct hits on several previously hidden German positions. By early October the following procedure described by the staff of the I Corps prevailed throughout the BEF: "The hostile batteries are first located as accurately as possible by aeroplane; these results are then communicated to divisions and an hour at which fire is to be opened is fixed. At that hour the aeroplane again goes up, observes the fire, and signals any necessary corrections

FIGURE 15. Interest in aerial photography grew as aviators acquired photographic souvenirs for loved ones such as this shot of the famous Chartres Cathedral. Source: Service Historique de l'Armée de Terre (SHAT).

by wireless."[159] However, despite these significant successes, the equipment was a liability over time. A few weeks later when the British advanced to the Ypres sector, the radio equipment began to malfunction. It required extensive maintenance with each sortie.[160]

The genesis of aerial photography within French aviation circles involved a mixture of innovation, mission necessity, and personal

---

[158] Col George O. Squier, "Intelligence Services of the British Army in the Field," 16 February 1915, 5, Squier Papers, USAMHI; Jones, II, 85-87.

[159] Gardner, 93.
[160] Anthony Farrar-Hockley, *Death of an Army* (London: Arthur Barker, Ltd., 1967), 110.

Chapter 1: The Evolution of Aerial Reconnaissance as a Force Multiplier

FIGURE 16. **Capitaine Barés was the first chef de l' aéronautique à GQG. However, his animosity toward aerial photography in the beginning of the war did not aid Bellenger's attempts to make aerial reconnaissance more effective.** Source: SHAA, photo contained in Christienne and Lissarague, *A History of French Military Aviation.*

detect and locate the batteries. The results were beneficial, alerting the French GQG that aerial reconnaissance was better served with a camera on board.[162]

While success was demonstrated with artillerymen on board the aéroplane, the actual liaison with the artillery unit was challenging. The pilot tried conducting various maneuvers with the aéroplane to link up with the battery. That proved confusing at first. Subsequent means of controlling the rounds included using a specific brand of tracer round to allow the aerial observer the ability to track the shell toward impact. However, attention to the challenge soon met with success.[163] Still in September 1914, French pilots succeeded in spotting the artillery of a German army corps in maneuver. They identified the location for the French artillery at Thiaucourt (Thiaucourt-Regniéville), whose subsequent barrage destroyed half of the corps, a feat recognized and cited by Général Joffre.[164]

The stalemate at the Aisne set the stage for significant evolution of aerial reconnaissance. Taking aerial photographs was on the minds of several RFC aviators. On 15 September 1914 an RFC No. 3 Squadron pilot, Lt. G. Pretyman, took five photographs of German gun positions on the Aisne. Photo quality at this early stage was not impressive, but the experiment demonstrated that aerial photographic technology was possible in a combat environment.[165] Major H. R. M. Brooke-Popham, commander of the RFC No. 3 Squadron, was the driving force for his squadron's efforts to employ photography. His pre-war photographic trials laid the groundwork for the first aerial photographs of the German forces.[166] However, existing camera technology did not function well in the new combat environment.

motives. The first aerial photographers were amateurs. Their intent was not to confirm or complement aerial observation in progress. It was to generate souvenirs for loved ones showing off the "pretty landscapes" of the front lines. Such acts of bravado soon caught the attention of artillery staff, who saw the opportunity of using photography as a means of "investigating German batteries."[161] French aviation also applied its aerial resources to artillery spotting. By mid-September, as the French faced a standoff against German forces at the Reims-Vosges sector in eastern France, French artillery personnel demonstrated an important initiative. Artillery personnel flew with the escadrilles to gain a better idea of the German artillery positions. It was during these sorties that the French artillery observers carried their own personal cameras to

---

[161] Labussière, in de Brunoff, 183 (translation provided by James Davilla).

[162] Alain Dégardin, "Un Observateur de la Guerre 1914-1918: Eugène Pépin," in *Vues d'en Haut: La Photographie Aérienne pendant la Guerre de 1914-1918* (Paris: Musée de l'Armée, 1989), 17 (translation provided by Commandant Marc Rivière).

[163] Weiller, 68.

[164] Christienne and Lissarague, 80.

[165] Nicholas Watkis, *The Western Front from the Air* (Stroud, UK: Sutton Publishing, Ltd., 1999), 8-9; Jones, II, 88-89; Edmonds, *1914*, I, 420; A. J. Insall, *Observer: Memoirs of the R.F.C., 1915-1918* (London: William Kimber, 1970), 152.

[166] Jones, II, 88-89.

The "press" type cameras of the Pan-Ross pattern became available later that year.[167]

French acceptance of aerial photographic reconnaissance commenced after British recognition of its value. Despite the notable success with the Marne observations, Capitaine Bellenger still met resistance from GQG staff. He continued his struggle to institutionalize aerial photographic reconnaissance. In October 1914, he attempted to create a new photo service, promising to provide maps of the enemy. To some, aerial photography represented a fad, not an integral part of the military. His counterpart at GQG, Capitaine Barès, chef de l'aéronautique a GQG, responded to one query with "use a Kodak that you can purchase from the local shop. Don't ask the government to pay for this."[168] Bellenger continued to find cameras, organize a lab, create a team of photographic interpreters, and teach aerial observers the techniques of aerial photography. All were essential, but advocacy for his efforts was still absent.[169] In post-war reminiscences, Bellenger recalled his confrontations with GQG. In December 1914, in an attempt to gain favor with Général Henri Berthelot, 2e Bureau, by showing aerial photos from various missions, Bellenger was told with a sarcastic comment that "he already had a map." Berthelot concluded the conversation with "I don't care about your pictures."[170]

The solution to GQG's intransigent attitude was found by Bellenger's counterpart, Lieutenant Grout of the French Artillery. Grout developed the right contacts at GQG and proceeded to establish the seminal French aerial reconnaissance program. While flying as an observer on a reconnaissance mission on 7 October 1914, Lieutenant Grout photographed German batteries threatening Fort Douaumont in the Verdun sector. The photographs aided French artillery in subsequent targeting. Grout also examined methods for transferring the information onto a map. The success of the mission resulted in Grout being placed in charge of an elite element to establish aerial photography's role. He proceeded to test cameras on aérostat platforms. One such

FIGURE 17. **Lieutenant Maurice Marie Eugène Grout, the leading French pioneer of aerial photography, acquired command trust early in the war, resulting in his establishing the French Section photo-aérienne (SPAé).** Source: SHAA.

design evolved into the mainstay 120 cm camera. Another long-term legacy from this advance group was the introduction to aerial photography of one of the greatest aerial photographic interpreters of the war, Lieutenant Eugène Marie Edmond Pépin.[171] Grout's persistence in proving aerial photographic reconnaissance continued into the next year, providing a successful example for not only the French staff, but an increasingly curious British staff.[172]

As the Marne campaign came to its conclusion, aerial reconnaissance was also on the minds of the German General Staff. General von Kluck

---

[167] Insall, 151-152.
[168] Capitaine Barès quoted in Hodeir, 109.
[169] Hodeir, 109.
[170] Hodeir, 8.

[171] Dégardin, in *Vues d'en Haut*, 18.
[172] Labussière, in de Brunoff, 183; Carlier, 16.

Chapter 1: The Evolution of Aerial Reconnaissance as a Force Multiplier

blamed the campaign's failure on several issues including the lack of critical information from aerial reconnaissance. "Both cavalry and air reconnaissance have failed during the past few days."[173] Von Kluck was relieved from command along with the senior German commander, General Helmuth Johannes Ludwig von Moltke. Dismissal did not result in a transfer for these senior officers. Von Moltke was ordered to stay in the background while General Erich von Falkenhayn commenced command of the Aisne campaign.[174]

The stalemate at the Aisne continued into late September with British commanders resolved to transfer the BEF to the left of the Allied line. If the war was to go in favor of the Germans, they wanted to be in place to best defend British interests. Their choice for the remainder of the war was to defend the coast and critical ports. On the afternoon of 1 October, GHQ directed the Army to move north to Flanders, ordering three British corps to withdraw in succession.[175] In preparation for the move, Field-Marshal French directed the RFC Commander, Brigadier-General Henderson, to establish aerial reconnaissance toward Antwerp. Field-Marshal French then expedited the move of all the British forces to the northern theater.[176]

The First Battle of Ypres signified the termination of mobile warfare on the Western Front for the next four years. The rapidly evolving battlefield demonstrated to commanders on both sides that mobility was a secondary consideration to firepower. As the Germans headed north in the "Race to the Sea" toward the British lifeline of the Channel ports, they were stopped through an effective combination of artillery and infantry fire. Artillery preparation had assumed the dominant position in warfare.[177]

The German General Staff had envisioned the Flanders plain as ideal territory for enveloping the Allied armies. The plain consisted of an abundant network of roads, railways, and canals that could transport and supply a great army.[178] However, geological and topological factors were the ultimate gauge of how the battle would be fought. A clay formation typified the Flemish landscape, which when wet became heavy, sticky mud.[179]

For the next four years, Flanders became the stereotype of all the horror associated with the Great War. The German attempt to take Ypres led to a series of catastrophic battles fought over the worst imaginable terrain. Damage from artillery fire was greatly reduced when shells exploded in the mud. Shell holes filled with water that did not drain away, turning the battlefield into an almost impassable morass that prevented any advance prepared by the ceaseless bombardment. Flanders was a logistical nightmare. Munitions and other supplies could not be moved in time to support an advance properly. Reinforcements floundered in the mire, while attacking forces were forced to relinquish hard-fought positions. Artillery suffered from an inability to operate off the roads. Light field artillery required macadam-like material to convert the shell-torn route to one meeting the weight and bulk demands for its movement. A British artillery officer, reflecting on the continual challenge, remarked, "I am carrying forward my guns and ammunition, the material for making my road as I go along, and the material for fortifying my new position.... I am half expecting orders to bring along an acre of ground with me, too."[180] "Stationary warfare now the rule" summed up the condition for most of the war on the Western Front.[181] In light of the topological horror, aerial reconnaissance assumed prominence. It served as the catalyst for the aerial photograph.

As positional war established itself with networks of trenches from the Belgian coast to the Swiss border, aerial observation assumed a permanency with employment of aérostats. The French had originally discontinued their efforts in developing captive balloons (captif ballon) in 1911 in favor of aéroplanes. The Germans had

---

[173] Von Kluck, 166.

[174] Macdonald, *1914*, 310.

[175] Gardner, 89.

[176] Field-Marshal French, 189.

[177] J.B.A. Bailey, *Field Artillery and Firepower* (Oxford: The Military Press, 1989), 128-129.

[178] Douglas Wilson Johnson, *Battlefields of the World War, Western and Southern Front: A Study in Military Geography* (New York: Oxford University Press), 7.

[179] Johnson, *Battlefields of the World War*, 11.

[180] Johnson, *Battlefields of the World War*, 23-24.

[181] Count A. E. W. Edward Gleichen, ed., *Chronology of the Great War, 1914-1918* (3 vols., London: Ministry of Information, 1918-20; reprint, 3 vols. in 1, London: Greenhill Books, 2000), 38.

FIGURE 18. **Race to the sea, September — October 1914.** Source: *West Point Atlas*, map 13. Courtesy, Department of History, U.S. Military Academy.

continued to develop a captive balloon variant known as the Drachen. These proved of great value to the Germans when the war commenced in August 1914. The aerial pioneer behind manned kite observation, Captaine Saconney, quickly rectified the shortfall in French balloon observation (ballon observateur) by assembling an initial set of aérostats to support French armées engaged in battle against the Germans. By October 1914, the French had assembled a force of 30 aérostats (3 sections of 10 captif ballon)

providing the front lines with a fixed platform to monitor the Germans and support artillery. By early 1915 the French had an additional 10 captif ballons at the front.[182] The innovative aerial pioneer Capitaine Saconney not only led the design of the ballon observateur but also configured its operational employment for combat, determining suitable missions such as observation, artillery ranging, verification of demolitions, and sector reconnaissance.[183] The aérostat also

[182] Christienne and Lissarague, 69.
[183] Christienne and Lissarague, 70.

Chapter 1: The Evolution of Aerial Reconnaissance as a Force Multiplier

had an advantage over the aéroplane. It could be connected directly to the headquarters or artillery battery via telephone, reducing communication time to a minimum. The best captif ballon used in the Great War, the Caquot (designer Capitaine Albert Caquot), was designed and deployed to the front in early 1916. The Caquot became the standard for balloon observation for the remainder of the war.[184] The British Army acquired its first balloons from the Royal Navy and fielded its first balloon observation unit in May 1915.[185]

With the decline and eventual termination of mobile warfare, observation by aéroplane assumed a more vigorous role. The French Aviation Militaire expanded from 31 flights to 65, most of which served the reconnaissance mission. Each French flight consisted of approximately six aéroplanes. By March 1915, the French had 53 flights of aéroplanes.[186] The Aviation Militaire now comprised 16 army reconnaissance and pursuit flights, 16 aerial bombardment flights, and 30 army corps observation flights.[187]

The last phase of mobile warfare cemented a relationship that continued for the remainder of the war. As the forces adopted positional warfare, there was an impetus for greater cooperation between aerial observation and the traditional infantry and artillery forces. The principle that "Photography is the basis of good artillery" started to evolve.[188] After the war Air Vice Marshal (AVM) Geoff Salmond stated that aerial photography owed its existence to radio and artillery.[189] His seminal efforts with Captain Lewis established a base for subsequent aerial observation efforts to support artillery. However, officers from the artillery arm were still slow to accept the critical role of aerial observation, despite the successes at the Aisne. Greater liaison was required to communicate aerial reconnaissance capabilities to both artillery and infantry senior officers and staff.[190] The pioneer in British aerial photography, John Theodore Cuthbert Moore-Brabazon, reflected later in life that the artillery culture felt that its ballistics were an exact science and did not require assistance from the aviation community. Moore-Brabazon related that it took one of the first British aerial celebrities, Major Harvey-Kelly, to drive home the value of aerial reconnaissance for the artillery. One day during the Battle of the First Ypres, Harvey-Kelly transmitted via radio a "very curious message." The British had moved several large mortars, the pride of the artillery, to the front. Near the Ypres battleground was a large lake (Bellewaarde Lake) well within RFC aerial coverage. During a mortar barrage, Harvey-Kelly commented on the accuracy of the mortar fire: "If anybody is firing on the middle of Bellewaarde Lake, he is hitting it." Moore-Brabazon stated that this dry assessment did more to convince the British Army to rely on British aviation to help direct artillery fire than any other effort.[191]

The experiences of the first five months of combat did little to impress British commanders of the value of their aerial reconnaissance. By the time the First Battle of Ypres had commenced, it was clear among the members of the staff that intelligence and operations had to learn to coexist. The BEF's first senior intelligence officer, General Macdonogh, was probably the most brilliant of any who served in the forces for the duration of the war. Despite conclusive information provided to British commanders, there was always an air of suspicion. When Field-Marshal French was informed that the Germans had reinforced their position at Ypres with three new reserve corps, he flew into a rage at Macdonogh: "How do you expect me to carry out my plans if you will bring up these bloody divisions!"[192] It took technological advancement in aerial photography to lend credibility to the assessments and eventually convince the operators to accept the information provided.

In early 1915 the U.S. military attaché to Great Britain, who later commanded the U.S.

---

[184] Christienne and Lissarague, 69-70.
[185] Edmonds, *1914*, I, 303.
[186] Christienne and Lissarague, 82.
[187] Christienne and Lissarague, 82.
[188] Unknown British officer quoted in Harold Porter, *Aerial Observation: The Airplane Observer, the Balloon Observer, and the Army Corps Pilot* (New York: Harper & Brother Publishers, 1921), 167.
[189] "Papers Collected by Salmond," TNA, PRO: AIR 20/705.

[190] Jones, II, 82; Lamberton, 10.
[191] J. T. C. Moore-Brabazon, *The Brabazon Story* (London: William Heinemann, Ltd., 1956), 88.
[192] Occleshaw, 28.

Army Signal Corps for the remainder of the war, Colonel George O. Squier, commented in his report on the changing face of battle:

It is strange, this modern war, when a [modern] strong fortress like Antwerp falls in ten days and then a simple trench dug in the open field can completely stop the German Army at its best. At Ypres 4 corps stopped something like 8 or 10 corps, including the Prussian Guards. What are we going to do about fortresses in the future? One thing is clear, concealment comes first, and protection is secondary.[193]

Squier's comments were prophetic. The evolution of warfare in the coming year brought aerial reconnaissance to the point of threatening the prevailing military mindset. The battlefield had been transformed.

---

[193] Squier, "Intelligence Services," Squier Papers, USAMHI.

Chapter 1: The Evolution of Aerial Reconnaissance as a Force Multiplier

LATE 1914 TO OCTOBER 1915:
AERIAL PHOTOGRAPHIC RECONNAISSANCE TAKES THE STAGE

Evolution of British Aerial Reconnaissance Operations

Leadership among the Allies was not easily convinced of the value of photos. Aerial photography involved trial by error, with lessons learned at the grass roots, not directly convincing the leadership of its value to intelligence and battle planning. Early in the war the commanders sent out cavalry as their eyes and ears, and quickly found this too costly. Even the cavalry leaders saw the preeminence of the air photo. Photographers quickly became a valuable adjunct to battle, particularly to artillery, where information miles back from the front—provided the location of support elements, of trenches, dugouts, boyaus, observation posts, machine guns, barbed wire, rails, trails, and more.[1]

The British Army underwent an evolution in thinking during this first year of the war. Despite the fact that they were seasoned veterans from combat in South Africa and engaged in a variety of military operations around the world, the British had to come to terms with major combat involving large formations against an equivalent adversary. They became subject to the conventional military thinking of the early

20th century as defined by the French and Germans. When the BEF commenced its campaign in France its initial maneuvers transitioned to holding ground at all costs. Departing significantly from its experiences in previous military campaigns, where the British commander and staff were in the middle of the fight, its leadership and thinking were now away from the battlefield in a protected sanctuary. Positional warfare prolonged this configuration. Access to information to make the necessary decisions now came through evolving aerial observation technology, to include the aerial photograph.[2]

The changeable role of aerial observation witnessed in the opening months of the campaign quickly settled down to established operations and a refinement of the aerial organization. By the end of 1914, the RFC established its Wing organization to support the ongoing mission of aerial reconnaissance in a positional war. Each wing, commanded by a lieutenant colonel, was charged with the formation and training of squadrons capable of reinforcing the air units already operating in the field. The institution of RFC wings now provided a structure that aligned with the British Army being supported, providing both reconnaissance and offensive mission capability. The British Corps commanders were the responsible echelon to

---

[1] Grand Quartier Général des Armées du Nord et du Nord-Est, État-Major, *Study and Exploitation of Aerial Photographs* (Trans. and issued by the U.S. Army Division of Military Aeronautics; Washington, DC: GPO, 1918), 7.

[2] Farrar-Hockley, 54-56.

task the wing for tactical reconnaissance.[3] The RFC now saw its resources providing reconnaissance beyond the front lines into the enemy rear echelons. To gain an appreciation of the extent of the operation, the RFC directed that each unit keep a "War Diary" on missions flown and other significant events of the day. The wing also provided any information on landing ground locations should the squadrons be required to move.[4]

As the RFC moved to support the Army and Corps, it further demonstrated the aeroplane's ability to go beyond the front lines and gather strategic information necessary to define the German adversary's intention. The initial five operational RFC squadrons (Numbers 2, 3, 4, 5, 6) that had deployed to France in August were now tasked to search for rolling stock at all railroad stations in the region so that commanders could have a possible indication of offensive buildup in the Ypres sector.[5] This function demonstrated a strategic purpose that would remain a priority for aerial observation.

Refining the aerial observation operations also called for a greater understanding of the army echelons that required information. In December 1914, the RFC imposed rules of operation so that the missions comprised both artillery and tactical artillery reconnaissance, with artillery support being preeminent. The squadron landing ground was to be as close to the artillery headquarters as possible. The RFC also encouraged division counterparts to locate their headquarters as close to the landing ground as possible. Aerial reconnaissance communication with British divisions was accomplished through the RFC liaison at the location, using a variety of communication devices to include dropping a message, communicating by radio or lamp, or having the aeroplane fly vertically (directly above) the target and drop

a smoke ball.[6] The RFC liaison was assigned with the advance guard and provided with a light tender (truck) and two motorcyclists. The officer reconnoitered landing grounds at intervals of five miles along a road over which the division was to advance. When a landing ground was selected, a "T" was placed on the ground and a report of the location forwarded to the division headquarters.[7]

French Advances in Reconnaissance

Developments in the first months of the war led to rethinking the role of aerial observation resources. The existing fleet of aérostat dirigibles was relegated to the background and soon disappeared from the scene. As the immediate postwar French assessment stated, "The science of aeronautics was reduced to that of aviation."[8] In 1915, captif ballons became a common feature of the stagnant front lines. The captif ballon also employed a new technique for aérostier [balloon observers] survivability, the parachute. Aerial observation now had a permanency with the aérostat platform.[9]

The French commenced organizing their aviation resources to suit the changing parameters of warfare. Aviation Militaire supporting the GQG now had a permanently assigned chief (chef) of the Service Aéronautique. The senior aviation presence was further established with each armée acquiring a chief of the Service Aéronautique on its staff.[10] Aviation Militaire determined that aerial reconnaissance resources were to be assigned within the French armées to better support operations. Each armée acquired two strategic reconnaissance escadrilles equipped with either MF 11s or Morane-Saulnier L's.[11] An armée cooperation escadrille was also assigned to each CA along with a company of ballon observateurs.[12] The French would later expand escadrille responsibilities to support artillery regiments with

---

[3] Insall, 18; "Memorandum on New Organization of the Royal Flying Corps," 29 November 1914, TNA, PRO: AIR 1/751/204/4/8.

[4] "Memorandum of New Organization of RFC," TNA, PRO: AIR 1/751/204/4/8.

[5] "Orders for Reconnaissance from 24th Oct. 1914 to 28th Nov. 1914," TNA, PRO: AIR 1/751/204/4/8.

[6] "Organization of the Royal Flying Corps British Expeditionary Force, December 1914," TNA, PRO: AIR 1/751/204/4/8.

[7] "Organization of the Royal Flying Corps, BEF," TNA, PRO: AIR 1/751/204/4/8.

[8] "Aeronautics," June 1921, NARA, RG 120, Box 819, 1-2.

[9] "Aeronautics," June 1921, NARA, RG 120, Box 819, 2.

[10] "Aeronautics," June 1921, NARA, RG 120, Box 819, 3.

[11] Davila and Soltan, 3

[12] "Aeronautics," June 1921, NARA, RG 120, Box 819, 3.

Caudron G.3 and G.4 aéroplanes.[13] As the campaigns of 1915 progressed, they realigned aerial resources to provide fighter support. In an interesting twist, a few multi-seat Caudron G.4 and Nieuport 11 aéroplanes were assigned to a new unit, the *Groupe de Chasse de Malzéville*, to defend other escadrilles from German bomber attacks.[14] As the year progressed, the existing line of aerial reconnaissance platforms fell victim to improved German fighters. French industry was producing an early type of aerial reconnaissance platform; designs for multi-seat, long-range reconnaissance aéroplanes such as the Caudron R.4 and G.6 were not produced until 1916. As 1915 concluded, this situation proved deadly for the units on the line flying older airframes.[15]

The French developed a more effective infrastructure for aerial photography in late 1914. The success of Capitaine Grout's efforts with aerial photography and the inclusion of French artillerymen serving on aéroplanes with cameras soon caught the attention of senior French

FIGURE 19. **Allied reconnaissance acquired a new generation of aeroplanes such as the Caudron G3 to support artillery targeting and battle planning.** Source: Jim Davilla, MA35860.

commanders.[16] Général Beliu, Director of the Service Aéronautique, approved a directive establishing *Section photo-aérienne du Group des divisions d'entraînement* (SPAé du GDE), one assigned to each armée. It advised that personnel with a background in photography should be considered for this assignment.[17] Grout established the initial SPAé architecture and commenced operations on 1 December 1914. The SPAé brought significant change to the production of photographic products for military operations and achieved even greater benefit by clearly demonstrating the potential of aerial photographic reconnaissance for senior officers

---

[13] Davilla and Soltan, 3.
[14] Davilla and Soltan, 4.
[15] Davilla and Soltan, 4.

[16] Dégardin, in *Vues d'en Haut*, 17.
[17] Grand Quartier Général Défenses et Différents Points du Territoire … Dossier 7, "Service Aéronautique, No. 5034," SHAA, A19.

and staffs.[18] Manning for each SPAé consisted of an officer, a draftsman (British term: draughtsman), three photographers and a driver.[19] With Capitaine Grout's SPAé now in operation, several initiatives became reality. The French hand-held 26 cm camera (13 x 18 cm photo plate) became operational after several months of development. The 26 cm was followed by aerial cameras of greater capability that became the mainstay of French (and later U.S.) aerial photography—the 50 cm camera and 120 cm camera. To further equip the SPAé's to support the operations near the front, the French developed a mobile photographic laboratory configured on a *camion* (truck). By the start of 1915, the Section photo-aérienne (SPAé) concept not only was taking hold within the French armées; it served as well as an intellectual catalyst for the British.[20]

The British became aware that the French were collecting information on trenches from aerial photographs and were transposing sketches from aerial observation onto their tactical maps. When trench warfare commenced, the first maps of the battleground were crude imitations of French and Belgian maps that captured topographical and tactical detail. Later, aerial photography contributed details to the map features.[21] As a courtesy, the French started to forward their aerial photographs to the British GHQ, labeled as an "aerial map." They showed the British that the French were earnest about aerial photography and were making major progress in its support of ongoing military operations. As a result, RFC Headquarters sent the innovative Major Geoff Salmond to visit the French unit responsible for the aerial coverage.[22] Besides observing French progress in camera technology, Major Salmond quickly recognized that the French were resolute about integrating aerial photography into their battle planning.[23] Grout's seminal French SPAé program successfully demonstrated that aerial photography served the Allied effort. The British were spurred to follow suit and develop their own program.

The French realized that their battlefield maps were inadequate to keep up with the significant changes under way in the field. Sketches from aerial observers were insufficient. Accuracy was called for and the memory of the air crew was limited at best; they could not enhance the results from the primitive hand-held cameras some used. The need for more information on the German artillery increased the demand to improve aerial reconnaissance. French staffs came up with a solution. They expanded the role of the *Plan Directeur*, a basic artillery map that became the mainstay of French intelligence and operational targeting for the remainder of the war.[24] With the Plan Directeur, battlefield information now provided a framework for operations. As post-war French assessments of this period reflected, "aerial combat became more and more general but the escadrilles were not yet specialized in pursuit, bombing, or observation."[25] French aerial observation now included hand cameras to record enemy troop movements. Artillery spotting became more refined compared to the previous attempts at signalling through unique maneuvers. French air crews initiated the use of either flares (*fusées*) or colored flags to signal the French artillery units to correct their aim. Also, French radio known as *télégraphie sans fil* (TSF) commenced operation to provide the air crews with a means to rapidly signal any necessary alterations of fire. TSF became the primary means to conduct artillery spotting for the remainder of the war. TSF experienced problems like any new technology, with unintelligible or incomplete transmissions during the sortie.[26]

Procedures institutionalized in 1915 increased the effectiveness of the SPAé's ability to interpret aerial photography and disseminate the information quickly to the combatant. Plan-

[18] Carlier, 17, 19; Hodeir, 110.

[19] Labussière, in de Brunoff, 183.

[20] Carlier, 110.

[21] Peter Chasseaud, "1:10,000 Regular Series Trench Maps," in *British Western Front Mapping 1914-18: Summary of Geodetic Situation with Reference to the Operations Maps Actually in Use in 1918*, in *The Imperial War Museum Trench Map Archives CD-ROM* (London: The Naval & Military Press and The Imperial War Museum, 2000).

[22] "Papers Collected by Salmond," TNA, PRO: AIR 20/705. Peter Mead, *The Eye in the Air: History of Air Observation and Reconnaissance for the Army, 1785-1945* (London: Her Majesty's Stationery Office, 1986), 66.

[23] Jones, II, 88.

[24] Weiller, in de Brunoff, 64-68.

[25] "Aeronautics," June 1921, NARA, RG 120, Box 819, 3.

[26] Weiller, in de Brunoff, 63, 68; Davilla and Soltan, 220.

ners for aerial photographic missions strove to achieve a common map reference scale to allow information from the print to be quickly transferred to the combat map. The scale of choice became the 1/10,000. The timeliness of the Plan Directeur targeting map soon benefited from this procedure.[27]

The mainstay French aéroplanes employed for aerial observation were the Henri Farman (HF) 20 and Maurice Farman (MF) 11. Both were ideal designs for aerial reconnaissance and artillery spotting, with the cockpit forward of the wings, yet vulnerable due to limited armament and a slow operating speed.[28] Both aéroplanes exemplified the

state of aerodynamic art. Their airspeed was relatively slow (HF 20: 165 kilometers per hour/102 miles per hour; MF 11: 118 kilometers per hour/73 miles per hour). However, they both possessed respectable mission endurance for observation, each being able to operate for around three hours.[29] Barring any threat, aerial observation could be maintained for extended periods of time. Examples of French aerial photographic work in early 1915 reflected the manner by which the escadrille functioned. On 30 January 1915, an HF 20 escadrille flew numerous reconnaissance sorties over enemy batteries at Harville, took aerial photographs over Eparges and Saint Rely, and used a TSF-equipped machine to direct artillery fire over the I[ème] Armée sector.[30] In a single day in February 1915, one MF 11 aéroplane flew two reconnaissance missions, three artillery spotting missions, and took several photographs of enemy camps.[31]

[27] Carlier, 18.
[28] Davilla and Soltan, 220.

[29] Davilla and Soltan, 211.
[30] Davilla and Soltan, 207.
[31] Davilla and Soltan, 220.

The British Adopt Aerial Photography

French military seniors were quick to share the aerial photographic experience with their British counterparts. French advances in aerial photography would prompt the British, as traditional competitors, to keep up and demonstrate an equal proficiency. The genesis of the British aerial photographic program stemmed from the accomplishments of two "civilians" who had come on board with the British military at the first call. Lieutenant J.T.C. Moore-Brabazon from the RFC and Lieutenant Charles Duncan Miles Campbell from the Intelligence Corps, GHQ, comprised the core team that institutionalized British aerial photography. Moore-Brabazon was a leader in the British aviation community, winning the 1909 Daily Mail prize for the first all-British machine that could fly a circular mile; Campbell was a photographic genius, later responsible for help-

FIGURE 21. **Charles Duncan Miles (C.D.M.) Campbell was the genius behind the British development of aerial photography. Together with J.T.C. Moore-Brabazon and Victor Laws, the British were able to establish a viable aerial photographic reconnaissance program in early 1915.** Source: Roy Nesbit, *Eyes of the RAF* (Phoenix Mill, UK: Alan Sutton Publ., 1996), 17-18.

ing the U.S. Air Service stand up a photographic capability.[32] At the start of the war, both Moore-Brabazon and Campbell had been assigned with the RFC's No. 9 Squadron, known for the application of new technologies such as the use of radio. They were ordered to RFC headquarters on 23 September 1914 to assist in the incorporation of new technologies in ongoing operations.[33] Also arriving at No. 9 Squadron was Sergeant-Major Laws, who was transferred from the anti-aircraft unit in December. He served a multitude of assignments such as carpenter, motor driver, and motor mechanic. His photography skills still remained in the background.[34]

Moore-Brabazon and Campbell's first challenge was to assuage the skepticism of a well-established British military culture. It required expert knowledge on the subject, an ability to educate an obstinate culture of military professionals, and the constant pressure of proving success every step along the way. Moore-Brabazon recalled the transformation under way within the British military. "Considerable difficulty was experienced at once in getting the Army to realize the full possibilities of photography, but slowly they came round to understand the advantages that were being put before them for a trench warfare proposition."[35] His subsequent memoirs provided further reflection on the transformation:

> The reluctance of the older Services to adopt new devices and inventions sprang from fundamental principles that were little understood, but were not unworthy. First of all, officers are up-to-date, progressive and technically minded; but they look upon the struggle with an enemy quite objectively, with no personal dislike at all, even though they might lose their lives at any moment. They take the greatest exception to an enemy who refuses to play according to the rules as understood or who, in their opinion, in-

[32] Raleigh, I, 170; Maj E. G. Toye, RFC, "History of Photography," TNA, PRO: AIR 1/724/91/1.

[33] Baring, 46.

[34] Nesbit, 16-18.

[35] Lt Col J. T. C. Moore-Brabazon, "Photography in the RAF," TNA, PRO: AIR 1/724/91/1.

Chapter 2: Aerial Photographic Reconnaissance Takes the Stage

dulges in a dirty trick.... Aerial photography was a thing that had not been done before, and to expose the whole set-up behind the enemy's lines was to invade a privacy that had always been accorded the enemy, never mind that it happened because nobody could do anything about it.[36]

The air crew eye was effective only up to a certain altitude. The ultimate gauge of effectiveness for the observation mission was the ability of the observer to detect and remember what was observed. In the early days pilots recorded their information by sketching on cavalry sketchboards attached to the forearm or on kneeboards. British air crews were to euphemistically refer to these "trench-sketching" sorties as "close reconnaissance and photography."[37] However, this did not adequately serve the information needs of the military commanders. Army demands for tactical and strategic information by far surpassed the initial capabilities of aerial observation. It was time to turn to available technology to serve the demand.[38]

The impetus for aerial photography improvement rested with the junior officers. Major Brooke-Popham's No. 3 Squadron was recognized for its role in demonstrating the utility of the aerial photograph. Lt. Pretyman's first attempt at photographing German artillery at the Aisne proved to the British that it could be done in a wartime environment.[39] With the coming of positional trench warfare, further refinement of aerial photography was accomplished. Again, the RFC No. 3 Squadron, now under the command of Major John Salmond (brother of Geoff Salmond), led the way. No. 3 Squadron at the time was working with the British 4th Corps in the Ypres sector. One of No. 3 Squadron's aerial observers, Lieutenant C.C.

Darley, had acquired an Aeroplex camera (with a 12-inch lens) and proceeded to take photographs from his aeroplane. His initial efforts were poor due to fogged plates and surface scratches on the film surface caused by metal plate holders. What impressed everyone was Darley's outstanding initiative. He conducted the entire process on his own. Not only did he take his own photographs, he also established his own photographic laboratory to produce the prints from his sorties. Darley purchased his own chemicals in Bethune, developing the slides in an emergency dark room converted from the stables of the château where he and several squadron personnel were billeted. He had one assistant, "who knew nothing about photography." When Darley finished developing his own photographs, he completed his own interpretation of the prints. Darley persevered in his efforts to get aerial photography recognized by spending every evening personally showing the results to staff members at the nearby Corps Headquarters or Divisional Headquarters.[40] Darley later recalled that his photography improved immensely thanks to Campbell's loaning him a Pan-Ross camera with a Mackenzie Wishart plate holder.[41]

In January 1915, Major Geoff Salmond recognized that an aerial camera was a significant improvement over the array of personally owned cameras being employed. Salmond selected Moore-Brabazon, Campbell, Flight Sergeant Laws, and 2nd Air Mechanic W.D. Corse to build a photo section equivalent to what the French had established under Grout.[42] They were instructed to work out with the wings the best form of organization and camera for air photography. Besides Geoff Salmond, the British team was supported by two influential members of the senior RFC staff. Colonel (later General) Hugh "Boom" Trenchard, RFC commander after Henderson, became impressed with the military potential of aerial photography. Moore-Brabazon recalled Trenchard going "about with these photographs in his pocket, trying to make people use them."

[36] Moore-Brabazon, *The Brabazon Story*, 92-93.

[37] Malcom Brown, ed., *The Imperial War Museum Book of the First World War: A Great Conflict Recalled in Previously Unpublished Letters, Diaries, Documents, and Memoirs* (London: Sidgwick & Jackson; and Norman, OK: University of Oklahoma Press, 1991), 134.

[38] Lee Kennett, *The First Air War, 1914-1918* (New York: The Free Press, 1991), 36-37; Jones, II, 87; James Barnes, *From Then Till Now; Anecdotal Portraits and Transcript Pages From Memory's Tablets* (New York: D. Appleton-Century Company, 1934), 426.

[39] Jones, II, 88-89.

[40] 1st Lieut C. C. Darley, "Notes on Photography in No. 3 Squadron, Royal Flying Corps, December 1914 - End of February, 1915," TNA, PRO: AIR 1/2395/255/1; Insall, 154.

[41] Darley, "Notes on Photography in No. 3 Squadron," TNA, PRO: AIR 1/2395/255/1.

[42] Raleigh, I, 170; Toye, "History of Photography," TNA, PRO: AIR 1/724/91/1.

FIGURE 22. **One of the greatest aeronautical figures of the Great War, Colonel (later General) "Boom" Trenchard was an influential promoter of aerial photography, supporting Moore-Brabazon's and Campbell's initial efforts.** Source: Imperial War Museum (IWM), courtesy of Nicholas Watkis.

He gave Geoff Salmond's section every encouragement.[43] Moore-Brabazon recalled his possessing a "quite terrifying" personality. Trenchard was a large man, possessing an enormous voice, by which he earned his nickname, "Boom."[44] It was said that junior officers were reduced to abject misery when rebuked by Trenchard.[45] The other was the RFC General Staff Officer, Colonel (later General) Frederick Sykes, who acquired support for the team to establish the first British Photo Section.[46]

One of the first objectives for the British photo section was establishing an effective role for aerial photography within the RFC as well as deciding on the best type of camera for aerial operations. Moore-Brabazon, Campbell, and Laws were ordered to the RFC 1st Wing on 16 January 1915. The initial plan was to first have the team work with the 1st Wing for a month, then proceed to the 2nd Wing for another month. Following the two visits, they were to put forward a scheme to RFC Headquarters on the best course of action for aerial photography implementation. The team accomplished its purpose early while at 1st Wing. Based on the recommendations of Laws, the three produced an assessment that each RFC headquarters should include a Photo Section assigned at the Wing. The Photo Section was to be equipped with a newly configured photographic lorry. The success of Lt. Darley in demonstrating aerial photography helped influence the team to determine that the responsibility for taking aerial photographs was to be levied on the aerial observers. Each RFC squadron was to have a camera available at all times for supporting ongoing operations as well as acquiring photos of any targets of opportunity. The RFC flight echelon acquired two cameras for ready aerial reconnaissance missions. After each sortie, all the photographs taken by squadrons were to be sent to the Photo Section at Wing Headquarters for development, fixing, printing and distribution.[47] The question of where photographic plates were to be developed prompted the decision of what echelon should serve as the photographic hub. Based on discussions between Moore-Brabazon, Campbell, and Darley, the decision was made by Colonel Trenchard that RFC-manned wing (not squadron) Photo Sections were to support each British Army.[48]

In January 1915, duties of the RFC's Photo Section were set to include: general control of all photographic work under the instruction of the Wing Commander; developing and printing plates at the Wing Headquarters; keeping a record of every negative and every print's date,

[43] Trenchard was later called the "Father of the RAF." Jones, II, 88; Richard T. Bickers, *The First Great Air War* (London: Hodder & Stoughton, 1988), 72; Mead, 66; Watkis, 9; Babington-Smith, 10; Moore-Brabazon, *The Brabazon Story*, 94.

[44] Moore-Brabazon, *The Brabazon Story*, xx.

[45] Nesbit, 22.

[46] Photo Section became the term that was used by the British. Moore-Brabazon, "Photography in the RAF," TNA, PRO: AIR 1/724/91/1.

[47] "Capt. [C. D. M.] Campbell's Notes on Aerial Photography," TNA, PRO: AIR 1/7/6/98/20; Nesbit, 22.

[48] Darley, "Notes on Photography in No. 3 Squadron," TNA, PRO: AIR 1/2395/255/1; "Papers Collected by Salmond," TNA, PRO: AIR 20/705.

hour, and place of exposure; height at which the photograph was taken; condition of the atmosphere and light; speed of shutter; and photographic stop used. The Wing Headquarters also kept a map showing battleground locations photographed and cross-referenced to files.[49] The initial success of establishing the RFC's Photo Section at 1st Wing led Moore-Brabazon and Campbell to be recognized for their astute assessment of what best served RFC aerial photographic reconnaissance. They produced the standard for what constituted the equipment and personnel for the photographic laboratory.[50] As Moore-Brabazon remembered, the results were so good that the whole of the Army began to "scream for more and more photographs." [51]

As aerial photography's popularity increased, it became necessary to expand production by adding a second photo section under the direction of Moore-Brabazon at the RFC's 2nd Wing. With the RFC's photographic support architecture quickly coming into place, Campbell was transferred back to London to establish an aerial photographic function for the Ministry's War Office. What was needed for the British military was an RFC training program for aerial photography and established personnel requirements for photographic officers. It became an arduous assignment for Campbell. The War Office was not attuned to the need for aerial photography, resulting in lack of sponsorship to the challenges that lay ahead.[52]

The Aerial Photographic Breakthrough

Throughout this period the RFC aggressively carried out reconnaissance and artillery spotting, despite unfavorable winter weather. Hand-held photographs covered the front lines to a depth of some 1,500 yards. It was a period of transition for the GHQ. Skeptics still were unconvinced that aerial photographs could generate a detailed picture of German trenches and barbed wire. It was Allied planning for an early offensive in 1915 that spurred acceptance of aerial photography. The RFC's No. 3 Squadron, commanded by Major John Salmond, and including the innovative aerial observer, Lt. C.C. Darley, started receiving queries on the layout of German trench networks opposite the British sector. It fell on Lt. Darley to accomplish this objective. He constantly updated his aerial map with each additional sortie. In the first days of February, Darley's photographs were provided to French and British staff officers planning an operation south of the town of Neuve Chapelle. The battleground comprised the brickfields and railway triangle south of La Bassée canal.[53] A significant finding was construction of a new German trench that would evidently serve as a launch point for a subsequent attack. The discovery created a major impression, resulting in the senior staff's modifying the plan of attack. The photographs also significantly aided the planning by determining the precise junction between the attacking Allied troops. On 6 February, the Allied attack commenced and achieved its objectives in capturing important ground and acquiring a considerable number of German prisoners.[54]

Momentum toward imputing value to aerial photography had significantly increased. The success of Lieutenant Darley's photographs at the La Bassée Canal sector prompted a vigorous effort by the RFC to employ aerial hand-held cameras to acquire as much aerial coverage of the battleground as possible. Following the initial proselytization about the potential of the aerial photograph, the GHQ staff became the strongest proponent, maintaining "an unswerving loyalty to Air Photography, and were ever pressing the R.F.C. for more and more photographs."[55] By the second week of February, Darley was acquiring excellent photos with his hand-held camera of the Neuve Chapelle area and fusing them together to develop an "aerial map" mosaic. Darley's format was immediately

[49] HQ, Royal Flying Corps, "H.Q. R.F.C. c/165/1," TNA, PRO: AIR 1/834/204/5/240.
[50] Toye, "History of Photography," TNA, PRO: AIR 1/724/91/1.
[51] Moore-Brabazon, "Photography's Part in the War," TNA, PRO: AIR 1/724/91/2.
[52] Toye, "History of Photography," TNA, PRO: AIR 1/724/91/1.

[53] Darley, "Notes on Photography in No. 3 Squadron," TNA, PRO: AIR 1/2395/255/1.
[54] Darley, "Notes on Photography in No. 3 Squadron," TNA, PRO: AIR 1/2395/255/1; Jones, II, 88-89; Insall, 152-153.
[55] Toye, "History of Photography," TNA, PRO: AIR 1/724/91/1.

FIGURE 23. **Initial aerial reconnaissance mapping at Neuve Chapelle was accomplished by aeroplanes such as those observed at the RFC No. 4 Squadron's St. Omer aerodrome.** Source: Peter H. Liddle, *The Airman's War, 1914-18* (Poole, UK: Blandford Press, 1987), 41.

accepted by Major John Salmond and taken to the sector army headquarters (recalled by Darley to be the Indian Corps Headquarters) where it generated considerable interest. Colonel Trenchard now got involved. He escorted Darley to a conference of British and French generals deliberating on Neuve Chapelle. Général Joffre was so impressed with the photographic array that he requested that he be included in future distribution of photographs taken by the RFC.[56] Darley's initiative accomplished one of the most significant intelligence production feats of the war. He clearly demonstrated to a British staff lacking training and awareness of aerial photography that an aerial map created from a mosaic of photographs did an excellent job of portraying the battlefield and significantly improved battle planning. The timeliness of aerial photographs contributed to a last-minute alteration of the Allied attack plan and spurred both French and British to collaborate on aerial photographic techniques. Not only did the hand-held photographs show the extent of German preparations; they also served as the catalyst for con-

structing the first British trench map. There was another result attributable to Darley's initiative. It prompted the British command to task Moore-Brabazon and his team of photographic experts to build the prototype "A" Type camera that became the breakthrough for British aerial photographic technology.[57]

Neuve Chapelle—The First Imagery-Planned Battle

After 180 days of conflict, the Allies started to institutionalize their preparation of the battlefield with photographic coverage. The initial pho-

---

[56] Darley, "Notes on Photography in No. 3 Squadron" TNA, PRO: AIR 1/2395/255/1; Jones, II, 88-89; Insall, 152-153.

[57] Insall, 152-153; Jones, II, 89.

FIGURE 24. **Stabilized Front at Neuve Chapelle and Ypres.** Source: *West Point Atlas*, map 32, Courtesy, Department of History, U.S. Military Academy.

tographic successes by the British design team were timely. Field-Marshal French recognized that a 1915 spring offensive in a location where the British had a tactical advantage was necessary. The decision was made to conduct an offensive at Neuve Chapelle, just south of the Belgian-French border.[58] Field-Marshal French appointed General Douglas Haig to command the British forces. His senior intelligence officer, Brigadier-General John Charteris, played a major role in the BEF's acceptance of aerial photography. Charteris was initially overwhelmed by the aerial photographic source. His 24 February 1915 diary entry mentioned that intelligence preparation for the upcoming battle at Neuve Chapelle

now included this new significant source. "My table is covered with photographs taken from aeroplanes. We have just started this method of reconnaissance, which will I think develop into something very important."[59]

The aerial photographic trench map (mosaic) covered the German trench network to a depth of 700 to 1,500 yards facing the British First Army.[60] The "big picture" planning base became a precedent for combat operations in the war.[61] Moore-Brabazon recalled, "At first, the R.F.C., in order to show the real value, made actual maps of the trenches from their photographs, and sent them out in large numbers. Map-making not, however, being the work of the R.F.C., this was eventually handed over to the Army, and we supplied the photographs from which they marked in the trenches."[62] Constructing the trench map also involved the traditional map-making element of the British Army, the Royal Engineers. Their field surveys soon complemented the aerial coverage.[63] Mosaics were carefully traced to a corresponding 1/5,000 scale map that included a detailed plan of attack as well as details for artillery targets. An impressive 1,500 copies of the trench map were sent to each corps prior to the attack. It proved a masterful stroke for intelligence. Analysts now could study the battleground and make assessments on the potential main line of approach of a German attack. For the first time in the history of the British military, the British Army went into action with a total picture of the hidden intricacies of the enemy defenses. When the first assault commenced, British bombing parties were able to make their way without loss of time to their separate objectives.[64]

The first day of fighting showed the benefits of the careful cartographic planning based on the mosaic. Charteris commented on the Neuve Chapelle battle, "Our Intelligence show was successful, in that we found the Germans exactly as we had located them, and their reinforcements arrived to the exact hour that we had predicted they

[58] Brig Gen John Charteris, At *G.H.Q.* (London: Cassell and Company, Ltd., 1931), 77.

[59] Charteris, At *G.H.Q.*, 77.
[60] Jones, II, 90-91.
[61] Babington-Smith, 9; Lamberton, 10; Watkis, 2.
[62] Moore-Brabazon, "Photography in the RAF," TNA, PRO: AIR 1/724/91/1.
[63] Charteris, At *G.H.Q.*, 77.
[64] Jones, II, 90-91; Edmonds, *1915*, I, 85-86.

would."[65] For the first time in the war, a British artillery barrage was employed to help the infantry advance, resulting in the immediate objective being attained with minimal losses. At a critical juncture of the battle, an RFC airman made a very useful report on the location of the advancing British infantry, which enabled the forces to penetrate deeper into enemy territory.[66] Despite the significant gains in planning made from employment of aerial photography, victory was not secured. Neuve Chapelle's failure was credited to obstacles that remained in place despite a heavy artillery barrage. The experience led the British commanders to consider a strategy of annihilation: destroying everything in the path of the attacking infantry regardless of damage to the sector terrain or the absence of surprise.[67] Artillery was now the key weapon in the arsenal for subsequent campaigns and aerial reconnaissance became an integral partner to ensuring success.

Despite the disappointment at Neuve Chapelle, British intelligence gained a positive reputation. Charteris mentioned for the first time the growing influence of photographic interpretation on the evolving battlefield: "I have now two regular majors under me, and three temporary officers—a barrister, a diplomat, and a stockbroker. They are all good linguists, keen and clever, so my work grows easier—only it never stops. The barrister's especial job is studying air photographs, at which he is getting extraordinarily expert; finding out all manner of things, some very important, from them."[68] Neuve Chapelle also initiated a standard that carried through the remainder of the war. The British and their Canadian Commonwealth counterparts crafted their first intelligence summary to support operations at the front. This was the first time that a British division generated a regular daily intelligence summary for its combatants on the line.[69]

The British improved their production and dissemination of intelligence to serve the increasing demand. British aerial reconnaissance

FIGURE 25. **The success of the "A" Type camera provided the British with their first trench map derived from aerial photography.** Source: Nicholas Watkis.

now started producing panoramic photographs that enabled the cartographer to draw out the current features of the landscape. Once that was accomplished, the British produced lithograph templates. Colonel Squier, U.S. attaché, reported that the daily cycle had aerial photographic coverage arriving around 2130 hours. During the night the staff completed a master copy and readied 100 copies for distribution by 0600 hours the following morning.[70] The distribution was extensive and included the lowest echelons of the British forces. In the British sector during the battle of Givenchy (Givenchy-lès-la-Bassée), every pla-

---

[65] Charteris, *At G.H.Q.*, 82.
[66] Lamberton, 10.
[67] Bailey, 131.
[68] Charteris, *Haig*, 82.
[69] Maj J. E. Hahn, *The Intelligence Service within the Canadian Corps, 1914-1918* (Toronto: The Macmillan Company of Canada, 1930), xv-xvi.

[70] Col George O. Squier, "The Map Room and Printing Room," 20 April 1915, Squier Papers, USAMHI.

50 • SHOOTING THE FRONT

Chapter 2: Aerial Photographic Reconnaissance Takes the Stage

toon commander and all staffs from battalions rearward acquired copies of an intelligence-produced panoramic sketch of the battleground.[71]

The Second Battle of Ypres

Following Neuve Chapelle, the next major battle took place to the north at Ypres in April 1915. This battleground witnessed some of the cruelest fighting of the war. Ypres took warfare to another dimension: mass casualties were inflicted through modern technology. Ypres acquired the reputation as the first battleground to witness the widespread use of chemical warfare on the Western Front. To the total surprise of the Allied combatants, the Germans had released heavy, asphyxiating chlorine gas from the trenches. The wind carried it onto the French line held by a territorial division and African troops. This innovation in warfare was observed by aeroplanes from the No. 6 Squadron based at Poperinghe (Belgium). However, the observations were of no consequence.[72] What intelligence had been collected on the chemical threat had not benefited the defenders. Despite the chaos caused by the gas attack among the Allies, German forces were unable to conduct a breakthrough. The legacy of chemical munitions became another sad fact that contributed to the overall misery of positional war. Only now it meant increased casualties without an appreciable gain in territory.

It was at Ypres that intelligence at the front was put to the test. When the Germans did advance under the chemical cloud, intelligence was reduced to a flurry of hurried telephonic exchanges to figure out what was occurring. It took reliance on aerial photography and map distribution to provide structure for intelligence under these extreme conditions. British intelligence officers at battalion, brigade, and division were now sensitive to acquiring as much information as possible not only to prepare for the battle but also to ensure that there was enough intelligence to preempt any further disruption caused by new and more dangerous weapons such as chemical munitions.[73] It was intriguing to note senior British staff confidence in locating chemical munitions through aerial photographic coverage. On 28 April 1915, Charteris remarked:

> We have had to take over some more of the French line, and have not yet regained all the ground that was lost. It will take some considerable time before we get things straight again in that part of the line. It does not, however, immediately concern our own army – except that we must now expect to have the same methods used against us; that is mainly a medical job. As far as I am concerned it involves only another thing to look for in air photos – and fortunately preparations are easily distinguishable in these photos – and a careful record of wind currents, for this gas depends entirely upon a favorable wind. We shall of course now have to use gas ourselves, as soon as we can get it going.[74]

Ironically, the surprise attack at Ypres eroded the good will between the RFC photographic section and army staffs that had been established from preplanning experience at Neuve Chapelle. Survey officers from the Topographical Sub-Section of the General Staff, also known as Section I(c) or "Maps GHQ," were competing with aerial photography for accurate replication of the front.[75] Moore-Brabazon reflected on the strife within the staff:

> After the first gas attack on Ypres, the line was pretty fluid. The British photo team accomplished a map of the enemy trenches. It took an extensive effort, aided by Captain [Harold] Wyllie [son of the great British marine artist]; who took an enormous risk to his own safety by flying very low over the trenches in order to identify the uniforms of the occupants. A map of the German lines was prepared. The photo

---

[71] Hahn, xvii.
[72] Nesbit, 27.
[73] Hahn, xvi-xvii.

[74] Charteris, *At G.H.Q.*, 88-89.
[75] Peter Chasseaud, *Topography of Armageddon: A British Trench Map Atlas of the Western Front, 1914-1918* (Lewes, UK: Mapbooks, 1991), 8; John R. Innes, *Flash Spotters and Sound Rangers: How They Lived, Worked and Fought in the Great War* (London: George Allen & Unwin, Ltd., 1935; reprint, Trowbridge, UK: Redwood Books, Ltd., 1997), 36.

FIGURE 26. **Royal Naval Air Service aerial reconnaissance was accomplished by floatplanes such as the Short 184. Hand-held cameras such as the "A" Type were acquired in 1915.** Source: Nesbit, *Eyes of the RAF*.

team then started to circulate the map, causing extensive commotion among the army staffs. Trenchard told Moore-Brabazon to stop "butting into affairs I had nothing to do with. Maps were to be done by Maps GHQ and nobody else had any right to go making them, and it was a disgraceful thing, and I ought to be ashamed of myself." Obviously he had been told by GHQ to "strafe" me, and that he had done. However, Trenchard followed with a positive burst, "That's the spirit; I am too delighted for words at what you have done—magnificent! But you know what the Army is, so now do you mind getting in touch with GHQ and going hand in hand together?"[76]

Positional warfare confounded the prevailing military mindset. Being stuck in a front line sector for extended periods of time was not something experienced over the past quarter century. Information regarding location and possible enemy intentions came traditionally from sources such as cavalry. Now technology was supplanting the human resource for information. Evolving strategies toward containing the enemy turned to using aerial reconnaissance as routine insurance

---

[76] Moore-Brabazon, *The Brabazon Story*, 95.

Chapter 2: Aerial Photographic Reconnaissance Takes the Stage

against surprise.[77] The combatants now engaged in active deception to counter the risk posed by aerial reconnaissance platforms. It did not take long for both sides to develop their own security policy for strategic cover. A German "Order of the Day" commented:

> According to the report of a squadron of Airplane Observers, our troops are very easy to mark in fighting, in spite of their grey uniforms, because of the density of their formation, while the French know apparently how to protect themselves perfectly against aerial reconnaissance. During a fight it is necessary that our troops should make the task of aerial reconnaissance more difficult by more careful use of the country – making use of narrow files along trees, edges of villages, shelter of houses, avoiding mass formations…. At the approach of an airplane all movements ought to cease…. Upon the approach of an enemy airplane there should be no firing, for the flash of the gun betrays the position from afar.[78]

The Royal Naval Air Service

British forces maintained two separate photographic programs until the formation of the RAF in 1918. In 1915, Royal Naval Air Service (RNAS) aeroplanes equipped with a variety of hand-held cameras, to include the "A" Type camera, operated out of Dunkirk and photographed significant targets along the coastline to a depth of four miles.[79] They maintained aerial reconnaissance on all known German defense systems from Nieuport to the Dutch border, to include determining detailed characteristics of the coast and inland batteries, the general topography, and information on slopes of beaches, and locations and heights of sea walls. Aerial photographs provided the necessary detail to map the coastal region. Analysis on enemy dispositions along the Belgian coast was forwarded to the Admiralty's Intelligence Department of the Naval Staff.[80]

The relations between the RFC and RNAS concerning photography were positive. Captain Campbell worked very closely and harmoniously with his leading RNAS photographic officer counterpart, Lieutenant Charles W. Gamble. Both realized that cooperation was essential, saving on duplication of work, time and money.[81] By the autumn of 1915, close cooperation between the RFC and the RNAS had become the order of the day.[82] Both RFC and RNAS treated aerial photography as a sensitive program, requiring the utmost security. Security policies such as that posted by the RNAS Station commander working with the RFC Photographic Branch at Chingford, England, mandated that all personnel keep the material confidential and an officer be on duty at all times, "never to leave the building on any pretext whatever."[83]

Advances in Artillery Spotting

Positional warfare settled down to a routine in the spring of 1915. All the major elements of aerial observation comprising aeroplane and ballon observateur resources were now operational and employed throughout the front. The emphasis on aerial observation covering the German artillery batteries started to have a major impact in 1915. Artillery batteries became concerned by their vulnerability and proceeded to employ extensive camouflage materials and procedures to cover themselves from aerial observation.[84] In addition to aerial observation from aeroplanes, aerostat activity increased throughout the front. In May 1915, during the French operations in the Artois sector, ballon observateurs were employed on a large scale for the first time. One of the first aerial observation successes from the ballon observateurs was achieved by Sergeant

---

[77] Jones, II, 80.

[78] German report quoted in Porter, 117.

[79] Gamble, "Technical Aspects of British Aerial Photography," TNA, PRO: AIR 1/2397/267/7; Jones, IV, 107.

[80] Jones, IV, 102; Edgar Charles Middleton, *The Great War in the Air* (4 vols., London: The Waverly Book Company, Ltd., 1920), III, 114-115.

[81] Lieut Charles Gamble, "Photographic Section of the French Flying Corps," TNA, PRO: AIR 1/404/97/1917.

[82] Toye, "History of Photography," TNA, PRO: AIR 1/724/91/1.

[83] Squadron Commander Letter, 4 September 1915, in Gamble, "Photographic Section of the French Flying Corps," TNA, PRO: AIR 1/404/97/1917.

[84] Weiller, in de Brunoff, 69.

FIGURE 27. **The French pioneer aerial photographic team of Capitaine Grout and Lieutenant Pépin, using a pre-war design Swiss Douhet-Zollinger film camera (above lens apparatus; below film magazine) convincingly demonstrated the value of aerial photography for targeting German artillery.** Source: Andre H. Carlier, *La Photographie Aerienne Pendant la Guerre* (Paris: Librairie Delagrave, 1921).

Toutay, a French pioneer aérostier. During one ascent, Toutay reported to his assigned battery that he observed German convoys, which were subsequently destroyed. Another French pioneer aérostier, Warrant Officer Arondel, accomplished twenty-five artillery rangings in the course of five and a half hours, an uncommon feat in the course of the war.[85]

While the British were fighting at Neuve Chapelle, Grout's SPAé advanced the role of aerial photography in targeting artillery. In April

1915, Grout and his subordinate Pépin attached the Douhet-Zollinger film camera to a Voisin 5 and tasked the sortie over the Verdun sector. The mission was a major success. It acquired the most comprehensive coverage to date of a battle area from one aerial sortie. The coverage proved deadly for German artillery in the Verdun sector, for the photographs provided accurate target locations for French counterbattery operations. Subsequent missions showed that German artillery suffered extensive losses from the barrage. However, it prompted new courses of action involving extensive camouflage and greater attention to deception techniques.[86] The initial success experienced by the Douhet-Zollinger camera was soon eclipsed by its operational limitations. The camera's limited focal length made aerial observation more vulnerable to ground and antiaircraft fire. A few more sorties were attempted that year with the Douhet-Zollinger camera in mapping the Verdun and Champagne sectors. However, the camera was soon replaced by the sturdier and more effective range of plate cameras, the French 26 cm, 50 cm and 120 cm.[87]

The British also started emphasizing aerial photographic coverage against artillery as a means to detect German camouflage.[88] Charteris made this bold claim:

> The Germans can quite easily cover up gun positions and other defenses, so that the observers in aeroplanes cannot detect them. It is next to impossible to conceal them from the camera. There is the negative result also, that these air photos teach us how to conceal our own gun positions, though as far as we know at present the Germans are not using air photographs. The plans for the battle were all worked out on maps, brought up to date from air photographs for the first time in the war.[89]

[85] Christienne and Lissarague, 71.

[86] Dégardin, in *Vues d'en Haut*, 20-21; Eugène Pépin Papers, MA&E, Paris (translation provided by Commandant Marc Rivière); Carlier, 18.

[87] Pépin Papers, MA&E, Paris; Carlier, 18.

[88] Watkis, 9-10.

[89] Charteris, *At G.H.Q.*, 82.

FIGURE 28. **The Voisin 5 served as the aeronautical testbed for the Douhet-Zollinger camera.** Source: SHAA.

It was then that individual initiative within the RFC came through with a more accurate means of guiding artillery toward the intended target.[90] Again, the innovative thinking of Captain D. S. Lewis from RFC No. 3 Squadron helped the British artillery to refine its targets. Lewis, having initiated the squared map during the Battle of the Aisne, further refined targeting through the "clock code."[91] The "clock code" took the target as being the center of a clock face, with 12 o'clock pointing true north. Imaginary circles with the target as center at radial distances of 10, 25, 50, 100, 200, 300, 400, and 500 yards from the target were lettered Y, Z, A, B, C, D, E, and F respectively. The RFC pilot conducted the "shoot," noting shell bursts with reference to the imaginary circles and clock hours, and signaling the result by giving the letter of the smallest circle within which the shot fell, followed by the hour of the clock indicating its direction from the target. Thus a shell which fell 90 yards west of the target was reported as B9—that is less than 100 yards from the target and due west of

it. The "clock code" proved to be a highly successful tool for aviation and artillery throughout the war.[92]

The "clock code" was described by one observer as an integral ingredient for artillery spotting:

> Working with the wireless required a standard procedure be put in place. Having reached a height of some 1,500 feet, one would let the aerial down, all the approximately 100 feet of it, and start calling up the home W/T station on the aerodrome and check the strength of one's signals. One would then make sure that the little sheet of

[90] Edmonds, *1915*, II, 142-143.

[91] Squier, "Intelligence Services," Squier Papers, 5, USAMHI; Jones, II, 85-87; Capt. D.S. Lewis, "Procedure of Ranging," 25 January 1915, TNA, PRO: AIR 1/834/204/5/240.

[92] Lamberton, 9-10; Lewis, "Procedure of Ranging," TNA, PRO: AIR 1/834/204/5/240.

FIGURE 29. **Captain D. S. Lewis in his January 1915 correspondence to a colleague drew a "clock code" describing how aerial targeting support for artillery can be accomplished.** Source: UK National Archives, Public Records Office (TNA, PRO): AIR 1/834/204/4/240.

FIGURE 30. **The clock code was a remarkably simple device. It correlated the location of the intended target to the center of the clock and allowed the aviator to radio the actual impact point to the superimposed clock face.** Source: TNA, PRO: AIR 1/1211/204/5/2627.

mica or celluloid, bearing the six concentric circles scratched and inked upon it (in a surrounding bolder circle representing a clock-dial, with the hour numbers indicated), was properly positioned securely, with its center-mark over the first target to be dealt with, and the "12 o'clock" mark pointing due north, before sitting back and relaxing. Each of the inner circles represented actual distances in yards from the center, the innermost circle indicating 50 yards and the next larger circle 100 yards, and so on.[93]

Once the preparation for the targeting process was in place, the observer commenced observation procedures:

Flying at 3,000-4,000 feet, the observer approached the line. The observer would go through the preamble and the battery being supported would be

ready to fire a sighting shot. In ranging a battery on a target, it was very necessary for the observer to be so placed as to be able to watch the entire cycle of operations undisturbed by any change of direction on the part of the aeroplane, and it behooved him and his pilot to agree upon a course that would give him a direct view of battery and target up to the moment of sending down corrections. The pilot would usually steer an oval course, so arranged that both battery and target would be in full view during the aeroplanes' advance along one leg of the oval, thus allowing time for the sending of corrections and for the battery-crew to make the necessary sighting adjustments called for while the artillery was returning along the other leg. Needless to say, once a shoot had begun, it was highly desirable not to deviate from this course, or alter the rhythm adopted. The occupants of the observing aeroplane were at the mercy of those enemy antiaircraft gunners who were

---

[93] Insall, 171-172.

Chapter 2: Aerial Photographic Reconnaissance Takes the Stage

gathered around their guns waiting for the operation to start.[94]

Captain Lewis did not survive the war. Later that year, while flying over the front lines to show a Guards officer the view of the front, his Morane Parasol aeroplane was destroyed by a direct hit from "Archie."[95]

The French did not employ the "clock code." Their artillery spotting process involved:

> Corrections being given as such and such a distance long, short, right or left (or in the event of a battery's position being unknown, North, East, South or West of the target). For corrections in hundreds of meters the unit figure is always given the same as the hundred figure (that is, "200 in right") would be sent down as 202 "in right" in order to check any possible error of transmission of the hundreds. For corrections in tens a 3 figure number beginning with 0 is used to avoid confusion with code signals which are two figured. Moreover the tens and units are given the same. For example "60 meters left" would be sent as "066 meters left."[96]

RFC Modifications to Aerial Observation

By the summer of 1915, the RFC assigned its wings to each British Army. General Haig's First Army now had the services of the 1st Wing commanded by Lieutenant Colonel E.B. "Splash" Ashmore. 1st Wing comprised four squadrons (RFC Squadron Numbers 2, 3, 10, and 16) and two Kite Balloon Sections (Numbers 6 and 8). The primary British aerial observation aeroplane was the ubiquitous BE 2c. Allocation of aeroplanes showed emphasis on the artillery observation mission with all possessing a radio transmission capability. Artillery spotting procedures were refined to include distinct use of radio to prevent jamming fratricide between aeroplanes. All aeroplanes cooperated with the ground forces within the squadron's assigned sector. Aerial photography was now a regular feature, particularly to assist artillery commanders in their choice of targets. Additionally, each squadron included one single-seater to provide standby pursuit or interceptor duty.[97] RFC Squadrons No. 2 and No. 3 each had two flights detailed for counterbattery work and one for observing trench bombardment. No. 10 Squadron had one flight for long distance reconnaissance and two for artillery observation. No. 16 Squadron had one flight for tactical reconnaissance, and two for artillery observation.[98]

Along with the ongoing evolution of the squadrons, the experiences of the RFC Photo Sections over the first six months now provided seniors with an appreciation of aerial photography's potential. During July 1915, the RFC conducted a conference at the War Office in London to discuss improving aerial photography. Attendees included the representative from the General Staff, Lieutenant Colonel C.C. Marindin, Captain J.T.C. Moore-Brabazon, and Captain Campbell. The summary of the conference highlighted the need for extensive modifications:

> Photographic work in the Royal Flying Corps is at present in a somewhat chaotic state, and that as means exist for co-ordinating it or for inter-communication of results obtained at home and abroad. Further, that it is difficult to initiate or develop useful experimental work at home unless the requirements of the Expeditionary Force are more fully known. The best means of co-ordinating photographic work would be through (1) appointment of an equipment officer for photography at the headquarters; (2) appointment of a photographic expert at the War Office; (3) appointment of an assistant equipment officer in charge of a photographic experimental section; (4) standardization should be tried for as

---

[94] Insall, 171-172.

[95] "Archie" was the slang term used by British aviators for antiaircraft artillery. Baring, 306-307.

[96] Maj J. P. C. Sewell, "Notes … on French Corps Aviation," TNA, PRO: AIR 1/475/15/312/201.

[97] Edmonds, *1915*, II, 143; Insall, 63.

[98] Insall, 63.

Les Tentes

far as possible; (5) all officers at home, both pilots and observers, should be taught something of photography [Their notes as to the conditions under which photographs are taken would then be of great assistance to the Photographic Section]; and (6) establish the requirement for testing all apparatus and material in the Field before its final adoption.[99]

The discussion at the War Office had an impact. The RFC's Wings commenced assigning photographic officers to the headquarters staff. As the British armies increased their demand for aerial photography in the subsequent months, emphasis was made to provide Photo Sections for all squadrons assigned at corps echelon. This led to the establishment of the Army Reconnaissance Squadron, the most definitive unit established in the war for strategic coverage.[100] As for the issues raised in the conference, the desire to field a fully aware aerial observation force would remain in committee. The British aerial culture

FIGURE 31. French aerial reconnaissance won converts by confirming to a skeptical senior staff that the French infantry occupied the sector known as the Tranchée des Tentes. Source: Capitaine Paul-Lewis Weiller photograph in *L'Aéronautique pendant la Guerre Mondiale, 1914-1918.* Ed. Maurice de Brunoff (Paris: M. de Brunoff, 1919).

soon gravitated toward greater emphasis on the combat role.[101]

At the front, the British and Commonwealth forces were refining their intelligence infrastructure to accommodate the new sources of intelligence such as aerial photography. A direct channel of information was now established to ensure reports passed from the Battalion Intelligence Officer through Brigade to Division. The British increased intelligence manning at the Corps to improve coordination and support.[102] The ad-

---

[99] Lieut Col Marindin, "Conference Notes, 23 July 1915," TNA, PRO: AIR 1/127/15/40/147.
[100] Insall, 155.

[101] Lieut Col Marindin, "Conference Notes, 23 July 1915," TNA, PRO: AIR 1/127/15/40/147.
[102] Hahn, xvii-xviii.

dition of personnel to the intelligence staffs now provided each echelon with an improved capability to handle the increasing volume of aerial photographs. A new function was added to the intelligence ranks known as the draughtsman. This position helped in the interpretation of the photograph as well as tracing key information for the command maps.[103]

Defining Lessons from the Artois (Loos) Battle

Throughout 1915 the Allies refined their entire aerial observation program to accommodate the lessons learned from the initial campaigns. RFC strength had expanded to meet the demands for aerial observation and photography. The three RFC wings now comprised 160 aeroplanes, backed by 40 aeroplanes in reserve at two aircraft parks. Each Photo Section supporting the wings now sported mobile darkroom vans on lorries. These additions complemented the darkrooms at various buildings in the area and provided direct service to arriving aeroplanes at the landing ground.[104] The Battle of Artois (referred to by the British as the battle of Loos, which is located south of Neuve Chapelle) commenced on 25 September 1915. The French also commenced an offensive along the Champagne front. Loos was fought on a larger front sector than that of the March 1915 Neuve Chapelle offensive. However, the number of British artillery pieces covering the wider sector was approximately the same as that employed earlier. To achieve the appropriate level of destruction as envisioned by the planners, a longer period of fire was conducted. The four days of artillery barrage accomplished an appropriate level of damage, but surprise was totally forsaken. The British artillery also applied a new artillery tactic called the "lifting barrage" against the Germans. Artillery fire concentrated on one trench at a time. In the ongoing 1915 Artois campaign, 16 reconnaissance escadrilles were assigned to cover a 35-kilometer front.[105] However, despite the use of aerial observation, the attack was effectively countered by the German forces. Thanks to a lack of surprise at the commencement of the offensive, the Germans were able to regroup their reserves and mass against the attacking Allies.[106]

The role of French aerial observation, reconnaissance, and artillery spotting was practically codified after the Battle of Artois. The experience gave Aviation Militaire the chance to clearly review what aerial reconnaissance provided to positional war. It was concluded that military aviation was most useful to armée commanders when providing tactical information such as location of enemy troops and regulation of artillery fire. Also, aerial reconnaissance reports on location of French troops were clearly demonstrated and strongly endorsed. The basic unit for aerial operations would be the Armée, cooperating with the escadrille assigned to the Corps d'Armée. Escadrilles supporting heavy artillery were to closely coordinate their operations with CA escadrilles. Finally, Aviation Militaire decided that each CA would require one aéroplane for photo reconnaissance, two for army cooperation duties, and one for artillery regulation (*avion de réglage*).[107]

Aerial photographic reconnaissance was now integral to the evolving battleground with a modern equipment suite, to include cameras, plate photographs, and mobile field laboratories. Air-to-ground liaison was expanding with an array of capabilities to include telegraphic sans file (radio) with one-way Morse code transmission, cloth panels, and new procedures for dropping messages. Despite improvements in components, improvements in French airframe and power plant design remained static. Their hesitation to advance aeronautical design translated directly into new vulnerabilities against a rapidly improving German pursuit force being fielded in the coming months.[108]

The defining moment for French aerial reconnaissance occurred during the Artois offensive. It showed that skepticism had lethal consequences for the French military. On 25 September, a French company had succeeded in taking a German trench network known as *Tranchée des Tentes* (Tent Trench). A German counterattack

---

[103] Hahn, xviii.
[104] Nesbit, 30.
[105] Weiller, in de Brunoff, 71.

[106] Bailey, 132.
[107] Davila and Soltan, 5.
[108] Christienne and Lissarague, 91.

Chapter 2: Aerial Photographic Reconnaissance Takes the Stage

FIGURE 32. **Capitaine Paul-Louis Weiller, legend of French aerial reconnaissance in World War I.** Source: SHAA.

forced most of the French troops to withdraw, but the forward unit, which had no warning of the retreat, stubbornly held on. The French command, unaware of the French forward unit's remaining presence, commenced general artillery fire on the position. Throughout this barrage, French aerial observation began to detect the ground signals laid out in desperate fashion by the forward unit. The aerial observation proceeded to notify the CA Post of Command (PC) that French soldiers were still in place in the sector. Tragically, the PC did not believe the reports. For the next three days, French artillery bombarded the position. Only after a French officer of the unit managed to safely escape and make it back to the French lines to personally relay the fratricidal horror taking place was the French command convinced of the forward unit's location. The incident did make the case that aerial observation was a credible source for gauging the battle. For French aerial observation, the Tranchée des Tentes served

as the last serious challenge by French military skeptics in the war.[109]

An Enduring Legacy of French Aerial Observation

Several French masters matched the demonstrated initiative of British aviators in evolving the role of aerial reconnaissance. Most notably, Capitaine Paul-Lewis Weiller was a leader in developing French aerial observation and photographic reconnaissance. Like the RFC's Captain Lewis, Weiller came from an artillery background. In the first year of the war, he was instrumental in exploring aerial photographic reconnaissance possibilities. Flying as an MF 11 observer, Weiller took numerous aerial photographs with his personal camera. Weiller was one of the leading proponents for establishing the French military's restitution process that transferred important information from the aerial photograph to the map. His efforts encouraged the French staff to rethink the role of aerial photography in updating maps. While assigned to a Voisin escadrille, Weiller worked with engineers in establishing a method of updating maps that became the standard for the French *Service Géographique*.[110]

In 1915, Weiller acquired a pilot's license and assumed command of a Caudron escadrille flight (C224). While assigned to C224, he established the process for achieving the longer-range armée reconnaissance mission profile, determining specific altitudes and ranges for the existing French aéroplane inventory. Weiller was the strongest of advocates for aerial photographs and reconnaissance. He recognized the prevailing skepticism that came with aerial observation, reminding colleagues that military seniors "were always incredulous when given simple oral reports." Weiller's operational experience proved invaluable in assisting the French to design one of the most important aerial cameras of the war, the 120 cm. The impetus for the longer focal length design was to have a camera "that could satisfy Général Charles Marie Emmanuel Mangin, his armée commander, who wanted 'to see

---

[109] Christienne and Lissarague, 91; Weiller, in de Brunoff, 75.

[110] Christienne and Lissarague, 181.

some Boches' on the negatives."[111] Weiller's career in aerial observation was legendary. He was a risk taker, flying low over German lines and experiencing wounds as a result. On one dangerous sortie, Weiller proved to seniors that an artillery barrage meant to prepare a French attack on a German installation had not succeeded. This resulted in the French commander's canceling the attack and saving many lives in the process.[112] The lessons of 1915 honed his aerial observer skills for the remainder of the war, establishing an example of aerial reconnaissance excellence that became recognized at the highest levels of the French military.

Aerial Observation in Ascendancy

The ascendancy of aerial observation coincided with the introduction of the pursuit fighter. Aerial combat now became a common fixture of the war, impacting all facets of aerial reconnaissance. During the late summer and autumn of 1915, British aerial reconnaissance beyond the front lines now started to come into contact with a new type of German aeroplane. RFC thinking up to that time had not placed emphasis on aerial combat. It was not until the battle of Artois (Loos) that it became a serious and permanent part of the aerial scheme.[113] In November of 1915, the British encountered a Fokker monoplane in the Cambrai area. A Vickers aeroplane was accomplishing army reconnaissance deep inside the enemy's lines. A brief fight ensued, but no casualties came from the engagement.[114] Aerial combat transformed aeronautics and established aviation's primary military purpose for the 20th century. While aerial combat became refined in 1916, aerial observation now entered into the time of its greatest prominence. It took the horrors of two cataclysmic battles, Verdun and the Somme, to determine the limits of aerial observation for refining positional war's potential. For the remainder of the war, the impact of aerial reconnaissance became dependent on the seniors who employed the information.

FIGURE 33. **The RFC expanded its aerial reconnaissance role in 1915 through deployment of a new line of British-produced aeroplanes such as the Vickers F.B.5. The photograph shows the observer receiving the hand-held "A" Type camera for the sortie.** Source: Nesbit, *Eyes of the RAF.*

---

[111] Christienne and Lissarague, 181. "Boche" was a derogatory term applied by the French to German soldiers.
[112] Christienne and Lissarague, 181.
[113] Edmonds, *1915*, II, 142-143.
[114] Insall, 73.

OCTOBER 1915 – OCTOBER 1916:
FORTIFICATIONS ACROSS THE FRONT LINE

The year 1916 is remembered for the climactic battles that culminated in catastrophic loss of life, yet with no discernable gain. For nearly a century Verdun has symbolized the cost of war to the French nation. Likewise, the Somme was to be Britain's benchmark for military planning gone horrifically wrong. Aerial photography was a novelty in its first year. By 1916, aerial reconnaissance had become a standard fixture of the operational mission. Decisions were made based on aerial photographic validation. However, a failing doctrine overshadowed the potential that aerial reconnaissance provided. The application of mass against well-established defenses proved catastrophic throughout the second year of conflict. *Étude et Exploitation des Photographies Aériennes* describes the transformation at the front lines as the traditional first line of defense became just one of many obstacles against an advancing Allied assault.

Photographs of the German defenses taken during the winter of 1915-1916 show that important fortifications had been built along nearly the whole front. The experience acquired as a result of our September offensive had borne fruit. The lines had been reorganized, with reference to the three following points of view:

Economy of forces.
Reduction of losses.

Logical utilization of terrain.

Economy of forces was obtained by the depth arrangement. The first line no longer consisted of two trenches, but of three, all provided with dugouts. Back of this was an intermediate line, the line of artillery protection; farther back, a second line, consisting of two trenches with dugouts, one in front of the crest, and the other on the opposite slope. (Redistribution of first line troops according to the Stein arrangement, in case of attack—Report la No. 1797 of Sept. 8, 1916—first line trenches, defense troops; second line trenches, defense and counteroffense troops; third line trenches, counteroffense troops.)

Reduction of losses was sought in:

(a) Deepening and widening the trenches—whence the disappearance of the circulation trenches and of the firing notches in unprotected trenches.

(b) Widening communications trenches.

(c) Reenforcing the covered dugouts and especially in replacing them by underground dugouts.

(d) Building narrow-gauge railways (0.6 and 0.4 meters) to serve the front lines.

(e) Constructing casements to replace the old breastworks.

Utilization of the terrain was carefully studied for the purpose of an obstinate defense. They endeavored to render impossible the breaking of their lines, or at least to limit our progress beyond their first line by successive supporting lines, generally continuous oblique organized trenches or boyaus ("suspenders") connecting the first and second lines.[1]

Verdun

Verdun was "the crucible in which the aviation of the French was fired."[2] Prior to that battle, French military leadership maintained a very narrow view of aviation's role in operations. Fighter/pursuit aircraft were employed to

FIGURE 34. **Verdun.** Source: *West Point Atlas*, Map 33. Courtesy, Department of History, U.S. Military Academy.

provide a protective escort for aerial observation, but aerial operations over the Verdun sector were concentrated in a small area. The consequence was that this allowed German fighters to marshal their pursuit forces sufficiently to gain air superiority.[3] At the end of 1915, German pursuit aviation led by the Fokker Eindecker forced a transformation of aerial operations over the battleground. The Allies had to contend with the realization that German pursuit aviation was dominant. The existing pusher aeroplane configuration, ideal for aerial observation, was no match for the more maneuverable tractor (aeroplane engine in front of the fuselage) fighter aircraft with synchronized machine guns. French aerial observation aéroplane performance was mediocre at best. Its average engine power plant could achieve a ceiling of only 3,000 meters car-

---

[1] *Study and Exploitation of Aerial Photographs*, 7.
[2] Henri Pétain, *Verdun* (New York: The Dial Press, 1930), 192.

[3] Christienne and Lissarague, 97.

Chapter 3: Fortifications Across the Front Line

DOUAUMONT   O. THIAUMONT   E. DE VAUX   R. DES VIGNES

FIGURE 35. **A panoramic northeast view of the Verdun battlefield taken from an altitude of 800 meters.** Source: SHAT.

rying a small load. By the end of 1915, several French prototypes were in the testing stage, but replacements were slow in coming.[4]

The battle of Verdun commenced on 21 February 1916. German preparations leading up to the first salvos were extremely effective. Warning signs varied with each intelligence source. However, German deception effectively masked critical signatures prior to the offensive. The combination of bad weather over the battleground and German aerial supremacy from Fokker Eindeckers denied the French aerial access to establish the more expansive strategic aerial picture needed to determine indications of an attack. Aerial photography was now integral to German battle plan-

ning. Coverage went beyond Verdun to strategic French locations 25 miles deep within the rear echelon.[5] The Germans recognized that an offensive in the Verdun sector was a major challenge. The attack plan had to contend with a maze of ridges that allowed the French to command practically every avenue of attack. The other significant topographical feature was the plain of the river Woevre and its dominating plateau scarp. It forced the Germans to attack from the north. In the end, the geographical obstacle proved one of the final determinants of French victory.[6]

German planning at Verdun established an effective strategic camouflage and deception program that brought into question the credibility of the entire French aerial reconnaissance and photographic interpretation effort. French aircraft three days before the offensive commenced were only reporting German forces far from the Verdun front lines. Their short-range tactical coverage did not pick up any unusual activity commensurate with the offensive, such as indications

---

[4] Christienne and Lissarague, 90.

[5] Lamberton, 11.
[6] Johnson, *Topography and Strategy*, 44-47.

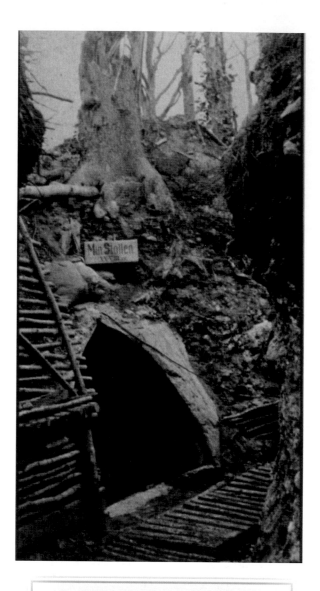

FIGURE 36. **Entrance to a _Stollen_ tunnel housing the first wave of German infantry prior to the 21 February commencement of the battle of Verdun.** Source: Bibliothek für Zeitgeshichte photo in _Tanks & Weapons of World War I,_ ed. Bernard Fitzsimons (New York: Beekman House, 1973).

Stollen were faulty, assuming the activity represented an upgrade in defensive works. German strategic camouflage was now playing a major role, masking construction activity. The Germans worked at night and effectively disposed of the removed earth material. When the Verdun battle commenced, the Stollen had served their purpose. The numbers of German shock troops positioned in the front lines far exceeded anything the French believed possible. The advance stockpiles were masked, and contained new technical weaponry, such as flame-throwers. [8]

The German chief of staff at Verdun, General von Falkenhayn, also intended to blind the French artillery from the start by depriving them of their ballon observateur and CA aéroplanes. His tactic for eliminating the French ballon observateur was to move heavy artillery up to the front lines as close as possible under the cover of darkness and extensive camouflage. When the barrage started, German long-range guns were fired as a pair, one firing time-fused shells at a ballon observateur already aloft and the other firing percussion shells at the winch on the ground. French aérostiers were trained in the classical evasive movement called the "cartesian diver." Upon observing the fire, the aérostier counted on a lead time of about 45 seconds, whereupon the winch operators were contacted via telephone to raise or lower the ballon observateur. The descending rate averaged five meters a second. Given a successful maneuver, the shell burst either too high or too low from the ballon observateur. However, the German tactic at Verdun cut the response time, resulting in the descending maneuver becoming fruitless. The opening German salvos went unrestricted. The French were faced with even greater urgency to regain air superiority so that they could reclaim the artillery spotting advantage.[9]

In a simultaneous show of aerial force, von Falkenhayn created an effective aerial blockade against French aviation through a concentration of Fokker Eindecker fighters. The Germans flew parallel to the front lines, countering or destroying any French reconnaissance aéroplanes attempting to "see" the battleground. Additionally,

of increasing supply dumps or logistical activity. It took cross-referencing prisoner interrogations with subsequent aerial coverage to discover German construction of _Stollen_, or tunnels, which secretly conveyed the troops to the jump-off point.[7] Initial French intelligence assessments of

---

[7] Porch, 96-97, 103.

[8] Porch, 102-103.
[9] Christienne and Lissarague, 72.

the German fighters suppressed French planes from taking off from nearby landing grounds. Those French aéroplanes that did arrive were met with formations of three or four German aeroplane patrols. Verdun's first day culminated in two significant gains for the German advance. They possessed air superiority for the first time and countered French attempts to gain the "high ground" for aerial observation.[10] French post-war recollections of their aviation losses were stated to the point: "They paid dearly for this disregard of economizing of effectives, and in spite of their heroism they were wiped out by the German air force at the beginning of the battle of Verdun."[11] Verdun's lessons learned reinforced critical facets of military aviation in general. Pursuit needed to be advanced to protect aerial observation missions. If artillery were to remain effective in targeting, it required closer liaison with an Aviation Militaire that possessed greater authority to designate objectives and regulate fire. At the same time, Aviation Militaire desired a more effective liaison with the infantry to provide a greater awareness of the battleground. Aéroplanes operating over enemy lines were now required to place greater emphasis on formation flying. Finally, French headquarters needed more aviation-experienced personnel on the staff to support planning as well as judiciously apply aerial resources to CA operations.[12]

With the serious setback of the first days of the German offensive, the French military realized it had to react immediately and decisively. The chef de l'aéronatique at GQG at this time, Commandant du Peuty, stressed a more aggressive combat role with greater presence of pursuit fighters in protection of aerial reconnaissance. He also stipulated that aerial observation was not to be flown solo over the front lines. The French also changed their aviation organization to be more responsive to the ground commander and the threat. In each CA, an aerial element, the *Secteur Aéronautique,* was established to centralize the use of aeronautic units working mis-

sions supporting infantry and artillery.[13] In turn, Général Joffre called upon Commandant Tricornot de Rose, escadrille commander of Moraine Saulnier (MS) 12, and gave him authority to take whatever steps necessary to regain air superiority and reestablish aerial observation. De Rose quickly responded by assembling 15 flights of elite pursuit escadrilles (*groupes de chasse*), tasked with "sweeping the sky." In the weeks that followed, the elite pursuit units proved successful, regaining air superiority to the point that German aviation was incapable of penetrating the French sector. Aerial observation rebounded with the resumption of French air superiority.[14]

The French also made a significant change in supporting heavy artillery targeting. Elite reconnaissance air crews were assigned to *premières escadrilles d'Artillerie lourde* (AL) to detect and photograph significant targets for the most powerful artillery units.[15] The French numerically designated the escadrilles from 201 through 228. The aerial reconnaissance specialists were experts, forwarding essential information to longer-range heavy artillery units capable of delivering more lethal firepower.[16] Such was the case on 2 April 1916 when one French aerial observer reported Germans rapidly advancing in a certain sector. His timely updates on the exact positions contributed to a massive French artillery barrage that was quickly followed by a ground attack. Germans taken prisoner reported the French barrage "littered the railroad track with German cadavers."[17] The concerted effort of the entire French military to do whatever it took to halt the German advance at Verdun finally saw its efforts rewarded. The German advance halted.

As the Verdun campaign entered its third month, the French military made demands on the government to produce a new line of more effective aéroplanes to counter any future German aviation dominance. Général Joffre personally requested the government halt production of

---

[10] Christienne and Lissarague, 95; Lamberton, 11.

[11] "Aeronautics," June 1921, NARA, RG 120, Box 819, 4.

[12] "Aeronautics," June 1921, NARA, RG 120, Box 819, 4-5.

[13] "Aeronautics," June 1921, NARA, RG 120, Box 819, 4-5; Jones, II, 165.

[14] Christienne and Lissarague, 72; Davilla and Soltan, 7.

[15] Hodeir, 115. This was also known as *Section Artillerie Lourde* (SAL).

[16] Alan D. Toelle, *Breguet 14* (Berkhamsted, UK: Albatros Productions, Ltd., 2003), 2.

[17] Christienne and Lissarague, 72; Davilla and Soltan, 7.

obsolete aéroplanes such as the HF 7 and MF 11 and replace them with aéroplanes with the engine in front to better accommodate rear defenses.[18] The French aeronautical industry was in a quandary. A revolution in design was called for to both keep ahead of any future German fighter planes as well as supply the numbers necessary to maintain superiority. Verdun became the catalyst for all of France to do whatever was necessary to stop the German advance and regain lost territory. The pervasive influence of the battle culminated in a significant upgrade for French aviation in the war.[19]

The French adopted a new intelligence strategy that modified aerial photography's role to be more readily available and have sufficient quantities of aéroplanes to meet any demand. The battle cry for intelligence became, "Follow the Attack," supporting the infantry and artillery with large numbers of aerial photographs.[20] Further supporting the realignment of reconnaissance expertise was the addition of new SPAé. This increased the numbers of intelligence personnel supporting the aeronautical sectors, in addition to those supporting the armée.[21] Mobile SPAé were set up at landing grounds near CA headquarters, allowing the air crew to photograph the target, land, quickly download and develop the photographic plates, produce prints, and personally distribute the intelligence products to the corps commander within an hour. Other recipients included artillery batteries and infantry companies responsible for the success of the battle under way. The surge in emphasis was illustrated when one French SPAé was credited with producing 5,000 prints in one day.[22]

The French took steps to increase the timeliness of their aerial reconnaissance force by assigning dedicated additional aéroplanes to respective units. Three photographic reconnaissance aéroplanes were attached to the division to photograph the German trench system and enemy batteries. Determining the extent of destructive fire required a minimum of eight aéroplanes (fit-

ted with radio) and two ballon observateurs (the famous Caquot captif ballon was introduced) to provide constant updates. A "sentry" aéroplane was assigned to search for rear echelon German reinforcement activity and reported via TSF any indications that the enemy was preparing a counterattack. Each French counterbattery artillery unit was assigned two radio-equipped aéroplanes. Any information of significant priority acquired through the aerial reconnaissance was telephoned immediately to the respective centers upon landing.[23]

Another factor for improving French aerial observation was the emphasis on "continuity" by sector. Verdun was now divided into air sectors, each covered continuously by the same observers. This enabled the observation officers to have an exact knowledge of the sector, an essential ingredient for maintaining an intelligence baseline to better support the ongoing Verdun campaign.[24] By the second month of fighting, the French aerial campaign under Commandant de Rose was regaining supremacy. French aviation in the sector improved, through pursuit to counter the Fokker Eindecker threat, and through aerial observation to supply more targeting information to support the aggressive artillery employment behind the counterattacks. The fighting was still bitter, but now it was in German-held territory. In May 1916, after months of intensive combat, the French key for the Verdun campaign, Fort Douaumont, was retaken and the German advance was finally halted.[25] Regaining Fort Douaumont also included a significant achievement for aerial photography. On 22 May 1916, 40 minutes prior to the French attack, aerial photographic interpretation discovered German troops at a position critical to the French attack.[26] The French commander, Général Mangin, acquired prints that had been quickly processed and flown to his advanced headquarters for review. Based on this information, he took decisive action, quickly modifying the attack plan and launching an assault on the sector. Mangin credited aerial observation as

[18] Christienne and Lissarague, 106.
[19] Christienne and Lissarague, 77.
[20] Lieut Paul-Louis Weiller quoted in Hodeir, 116.
[21] Hodeir, 115-116.
[22] Hodeir, 115-116; Jones, II, 176-177.

[23] "Notes on the French System of Intelligence during the Battle of the Somme," 23 September 1916, 4-5, TNA, PRO: WO 198/983.
[24] Hodeir, 115; Christienne, 98.
[25] Christienne and Lissarague, 72.
[26] Hodeir, 116.

FIGURE 37. The destruction of Fort Douaumont was symbolic of Verdun's horror. The devastation is clearly discernable in late 1918. The dark area in the foreground is all that remains of the fort. Source: Gorrell Report, National Archives and Records Administration (NARA).

his "eyes" throughout the attack.[27] Mangin's confidence was soon curtailed. His attack ultimately failed due to an inability to sustain the offensive. A fierce German rearguard action from underground passages into the fort ultimately brought defeat to the French operation.[28] Despite the setback, aerial reconnaissance and photographic interpretation had successfully served its purpose. Commanders such as Mangin trusted the intelligence they saw.

German regimental histories of Verdun recalled the aggressive French reconnaissance over the front lines. Both Prussian Guards and Bavarian forces recalled having to stay undercover as the French observation aéroplanes circled overhead, calling in artillery against any observed movement. "The French observation and artillery fire direction from the especially low, swaying aircraft were so accurate and skillful that throughout the course of the afternoon of May 28, their fire crept toward our positions.... The impact of three heavy shells — direct hits — annihilated the battalion staff."[29] A few days later, the Royal Bavarian 20th Infantry Regiment recalled:

> As so often happened — especially at Verdun — the brilliantly carried out attack was not the worst. Already by the evening of June 1, the presence of a circling French flyer over the captured ground warned us that the enemy was not about to take the loss lightly. In the early morning of June 2, the retaliation fire began. This quickly swelled and grew into a powerful bombardment of annihilation.[30]

---

[27] Weiller, in de Brunoff, 79; Jones, II, 177.

[28] David Mason, *Verdun* (Gloucestershire, UK: The Windrush Press, 2000), 144.

[29] *The History of the 6th Garde Infantry Regiment* (n.p., 1931) (translation provided by Tom Gudmestad).

[30] Colonel Höfl, *The History of the Royal Bavarian 20th Infantry Regiment*, "*Prinz Franz*" (Munich: n.p., 1929) (translation by Tom Gudmestad).

Général Henri Philippe Pétain

Général Henri Philippe Pétain is one of history's greatest military enigmas. His successes in the First World War are clouded by his later capitulation to Nazi Germany and the repugnant Vichy government. Despite that disgrace, Pétain was a positive force behind the French victory in the First World War. His military legacy was forever established thanks to his leadership at Verdun. He reconstituted the French Armée to withstand the Verdun horror and achieve the ultimate victory, rightfully earning him the sobriquet as the Hero of Verdun. In the following year, Pétain again rose to the occasion following the debacle of the failed Nivelle offensive. On the strength of his stature, he kept the French Armée in check during a wave of mutinies and desertions, achieving a force balance while awaiting the arrival of the Americans. Within the environment of aerial photography, it was Pétain's understanding and recognition of its intelligence value that influenced the senior leadership and staff to take action based on a photograph.

FIGURE 38. Général Pétain, the Allied commander who used aerial photography to great advantage in the war. Source: Bibliotheque de Documentation Internationale Contemporaine (BDIC).

Général Pétain personified the best of military leaders, committed to the mission without needlessly sacrificing troops in the process. His brilliance lent credibility to aerial photographic reconnaissance attempts to influence decision-making in an environment beset with outdated doctrinal procedures. He led French development of the art and applied it to the operations for which he was responsible. In a post-war reflection on aerial reconnaissance, Pétain made it clear that structure gave credibility to the entire process, a credibility that both saved lives and achieved victory:

> Observation planes of the Farman and Caudron types now guaranteed with the greatest exactness the operation of liaison with the infantry, of the photographic service, and of the timing of the artillery. They were constantly fighting the pursuit planes of the enemy, were hampered many times by unfavorable atmospheric conditions under the lowering gloomy sky of Verdun, as they skimmed over the pockmarked and tumbled crests of the hills, and suffered heavy losses, but never failed in their mission."[31]

The "greatest exactness" became the standard by which French aerial reconnaissance proceeded for the remainder of the war.

---

[31] Pétain, *Verdun*, 191.

FIGURE 39. A new generation of longer-range aéroplanes such as this Caudron G6 entered service to provide increased aerial reconnaissance and firepower. Source: SHAA, B83.5656.

Pétain had a passion for detail that impressed all of his counterparts.[32] He was methodical in his leadership. He personally visited with all echelons to better gauge the potential of the unit as well as to demonstrate a deep personal commitment to his troops. He questioned regimental officers and NCOs to make sure they knew they were clear as to their individual role.[33] This attention to detail provided the impetus for legitimizing aerial photographic reconnaissance. Soon Pétain established a select group of aerial reconnaissance experts to both provide him with a better understanding of the battleground as well as educate the remaining staffs to this new art. One of the leading figures of this effort was Capitaine Grout's deputy for the SPAé, Lieutenant Eugène Pépin. Pétain organized an elite group of brilliant and proven experts to introduce new methods of conducting warfare to senior staffs supporting Pétain's *groupe des armées du centre* (Army

Group Center [GAC]). These experts were central to Pétain's objective of successfully integrating new technologies within the *armée*.[34] Pétain directed Pépin to train staffs and unit commanders on the use of aerial photography. The effort culminated in the publishing of *Études et Exploitation des Photographie Aériennes*, one of the first manuals on the art of photographic interpretation. Pépin also served as an advisor to Pétain on acquiring the maximum benefit from analysis of the aerial photograph. It marked a professional relationship that benefited aerial reconnaissance for the remainder of the war.[35]

Transformation within the Royal Flying Corps

Like the French, the British also had to contend with the threat posed by the introduction of the Fokker Eindecker. On 14 January 1916, RFC headquarters mandated that any aeroplane working aerial reconnaissance had to be escorted by at least three fighting machines in close formation. Shortly afterward they extended formation flying to bombardment missions. British aerial combat was now becoming specialized, profiting from the French experiences at Verdun. It became an established policy that, in order to win freedom of action for the three key missions of aviation (reconnaissance, artillery observation, and bombing), a new priority had to be established.

---

[32] Francis Martel, *Pétain: Verdun to Vichy* (New York: E.P. Dutton & Company, Inc. 1943), 37.

[33] Basil H. Liddell Hart, *Foch: The Man of Orleans* (Boston: Little, Brown, and Company, 1932), 181.

[34] Dégardin, in *Vues d'en Haut*, 22.

[35] Pépin Papers, MA&E, Paris.

The enemy had to be denied freedom to operate in the air. The British now committed to conducting a relentless and incessant aerial offensive.[36] In March, the new RFC Commander, Brigadier-General Trenchard, reinforced this policy: "It is now necessary to provide protection in the form of patrols for machines doing artillery work. The demands of Corps for artillery work, photography and close reconnaissance are now such that they occupy the entire services of a squadron. The aeroplanes of artillery Corps squadrons are therefore not available for other duties, without impeding the work for which they are now intended."[37]

More aircraft were being committed to controlling the sector, with the 12 squadrons assigned in October 1915 increased to 27 squadrons at the commencement of the Somme battle. The squadrons were better equipped, better armed, and better trained.[38] Trenchard advocated that the aeroplane establishment of artillery squadrons be increased to 18, providing three single-seat fighters with engines of the same type. Once the artillery squadrons had received their complement of 18, an equivalent number of aeroplanes was assigned to newly established Army and GHQ squadrons.[39] In April 1916, British RFC commanders made a critical shift in controlling the airspace of the battlefield. All fighting machines at Corps squadrons were now reassigned to Army squadrons. Throughout the remainder of the war, air fighting was the duty of specific squadrons of higher-echelon wings subordinate to the British Army.[40]

The demands on aerial reconnaissance increased with new artillery tactics being applied at the front. The characteristic straight barrage of 1915 was now replaced with the "piled-up barrage," a barrage that employed parallel lines of fire which shifted to firing at irregular intervals along the line. The advancing barrage would then "pile up" on the German position simultaneously. The infantry would not advance until the entire German line was engaged by fire. Those soldiers requiring the longest advance had to depart the trench first. The effect was to have British forces reach the German trenches at the same time. The idea of mass concentration had its perceived benefits. However, the dilemma was that British forces were thus more vulnerable to unidentified enemy positions. Dependency on intelligence from aerial reconnaissance was now even greater.[41]

Artillery was transformed with the increased targeting information. Still, changing technology required significant and continual refinements and improvements. Communications between aeroplane and receiving station were short-range and sporadic. Increased reliance on Captain Lewis' clock code necessitated more accurate target materials. Trench maps derived from aerial photography were in greater demand. However, mapping accuracy was hampered by camera distortion from motor/engine vibration. The lack of precise coordinates from the aerial maps prompted artillery units to demand continued registration from the aerial platforms. Increased Allied aerial observation spurred the enemy to respond with more lethal defenses.[42] Although the demand was great, the RFC lacked experienced aerial observers. Despite the array of challenges, artillery received more targeting information. British artillery tactics evolved with the changing dynamic. Artillery now focused on a massive bombardment to "crush all resistance." Infantry mobility could resume once the opposition was annihilated. It was time to apply the new strategy and achieve the breakthrough.[43]

Far from being challenged like the French at Verdun, the British RFC dominated their sector. The RFC further enhanced its support to the British armies by establishing the brigade echelon. Each RFC brigade was able to meet the increasing demands for close reconnaissance, photography, and artillery cooperation on the immediate front. It also met the increasing need for longer range reconnaissance beyond the Corps area of responsibility. The brigade comprised a "corps wing" to accomplish short-distance reconnais-

---

[36] Edmonds, *1916*, I, 86-87.

[37] "Proposals for a Long Distance Machine," 9 March 1916, encl. 1A to "Letter from Col R.F.C. E. F. D. 28/2," TNA, PRO: AIR 2/16

[38] Jones, II, 146-147; Edmonds, *1916*, I, 85.

[39] "Proposals for a Fighting Machine," TNA, PRO: AIR 2/16.

[40] Edmonds, *1916*, I, 86-87.

---

[41] Bailey, 133.

[42] Bailey, 134.

[43] Bailey, 135.

sance, photography, and artillery cooperation missions within five miles of the front line. An "army wing" was also created to better support the Army commander, with aerial resources beyond the first five miles of front lines, and with long-distance reconnaissance, air fighting, and photography. Since Army Wing responsibilities required an extended radius of action, British aeroplanes that possessed the greatest performance and firepower to better protect themselves were assigned at that echelon. The RFC also established a new wing, the 9th Wing, allotted to the GHQ with air assets to conduct strategic work and a host of special missions that included destruction of kite balloons and close-in photography. Finally, the RFC headquarters staff was strengthened and reorganized on the model of a corps staff.[44]

The changes under way in British aviation also positively affected the establishment of aerial liaison to the battlefield commander. Close cooperation, practice, and constant communication between aerial observers and artillery battery commanders became normal practice. British radio technology was refined to better support the ground combatant as well as counter German electronic jamming. British transmissions now included a "clapper break" which varied the pitch or tone of the note sent out by the aeroplane transmitter. The clapper break allowed the ground receiver to distinguish one aeroplane's signal from another and increased the number of aeroplanes that could operate in a given sector without jamming each other's transmissions.[45]

By the spring of 1916, British army and artillery demand for aerial photographs became so enormous that the traditional photographic plate processing and print development centers at the wing were overburdened, resulting in critical delays in print dissemination. Moore-Brabazon recalled:

The demands for photographs increased out of all proportions to the possibilities of being able to deal with

it from the point of view of hand-held and hand-changing cameras, so that a semi automatic device was got out, whereby the camera was fixed to the machine, and by a simple movement of the hand the plate was changed, the shutter wound and the photograph taken. This increased the number of photographs enormously, and although the development, printing and identification of them were at the time done at Wing Headquarters, the proposition soon became so big that it was decided, during 1916, to departmentalize down photography and make it a Squadron proposition.[46]

This was especially true for artillery, which required a constant update of photographs to supplement its firing maps. Increased aerial coverage was necessary for ongoing and future planning, especially in preparation for the upcoming offensive at the Somme. With the increase in aerial photographic support came an increase in manning establishment for British intelligence. Now every squadron with an observation and photographic reconnaissance mission possessed an intelligence section (manning included one intelligence officer, two draftsmen, and one clerk). A photo section was also added to each RFC corps, and army reconnaissance squadrons were augmented with a photo section manned with an NCO and two draftsmen.[47] Brigadier-General Charteris commented on the expansion under way: "On the Aisne (1914) each corps only had one officer for "I" work. Now there is one with each brigade and division, and altogether seventeen at Army Headquarters and every corps is asking for a larger staff."[48]

Back in England, Captain Campbell worked with the Ministry to keep pace with the demand for photographic expertise. The RFC School of Photography focused on training a complete photo section (1 officer, 1 NCO, and 5 men). The personnel were busy loading magazines with unexposed plates, uploading and down-

[44] Jones, II, 147; Lamberton, 11; Edmonds, *1916*, I, 85.

[45] Edmonds, *1916*, I, 87-88; Gerald Gliddon, *The Battle of the Somme* (Phoenix Mill, UK: Sutton Publishing, 1987), 427.

[46] Moore-Brabazon, "Photography in the RAF," TNA, PRO: AIR 1/724/91/1.

[47] Jones, II, 177; Edmonds, *1916*, I, 88; Mead, 76.

[48] Charteris, *At G.H.Q.*, 155.

FIGURE 40. **Brigadier-General Charteris was in charge of "I" work for Field Marshal Haig until late 1917.** Source: John Charteris, *At G.H.Q.* (London: Cassell and Company, 1931).

lots and observers were not inclined to take instruction from anyone, particularly an NCO. His prior experience with squadron air crews showed their attention to developing and printing was not always confined to aerial work (these unofficial or extraneous photos are also known as "happy snaps"), resulting in a wastage of material. Campbell concluded that in light of aerial photography's increased importance, "the flying officer should undergo a practical examination to include *taking a good photograph of a given area*. If this suggestion be adopted, a good deal of our present difficulties in getting work done at home would vanish."[49] Grooming pilots and observers to become more involved in the correct process of working aerial photography became an obsession for Campbell and his Air Ministry counterparts. Campbell made it clear in his report to the Ministry: "In conclusion, the training of photographic personnel is in good working order, but it is regretted that despite the efforts of the photographic Officers at Wings, the training of Pilots and Observers in Aerial Photography still leaves much to be desired. Very few photographs are taken, and consequently success is not always attained when the squadrons or drafts arrive overseas."[50]

The report went through the Ministry, prompting the Deputy Director of Military Aeronautics, Lieutenant Colonel C. C. Marindin, to echo, "I am directed to call your attention to the necessity of training all pilots in the handling of cameras and in taking aerial photographs before they proceed abroad, and to request you to take such steps as will ensure this being carried out in all service units under your command."[51] It is interesting to note that the concern lingered on throughout the remainder of the war. The American photographic expert, Major Edward Jean Steichen, commented on this very issue in his post-war critique:

The Photographic Section was rarely asked to make assemblages except

loading aerial cameras to the aeroplanes prior to and after the flight, and working on the photographic negatives (developing, washing, drying, and plotting). Several men were constantly engaged in the enlarging room. Campbell was faced with a need to orient pilots and observers to aerial photography. He observed that pi-

[49] Campbell, "Notes on Aerial Photography," TNA, PRO: AIR 1/7/6/98/20.

[50] Capt C. D. M. Campbell, "Progress of Photography in Royal Flying Corps at Home, to 31st December, 1915," 22 January 1916, TNA, PRO: AIR 1/724/91/1.

[51] "The General Officer Commanding, 6th Brigade," 3 February 1916, TNA, PRO: AIR 1/724/91/1, 87/7298.

Chapter 3: Fortifications Across the Front Line

for office ornaments. Stereoscopic prints were only occasionally called for. Not once was a large assemblage requested of an entire sector. Initiative in these directions on the part of the Photographic Sections was discouraged and there was a general atmosphere concerning these things which suggested that it was none of our affair and did not conform to Army Intelligence Regulations.[52]

The Somme

With transformation well in place within the British military hierarchy, the stage was now set for the Somme offensive, one of the greatest military operations of the war. The battle of the Somme was a defining moment for the British in World War I. Its horror culminated in the greatest number of casualties ever experienced by the British Army in one day of fighting. The Somme battleground featured extensive open country with unobstructed vision and broad fields of fire. Geology favored the defenders, with extensive areas of solid chalk reinforcing the trench lines better than the soil on most sectors of the Western Front. Additionally, the region's dense clusters of houses formed veritable forts, which became the strongpoints for the Germans' defensive system.[53] The most striking characteristic of the Somme battlefield was its monotonous succession of low, rolling plains.[54] The British had commenced planning for the Somme offensive as early as 1915, acquiring aerial photographs that detailed the first and second line networks. The total concentration of the RFC for the Somme was evidenced by its complement of 185 aeroplanes. In the opening phase of the battle, the German Air Service was considerably outnumbered and remained so until the middle of July. During the buildup and first days of the offensive, the RFC reinforced protection of corps reconnaissance through a continuous line of patrolling pursuit aeroplanes. Aerial activity increased that spring with more units augmenting the sec-

tor, to include the RFC's 9th Wing, configured for special operations. The 9th comprised four squadrons (Numbers 21, 27, 60, and 70). In addition to increased strategic reconnaissance of the region, the RFC increased its attacks against German aviation and conducted bombardment of communication networks.[55] The RFC preparation strategy for the Somme offensive worked. In the preparation for the battle, not one German aeroplane came over the Fourth Army zone either to bomb the British marshalling areas, direct enemy fire, or observe or photograph the preparations.[56]

The RFC had honed its aerial reconnaissance skills right up to the kickoff of the offensive. The effort to achieve timely photography for the commander was clearly demonstrated through a "speed test." The RFC's 1st Brigade had three squadrons from 1st Wing, 1st Brigade, acquire coverage of German targets with amazing results. A BE 2 from No. 9 Squadron took an aerial photograph over the front on 10 June at 0750 hours, landed 20 minutes later, and had the first print dispatched to I Corps via motorcycle at 0832 hours. Seven minutes later the prints arrived. Total time from aerial photograph to receipt of coverage at the Corps was 49 minutes. On 16 June, FE 2b's from No. 18 Squadron conducted a similar test. The photograph was taken at 1706 hours. The FE 2b landed with the camera quickly downloaded and the first print developed 21 minutes later, an incredible accomplishment in a wartime aerial battleground environment. Ten prints were handed to the motorcyclist and arrived at IV Corps Headquarters approximately 37 minutes after producing the first print. Finally, a BE 2c from No. 10 Squadron on 18 June photographed the German target, arrived at the landing ground, developed a print, and delivered it to XI Corps Headquarters in an astonishing 30 minutes.[57] The speed tests showed the staff that aerial photographic reconnaissance was dependable in providing the battlefield commander with timely information as the campaign progressed.

---

[52] Maj Edward Steichen, "Aerial Photography: The Matter of Interpretation and Exploitation," Gorrell Report, ser. G, r. 24, NARA.

[53] Johnson, *Battlefields of the World War*, 111-112.

[54] Johnson, *Battlefields of the World War*, 96.

[55] Edmonds, *1916*, I, 268.

[56] Edmonds, *1916*, I, 286-287.

[57] No. 2 Squadron flew both BE 2c and BE 2d variants. Author discussion with Michael Mockford. Campbell, "Notes on Aerial Photography," TNA, PRO: AIR 1/7/6/98/20; 2nd Lt V. F. Bryce, Photographic Officer, 1st Brigade, BEF, Report, 1 June 1916, TNA, PRO: AIR 1/7/6/98/20.

FIGURE 41. The Somme. Source: *West Point Atlas,* map 34. Courtesy, Department of History, U.S. Military Academy.

Such preparations contributed to a growing confidence in the upcoming battle.

The RFC took excellent photographs daily, which were in the hands of the artillery commanders the same night. This greatly helped in determining the results of the fire.[58] The aerial reconnaissance did report new and more formidable defenses being built, to include the discovery of a third German defense line. The British soon acquired aerial coverage of the entire German trench network in the Somme region facing the British Fourth Army. Ten days prior to the actual offensive, British aerial photography of the entire

sector was again acquired. The preparation had gone well. Aerial coverage had reinforced British military confidence to proceed as planned. The British commander-in-chief, General Haig, notified Général Joffre that the British would "continue the battle with such vigour as will force the enemy to abandon his attacks on Verdun."[59]

During the last six days of June, the Allies continuously bombarded the German positions. Aerial reconnaissance was in constant demand. On 26 June, the bombardment was stopped in order to allow the RFC to photograph the area and obtain an exact record of fire for the artil-

---

[58] Edmonds, *1916*, I, 300.

[59] Jones, II, 197.

Chapter 3: Fortifications Across the Front Line

lery. Aerial photographs not only showed how the heavy shells had fallen, but also provided insight on the status of the defensive wire entanglements around the German trench networks. The coverage showed the artillery was accomplishing its objective.[60] One of the corps commanders remarked, "The aeroplane photographs showed admirably the effect of the bombardment both on the wire and on the trenches and were of the greatest value."[61] The weather in the region hampered aerial reconnaissance coverage for the next two days. Despite the interruption, aerial observation continued whenever there was a break in the clouds.[62]

On the eve of the battle, Charteris predicted, "We do not expect any great advance, or any great place of arms to fall to us now. We are fighting primarily to wear down the German armies and the German nation, interfere with their plans, gain some valuable position and generally to prepare for the great decisive offensive which must come sooner or later, if not this year or even next year. The casualty list will be big."[63] On 1 July, the British Army suffered a catastrophic 60,000 men killed and wounded.

Throughout that first day of the Somme campaign, the RFC maintained command of the air. Although 110 pilots were in the air for a total of 408 hours, there were only nine recorded aerial combat engagements with the Germans. Infantry contact sorties tried their best to report the progress of the infantry. Ongoing artillery spotting missions searched for targets. However, the sheer volume of artillery masked the ability to determine impact with accuracy. Strategic aerial reconnaissance discovered very little activity on the roads and railways behind the German lines. A fair number of aerial photographs were taken, including some of the German third line of defense.[64] After a week, the Fourth Army had yet to secure the important preliminary Somme campaign objectives of Trones Wood, Mametz Wood, and Contalmaison. The British Fourth Army commander, General Sir Henry Seymour Rawlinson,

FIGURE 42. **The BE 2d variant, shown here, delivered intelligence to the headquarters within 30 minutes of acquisition of the target.** Source: Gorrell Report, NARA.

issued a preparatory order for the attack against the German second position, to be launched on 10 July. The preparations were similar to what had transpired before the first major assault on 1 July with aerial reconnaissance acquiring coverage of new objectives, to include the newly discovered German third line of defense.[65]

---

[60] Edmonds, *1916*, I, 303.
[61] Jones, II, 209.
[62] Edmonds, *1916*, I, 304.
[63] Charteris, *At G.H.Q.*, 77.
[64] Edmonds, *1916*, I, 477.

[65] Edmonds, *1916*, II, 62.

The resultant Somme campaign did not lack for intelligence from aerial photographs. In the five months of battle, the RFC took more than 19,000 air photographs and generated 430,000 prints for the combatants.[66] British planning for the 14 July attack was aided by aerial photographs that revealed additional enemy positions. However, quality of analysis was now becoming suspect due to unforeseen enemy resistance. Aerial reconnaissance reports were losing credibility; claims of limited enemy resistance were not being believed. The situation did not improve. Charteris commented in a letter to Macdonogh at the Air Ministry 28 days after the Somme campaign commenced, "Air reconnaissance as a battle means of information has failed us. Aeroplanes have to go too high now to do much good, and in any case the number of machines is very limited and the information they give meager and amateurish."[67] It is interesting to note that German recollections reflected just the opposite view. Allied reconnaissance, in their view, was effective. One German veteran of the Eastern Front remarked on his time during the August campaign at the Somme:

What I have been through during this time surpassed in horror all my previous experiences during the second

year of the war.... How the English, with the aid of their airmen, who are often 1,500 feet above the position, and their captive balloons, have exactly located every one of our batteries and have so smashed them up with long-distance guns of every caliber that the artillery here has had unusually heavy losses both of men and material.[68]

After the war, the Quartermaster-General of the German Army, General Erich Friedrich Wilhelm Ludendorff, reflected that Allied aeroplanes made "the troops feel that they had been discovered in places which heretofore they had thought afforded safe cover."[69]

The Somme campaign continued for months. Prior to the British assault of 15 September, Army reconnaissance of the rear German sec-

[66] Watkis, 11.

[67] "Brig-Gen John Charteris to Gen Macdonogh, War Ministry," 28 July 1916, TNA, PRO: WO 158/897; Charteris, *At G.H.Q.*, 159.

[68] Friedrich Steinbrecher quoted in Robert B. Asbrey, *The German High Command at War: Hindenburg and Ludendorff Conduct World War I* (New York: William Morrow and Company, 1991), 245-246.

[69] Ludendorff quoted in Porter, 17.

tor revealed no abnormal activity upon the roads and railways in the area. The RFC monitored key cities behind the German lines for signs of troop buildup and reinforcement, but did not discover any sign of activity. From the opening of the Somme offensive, British Intelligence employed all sources to determine any change in the German order of battle. British analysis showed 32 enemy divisions had been fighting since the commencement of the campaign on 1 July. By September, 19 enemy divisions had departed to other fronts.[70] When the British started their 15 September offensive, the RFC flew more hours and experienced more fighting than on any day since the war began. Artillery spotting in support of the Fourth Army front revealed the location of 150 batteries, 70 of these being engaged. At the same time the RFC's Army Squadron sorties over German rear echelons did not detect any abnormal movement.[71]

The British Army fully accepted the need for extensive aerial coverage to conduct its campaign. The demand impacted the entire aerial photographic community. British photographic training was well in place, producing photo section staff necessary for the campaign. The pioneers of British aerial reconnaissance, to include Moore-Brabazon, introduced measures to orient staffs and combatants to photographic interpretation with the first British manual on aerial photographic reconnaissance, *Notes on the Interpretation of Aeroplane Photographs*.[72] Improvement in camera and mount technology was accompanied by a greater awareness of the potential of aerial coverage. Lieutenant Victor Laws was in the process of developing the prototype "L" Type camera, the best British aerial camera of the war.[73] Better designs for mounting aerial cameras had been developed, eliminating many problems associated with vibration

from the aeroplane motor.[74] Innovation on the battlefield was on the rise as the combatants entered into the third year of the conflict. Stabilization was addressed and solutions were found. Captain Campbell had developed a new mounting device for the aerial camera, using rubber sponges inside the fuselage to reduce vibration. He had even purchased the entire stock of rubber sponges in St. Omer for this purpose.[75]

The United States Military Commences Aerial Observation

The American military studied aerial reconnaissance while the war progressed in Europe. The War College Division sponsored studies in 1915 to "consider various aeronautical appliances in regard to their practical value in campaign."[76] The aerial reconnaissance role earned primary consideration. In the early stages of the conflict, assessment of photography's role paralleled cartographic construction. In the American staff assessment of 1915, photography was "utilized to the greatest extent possible in aerial reconnaissance."[77] The Americans recognized that timely development and production was essential to the value of the aerial photograph, and that institutionalizing the interpretation process was necessary: "The plates or films thus made are rapidly developed and are thrown on a screen by means of a stereopticon, when all details are magnified to any extent desired and details invisible to the naked eye are brought out plainly. These details are then entered on the maps of the officers concerned."[78] Cartography also benefited from the coverage. "As the height at which an aeroplane is flying can be taken from the barograph, and as the focal angle of the lens of the camera is known, a scale can easily be

[70] Edmonds, *1916*, II, 304.

[71] Edmonds, *1916*, II, 347.

[72] Great Britain, General Staff (Intelligence), General Headquarters, *Notes on the Interpretation of Aeroplane Photographs* (Paris, France: Army Printing and Stationery Services, November 1916). Hereafter, the three editions of this work will be distinguished by their Stationery Services numbers: S.S. 445 (1916), S.S. 550 (1917), and S.S. 631 (1918).

[73] Nesbit, 40.

[74] Toye, "History of Photography," TNA, PRO: AIR 1/724/91/1.

[75] Toye, "History of Photography," TNA, PRO: AIR 1/724/91/1.

[76] "Military Aviation," in Maurer Maurer, ed., *The U.S. Air Service in World War I* (4 vols., Washington, DC: The Office of Air Force History, 1978), II, 41.

[77] "Military Aviation," in Maurer, ed., *U.S. Air Service*, II, 41.

[78] "Military Aviation," in Maurer, ed., *U.S. Air Service*, II, 49.

worked out and the views form good maps of the terrain photographed."[79]

Military employment of American forces on the Mexican border following the 1916 attack by Pancho Villa on Columbus, New Mexico, showed an acute lack of U.S. military preparation. However, the subsequent campaign against Pancho Villa highlighted aviation's potential for information gathering. Major Benjamin D. Foulois and the First Aero Squadron provided the limited aerial support in the campaign. Photographic expertise was available to support the fledgling effort. James Bagley, a world leader in photographic mapping and exploration, was assigned to Pershing's staff to share his expertise. The dimension of the ongoing campaign proved a challenge for any reconnaissance effort. Pershing's forces operated in a 19,000 square mile area.[80] Despite the opportunity, the U.S. mili-

FIGURE 44. **A detailed oblique aerial photograph of French troops on the attack at the Somme on 10 October 1916.** Source: SHAA, photo in Christienne and Lissarague, *A History of French Military Aviation.*

tary was not prepared for the demands associated with modern warfare awaiting it upon entering the European war in 1917. The Americans lacked the knowledge to exploit aviation, particularly in aerial photography. America's entry in the war exposed its woeful lack of preparation, forcing it to depend upon Allies who already were strained beyond capacity.[81]

---

[79] "Military Aviation," in Maurer, ed., *U.S. Air Service*, II, 49.

[80] Brig Gen George W. Goddard, *Overview: A Life-Long Adventure in Aerial Photography* (Garden City, NY: Doubleday & Company, 1969), 10.

[81] Benedict Crowell and Robert F. Wilson, *The Armies of Industry: Our Nation's Manufacture of Munitions for a World in Arms, 1917-1918* (2 vols., New Haven, CT: Yale University Press, 1921), II, 419.

Chapter 3: Fortifications Across the Front Line

CHAPTER 4
OCTOBER 1916 – NOVEMBER 1917:
POSITIONAL WARFARE AT ITS ZENITH

The Aerial Photographic Institution

During the third year of the Great War, aerial reconnaissance and photographic interpretation were fully integrated with operational planning and execution. There was no longer a debate with the military staff and combatants on capabilities and potential. The past year had proved that aerial observation, validated by the photograph and transformed into a map, was the most lucrative source for defining the battlefield. With that process fully institutionalized, the Allied aviation establishment now gravitated to developing pursuit resources to maintain air supremacy. Experienced aerial reconnaissance and photographic interpretation personnel were now in place at all echelons. Aerial reconnaissance and photographic interpretation both underwent substantial evolution in the final two years of conflict. The quantity and quality of photographic production enjoyed substantial incremental increases, providing the combatants with an excellent overview of what confronted them on the battlefield. The second key ingredient was improvement in aeroplane design. With fuselage, propeller, engine, and other design changes, reconnaissance aeroplanes could operate at higher altitudes, above the range of air defense cannons and enemy pursuit.

Aerial observation remained a critical priority for both sides, but emphasis was shifting toward achieving air superiority. German General Fritz von Below, Commander of the First Army described the German aerial posture against the Allies in his January 1917 memorandum, "The main object of fighting in the air is to enable our photographic registration and photographic reconnaissance to be carried out, and at the same time prevent that of the enemy. All other tasks, such as bombing raids, machine gun attacks on troops, and even distance reconnaissance in trench warfare must be secondary to this main object."[1] Von Below's comments governing the offensive accurately prophesied things to come: "It is this principle that the enemies have now realized and are now acting upon. What we need to defeat their application of it is a sufficient quantity of efficient weapons; that is to say, a sufficient quantity of fast fighting machines."[2] *Study and Exploitation of Aerial Photographs* discussed some salient points from the French perspective:

> After the hard battles of 1916 at Verdun and on the Somme, the German staff published in November and December 1916, "New Regulations for Stationary Warfare." The first part (General Instructions on the organizations of positions and the details of organization) and the eighth part of these regulations (Principles for conducting defensive battles) are of great interest.

---

[1] General von Below quoted in Baring, 200.
[2] General von Below quoted in Baring, 201.

FIGURE 45. **A new generation of aerial reconnaissance aeroplanes such as the French AR 1 were deploying to front sectors. The AR 1 is acquiring a 50 cm aerial camera for the sortie.** Source: SHAA, photo in Christienne and Lissarague, *A History of French Military Aviation.*

A. The following are the salient points:

(a) Maximum utilization of the reverse slope.

(b) Organization of extensive fortified areas, several lines deep and thoroughly organized.

(c) Distribution on the terrain of flanking machine guns (checkerboard arrangement) and dugouts forming the skeleton of all the infantry fighting lines.

(d) Successive lines of troops in depth — Small garrison in the front line, with shallow concrete shelters so far as possible, the underground dugouts being reserved for the rear lines. (One

about every 150 meters for a group of 8 men, on the Hindenburg line.)

(e) Extensive use of diagonal defensive trenches, especially near the sector limits.

(f) Execution of urgency works, picketing the lines, narrow gauge railways, flanking sections and dugouts (position framework), observation posts, headquarters, auxiliary defenses, ammunition depots, drainage, etc.

B. Regarding construction and organization details, the above-mentioned regulations recommend:

(a) Giving to the auxiliary defenses an irregular outline and arranging them in sections separated by spaces, in such fashion that they may be effectually flanked by machine guns.

(b) Still further widening the trenches and boyaus. This width attains 3.2 and 3.4 meters on the Hindenburg line in front of the British.

(c) To dispose the mortars outside of the firing trenches.

(d) To establish a large number of observation posts at successive intervals from the front.[3]

It was in accordance with these principles that the Hindenburg line was constructed, during the winter of 1916-1917.

The GQG vision for *Aviation Militaire* at the commencement of 1917 was to increase its aeronautical strength to 187 escadrilles, each with a nominal count of 10 aéroplanes. The emphasis was on the reconnaissance mission protected by pursuit.[4] In addition to this realignment in thinking, *Aviation Militaire* came to terms with the eroding quality of its aerial reconnaissance force. New enemy fighter aeroplanes were being introduced

---

[3] *Study and Exploitation of Aerial Photographs,* 7-8.
[4] Davilla and Soltan, 10.

Chapter 4: Positional Warfare at Its Zenith

FIGURE 46. **Three-seat, long-range reconnaissance aéroplanes such as the Morane-Saulnier T provided both aerial reconnaissance and additional protection for other allied aéroplanes operating over the sector.** Source: Jim Davilla.

and raising havoc throughout the front. France's existing fleet of Sopwith 1 A2 (French variant of the British Sopwith 1½ Strutter, two-seater reconnaissance and bombardment aeroplane), A.R.1, Caudron G.6, Salmson-Moineau S.M.1's and Morane-Saulnier T's suffered from technical limitations. The GQG decided to reorganize aerial resources. A 16 March 1917 memorandum directed that many three-seat, long-range reconnaissance aeroplanes (Caudron G.6, R.4, Salmson-Moineau S.M.1s, and Morane-Saulnier T's) disperse across Aviation Militaire units due to "serious inconveniences" being imposed on escadrille personnel. Maintenance downtime and landing ground overcrowding prompted the new arrangement. Rearranging long-range reconnaissance throughout the escadrilles of the Aviation Militaire had a consequence for aerial reconnaissance. The mission was integral to all of French aviation and remained in place throughout to the conclusion of the war.[5]

In 1917 British aerial reconnaissance enjoyed a resurgence caused by the arrival of a new generation of aeroplanes that served until the end of the war. Key to aerial reconnaissance was the Reconnaissance Experimental (RE) 8 and Airco DeHavilland (DH) 4. One of the most famous of the RFC (and RAF) units was No. 55 Squadron. They were the first to acquire the DH 4 in March 1917 and achieved an impressive strategic bombardment and long-range reconnaissance record.[6]

The reconnaissance mission permeated the work environment of RFC squadrons. By the early part of 1917 every aerodrome at the landing ground had its map room, the walls of which

---

[5] A.R. was the primary designation of the A.R.1. *Aviation Militaire* referred to it as "*Avion de Reconnaissance*." The Renault firm called it "*Avion Renault*" or "*Avant Renault*." Finally, the French production directorate *STAé* just called it A.R. 1. Davilla and Soltan, 9-10.

---

[6] J. M. Bruce, *The de Havilland D.H. 4* (Leatherhead, UK: Profile Publications, Ltd., 1965), 5.

were adorned with sections of maps and photographic mosaics. The maps and mosaics enabled air crews to quickly study the terrain and identify critical landmarks.[7] With the increased demand for aerial reconnaissance came the need for more intelligence personnel to ascertain what was observed and photographed. This led the British to increase intelligence training at their schools in the United Kingdom and within the BEF. The Somme campaign generated large volumes of information without much benefit, resulting in the British turning to their French counterparts for another view of interpreting and processing information. The French experience in 1916 had clearly demonstrated the benefits of integrating intelligence personnel at the escadrilles. A British study of the French intelligence process entitled *Notes on the French System of Intelligence, 23rd September 1916*, outlined the French method of acquiring and disseminating aerial reconnaissance and photographic interpretation information during a major campaign. The analysis was published and disseminated to British staffs.[8] The next step was to learn from the French experience and modify to suit what worked best for the evolving British program. In October 1916, Major-General Trenchard proposed that British Intelligence Sections be established in certain squadrons and wings where the Intelligence Officer could be in intimate touch with the flying and photographic personnel.[9] This was approved and instructions issued to the British forces in December 1916. In a step taken to retain intelligence personnel, the RFC established its own Branch Intelligence Sections at each corps squadron and Army wing. Trenchard preferred that the intelligence units remain integral to the RFC, but he was overruled by seniors at GHQ who decided that intelligence must remain under the Army Intelligence Chief.[10]

In the fall of 1916, senior factions of the Royal Artillery and RFC debated the predominant role of the aviator. The Royal Artillery made demands on the British RFC to allocate more aerial observer resources to its artillery-spotting mission. British artillery was upgrading with greater numbers of heavy artillery and howitzers to fire larger and more lethal munitions against an increasingly fortified German adversary.[11] The premise was simple: Increases and improvements in artillery required more dedicated artillery spotting aerial platforms. Improving radio capabilities also added to the allure of acquiring more aeroplanes. British aerial priorities had committed twice the number of aeroplanes to artillery spotting over the previous year.[12] With these trends, the British military high command in October 1916 proposed that the control of the Corps squadrons should pass to the Artillery. General Rawlinson made his move to reorganize the aviation assets; "To ensure perfection, we require: The observers must be highly skilled. Aeroplane observation for artillery purposes is skilled work of a very high order. With an unskilled observer the best trained and best equipped battery is useless."[13] Trenchard fought Rawlinson's suggestion with a dose of aviation reality, "Artillery work is not the entire duty of the Corps Squadron, which is also charged with contact patrol work, trench reconnaissance, and trench photography. Nor are Corps Squadrons at present equipped with machines of a suitable type to do all the work required by the artillery, such as photography, at a distance behind the lines which must be done by fighting machines."[14] Trenchard won this battle. The allocation of aeroplanes remained within the jurisdiction of the RFC.

The Siegfried Stellung (Hindenburg Line)

The lessons of Verdun and the Somme made an indelible mark on both sides. The human casualties from positional warfare greatly exceeded every known estimate. British and French leaders considered their tactics of destruction successful, despite the incredible cost. They assumed that sufficient artillery could acquire any limited objective. Planning a successful campaign required longer-range artillery and more effective

[7] Maj Charles C. Turner, *The Struggle in the Air 1914-1918* (New York: Longmans, Green & Co., and London: Edward Arnold, 1919), 203.

[8] "Notes on the French System of Intelligence," TNA, PRO: WO 158/983.

[9] Jones, III, 314-315.

[10] Jones, III, 315.

[11] Edmonds, *1917*, I, 11.

[12] Edmonds, *1917*, I, 15.

[13] Jones, III, 307.

[14] Jones, III, 308.

FIGURE 47. **Siegfried Stellung at Bellencourt. "Held by an Army of unimpaired morale, it would have been wellnigh impregnable."** Source: Great Britain, General Staff (Intelligence), *Illustrations to Accompany Notes on the Interpretation of Aeroplane Photographs* (S.S. 631a) (France: Army Printing and Stationery Services, 1918).

counter-battery fire. These objectives depended more than ever on aerial reconnaissance.[15]

By the close of 1916 the German OHL had become deeply disturbed by the impact of the allied offensives in the Somme region. Because General Ludendorff feared the German Army might not stand up to a similar offensive in the coming spring, the decision was made to transform the front to the most intricate defensive system ever devised. The Germans called their master network the *Siegfried Stellung*, but to the Allies it was known as the Hindenburg Line.[16] Charteris viewed the obstruction with awe: "Held by an Army of unimpaired morale, it would have been well-nigh impregnable."[17] The Hindenburg Line prompted many improvements in Germany's approach to positional warfare, to include more elaborate tank maneuvers, unregistered artillery bombardments, elastic defenses, and the use of storm troops to infiltrate enemy lines.[18]

The Siegfried Stellung returned the Western Front to a more strategic posture of elaborately built networks of defense. The German OHL decided to build five such strategic systems. The *Flandern* Line ran from the Belgian coast via the Passchendaele ridge through the Messines salient to Lille. The *Wotan* Line extended from

---

[15] Bailey, 139.

[16] David French, "Failures of Intelligence: The Retreat to the Hindenburg Line and the March 1918 Offensive," in *Strategy and Intelligence, British Policy during the First World War*, eds. Michael Dockrill and David French (London: The Hambledon Press, 1996), 68.

[17] Charteris, *Haig*, 131.

[18] Peter Oldham, *The Hindenburg Line* (London: Leo Cooper, 1997), 9-10.

Lille to the rear of the Loos-Arras-Vimy and Somme battlefields. The *Siegfried* Line began at Arras and proceeded west of St-Quentin and Laon to the River Aisne east of Soissons. The *Hunding* Line began near Peronne on the Somme and ran to Étain on the Meuse and then north of Verdun. The fifth line, the *Michael* Line (The Germans called it the *Michael I* Zone) covered Étain to Pont-à-Mousson on the River Moselle.[19] The Siegfried Stellung also helped the Germans' strategic objectives in the other theaters. They traded a seemingly impregnable defense network for the ability to more effectively move personnel throughout the theater. The Siegfried Stellung allowed German staffs to effectively transfer thirteen German divisions and fifty batteries of heavy artillery to the Austrian southern front opposite the Italians without experiencing a major shortfall in manning.[20]

The first indication of construction was acquired by British aerial reconnaissance toward the end of October 1916. Fresh earth was discovered near Queant (12 miles south-east of Arras

FIGURE 48. **Within the La Malmaison sector near the city of Reims, the Germans' Hunding line shows the symmetry of the network of traverses.** Source: France. General Headquarters, Grand Quartier Général des Armées du Nord et du Nord-Est, Etat-Major, *Étude et Exploitation des Photographies Aériennes* (Paris: Imprimerie Nationale, 1918).

and 14.5 miles east of the front line at Monchy au Bois). Suspicions were raised anytime defensive network construction was discovered, especially when it was observed well behind the existing front line. A special reconnaissance was ordered. On 9 November 1916, the first aerial reconnaissance report was generated, describing trench construction through Queant and Bullecourt, crossing the Sensée and the Cojeul and linking up to the Germans' rear third line east of Neuville Vitasse.[21] Despite noticeable construction activity in several sectors, the Allies were slow in recognizing the overall strategic implica-

---

[19] David French in Dockrill and French, 76-77; Jones, III, 305-306.

[20] David French in Dockrill and French, 77.

[21] Edmonds, *1917*, I, 87-88; Jones, II, 318.

Chapter 4: Positional Warfare at Its Zenith

FIGURE 49. Companion line drawing of the network at la Malmaison.
Source: *Étude et Exploitation des Photographies Aériennes*.

tions. When construction commenced, the large number of gaps in construction did not suggest a masterful defense network. A December aerial reconnaissance of the eventual location of the Siegfried Stellung near the French town of Marcoing "observed no unusual activity."[22] The Allies did share what they knew of the activity. On 2 January 1917, the French commander-in-chief, Général Robert Nivelle, prompted by reports from agents and repatriated civilians, instructed his aviation services to cooperate with the British in reconnaissance of the system of defense. Later that month, the British GHQ Intelligence Summary mentioned in the report of French "rapatriés" that the Germans were constructing a line of defense, "from Arras to Laon."

Although the Siegfried Stellung did not follow that very same course, it did show extensive activity in the strategic rear areas.[23] Additional reports from prisoner interrogations were treated as unconfirmed rumors at Haig's GHQ. Analysis continued, but elicited a consistent, "Confirmation is required."[24] Général Nivelle received more reports from agents and repeated his order for more reconnaissance.[25] Through the remainder of the winter, the British monitored the construction while their armies slowly advanced on the Somme front. However, the aerial superiority was now turning in favor of the Germans.[26]

The "very combative" attitude of German aircraft that prevented both aerial reconnaissance and photography complicated the Allies' ability to effectively gauge the extent of construction. The lack of aerial reconnaissance validation of human intelligence in January resulted in the French 2e Bureau still deliberating over the Siegfried Stellung's ultimate purpose. Effective

---

[22] Edmonds, *1917*, I, 88-89.

[23] Edmonds, *1917*, I, 88-89.
[24] David French in Dockrill and French, 77-78.
[25] Edmonds, *1917*, I, 88-89.
[26] David French in Dockrill and French, 78.

reconnaissance did not resume until the Germans had departed their forward areas for the Siegfried Stellung in mid-March. French postwar analysis later confirmed their frustration that the "General-in-Chief was thus not informed of the situation of the Hindenburg Line."[27] German General von Below's remarks of January 1917 reflected a sensitivity to the effectiveness of the Allied reconnaissance and a determination to neutralize their efforts:

> The beginning and the first weeks of the battle of the Somme were marked by a complete inferiority of our own air forces. The enemy's aeroplanes enjoyed complete freedom in carrying out distant reconnaissances. With the aid of aeroplane observation the hostile artillery neutralized our guns, and was able to range with the most extreme accuracy on the trenches occupied by our infantry; the required data for this were provided by undisturbed trench reconnaissance and photography.[28]

FIGURE 50. **The wide trench network of the Seigfried Stellung served as obstacles against a tank attack. Most of these 3.20 to 3.40 meter wide trenches were in sectors opposite the British.** Source: *Étude et Exploitation des Photographies Aériennes.*

Aerial reconnaissance provided a piecemeal picture reflecting the nature of the target. On 2 February the British reported from one sortie south of Queant that "There appears to be a complete system of trenches around the town. On the south east corner of the town there is a short line about ¾-1 mile running up through Itancourt. On the north side, running east of the canal, is a fairly continuous line with strong points at about ¼ mile intervals. Between Bellicourt and Bellenglise the line of trenches is very broken."[29]

Strategic analysis of the Siegfried Stellung tested the analytical skill of Allied aerial photographic interpreters. Aerial photographic inter-

---

[27] Edmonds, *1917*, I, 88-89.
[28] Von Below quoted in Baring, 199.

[29] Reported by Lieut Peters and Lieut Balfour of RFC No. 70 Squadron, in Oldham, 9.

pretation eventually confirmed that the Siegfried Stellung was a masterful work of defense. The Siegfried Stellung defenses, though they varied in different sections, represented the application of mass production to fortification. Comparatively shallow dugouts of ferro-concrete (steel-reinforced concrete) were constructed according to a fixed pattern beneath the parapet for each squad. Mined dugouts were spaced throughout. The Siegfried Stellung's formidable barbed-wire obstacles included three belts, each ten to fifteen yards in depth and five yards or more apart and in front of the fire trench, configured in a zig-zag pattern. This allowed machine guns to sweep the sides.[30] Adding to the defenses were a number of small forts and strong points configured along the line.[31] In each sector, trenches were configured for transversal stopping positions (*Querstellungen*). Narrow gauge railways; flanking organizations and shelters; observatories; defenses for PCs; munitions depots; and drainage works were constructed in elaborate configurations. Defenses were now irregular and dispersed in several bands. The non-continuous entanglement supported any requirement for a German counterattack against the allied forces. This allowed for more effective emplacement of machine guns.[32] These "centers of resistance" provided places to which the garrisons could retire and hold out until reinforcements arrived. They were skillfully built and sited, designed for deliberate use after the enemy broke through the adjacent lines. Once past, the Germans could attack from the rear with machine gun and rifle fire.[33] Many trenches were widened to entrap attacking tanks. Tank pits were dug in the road and covered with camouflage to provide additional obstacles. Opposite the British, the average Siegfried Stellung trench measured between 3.20 and 3.40 meters in width. The German trench mortars (*minenwerfer*) were placed outside of the firing trenches. Finally, a network of observation stations was placed throughout, echeloned in depth to handle the vast contingencies of an experienced army, well versed in positional warfare.[34]

The German withdrawal back to the Siegfried Stellung also challenged aerial photography's support to artillery targeting. Additional detailed maps were required of the new sector. Triangulation targeting through flash-spotting and sound-ranging had to be moved forward and accurately positioned. Long-term reliance on cartographic data suddenly required a major overhaul.[35] The demand on aerial photography increased as analysts scrambled to acquire detailed information that would explain the complexities of the new front line to a host of consumers, to include artillery and infantry. German aerial resistance to reconnaissance of the Hindenburg Line is the basis of legends. The sector was the domain of most of Germany's top fighter pilots. The elite German ace, Manfred Freiherr von Richthofen, operated his *Jagstaffel* out of Douai, a key part of the Siegfried Stellung.[36] The RFC repeatedly paid the ultimate price throughout this transition. On 15 April alone, Richthofen and his unit shot down six reconnaissance aeroplanes on photographic missions over the Siegfried Stellung.[37]

By early February, the Siegfried Stellung was ready for occupancy. German forces commenced their withdrawal about 9 February 1917, moving both their own forces and the French civilians out of the front areas. They commenced a scorched earth policy, abandoning the former front line sector, leaving the Allies with an unusable countryside. The Germans methodically destroyed 264 villages and 38,000 houses in the region. Trees were sawed to the base, wells were clogged up, and landing grounds for aeroplanes were plowed up and further rendered ineffective with mines. The transformation was accomplished by forced labor from French civilians as the workforce. Aerial reconnaissance failed in its inability to successfully determine the extent of the withdrawal. By the end of February, the German Army had withdrawn its front line on the Somme battlefield

---

[30] Edmonds, *1917*, I, 92.

[31] Jones, III, 305-306.

[32] *Study and Use of Aerial Photographs*, 15 January 1918, sec. I, 10, NARA, RG 120, Box 819.

[33] Maj Joseph M. Hanson, ed., *The World War through the Telebinocular* (Meadville, PA: Keystone View Company, 1928), 24.

[34] *Study and Use of Aerial Photographs*, 15 January 1918, sec. I, 10n, NARA, RG 120, Box 819.

[35] Chasseaud, *Topography of Armageddon*, 11.

[36] Edmonds, *1917*, I, 88-89.

[37] Edmonds, *1917*, I, 90.

twenty miles to the east and occupied the Siegfried Stellung. It had totally disengaged from the English Fifth Army and moved east. Two weeks later, the sector opposite the French IIIème Armée was evacuated. The remaining lines did not finalize until the last withdrawal of German troops took place on 8 April 1917.[38] The withdrawal had strategic implications for the conduct of the war. The German move to the east successfully complicated Anglo-French plans for a spring offensive.[39]

Well into the final weeks of the war, the Siegfried Stellung remained the subject of much aerial photographic interpretation scrutiny:

> The relationship of the different German defensive positions to each other and the places of each in the general scheme of defense and even a description of the forward positions was published for battlefield preparation on 5 September 1918. The Michael I Zone that covered the area at Pagny on the Moselle River, west through Rembercourt to Pareid was analyzed from two to four kilometers. The strategic sector was further analyzed from the outpost line to the rear sector from 100 to 400 kilometers in depth. Wire was plentiful but there were practically no trenches. Concrete dugouts were numerous and the new work noted during the period included many additions to the number. The Hindenburg Line took advantage of counter slopes.[40]

The Nivelle Offensive

The enduring legacy of the French Armée in 1917 was the failed Nivelle Offensive. Général Nivelle had replaced Général Joffre as Général Commandant en Chef de les Armées. Nivelle enthusiastically supported his own master strategy to defeat the Germans, the high point of which was a quick, decisive offensive with imposing

tank forces achieving the breakthrough. Convinced that a breakthrough would outrun the reconnaissance, he did not value aerial photography like Pétain. However, his tanks quickly fell victim to German defenses that had been configured with three meter deep trenches to counter any forward movement. When Nivelle's offensive commenced on 17 April at Chemin des Dames, the Aviation Militaire was assigned the spearhead role to destroy German aerial reconnaissance and bombardment over the advancing sectors. Under a newly established *Groupement de Combat de la G.A.R.*, approximately 100 fighters were assigned to the IVème Armée to protect the reconnaissance. Despite the realignment, the French armée cooperation escadrilles suffered extensive losses.[41]

The British at Cambrai subsequently learned from this lesson in preparing for their tank offensive that fall. British armor attacked with bales of timber serving as self-contained trench fillers. Upon arriving at the trench obstacle, the tanks offloaded the bale and continued the attack. However, such precautions were not always successful.

Besides generating 100,000 French casualties, the Nivelle offensive in the Chemin des Dames sector broke the spirit of the French Armée and generated mutinies throughout the military. Général Pétain was quickly brought back to assume command of the French Armées before the surge of discontented manpower got out of control. Pétain's confidence in employing aerial photography helped maintain stasis in the battlefront. By increasing reconnaissance, he was able to gauge in which areas the French Armée could maintain presence without a major commitment to battle. This allowed for more effective control during this critical time. The French Armée had failed in the Nivelle offensive, but Pétain was now extending its life through a more judicious use of resources. Intelligence from aerial reconnaissance reinforced the operational picture, eliminating the fruitless assaults against a clearly defined German defense.[42] Pétain also decentralized the groupes de chasse to better support missions such as aerial reconnaissance.

---

[38] Christienne and Lissarague, 111.

[39] David French in Dockrill and French, 68.

[40] Assistant Chief of Staff for Intelligence, G-2, to Chief of Staff, "Account of the Operation from the Standpoint of Enemy Works," 51, Drum Papers, Box 14, USAMHI.

[41] Davilla and Soltan, 12.

[42] Pépin Papers, MA&E, Paris.

FIGURE 51. **Nivelle Offensive.** Source: *West Point Atlas*, 60. Courtesy, Department of History, U.S. Military Academy.

For Aviation Militaire, reinforcement of traditional missions supplanted aerial supremacy for the remainder of the year.[43] Pétain reemphasized the *Groupe des Armées du Centre* (GAC) role in reinforcing the use of aerial photography in battle planning. He ordered Général Estienne, commander of France's newest combat arm, *les chars d'assaut* (tank force), to work directly with Lieutenant Pépin to ensure that aerial photographic interpretation became an integral part of chars d'assaut planning operations.[44]

The remaining problem for the French Armée in 1917 was exhaustion. There was little energy left in the force to maintain any offensive action. The only positive note was that America's declaration of war equated to a fresh new army that soon arrived to help continue the fight. The most intriguing feature at this stage

was the incredible oversight by German intelligence in failing to recognize the precarious state of the French Armée. In the end, this oversight proved fatal.[45]

Vimy Ridge

One of the most decisive battles in favor of the Allies was the Canadian offensive at the strategic heights of Vimy Ridge. A model for planning at the time, it involved all facets of intelligence and operations. Planning commenced in January for acquiring in-depth aerial photography of the ridge and German rear echelons.[46] German defenses on the ridge and rear echelons were completely photographed weeks before the opening of the bombardment, creating an accurate map of the entire sector. The map not only formed the basis of the artillery preparation, but also enabled each stage

---

[43] Davilla and Soltan, 12.
[44] Dégardin, in *Vues d'en Haut*, 22.

[45] David French in Dockrill and French, 69.
[46] Edmonds, *1917*, I, 305.

of the infantry advance to be rehearsed in detail. All key targets in the German sector were carefully tabulated for the artillery. The bombardment was directed especially against trench junctions, dugouts, concrete machine gun emplacements, strong points and entrances to tunnels; also against road junctions, ammunition dumps and light railways to a depth of four to five thousand yards behind the German front.[47] The RFC assigned No. 16 Squadron to the Canadian Corps for reconnaissance operations. The No. 2 Squadron, attached to the I Corps, provided additional aerial coverage. The RFC units were exemplary in their efforts, ensuring that good coverage was acquired.[48] Low clouds and bad weather curtailed most RFC aerial coverage opportunities. Sorties flew whenever visibility permitted. Photographs taken on 24 March and four days in the first week of April disclosed the obliteration of the front line system of defense, the destruction of long stretches of communication trenches, and the cutting of lanes in dense wire entanglements both in front of and behind the strategic town of Thelus. Aerial photographic interpretation detected the wire entanglements after a snowstorm brought out the features. Aerial photographs of the region were exemplary in detecting German active battery positions. Some 190 German batteries were identified for subsequent targeting.[49] Final details were applied to the plasticine model used by officers and noncommissioned officers for extensive study of operational roles. During this battle and the preparation that preceded it, the systematic recording of targets for destruction, and coordination of all arms for destructive shoots, were successfully accomplished. This resulted in a corresponding reduction in waste by elimination of overlapping tasks.[50]

Vimy Ridge successfully demonstrated that "destruction" still achieved results. The downside was that the devastated terrain and road system were unable to support subsequent exploitation of the victory. Despite the ability of the Germans to counter any deep penetrations, the Allies still clung to the perception that "destruction" was the best course. This was the case with

the failed Nivelle offensive, Vimy Ridge and subsequent campaigns.[51] With the continued dependency on artillery to achieve this goal, aerial observation required continued improvement and refinement of aerial resources. Each complemented the other in the coming months.

As was the case with the Siegfried Stellung, RFC aerial reconnaissance losses were significant in trying to cover Vimy Ridge. The German aviation resurgence culminated in "Bloody April," where the Allies suffered major losses of aeroplanes of all types. The state-of-the-art German aircraft such as the Albatros (DIII) and Pfalz pursuit aeroplanes wrought havoc on Allied aircraft. "Bloody April" spurred Allied aircraft industries to design and field more effective aircraft, both pursuit and reconnaissance.[52]

Messines

The first half of 1917 held few redeeming qualities for the Allies. The eastern front was a disaster as the Russian military disintegrated into chaos. The Nivelle offensive had crippled France's armée. British Commonwealth successes at Vimy Ridge demonstrated in-depth planning could achieve positive results. The most important development was not military, but political. The United States had declared war on Germany and her allies Austria-Hungary and Turkey on 6 April 1917. Now the Allies could draw on the tremendous American reserves. However, almost a year passed before American forces were noticeable on the front lines. Besides, the Americans had to be trained to the realities of positional warfare. That drew further resources from the already strapped British and French staffs.

The British realized that this was a critical time to consolidate their position on the continent while awaiting reinforcement from the United States. They decided to concentrate on further protecting the Belgian coastline, the one area that presented the greatest risk to their strategic lifeline. The British decided to attack the Messines-Wytschaete Ridge south of Ypres, one of the enemy's most important strongholds on

[47] Edmonds, *1917*, I, 312-313.
[48] Edmonds, *1917*, I, 311.
[49] Edmonds, *1917*, I, 314.
[50] Hahn, xix-xx.

[51] Interestingly, Bailey entitles this segment "1917: Destruction Reaches Its Zenith," Bailey, 140.
[52] Mead, 100.

FIGURE 52. **Messines.** Source: *West Point Atlas*, map 59b. Courtesy, Department of History, U.S. Military Academy.

radio intercept operations and intelligence staff also improved on its ability to monitor German aerial observation radio transmissions, providing the RFC with a general picture of the enemy's aeroplane and artillery activity. The volume of observed radio activity correlated to any buildup or decrease of enemy artillery in the sector.[56]

The improvements in British signals intelligence at Messines also served as the genesis for aerial command and control in the creation of Compass Stations. Compass Stations provided indications of German aerial observation within the respective center of operation.[57] When the Americans arrived in theater, they also assumed a similar network to track German aerial operations. Known as the Airplane Information Service, it comprised a network of radio detection and monitoring units called goniometric stations. When the enemy aeroplane commenced radio transmissions for artillery spotting, the goniometric units intercepted the message, telephoned the unit that was to be targeted, and contacted Allied artillery to commence counterbattery fire. It became an important function during positional war. However, when mobile war commenced in the final weeks, the process was discontinued.[58] The Germans' Messines-Wytschaete network of

the Western Front. The ridge at Messines completely overlooked the British positions in the Ypres sector. The carefully planned offensive resulted in a significant victory for the British and was subsequently labeled "a perfect operation of siege warfare."[53] Success at Messines required British artillery to dominate the German batteries through greater accuracy. The burden was on the RFC to ensure that their artillery-spotting mission dominated the information battleground.[54] All intelligence elements were put to the test. The first known use of signals deception on a large-scale occurred at Messines. GHQ manipulated the patterns of their radio traffic, leading "the enemy to believe that Corps which were on any given front, now unimportant, are still there, and also that no increase has been made in the No. of Corps on the front of importance." The British signals security effort had successfully masked the order of battle work of the German traffic analysts.[55] The British

---

[53] Mead, 85-86; *Artillery Operations of the Ninth British Corps at Messines, June, 1917* (Washington, DC: GPO, 1917), 116.

[54] Jones, IV, 113-114.

[55] John Ferris, "The British Army and Signals Intelligence in the Field during the First World War," *Intelligence and National Security* 3, No. 4 (October 1988): 39.

[56] A "blacklist" was compiled of the various sources, Jones, IV, 117.

[57] Jones, IV, 115-116.

[58] Brig Gen Dennis Nolan, HQ AEF G-2, later concluded that the Air Service's goniometric role was useful only while the army engaged in trench warfare. He expressed the remarkable assumption that "the service lost much of its value, and it is doubtful that in any future war that its duties will again fall on the intelligence," and he amazingly concluded that "We fell heir to it, as we did to many other things, because it was new and the Intelligence Section seemed as good a place as any for it." Nolan, "Codes & Ciphers," 15, Nolan Papers, USAMHI.

FIGURE 54. The German lines at Messines experienced the largest mine explosion in history shortly before this aerial photograph was taken. Source: Liddle, *The Airman's War 1914-18.*

defenses exemplified positional war at its zenith. They held the higher ground reinforced with artillery and infantry. The German forward defenses on the Messines-Wytschaete Ridge consisted of an elaborate and intricate system of well-wired trenches and strong points forming a defensive belt over 2,000 yards in depth.[59] Impenetrable defenses included an array of concrete bunkers providing cover for machine gun emplacements, observation posts, and large dugouts. Ongoing RFC aerial photography confirmed many of the bunkers were resisting British artillery shellfire.[60]

The British commenced the attack with systematic trench bombardment and wire cutting on 21 May 1917. RFC aerial artillery spotting was active supporting British 18-pounders and 6-inch howitzers. During the final phase of preparing the battlefield, the British also conducted extensive artillery night firing. Billets, headquarters, and villages in back areas were shelled by long-range pieces and a continuous barrage was maintained on the enemy's communications.[61] The legacy of Messines was the initial British offensive. On 7 June 1917, 19 deep mines containing an aggregate of 937,000 pounds of explosives were detonated under the German trenches. The massive explosion blew up large portions of the enemy's front and support line.[62] Mining operations were an integral feature of positional warfare. Aerial reconnaissance was continually looking for any signs of excavation that indicated this activity. The British had nine tunneling companies in 1915, expanding to a total of 25 from 1916 to 1918. In 1916, 48 of 128 kilometers of the front

held by the BEF were protected by underground galleries, in several instances at more than one level. But mining was effective only against a strongly held front line, and by the close of 1917 it became a recognized principle to hold the front by firepower rather than manpower. Troops were deployed in depth and protected from bombardment by dugouts, subways, and other subsurface excavations. Despite the increase in tunneling companies, as offensive mining declined, the companies were increasingly diverted to the construction of dugouts.[63]

British artillery was active from 21 May to 6 June. With supporting aeroplane observation it carried out 297 trench bombardments. Wire was cut along front and support lines by trench mortars and 18-pounder batteries, and on rear lines by 6-inch howitzers with aeroplane observation.[64] On 5 June 1917, British artillery engaged in intense counterbattery work. Every available howitzer from bombardment groups was to be used for intense and destructive counterbattery work. "Maximum value from aeroplane and balloon observation" was to be arranged. Gas shelling was planned against the German batteries during the three to four nights before the assault in sufficient quantity to ensure the German artillery personnel were to be forced to use their masks and be kept awake and become exhausted.[65]

---

[59] *Artillery Operations of the Ninth British Corps at Messines,* 115-116.

[60] *Artillery Operations of the Ninth British Corps at Messines,* 117.

[61] *Artillery Operations of the Ninth British Corps at Messines,* 115-116.

[62] Mead, 85-86; *Artillery Operations of the Ninth British Corps at Messines,* 116.

[63] E. P. F. Rose and M. S. Rosenbaum, "British Military Geologists through War and Peace in the 19th and 20th Centuries," in James R. Underwood and Peter L. Guth, eds., *Military Geology in War and Peace* (Boulder, CO: The Geological Society of America, Inc., 1998), 32-33.

[64] *Artillery Operations of the Ninth British Corps at Messines,* 1.

[65] *Artillery Operations of the Ninth British Corps at Messines,* 35.

Prior to the actual attack, the RFC's No. 53 Squadron was tasked to keep three planes in the air throughout the hours of daylight to conduct artillery work. Normally, two planes were employed on counterbattery work. The third plane carried out observation of the effect of trench bombardments and wire cutting as well as providing registration in support of the heavy artillery. The RFC was required to photograph the entire trench area within the flank limits of the British IX Corps once a day. No. 53 Squadron was responsible for delivering proof copies to IX Corps heavy artillery one hour after the aerial reconnaissance aircraft landed, with secondary distribution going to the divisions and IX Corps headquarters. Aerial photographs of hostile battery positions were to be taken as soon as possible after the completion of a destructive artillery barrage, with copies delivered to the counterbattery office. Every evening the counterbattery staff officer issued the program of destructive targets for

the next day. An effective liaison network was accomplished when No. 53 Squadron assigned the same air crew to support a designated artillery battery throughout the campaign.[66] An example of artillery spotting work accomplished by No. 53 Squadron on 18 May 1917 shows the extensive effort during the battle: "Battery 405th

---

[66] *Artillery Operations of the Ninth British Corps at Messines*, 51.

Siege firing on target Ochre Trench, O 26 c 11.42 to 05.55. Successful. About 60 rounds observed. 2 OK's, 6 Y's, 8 Z's. Battery shooting well when machine left. Several rounds fell very close to trench, one causing a fire, smoke of which lasted 10 minutes."[67]

The RFC's IInd Brigade provided vital support throughout the campaign. Most of the German batteries were out of sight from the ground artillery observers. The Brigade's 300 serviceable aeroplanes successfully carried out the essential artillery observation and aerial photographic missions, acquiring daily coverage of German defenses during the bombardment period as well as coverage every other day of the counterbattery area.[68] The RFC at Messines averaged a daily flying rate of 612 hours, accomplishing a total of 716 zone calls against German targets.[69] Observation balloon operations monitoring the German rear areas at the Messines Ridge were connected via telephone to most of the heavy artillery groups of the British IX Corps. These resources worked sector observation reporting intensity and extent of enemy barrages, updating progress of Allied barrages, and locating any tanks in the sector.[70]

The British aggressively conducted systematic aerial photography to determine the effect of artillery fire. The demand for increased coverage was levied on all flights. This was backed by the proliferation of photographic sections assigned at the squadrons. The schedule of coverage was continuous to satisfy corps requirements. British corps increased their demands, prompting the squadrons to continue to provide coverage from the front line to 5,000 yards beyond. To ensure timeliness, the squadrons were responsible for distribution. Photographs of lower priority targets were forwarded to the Army Printing Section at Hazebrouck for additional printing.[71] Army reconnaissance covered the Germans' main railway communications farther to the east,

FIGURE 56. **Captured German aerial photograph of British Mark IV tanks at Cambrai.** Source: Edgar Middleton, *The Great War in the Air* (London, 1919).

to include Bruges, Ghent, Grammont, and Ath. Particular attention was paid to the rail lines converging on Courtrai and Menin. DH 4 aeroplanes of No. 55 Squadron, fitted with cameras and flying at high altitudes between 16,000 and 20,000 feet, usually accomplished the more distant reconnaissance. The closer and more detailed strategic reconnaissance was made by formations of Sopwith 1½ Strutters of No. 70 Squadron, escorted by a flight of pursuit fighters.[72]

Messines was a major success story for British military operations, "a tactical masterpiece of its kind."[73] The British Second Army advanced 2 ½ miles in a single day, capturing the objective. The cooperation between the aerial observer and battery was recognized as outstanding, allowing the artillery to effectively target and destroy the enemy artillery. It did experience problems with

[67] *Artillery Operations of the Ninth British Corps at Messines*, 95.
[68] Edmonds, *1917*, II, 42-43.
[69] *Artillery Operations of the Ninth British Corps at Messines*, 52.
[70] *Artillery Operations of the Ninth British Corps at Messines*, 118.
[71] Jones, IV, 118-119.

[72] Jones, IV, 122.
[73] Jones, IV, 135.

fleeting targets, a premonition of future challenges as the battleground transitioned to mobile warfare. However, the relationship between aviator and artillery reflected the growing sophistication of communication technology, resulting in effective results.[74]

June 1917

The French-English 1917 spring offensive led the German General Staff to publish, on 10 June 1917, a Supplement to the Regulations for Stationary Warfare, in which it summarized the most important principles in these regulations. This supplement was annotated and enlarged by General Friedrich Sixt von Armin (commander of the Fourth Army) in an Army order dated 30 June 1917. This order fell into Allied hands, and some essential extracts include:

Camouflage necessity—"Strength in a defensive battle depends essentially on the precautions taken to con-

FIGURE 57. **Aerial photography of World War I tanks represents the first photographic interpretation of mobile armored equipment in history.** Source: Elmer Haslett, *Luck on the Wing: Thirteen Stories of a Sky Spy* (New York: E.P. Dutton and Company, 1920).

ceal from the eyes of the enemy all our means of fighting. These fighting means (trenches, dugouts, machine gun and battery emplacements) will surely be destroyed, if they appear on the enemy's aerial photographs."

Depth organization—"There must be substituted for the old system of position, which may be plotted and destroyed by the enemy, a defensive zone organized in depth."

Utilization of shell holes by the fighting line—"During a battle it is no lon-

---

[74] Jones, IV, 135-136.

ger necessary to have continuous trenches in the front line. They may be replaced by shell holes held by bunches of men and isolated machine guns, arranged in checkerboard.

"In front of the first row of shell holes will be placed an irregular barbed-wire entanglement, as continuous as possible. It is also advisable to protect with barbed wire the holes in the front of the first line, to prevent their occupation by the enemy.

"Farther back, it is preferable to organize isolated defensive works, by surrounding the shell holes with auxiliary defenses in such a way as to leave passages for counterattacking troops."

Placing supporting troops and reserves—"A large part of the supporting troops and of the reserves will be sheltered in the open field, in shell holes, woods, ravines, anywhere to avoid aerial observation. (Villages must be avoided, as they draw the enemy's fire.) These troops assist in the formation of a continuous line, avoiding so far as possible the view of the enemy. Thus a supporting line is established for the defense troops placed at successive intervals in front of it."

First-line defenses—"These must include several lines of trenches, protected by a strong barbed-wire entanglement, with passages for assaulting troops. Deep dugouts will be constructed only on the second and third lines. The first line will have only small dugouts, capable of holding about one-sixth of the occupants of this line."

New-line defense—"The organization of new lines back of the first will be governed by the same principles as above. If possible, the construction of dugouts for the garrison must be undertaken in succession for the whole depth of the zone. (For one-sixth of the men in the first trench, two-sixths in the second trench, three-sixths back of the second trench as far as the line of artillery defense.)

By the creation of numerous shelters in the rear of the lines, preparations are made for the opening of the defensive battle, the orderly retreat of the troops in the trenches, and their redistribution on the intermediate terrain.

Order of urgency of the works — Staking out the works, placing auxiliary defenses, bomb-proof shelters, digging trenches.

Machine gun emplacements — Machine gun locations should not be chosen in front positions, but on the sides of hills or in depressions, at points convenient for flanking. The enemy should come upon machine guns unexpectedly. Therefore, it is not desirable to install them in salients, but to the right or left or in the rear. In the salients only fake emplacements should be constructed.

Laying out boyaus — In order to prevent the enemy from forming an exact idea of our system of defense, the boyaus connecting the different lines may be given an oblique direction. This arrangement gives the appearance of the meshes of a net, in which the boyaus, provided with auxiliary defenses and organized as firing trenches, have at the same time defensive functions. [Riegel]

Everywhere must be kept in mind the necessity of escaping aerial observation.[75]

The British victory at Messines had spurred the Germans to develop a new defensive posture. Allied aerial observation remained a major concern to German military thinking. Newer tractor (engine in front) aircraft such as the RE 8 and longer focal length cameras such as the

_____
[75] *Study and Exploitation of Aerial Photographs*, 9-10.

"L" Type camera were fielded, allowing aerial observation to operate at higher altitudes and acquire the same quality coverage, particularly with stereo photographs. Intelligence discovered that the Germans were modifying their defenses at the front. The Germans' new line of strong points using shell holes further complicated Allied operations. Aerial photographic review of the front sectors soon identified the network and provided in-depth information for subsequent artillery targeting. The shift in fire toward these fortifications both dramatically increased German casualties and caused a rift in their overall defensive network.[76]

During the summer the RFC developed a strategy for air superiority over the Western Front from the Lys sector to the coast. RFC pursuit fighter strength was on the increase. They prosecuted the enemy to a depth of five miles from the German front line back to the observation-balloon line. It became a clear challenge for air mastery over the battlefield. Aerial observation conducted more operations as the battle for aerial supremacy fueled the largest air battles of the war. Massive dogfights with thirty aircraft on either side commenced. It culminated on the evening of 26 July above the Ypres battleground. An air battle took place involving at least 94 single-seat fighters flying furiously at heights from 5,000 to 17,000 feet. Despite the incredible numbers of fighters engaged, no decisive results were recorded. In fact, while the dogfight was in progress, four German aerial observation aeroplanes took the opportunity to fly over the British lines and conduct a reconnaissance of the Ypres sector.[77] At 8,000 feet, thirty Albatros Scouts fought seven DH 5's; at 12,000 to 14,000 feet, ten Albatros Scouts fought approximately thirty British single-seater fighters; at about 17,000 feet, ten Albatros Scouts engaged seven British naval Sopwith triplanes. Below the entire dogfight, a few British two-seaters flew at 5,000 feet.[78]

August 1917

In the American translation of *Étude et Exploitation des Photographies Aériennes*, the fi-

nal description of changes under way of the front highlighted the Germans' depiction of front sectors as fighting zones:

> The supplement of June 10, 1917, appeared a little in advance of a new edition of the First Part of the Regulations for Stationary Warfare, which reaffirmed the necessity, for all defensive works, of organization in depth for a mobile and active defense.

> Fighting zones — But where, in the appendix of June 10, 1917, it was written: "The fight in or for the first line has become the fight for the first position," the new regulation reads: "The fight must be conducted not about the lines, but in the fighting zones."

> The fighting zone comprises a number of organizations (trenches, boyaus, supporting points, etc.) designated to provide for the defense by infantry and artillery, lines of communication, replenishment and good conditions of living. Its depth could reach several kilometers. Its defense was to be organized by sectors.

> Several fighting zones will be constructed, at least 3 km. from each other so that artillery preparation cannot be made on two zones at the same time. A fighting zone should include:

> (a) An ordinary fighting zone, organized to repel any surprise attack and considered as the covering zone (*Vor-feld-zone*).

> (b) A grand fighting zone (*Grosskampfzone*). It is in this that enemy attacks, even the most violent, must be stopped. It may coincide with the ordinary fighting zone. If, however, the latter zone is unfavorably located, the grand fighting zone will be located and organized further back. The grand fighting zone should be constructed in the ordinary fighting zone but with much more care and thoroughness. Still further back,

---

[76] Occleshaw, 66-67.
[77] Jones, IV, 156-157.
[78] Jones, IV, 156-157.

at least one rear fighting zone (*Rueck-waertige Kampfzone*).

The principles already stated for selecting trench locations also apply to selecting zone locations:

Need for good rear communications,

Need for good artillery observation,

For trenches, the use of opposite slope, wherever compatible with good artillery observation.

Location of batteries—The regulations of August 17 insist upon the necessity of making shelters for the men, munitions and artillery. Mobility being the best protection against enemy fire, it prescribes the organization, in advance, of extra emplacements with dugouts. It goes even further, and this is new, in saying that "during a battle, or for special objects, the use of unprepared locations is often advisable."

Order of Urgency of Defensive Works—The order of urgency of the works has not been changed: flanking positions and dugouts, observation stations and headquarters, barbed-wire entanglements, communications (liaisons). Earthworks (*terrassements*) are only made as a last extremity.

The historical sketch just given shows the evolution of the German theory of defense. The fighting in or for the first line has become the fight in the fighting zone. This doctrine may be modified in the future.

Whatever changes may be made, it is probable that aerial photos and information from prisoners, observation stations, etc., will enable us to keep pace with them. Perhaps the difficulties encountered by the officers who have to interpret the photos will become greater. They will always be less

than those of our adversary to conceal his system of defense.[79]

Positional war transformed aerial reconnaissance from fledgling status in 1914 to a well-refined knowledge source serving the final year of combat. British military aviation pioneers such as Trenchard and the Salmond brothers proved aerial reconnaissance to be an integral part of the battle and they now held senior positions of command. These officers created the foundation for aerial operations in the final year of combat, giving the RFC the direction it required to both refine aerial observation and increase pursuit roles necessary to maintain aerial supremacy. French aviation also clearly demonstrated innovation and leadership in the ranks, but seniority was limited at best. Despite the influence of aviation on French military operations for the first three years of combat, the most senior French rank in the Aviation Militaire (chef de l'aéronautique a GQG) at this time was commandant (Major).[80] Despite the absence of seniority, Allied expertise within the ranks of intelligence and aerial photographic interpreters constituted an impressive capability. The outcome of three years of intense analytical effort interpreting aerial photographs created a sound resource on which to base the interpretation of German military doctrine and practice. In many respects, the aerial photographic interpreters became the most knowledgeable experts on how the adversary put to practice the operational art of positional war.

One important feature of Allied aerial reconnaissance at this stage of the war was the introduction of a new generation of state-of-the-art aeroplanes that could both meet the demands of lower-altitude missions against the threat of enemy pursuit as well as operate at high altitude beyond the limits of fighters and antiaircraft artillery. Allied aerial reconnaissance units now started to acquire Breguet 14 A2, Salmson 2 A2, and DH 4 aeroplanes. One outstanding aeroplane of the era, the Bristol F.2B, was initially designed for fighter-reconnaissance. It would subsequently serve the RFC/RAF as one of the

---

[79] *Study and Exploitation of Aerial Photographs*, 11-12.
[80] Christienne and Lissarague, 110; Davilla and Soltan, 9.

best pursuit fighter aeroplanes of the war. On one mission in August 1917, a flight of Bristol F.2Bs from 48 Squadron flew a photo-reconnaissance mission at an impressive altitude of over 19,000 feet. The flight leader, Capt B.E. Baker, reached an altitude of 22,000 feet during the sortie.[81]

The year 1917 concluded with the battle at Cambrai, most noteworthy for the extensive employment of tanks in battle. Tanks revolutionized artillery close support and provided new tactics and strategies for the battle. Surprise would be employed in breaching the Siegfried Stellung's extensive defense network. This time a mass assault of tanks drove the British through the German fortifications. The shock effect of the armored advance was determined to have been sufficient to neutralize any infantry in the way. Artillery assumed a new role at Cambrai. Instead of delivering destruction, it supported mobility

FIGURE 58. One of the finest aerial reconnaissance aéroplanes of the war, the Breguet 14 A2 arrives at the front on August 1917. This aéroplane was assigned to the first Breguet-equipped escadrille, BR 7. Source: SHAA, B78.917.

by neutralizing enemy artillery and any infantry firepower that the tank did not eliminate. To further accomplish the objective of surprise with armor's mobility, the British withheld the traditional precursor to the attack with a heavy artillery barrage, as explained below.[82]

The British paid particular attention to a new technique of "shooting by the map," in which "unregistered" or "predicted" fire to gain accu-

---

[81] Lamberton, 62.

[82] Johnson, *Battlefields of the World War*, 166-167; Bailey, 142.

FIGURE 59. **Cambrai.** Source: *West Point Atlas*, 60b. Courtesy, Department of History, U.S. Military Academy.

rate range and bearing was accomplished in advance for each artillery piece. The lack of a preliminary bombardment and associated analysis gained surprise and eliminated several German batteries at the start of the offensive.[83] The Cambrai sector was selected as the point of attack because the plain was especially favorable for tank operations. Additionally, the sector had the necessary natural cover with Havrincourt Wood, to

mask the assembly of equipment prior to the advance.[84] RFC operations laid the groundwork for the offensive, providing important reconnaissance information.[85] At dawn on 20 November, screened by artificial smoke clouds but without artillery preparations, a veritable tank army crawled across the rolling plain, smashing its way into the German lines.[86] However, the weather

[83] Chasseaud, "1914-18 Trench Maps."

[84] Johnson, *Battlefields of the World War*, 167.
[85] Edmonds, *1917*, III, 230.
[86] Johnson, *Battlefields of the World War*, 168.

Chapter 4: Positional Warfare at Its Zenith

during the attack was not conducive for supporting effective aerial reconnaissance. "Air observation was impossible at first, dangerous later and always unreliable."[87] When they did get airborne, the British Army squadrons did conduct aggressive attacks against German airfields, batteries and infantry. However, this time German aviation reacted quickly with newly arrived squadrons of fighters. In two days of intense struggle they had converted RFC air supremacy into "air parity." German aviation also effectively integrated with the army battle organization providing effective aerial reconnaissance and artillery support in the counterattack.[88]

The ineffectual analysis by British Intelligence at GHQ under Brigadier-General Charteris had bothered the British Prime Minister, Lloyd George, for a long time. Despite Charteris' strong influence on Haig, the time had come for dismissal. Charteris' promulgation of the idea that the Germans were defeated in will and capability was consistently wrong, culminating in the successful German counterattack at Cambrai. It proved to be the final straw. In December 1917 Lloyd George took action and had General Macdonogh's nominee, Brigadier-General Edgar Cox, relieve Charteris. BEF intelligence remained under the influence of the Ministry's Directorate of Military Intelligence for the remainder of the war.[89] As for Charteris, Haig's loyalty saved him from total humiliation. He was retained as the GHQ's Deputy Director General of Transportation and continued to have the ear of Haig.[90]

Cambrai demonstrated that infantry now could depend on armor to assist in an offensive. Artillery was still vital for all remaining campaigns in the war, but its dominance had to adjust for advances associated with mobility. The tanks also depended on artillery to assist in their advance. The critical development was that artillery could now concentrate on supporting the breakthrough, leaving armor to breach the front lines.[91] Despite Cambrai's legacy as a relatively successful massive tank attack on the Western Front, the breakthrough did not occur. The siege of the Western Front continued on with more massive casualties for another year. The impact on aerial reconnaissance was increasing requirements for aeroplanes that could better support the demand for intelligence on the rear echelon. Positional war was giving way to mobility.

---

[87] Mead, 92-94.
[88] Mead, 92-94.

[89] Lyn Macdonald, *To the Last Man, Spring 1918* (New York: Carroll & Graf Publishers, Inc.), xxxii-xxxiv.
[90] Occleshaw, 349; Macdonald, *To the Last Man*, xxxiv.
[91] Bailey, 143.

1918: AERIAL PHOTOGRAPHY REFINED

Preparations for the Michael Offensive

The fall of the Russian Government and the subsequent release of German divisions from the Eastern Front provided the Germans with an opportunity to make a major strategic move in the west, leading to one of the most decisive battles in the war. The Allies were in a quandary, for they knew that German reinforcements were soon to be arriving. The question was where and when the forces would be committed. The status of American reinforcements was also a source of anxiety. Despite the United States having been in the war since April 1917, it had too little military presence in theater to make a difference. The potential was there, but only four divisions had arrived by the end of that year. Of those four, only two divisions had experienced the front lines when the Germans commenced their offensive.

Indications of the impending offensive grew throughout February 1918. What intelligence could be acquired by RFC aerial reconnaissance in the winter months focused on rear echelons. Aerial reconnaissance and photographic missions had observed abnormal amounts of railway traffic, construction of new aerodromes, dumps, railway sidings and hospital camps. In January alone, 14 new German aerodromes had been established just opposite the British Fifth Army sector.[1] Leadership changes had just taken place in the RFC. Major-General John M. Salmond assumed command of the RFC from Major-General Trenchard.[2] Salmond directed the RFC headquarters reconnaissance unit, No. 25 Squadron, to concentrate its aerial observation efforts east of the British Fifth Army reconnaissance area. Subsequent reporting provided further indications of increasing German rail and road movements behind the Third and Fifth Army fronts, as well as more sightings of new dumps, aerodromes, and emplacements. The signatures for a buildup were multiplying, leaving little doubt in the mind of many commanders, including Général Foch and General Haig, that something was going to break loose.[3] Later that month, Salmond assembled his RFC Brigade commanders and gave them instructions as to the importance of obtaining evidence, generating more sorties from available aeroplanes, and increasing the reconnaissance effort to help substantiate further evidence of enemy intentions. Air reports and aerial photographs generated at the end of February revealed a marked increase in German road and rail movements and further

---

[1] Edmonds, *1918*, I, 108.
[2] Salmond's illustrious career from the first days as an aerial observer to his appointment as RFC commander on 18 January 1918 was an important statement on the role that reconnaissance played in determining the leadership of British aviation. His counterpart, Trenchard, had returned to England to serve with the newly created Air Ministry. Jones, IV, 266; Edmonds, *1918*, I, 108-109.
[3] Jones, IV, 266-268.

signs of the mounting of the offensive, including daily extension of the network of light railways.[4] Despite the growing indications, it was intriguing that British aerial observation was not being heavily tasked to glean any indications of German intentions. A British aerial observer, Lieutenant Thomas McKenny Hughes, commented that "there are not a great number of shoots to do as a rule now and the Corps are quite exemplary in the smallness of their demands for photographs."[5] However, British BEF GHQ had not come to a definite conclusion as to where and when the attack was to commence.[6]

Four years of positional war had accustomed the German combatants to the risks associated with aerial reconnaissance and photographic interpretation. They always assumed the potential intelligence value of the photograph. Moreover, preparation for the *Michael* offensive included taking steps against aerial observation. The German OHL chief of staff, General Ludendorff, personally signed off a memorandum entitled, "Protection of Artillery Positions from Air Observation" that portrayed senior concern with Allied aerial observation:

> The constant observation of our organizations by the enemy's aeroplanes in trench warfare, and the technical improvements introduced in aerial photography, compel us to hide our artillery positions from air observation to an increasing degree. Experience has shown that the type of work carried out by our troops up to the present has not led to the desired results. In all camouflage work, greater endeavors than in the past must be made, not only to avoid the effect of light and shade, but also to assimilate the whole emplacement to the color of the ground. The plates employed for photography from great heights are extraordinarily sensitive to colors and show up clearly the slightest difference in shades, even those imperceptible on the ground. Effective camouflage is only possible if,

FIGURE 60 (OPPOSITE PAGE). **Michael Offensive, less commonly called the Somme Offensive.** Source: *West Point Atlas*, map 63a, Courtesy, Department of History, U.S. Military Academy.

before the emplacement is built, the coloring of the surrounding ground is carefully taken into account. The necessary data can only be furnished by air photographs.[7]

General Ludendorff and the senior OHL staff had at their disposal one of the most important documents on the subject of aerial photography. During the Cambrai counter-offensive of November 1917, the Germans had acquired the British 1917 edition of *Notes on the Interpretation of Aeroplane Photographs* (S.S. 550). With the manual the Germans were able to speak to the Allied method of accomplishing aerial photographic interpretation with clarity. Ludendorff's directive continued, "The following extract is of interest, 'It is evident that increasing care is taken to conceal emplacements and to defeat the camera. As, however, the Germans usually start to construct camouflage after a battery emplacement has been completed, their attempts are rendered abortive, owing to the fact that the emplacement will probably have been photographed several times during the various stages of construction'."[8]

Ludendorff issued his directive to the forces in final preparation for the Michael offensive. Steps to be taken during the offensive included:

> 1. Whenever an emplacement is to be built, a specially detailed Divisional Artillery Staff Officer will be responsible for furnishing the battery with air photographs showing all necessary details as regards light effects and coloring."

---

[4] Edmonds, *1918*, I, 109.

[5] Lieut Thomas M. Hughes quoted in Brown, 136.

[6] Jones, IV, 266-268.

[7] "Protection of Artillery Positions from Air Observation," captured German document, TNA, PRO: AIR 1/2124/207/74/3.

[8] "Intelligence Summary," 19 August 1918, TNA, PRO: AIR 1/2124/207/74/3.

WESTERN FRONT, 1918
SOMME OFFENSIVE
(FIRST GERMAN DRIVE)

Situation 21 March and Operations
to 4 April

0   5   10
SCALE OF MILES

a

2. Photographs will be taken repeatedly during the stages of construction, in order to test the camouflage. The staff officer mentioned above will make the necessary arrangements with the divisional flight concerned.

3. Once the camouflage is complete, the emplacement should, whenever possible, be again photographed before it is occupied.

4. The same precautions will be taken in the construction of alternative emplacements, and of positions built in the rear in view of possible retirements.

5. The staff officer mentioned in para. 1 is responsible for testing by frequent photographs the camouflage of occupied battery positions.

6. Aerial photography became an integral test of the impending offensive. The German reconnaissance force would photographically validate what was perceived to be on the print acquired by the allied reconnaissance plane.[9]

Allied reconnaissance now had to contend with an even more alert adversary. On the eve of the battle, from 17 to 20 March, early morning reconnaissance reflected a calm before the storm. German aerial activity was minimal with Allied aerial observation activity detecting nothing of interest, a reflection of adherence to the Ludendorff directive.[10] Night reconnaissance was called for. British sorties were generated, but nothing was detected. German march discipline was at its peak. Whenever the British airmen dropped flares to detect activity, "all traffic stops, and the troops crouch lifeless under the shelter of trees and houses."[11] Aerial reconnaissance was not enough to determine German in-

tentions prior to the Michael offensive. The Allies had been successfully deceived by German operations prior to the offensive. Order of battle estimates showed 190 German divisions in France, supported by logistics flowing from the eastern front to the West. Many of these battle-experienced troops were relocated to the Hirson-Mézières region, over a hundred kilometers from the Western Front. The Germans had proven from fighting the Russians at Riga (Baltic State of Latvia) that they could stage their forces for an offensive far from the front. French intelligence had conducted a major assessment of that battle and was aware of the strategy. Their armée escadrilles discovered new railway lines leading toward the British sector to reinforce a possible operation. However, the indications did not help reinforce the Allied line.[12]

British artillery had been active prior to the German attack, firing conventional and gas rounds into the German lines. During one barrage, the British Third Army fired on a target discovered from aerial photography: a number of small white objects in pits east of Bullecourt. The British fired 9.2-inch howitzer rounds, resulting in a massive explosion. The objects had been piles of ammunition boxes. The British quickly followed up with a general bombardment that created over a hundred explosions, large and small. Similar objects were noticed on aerial photography, found in the hollows and valleys of the German sector opposite the British Fifth Army. The initial thought was that the covered objects were tanks, until the artillery rounds verified they were munitions under wraps.[13]

Keeping to the Ludendorff directives, the Germans moved largely at night, and camouflaged their forces by day, thereby diminishing the value of aerial reconnaissance. The weather also was a factor. Four days immediately before the attack, the early morning reconnaissance flights were impossible due to thick cloud and rain. However, challenges from weather were not enough to prevent the British RFC from photographing some of the German preparations.[14] For this campaign, the Germans became masters in masking their ra-

---

[9] "Intelligence Summary," 19 August 1918, TNA, PRO: AIR 1/2124/207/74/3.

[10] Edmonds, *1918*, I, 109.

[11] Rudolf Stark quoted in William E. Fischer, Jr., *The Development of Military Night Aviation to 1919* (Maxwell AFB, AL: Air University Press, 1998), 104.

[12] Porch, 107; David French in Dockrill and French, 92.

[13] Edmonds, *1918*, I, 111.

[14] David French in Dockrill and French, 92.

dio network. They employed false signals to create a phantom army on the French front, imitating preparations for an offensive against the British in Flanders. By exercising effective radio transmission discipline—limiting communications to short messages—the Germans offered French direction-finding a small signature to work with, curtailing any ability to ascertain the German order of battle. Almost two weeks prior to the offensive, the Germans started to change their call signs daily. Complicating the picture was the frequent German use of ciphered communications, an important radio intercept signature, usually indicating impending operations. Meanwhile, German employment of artillery barrages and infantry raids to probe against the French and British lines lent to the confusion. It was impossible to tell if these actions were in preparation for the great blow or were simply feints.[15]

Artillery employment achieved prominence at this stage of the war as a result of bold initiatives by the brilliant German tactician, Colonel Georg Bruchmüller. Destruction was not the best strategy for ensuring victory in positional war. Instead, Bruchmüller advocated "neutralization" through demoralizing the enemy. The preliminary bombardment was not targeted against obstacles and troops in the trenches. Instead, Bruchmüller advocated that artillery strike the enemy's command and control networks comprising PC's, telephone exchanges and observation posts. A subsequent barrage of artillery fire would be applied to different sectors using a variety of weapons and munitions. The final artillery barrage comprised an intense fire on the front lines for ten minutes followed by a "creeping barrage" in front of the infantry attack.[16] It was intriguing to note that the Germans also limited artillery registration to add to the element of surprise. German aerial support to registration relied on other sources such as sound-ranging, accurate meteorological data and ammunition consistency.[17]

German artillery units honed their deception tactics prior to the offensive. One recollection portrays maneuvers specifically designed to confuse Allied observers:

> Our batteries had half their guns constantly on the move, appearing here, there and everywhere, firing at night a few shots into enemy territory: and when next morning British or French reconnaissance aircraft flew over to take photographs of the new battery positions, there it apparently was, but actually consisting of wheels of farm carts with a wooden beam, all scarcely camouflaged. The British artillery fired fiercely on these dummies and the next night, a few hundred yards away, a new "battery" popped up. And this deception maneuver went on for weeks from north to south, and especially on those parts of the front where no attack was intended to take place.[18]

Haig's former Intelligence chief, Brigadier-General Charteris, even provided his own estimate of the situation. Despite his new assignment working transportation issues, he was still able to access aerial photography and make his own deductions on the growing body of evidence. On 8 March he observed that "There was a good deal of shelling going on in the front line, and swarms of aeroplanes—mostly our own—out reconnoitering…. Our front there is pretty strong, and should give a good account of itself if it is attacked. The Third Army is rather concerned about some new marks on air photographs in the fields by the roadside of the German back area. The tracks leading to them mean some form of German tank. I think there are too many of them in one place to be tanks. The Fifth Army has something of the same sort on its photographs of areas near St. Quentin, and thinks it is ammunition brought up on caterpillar tractors. I am not sure that they are not large handcarts for the supply of small arms ammunition, but if so they must have particularly broad wheels. Whatever they are, they point pretty conclusively to a very early offensive."[19]

---

[15] Porch, 107-108; David French in Dockrill and French, 92.

[16] Bailey, 143-144.

[17] Bailey, 144.

[18] Stephen Westman quoted in Malcom Brown, *The Imperial War Museum Book of 1918, Year of Victory* (London: Sidgwick & Jackson, 1998), 38.

[19] Charteris, *At G.H.Q.*, 289-290.

The Michael Offensive

When the German offensive commenced on 21 March 1918 at 0615 hrs, 6,000 German guns opened an artillery barrage along almost fifty miles of front between Arras and La Fère on the Somme, held principally by the British Fifth Army and the French Ième Armée. The weather favored the attacking Germans as fog covered the southern Fifth Army sector, prohibiting any aerial reconnaissance of the advance. One sortie, from RFC No. 59 Squadron, did manage to track the German bombardment along the whole front of the IV Corps. Other RFC aircraft were launched to support British artillery counterbattery. By noon that day, six aeroplanes were generating countless radio transmissions to the artillery on a multitude of targets, to include artillery and large formations of infantry on the roads heading west.[20] The Germans had neutralized the sector communications and the artillery. The British Corps aeroplanes that could fly did not get airborne until noon and what little they could see was not of much consequence. When the fog cleared that afternoon, British aerial reconnaissance saw many targets, but the British artillery had been effectively neutralized.[21] The prevailing historical interpretation of the first day of the Michael offensive is that the Royal Artillery failed. The organization between artillery and aerial observation did not succeed in working through the challenge of the fog on the first day of the campaign. What was recognized was that "Contact patrol work and close reconnaissance were maintained by the Royal Flying Corps, and its reports often gave the corps staff the best information which they received as to the movements of the fighting troops and of the enemy's advance."[22] Despite the fact that the Germans were advancing so rapidly, the British did establish air superiority, allowing their aerial observation to continue without interference.[23]

The impact of the offensive was astounding. Within a week the Germans had driven the Allies back almost thirty-eight miles to Amiens. French intelligence was as stunned as the rest of

FIGURE 61. RFC units such as No. 15 Squadron were operating at peak levels during the Michael offensive. The squadron commander, Major H. V. Stammers, reviews fresh reports from the front. Source: Nesbit, *Eyes of the RAF.*

the Allied command. "By virtue of my job, I am the best-informed man in France, and at this moment I no longer know where the Germans are. If we're captured in an hour, it wouldn't surprise me," the head of GQG's 2e Bureau declared.[24] Ironically, the exemplary gains made by British forces at Messines Ridge the previous June were quickly overrun in the first days of the offensive. However, the British did generate a significant amount of intelligence at the front. When the Michael offensive was launched, the intelligence summaries of British divisions at the front were credited in post-war assessments as valuable, "so that an immediate appreciation of all the enemies' intentions was always available."[25]

The overwhelming German advance in the first days of the Michael offensive found British resistance to be disjointed. Post-war analysis determined that cooperation between the Royal Artillery and the RFC failed completely from the start. For long periods, not only in the fog of the first morning but throughout the British retreat, the communication between batteries and aero-

---

[20] Edmonds, *1918*, I, 163-164.
[21] Mead, 128.
[22] "Official History," in Mead, 129.
[23] Mead, 130.

[24] Unknown GQG intelligence senior quoted in David Kahn, *The Codebreakers: The Story of Secret Writing* (New York: The Macmillan Company, 1967), 341.
[25] Hahn, xx-xxi.

planes was ineffectual at best. British planners had attempted to establish a zone call system to meet the anticipated conditions of open mobile warfare. Major-General Trenchard had emphasized in his memorandum, "The Employment of the Royal Flying Corps in Defense," that

> Modern artillery plays such an important part in a defensive action that too much stress cannot be laid on the work of the corps machines. Counterbattery work without air observation is in most cases of little value. The best way, therefore, in which the Flying Corps can assist at this period [i.e., when the attack has begun] is by assuring a continuance in the air of artillery machines. If this object can be attained, it will be a far more effectual help to the infantry and artillery, though invisible to them, than any amount of low-flying or bombing against the enemy front line troops.[26]

Retreating British forces could not maintain effective communication between artillery batteries and artillery liaison. Artillery telephone lines and radio masts had been disconnected or not set up effectively. As the artillery batteries retreated westward, they were unable to set up and link to the artillery spotting aeroplanes for decisive targeting. Even when the retreating artillery units were able to erect their vital radio masts, receiver operators were often unaware of which zones were assigned to the battery. The roar of the artillery created such noise on the lines that voices could not be heard.[27]

The Michael offensive created a most desperate situation for the Allied commanders. They needed as much information on the Germans' intentions as could be acquired. Intelligence from aerial reconnaissance was deemed "intelligence that is of the greatest value in present circumstances." What information could be acquired had to be shared as quickly as possible by whatever means were available.[28] On 23 March 1918, the Supreme Allied Commander, Général

Foch, sent a personal memorandum to General Haig, — a comprehensive survey of the disposition of German forces — and summed up three possible German objectives. First, an offensive in a sector of the front between the sea and the Somme; a continuation of the attacks between Montdidier and Rheims, and a surprise assault on some other part of the front, in Champagne, at Verdun, or in Lorraine.[29] The French staff drew up detailed plans for the reconnaissance escadrilles to conduct both day and night reconnaissance of the railway systems to assess the density of the traffic along the whole German front between Flanders and Alsace. The British were to maintain a watch of the area opposite the British armies. The overall reconnaissance strategy focused on a systematic aerial photographic reconnaissance of enemy billeting areas. Maps were issued marking the billeting areas and likely maneuver areas for German artillery. Aerial observers were also instructed to keep a general lookout for extensive counts of trains and heavy artillery distant from the front.[30]

Three days into the attack against the British sector, Général Pétain alerted the British that there were definite signs that he was about to be attacked in Champagne and mentioned that aerial reconnaissance had found German camps, tents, and other facilities lit up that night.[31] The night reconnaissance from French aerial bombardment sorties in the sector led to the conviction that the Germans' preparations were defensive in nature. The usual signatures associated with an offensive buildup did not transpire. The Militaire Aviation did not convince GQG of their suspicions as it concerned German intentions against forces in Champagne. Even after the German attack commenced at the Somme, the GQG view that Champagne was still at risk did not abate. French bombardment aviation remained concentrated against Champagne. German deception also contributed to French confusion. On 23 March the French prepared to reinforce the British. However, the next day the order was revoked. A German captive balloon landed on the French lines

---

[26] Trenchard quoted in Edmonds, *1918*, I, 167-168.
[27] Edmonds, *1918*, I, 167-168.
[28] Jones, IV, 457-458.

[29] Author discussions with Dr. Michael Neiberg; Jones VI, 405-407.
[30] Jones, VI, 405-407.
[31] "Conference at Dury at 11:00 p.m., Sunday, March 24th, 1918," TNA, PRO: WO 158/48.

Chapter 5: Aerial Photography Refined   **SHOOTING THE FRONT • 111**

as if by accident. The gondola contained documents that referenced a German attack on 24 March against French armées in the Champagne sector to the south of the Somme. The deception worked, for the French ordered their bombardment units to operate away from the Somme. On 27 March the bombardment units finally returned to the Somme and commenced operations.[32]

Général Maxime Weygand, *chef d'état-major* (Chief of Staff) to Général Foch, followed up a week later in correspondence with the British staffs on maintaining a sense of urgency regarding strategic reconnaissance: "Reconnaissances to ascertain the direction of the enemy's main movements, and therefore his intentions, should extend at least as far as the line *ST. QUENTIN-CAMBRAI-DOUAI,* where he may detrain." Strategic reconnaissance remained critical: "To ensure that air observation covers every part of the area of approach to the battle zone, it will be necessary for the British Air Service to watch particularly the approach routes leading from Le Catelet to Peronne; Cambrai to Bapaume; Aubigny to Arras; Douai to Lens. The air units with Armies will undertake to follow up any movements, discovered in the back areas, as far as the battle front."[33] Foch's subsequent memorandum on the state of the Allied effort reminded all participants that whatever information was acquired had to be shared.[34]

In the midst of the Michael offensive, the Royal Air Force (RAF) was born. On 1 April 1918, the RFC and RNAS merged to create a new independent RAF. The decision did not impact aerial observation and reconnaissance because the new organization revolved around strategic bombing. The principal factor behind establishing the RAF was to unite the heavy bombers within the construct of an "Independent Bombing Force" to impose destruction directly upon the industries and population centers of the enemy. Major-General Trenchard was appointed the first RAF commander.[35] The merger of RFC

and RNAS did pose issues over standardized equipment for British aerial photography. All RFC and RNAS aeroplanes were assessed for aerial reconnaissance. Major Moore-Brabazon, representing the RFC, and RNAS Lieutenant Charles Gamble, discussed all aerial platforms to determine to what extent aerial photographic missions could be served by the existing aerial fleet. An exchange involving the ubiquitous Sopwith 1½ Strutter showed the RNAS preference. Gamble told Moore-Brabazon, "With respect to XXI (Sopwith 1½ Strutter listed in the memo), we like them for photography, but you do not. I understand the contract is expired and no more will be made. In any case I think they should be fitted for cameras."[36]

With the reorganization, concern surfaced in the Royal Navy over meeting the needs of seaplane stations, especially in continuing their ongoing anti-submarine operations. However, the photographic officers of both services were able to work together and resolve the differences. Standards were established on camera fittings. The table of equipment was also revised to suit the requirements of both the former RFC and RNAS. All the branches were "departmentalized" to allow for further expansion as the program required.[37]

When the German's Michael offensive started to show indications of winding down, ongoing aerial reconnaissance started to detect a shift in direction by the German forces, to include preparations for another offensive in the Lys salient.[38] Aerial photographs taken in the afternoon of 6 April showed the Germans were preparing an offensive north of Aubers, opposite the Portuguese left. Throughout the morning of 7 April aerial observers reported the main roads full of moving transport immediately opposite the Portuguese sector. Other intelligence sources reported more ammunition being moved into the German support lines. The impression conveyed by the combined air and ground reports was that the German

---

[32] René Martel, *L'Aviation Française de Bombardment (Des Origines au 11 Novembre 1918)* (Paris: Paul Hartmann, 1939), 317 (translation provided by Allen Suddaby).

[33] Jones, IV, 456-457.

[34] Jones, IV, 457-458.

[35] Mead, 127, Nesbit, 43.

[36] Lieut Charles Gamble, "Memorandum … to Major Moore-Brabazon," 4 February 1918, in "Re-Organisation of Photographic Activities," TNA, PRO: AIR 2/163.

[37] Toye, "History of Photography," TNA, PRO: AIR 1/724/91/1.

[38] "Summary of Indications of Enemy Preparations for an Offensive in Flanders," Conger Papers, Box 2, USAMHI.

Chapter 5: Aerial Photography Refined

concentration of forces was nearing completion.[39] Strategical (which evolved to "strategic during" the next several decades) reconnaissance kept headquarters aware of the flow of reinforcements into the battle. Throughout the day aerial observation reported the main roads opposite the Portuguese were full of moving transport. That evening, rail activity was observed increasing behind Lens and eastward from Lille.[40]

On 9 April the second phase of the German campaign, the St. George offensive, commenced against the Portuguese division on the front line. The steps required for preparing the Michael offensive attack were repeated for St. George. It began with an intense German artillery bombardment, to include the extensive use of gas directed at the Allied artillery, headquarters, and communications. Advancing German storm troops quickly followed. Aerial observation was limited due to fog in the battle areas. The impact of the Germans' drive through the front lines caused Portuguese resistance to fold. The Germans quickly reached the Lys salient. On the evening of 11 April, General Haig summed up the Allies' desperate situation with his "Backs to the wall" Order of the Day, one of the most profound statements of the entire war.[41]

Two days into the St. George offensive, aerial reconnaissance finally caught a break in the weather. Now the Allied air forces were acquiring observations, conducting infantry contact missions, and attacking German troops. On 12 April, weather over the battleground was excellent. RAF sorties were able to provide artillery spotting information and low altitude ground support against the German infantry. The advancing German divisions were now subjected to relentless attacks by the RAF squadrons. The effort was memorable. "More hours were flown, more bombs dropped and more photographs taken than on any day since the War began."[42] RAF aerial coverage that day produced an impressive 3,358 photographs.[43] Aerial reconnaissance was aggressive throughout this period. A daily average

of 40 sorties by the RAF alone provided extensive coverage. When weather got worse toward the end of the month, sortie generation dropped to an average of 23 per day.[44]

When the offensive came to a halt and the line stabilized at the end of April 1918, practically no work was done along the entire front beyond that which was immediately necessary. The Germans did not attempt to construct a properly organized trench system despite their tremendous gains. In the Lys salient, tractors or tanks were very extensively used for the transport of ammunition in the counterbattery area with the tracks of the vehicles becoming very conspicuous on the aerial photographs.[45] What caused the failure of the German offensive was that the size and depth of the British reserves halted the advance into the rear echelons. Both the Michael and St. George offensives clearly demonstrated that unique tactics could yield spectacular results. Artillery had to adjust to the new phenomena. Instead of massive and prolonged barrages along the front, artillery now resorted to sudden and annihilating concentrations of fire on demand. Excellent reconnaissance and initiative on the part of the artillery commanders were now required. Mobility was reestablishing itself in the thinking of the combatant.[46]

Establishing an American Presence

America's entry coincided with a flagging of the Allied force, exhausted after almost three solid years of unceasing combat. The addition of U.S. forces into the fray brought a heretofore untapped manpower source into play to sustain Allied objectives. The Americans, upon arrival in theater, were relegated to a novice role vis-à-vis their Allied counterparts in the art and science of positional war. Their own combat experience had primarily been fighting guerilla-type battles in diverse locations like the Philippines, the southwest United States, and Mexico. Positional war of any duration had not been experienced since the last year of the Civil War. American forces had not acquired or integrated the technologies

[39] Jones, IV, 368.
[40] Edmonds, *1918*, II, 144.
[41] Mead, 131.
[42] Edmonds, *1918*, II, 273-274.
[43] Mead, 131; Jones, IV, xxx.

[44] Edmonds, *1918*, II, 374.
[45] "Summary of Indications of Enemy Preparations for an Offensive in Flanders," Conger Papers, Box 2, USAMHI.
[46] Bailey, 147.

that had been developed by the combatants during the first three years of combat. A major industrial mobilization was required, but this was possible thanks to America's innate industrial might, to include a vibrant photographic industry. Despite the nation's potential to produce, maintaining an effective reconnaissance capability was a constant struggle right up to the Armistice.

The first missions for the newly created U.S. Air Service involved aerial observation. Aerial units were aligned with the French, who presided over initial training for conducting observation in the sector. The Americans received their first lessons in aerial photographic reconnaissance at Amanty (Meuse) in January 1918. The first class consisted of ten personnel. However, it was ineffective because of the language difficulties. French faculty and American students were unable to understand each other. The Americans were able to mutter only a few words of French, dealing mostly with things to eat. After a few weeks of stalemate, the French left the school to the on-scene Americans to work with their own available experts on the subject of aerial reconnaissance and photography. The initial student cadre soon became the instructors.[47] Despite this austere beginning, the American juggernaut picked up speed and proceeded to build an extensive force of aeroplanes and support operations. By the end of the war, the United States had 45 Aero Squadrons and 21 Photographic Sections assigned in theater. It was an impressive buildup for a military that had been devoid of any substantive aerial expertise when war was declared.

---

[47] Corporal Martin E. Friedmann, "History of Photographic Section #1, Air Service, U.S.A., 1918," 1, Gorrell Report, ser. G, r. 24, NARA.

The U.S. Air Service commenced aeroplane observation operations in April 1918. The German Michael offensive was concluding in the Somme sector. The United States established the 1st Corps Observation Group comprising two squadrons (1st and 12th) as well as a contingent of Photographic Section #1 near the front. The units were assigned the responsibility of covering the American divisions near Chemin des Dames. Both arrived for duty at Ourches flying Spad two-seaters on 5 April 1918.[48] Upon arrival, Major Royce of the 1st Aero Squadron and Captain Griffin, commanding officer of the photographic section, flew over the lines and took the first aerial photographs by Americans in a combat environment. However, they did not have the luxury of an established photographic laboratory infrastructure to work with. The first AEF aerial photographs were developed, washed, and prints made in a photo car parked along the side of the road. They had to make do while the photographic laboratory buildings and support barracks were being constructed.[49]

U.S. Air Service squadrons began active operations over Toul, a quiet sector of the front occupied by the American 26th (Yankee) Division. The 1st Corps Observation Group was the primary U.S. aerial unit in the region with two Aero Squadrons assigned. The 1st Aero Squadron conducted aerial photographic missions, while its counterpart, the 12th Aero Squadron, was assigned artillery spotting missions.[50] The 1st Corps Observation Group would eventually include the 9th Aero Squadron, 24th Aero Squadron and 91st Aero Squadron. The 91st Aero Squadron eventually became the most famous of the U.S. Air Service aerial reconnaissance units, supporting the AEF with long-range reconnaissance.[51]

The initial U.S. aerial photographic effort was abysmal. Almost all of the sorties attempted were either cancelled by weather or suffered aeroplane motor problems. What sorties were generated did not yield any coverage of value. Only 10 plates were acquired in a period of two weeks and were of no value in alerting the American

[48] Eric E. Dixon, *Diary of Eric E. Dixon, Whippany, N.J., U.S.A.: An American Citizen* (Whippany, NJ: n.p., n.d.), 49, Dixon Papers, USAMHI.

[49] Friedmann, "History of Photographic Section #1," 2, Gorrell Report, ser. G, r. 24, NARA.

[50] "Final Report of Chief of Air Service," in Maurer, ed., *U.S. Air Service*, I, 182.

[51] Friedmann, "History of Photographic Section #1," Gorrell Report, ser. G, r. 24, NARA.

FIGURE 64. The first operational presence of U.S. Air Service aerial reconnaissance was marked by the arrival of a SPAD XI group at Ourches. Source: Gorrell Report, NARA.

forces to German intentions. When the 26th Division fought the first major engagement by U.S. forces against the Germans at Seicheprey on 20 April 1918, U.S. aerial reconnaissance was totally ineffective.[52] Despite the lackluster start, the U.S. Air Service honed its skills with each campaign, ultimately supplying important information on the activities of the enemy by means of both visual and photographic reconnaissance.[53] It is noteworthy that the work of the 1st Corps Observation Group was seldom hampered by the presence of enemy pursuit aircraft. Thus, practically no experience in combat was gained. However, the enemy antiaircraft fire in the Toul Sector was exceedingly dense, active and accurate; it resulted in the pilots' becoming adept at evading antiaircraft fire after a month of operations.[54]

The 1st Corps Observation Group learned the aerial reconnaissance trade through extensive interaction with the French. It established an operations room at Group Headquarters to serve as an information and intelligence center. Large-scale maps of the Toul Sector and of the enemy's de-

fensive organization, charts, diagrams, and tabulations of all available tactical and technical information collected by the operations and intelligence officers were displayed in this room.[55] American aerial reconnaissance support for British units in the sector included a few squadrons assisting battle planning. Prior to the combined Australian-American attack on 4 July 1918 at the battle of Hamel, U.S. Air Service units provided 1,200 copies of aerial photographs. The first American operationally deployed photographic unit, Photographic Section #2, rounded out the 1st Corps Group, providing superior support throughout. The only threat to ground operations came from an occasional air raid from German aerial bombardment.[56] Edward Steichen

[52] HQ First Army Corps, A.E.F., Office of Chief of Air Service, "Report of Operations, For April 20, 1918,"Gorrell Report, ser. C, r. 12, NARA.

[53] "Final Report of Chief of Air Service," in Maurer, ed., *U.S. Air Service*, I, 210

[54] "Final Report of Chief of Air Service," in Maurer, ed., *U.S. Air Service*, I, 182.

[55] Sam H. Frank, *American Air Service Observation in World War I*, Ph.D. Dissertation (Gainesville, FL: University of Florida, 1961), 216.

[56] Friedmann, "History of Photographic Section #1," HQ, 1st Army Corps, Office of Chief of Air Service, "Report of Operations, for April 20, 1918," Gorrell Report, ser. C, r. 12, NARA.

later had high praise for the Photographic Section #2 organization. "I do not believe that there was a better or more efficient outfit for the producing of aerial photographs in any of the combatant armies."[57]

The Second Marne Campaign

The increasing arrival of fresh American forces to the front heightened German concerns and prompted new campaigns. The lessons from the Michael and St. George offensives showed the Allies still were vulnerable to a well-planned German operation. Michael had depleted the British Army to the point that the French Armée had to reposition its reserves to the northern sector of the Western Front. Ludendorff used this opportunity to generate a major offensive against the French VIème Armée, positioned on the Chemin des Dames ridge north of the river Aisne. The preparation for battle included 3,700 guns being massed on a thirty-eight mile front opposite the French. Aerial reconnaissance assets from both France and Britain were committed to the sector. The British sent their IX Corps south to the French-controlled Aisne sector, supported by RAF No. 52 Squadron. The squadron's RE 8 observation aeroplanes were successful in reporting the buildup, especially when they detected large dust clouds caused from forces and weapons on the move toward the front lines. Despite the indication of the German movement toward the sector, the French Armée's 2e Bureau was slow to respond. Early on the morning of 27 May, the Germans unleashed one of the fiercest bombardments of the war, followed by a rapid advance across the Aisne. Three days later the Germans captured Soissons and reached the Marne at Château-Thierry. Fierce resistance by two American divisions (2nd and 3rd) and French reserves managed to stop the German advance. Throughout the drive, German pursuit activity had been aggressive, keeping Allied aerial reconnaissance to a minimum.[58]

American exposure to the utility of aerial photography came quickly as the Germans advanced on Château-Thierry. The rapid German advance prompted fears within the GQG that it could be the final breakthrough to Paris. Artillery targeting in this sector was hampered by lack of any large-scale maps. French and American topographic troops were rushed to the sector and through the use of photography enlarged a smaller-scale map in a desperate attempt to provide rear echelon artillery with sufficient data. At the same time, rapidly acquired aerial photography created sufficient mosaics to create a more accurate larger-scale map to prioritize artillery targeting. It demonstrated to both Allies the value of the resource in applying force against the German thrust.[59]

On 9 June, the Germans conducted one of their last offensives against French forces in the Compiègne sector. This time, the offensive lacked surprise. French intelligence analysis had successfully determined the German intention. An intercepted message sent by German headquarters to the staff of the German Eighteenth Corps occupying the sector read, "Rush munitions Stop Even by day if not seen." The implication of the message was that the Germans were massing for an offensive from the town of Remaugies. The intelligence analysis estimated that Ludendorff was trying to salvage his salient by attacking southward on a line between Montdidier and Noyon toward Compiègne. Subsequent aerial reconnaissance and prisoner interrogations confirmed the intended maneuver. Fifteen German divisions engaged in the offensive advanced only six miles before a spirited counterattack led by five French divisions under Général Mangin stood their ground, forcing the Germans to retreat. The French IVème Armée commander, Général Gouraud, conducted a detailed analysis of the aerial photographs in his sector. He countered the German offensive in his sector with a remarkable defensive arrangement comprising two lines. The first line was a tripwire, lightly held and evacuated at the first signs of activity. Gouraud's forces then proceeded to a more powerful network on the second line, which was out of range of German artillery.[60] It proved to be Ludendorff's last chance to achieve decisive strategic results with his armies on the Western

---

[57] Maj Edward Steichen, "American Aerial Photography at the Front," 2, NASM, A30.2/24.

[58] Mead, 133.

[59] Brig Gen Dennis E. Nolan, "G-2-C Topography," 5, Nolan Papers, USAMHI.

[60] Christienne and Lissarague, 73.

Front.[61] It was now the Allies' turn to establish the final offensive.

GQG correctly ascertained German intentions concerning the July offensive, thanks to intelligence capabilities. Two weeks prior, French aerial photographic reconnaissance systematically covered the entire Marne salient, to include Rheims, Château-Thierry, and Soissons. The analysis led to the GQG's forecasting the German drive to within a forty-eight hour window, determining the exact axis of the main drive. German intentions were revealed through standard signatures of an offensive buildup, to include new second-line defenses, supply depots and ammunition dumps, and the enormous increase of traffic on the highways. Also, additional ammunition dumps were observed near the front. It all accumulated with a "sudden great increase in the activities on the roads immediately behind the German front lines; the construction of ramps and new roadways leading from battery positions and trenches to facilitate the egress of troops; and one particularly damning indication of attack, the fortunate location by French aerial observers of a German pontoon train, located not far from the Marne and just north of Dormans."[62] French ballon observateur activity complemented the ongoing observation. The sector had reinforced the observation posts (the French term for this function was *service des renseignements de l'observation du terrain* [SROT]) with additional telephone lines. When the Germans finally attacked, the French Command Post (PC) was immediately informed of the advancing forces and artillery activity.[63]

The Changing Dynamic of Aerial Reconnaissance

As the war reached its final months, aerial tactics reflected reactions to the threat posed by pursuit aeroplanes. "Reconnaissance planes may have to give battle," assessed a French post-war Aeronautics manual. A merger of the two missions became the focus of aéroplane development in the final years of the conflict. "Aviation was to seek out the destruction of enemy aeronautics,

assure use of aerial observation and impede enemy aerial observation. Aeronautical units were at the disposal of the army and placed in appropriate echelons."[64] This included A3 reconnaissance aéroplanes of long range subordinate to the armée and armée Group and reconnaissance aéroplanes of short range attached to the troops. However, the French discovered that the larger A3s (Letord, Morane-Saulnier T) complicated their management of assigned escadrilles. Aviation Militaire made the decision to disperse the long-range A3 category to individual reconnaissance and, in some cases, pursuit escadrilles, to provide each unit with a reconnaissance function to better support armées or CA as necessary.[65]

The final year of the conflict saw a concerted effort by all of the Allies to establish a strong pursuit presence in support of aerial reconnaissance. British pursuit squadrons assigned greater numbers of aircraft to escort aerial observation, in order to ensure continuation of the observation mission.[66] Aerial reconnaissance mission planning followed a routine that included a rendezvous with the protecting pursuit squadron.[67] As the war neared its conclusion, the Americans eventually determined that their best observation formation was several aerial photographic aircraft flying together. State-of-the art aeroplanes such as the Salmson 2 A2 and DH 4 made this configuration defendable. The lead aeroplanes accomplished the photo mission; the remaining aeroplanes conducted defense. However, there was no denial that additional Allied pursuit planes in the area also benefited the mission.[68] A post-war French assessment conveyed the prevailing attitude that, "Combat planes may sometimes bring back valuable information to the Command."[69]

German aerial defense was at its limits in the final months. There were not enough aeroplanes to engage the burgeoning Allied offensive. The

<hr>

[61] Porch, 110-111.
[62] Knappen, 199-202.
[63] Christienne and Lissarague, 73.

[64] "Aeronautics," June 1921, 8-9, NARA, RG 120, Box 819.
[65] Author conversation with Dr. James Davilla.
[66] J. T. C. Moore-Brabazon, "Photography's Part in the War," TNA, PRO: AIR 1/724/91/2.
[67] John W. Stuart Gilchrist. *An Aerial Observer in World War I* (n.p.: privately printed, 1966), 127.
[68] "Final Report of Chief of Air Service," in Maurer, ed., *U.S. Air Service*, I, 207.
[69] "Aeronautics," June 1921, 8-9, NARA, RG 120, Box 819.

lack of air superiority also impacted German infantry. One such indication of concern came from a published order:

> All regiments have repeatedly complained that low-flying enemy aeroplanes are not interfered with by our fighter machines. In reply to these complaints, the Group points out that its resources in aircraft are so low, and those available are so busily engaged on reconnaissance work, that they cannot also be expected to engage enemy machines carrying out low reconnaissance over our lines. The infantry must arrange for its own defense against enemy aircraft to a greater extent than heretofore.[70]

At the same time greater emphasis was placed on masking infantry operations. The German 2nd Guards Reserve Division issued the following directive on 1 August 1918: "The camp, viewed from the air, should produce the impression of being deserted. Tracks will be definitely marked out; all tracks leading into a camp will be continued through it and will lead into other tracks or roads. Camouflaged netting is to be put up over tracks at frequent intervals."[71]

The Summer Offensives

The last months of the war demonstrated aviation's dynamic role as the conflict transitioned from the stalemate of positional war to maneuverability in the final weeks. All allied combatants pushed their respective air forces to be fully engaged in combat. For the French, the Aviation Militaire committed its escadrilles to an aggressive campaign of long-range bombardment, night and day aerial reconnaissance, infantry contact and fighter patrols in group (*groupe de chasse*). The French possessed more aéroplanes than any other aerial combatant and it was clearly demonstrated in the final weeks of conflict.[72] An in-

FIGURE 65. **Capitaine Paul-Louis Weiller led development of French strategical aerial reconnaissance.** Source: de Brunoff, ed., *L'Aéronautique.*

depth experience base of aviators accompanied the state-of-the-art aéroplanes now in use.

The noted French aerial reconnaissance leader, Capitaine Paul-Louis Weiller, exemplified the aerial reconnaissance elite. Weiller took the lead in advancing the role of strategical reconnaissance with the new Breguet 14 A2. He commanded escadrille BR 202 and put his strategical vision to work, demonstrating aerial reconnaissance potential well behind the front lines. Weiller was recognized for his efforts with control over two more Breguet 14 A2 escadrilles, BR 45 and BR 220. The resulting formation was called the Weiller Grouping.[73] Not only did he prove the airframe's ability in flying long-range

---

[70] "Intelligence Summary," 9 August 1918, TNA, PRO: AIR 1/2124/207/74/3.

[71] "Intelligence Summary," 19 September 1918, TNA, PRO: AIR 1/2124/207/74/3.

[72] Author conversation with Dr. James Davilla.

[73] Christienne and Lissarague, 181.

strategic reconnaissance, he personally shot down two German aeroplanes in one day (9 July 1918) during the French Xème Armée offensive in the Ypres sector at Mont Kemmel.[74]

The reassignment of American forces from the Toul sector to Château-Thierry commenced the beginning of large-scale American military operations against the German lines. The German assault on Paris in June culminated in their forces being stopped at Belleau Wood and Château-Thierry. The Americans followed up with their first offensive at Aisne-Marne in mid-July. This involved five American divisions working

FIGURE 66. The Weiller Group made strategical reconnaissance a successful effort to determine enemy intentions. The map shows key German targets in the rear echelon. Source: de Brunoff, eg., *L'Aéronautique*.

in concert with three French divisions. Aisne-Marne represented the first of many strategical offensives, countering the last efforts by the Germans to establish an offensive strategy and set the stage for the conclusion. More resources and better weather aided aerial photographic reconnaissance. The initial dismal performance by the

[74] J. M. Bruce and Jean Noel, *The Breguet 14* (Leatherhead, UK: Profile Publications, 1967), 7.

FIGURE 67. **BR 202 Escadrille was assigned to the Weiller Group for strategical reconnaissance.** Source: Jim Davilla, MA7180.

U.S. Air Service was quickly forgotten as aero squadrons increased their sortie rate and acquired more relevant coverage for ground operations. More effort was also placed on distributing photographs in a timely manner. The 1st Army Corps placed photographs into categories of "First Needs" that, delivered by aeroplane, dropped the packet of prints to the PC's for Corps and Divisions. Recipients included intelligence (G-2), operations of Corps HQ, and intelligence offices supporting key divisions in the Corps (42nd, 77th, 82nd, 90th). "Second Needs" distribution went to echelons below division.[75]

American forces commenced planning to regain Soissons and drive the Germans from the Aisne salient. On 18 July, the Allies proceeded to launch a counter-offensive between Soissons and Château-Thierry. It was the first sign of a shift from positional war to mobile war. The resulting mobile campaign complicated the well-established ground and air liaison. Infantry contact patrols now gave way to the more important aerial mission, with aerial photography assuming a less critical role. It also impacted on the traditional artillery spotting role due to batteries maneuvering on a more frequent basis.[76] Continued success prompted the Allies to reconsider aerial reconnaissance roles. As the 2nd Marne progressed and the Allies began achieving their objectives, the Supreme Allied Commander, Maréchal Foch, reviewed plans to increase pressure on the Germans through coordinated, local ground and air offensives, achieving definite but limited objectives. The RAF also modified its aerial reconnaissance strategy. No longer did it concentrate on static billeting areas. Coverage of interior

---

[75] G-2, 1st Army Corps, "Distribution of Photographs made by the Aviation Section of the Corps," 11 August 1918, Gorrell Report, ser. C, r. 12.

[76] Frank, 297.

WESTERN FRONT, 1918
REDUCTION OF THE AMIENS SALIENT
Situation 8 August and Operations
to 4 September

0   5   10
SCALE OF MILES

railway networks became the priority to help gauge German efforts to sustain the fight.[77] The U.S. Air Service now emphasized aerial reconnaissance as an integral part of American battle planning. Within the 1st Observation Group, the 1st Aero Squadron accomplished long-distance photographic missions, adjustment of divisional heavy artillery fire, and long-distance visual reconnaissance. The 12th Aero Squadron and the 88th Aero Squadron conducted short-range visual reconnaissance, short-range photographic missions, adjustment of light artillery fire, and infantry contact patrols.[78]

The British commenced their counter-offensive in August. Armed with more flexible use of both artillery and infantry, their strategy now brought major gains. The artillery would forsake preliminary bombardment in favor of surprise. Batteries were deployed at night, ammunition dumps concealed from aerial observation, and more accurate surveys of the rear echelons accomplished to ensure greater accuracy of fire.[79] Allied offensives now had purpose. The Germans were overcome at Amiens as the British withheld the preliminary bombardment and focused on rear-echelon artillery targets. They had attempted to diversify and conceal machine gun locations throughout the battlefield to stem the British advance. However, the Allied offensive broke through.[80] General Ludendorff's memories of this moment would be forever engraved in his-

tory. "August 8 was the black day of the German Army in the history of the war."[81]

Artillery staffs now focused on striking deeper targets. The concept of strategic surprise gained respect as they proceeded to annihilate rear echelons.[82] The next major battle was the breakthrough of the Siegfried Stellung at Drocourt (east of Vimy Ridge) in September. Additionally, Cambrai was finally breached without a German counterattack. The sudden access to mobile operations impacted Allied Intelligence. Intelligence no longer followed a well-established routine, as it had in collecting against a fixed geographical point on the battlefield.[83] The last months of the conflict strained French and British air crews. The near fatal effect of the Michael offensive with its long-term critical engagement had severely impacted the Allies' ability to generate aeroplane sorties. The shift from a positional mode of operations to a much more flexible mobile war concept, reminiscent of the first months of 1914, placed additional burdens on routine reconnaissance missions. In 1914, aerial operations covering a mobile battlefield were limited in scope, reflecting the limited available resources. The concluding military operations were much more massive in scale, requiring extensive coordination to ensure the best use of an overstrained resource. Accommodating the requirements of the last months of the British offensive on the northern front with aerial reconnaissance was described as "being very difficult at times."[84]

---

[77] Jones, VI, 415.

[78] Frank, *American Air Service Observation*, 218; "Letter to the Director of Air Service, French Sixth Army from the Chief of Air Service, I Army Corps, American Expeditionary Forces, July 9, 1918," in U.S. Army, Office of Military History, *United States Army in the World War, 1917-1919* (17 volumes, Washington, DC: GPO, 1948; reprint, Washington, DC: U.S. Army Center for Military History, 1988-92), III, 397-398.

[79] Bailey, 148.

[80] Edmonds, *1918*, I, 12.

[81] Erich von Ludendorff, *Ludendorff's Own Story, August 1914-November 1918: The Great War from the Siege of Liege to the Signing of the Armistice as Viewed from the Grand Headquarters of the German Army* (2 vols., New York: Harper & Brothers Publishers, 1919), II, 326.

[82] Bailey, 149.

[83] Hahn, xxi.

[84] "Squadron Leader F.C.V. Laws O.B.E. to G.O.C., Advanced Operations," 18 November 1918, TNA, PRO: AIR 1/724/91/2.

The American Air Offensive at St. Mihiel

Ongoing battle experience over the summer helped solidify AEF appreciation of the value of aerial reconnaissance. In early August, the American 3rd Corps participated in a minor offensive with the French VIème Armée along the River Vesle. Aerial photography was acquired by the 88th Aero Squadron assigned to 3rd Corps.[85] U.S. Air Service aerial reconnaissance successfully accomplished vertical and oblique coverage of the entire River Vesle sector to a depth of seven and a half miles. American field commanders were very impressed with oblique coverage, resulting in more requests for that product to aid their battle planning.[86]

The Americans had been at war for almost 17 months before they were ready to conduct their own campaign against the Germans. Now the AEF had an opportunity to clearly demonstrate its value to the Allies by planning a major operation against the St. Mihiel salient, held by the Germans since 1914. St. Mihiel had been a battleground many times, with the strategic city of Metz as the ultimate objective, as it served as the logistical lifeline for German forces. However, AEF planning focused on the first objective of liberating St. Mihiel and the immediate area. Recapturing the strategic city of Metz with its vital railway hub would come later. The intelligence base comprised French Plan Directeur and other army maps. The U.S. Air Service was immediately tasked to acquire the necessary aerial photographic coverage.[87] St. Mihiel stirred the imagination of the American planners, both infantry and aviation. Of the latter, Brigadier General William "Billy" Mitchell envisioned a dynamic role for aviation employing around 1,500 aeroplanes to engage the enemy not only with bombardment and infantry contact missions, but also with an extensive aerial reconnaissance role as well. During the early part of September, a large amount of aerial photographic work was accomplished throughout all hours of daylight.[88] The AEF G-2-C Topography unit alone generated and distributed 2,320 oblique prints of the battleground prior to the offensive.[89] Additionally, the planning included extensive preparation of maps, charts, assemblages, and clay reliefs of the territory over which the AEF advanced. The level of effort was impressive. In one day, a single American photographic production facility (Photographic Section #4) processed 250 plates and produced 11,212 prints.[90]

By September 1918, the AEF Air Service was made up of one army observation aero squadron, seven corps observation aero squadrons, a day bombardment aero squadron and fourteen pursuit aero squadrons. In anticipation of the St. Mihiel offensive, the French placed a large number of pursuit and day bombardment escadrilles at the disposal of the Americans and under Mitchell's command. It became the largest aggregation of aeroplanes assembled for a single operation on the Western Front during the entire war. A total of 1,481 aeroplanes comprising 701 pursuit, 366 observation, 323 day bombardment, and 91 night bombardment machines supported the offensive.[91] The Americans had finally arrived. For the first time they fielded an aerial force larger than the Germans.[92]

Army reconnaissance sorties monitored strategic targets up to the city of Metz, covering aerodromes, hospitals, ammunition and supply dumps, roads, railroads and rear area works of all kinds.[93] One pilot, Lieutenant Lawrence L. Smart, of the 135th Aero Squadron, remembered flying every day that the weather allowed, accomplishing aerial photography, observation, and *avion de réglage*. Both Corps and Army Headquarters wanted every inch of the sector photographed daily to enable them to tell if the Germans were anticipating an attack, or if they

[85] "Final Report of Chief of Air Service," in Maurer, ed., *U.S. Air Service*, I, 221-223.

[86] Frank, *American Air Service Observation*, 266-267; "Final Report of Chief of Air Service," in Maurer, ed., *U.S. Air Service*, I, 226-228.

[87] G-2 to Chief of Staff, "Account of the Operation," 7, Drum Papers, Box 14, USAMHI.

[88] "Final Report of Chief of Air Service," in Maurer, ed., *U.S. Air Service*, I, 239.

[89] Nolan, "G-2-C Topography," 12, Nolan Papers, USAMHI.

[90] Maj James Barnes, "History of Photographic Section #4, Air Service, U.S.A. 1918," Gorrell Report, ser. G, r. 24, NARA.

[91] Frank, *American Air Service Observation*, 312.

[92] Frank, *American Air Service Observation*, 342.

[93] G-2 to Chief of Staff, "Account of the Operation," 51, Drum Papers, Box 14, USAMHI.

FIGURE 69. **St. Mihiel.** Source: *West Point Atlas*, map 68, Courtesy, Department of History, U.S. Military Academy.

were digging any new trenches, barbed wire or gun emplacements, or preparing troop movements. Smart recalled, "By comparing daily photographs of a sector, new construction or movements of large groups of men could be detected with accuracy."[94] They had photographed the objectives many times. Intelligence was very busy studying photographs taken constantly by the observers, and studying them for machine gun emplacements, battery positions, and anything of unusual significance, such as new defenses and troop concentrations.[95]

Another aerial observer, 2nd Lieutenant G. T. Lindstrom, recalled his role with photographic reconnaissance preparations in support of one of the American divisions. His aeroplane flew at an altitude of 2,000 to 2,500 meters about

15 kilometers to the rear of the German lines. When the St. Mihiel attack commenced, Lindstrom flew low-altitude missions at 350 meters taking oblique photographs of the German front line positions. A formation of other aeroplanes from his aero squadron as well as pursuit fighters from other aero squadrons rounded out the mission, providing protection. Lindstrom recalled that aerial photographic reconnaissance required concentration on four objectives, the course of the plane, where the enemy pursuit planes were flying, location of enemy antiaircraft fire, and the whereabouts of the protection aeroplanes.[96]

Bad weather curtailed coverage during the initial drive. However, other intelligence sources came into play. American radio intercept stations (goniometric service) were able to locate the position of all enemy radio stations. These stations

[94] 1st Lt Lawrence L. Smart, *The Hawks that Guided the Guns* (n.p.: privately Printed, 1968), 44.

[95] Smart, 45.

[96] G. T. Lindstrom, "Photographic Missions," Gorrell Report, ser. N, r. 53, NARA.

were usually located close to the enemy's headquarters, providing the intelligence analysts with not only the approximate location of the command center, but also an estimate of the numbers of enemy regiments and battalions in the sector. All the combatants waged a different kind of war when it came to goniometric operations. Deception techniques were common, for example generating intense radio traffic in quiet sectors and curtailing radio activity in the area where a surprise attack was planned. Just before the attack at St. Mihiel, intelligence suspected German forces had withdrawn. However, goniometric analysis determined that German radio stations were still active in the sector. Armed with that evidence, Pershing directed that the attack follow a heavy artillery bombardment.[97] The second day of the offensive allowed some sorties to acquire low-level oblique coverage of key towns in the area. However, the overall lack of aerial reconnaissance stifled analysis of enemy locations and intentions. During the final hours of the St. Mihiel campaign, the Americans were not able to confirm the withdrawal of the Germans from the sector. This posed problems with where to commit forces as well as how to determine the extent of the German retreat.[98]

Allied aerial reconnaissance aeroplanes accomplished an enormous amount of aerial photographic coverage of the forward area. Between 21 and 24 September, AEF staffs sorted and distributed approximately 8,500 oblique and 20,000 vertical photos. French photographic interpreter support was a crucial part of the overall effectiveness of the operation. They established a special distribution of photos in preparation for the offensive. This was planned and carried out under the direct supervision of France's leading photographic interpreter, Capitaine Pépin. Photographic packages were furnished to French chars d'assaut headquarters in sufficient number to give each French and American tank unit oblique photographs of their assigned sector as well as a set of about 30 vertical shots.[99] The St.

Mihiel battle planning had photo sections producing prodigious amounts of maps, charts, assemblages, and clay reliefs of the territory over which the American Army advanced. When the offensive commenced, photo sections compensated for the bad weather and produced extensive, low-level, oblique coverage for the rapid advance of the Allies to cut off the Germans at the salient.[100] In spite of the impressive statistics, post-war reflections on the lessons learned by America's aviation effort at St. Mihiel suggested disappointment with the lack of accomplishment with aerial photography. "In general our back-area photographic information was unsatisfactory, owing to the rapidity of our advance and the bad weather, which combined to keep our Squadrons photographing the areas just ahead."[101]

St. Mihiel proved the AEF's ability to conduct a major offensive against the Germans. The performance of U.S. Air Service aerial reconnaissance reinforced Allied confidence in the ability of American forces to proceed to more demanding campaigns. After St. Mihiel, Maréchal Foch had his staff receive and examine aerial photographs of the sector to confirm the nature and strength of the new Allied line established by the victorious Americans. The evidence was conclusive and the verdict was made in Pershing's favor. Foch approved the next offensive at the Meuse-Argonne.[102]

Meuse-Argonne

The Meuse-Argonne campaign was the last major Allied offensive in the war. The movement of men and material was made entirely under cover of darkness, all activity being suspended and the men kept in concealment during daylight hours. Consequently, the roads leading into the area were scenes of activity at night as troops and artillery, ammunition, and supplies moved forward. French soldiers within the sector remained in the outpost positions until the last minute in an effort to hide Allied intentions from German

---

[97] Nolan, "Codes and Ciphers," 14, Nolan Papers, USAMHI.

[98] G-2 to Chief of Staff, "Account of the Operation," 7, Drum Papers, Box 14, USAMHI; "Final Report of Chief of Air Service," in Maurer, ed., *U.S. Air Service*, I, 239.

[99] "Historical Account of Organization and Functioning of Subdivision," 62, Drum Papers, Box 14, USAMHI.

[100] Barnes, "History of Photographic Section #4," Gorrell Report, ser. G, r. 24, NARA.

[101] G-2 to Chief of Staff, "Account of the Operation," 56-57, Drum Papers, Box 14, USAMHI.

[102] Steichen, "American Aerial Photography at the Front," 1, NASM, A30.2/24.

observation.[103] Battlefield preparation was extensive. Photographic mosaics were prepared for the AEF's 1st, 3rd, and 5th Corps, covering the front of each. A mosaic of the Meuse River was made for the 3rd Corps. Staff packages containing oblique coverage along the front lines were prepared for the commanders and staff.[104] The Meuse-Argonne became one of the largest battles ever fought by Americans, involving over 600,000 soldiers.

Planning preparation for Meuse-Argonne required extensive analysis of several high-interest German targets in the region such as parts of the Siegfried Stellung known as the *Kriemhilde Stellung* and *Freya Stellung*. As in the St. Mihiel operation, the weather for Meuse-Argonne was critical leading up to and during the offensive. There were occasional ideal flying days, but atmospheric conditions ranged from poor to impossible and proved a great handicap in carrying out extensive aerial operations. Haze and fog obscured the ground to a great extent in the early morning and late afternoon during the last four weeks of the offensive, greatly impacting not only available light but access to interpretable shadows as well. Aerial photography from 26 September to 11 November 1918 was in almost every case confined to taking photographs of well-defined areas of particular interest to the Intelligence (G-2) section of the Corps and Army staffs, rather than searching for targets of opportunity. All corps air services adjusted to the weather challenge, readying their aeroplanes for immediate launch, given a break in the atmospheric conditions.[105]

Throughout the campaign, the AEF G-2 continually asked the question, "Does the enemy intend a withdrawal, and if so, to what position?"[106] Initially, aerial photographic interpretation acquired during the battle convinced French and AEF interpreters that the Germans were making practically no progress in strengthening their Kriemhilde Stellung defense. However, at the same time, the photographic interpreters were unable to determine German intentions for staying put or withdrawing.[107] As the Meuse-Argonne battle brought the war to an end, tasking aerial observation and photographic coverage became an exercise in keeping pace with the rapidly advancing front line. The 1st Army assigned Corps area-of-interest information to the Corps squadrons and Corps intelligence. The Meuse-Argonne offensive prompted the army office to frequently determine the new front line, a phenomenon not seen since 1914.[108] Oblique coverage supported the advance of the infantry. Vertical coverage on the other hand was viewed as more appropriate for cartographic work.[109]

The Meuse-Argonne campaign clearly demonstrated the ability to acquire and produce aerial photography for the combatants. An impressive count of 56,000 prints was produced and distributed in four days by the American Photographic Sections.[110] Headquarters planning staffs had envisioned a maximum daily outlay of prints from a single production facility to be 10,000. In spite of the challenges posed by limitations to coverage due to the weather, an impressive number of plates were acquired and prints developed for the combatants. Photographic Section #5, supporting the 3rd Observation Group, produced 11,500 prints.[111] The AEF Tables of Organization initially had contemplated having one photographic section assigned to each observation group. The demonstrated volume of prints made a major difference in rethinking the manning necessary for the photographic section to sustain the rate of production. In the closing days, the AEF assigned two complete photographic sections to the 1st Army Observation Group to handle the volume.[112]

---

[103] Frank, *American Air Service Observation*, 345.

[104] "Historical Account," 61, Drum Papers, Box 14, USAMHI.

[105] "Final Report of Chief of Air Service," in Maurer, ed., *U.S. Air Service*, I, 249-250; Frank, *American Air Service Observation*, 353; G-2 to Chief of Staff, "Account of the Operation," 56-57, Drum Papers, Box 14, USAMHI.

[106] G-2 to Chief of Staff, "Account of the Operation," 48, Drum Papers, Box 14, USAMHI.

[107] G-2, 1st Army, "Account of the Operation," Drum Papers, Box 14, USAMHI.

[108] G-2, 1st Army, "Account of the Operation," 47, Drum Papers, Box 14, USAMHI.

[109] "Final Report of Chief of Air Service," in Maurer, ed., *U.S. Air Service*, I, 213; Frank, *American Air Service Observation*, 292.

[110] "Final Report of Chief of Air Service," in Maurer, ed., *U.S. Air Service*, I, 152.

[111] "Final Report of Chief of Air Service," in Maurer, ed., *U.S. Air Service*, I, 154.

[112] "Final Report of Chief of Air Service," in Maurer, ed., *U.S. Air Service*, I, 154.

WESTERN FRONT, 1918

MEUSE–ARGONNE OFFENSIVE

Operations 26 September–11 November

SCALE OF MILES

The effort by the American aerial reconnaissance elements was impressive. There was competition both from within and throughout the group. The aero squadrons were in a race to keep coverage coming in that would be of value to the staffs.[113] During the Meuse-Argonne advance the U.S. Air Service 24th and 91st Aero Squadrons acquired 1,098 photographs.[114] By the end of the war, one aeroplane out of every four flying on the Western Front was there to provide aerial photographic coverage.[115] The final mark of success was the impression that aerial photography made on the ultimate user, the infantry in battle. Steichen recalled two cases where the opinion was highly favorable. One American infantry colonel referred to the aerial photographs he received from the U.S. Air Service as the most vital assistance he had ever been given. The details available from studying the photographs had contributed mightily to the success of his unit's action and was as an important determinant in reducing casualties. Another post-battle critique came from a young lieutenant in speaking of his battle experiences near Vaux. He commented that the only data he had there that were worth a "tinker's damn" came from three aerial photographs some-one had "policed up" for him.[116] High praise for American aerial photography's contribution came from General Pershing: "No army ever went out with the information as to what was in front of it as the American army did at St. Mihiel and the Argonne."[117]

The Offensive to the Finish

A resumption of mobility in warfare in the final days of the war prompted rethinking of aerial reconnaissance practices. As the Allies advanced at a rapid rate, established procedures were determined to be ineffective. The AEF's 3rd Army Corps noted on 5 November 1918, in its Operational Report, that "Photography was not attempted as the rapidly changing situation did not warrant such missions."[118] Most of the aerial photographic missions from 26 September to 11 November focused on well-defined areas specified by the intelligence sections of the Corps staffs. The weather during this period determined target priorities, with sortie generation revolving around breaks in cloud coverage.[119] Oblique photographs continued to be a favorite of the advancing infantry, providing excellent views of the objective. German centers of resistance were the ongoing reconnaissance objectives assigned to elite flying units that were thoroughly familiar with the exact locality to be photographed, reducing the possibility of failure in trying to photograph the target.[120]

In the final days of the conflict, the Allies employed advance guards of all combat arms to follow the German forces. This advance team determined enemy positions of resistance so that the main body of follow-on forces avoided becoming entrapped. Weather remained a challenge to the end. To the north, British aerial observation met with little success in providing tactical coverage to support the advance team. A few aeroplanes were employed to report to the corps headquarters the whereabouts of the leading troops and the position of the front line hour by hour. In general, the final days of the war saw the RAF engaged in minor bombing sorties of railway junctions, cantonments, reserves and transport. Aerial observation played a role in determining enemy intentions, especially through observed massing of enemy reserves for counterattack, artillery spotting when possible, and spotting infantry contact

---

[113] G-2, 1st Army, "Account of the Operation," 63, Drum Papers, Box 14, USAMHI.

[114] G-2, 1st Army, "Account of the Operation," 14, Drum Papers, Box 14, USAMHI.

[115] Porter, 158.

[116] Steichen, "American Aerial Photography at the Front," 1, NASM, A30.2/24.

[117] Pershing quoted in Knappen, 212-213; Powell, 293.

[118] "Operations Report for November 5, 1918," HQ 3rd Army Corps, Office of Chief of Air Service, Gorrell Report, ser. C, r. 12, NARA.

[119] Frank, *American Air Service Observation*, 363-364.

[120] Frank, *American Air Service Observation*, 353.

FIGURE 71. **Detailed annotations by the 5th Photographic Section supporting the 99th Aero Squadron show threats against AEF forces at the Meuse-Argonne.** Source: USAFA McDermott Library Special Collections (SMS57).

on the roads.[121] British aerial photographic coverage was now attained at higher altitudes with more powerful cameras, acquiring greater detail of a broader area in a more rapid manner. Moore-Brabazon touted the capability to photograph the entire battle line in the short space of 2½ hours. The ability to image developments at this level was considered an important achievement in planning for the mobile battlefield.[122]

As the German armies withdrew in the final days of the war, concern arose over where a possible "last stand" might take place. Aerial photography was called on to determine possible lines of natural defense that could reinforce ongoing preparations for mobile warfare.[123] However, aerial

photography's primary purpose in the final days was to prepare the commander for rapid advance. Lines of communication networks were evaluated in detail, prepping the mobile battlefield for impending obstructions and points of resistance. Roads, railways, rivers, and key bridge crossings were subjected to analysis. Any networks that had been blown by mines were now the subject of interpretation, to include damage repair estimates. This cut down the time allotted to rapidly repair the network and ensure that momentum was not impaired. "Without such information the advance would have taken considerably longer than was the case."[124]

The war ended with the Armistice in November, followed by the peace treaty at Versailles the following spring. The Allies moved into the German Rhineland and prepared to advance farther should the peace negotiations at Versailles end in failure. Intelligence operations in the occupied Rhineland sought out information on Bolshevism creeping into the region. Aerial operations continued over the Rhine, providing an assessment of any signs of German forces near the border of the occupation sector and helping to maintain force readiness. Aerial photographs were acquired of the scenic views along the Rhine and Moselle Rivers; they were often used to grace the squadron walls. The six months leading up to the Treaty of Versailles witnessed personnel more focused on returning home and to civilian life than honing their skills in aerial photography. Occupation forces along the Rhine tried to maintain consistency, reviewing what had been published and retaining data for operations.

Such was the case with the Pépin study on aerial photographic interpretation. It remained filed away at the American headquarters at Koblenz along with other documents generated after the conclusion of the fighting. Other campaigns still active in the world, such as in Mesopotamia, would keep British aerial photography active. However, by the early 1920s the military seniors wondered if it was necessary to keep training in an art that had passed by. To many, positional warfare did not seem to have a future.

[121] Edmonds, *1918*, V, 576-577.

[122] Moore-Brabazon, "Photography's Part in the War," TNA, PRO: AIR 1/724/91/2.

[123] Moore-Brabazon, "Photography's Part in the War," TNA, PRO: AIR 1/724/91/2.

[124] Moore-Brabazon, "Photography's Part in the War," TNA, PRO: AIR 1/724/91/2.

PART TWO:
THE ARCHITECTURE OF ALLIED AERIAL RECONNAISSANCE AND PHOTOGRAPHIC INTERPRETATION

THE OPERATION OF INTERPRETATION

Aerial photography in the Great War encompassed three distinct operations: 1) location of enemy works on the print or glass plate (interpretation); 2) application of aerial photographic data to map construction (restitution); and, 3) exploitation of intelligence for subsequent operations against the enemy (such as adjusting artillery fire).[1] Allied dependence on these processes increased substantially as the aerial photograph became an accepted form of intelligence data. Interpretation established the science of photography as a legitimate source of intelligence, restitution served as the framework for cartography, and exploitation assumed the ultimate role of validation of the many sources of information that served the combatant.

The Basic Science of Photography

Aerial photography created a landscape of black and white images oriented to the points of the compass and a corresponding map. The first step behind interpreting a photograph required understanding sunlight direction so that the relationship of image and shadow cast could be correctly established.[2] Lessons in aerial photography introduced this requirement:

A photograph reduces the earth to a pattern of tones ranging from dark to light. This ground pattern is produced primarily by color, which in turn is enormously modified by light and shade. Embankments and hollow places produce shadow. In connection with light and shade, it should be understood that objects need not be of dark \color, or in shadow, to photograph dark. They may be light-colored and in full sunlight and yet the quality of their surface may be such that they contain enough shadow to photograph dark. In short, the most important factor in determining shadow, excepting contours and cavities, is texture [of the perceived image]. Any irregularity or roughness of surface produces shadow, and any flattening down or smoothing of surface reduces it.[3]

Understanding shadow was critical to the discipline. Without it an interpreter could easily confuse a hole from a mound.[4] One technique employed by the interpreter was to adjust the light

---

[1] Lt G.W. Gill and 1st Lt Thomas E. Hibben, "Preparation of Photographic Missions," Lectures given at 2nd Aviation Instruction Center, Gorrell Report, ser. J, r. 34, NARA; Solomon J. Solomon, *Strategic Camouflage* (New York: E.P. Dutton and Company, 1920), 1.

[2] Porter, 179; Hahn, 20.

[3] "Lecture on Aerial Photography," 25 April 1923, NASM A30.2/36.

[4] *Study and Use of Aerial Photographs*, 15 January 1918, sec. I, 34-35, NARA, RG 120, Box 819; "Aerial Photography for Pilots," 21 August 1918, 20, NASM, A30.2/2; "Lecture on Aerial Photography," 25 April 1923, NASM A30.2/36; *Notes on the Interpretation of Aeroplane Photographs*, March 1917 (S.S. 550), 5, and February 1918 (S.S. 631), 3; Solomon, 4; Hahn, 21.

source during the examination to simulate sunlight. This gave value to the shadows, enabling the reliefs of the hollows to be differentiated, and the height or the depth of the obstacles to be judged in comparison with the length of the shadows of known objects.[5] One post-war description further embellished the discipline:

> The interpreter must know shadows not as an artist knows them, but rather as a scientist knows them. The shadow is his best friend. By its length and shape he not only pictures to himself the object which cast it, but he can also judge the size and shape of other objects close by, whose own shadows are perhaps indistinct or misshaped. Without the shadow, he could hardly tell an embankment from a trench; and he certainly couldn't hope to distinguish between a gun emplacement and a haystack, unless somebody told him that one of them was shooting.[6]

FIGURE 72. Analyzing shadows was critical to the aerial photographic interpreter's discipline. Source: *Étude et Exploitation des Photographies Aériennes.*

Interpretation was rarely left to a beginner, even in wartime.[7] The interpreter had to know photographic reality. Light and shade did not directly relate to normal vision. The photographic image represented the amount of light reflected, rather than the degree of "actinic" (photochemically active radiation such as that produced from sunlight) effect of the objects reproduced.[8] Thick vegetation appeared dark while a smooth road surface showed as a white line on a print. Light reflection and absorption created the final image.[9]

---

[5] Hahn, 21.
[6] Porter, 184.

[7] Porter, 181.
[8] "Characteristics of the Ground and Landmarks in the Enemy Lines Opposite the British Front from the Sea to St Quentin," TNA, PRO: AIR 10/61.
[9] *Notes on the Interpretation of Aeroplane Photographs*, March 1917 (S.S. 550), 5, and February 1918 (S.S. 631), 3; Solomon, 4; Hahn, 21.

SCALE AND GROUND AREA COVERED BY LENSES OF GIVEN FOCAL LENGTH ON GIVEN SIZE PLATES

SIZE OF PLATE	13 X 18		18 X 24		18 X 24		18 X 24	
F.L. OF LENS	26		26		50		120	
AVAILABLE PLATE AREA	12 X 17		17 X 23		17 X 23		17 X 23	
ALTITUDE IN METERS	METERS COVERED	SCALE	METERS COVERED	SCALE	METERS COVERED	SCALE	METERS COVERED	SCALE
1000	461 X 654	1-3840	654 X 885	1-3860	340 X 460	1-2000	142 X 192	1-835
1250	575 X 817	1-4790	817 X 1105	1-4820	425 X 575	1-2500	177 X 240	1-1040
1500	691 X 981	1-5760	981 X 1328	1-5780	510 X 690	1-3000	213 X 288	1-1210
1750	805 X 1145	1-6710	1145 X 1550	1-6740	595 X 805	1-3500	248 X 336	1-1460
2000	922 X 1308	1-7680	1308 X 1770	1-7670	680 X 920	1-4000	284 X 384	1-1670
2250	1036 X 1470	1-8630	1470 X 1990	1-8650	765 X 1035	1-4500	319 X 432	1-1880
2500	1152 X 1635	1-9620	1635 X 2240	1-9620	850 X 1150	1-5000	356 X 480	1-2100
2750	1268 X 1798	1-10560	1798 X 2430	1-10580	935 X 1265	1-5500	391 X 528	1-2300
3000	1382 X 1960	1-11520	1960 X 2660	1-11540	1020 X 1380	1-6000	426 X 576	1-2505
3250	1498 X 2123	1-12480	2123 X 2875	1-12530	1105 X 1495	1-6500	461 X 624	1-2715
3500	1615 X 2209	1-13460	2209 X 3100	1-13020	1190 X 1610	1-7000	497 X 672	1-2920
3750	1690 X 2450	1-14090	2450 X 3320	1-14450	1275 X 1725	1-7500	533 X 720	1-3140
4000	1845 X 2620	1-15380	2620 X 3540	1-15550	1360 X 1840	1-8000	568 X 768	1-3340
4250	1960 X 2780	1-16320	2780 X 3760	1-16390	1445 X 1955	1-8500	604 X 815	1-3560
4500	2075 X 2942	1-17230	2942 X 3980	1-17360	1530 X 2070	1-9000	638 X 864	1-3750
4750	2190 X 3110	1-18250	3110 X 4210	1-18320	1615 X 2185	1-9500	675 X 912	1-3975
5000	2305 X 3278	1-19200	3278 X 4435	1-19300	1700 X 2300	1-10,000	710 X 960	1-4170

CHART No. 101   PHOTO SECTION-AIR SERVICE - A.E.F.

FIGURE 73. **Mission planning for aerial photography was an exact science. The AEF photogrammetry chart captures the key ingredients for all required data, to include camera lens, scale desired, desired overlap, and aeroplane altitude.** Source: Gorrell Report, NARA.

Planning the Aerial Photographic Mission

Extensive planning was required prior to conducting the mission. Every aspect of photography had to be considered before the aeroplane took off on the sortie. Preparation included selection of camera, determining the flight path (ground trace) of the aeroplane, altitude flown, and considerations for defense. The camera's configuration depended upon the aerial photographic mission and the type of coverage required. Aerial photography was a flexible medium thanks to a variety of focal lengths and plate sizes, providing the planner with accessibility to a broad range of photo scale to ground coverage.[10] Prior to each aerial reconnaissance sortie, the air crew and photographic interpreter would consult photograph charts to determine the altitude, camera lens, photographic plate size and speed of the aeroplane required to successfully cover the terrain to be photographed.[11]

Aerial Photographic Products

Aerial photographic plates produced an array of products by which the photographic interpreter could conduct analysis and dissemination of material for staffs and infantry combatants. Production included negatives, positives, photographic proofs, enlargements, mosaics and stereoscopic

---

[10] 1st Lt Thomas E. Hibben, "Interpretation of Aerial Photography," 49th Inf. Att. A.S., Gorrell Report, ser. J, r. 34, NARA.

[11] "Table of Information for Taking Aerial Photographs," Gorrell Report, ser. G, r. 24, NARA.

MAP AREA COVERED
FOCAL LENGTH OF LENS, SIZE OF PLATE
AND ALTITUDE GIVEN
DIMENSIONS IN MILLIMETERS.

SIZE OF PLATE	13 X 18			18 X 24			18 X 24			18 X 24		
F.L. OF LENS	26			26			50			120		
AVAILABLE PLATE AREA	12 X 17			17 X 23			17 X 23			17 X 23		
ALTITUDE IN METERS	MAPS 1:50000	MAPS 1:20000	MAPS 1:10000	MAPS 1:50000	MAPS 1:20000	MAPS 1:10000	MAPS 1:50000	MAPS 1:20000	MAPS 1:10000	MAPS 1:50000	MAPS 1:20000	MAPS 1:10000
1000	9 X 13	22 X 33	46 X 65	13 X 18	33 X 45	65 X 89	7 X 9	17 X 23	34 X 46	3 X 4	7 X 9	14 X 19
1250	11 X 16	29 X 41	58 X 81	16 X 22	41 X 55	81 X 110	9 X 12	21 X 29	43 X 58	4 X 5	9 X 12	18 X 24
1500	14 X 20	35 X 49	69 X 98	20 X 26	49 X 66	98 X 132	10 X 14	25 X 35	51 X 69	4 X 6	10 X 14	21 X 29
1750	16 X 23	41 X 58	81 X 115	23 X 31	58 X 78	115 X 155	12 X 16	30 X 40	59 X 80	5 X 7	12 X 18	25 X 37
2000	18 X 26	46 X 66	92 X 131	26 X 35	66 X 89	131 X 177	14 X 18	34 X 46	68 X 92	6 X 8	14 X 19	28 X 38
2250	21 X 29	52 X 74	104 X 147	29 X 40	74 X 100	147 X 199	15 X 21	38 X 52	77 X 104	6 X 9	16 X 21	32 X 43
2500	23 X 33	58 X 82	115 X 164	33 X 45	82 X 111	164 X 222	17 X 23	43 X 58	85 X 115	7 X 10	18 X 24	36 X 48
2750	25 X 36	64 X 90	127 X 180	36 X 49	90 X 122	180 X 243	19 X 25	47 X 63	94 X 127	8 X 11	19 X 26	39 X 53
3000	28 X 39	69 X 98	138 X 196	39 X 53	98 X 133	196 X 266	20 X 28	51 X 69	102 X 138	9 X 12	21 X 29	43 X 58
3250	30 X 42	75 X 106	150 X 212	42 X 58	106 X 144	212 X 288	22 X 30	55 X 75	111 X 150	9 X 13	23 X 31	46 X 62
3500	32 X 44	81 X 110	162 X 220	44 X 62	110 X 155	226 X 310	24 X 32	60 X 81	119 X 161	10 X 13	25 X 33	50 X 67
3750	34 X 48	85 X 123	169 X 245	49 X 66	123 X 166	245 X 332	25 X 35	64 X 86	128 X 173	11 X 14	26 X 36	53 X 72
4000	37 X 52	93 X 131	185 X 262	52 X 71	131 X 177	262 X 354	27 X 37	68 X 92	136 X 184	11 X 15	28 X 38	57 X 77
4250	39 X 56	98 X 139	196 X 278	56 X 75	139 X 188	278 X 376	29 X 39	72 X 98	145 X 196	12 X 16	30 X 41	60 X 82
4500	42 X 59	104 X 147	205 X 294	59 X 80	147 X 199	294 X 398	31 X 41	77 X 104	153 X 207	13 X 17	32 X 43	64 X 86
4750	44 X 62	110 X 155	219 X 311	62 X 84	156 X 211	311 X 421	32 X 44	81 X 109	162 X 219	14 X 18	34 X 45	68 X 91
5000	46 X 66	116 X 164	231 X 328	66 X 89	164 X 222	328 X 444	34 X 46	85 X 115	170 X 230	14 X 19	35 X 48	71 X 96

CHART No. 102. PHOTO SECTION·AIR SERVICE·A.E.F.

FIGURE 74. **Additional chart showing desired scale and ground area covered by French aerial cameras.** Source: Gorrell Report, NARA.

views.[12] Mission planning also specified the type of photograph that was acquired. The three formats, panoramic, vertical and oblique, became the most recognizable signature of the aerial photograph. Camera focal length was the key to mission planning. The shorter the focal length, the larger the area that could be photographed. The aerial photograph was further divided into three groups corresponding to the collection method. Continuous photographs were taken so that each succeeding photograph had enough overlap to show continuity of coverage. Separate pinpoint photographs were taken to acquire a specific target within the photographic plate. Finally, stereo coverage required the maximum amount of overlap in order to accomplish the necessary stereo effect.[13] Of the three, stereo coverage was the most useful format for detailed interpretation.[14]

When the Allied forces were introduced to a new sector, the best and most effective way of introducing the terrain and configuration was through the panoramic photograph. The first recorded panoramic was acquired by the French on 20 October 1914.[15] Panoramic photographs provided the necessary study of a sector ensem-

---

[12] Lieut Eugène Pépin, "A Lecture on the Study and Interpretation of Aerial Photographs," 10 December 1917, War Department, Office of the Chief Signal Officer, Information Section – Air Division, Washington, DC, Stencil No. 682, 1, NASM.

[13] Gill and Hibben, "Preparation of Photographic Missions," Gorrell Report, ser. J, r. 34, NARA.
[14] Ives, 40.
[15] Christienne and Lissarague, 70.

Chapter 6: The Operation of Interpretation

TABLE OF INFORMATION
FOR TAKING AERIAL PHOTOGRAPHS

0.26 CAMERA						0.50 CAMERA						1.20 CAMERA					
ALT.	GROUND COVERED LENGTH	WIDTH	SCALE	1"m ON PHOTO	TIME BETWEEN EXPOSURES 140x 160x 180x	ALT.	GROUND COVERED LENGTH	WIDTH	SCALE	1"m ON PHOTO	TIME BETWEEN EXPOSURES 140x 160x 180x	ALT.	GROUND COVERED LENGTH	WIDTH	SCALE	1"m ON PHOTO	TIME BETWEEN EXPOSURES 140x 160x 180x
1000	650	460	3847	3ᵐ84	9" 7" 6"	1000	440	330	1923	1ᵐ90	6" 5" 5"	1000	190	140	833	0ᵐ83	
1100	710	500	4231	4 23		1100	480	360	2115	2 10		1100	210	150	915	0 91	
1200	780	550	4616	4 60	11" 9" 8"	1200	530	390	2305	2 30	7" 6" 6"	1200	230	170	1000	1 00	
1300	850	600	5000	5 00		1300	570	420	2500	2 50		1300	250	180	1084	1 08	
1400	910	640	5385	5 38	13" 11" 10"	1400	620	460	2692	2 70	8" 7" 7"	1400	270	200	1166	1 16	
1500	980	690	5770	5 75		1500	660	490	2884	2 88		1500	290	210	1245	1 25	
1600	1040	730	6154	6 15	15" 13" 12"	1600	710	520	3070	3 07	9" 8" 7"	1600	300	230	1330	1 33	4" 3'5 3"
1700	1110	780	6539	6 56		1700	750	550	3270	3 27		1700	320	240	1415	1 40	
1800	1170	830	6924	6 90	17" 15" 13"	1800	790	590	3460	3 46	10" 9" 8"	1800	340	250	1500	1 50	4'5 4 3'5
1900	1240	880	7308	7 30		1900	810	620	3650	3 65		1900	365	270	1585	1 60	
2000	1310	920	7693	7 70	19" 17" 15"	2000	880	660	3840	3 84	11" 10" 9"	2000	390	290	1670	1 67	5" 4'5 4"
2100	1380	970	8077	8 07		2100	930	690	4032	4 03		2100	410	300	1755	1 75	
2200	1440	1010	8461	8 46	21" 18" 16"	2200	970	720	4230	4 23	12" 11" 9"	2200	420	310	1840	1 84	5'5 5 4'5
2300	1510	1060	8846	8 84		2300	1010	750	4420	4 42		2300	440	325	1915	1 91	
2400	1570	1100	9230	9 23	22" 20 18	2400	1060	790	4610	4 61	13" 12" 10"	2400	460	340	2000	2 00	6" 5" 4'5
2500	1640	1150	9615	9 61		2500	1100	820	4802	4 80		2500	480	355	2085	2 08	
2600	1700	1200	10.000	10 00	24" 21" 19"	2600	1150	850	5000	5 00	14" 12" 10"	2600	500	370	2170	2 17	6" 5'5 5"
2700	1770	1250	10 384	10 38		2700	1190	880	5190	5 19		2700	520	385	2255	2 25	
2800	1830	1290	10 769	10 76	26" 23 20	2800	1230	920	5380	5 38	15" 13" 12"	2800	540	400	2340	2 34	6'5 6" 5"
2900	1900	1340	11 151	11 15		2900	1270	950	5572	5 57		2900	560	415	2425	2 42	
3000	1960	1380	11 538	11 53	28" 25 22	3000	1320	980	5770	5 77	16" 14" 13"	3000	580	430	2510	2 51	7" 6'5 5'5
3100	2030	1430	11.925	11 92		3100	1370	1010	5762	5 76		3100	600	445	2595	2 59	
3200	2090	1470	12 307	12 30	30" 26 23	3200	1410	1050	6150	6 15	18" 15" 14"	3200	620	460	2680	2 68	7'5 7" 6"
3300	2160	1520	12 691	12 69		3300	1450	1080	6342	6 34		3300	635	470	2765	2 76	
3400	2220	1570	13 078	13 07	32" 28 25	3400	1500	1110	6530	6 55	19" 16" 14"	3400	650	480	2830	2 83	8" 7'5 6'5
3500	2290	1620	13 460	13 46		3500	1540	1140	6722	6 72		3500	670	495	2915	2 91	
3600	2360	1660	13 845	13 84	34" 30 26	3600	1590	1180	6920	6 92	20" 17" 15"	3600	690	510	3000	3 00	8'5 8" 7"
3700	2430	1720	14 229	14 22		3700	1630	1210	7112	7 11		3700	710	525	3085	3 08	
3800	2490	1760	14 612	14 61	36" 32 28	3800	1680	1250	7300	7 30	21" 18" 16"	3800	730	540	3170	3 17	9" 8'5 7'5
3900	2550	1800	14 998	14 99		3900	1720	1280	7490	7 49		3900	750	555	3255	3 25	
4000	2610	1840	15 385	15 38	38" 33 29	4000	1760	1310	7680	7 68	22" 19" 18"	4000	770	570	3340	3 34	9'5 9" 8"
4100	2680	1890	15 767	15 76		4100	1800	1340	7870	7 87		4100	780	580	3425	3 42	
4200	2740	1930	16 152	16 15	40" 35 31	4200	1850	1370	8065	8 06	23" 20 19	4200	800	590	3510	3 51	10" 9'5 8'5
4300	2810	1980	16 536	16 53		4300	1890	1400	8255	8 25		4300	820	600	3595	3 59	
4400	2870	2030	16 921	16 92	42" 37 32	4400	1940	1430	8450	8 45	24" 21" 19"	4400	840	620	3680	3 68	10'5 9'5 9"
4500	2940	2070	17 305	17 30		4500	1980	1460	8640	8 64		4500	860	630	3765	3 76	
4600	3010	2120	17 690	17 69	44" 38 34	4600	2030	1500	8832	8 83	25" 22 20	4600	880	650	3850	3 85	11" 10 9'5
4700	3070	2160	18 074	18 07		4700	2070	1530	9025	9 02		4700	900	660	3935	3 93	
4800	3130	2210	18 459	18 45	46" 40 35	4800	2120	1560	9215	9 21	26" 23 21	4800	920	670	4020	4 00	11'5 10'5 10"
4900	3200	2260	18 843	18 84		4900	2160	1590	9410	9 41		4900	940	680	4105	4 10	
5000	3260	2310	19 228	19 22	48" 41 37	5000	2210	1630	9600	9 60	27" 24 22	5000	960	700	4190	4 19	12" 11" 10"
5100	3320	2345	19 613	19 61		5100	2260	1660	9790	9 79		5100	980	710	4275	4 27	
5200	3380	2390	20 000	20 00	50" 43 38	5200	2300	1690	10 000	10 00	28" 25 23	5200	1000	720	4360	4 36	12'5 11'5 10'5
5300	3450	2435	20 385	20 38		5300	2340	1720	10 195	10 19		5300	1020	730	4445	4 44	
5400	3510	2480	20 770	20 77	52" 45 40	5400	2390	1750	10 385	10 38	29" 26 24	5400	1040	740	4530	4 53	13" 12" 11"
5500	3580	2530	21 155	21 15		5500	2440	1790	10 580	10 58		5500	1060	750	4615	4 61	
5600	3640	2570	21 540	21 54	53 46 41	5600	2490	1820	10 770	10 77	30" 27 25	5600	1080	760	4700	4 70	13'5 12'5 11'5
5700	3700	2620	21 923	21 92		5700	2540	1850	10 960	10 96		5700	1100	770	4785	4 78	
5800	3770	2660	22 310	22 31	54 48 43	5800	2580	1880	11 155	11 15	31" 28 26	5800	1120	780	4870	4 87	14" 13" 12"
5900	3830	2710	22 695	22 69		5900	2630	1910	11 345	11 34		5900	1140	790	4955	4 95	
6000	3900	2760	23 080	23 08	56 50 44	6000	2680	1940	11 540	11 54	32 29 27	6000	1160	800	5040	5 04	14'5 13'5 12'5

ble up to the horizon. Broad details such as the general form of the terrain, trench lines, study of routes, and the like were acquired from the photo angle. Using the standard camera (French 50 cm focal length, for example), a panoramic view of the sector provided a relief impression of the ground showing terrain features of valleys, hills, and natural lines of communication as well as locations and present state of woods and villages. The aérostat/captif ballon aerial

FIGURE 75. **Coverage to support restitution was planned according to the data portrayed on this chart.** Source: Gorrell Report, NARA.

AERIAL PHOTOGRAPHY CAMERA LENS

Showing area photographed by different focus Lens on 18cm x 24cm plate at same altitude.

A - Telescopic Lens - 120cm. F.L.
B - Ordinary Lens - 50cm. F.L.
C - Short focus or Wide Angle Lens

AREA COVERED

AREA COVERED

AREA COVERED

Center of photo vertical, but from center to edge of photo gradually tend towards an Oblique owing to very wide angle lens.

A
Giving enlarged detail within a very limited area

B
Good detail and covers considerable area without distorting vertical (or plan) photographs.

C
Covers a very large area with considerable distortion to vertical (or plan) photographs.

CHART Nº 111

PHOTO SECTION - AIR SERVICE - A.E.F.
SEPT. 19, 1918.

platform was the best source of panoramic photographs, providing a precise view of the opposing sector. The area beyond the coverage of the balloon could be marked off and acquired by aeroplane reconnaissance.[16] A panoramic view or photo mosaic of the sector soon decorated the squadron operations room.[17]

Oblique photographs differed from panoramic views in that they were acquired at

FIGURE 76. **The camera focal length available to the French and Americans acquired three areas of coverage such as displayed on the chart.** Source: Gorrell Report, NARA.

a lower attitude and covered less terrain than those cameras possessing a shorter focal length lens. It was the favorite of the line officer infantryman prior to an offensive, for it provided a view angle that approximated the sector to be attacked. The officer could now plan the itinerary for the attack. Oblique photographs were usually acquired by an observer either holding or mounting a camera on the machine gun turret rail and shooting laterally away from the

[16] *Notes on the Interpretation of Aeroplane Photographs*, March 1917 (S.S. 550), 10, and February 1918 (S.S. 631), 11; Gill and Hibben, "Preparation of Photographic Missions," Gorrell Report, ser. J, r. 34, NARA; *Study and Use of Aerial Photographs*, 15 January 1918, sec. I, 33, NARA, RG 120, Box 819; Pépin, "Lecture on the Study and Interpretation of Aerial Photographs," 10 December 1917, 1, NASM.

[17] "Provisional Manual of Operations," in Maurer, ed., *U.S. Air Service*, II, 272.

FIGURE 77. **Panoramic photographs provided a broad view of the battle terrain, such as this trench network in the Vosges Mountains.** Source: *Étude et Exploitation des Photographies Aériennes.*

Vue panoramique en pays de montagne.

Lignes allemandes

Lignes françaises

2. Région des Vosges _ 25.5.17 _ 350 ᵀ _ F:26

FIGURE 78. **The draughtsman's line drawing highlighted appropriate details for cartographic and intelligence review.** Source: *Étude et Exploitation des Photographies Aériennes.*

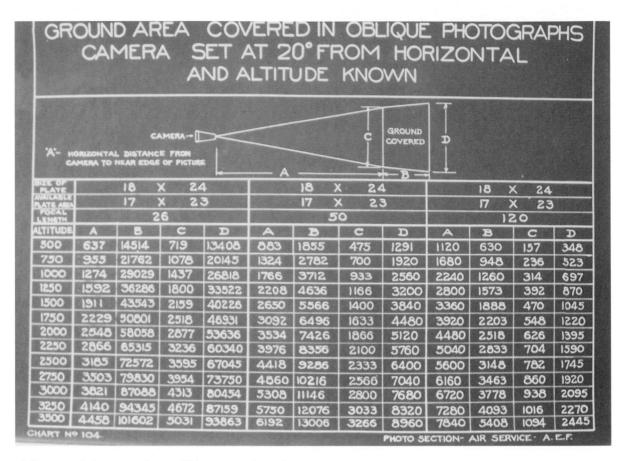

airframe of the aeroplane. This was a favorite technique used by French observers. The coverage provided the unskilled student with a better understanding of slopes, form of the terrain behind the trenches, depth of sunken roads, loop holes, entrances to shelters and dugouts and those works which were not apparent from vertical views. Oblique views were made at angles from 12 to 35 degrees from the horizon, aiding analysis of the details of shelters, gas installations, and trench configuration behind an abrupt slope not observable from the ground.[18] Oblique coverage was also an invaluable aid toward further detailing the features on a map.[19] Oblique photography required sensitivity to the parameters of flight by which the photograph was taken. An oblique photograph required a high shutter speed to eliminate the effect of rapid movement in the foreground.[20] Flying at a few hundred feet, leaning from the cockpit

FIGURE 79. **Mission planning for oblique coverage determined the altitude to be flown and the area required.** Source: Gorrell Report, NARA.

with a camera held so that its line of sight was from 12 to 45 degrees also contributed to the challenge of acquiring the photograph. It was a hazardous assignment, but one that was greatly appreciated when the infantry received the coverage.[21] The following is a good example of oblique reporting: "Photographic missions took 20 oblique exposures from Eply to Les Menils; 17 photographs from Moselle to Bois de l Voivrotte; 18 photographs in vicinity of Remenauville, Regnieville and Bois du Four; 12 exposures N. of Remenauville; 20 oblique exposures of front lines W. of Moselle."[22]

---

[18] Gill and Hibben, "Preparation of Photographic Missions," Gorrell Report, ser. J, r. 34, NARA; Porter, 176-177; Hart, 37; 1st Army Historical Files, NARA, RG 120, Box 22; Ives, 39-40.

[19] Hahn, 22.

[20] Ives, 39-40.

[21] Alan Morris, *Bloody April* (London: Jarrolds Publishers, 1967), 103.

[22] G-2, 1st Army Corps, "Summary of Intelligence," Nolan Papers, USAMHI.

Labels visible on the photograph:
R35d6958, R35d2565, R35d1449, R38d2396, Road to Ficheux, R35a9510, R35e7140, R35a8035, O.P. for periscope, 5b1575, R35a6073, R55a9396, probable M.G. Note extra large traverse, signs of movement & loopholes, R35a6177, R35a6290, R29c5219, R29c7828, DIRECTION OF FIRE

FIGURE 80. **A superb oblique shot of the German trench network with interpretation details.** Source: *Illustrations* S.S. 550a.

The vertical photograph was the most popular aerial photographic format used in the war, providing the most invaluable tool to intelligence for determining exact locations of key targets such as machine guns, minenwerfer, shelters, and frequented tracks. The vertical view was the primary source of photographs used in the restitution process.[23] Acquiring the pinpoint vertical coverage required a sufficient focal length of the aerial camera lens to secure an adequate size image, a shutter speed to counterbalance the speed of the plane, and a sufficiently wide lens aperture to give adequate exposure with the required shutter speed.[24] Photos taken from the perpendicular with respect to the surface of the earth, or directly overhead, were the most desirable for several reasons. As one post-war assessment stated: "All aerial photographs should be taken vertically; otherwise we would have distortion which makes the reading difficult and inexact."[25] Vertical photos were the "document most rich in every nature" and were used extensively to form mosaics, the photographic map at a desired scale.[26] It was important that the entire enemy area opposite each division be mapped to a considerable depth. Missions were assigned in such a manner so that the photographs would overlap and form a continuous mosaic map when pasted together.[27] An accurate mosaic required photos with an equivalent scale. To achieve this required a consistent photograph altitude and vertical alignment. Another concern was differences

[23] Gill and Hibben, "Preparation of Photographic Missions," Gorrell Report, ser. J, r. 34, NARA; Hahn, 36; Hart, 36-37.

[24] Ives, 39-40.
[25] Lieut Michel quoted in Porter, 173.
[26] "Lecture on Aerial Photography," 25 April 1923, NASM A30.2/36.
[27] Hart, 36-37.

VERTICAL OR PLAN PHOTOGRAPHS

MACHINE FLYING LEVEL

MACHINE BANKING

Area Covered

Area Covered

Pin Point

Pin Point

Pin point missed

CORRECT RESULT

Scale of Photograph the same
at all points.

BAD RESULT
Photographs taken Oblique instead of Vertical.
Scale of Photograph different at points
furthest and nearest from lens of camera.

CHART Nº 112

PHOTO SECTION - AIR SERVICE - A.E.F.
SEPT. 16, 1918.

in the time of the photograph, which could create shadow variance. Barring those abnormalities, the mosaic provided the interpreter with a comprehensive view of an enemy trench network as well as an automatic layout for a map.[28] With vertical coverage and mosaics, the military decision-maker now possessed a more precise medium to appreciate both the natural obstacles and hostile defenses.[29] As early as 1915, the mosaic became an important tool for planning. A British liaison to the French Aviation Militaire noted that "photographic maps are continually being made of the whole line, and when any important change is found a re-issue is made."[30]

FIGURE 81. **Photographic planning for vertical coverage showed the ideal coverage area to support the restitution process.** Source: Gorrell Report, NARA.

Stereoscopic photographs or stereographs were the most valuable aid in detecting terrain contours, relief, and an estimate of object height and depth. The view from stereo coverage exaggerated the feeling of the third dimension. The normal tool for interpretation was a magnifying glass. When stereo coverage was acquired, a stereoscope was employed. Stereoscopic viewing was acquired from two overlapping photographs taken at the same altitude, at the same hour covering the same points. Stereo coverage

---

[28] Hahn, 36-37.
[29] 1st Army Historical Files, NARA, RG 120, Box 22.
[30] Gamble, "Photographic Section of the French Flying Corps," TNA, PRO: AIR 1/404/97/1917.

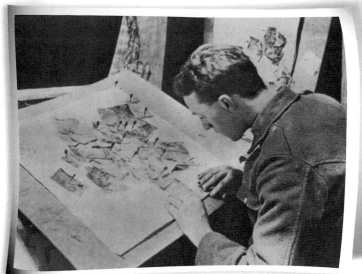

FIGURE 82. A draughtsman would assemble the photographs and align them so that the assembly would form a continuous mosaic map. The British aerial photograph format was 4" x 5," requiring a number of photos to cover a given sector. Source: IWM, courtesy Nicholas Watkis.

employed either vertical or oblique photos. The stereoscopic oblique photograph added value to mission planning by showing undulations of the ground which portrayed features of tactical importance that were not obvious from the map itself. Instructions for stereoscopic coverage required placing one photograph alongside of a companion photograph matching the coinciding features. As the photographs were drawn apart to the point that the eyes could directly focus on the views, a process aided by the simple stereoscope, objects stood up. The photographs required placement in the order in which they were taken. For example, the left-hand photo was positioned on the left-hand side of the viewing lens. Overlooking this simple requirement resulted in the features appearing reversed; obstacles such as houses appeared as cavities and cuttings became embankments.[31] The stereoscope was a well-established fixture of the photographic world long before the conflict, providing public and experts alike with a popular mode of experiencing photographic images.[32] By the mid-1800s, the stereoscope phenomenon became a topic of intense scrutiny, for it demonstrated to its practitioners new ways of seeing the world. A leading 19th century theorist of vision, Helmholtz, wrote at that time, "these stereoscopic photographs are so true to nature and so lifelike in their portrayal of material things, that after viewing such picture and recognizing in it some object like a house, for instance, we get the impression, when we actually do see the object, that we have already seen it before and

FIGURE 83. The stereoscope provided the photographic interpreter with the tool to determine important features from overlapping aerial photographs. Source: Gorrell Report, NARA.

---

[31] *Notes on the Interpretation of Aeroplane Photographs*, March 1917 (S.S. 550), 10, and February 1918 (S.S. 631), 11; Porter, 163; Hahn, 37-38.

[32] Crary, 117-118; Arthur W. Judge, *Stereoscopic Photography* (London: Chapman & Hall, Ltd., 1950), 14-15.

are more or less familiar with it."[33] About 70 years later, the stereoscope helped analysts discern battlefield reality from fabrication.

The demands of war promoted the application of physics and the science of color to further enhance the stereoscopic view. The leading British staff officer on aerial photography, Moore-Brabazon, recalled using slide projection (lantern slide) images tinted with red and green to highlight the stereoscopic effect of the terrain features. The photographic interpreter audience viewed the colored projections with red and green spectacles that produced a stereoscopic effect from the photographic pairs.[34] This interpreter technique continues to the present day.

Annotating Aerial Photographs

It became apparent from the beginning that aerial photography required a standard identification process to portray essential information describing the moment that the photograph was acquired. The British made reference to this as early as December 1914. Their direction specified a standard for each print: "Every negative and every print shall have the following marked upon it, viz., Date, hour, and place of exposure. A line indicating the approximate direction of true North. Height at which flying. Condition and atmosphere and light. Without accurate information on the above points, a photograph, no matter how good in itself, is likely to be useless for military purposes."[35] Since aerial photography was proving to be an invaluable information tool, clarifying information directly applied on the plate and print accentuated the value of the intelligence. Sortie information was compiled and processed as soon as possible, to include: Pilot Name; Observer Name; Date of Photograph; Time of Photograph; Altitude of the Aerial Platform; Mission; Camera Type; Camera Focal Length; x and y Coordinates of the Target; Number of Plates Exposed, Number of Magazines Used; Planned Itinerary; and Significant Observations.[36] Once the photo plates were developed, annotations were transcribed on the photographic plate and became the identification moniker for all subsequent prints. For French aerial photographs the data included: Name of location in the photograph; escadrille; principal target (trench, wood, village); coordinates of the photograph; focal length of the camera; date; hour of the photograph; altitude that the photo was taken; and north arrow.[37] The following is an example of French photographic annotation: "La Cheppe. (Location) F22. (Escadrille Farman 22) 454. Nap-Py. (Principal target); 536/725 (Coordinates of photograph) F=50 – (50 cm Focal Length) 22.8.16—(Date: 22 August 1916) 10H (1,000 hrs) NR 3,000m (Altitude that aerial photograph was taken)."[38]

British photograph annotations were aligned to 1/40,000 artillery maps. The maps were divided into 6,000-yard squares identified by capital letters A to X. The areas were further subdivided into 36 numbered 1,000-yard squares, which were further subdivided into four lettered (lower-case) 500-yard squares (abcd). Points within the 500-yard square were pinpointed by four figure coordinates, eastings (left to right), then northings (from bottom to top). A full-grid reference annotated on the photograph read as a series of alphanumeric symbols. The references were identical for larger-scale 1/10,000 and 1/20,000 maps derived from the 1/40,000 map.[39] An example annotation provides a breakdown of the aerial photograph's identity:

5AE 25 37	(Negative series number, Local serial of the print)
7.8.18 7am F 8 1/4	(Date, time, focal length of camera)
62D V25bd 26ac	(62 D [Map Sheet Number]; V [Identification of the 6000 yard square]; 25bd, 26ac [identification of 500 yard squares covered by aerial photographic print])[40]

[33] Herman von Helmholtz, *Treatise on Physiological Optics* (trans.; n.p., n.d.), quoted in Crary, 122-124.
[34] Moore-Brabazon, *The Brabazon* Story, 104.
[35] "Notes on Photography from Aeroplanes," 20 December 1914, TNA, PRO: AIR 1/836/204/5/268.

[36] Carlier, 76.
[37] Carlier, 76.
[38] Carlier, 76.
[39] Author discussion with Nicholas Watkis.
[40] Annotation example provided by Nicholas Watkis.

Some British annotations did not apply to the artillery map standard and reflected less data. The Squadron number; Wing (initial letters); serial number of the photographic plate; and date of photograph was provided.[41] For example, the 680th photograph taken by No. 30 Squadron, 31st Wing, 18 April 1918 was simply displayed on the photograph as: "30 C.A. 680, 18-4-18."[42]

The U.S. Air Service mostly adopted the French standard for annotating aerial photographs. The top margin of the plate/photograph would be marked with the following information: Corps number; Aero Squadron number; location of photograph; coordinates of the photo center; date; hour; altitude of photograph; and focal length. The location of the photograph included the village or farm in the vicinity. When appropriate a map number was assigned. Guidance suggested making interpretation marks on the photo, to include nature of the terrain (compared with the Plan Directeur), highlighting belts of wire and machine gun locations.[43] The photographic section sometimes included the serial number of the plate to further add detail to the annotation.[44] Here is an example of an American serial number photographic annotation: "U.S. 1AC (1st Army Corps) 1 Sq (1st Aero Squadron) Bg13 Eply (Target location) 3860.236.7 (coordinates of the center of the photograph) 29.8.18 (date of photograph) 16h, (hour that photograph was taken) 500 (altitude in meters photo was taken) 32 (focus)."[45]

[41] "Interpretation of Aeroplane Photographs in Mesopotamia," TNA, PRO: AIR 10/1001.

[42] "Interpretation of Aeroplane Photographs in Mesopotamia," TNA, PRO: AIR 10/1001.

[43] 1st Army Historical Files, NARA, RG 120, Box 22.

[44] Gill and Hibben, "Preparation of Photographic Missions," Gorrell Report, ser. J, r. 34, NARA.

[45] 1st Army Historical Files, NARA, RG 120, Box 22.

FIGURE 84. **Close-up of standard French aerial photograph annotation. The BR 202 escadrille was part of the Weiller Group that flew strategic reconnaissance in the rear echelon.** Source: Library of Congress, Brigadier General William Mitchell Papers.

History of Coverage

One of the foundations of aerial photographic interpretation was the ability to exploit the history of coverage of areas and targets. This technique, now known as negation and research, with negation being the ability to go back over time to see what in an image had changed, and research being the analysis of what happened, had its origins with aerial photography of World War I. The ability to analyze a target through a collection of photographs acquired over time became the mainstay for analysis. The French recognized this early on in the war and established a complete photographic and tactical dossier history of the sectors.[46] Target analysis was reinforced with each aerial photograph acquired and compared. The frequency of coverage was based on sortie availability and the sector. French policy regarding the cycle of coverage was discussed in postwar analysis: "Such work necessitates a constant supervision on the part of the aviation and the methodical taking of photographs of all the zone to be surveyed. In an Army Corps it may be accepted that the first position is to be photographed

[46] "Aerial Photography for Pilots," 21, NASM, A30.2/2.

on an average once a week and the rear area once a month."[47]

A post-war discussion described the added value that history of coverage provided the interpretation discipline:

> In order to obtain good results from a study of a photographic reconnaissance, one must not be content only to study the photographs of this reconnaissance but must complete them with photographs taken previously, which will allow one to see the small changes which are often of great importance. It is necessary to bring to this study a great deal of method and minute exactness. The whole surface of the photograph must be explored in a logical order; one must distrust his imagination and control it as often as possible.[48]

The following is an example of analysis from a history of coverage: "Region of Vilcey. No. 943 – 14/8/18 – 695-460. A comparison of this photo with one taken June 30, shows no marked increase of activity between the two dates. The collection of buildings at point 369.5-246 shows indications of being an important distributing point and might be perhaps a Pioneer headquarters."[49]

Filing and Distribution

The culminating experience showed that all information acquired through aerial photographs required careful archiving to make it accessible and quickly retrievable.[50] However, cataloging and filing were not without problems. Filing was accomplished at all echelons without a standard established. The French advocated that information be kept in a sector dossier. The dossier contained all vertical or oblique photographs concerning the sector covering both French and German areas.[51] British squadrons pasted photographs organized by serial number into a photo album-type book. They also maintained another file based on coverage of a given five-kilometer square. Despite the attempt to create order as the quantity of photographs increased, both systems were not without their critics. A review of French and British practices led the AEF Assistant Chief of Staff for Intelligence to comment in a memorandum that "One of the most serious problems of the office has been the photo filing system."[52]

The British established a separate filing and distribution process within each army. Branch Intelligence Section personnel assigned to the British Second Army prepared a daily chart showing the location of area coverage. Filing of photographs occurred after the decision was made as to what aerial photographs were to be retained. A daily summary along with a chart displaying the photos taken were forwarded to distribution centers. All negatives were compared with a baseline map recording the coverage (a record map). Plates that were deemed duplicative were then thrown out. The plates that were retained were given serial numbers according to the covered sector. As soon as the photograph was accepted, the area covered was blocked off on the daily chart and the photo number entered in the space. Photos were filed according to area and indexed under the category of area and serial number. Distribution was based on the requirements of the unit serving in the sector.[53] The British Fifth Army

[47] "Aeronautics," June 1921, 24-25, NARA, RG 120, Box 819.

[48] "Lecture on Aerial Photography," 25 April 1923, NASM, A30.2/36.

[49] G-2, 1st Army Corps, "Summary of Intelligence," Nolan Papers, USAMHI.

[50] *Notes on the Interpretation of Aeroplane Photographs*, March 1917 (S.S. 550), 5, and February 1918 (S.S. 631), 3; Hahn, 21.

[51] *Study and Use of Aerial Photographs*, 15 January 1918, sec. II, 22, NARA, RG 120, Box 819; "Depots de Munitions Ennemis, Woevre et Hauts de Meuse," Mitchell Papers, LC.

[52] "Historical Account," 57, Drum Papers, USAMHI.

[53] 1st Lt J. L. Stewart, "Report on the Organization and Operation of Intelligence 'A' at the British II Army (with Special Attention to the Photographic Section, Enemy Defenses and Rear Organizations)," 18-29 September 1918, Conger Papers, Box 2, USAMHI.

Box 60 Series 1st Wing

Neg. No.	Size	Date	Map Sheet		Plotting
√1488	5×4	23.9.15	36 c	9	6.c 13a
√1489	"	23.9.15	36 c	9	6.c 12a
√1490	"	23.9.15	36 c	9	5
√1492	"	24.9.15	36 c	9	15.16.21.22
✳1493	"	24.9.15	76 c	9	24.28.33.34

REMARKS. ✳ Not in box.

Box 60 Series 1st Wing

Neg. No.	Size	Date	Map Sheet		Plotting
✳1494	5×4	24.9.15	36 c	9	17.18.23.24
√1495	"	24.9.15	36 c	9	33.34 M 34
√1496	"	24.9.15	36 c	9	16.17.22.23

REMARKS. ✳ Not in box.

Box 61. Series 1st Wing

Neg. No.	Size	Date	Map Sheet	Plotting
√1511.	5×4	26.9.15	36 c	G.ba
√1512.	"	26.9.15	36 c	G.bd
√1515.	"	28.9.15	36 c	G.ba
√1516.	"	28.9.15	36 c	G.ba
√1517.	"	28.9.15	36 c	G.ba

REMARKS.

Box 65. Series 1st Wing

Neg. No.	Size	Date	Map Sheet	Plotting
√1513.	5×4	26.9.15	36 c	G.12a at
√1514.	"	28.9.15	36 c	G.bc

REMARKS.

Box 61 Series 1st Wing

Neg. No.	Size	Date	Map Sheet
√1556	5×4	30.9.15	36 c G.14
√1560		1.10.15	36 c G.12a
√1586		2.10.15	36 c G.29d 30c etc
√1587		2.10.15	36 c G.29d.30 etc
√1605		3.10.15	36 c G.30 etc

Box 61. Series 1st Wing

Neg. No.	Size	Date	Map Sheet
√1518	5×4	28.9.15	36 c G.b
√1521		28.9.15	36 c G.
√1522		28.9.15	36 c G.
√1525		28.9.15	36 c G.
√1540		30.9.15	36 c G.

REMARKS.

policy was to have all photographs on a specific target logged in and target records kept in alphabetical order. Photographs were filed in numerical order by squadron. Maps were annotated with the area covered by the photograph and the photo was filed according to the map section. A cross-index book was kept to provide ready reference to photos of particular objects (such as dumps, etc.) that were not displayed on the maps.[54]

Over time, the British adjusted their distribution to meet both the requirements of the combatants and the realities of the front line. The initial large quantity of photographs for the front line units was reduced in favor of intelligence being transmitted via message or communicated verbally. Whenever a sufficient number of changes warranted attention, the unit received a photographic mosaic and an accompanying document with explanations. The end result for British units was that they received more manageable amounts of aerial photographs with supporting information.[55] The standard British aerial photograph processing included the "rush copy," filing copy, and a copy for the dossier. The dossier copy was circulated and all relevant information was culled from the photograph.[56] The remainder of the prints, disseminated according to the prescribed squadron distribution, quickly followed the rough print. When tasking ordered a large number of prints beyond normal distribution, the squadron prepared and forwarded a transparency to army or corps photo centers.[57] Photograph distribution was arranged by squadron, each forwarding their material in separate envelopes.[58]

U.S. Air Service Corps aero squadrons were instructed to send an advance copy of aerial photographs for prompt study. However, the procedure was discontinued as "every squadron either discontinued the practice or carried it out so tar-

dily as to make it worthless." Photographic production and interpretation attempted to support all known functions that benefited from the analysis. The distribution differed with the assigned mission. "Each Corps Squadron sent us thirteen finished copies of every photo. Two were for our files, one for artillery information service, four for artillery observation group, c/c First Army Air Service, and six for Photographic Aérienne, French Second Army."[59] Even at the lower echelon squadron level, the distribution list was fairly extensive, including: 1st Army, A.E.F.; Headquarters, 1st Brigade Air Service; 96th Bombing Squadron; G.H.Q., A.E.F.; G-2, G.H.Q., A.E.F.; Observers and Pilots; and the Branch Intelligence Officer file.[60]

U.S. Air Service aero squadrons emphasized order and ready access. The AEF Assistant Chief of Staff for Intelligence praised the American x and y coordinates (measured to one tenth of a kilometer) filing system employed at the aero squadrons. A master photo file was established to retain the original copy and extra copies as required. Photos of enemy aerodromes and a key map were established to monitor the sector. A review of the process by the AEF G-2 was a reminder of what worked best behind a successful filing system: "Perhaps the best solution is a thoroughly competent and interested clerk in charge of this very important file."[61]

Post-war direction from Brigadier General Mitchell to U.S. Air Service aero squadrons reminded all that photographs required x and y coordinate filing in conjunction with the Plan Directeur process. In practice, a card catalog was established listing more information on the size of the camera, coordinates, index number, altitude, date, and a qualitative description of the photograph. A map was used to illustrate areas covered by photographic missions. Plate coverage was outlined, the index number and date attached, and the area covered by the mission colored. The maps illustrated the sorties accomplished during the week. Once a month a second map was pre-

[54] "Organization of Intelligence," HQ, British 5th Army, Conger Papers, Box 2, USAMHI.

[55] S. T. Hubbard, Jr., "Memorandum for Col Nolan, Subject: 'Report on Trip to British Front'," 3 January 1918, 6, Conger Papers, Box 2, USAMHI.

[56] Stewart, "Report on the Organization and Operation of Intelligence 'A'," Conger Papers, Box 2, USAMHI.

[57] "Aerial Photography. Statement Made by Squadron Leader F. C. V. Laws O.B.E. to Mr. A. J. Insall on 3rd June, 1924," TNA, PRO: AIR 1/724/91/2.

[58] Stewart, "Report on the Organization and Operation of Intelligence 'A'," Conger Papers, Box 2, USAMHI.

[59] "Historical Account," 63, Drum Papers, USAMHI.

[60] "Notes on Branch Intelligence," 91st Aero Squadron, 1 November 1918, Gorrell Report, ser. M, r. 40, NARA.

[61] "Historical Account of Organization and Functioning of Subdivision," 62, Drum Papers, Box 14, USAMHI.

pared displaying the entire area covered by aerial photographs.[62] The classification and filing of all aerial negatives became a post-war priority to archive the battleground. The objective was to have a complete set of photographic negatives to portray a different view of the war. Ground photographs of all the important points pictured in aerial photography were taken to clarify the aerial targets. Additional photos were acquired from French and British files.[63]

Evolution of the Science and Art of Photographic Interpretation

The earliest writings on aerial photographic reconnaissance clearly acknowledged that aeroplane photographs formed a most useful source of information for planning a military operation. Once the interpreter accomplished the review of the photograph, he had at his disposal a visual framework for understanding the enemy's defensive organization, its topographical location, and a comprehensive reference to the evolving military formation. By the end of the conflict, those well experienced in the interpretation discipline considered the aerial photograph to be an "inexhaustible mine of information" contributing to an understanding not based on theory but purely empirical data.[64] Three phases for interpreter analysis were developed. The preparatory period involved studying the target area and applying the research to the plan of attack. The destructions period determined the state of progress of the Allies' impact on enemy works. Finally, the execution period comprised analysis of the attack to determine the extent of Allied occupation.[65]

Intelligence acquired a definitive perspective on the threat thanks to aerial photography. The earliest aerial photographic interpretation manuals written in 1915 reflected this attitude. The overhead image of the battleground was "now visible, except machine guns and guns placed in trenches and covered over."[66] The interpreter's analysis went beyond the visual cues and developed a perception of reality through the exercise of deductive logic. Data that were not relevant in determining the threat were to be eliminated from the mental process. Upon completion of this phase of deliberation, the interpreter had to pass the intelligence to the staff in a timely manner so that operation orders for both artillery and infantry could be generated.[67]

Establishing an aerial photographic reconnaissance-aware military culture remained a challenge throughout the war. The experiences of the British and French showed that it took several years of aggressive promotion on the part of a few advocates to gain support from command, staff, and eventually the military forces being supported. By 1916, aerial photography was recognized as essential to the conduct of the campaign. However, when American forces started arriving in Europe in late 1917, the same challenges resurfaced. Major Steichen ruminated on the issue that confronted interpretation:

> Photographic reconnaissance is a most difficult and ungrateful part of aerial observation. It gets more recognition and credit from the enemy than any one else. Captured enemy documents indicate that their General Staff was very much worried about Allied aerial observation, and particularly the planes with the all-recording camera soaring miles up in the air overhead.[68]

The key behind the conversion of skeptics to aerial photography and interpretation was education. The French led the way in determining the purpose of aerial photography from an academic standpoint. French photographic

---

[62] "Provisional Manual of Operations," in Maurer, ed., *U.S. Air Service*, II, 272.

[63] The location of this postwar archive is unknown. Some files of divisional photographs exist, albeit incomplete. It has been suggested that the WW I glass negatives were recycled in the 1950s for silver recovery; see "Final Report of Chief of Air Service," in Maurer, ed., *U.S. Air Service*, I, 154-155.

[64] "Conference du SLT [Sous-Lieutenant] Pouquet sur le Fonctionnement du Service d'Interpretation des Photographies dans un Secteur Offensif faite au G.D.E., le 27 December 1916," SHAA; transl. as "Working of the Service of Interpretation of Photographs in an Offensive Sector (Conference by Sub/Lieutenant Pouquet)," 1, NARA, RG 120, Box 819; Coleman, "Interpretation of Aerial Photographs," 1921, NARA, RG 120, Box 819.

[65] Pouquet, "Working of the Service of Interpretation of Photographs," 1, NARA, RG 120, Box 819.

[66] *Illustrations to Accompany Captain De Bissy's Notes*, 1.

[67] *Illustrations to Accompany Captain De Bissy's Notes*, 1.

[68] Steichen, "American Aerial Photography at the Front," 2, NASM, A30.2/24.

experts related it to prevailing military thinking. Leading the effort was Capitaine Jean de Bissy. His initial pamphlet, *Note concernant l'interprétation méthodique de Photographies Aériennes*, 19 November 1915, helped establish the precedent for what was to become the foundation of aerial photographic interpretation training.[69] A team of French photographic interpreters (Couderc, Pépin, Rousselet, and Jaulin et Paulon) subsequently produced the first known photographic manual. Published 7 January 1916, the *Bulletin du Service de la Photographie Aérienne aux Armées* provided a brief introduction to the experiences on the Western Front as conveyed through aerial photography. The U.S. version was published in 1918, and entitled the *Bulletin of the Aerial Photography Department in the Field 1918*. It was an intelligence document, compiled from various captured German documents that directed standards for military structures, and from line drawings of German trench networks found on the body of a dead German soldier. The manual provided a glimpse of the German policy that governed their operations at the front. The seminal work would serve as the intelligence foundation for subsequent published manuals.[70] In 1916 Capitaine de Bissy produced the first comprehensive manual that correlated text with photographic templates of relevant targets.

The baseline French aerial photographic interpreter manual for the last two years of the war was *Étude et Exploitation des Photographies Aériennes*. This work became a critical source for explaining to the intelligence community the role and science of the aerial photograph.[71] Authorship was not specifically credited in the text, but the preponderance of evidence from a selection of writings shows the primary author to be *Lieutenant* Eugène Pépin. This brilliant academic provided a textual foundation for the philosophy behind aerial photographic analysis, combined with descriptions of the entire battlefield. Pépin was recognized later for galvanizing the American photographic interpreter effort during the final months of the war.

Brigadier-General Charteris spearheaded British aerial photographic interpretation training support based on exchanges with the French during their ongoing effort to create doctrinal manuals. Charteris took their insights and commenced producing a similar training manual for British forces. The British lead for aerial photographic interpretation, Moore-Brabazon, recalled that the Intelligence staffs were not getting enough information out of "our photographs." Moore-Brabazon proceeded to acquire the services of the British portrait painter, Sir Oswald Birley, to lead the assembly of the manual of instruction.[72] The Army Printing (AP) and Stationary Services (SS) served as the production facility for the manuals. AP and SS were well known by BEF staff on account of the rapidity with which they turned out printing, including illustrations. The AP and SS also reproduced aerial photographs in large quantities.[73] The effort culminated in the publication of the first British manual for Photographic Interpretation, S.S. 445, *Notes on the Interpretation of Aeroplane Photographs,* and the companion S.S. 445a, *Illustrations to Accompany Notes on the Interpretation of Aeroplane Photographs* in November 1916.[74] Moore-Brabazon gave his intelligence counterparts credit for the final publication. "They produced during the war one of the finest works on the interpretation of aerial photographs I have ever seen. It was a great show."[75]

The second British photographic manual, S.S. 550, *Notes on the Interpretation of Aeroplane Photographs* and companion, S.S. 550a, *Illustrations to Accompany Notes on the Interpretation of Aeroplane Photographs* were published in March 1917. The distribution was extensive, down to the British battalion, machine gun company, and trench-mortar battery. The War Office

---

[69] Capt Jean de Bissy, "Note Concernant l'Interpretation Méthodique de Photographies Aériennes," 19 November 1915, SHAA.

[70] *Bulletin du Service de la Photographie Aérienne aux Armées*, 7 January 1916 (Paris: Imprimerie Nationale, 1916), 7; *Bulletin of the Aerial Photography Department in the Field* (Washington, DC: GPO, 1918).

[71] *Étude et Exploitation des Photographies Aériennes*, 1918.

[72] Occleshaw, 66.

[73] Edmonds, *1916*, I, 132.

[74] *Notes on the Interpretation of Aeroplane Photographs*, March 1917 (S.S. 550), 4; Watkis, 11-12.

[75] Moore-Brabazon, *The Brabazon* Story, 95-96.

Chapter 6: The Operation of Interpretation

in London alone received 3,100 copies.[76] *Notes on the Interpretation of Aeroplane Photographs* was also exchanged with the Allies. American recipients included the American Day Bombardment School at Clermont-Ferrand.[77] The British published the third and final version, S.S. 631, in February 1918.[78] Later that summer the Americans published additional copies of the S.S. 631 text through the Government Printing Office. It was a sensitive document showing the quality of the coverage, the ability to pick out key German targets in the trenches, and details provided by draftsmen. The reader was warned: "This document is the property of the United States Government, and the information in it is not to be communicated, directly or indirectly, to the press or any person not holding an official position in the Government service."[79]

The arrival of the Americans pointed out the urgent need to educate them about the role and purpose of aerial photography, to introduce staff officers and senior leaders to its potential in battle planning, and, most importantly, to integrate them quickly into Allied operations. At the end of 1917, two intelligence conferences attended by Allied aerial photographic experts and staffs recognized that need, especially for current aerial photographic interpretation manuals. The French provided the AEF with its *Étude et Exploitation des Photographies Aériennes*. With this document in hand, the pioneer American photographic interpreter team of Major James Barnes and 1st Lieutenant Edward Steichen became the primary catalyst in standing up the first American aerial photographic interpretation teams using this manual and whatever other manuals and handbooks they could acquire. Their efforts resulted in two American translations of the French document. A translation by members of the AEF staff, titled *Study and Utilization of Aerial Photographs*, appeared

as a field manual in July 1918.[80] A companion version was produced by the Army's Division of Military Aeronautics and published through the Government Printing Office entitled *Study and Exploitation of Aerial Photographs*.[81] A final literal translation, titled *Study and Use of Aerial Photographs*, was produced after the war by the American Mission with the Commanding General Allied Forces of Occupation, Mainz.[82]

The initial American lack of analytical expertise on positional warfare was clearly discernable. In retrospect, shortly after the Armistice, the Assistant Chief of Staff G-2, 1st Army, AEF, recommended that "The officers charged with the duty of interpretation of photos found themselves handicapped by their ignorance of actual conditions. Of many of the objects which they learned to recognize on photos they had never seen an example on the ground. It is thought that if a photo intelligence officer is without actual experience in the combat areas, he should be sent forward on a tour of observation. A few trips in an airplane would also assist in giving him the point of view of the air."[83] Steichen echoed the sentiment. Access to the training manuals was not enough. The lessons learned in the conflict showed that the art of interpretation required an intense knowledge of the battlefield:

The mistakes that are [made] by a student in interpretation whose knowledge has been gained entirely from the study of books and pictures are flagrant; a few hours spent on the battlefield studying the ground and organizations in connection with aerial photographs previously, arc of more value than any amount of classroom work. The interpretation of photographs is in no sense

---

[76] "Scale of Issue of Periodical Publications," Conger Papers, Box 2, USAMHI.

[77] "Report on Day Bombardment Training," Gorrell Report, ser. J, r. 35, NARA.

[78] *Notes on the Interpretation of Aeroplane Photographs*, February 1918 (S.S. 631), 1.

[79] *Notes on the Interpretation of Aeroplane Photographs* (Washington, DC: GPO, 1918), reprint of February 1918 (S. S. 631).

[80] *Study and Utilization of Aerial Photographs* (transl., [France]: Headquarters American Expeditionary Forces, France July, 1918), NARA, RG 120, Box 6202.

[81] GHQ, [French] Armies of the North and North East, *Study and Exploitation of Aerial Photographs*, Translated and Issued by the Division of Military Aeronautics, U.S. Army (Washington, DC: GPO, July 1918).

[82] GHQ, [French] Armies of the North and North East, *Study and Use of Aerial Photography* ([Washington, DC: GPO?], November 1921), copy in Part XLIII, sec. 5, in American Mission with the Commanding General, Allied Forces of Occupation, Mainz, Germany, "A Study of the Organization of the French Army ...," NARA, RG 120, Box 819.

[83] G-2, 1st Army, "Account of the Operation," 67, Drum Papers, Box 14, USAMHI.

an exact science, but is largely a matter of astute deductions, and men picked for this work must have qualifications that will make it possible for them to develop along such lines.[84]

The process of photo interpretation for operational purposes was clearly established in the Great War. At war's end, aerial photography was institutionalized throughout with an infrastructure that assured timely acquisition of required information and dissemination to the combatants. Mission planning, annotating photographs, distribution, and production of manuals became integral to the manner in which the photograph was employed. The interpretation operation achieved a permanence that would support military operations for the remainder of the century. The cartographic process became the next operation that evolved with aerial photography's ascendance.

---

[84] Steichen, "Aerial Photography," Gorrell Report, ser. G, r. 24, NARA.

CHAPTER 7

THE FRAMEWORK OF THE AERIAL PHOTOGRAPH

Cartography at the Beginning of the Conflict

When the fast-paced mobile campaign of the first Battle of the Marne shifted to the trenches on the Aisne, it set the stage for aerial photography to become the standard for planning and conducting the battle. Integral to the entire planning process of the war was the map, supporting a range of purposes from firing charts to geologic surveys.[1] Prior to the Marne battle, the only way a combatant could acquire a remote understanding of the terrain was through ground observations displaced on a map. Details of the earth's surface selected to define a map varied with whoever conducted the survey. When the BEF arrived on the continent in August 1914, the maps of the impending battlefield were based on Napoleonic-era French maps and Belgian surveys. Both were found to be inadequate and unreliable for supporting accurate artillery fire.[2] Aerial photography created an information breakthrough when its results were applied to the map format. It was the ideal medium to illuminate intelligence based on visual observation. As one cartographic lesson suggested, "The map is a guide for traveling over the terrain."[3]

The map provided all combatants the means to prepare for battle by studying the terrain from a perspective that could not be achieved from traditional viewing angles. Thanks to the aerial photograph, "the other side of the hill" no longer remained a permanent mystery.

Effective targeting for artillery spurred on the need for cartographic accuracy. Before 1914, British coast defenses using Ordnance Surveys established a high standard for target surveys using instruments that accurately fixed on a target and measured the location. German pre-war targeting included rudimentary flash-spotting triangulation and measurements. The French established the *canevas de tir* or artillery board to enhance their targeting. The canevas de tir was a rigid, gridded board with the location of artillery, SROTs, and enemy targets plotted with range and bearings applied. It was the aerial photograph, however, that would soon revolutionize the entire process.[4]

Cartographic accuracy was further complicated by the fact that none of the Allies shared a cartographic standard before the war started. Moreover, a consistent map scale did not exist. In 1914, the British standard for maps of the impending battleground consisted of an array of smaller scales to include 1/250,000, Belgian 1/100,000, and French 1/80,000.[5] The 1/80,000

---

[1] Pouquet, "Working of the Service of Interpretation of Photographs," 3, NARA, RG 120, Box 819.

[2] Gill and Hibben, "Preparation of Photographic Missions," Gorrell Report, ser. J, r. 34, NARA.

[3] "Balloon Training," slide 59, Gorrell Report, ser. F, r. 23, NARA.

[4] Chasseaud, *Topography of Armageddon*, 8.

[5] Author discussion with Dr. Peter Chasseaud; Squier, "Map Room and Printing Room," Squier Papers, USAMHI.

Carte d'État Major was the universal topographical map representing the whole of France and based on the Cadastral Plans (large-scale land registration plans). The entire map consisted of 274 sheets, each sheet having a name and number, the name being that of the most important town on the sheet. The names of the four adjacent maps were printed in the center of each side of the border. The 1/80,000 scale was hardly adaptable to calculations.[6] At the end of 1914, the French enlarged their 1/80,000 map to 1/20,000 scale. However, it proved a useless endeavor for the details were inaccurate and out of position.[7] The French 1/20,000 map was produced by the *Service Géographique* by expanding the 1/80,000 series. Prior to the war, a comprehensive Belgian national survey provided a

> **FIGURE 86.** The 1/80,000 Carte d'État Major universal topographical map of France. The map was labeled by the most important city contained on the sheet. Gorrell Report, NARA.

cartographic foundation for operations at Ypres and the surrounding area. The maps were fairly detailed for the time. As befitted the Low Countries' flatter terrain, vertical contours on the map were measured in single meters, rather than the normal 5-meter interval. The Belgian 1/10,000 scale drawings had been evacuated from Antwerp in 1914 and were subsequently reproduced for Allied use.[8] Man-made changes totally transformed cartography in the Great War. The destruction virtually eliminated topographical landmarks in the battle area. In some sectors

---

[6] 1st Lt Thomas E. Hibben, "Topography, Lecture delivered at the Second Aviation Instruction Center," Gorrell Report, ser. J, r. 34, NARA; "Balloon Training," Gorrell Report, ser. F, r. 23, NARA.

[7] Chasseaud, *Topography of Armageddon*, 8-9.

[8] Chasseaud, "1:10,000 Regular Series Trench Maps," in *British Western Front Mapping*.

forests were decimated, leaving no visible trace. Cartography was challenged by the obliteration of man-made features such as buildings and roads. Traditional surveying became seriously challenged by the elimination of common trigonometrical points such as church steeples. With each barrage, maps of the region became obsolete, a factor that added to the inevitable "fog of war." Aerial coverage became the sought-after solution to maintain a common cartographic standard with each daily round of devastation.[9]

The Discipline of Restitution

Restitution, the method of transferring information from the photograph to a map, became an integral part of the cartographic process in support of daily operations and offensive planning. It was a demanding process, requiring pinpoint accuracy to meet artillery targeting requirements.[10] Maps updated by this process were critical to intelligence analysis. In a post-war analysis, Brigadier General Dennis E. Nolan, AEF G-2, wrote that "There is no part of a system of military intelligence more important than is the furnishing of maps and topographic information to the army and the nation."[11] It served all combatants throughout the conflict. The prolonged stasis of positional war encouraged the demand for battleground detail on the enemy. The science of restitution served both map construction and aerial photographic interpretation. The aerial photograph became the primary template for configuring the map. In turn, the map, augmented through the restitution process, guided the aerial photographic interpreter throughout his exploration of the photograph. Traditional sources for map development such as surveys and cadastral plans were further complemented by the data derived from aerial photography.[12] If restitution was to be effective, it required expertise in determining the appearance of objects as viewed from above.

Prior to the examination of a photograph, the best available map required intense study to gain knowledge of both the ground configuration and prominent features in the area. Given an accurate baseline of existing survey control, the scale of distances was determined by taking a known distance between two points on the map and applying it to the same two points on the photo. The intimate relationship between aerial photograph and the corresponding map became an important feature of the evolving reconnaissance process, for each legitimized the other.[13]

An in-depth knowledge of the battlefield's terrain was essential for all combatants, requiring restitution to clarify the topography and to accomplish effective planning. An understanding of relief, height, slopes and identifying both natural and artificial objects on the surface became key to conducting the positional war campaign. The battleground required a responsive map development process to portray what the aerial photograph revealed.[14] Positions of strength, flanks, protection from enfilade fire, points of command, and the like became a dynamic part of the cartographic ensemble. Every opportunity had to be exploited in studying ground objects similar to those identified on a photograph. Restitution also included the interpretation of man-made arrangements such as terrain within villages, sunken roads, slopes, earth prints, earthworks, breastworks, intersections of routes and railways. Restitution's exigent nature converted captured hostile trenches and positions into classrooms for the aerial photographic interpreter's on-scene and in-depth analysis.[15] Restitution's dominance remained a chief influence on French decisions on how to portray intelligence information, as the ability to "put [information] in the form of a map or a sketch … is preferable to any others."[16]

---

[9] Porter, 167; Middleton, III, 123; Meade, 62.

[10] *Study and Use of Aerial Photographs*, 15 January 1918, sec. I, 18-19, NARA, RG 120, Box 819; "Aeronautics," 22, June 1921, NARA, RG 120, Box 819; "Lecture on Aerial Photography," 25 April 1923, NASM A30.2/36.

[11] Draft notes show that "and the nation" was subsequently deleted from the text. Nolan, "G-2-C Topography," Nolan Papers, USAMHI.

[12] Author discussion with Dr. Peter Chasseaud; "Aerial Photography for Pilots," 19-20, NASM, A30.2/2.

[13] Porter, 179.

[14] *Study and Use of Aerial Photographs*, 15 January 1918, sec. I, 19, NARA, RG 120, Box 819; "Balloon Training," Gorrell Report, ser. F, r. 23, NARA.

[15] *Study and Use of Aerial Photographs*, 15 January 1918, sec. I, 19, NARA, RG 120, Box 819; Pouquet, "Working of the Service of Interpretation of Photographs," NARA, RG 120. Box 819; *Notes on the Interpretation of Aeroplane Photographs*, March 1917 (S.S. 550), 9.

[16] Maxel, "Instructions on the Intelligence Service," Conger Papers, Box 2, USAMHI.

Map Scale and the Portrayal of the Battleground

The level of detail described on a map was in direct correlation to the purpose and the scale. Years of experience on the same battleground institutionalized battlefield map development. Both French and British maps were produced at a range of scales to accommodate the respective operational mission. Smaller-scale maps provided a broad overview of terrain. Larger-scale maps provided the reader with intimate details. Thanks to aerial photography, a more accurate standard was attained. French maps of the battleground gained notoriety for being so accurate that advancing infantry consulted them to determine the exact tactic to be employed against key German defense points such as machine gun nests. Artillery planning used maps to know in advance where they were to target the barrages.

Reserve forces also employed maps to organize their operations in support of the offensive.[17]

Core Allied maps comprised the French Plan Directeur and the British Firing Map (also known as the Trench Map). Both served the same purpose, providing the commander of the battlefield with a situation update. The maps ranged in scale from 1/5,000 to 1/50,000, together creating a general map of operations throughout the

---

[17] Porter, 121-123.

FIGURE 88. The extrait du Plan Directeur illustrated the intelligence source, verified by aerial photography. Source: SHAT.

battlefields of France, Belgium, and even into Germany.[18] The Plan Directeur became the focal point for French battle planning. Général Pétain reinforced the role of the Plan Directeur in developing his priorities for daily operations. He stipulated that the level of detail be commensurate with the map scale.[19] This meant that no one map scale sufficed for the conduct of the campaign. Large-scale 1/5,000 maps were designed as infantry maps for use in attacks within a given sector, showing the German trench organization in fine detail.[20] The 1/5,000 version was derived from aerial photographs, aerial and ground observation, and prisoner interrogations.[21] The large scale provided a schematic study of the enemy disposition from the defensive point of view, whereby the probable distribution of the troops in the various trenches and shelters was emphasized, to include the halting points, the emplacements of the reserves and the probable directions of counterattacks. With each annotation, an explanatory notice was attached to each study or printed directly on the bottom of the card. The

---

[18] Hahn, 96.

[19] Général Henri Pétain, French General Staff and 3e Bureau, No. 1077/3, "Notice about Maps and Special Plans to be Drawn by the Armies," Conger Papers, Box 2, USAMHI.

[20] Hibben, "Topography," Gorrell Report, ser. J, r. 34, NARA.

[21] Hibben, "Topography," Gorrell Report, ser. J, r. 34, NARA.

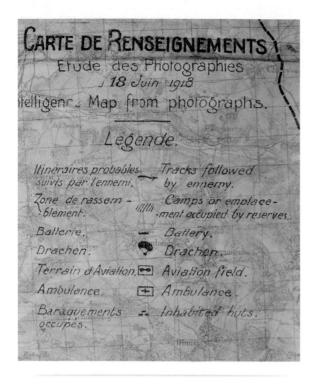

photographic information was applied by hand-drawing the perceived information, and then kept up to date. Distribution was limited, so that only a select few such as the battlefield commander received timely copies.[22]

The first British maps were devoid of any depiction of the British lines, due to security concerns associated with maps at the front lines falling into the hands of the Germans. Confusion set in as troops in the trenches tried to figure out their own sector. The British then resorted to field-generated maps that not only portrayed the trench, but also included additional sensitive information. The situation got out of hand when the troops depended on captured German maps to show their own lines. In September 1915, while preparing for the offensive at Loos, the BEF established a limited edition map of its own trenches. Distribution was limited only to

the Brigade Headquarters and above. The impact of aerial photographic reconnaissance and restitution proved that maps had to include both sides if they were to be of value. By the end of 1916, the British published such maps for general distribution.[23] Special planning revolved around the 1/10,000 French Plan Directeur and British Firing Map. Pétain himself labeled the 1/10,000 as the "complete document which enables the [assault unit commanders] to issue detailed orders with all desirable precision.[24] Both maps had similar purposes, meeting the needs of the infantry at the front. It was a working map, providing the forces with a large-scale plan of villages and important strong points. Some maps annotated the front line trenches and communication trenches by their relative importance. The 1/10,000 Plan Directeur map included additional detail, covering a range of significant data on the enemy forces

FIGURE 90. **Map highlighted in blue shows the German targets and networks.** Source: Massachusetts National Guard Museum.

[22] Pouquet, "Working of the Service of Interpretation of Photographs," 1, NARA, RG 120. Box 819; "Balloon Training," Gorrell Report, ser. F, r. 23, NARA.

[23] Chasseaud, *British Western Front Mapping.*

[24] Pétain, "Notice about Maps and Special Plans," Conger Papers, Box 2, USAMHI.

FIGURE 91. W.B. Prince, then an NCO with American Army Intelligence, saved this guide he prepared in 1918. Source: W.B. Prince Collection, Map Library, Library of Congress.

to include vital organizations or points, shelters, flanking organizations, command posts, ammunition depots, optic and telephone stations.[25] The 1/10,000 map was also used by artillery and staff to show details for accomplishing accurate fire against wire, obstacles, dugouts, trails, and other important components of the trench network organization. They were marked with the date of information. Without the date, these maps were

of little or no value.[26] By 1916, the 1/10,000 series would serve as the most accurate targeting map for the artillery. Sound-rangers and flash-spotters used it to plot their triangulated data to determine locations of German artillery.[27] The Allies also used the 1/10,000 to show their offensive organization.[28]

The Lambert method of projection, with Lambert Kilometric coordinates, was used for firing maps. The Lambert method was one of three survey processes, which included the Polyhedric Projection and Bonne's (*Projection du Depot de la Guerre*) method.[29] When Foch became Supreme Allied Commander, he directed

[25] Pétain, "Notice about Maps and Special Plans," Conger Papers, Box 2, USAMHI; "Notes on the French System of Intelligence," 6, TNA, PRO: WO 158/983; Marie-Anne de Villèle, Agnès Beylot, and Alain Morgat, eds., *Du Paysage à La Carte: Trois Siècles de Cartographie Militaire de la France* (Vincennes, FR: Ministère de la Défense, SHAA, 2002), 129-130 (translation by Commandant Marc Rivière).

[26] Hibben, "Topography," Gorrell Report, ser. J, r. 34, NARA; "Balloon Training," Gorrell Report, ser. F, r. 23, NARA.

[27] Chasseaud, "1:10,000 Regular Series Trench Maps," in *British Western Front Mapping*.

[28] Hibben, "Topography," Gorrell Report, ser. J, r. 34, NARA.

[29] "Balloon Training," Gorrell Report, ser. F, r. 23, NARA; Chasseaud, "1:10,000 Regular Series Trench Maps," in *British Western Front Mapping*.

FIGURE 92. **1/10,000 scale map of the key city of Ypres.** Source: Map Library, Library of Congress.

that mapping become uniform among the Allies. 1/20,000 maps were produced based on the Lambert projection, to include a grid overlay that became the standard map reference. The changes were late in coming; actual implementation took place after the Armistice.[30] The vital role of targeting artillery was the domain of the 1/20,000 map. The French Plan Directeur 1/20,000 served as the primary map scale for planning artillery objectives as it showed both battery location with calibers and used different colors to reflect levels of activity. The map included an area of at least five kilometers inside Allied lines and the first ten kilometers of German-occupied territory. Artillery planning used the modified scale map with pasted-on sheets marked with spe-

cific updated details.[31] Likewise, French tracking of German activity in the rear echelons included the process of updating sections through pasted notes. The rear echelons were marked on the 1/20,000 scale, with updates acquired from aerial photography on key installations such as munitions dumps, railroad activity, and any observed change in German defensive organizations. The French Armée headquarters used the 1/20,000 as its principal scale to evaluate the

---

[30] Chasseaud, *Topography of Armageddon*, 11.

[31] Pétain, "Notice about Maps and Special Plans," Conger Papers, Box 2, USAMHI; "Notes on the French System of Intelligence," 6, TNA, PRO: WO 158/983; Villèle, 129-130 (translation by Commandant Marc Rivière).

FIGURE 93. British maps portrayed extensive detail to support artillery operations.
Source: Peter Chasseaud, *Artillery's Astrologers: A History of British Survey and Mapping on the Western Front 1914-1918* (Lewes UK: Mapbooks, 1999).

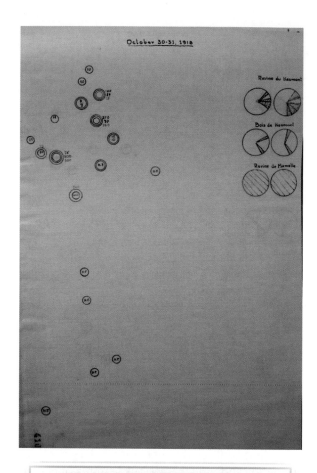

October 30-31, 1918

Ravine du Haumont

Bois de Haumont

Ravine de Mamelle

FIGURE 94. **Details of artillery round impacts were plotted on maps. This 26th Division overlay shows the level of detail attained.** Source: Massachusetts National Guard Museum.

In 1916 at the Somme, a "positions" map was created showing all enemy battery positions located from all collection sources, to include aerial photography, flash-spotting, and sound-ranging. Each gun emplacement was marked on the map and used for directing counterbattery fire.[34] Later a Hostile Shelling Map was created for tracking the extent of daily enemy artillery. Unlike the majority of information acquired from aerial photography, this map was primarily compiled at the division level. The 1/20,000 map helped portray where artillery was being directed within a particular sector of the front. Reports were forwarded by units in the line through the brigade headquarters showing the numbers of rounds fired, the caliber of the shell, and the area shelled.[35] The Hostile Shelling Map was kept for one week. The weekly updates were compared, providing an accurate estimate of the distribution and volume of enemy fire. If the Hostile Shelling Map identified a certain number of rounds being fired for several days in succession against a small section of trench or wire, it suggested that wire-cutting prior to a projected enemy raid was in progress. The unit in the line was warned accordingly. When German artillery fire covered a certain divisional sector or was noticed being directed against trench junctions and communications, it suggested either normal harassing activity or a possible registration of new guns. Any increase in the general volume of fire directed against the divisional front as a whole as well as any marked change in distribution of fire became apparent from the map.[36]

The French and British employed different scale maps as the area coverage increased and the scale decreased. The British maintained a daily map of the Army area (1/40,000) on which all photos taken in one day were plotted, and within each square covered by one photo is marked the photo number. There was a standing order that the entire army area, extending from 4,000 to 18,000 yards behind the enemy front line, was to be photographed once each fortnight. As soon as negatives were developed they were compared with the record map. Many plates were thrown out on account of duplication. Only those accepted were

battle.[32] As early as the 1914 Battle of the Aisne, the French produced a 1/20,000 Plan Directeur derived from pre-war surveys and enhanced by visual aerial reconnaissance and aerial photographs. The British had lithographed copies made for use by the artillery and the RFC. Targeting data marked on the maps included German trench and battery positions.[33]

British efforts to chart all enemy artillery reflected the information sources at their disposal.

[32] Maj Kerr T. Riggs, "Memorandum to Chief of Intelligence 'A,' 14 February 1918, Subject: 'Memorandum Report of Visit to HQ 1st French Army," Conger Papers, USAMHI.

[33] Author discussion with Dr. Peter Chasseaud.

[34] Chasseaud, *Topography of Armageddon*, 11.

[35] "Balloon Training," Gorrell Report, ser. F, r. 23, NARA.

[36] Hahn, 121-122.

given serial numbers according to the sector. As soon as the photograph was accepted, the area covered was blocked off on the daily chart and the photo number entered in the space.[37] British long-range railway guns used the 1/40,000 scale map for their operations.[38] The British also used the 1/40,000 to track German artillery positions opposite the British front. It was updated "fortnightly."[39]

The French GQG used the 1/50,000 scale to show the strength of the infantry and artillery to be used in the battle. A similar scale map portrayed the details of the enemy organization.[40] Sketch maps showed active batteries as well as previously occupied or possible emplacements. The French considered the 1/50,000 scale the best source for portraying defensive organizations and the logistical networks necessary to sustain their operation.[41]

American processes paralleled those of their French counterparts. Information flowed to the Army Headquarters in the same manner as for the French Plan Directeur. The AEF Army Headquarters photo office served as the office responsible for all information on enemy works, regardless of the source (including captured enemy photographs). A primary source was interpretation of vertical photographs for determining new activity or changes with the existing works. All changes were noted on the works chart, a tracing created over a 1/50,000 map. A master Plan Directeur was kept in triplicate and updated at all times.[42]

Aerial bombardment relied on the 1/80,000 ensemble map with all objectives in the target area sketched out. When planning bombardment, more detailed 1/10,000 tracings from aerial photographs were drafted onto the map to provide the air crews with more detailed descriptions of the targets. The map and annexed tracings were produced by 2e Bureau and coordinated with the Service Aéronautique and the *Groupe de Canevas de Tir*.[43]

Cartographic Updates

Plotting daily coverage became a well established process for all echelons. For operations in the front sector, maps provided the most effective way to track the changing situation.[44] "Enemy Work" reflected enemy defenses portrayed on a map covered by a sheet of tracing paper marked in squares with a letter to identify the location. Once information on the enemy was confirmed by various sources, the data were marked on the tracing paper. New trenches under construction, trench improvement, construction of new switch lines, or organized shell hole defenses were traced by the draughtsman and applied to the map. It was reviewed weekly. The tracings of the preceding weeks were reviewed, providing an indication of any observed activity being offensive or defensive in nature, as well as providing additional targets for artillery.[45] All information showing the various features of enemy activity in a given sector were confirmed by the aeroplane photograph.[46] The French annotated new enemy works on tracing paper covering a small-scale map known as *Croquis de reconnaissance*. Prints were then produced on bromide paper, and forwarded to headquarters for staff awareness of ongoing changes and further distribution to the army sector of interest.[47] When a new division came into the sector, one of the first actions was to transfer that information to an up-to-date map of the battleground.[48]

The daily restitution method that was acceptable to the British Photo Sections was to use tracing paper that had lines corresponding to the 1/20,000 scale map of the area. The tracing paper was marked with the number and description of the map used, the scale of the map, the date the photograph was taken, and an identifying

[37] Stewart, "Report on the Organization and Operation of Intelligence 'A'," Conger Papers, Box 2, USAMHI.

[38] Chasseaud, *British Western Front Mapping*.

[39] Hubbard, "Report on Trip to British Front," Conger Papers, Box 2, USAMHI.

[40] Hibben, "Topography," Gorrell Report, ser. J, r. 34, NARA.

[41] Pétain, "Notice about Maps and Special Plans," Conger Papers, Box 2, USAMHI.

[42] G-2, 1st Army, to Chief of Staff, "Account of the Operation,"47, Drum Papers, Box 14, USAMHI.

[43] Pétain, "Notice about Maps and Special Plans," Conger Papers, Box 2, USAMHI.

[44] Hahn, 96.

[45] Hahn, 124.

[46] Hahn, 125.

[47] "Aerial Photography for Pilots," 21, NASM, A30.2/2.

[48] Hahn, 126.

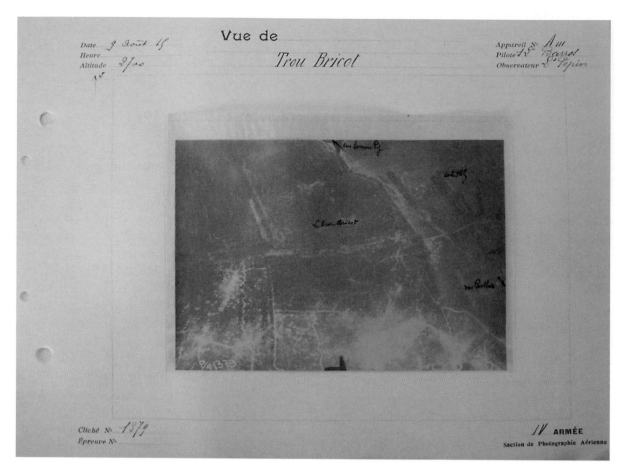

FIGURE 95. Annotations of new enemy works accomplished on tracing paper. The French called this the "Croquis de reconnaissance." Source: Eugène Pépin Papers, Musée de l'Air de l'Espace (MA&E), le Bourget, France.

large "square" letter that corresponded to a similar square on the photo being examined. Further lines were drawn on the tracing paper to equate to the number of the small squares found on the map area covered by the aerial photograph. These steps allowed the photograph to be "placed" on the map. The tracing paper was then attached to the photograph and forwarded on to the party of interest for a clear understanding of correlation between print and map.[49] The British also plotted on a 1/40,000 map all relevant information gained from the photographic analysis. In addition to the 1/40,000 map, there was a smaller format 1/100,000 map covering the same area. The 1/100,000 map was used to produce tracings for publication.[50] The Americans had each aero squadron send a key map along with the photographs to show where the coverage had been acquired. After a few days, the key map tracings underwent a color change to show the interval since the last date of coverage. This process assisted the squadron in prioritizing the coverage requirements for each sortie.[51]

The maps showed all enemy batteries that had been seen in action, or were known to have been in action, during the previous twenty-four hours. All escadrilles and ballon observateur companies received their copy of the Plan Directeur map every morning. In addition to the Plan Directeur, objective maps were also made, indicating in different colors every foot of enemy entrenchment, every weapon of defense, every item of military

---

[49] "Photographs and the Map, Appendix D," in Campbell, "Notes on Aerial Photography," TNA, PRO: AIR 1/7/6/98/20.

[50] Stewart, "Report on the Organization and Operation of intelligence 'A'," Conger Papers, Box 2, USAMHI.

[51] G-2, 1st Army, to Chief of Staff, "Account of the Operation,"48, Drum Papers, Box 14, USAMHI.

value. The objective maps were objects of extensive preparation and were constantly revised, re-edited and reissued to the combatants. Every feature of the German trenches, to include paths, approaches, dugouts, barbed-wire entanglements, machine guns, trench mortars, and PCs were repeatedly examined and updated. The information was recorded on countless photographs under a variety of lighting conditions, altitudes, and time frames.[52] The Plan Directeur was updated by the plan novette, a 1/20,000 scale map showing both

enemy and Allied trenches, barbed wire, dugouts, PCs, and other points of interest.

The photographic role was to acquire vertical coverage of a general view of the trench lines (small-scale); details of enemy organization (large-scale); and oblique photographs of the rear areas. Visual reconnaissance and aérostat observations were to complement the photographic analysis with traffic and movement reports on roads and enemy artillery.[53]

Color Schemes for Military Cartography

Cartography added to the dimension of the battleground by establishing an extensive color scheme that portrayed every major facet of the terrain and the threat. From the initial stages of the conflict, the maps became an array of hues that portrayed a clearly defined network of trenches labeled with key symbols of significant weapons systems or centers of resistance.

[52] *Study and Use of Aerial Photographs*, 15 January 1918, sec. I, 19, NARA, RG 120, Box 819.

[53] "Aeronautics," June 1921, 22, NARA, RG 120, Box 819.

Everything displayed on a map had to be visually clear and obvious, while at the same time not overwhelming the reader with detail. Color schemes applied to all maps, from the large-scale infantry maps to the small-scale staff maps, remained consistent to allow quick identification of the targets of interest. The maps that evolved during the war imparted significance and value to each element of terrain and enemy work. Various techniques were applied to include adding bright colors applied with a copying brush or hand-drawn on specific targeting maps.

The basic color schemes in relation to the map feature varied among the Allies. The French used blue for German (enemy) trench networks and fire lines; red for Allied trench networks and traffic routes; green for shelters and bivouacs; yellow to illustrate wire entanglements; brown for railways, and red to highlight key threat locations such as a machine gun emplacement. The British showed the German trench network in red and the Allied lines in blue. In 1918, they changed to conform with the French standard.[54] Smaller-scale maps had different color schemes. The color scheme for the French 1/200,000 series had roads printed red, railroads black, rivers blue, and contours brown.[55] Map symbols were colored to illuminate high-value targets such as machine gun locations, mines, points of resistance, PCs and ground observation points. A brown-shaded circle highlighted artillery targets such as junctions of fire trenches and principal communication trenches. Those targets that combined features were identified with multiple colors. A communication trench adapted for fire was described by a red line followed by a blue line on the side of the firing parapet. A blue line coupled with a green line represented a trench with deep dugouts.[56]

Cartography also became a means for identifying earlier aerial photographic information. Some centers traced their maps in a different color scheme so that the reader understood that the information depicted on a given location was dated.[57] French interpreters used intensive shading with red ink to display the effect of artillery fire. Those areas shaded heavily by hachure or lines drawn close together portrayed completely bombarded and destroyed areas. When artillery was less effective, the area was slightly shaded or a circle drawn in red ink around the area. The finished map was forwarded to the artillery units to help them gauge the effectiveness of fire. The ultimate objective was to demonstrate total destruction of the enemy.[58]

The analysis of the battlefield also included a color scheme to trace historically the impacts of incoming artillery rounds in a given sector. Different colors represented the different calibers of enemy shells, particularly the smallest guns such as the 77 mm. One dot of the color indicated the caliber of the round and was marked on the map at the place where the shell exploded.[59]

Cartography's Evolution for Portraying Future War

Cartographical support of positional war adopted a routine that became an institution. As soon as the GQG staff had committed to go ahead with an offensive, the ground in front of the army was carefully studied, mapped, and photographed. The analysis went beyond the front sector to the rear echelon.[60] British firing maps made good use of aerial photography to help establish a reference baseline that was of value even when a rapid advance or retreat caused a major shift in the front line.[61]

Advances in the use of tanks, followed by the breakthrough of the German lines in the last months of the war, forced the cartographic process to change. Aerial photography provided a foundation for determining the topological base; however, the sub-surface geological makeup of the battlefield now had to be considered. The first

---

[54] Chasseaud, *British Western Front Mapping.*

[55] *Illustrations to Accompany Captain De Bissy's Notes*, 3.

[56] Post of Command (PC) was translated from the French term for command post; the AEF adopted that term for operations at the front. *Illustrations to Accompany Captain De Bissy's Notes*, 3; Pouquet, "Working of the Service of Interpretation of Photographs," NARA, RG 120, Box 819.

---

[57] "Historical Account of Organization and Functioning of Subdivision," 57, Drum Papers, Box 14, USAMHI.

[58] "Aerial Photography for Pilots," 22, NASM, A30.2/2.

[59] Hahn, 121.

[60] Porter, 121-122.

[61] 1st Lt Thomas E. Hibben, "The Importance of Aerial Photographs in Intelligence," Lecture given at 2nd A.I.C., Gorrell Report, ser. J, r. 34, NARA.

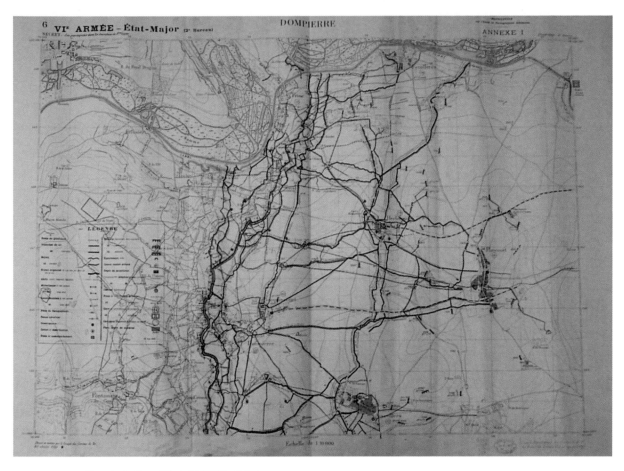

studies focused on analysis of water sources to determine the impact of the existing water table on the planned trench network. When positional war started to ebb in favor of mobile war, additional consideration was paid to determining "passability" limits for heavy pieces of equipment such as the tank in the countryside.[62] When the British fought the Battle of Passchendaele in late 1917, the conditions of the terrain were abysmal. The mud made mobility impossible for both human and motorized activity. However, the British Tank Corps introduced the first "going" map, which portrayed the hazardous areas in the sector that were most likely to be flooded or boggy, and to be avoided by tanks at all costs. In some cases, even the best of surveys did little good. Tanks, infantry, and artillery not only bogged down in the horror that was the mud of Passchendaele; some even disappeared without a trace.[63] In the last year of the war, the French were the first to produce a "passability" map to support military operations. Several prominent French and Belgian geologists were attached to the *Service Géographique* to prepare "tank maps" that delineated the physical conditions produced by the surface and near-surface soils and materials of future battlegrounds to prepare forces for maneuvers.[64] When mobile warfare commenced in the final months of 1918, the French employed 1/20,000 maps to provide the necessary detail to support faster tempo operations.[65] Another challenge to mobile operations

[62] Brooks, 93; G. A. Kiersch and J. R. Underwood, Jr., "Geology and Military Operations, 1800-1960: An Overview," in Underwood and Guth, 12; Alfred H. Brooks, "The Use of Geology on the Western Front," in D. White, ed., *Shorter Contributions to General Geology, 1920* (Washington, DC: GPO, 1921), 93.

[63] Chasseaud, *British Western Front Mapping.*
[64] Brooks, in White, 93; Kiersch and Underwood, in Underwood and Guth, 12.
[65] de Villèle, 129-130 (translation by Commandant Marc Rivière).

FIGURE 98. **Detailed 1/80,000 scale map of the St Mihiel battleground used by the 26th Division for planning. Note the German trenches are outlined in blue.** Source: Massachusetts National Guard Museum.

was that the larger-scale 1/10,000 map did not sufficiently cover the rapid advance of the forces. After the Battle of Amiens, the British dropped the 1/10,000 scale and the 1/20,000 on occasion since their forward momentum precluded benefit. They had to resort to a smaller scale of 1/40,000 or greater.[66] With the transition to more mobile operations, the cartographer added to the confusion of the moment. Now the color scheme varied, with both German and Allied organizations being portrayed in both red and blue.[67] Fortunately, the confusion was reduced by the coming of the Armistice.

The cartographic institutions lasted well beyond the time of the Armistice. Knowledge of terrain, topology, and the geology that defined the battlefield for this war guided the vision for future conflicts. In the post-war era, aerial coverage soon equated to reinforcing the defensive strategy, requiring more detail on the future zone of combat. For France, it only extended the battle line within the confines of front fortresses. The self-fulfilling prophecy for future war expressed by map development culminated in a formidable defense strategy that spurred the construction and operation of the Maginot Line of the 1930s.

---

[66] Dr. Chasseaud states it best on the challenge of mobile operations: "The faster the movement, the smaller the scale – otherwise units and formations would be off the sheet before they received it!" Chasseaud, "1:10,000 Regular Series Trench Maps," in *British Western Front Mapping.*

[67] de Villèle, 129-130 (translation by Commandant Marc Rivière).

Chapter 7: The Framework of the Aerial Photograph

Passchendaele, 16th of June 1917

Passchendaele, 5th of December 1917

FIGURE 99. **Future war would never see the likes of Passchendaele. Cartography had to decipher the topography of destruction.** Source: IWM, *Passchendaele — Before and After*, reproduced in Sholto Douglas, Years of Combat (London: Collins, 1963), 245.

THE EXPLOITATION OPERATION

American lectures to AEF personnel on the role of intelligence at the front reinforced the prevailing thinking among the Allies as to the value of aerial photographs.

The maximum efficiency in gathering intelligence can be attained only by a balanced and thorough distribution of the different missions of information; so that a complete coordination of work may bring about a complete surveillance of the enemy, and so that eventually all information may come to a single head where it may be checked for error. Photographs are one of these sources of information and because of the great mass of detail presented with a maximum of accuracy they are to be considered the most important.[1]

The Intelligence Role

Interpretation and restitution operations were indispensable, but were not enough to extract meaning from the intelligence source. The measure of effective exploitation went beyond the recording accomplished in these initial steps. Effective exploitation went to the heart of the matter by seeking a greater depth of understanding of the situation, nature of the events in progress, the value of the intended operation

FIGURE 107. **French photographic interpreters engaged in analysis. Their ultimate objective was to legitimize all military activity against the enemy.** Source: SHAA, photo contained in Christienne and Lissarague, *A History of French Military Aviation.*

and the details of the enemy forces committed to the operation. Determining the reason why was the constant theme for analysis. Discussion of the art of photographic interpretation now concentrated on ascertaining the enemy plan of defense or the intentions of attack by taking into account the German methods of combat. Exploitation exemplified the "duty of the General Staffs (2ᵉ Bureau)." How this process was accomplished varied for each Allied nation. The

---

[1] Hibben, "Importance of Aerial Photographs," 1, Gorrell Report, ser. J, r. 34, NARA.

ultimate objective was legitimizing all military activity against the enemy.[2]

Through consistent and persistent analysis, intelligence could determine what constituted the status quo on the front lines, thereby allowing the defenders to "permit the plans of the enemy to be discovered in time." Searching for signatures associated with an offensive operation was a critical focus of information collection. Telling signatures included: construction of roads and railroads, increased presence of supply depots, sightings of new artillery battery positions, and new trench work into No-Man's Land. Planning for the "period of elaboration" required currency at all times. Exploitation showed that offensive preparations required a considerable amount of time, and proper surveillance and intelligence ensured that the enemy "cannot pass by unperceived."[3]

Determining enemy intentions went beyond "role playing" the adversary. For commanders, it also meant extensive interaction with colleagues in the intelligence discipline.[4] The experience of positional war showed the participants that extensive knowledge of defensive tactics was essential. The French pioneer interpreter Capitaine de Bissy succinctly discussed the methodology for analysis: "In order to determine accurately the existing defensive organization, it is therefore necessary to exercise one's discretion and to eliminate."[5] French analysis promulgated the view that the German adversary was methodical and closely followed senior policies. Interaction among the Allied experts became a recognized medium to further understand enemy intentions and trends in analysis. Conferences served as a primary medium among intelligence and photographic specialists to share ideas and techniques for intelligence collection and analysis. The more senior the rank of the participants, the broader the scope of information that was shared. A valuable outcome of the meetings was that a closer cooperation was established between the infantry combatant and the affiliated arms, to include artillery and aviation.[6]

Sources of Intelligence

Successful exploitation of intelligence required knowledge of what sources were available to provide the most complete portrayal of the enemy. Prior to the outbreak of the Great War, intelligence was rudimentary, primarily derived from human sources, compiled from espionage, military attachés, and repatriated persons. By 1918, intelligence was an expanding discipline covering traditional methods and a host of new technologies. Sector surveillance of the positional battlefield had become the established domain for intelligence exploitation.[7] Aerial photography exploitation was viewed as the most significant of the intelligence disciplines, for it governed 11 primary sources, to include prisoner interrogations; information from repatriated men; spies; patrol reports; aerial observation from aeroplanes and balloons; ground observation reporting from infantry and artillery; sound-ranging; flash-spotting; captured documents; and radio intercept/direction finding (radiogoniometry).[8] French description suggests the value of a fusion of sources:

> The intelligence service obtains much information of value to the interpreter, through prisoners, deserters, sounding boards, sounding telephones and documents. Prisoners and deserters give first hand the location of machine guns and works of the front lines in general, and often of rearward positions. Sound boards (sensors that triangulated sound waves from artillery fire) tell us where to look for batteries, for a matter of fact it is not the duty of the interpreter to discover batteries but to locate them exactly in a given area. Or-

[2] *Study and Use of Aerial Photographs*, 15 January 1918, sec. I, 20, NARA, RG 120, Box 819.

[3] "Aeronautics," June 1921, 24-25, NARA, RG 120, Box 819.

[4] Hahn, 263

[5] *Study and Use of Aerial Photographs*, 15 January 1918, sec. II, 1, NARA, RG 120, Box 819; *Bulletin du Service de la Photographie Aerienne*; *Bulletin of the Aerial Photography Department*, 7; *Illustrations to Accompany Captain De Bissy's Notes*, 1.

[6] Hahn, 263.

[7] Hibben, "Importance of Aerial Photographs," Gorrell Report, ser. J, r. 34, NARA.

[8] Hibben, "Importance of Aerial Photographs," Gorrell Report, ser. J, r. 34, NARA.

ders are tapped from the enemy telephones through sounding telephones. Finally we have the documents captured from the enemy; complete rules regarding the construction of field positions have been obtained in this way.[9]

Daily updates for determining enemy intentions and operations revolved around human intelligence, acquired primarily from prisoner and deserter interrogations. Both French and British relied on this medium to substantiate ongoing analysis. At the same time, aerial photography was both a dominant and subordinate complement to the information acquired from prisoners. Charteris described the British process for prisoner interrogation: "Most of the information which a prisoner has is information in detail regarding the enemy defensive works on his own immediate front. To extract this information from him requires time. It is sometimes necessary to take the prisoner back in the front line trenches, or to Observation Posts and almost always necessary to examine him with the assistance of aeroplane photographs."[10] An American G-2 staff member recounted the French prisoner interrogation process:

The Chief of the Bureau calls his interpreters (who are all officers) into conference and carefully explains to them the nature of the operation which resulted in the capture of the prisoners; shows them on Plan Directeurs and relief models where the action was carried out, and makes clear just what information he is particularly anxious to get and to get first. He then charges one interpreter with the examination of minenwerfer, another with machine gunners, signal men, telephone listeners or riflemen, and so forth. This done, each interpreter goes to his office, where with map and aerophotograph at hand, he proceeds to examine the prisoners who have, in the manner indicated above, been selected as

qualified to give the particular kind of information he is after. These interrogations consume a great deal of time, usually from fifteen to forty-five minutes for each prisoner, and in case the interpreter gets into a friendly visit or an argument with a German, it may last even longer.[11]

Prisoner interrogation used the mosaic to portray the sector in explicit detail. Armed with these data, the interrogator could trace with the source (prisoner or deserter) the itinerary taken from the rear to the front line trench network, confirming the interrogation with specific details from the photo to include an isolated tree, house, or any other visible feature. The prisoner's cross examination could describe myriad targets such as railroad stations, platforms, switches, stores; itinerary routes, tracks; rest camps, ration depots, distribution depots; narrow tracks; as well as the identification of the enemy's command leaders (captain through colonel ranks). Other significant outcomes from interrogation led to location of machine guns; limits of the sector; distribution of the units; and orders in case of alert, the latter enabling the supporting points (Stutzpunkte) to be located and further analyzed. Further interrogation focused on those prisoners associated with the artillery to acquire more information on battery emplacement, observation post locations, and the associated echelons of command.[12] The limits of aerial photographic validation of interrogations came when "invisible" targets such as "organizations under wood," Stollen, tunnels, and mine works were mentioned. This meant interrogation was a sole source of information for many critical issues.[13]

Prisoners and raids on enemy territory often became a source of personal letters and correspondence. Both the British and French kept thorough lists of enemy postal details to include addresses, postal sectors and other units mentioned

---

[9] "Interpretation of Aerial Photography," 2, NASM, A30.2/28.

[10] Charteris quoted by Occleshaw, 100-101.

[11] 2nd Lt Arthur A. Zimmerman, "Report on Visit to VIIIth French Army, February 22 to March 2, 1918," 7 March 1918, 4-6, Nolan Papers, USAMHI.

[12] *Study and Use of Aerial Photographs*, 15 January 1918, sec. I, 37, NARA, RG 120, Box 819.

[13] *Study and Use of Aerial Photographs*, 15 January 1918, sec. I, 38, NARA, RG 120, Box 819.

FIGURE 101. **Aerial photographic mosaic of a German regimental sector. The interpreter would construct the intentions of the adversary once the sector was described**. Source: *Étude et Exploitation des Photographies Aériennes.*

Chapter 8: The Exploitation Operation

FIGURE 102. **The companion line drawing of the German regimental sector.** Source: *Étude et Exploitation des Photographies Aériennes.*

in material acquired from prisoners.[14] An additional source of human intelligence emerged from interrogating repatriated civilians as they made it to Allied lines from German-held territory. Interviews were normally conducted by intelligence personnel at the sector and focused on uncovering German activity and intentions.[15] One example of a valuable interrogation of repatriated civilians:

> The 2 French civilians who came into our lines near Pont-a-Mousson on Sept 2, have described in detail a water supply system by which water from the Fontaine du Soiron, 66.8-48.3, is pumped to reservoirs at 3 points, each about 1 km. Distant (N.W., S.W and S.) whence it is to be piped to points on the Hindenburg line from Dommartin, S.E. to Mont Plaisir Farm, for use in concrete work. This system is partly visible on photos, where it has the appearance of buried cable trenches, and it has been so represented on maps. The civilian's statement is entirely consistent with the photographic evidence and indicates that the further strengthening of the Hindenburg line is to be looked for at the points indicated.[16]

Intelligence gathering took place throughout the front sector at all echelons. Each Ally had its own patrol procedures to collect and disseminate information. When information was necessary for refining last-minute operations, a unit was sent on a trench raid either to capture prisoners for interrogation, gather available evidence from the enemy trenches, or both. Information from observation posts, patrols, sentries on the line, and artillery liaison officers was forwarded to higher headquarters for further analysis and dissemination. Aerial photographic reconnaissance was called in to verify significant reporting.[17] French SROT support to either artillery or command forwarded information to a central office (2e Bureau) and the appropriate commander. Sectors were monitored and activity tracked via the Plan Directeur. Prior to an offensive operation intended to penetrate deeply into the German lines, SROT were located on the heights having a visual command, "not only in front of the lines but also of the intermediate and rear zones."[18]

Sound-ranging (French term was *section de repérage par le son* [SRS]) used acoustical principles to locate enemy artillery. As sound traveled at the rate of 1,100 feet per second, it created an arc which was measured by several stations emplaced along the front. The time interval of the sound arc was triangulated and plotted on a map.[19] The British used a six-microphone configuration along a 9,000-yard sector to compile the information. Integral to the operation was a forward observer who could recognize the artillery piece being fired by its sound, and phone to headquarters any specifics regarding the weapon and location. The back-up microphone sensors would then be analyzed for sound wave characteristics and triangulated. Targeting information was passed on to the counterbattery artillery.[20]

Flash-spotting applied optical measurement to determine the location of enemy artillery. The essential equipment for flash-spotting control at headquarters was the flash and buzzer board and the plotting board which synchronized observations from spotting posts. A telephone switchboard provided connectivity to the posts.[21] The plotting board employed a 1/10,000 map that traced each response from the posts. All calculations on identified artillery batteries were forwarded to artillery for counterbattery operations.[22] In some cases, flash-spotting supplemented the work of the ballon observateur.[23] The combination of sound-ranging and flash-spotting became a vital part of the intelligence network in place to support targeting. Aerial reconnaissance was an integral player in confirming the locations of the optical and acoustical sensors.

[14] Hubbard, "Report on Trip to British Front," Conger Papers, Box 2, USAMHI.

[15] *Study and Use of Aerial Photographs*, 15 January 1918, sec. I, 38, NARA, RG 120, Box 819.

[16] 1st Army Corps, "Summary of Intelligence," Nolan Papers, USAMHI.

[17] Hahn, 188.

[18] *Study and Use of Aerial Photographs*, 15 January 1918, sec. III, 15, NARA, RG 120, Box 819.

[19] Innes, 129-130.

[20] Innes, 132.

[21] Innes, 99.

[22] Innes, 100.

[23] Innes, 67.

Captured documents were considered the ultimate tool for "perfect interpretation," particularly if aerial photographs were available showing coverage on the date of the document. Sketches contained within the document often included notes regarding machine guns, minenwerfer, dummy complexes and other projects of interest. By correlating the aerial photograph with the captured document, the analyst could identify obscure features. The interpreter's art required a perfect knowledge of the details of the trench organization, such as that found in the published German regulations. Captured documents were forwarded to the photographic interpreter for in-depth examination. The interpreter's appreciation opened the door to understanding enemy intentions, followed by a broader strategic analysis accomplished by the staff. Both sources of analysis depended on various offices for translating documents. The French-German language translation challenge was the responsibility of both the GQG's 2^e Bureau and the Technical Section of the Engineers. The interpreter and 2^e Bureau colleagues "role-played" to better understand enemy decision-making. As the French manuals reminded their readers, the commander's responsibilities included providing for every possible phase of attack, and for successive lines of defense and all enemy lines of approach. To do so best positioned the French defense to counterattack and eject the enemy rapidly from any captured territory.[24]

The successes at Tannenberg and the Marne clearly illustrated the value of radio intercept and radiogoniometric (direction finding) to combatants throughout the war. A Radio Intelligence Subsection served as the unit designed to accomplish both radio interception and goniometric functions. A wire-tapping section also intercepted German ground telegraph lines (the French term was *télégraphie par le sol* [TPS]). Radiogoniometric units determined enemy order of battle by measuring the direction from which radio signals emanated. Traffic analysis focused on identifying enemy radio procedures and call signs. This analysis was a highly favored method for confirming enemy order of battle and determining the depth of echelons in a given sector. Enemy movement was also revealed by radio intercept. It allowed Allied forces to position their own forces to provide an effective counter against an enemy attack.[25]

The Ultimate Arbiter of Intelligence

The early French writings on aerial photographic analysis provided explicit descriptions of the intelligence exploitation role. These seminal documents made it clear that fusion of information both legitimized the intelligence medium and proved the ultimate value of aerial photographic interpretation. Everything on a photograph was of intelligence interest. The snapshot would "succeed in penetrating the thought of the German commander, to live the life of the men holding the trenches, and to foresee the action that they will instinctively take in case we attack."[26] Those who collected and utilized intelligence data were obligated to read and interpret aerial photography. In case of conflicting information or data, the photograph was acknowledged by the French as the source that settled the discrepancy.[27] The intelligence value of aerial photography was starkly demonstrated in how it was exploited, regardless of source. The medium had critical value because it showed collection priorities as well as target details. Whenever an enemy photographic reconnaissance aeroplane was recovered on the Allied side, intelligence personnel acquired the plates or film and processed it for analytical review.[28]

When the Americans arrived in theater and tried to establish an effective intelligence architecture to support AEF operations, the AEF G-2 staff made extensive visits to both French and British headquarters. The subsequent reports echoed the prevailing attitude toward aerial photography's

---

[24] *Study and Use of Aerial Photographs*, 15 January 1918, sec. II, 1, NARA, RG 120, Box 819; *Bulletin du Service de la Photographie Aerienne*; *Bulletin of the Aerial Photography Department*, 7; *Illustrations to Accompany Captain De Bissy's Notes*, 1.

[25] William A. Morgan, "Invasion the Ether: Radio Intelligence at the Battle of St. Mihiel, September 1918," *Military Affairs* 51, No. 12 (April 1987): 57-61.
[26] *Illustrations to Accompany Captain De Bissy's Notes*, 1.
[27] Pépin, "Lecture," 1917, 1, NARA.
[28] Dixon, *Diary*, 52; Maj David M. Henry, "Report on my Visit to the British Army for the Purpose of Observing the Work of the Intelligence Section of the Royal Flying Corps," 7 March 1918, 8, Conger Papers, USAMHI.

FIGURE 103. **Example of French escadrille target folder with photograph and croquis de intelligence line drawing.** Source: Pépin Papers, MA&E.

leading role. An AEF Intelligence staff officer (Major Riggs) described the sentiment while visiting the headquarters of the French I^ème Armée in February 1918:

> It was continually impressed upon me by all the officers of the 2e Bureau (G-2) that information obtained from photographs was the most important information obtained and constituted the greater part of the total information used by the Bureau. In fact, I got the impression that information of the battlefront from other sources was considered unreliable unless it could be verified by photographs. The study of photographs was considered all important, not only for information concerning defensive works, but also for information of the enemy's intentions, as deduced from indications of routes of circulation, new camps, etc., in the rear.[29]

The final arbiter for any debate was the GQG's 2^e Bureau. This office was acknowledged as the most definitive interpreter of aerial photographs for intelligence purposes.[30] The photographic medium was important, but it was clearly understood by those interpreting the photograph that full exploitation required staff coordination with other intelligence acquired by 2^e Bureau.[31] The process was termed "a drawn summary of a reconnaissance."[32]

---

[29] Riggs, "Memorandum Report of Visit to Headquarters 1st French Army," Conger Papers, USAMHI.

[30] *Study and Use of Aerial Photographs*, 15 January 1918, sec. I, 24, NARA, RG 120, Box 819.

[31] *Study and Use of Aerial Photographs*, 15 January 1918, sec. I, 18, NARA, RG 120, Box 819.

[32] "Lecture on Aerial Photography," 25 April 1923, NASM A30.2/36.

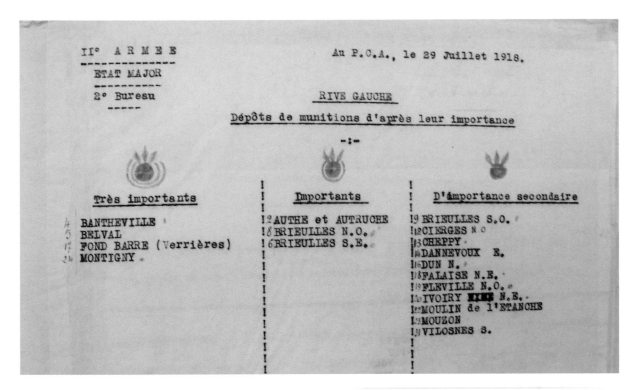

II° ARMEE
ETAT MAJOR
2° Bureau

Au P.C.A., le 29 Juillet 1918.

RIVE GAUCHE

Dépôts de munitions d'après leur importance

-:-

Très importants	Importants	D'importance secondaire
4 BANTHEVILLE	12 AUTHE et AUTRUCHE	19 BRIEULLES S.O.
5 BELVAL	18 BRIEULLES N.O.	112 CIERGES N O
17 FOND BARRE (Verrières)	16 BRIEULLES S.E.	113 CHEPPY
21 MONTIGNY		114 DANNEVOUX E.
		116 DUN N.
		118 FALAISE N.E.
		119 FLEVILLE N.O.
		110 IVOIRY XXX N.E.
		111 MOULIN de l'ETANCHE
		113 MOUZON
		111 VILOSNES S.

Aerial photographic interpretation was a team effort throughout all three phases of exploitation. The Intelligence Officer usually reviewed one set of photographs, while a draughtsman compared a duplicate set of the photographs with the history of coverage (earlier photographs of the same area) to detect any new works or defenses created in the meantime.[33] The exploitation process at both these phases was accomplished by attaching a piece of tracing paper to the photograph and highlighting objects that required further attention. When the first prints were produced in the photograph laboratory, the draughtsman created sketches of key objects on the tracing paper. The sketches were promptly completed and delivered along with the prints. The draughtsman accelerated the interpretation by highlighting the features of new positions and points of interest. This was accomplished in coordination with the aerial observer who flew the mission.[34] These "short notes" attached to the maps also included impressions of the enemy's organization gained from the study of photographs and of the ground.[35] The process of generating intelligence products, or the third phase of exploitation employed a broad array of specialists. The main product for the French (and U.S. staffs working

FIGURE 104. Unique symbols show the order of priority for the target. Source: Library of Congress, Mitchell Papers. Figures 104 through 106 show examples of products included in the target dossier.

within the French sector) was the visual array created from aerial photography. Pépin outlined the list of products in his lectures to the AEF staff, as shown in Figure 107.

Intelligence in Retrospect

It became obvious by 1917 that aerial reconnaissance and photographic interpretation had become critical information sources for Allied decision-makers. However, what plagued intelligence analysis was the weight given to determining German order of battle as the basis for gauging enemy intentions. British operational intelligence (British military parlance mentioned the function as "I(a)") emphasized order of battle, to determine the German fighting configuration in a given sector.[36] A senior British analyst explained "As everyone knows, the basis

---

[33] Hahn, 260.
[34] "Aerial Photography for Pilots," 21, NASM, A30.2/2.
[35] *Illustrations to Accompany Captain De Bissy's Notes*, 3.

[36] Occleshaw, 37.

FIGURE 105. **The highest-priority target for munitions depots in the target dossier was marked on the 1/80,000 map.** Source: Library of Congress, Brigadier General William Mitchell Papers.

Chapter 8: The Exploitation Operation

FIGURE 106. **A high-resolution aerial photograph was included in the target dossier.** Source: Library of Congress, Mitchell Papers.

[of intelligence work] is the building up of the enemy's order of battle, for when this has been done the identification of one unit is prima facie evidence of the presence of the division to which it belongs and possibly also of the corps or even army."[37] This flawed inferential methodology led to continued frustration for the Allied forces. It took a breakout from the positional war to re-evaluate what constituted good analysis of enemy intentions.

After the war, the French remained the strongest advocates for aerial photography exploitation. As one French staff officer described the prevailing sentiment:

The information [data] that aerial reconnaissance can furnish and which are the most useful for the study of the intentions of the enemy are those concerning the organization of the terrain, the batteries, the depots, the aviation fields, the camps, the vehicle parks, the circulation on roads, the intensity of movement on the railroads, the activity in the railroad stations, etc. It is readily seen, that the possibility of a minute examination of the photograph of the region flown over, permits a much more detailed examination of the ground than the one made in the course of a visual reconnaissance. In addition, the photographic documents give to the information an unquestionable authenticity and great accuracy.[38]

Despite the effort made to acquire and disseminate exploitable information, the real value of intelligence as process lay in its ability to apply

---

[37] Kirke, senior GHQ intelligence officer, quoted in David French in Dockrill and French, 76.

[38] Lieut Estienne, "Army Photographic Reconnaissance as it Should Be," 29 March 1923, 2, NASM, A30.2/34.

| PHOTOGRAPHIC INTERPRETATION PRODUCTS ||
STUDIES	RESULTS
1. A study of the general organization of the German Forces.	A colored schematic map showing sectors, headquarters, supply centers and lines of communication; plus a collection of photographs annotated for each sector.
2. A study of the enemy defensive (perhaps offensive) system.	A map showing the lines of defense, sheltered zones or arms caches and the possible directions of counterattacks.
3. Investigation of new works.	Annotated sketches and photographs.
4. A detailed study of Infantry organizations	A large-scale map showing machine guns, bomb throwers, etc. and annotated photographs.
5. Investigation of battery Emplacements.	Description or sketches of batteries.
6. A study of the German Artillery (with its observation posts, telephone centers, etc.)	A map of the artillery showing the principal groupings, etc.
7. A study of sensitive points, of possible targets for our artillery.	
In times of great activity:	
8. A verification of all destructions.	Rough sketches.
9. Reports of Infantry advance. (lines of march, etc.)	Sketches.

FIGURE 107. **French photographic interpretation products.** Source: Lieutenant Eugène Pépin, "A Lecture on the Study and Interpretation of Aerial Photography," 1917, War Department, Washington, DC. National Air and Space Museum.

reason to the information. However, such reasoning was imperfect. Allied Intelligence throughout World War I had mixed results. Detection of critical maneuvers through aerial observation at the Marne, seminal aerial photographic coverage for Neuve Chapelle, responsive actions at Fort Douaumont following timely analysis of important photographs, and the infusion of aerial photographs that countered German maneuvers in the final months of combat in Champagne contributed to the final victory. Yet, the negative legacy was equally significant. The inability to detect Stollen at the onslaught of the Verdun campaign in 1916 as well as the dramatic breakthrough of the Michael offensive of 1918 clearly demonstrated that analysis of enemy intentions was not effectively determined and acted upon. In the end, progress made with aerial reconnaissance using traditional observation methods, and rapidly evolving photographic capabilities, produced a major flow of information that filtered down to the lowest echelon. The challenges facing the rapidly evolving collection process centered on establishing a well-honed routine.

With every new dimension of collection came an effective counter by the adversary through changes in operational procedure or new techniques in camouflage and deception. The environment for intelligence from aerial reconnaissance remained dynamic throughout the war up to the Armistice.

CHAPTER 9

FRENCH INTELLIGENCE AND PHOTOGRAPHIC INTERPRETATION

Of the nations fighting on the Western Front, the French had the greatest stake in aerial reconnaissance and photographic interpretation; it was their soil that had been invaded and devastated. The number of reconnaissance aircraft produced and operated throughout the war reflected French intention to keep their eyes firmly on the Germans. Further testament to French commitment to the art of aerial observation and photographic interpretation came from the priority placed on reconnaissance following the war. French aeronautical doctrine made it clear that the primary role of the aeroplane was to "assist the Infantry to conquer and hold terrain. Like the Cavalry, it fulfills its role by fighting and by furnishing information." The air arm assured security, "both near at hand and at a distance of the great Units, by furnishing them with detailed information regarding the positions of the enemy, of the arrangement of artillery, of the occupation of camps bivouacs, and aviation terrains, and by informing the chiefs in the course of the battle of the general progress of the battle, the attitude and movements of the enemy, and preparation for counter-attacks. These two types of missions necessitate reconnaissance at more or less long range, at sight, and by photographs."[1]

For French aerial reconnaissance, command and control commenced with the Grand Quarter Général, commanded by a senior général such as Général Joffre, Général Pétain, and Maréchal Foch. GQG directorates included both a 2e Bureau and 3é Bureau (Operations). The commanding général was supported by the Aviation Militaire *chef d'état-major* (chief of staff) for all issues concerning aviation. The Aviation Militaire chef d'état-major commanded all pursuit and bombardment aviation and a certain number of reconnaissance ballon observateurs and escadrilles. In addition, he was also responsible for logistics supporting aeronautical missions.[2] The Aviation Militaire played an important role in managing the French Intelligence process, especially when collection involved aeronautical resources. The Directorate controlled photographic and intelligence services to both "clarify and facilitate the work" of the reconnaissance escadrilles. The Aviation Militaire photo reconnaissance staffs worked on aerial routes in support of bombardment as well as the assembly of aerial maps of entire sectors.[3] Since the Aviation Militaire was involved in acquiring intelligence, the branch also was responsible for processing and disseminating that information. The primary Aviation Militaire office responsible for managing the aeronautical resources assigned to the reconnaissance mission was the Aeronautical Intelligence Service (*Service de Renseignements*

---

[1] "Aeronautics," June 1921, 7-8, NARA, RG 120, Box 819.

[2] *Aviation Militaire* was also referred to as either *Director of Service Aéronautique* or the Aeronautical Command at GQG; "Aeronautics," June 1921, 20, NARA, RG 120, Box 819.

[3] Martel, 268.

FIGURE 108. Général Maurice Duval served as *le Chef du Service Aéronautique au GQG* under Pétain and Foch. He led the use of airpower thinking in the final year of the war. Source: SHAA, photo contained in Christienne and Lissarague, *A History of French Military Aviation*.

Bureau ongoing battle planning.[4] The underlying idea in this architecture was that the Aviation Militaire chef d'état-major was the final authority on determining the extent to which information was acquired from aeronautical sources, to include photography. No document could be printed and distributed without chef d'état-major approval.[5] Cooperation was key to success at Aviation Militaire.[6]

The position of Aviation Militaire chef d'état-major represented the most senior pilot-aviator to assist the French commander. Général Joffre selected Capitaine Barés to the first position of chef de l'aéronautique at GQG in 1914. The position was conceived as "new blood into an organization whose principal qualities would be deliberate audacity and intense activity."[7] His staff included a number of capitaines who were cited as "a bold young crew with inquiring minds, which constitutes a veritable intellectual center oriented toward the practical problems posed every day by the air war and the unexpected developments of the ground operations."[8] Barés was followed by Commandant du Peuty as chef d'état-major. De Peuty was an aviator full of enthusiasm for fighting, but lacked the necessary staff expertise.[9] When the Nivelle offensive failed, Général Pétain assumed command and replaced du Peuty with the most dynamic person to occupy the position for the entire conflict, Colonel Duval. Despite being a certified pilot-aviator, du Peuty left aviation to assume a command in the infantry. He would die at the end of the year leading his men in an assault.[10]

Despite the appointment to the highest aviation position on the GQG staff, Colonel Duval did not have flying experience. Prior to this move, Duval served as commander of a light infantry brigade. Colonel Duval provided an intellectual rigor to the allocation of aerial resources. His daily rou-

de l'Aéronautique [*S. R. Aéronautique*]). S. R. Aéronautique served as the French authority on intelligence involving aviation topics, to include German aviation activity, aeronautical establishments, aviation tactics, organization and materiel (aviation) and destruction of organizations. The office also addressed a broad spectrum of intelligence issues such as German troop movements, artillery activity, and determination of extent of destruction. S. R. Aéronautique acquired intelligence analysis from the 2ᵉ Bureau to manage the aeronautical resources and to provide refined information to the GQG's 2ᵉ Bureau and 3ᵉ

---

[4] Maxel, "Instructions on the Intelligence Service," Conger Papers, Box 2, USAMHI.

[5] *Study and Use of Aerial Photographs*, 15 January 1918, sec. I, 29, NARA, RG 120, Box 819.

[6] "Instructions on the Employment of Aerial Observation in Liaison with Artillery," in Maurer, ed., *U.S. Air Service*, II, 181.

[7] Martel, 19-20.

[8] Martel, 20.

[9] Christienne and Lissarague, 141.

[10] Martel, 156.

Chapter 9: French Intelligence and Photographic Interpretation

tine made it a point to acquire the viewpoints of a broad range of experts. Duval envisioned that a mobile battlefield would return along with a mobile aerial front. Air supremacy would be his hallmark. Colonel Duval was noted for his interest in the use of airpower. He directed his organization with an unwavering will by working toward compromise through persuasion and a flexible attitude. He would tirelessly examine arguments and demand as many facts as could be found. His hallmark within GQG was a series of conferences that included the senior staff. They would air their views and Duval would respond with what he had planned. The meetings were cited as being both very informative and productive.[11] Duval's stature would increase as he continued in his position. He would ultimately be promoted to *aide-major général* (assistant major general).[12]

The Culture of the Daily Conference

The daily flow of intelligence for the French revolved around key senior intelligence personnel, who discussed every evening key events and the information acquired.[13] The meeting was labeled the "daily reunion of the 2e Bureau."[14] The chef, 2e Bureau, normally presided over a conference of intelligence officers from all the staffs, to include artillery, aeronautical staffs, radiotelegraphical (*radiotélégraphie*) units, and corps radio officers. The daily discussion revolved around the update of a variety of Plan Directeur maps that portrayed enemy order of battle and dossiers that described German defensive organization, artillery, aviation, and mine locations. As the battle became more intense, the frequency of discussion increased among the staffs.[15] A similar pattern took place at all French sectors at the front. The analytical process became so well established within the French ranks that the British became aware of and adopted some of the more productive processes. British commentary concerning the manner by which the French established their intelligence role by 1916 referred to

an extensive and continuous coordination effort, "to a certain extent automatically"[16] between the various intelligence branches and throughout the various headquarters echelons. Cooperation was a prominent feature of the ongoing dialogue, thanks in part to the culture that developed from the close proximity of the various offices. It also facilitated rapid tasking and collection of aerial reconnaissance as the situation demanded. A daily dialogue on ongoing operations produced a plan of investigation (a collection plan in today's parlance). The participants worked on the appropriate agreement and the plan was subsequently carried out.[17]

By 1918, American G-2 staff observations on French intelligence reflected the same pattern. The French VIIIème Armée held daily conferences between the 3e Bureau and 2e Bureau, with the chef, 2e Bureau leading the discussion. The atmosphere was described by the American visitor as enthusiastic. This scheme of intimate coordination was greatly enforced by the daily schedule of three meals attended by Intelligence and Operations personnel, with the discussion of the day's work a central topic.[18] Daily conferences with the photographic interpreter also helped develop priorities and an awareness of campaign progress.

Daily conferences at 2 p.m. are the means by which the Chief of the Bureau keeps in touch with the interpreters as a group and keeps things well in hand and moving. Here each interpreter makes an oral report on what he has done and learned. Many discussions between the Chief and some interpreter or between a couple of interpreters take place. Thus matters of detail are thrashed out, but the Chief with his ever-recurring admonition of "Hurry Up!" (*activez vous*) kept business moving as expeditiously as possible. When the interpreters are done with their work, they shift to other subjects.[19]

---

[11] Martel , 250-252.

[12] Martel, 244.

[13] "Notes on the French System of Intelligence," 6-7, TNA, PRO: WO 198/983.

[14] Maxel, "Instructions on the Intelligence Service," Conger Papers, Box 2, USAMHI.

[15] Maxel, "Instructions on the Intelligence Service," Conger Papers, Box 2, USAMHI.

[16] "Notes on the French System of Intelligence," 9, TNA, PRO: WO 198/983.

[17] "Notes on the French System of Intelligence," 9, TNA, PRO: WO 198/983.

[18] 1st Lt Colman D. Frank, "Report of a Visit to VIIIth Army Headquarters to Attend the Interrogatory of Prisoners Taken in the Coup de Main on the Lorraine Sector," 20 February 1918, Conger Papers, USAMHI.

[19] Zimmerman, "Report on Visit to VIIIth French Army," 2-3, Nolan Papers, USAMHI.

French military intelligence excelled in the daily preparation of the Plan Directeur map. Its well-established process gained the favor of the leading generals. Général Pétain commented in 1917 while reviewing the map production process that instructions regulating Plan Directeurs "have always given full satisfaction; it seems therefore there is no reason to bring any modification to them."[20] It was a well-organized team of experts that produced the French targeting plan. 2e Bureau, S. R. Aéronautique, artillery and other staffs met, providing a definitive restitution on maps and sketches that reflected the most current and agreed upon intelligence.[21] Attention to the intelligence source was also indicated on the Plan Directeur. The whole system depicted successive enemy lines by their respective strength, taking into account any intelligence at hand. Intelligence indications not confirmed by photographs or other precise documents were highlighted by special signs.[22] Aerial photographic interpreters not only helped in the daily production of the Plan Directeur, but also generated written intelligence reports every evening.[23] The Plan Directeur's list of artillery targets was drafted every evening. The process also served as tasking for the escadrilles to accomplish subsequent observation. When conflicts arose over photographic interpretation of a given target area, the chef d'état-major was called in to decide on the final position prior to approving the target list.[24] Draftsmen were employed to inscribe the latest changes based on the latest intelligence on the master Plan Directeur. At midnight, the original, completed up-to-date master was sent to Paris where the *Service Géographique* completed the printing by the early morning. By 0400 hours, the first thousand copies were to be delivered to the respective units involved in the operation.[25]

British assessments of the process showed a respect for the way the French attended to detail in the various intelligence elements. In late 1916, maps produced for French operations at the Somme represented a compilation of intelligence gleaned over time. The information was extremely comprehensive, providing the artillery with detailed targeting for the initial offensive. Targets included the most vital points of the enemy's defenses (battle headquarters, observation posts, telephone exchanges, supply centers, routes used for bringing up reinforcements). The British commented that the accuracy and efficacy of French artillery "surprised our opponents."[26]

Staff Responsibilities

The French intelligence network was an organization based on the personality of those involved. The merger of intelligence was the dominant feature of Plan Directeur map production.[27] At the armée echelon, all 2e Bureau information relative to the German defensive organization was forwarded to the *chef d'Cartographie* who was the acknowledged French expert on the sector. An American G-2 staff officer visiting the French headquarters described the chef d'Cartographie as one who clearly understood the battleground, possessing a very intimate acquaintance with the terrain and its organization along the entire armée sector. The officer personally made visits "going not only into the foremost observation posts but even into No-Man's Land."[28] The chef d'Cartographie reviewed all available aerial photographs, prisoner interrogations, daily reports and summaries appropriate for the given sector. Since the crux of the French intelligence effort was aerial reconnaissance and photographic interpretation, knowledge of aerial photography gave the chef d'Cartographie a special stature among intelligence counterparts from the other disciplines. The chef d'Cartographie possessed great skill in the interpretation of photographs, scanning very quickly large num-

---

[20] Pétain, "Notice about Maps and Special Plans," Conger Papers, Box 2, USAMHI.

[21] *Study and Use of Aerial Photographs*, 15 January 1918, sec. I, 24, NARA, RG 120, Box 819.

[22] Pétain, "Notice about Maps and Special Plans," Conger Papers, Box 2, USAMHI.

[23] Zimmerman, "Report on Visit to VIIIth French Army," 2-3, Nolan Papers, USAMHI.

[24] "Notes on the French System of Intelligence," 6-7, TNA, PRO: WO 198/983.

[25] "Notes on the French System of Intelligence," 6-7, TNA, PRO: WO 198/983.

[26] "Notes on the French System of Intelligence," 9, TNA, PRO: WO 198/983.

[27] "Lecture on Aerial Photography," 25 April 1923, NASM A30.2/36; Hibben, "Topography," Gorrell Report, ser. J, r. 34, NARA; "Historical Account of Organization and Functioning of Subdivision," 57, Drum Papers, Box 14, USAMHI.

[28] The U.S. report referred to the *Chef d'Cartographie* as Head of the Cartographie. The more correct French term is used hereafter. Zimmerman, "Report on Visit to VIIIth French Army," 2-3, Nolan Papers, USAMHI.

FIGURE 109. **French 2ᵉ Bureau analysis and reporting under way. Note the Plan Directeur map is being updated.** Source: BDIC.

bers of aerial photographs in search of evidence of new works, various enemy activities and enemy intentions. He directed the photographic interpretation effort within the respective sector. When aerial photography discovered a new battery, railway, or other targets of significance, the chef d'Cartographie personally annotated the master Plan Directeur. Other intelligence sources such as prisoner interrogations were validated by the chef d'Cartographie through other interpreters or through personal interrogation of the more intelligent prisoners. Again, intelligence gleaned from these sources was annotated on the Plan Directeur. Daily reports from the array of functions at the front, intelligence summaries, and miscellaneous sources of all sorts were transferred onto the Plan Directeur. Once the chef d'Cartographie approved, the Plan Directeur was then turned over to the draftsmen along with final verbal guidance to ensure the final map portrayed the exact vision of intelligence.[29]

The manner by which the Plan Directeur was assembled demonstrated the significant role of aerial photographic intelligence in supporting artillery. One of the offices involved in the development of the final Plan Directeur was the Army Topographical Section, known as the *Groupe de Canevas de Tir des Armées* (GCTA).[30] The GCTA received the results of the deliberations among intelligence seniors and conducted precise and final restitution of the aerial photographs being applied to the Plan Directeur. A cell of officer photographic interpreters provided quality control for work furnished by the 2ᵉ Bureau of the subordinate CA

---

[29] Zimmerman, "Report on Visit to VIIIth French Army," 2-3, Nolan Papers, USAMHI.

[30] Canevas de Tir literally means "triangulation for the direction of artillery fire."

concerning targets deep in the rear zone of the enemy's front, to include determining withdrawal positions, communication nodes, targets for both artillery and air bombardment, military establishments, and other areas of interest. This information led to the final restitution of the information onto the artillery-firing map.[31] Pétain made it clear in his 1917 instruction that the GCTA "should be entrusted with the drawing of all maps for which a certain amount of accuracy and technical knowledge are required."[32]

Assisting GCTA in restitution of topographical work accomplished at echelons below the GQG and French Armée were the offices of the *Service Topographique Corps d'Armée* (STCA) and Divisional Topographical Section. The French intelligence architecture was repeated at the CA level. The CA Intelligence Service comprised the 2e Bureau, Artillery Intelligence Service (*Service de Renseignements de l'Artillerie*

[SRA], French designation; AIS, British designation), S. R. Aéronautique and the Radio-Telegraphical Intelligence Service. Each CA element was responsible for its respective source of intelligence. They worked together on synthesizing key elements of enemy activity, to include the order of battle, troop movements, situation of enemy artillery, defensive organization, destruction, aeronautical activity, etc. CA information resources such as reconnaissance escadrilles forwarded their information to the 2e Bureau.[33]

The CA chef d'état-major assigned primary responsibility for fusion of the respective intelligence sources to the chef, 2e Bureau des CA, who in turn directed the research and ensured coordination among the members. The officer in charge of STCA worked under the immediate

---

[31] *Study and Use of Aerial Photographs*, 15 January 1918, sec. I, 25, NARA, RG 120, Box 819; "Historical Account of Organization and Functioning of Subdivision," 57, Drum Papers, Box 14, USAMHI; "Notes on the French System of Intelligence," 6-7, TNA, PRO: WO 198/983.

[32] Pétain, "Notice about Maps and Special Plans," Conger Papers, Box 2, USAMHI.

[33] "Instructions on the Functions of the Corps Intelligence Service," Conger Papers, USAMHI.

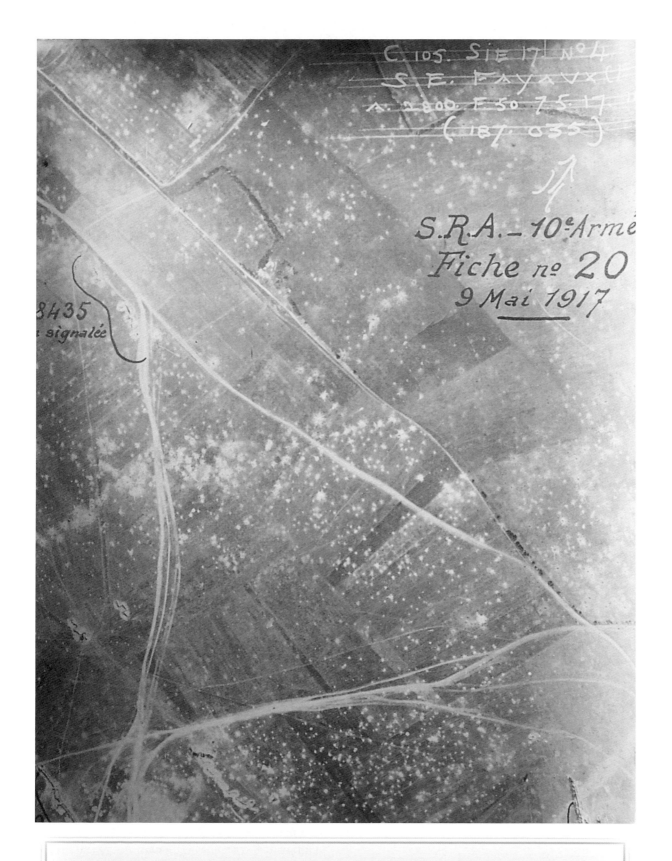

FIGURE 111. *Service de renseignements de l'artillerie (SRA)* provided intelligence support to the artillery. The aerial photograph was used to further determine German artillery locations and associated target locations. Source: Pepin Papers, MA&E.

supervision of the chef, 2ᵉ Bureau des CA. The STCA served as an intelligence hub in its own right, acquiring information from headquarters, Aviation Militaire, and the artillery staffs. Within the respective CA sector, aerial photographs relevant to Corps' objectives were processed by the STCA for restitution.[34] This office also applied topographic details as well.[35] The STCA served as the logical centerpiece for graphically depicting the fusion of intelligence on the CA Plan Directeur. The STCA sometimes produced more timely maps to reflect the current battle situation. By 1916, cartographic information portraying enemy defenses was being produced on an hourly basis.[36] It remained a very dynamic process as the STCA interpreted aerial photographs, revised artillery plans, and drafted special plans as ordered by the chef d'état-major. The STCA was usually collocated with the 2ᵉ Bureau offices near the landing ground of the assigned escadrilles, pro-

FIGURE 112. **The map key used in 1918 by the French working with the U.S. 26th Division illustrates the source and certainty of the information behind the target.** Source: Massachusetts National Guard Museum.

viding a model to the British on possible roles for the Branch Intelligence Officer (BIO) function at the squadron. The British saw great value in the manner by which the STCA operated close to the front where the escadrilles operated. This eliminated crowded offices at headquarters as well as reinforcing the aerial photographic interpretation process.[37] One British visitor commented on the STCA's operation in glowing terms: "At Verbery the arrangements are for general photographic work in connection with distribution mapping, and analysis of photographs for the Army Corps. Here the mapping was splendid and carried out

---

[34] "Lecture on Aerial Photography," 25 April 1923, NASM A30.2/36.

[35] "Notes on the French System of Intelligence," 9, TNA, PRO: WO 198/983.

[36] "Notes on the French System of Intelligence," 6-7, TNA, PRO: WO 198/983.

---

[37] "Notes on the French System of Intelligence," 6, TNA, PRO: WO 198/983; Maxel, "Instructions on the Intelligence Service," Conger Papers, Box 2, USAMHI.

Chapter 9: French Intelligence and Photographic Interpretation

with the greatest care for detail. The work was very strong in stereo photography."[38]

Intelligence for Artillery

The French SRA centralized all intelligence concerning artillery targets. In practice, the officers of this branch dealt almost exclusively with the enemy's batteries and observation posts. In several CA, the SRA functioned like the 2[e] Bureau, operating near the landing grounds of aerial observation escadrilles.[39] The SRA further studied batteries and associated target sets such as cantonments, bridges, stations, munitions depots, etc. SRA officers were responsible for working out their own means of obtaining intelligence or other means placed at their disposal such as SROTs, artillery spotting, sound-ranging and observation sections. The ongoing interpretation of photographs stopped only after approval of the chief of the 2e Bureau. Additionally, the SRA assisted the French batteries in determining the accuracy of their fire.[40] Sound-ranging and observation sections were armée-level responsibilities, but they were authorized to support the CA with intelligence directly emanating from the assigned sector. The SRA personally ensured the rapid exchange of intelligence among the various artillery sections.[41]

Restitution of aerial photographs noting enemy defenses in the sector was a daily event.[42] The SRA attended the daily 2[e] Bureau des CA conferences to assist in the compilation of battery target lists. Once the targets were selected, they were forwarded to higher headquarters offices for validation. Despite their intimate involvement with the targeting process, the CA staffs were considered incapable of accurately calculating target coordinates with sufficient accuracy. The armée staffs replied as soon as possible with final coordinates to allow the CA to con-struct their final battery list for their own artillery units. In turn the armée forwarded the definitive target locations for publication with the armée's SRA Summary. This helped avoid duplicate target assignments.[43]

At the end of every day, especially during active periods, the process for producing the Plan Directeur helped both observation and artillery to prioritize the extent of destruction to be accomplished in the next barrage. Artillery planning also took into account, from aerial photography, what shots had struck outside of the planned destruction zone.[44] Artillery targeting information was extensive. CA SRA received various reports from intelligence sources throughout the sector, to include sound-ranging and observation sections. A daily battery list was prepared that provided coordinates of batteries (in action) and confirmed locations of enemy observation posts. Diagrams were then constructed showing the general disposition of the enemy's artillery.[45]

The common cartographic baseline also served as the foundation for planning an offensive operation. French assault unit commanders used the Plan Directeur document to issue detailed orders "with all desirable precision." The Plan Directeur met the map requirements for "artillery objectives which appear to be specially signaled on the Division front." The Plan Directeur also enabled the various artillery commands to set up "action plans."[46] In the period of preparation for an offensive, rough sketches accomplished by the aerial unit (escadrille or aéro-stat) were drawn from the aerial photographs and provided expeditiously to the 2e Bureau offices. After examining the photographs, the CA compiled reports of artillery and aerial observation, and sketches of the new battleground. They were edited by the STCA and distributed the very

---

[38] Gamble, "Photographic Section of the French Flying Corps," TNA, PRO: AIR 1/404/97/1917.

[39] "Notes on the French System of Intelligence," 5-6, TNA, PRO: WO 198/983.

[40] Study and Use of Aerial Photographs, 15 January 1918, sec. I, 26-27, NARA, RG 120, Box 819.

[41] "Notes on the French System of Intelligence," 5-6, TNA, PRO: WO 198/983.

[42] Study and Use of Aerial Photographs, 15 January 1918, sec. I, 24-25, NARA, RG 120, Box 819.

[43] "Notes on the French System of Intelligence," 5-6, TNA, PRO: WO 198/983.

[44] Pétain, "Notice about Maps and Special Plans," 5, Conger Papers, Box 2, USAMHI; Aerial Observation for Artillery, Based on the French Edition of December 29, 1917 ([Washington, DC: GPO?], May 1918), 8.

[45] Study and Use of Aerial Photographs, 15 January 1918, sec. I, 16-17, NARA, RG 120, Box 819.

[46] Pétain, "Notice about Maps and Special Plans," 1-2, Conger Papers, Box 2, USAMHI.

same night to artillery staffs down to and including Group Commanders.[47]

French 2e Bureau des Armée staff interaction with the CA 2e Bureau was carried out through orders, instructions, and personal liaison existing between the officers of both echelons. Staff visits between the two headquarters were frequent. When a CA was assigned to a certain armée, the chef, 2e Bureau des CA, was personally attached for two or three days to the 2e Bureau des Armée to help personalize the staffs' relationship. When the time came for the CA to proceed to the front line, the CA staffs were familiar with the *armée's* headquarters methods and procedures.[48]

The French intelligence architecture maintained a similar structure to support divisional operations. The division's 2e Bureau officer worked under the direction of the 2e Bureau des CA. The pattern of interaction repeated itself. French division staff coordinated with several offices to concentrate on key issues concerning the division's sector. Coordination was accomplished with the SRA, the division's own Topographic Service (*Section Topographique de Division d'Infanterie* [STDI]), STCA, and S. R. Aéronautique.[49] At the division, the photographic interpreter examined front-line enemy organizations and tabulated all information supplied by the troops in sector and maintained frequent liaison with the unit intelligence officers at the front. Reports of patrols, prisoner interrogations, verbal reports from listening posts, repatriate information, and aerial photographs taken by the CA and armée escadrilles flowed down to the division as appropriate. The French division also employed a photographic interpreter to work for the 2e Bureau and Topographical Service. Staff instructions to the division included directions to ensure all divisional elements were provided with maps, sketches, photographs, and Plans Directeur. The French emphasized that no information furnished by any source was in itself complete. All infor-

mation received was to be compared with the information of the same nature already at hand and with the general situation already known.[50]

The Network of French Aerial Reconnaissance

French aeronautical doctrine emphasized the urgency of timely reconnaissance and analysis for aviation resources. At the moment of the attack, information required immediate transmission and circulation to the infantry commanders. Aérostats, aeronautic liaison, and observation aéroplanes were three main resources to accomplish this requirement. Order of battle resources for the two phases included an infantry aéroplane (*avion d'accompanement de l'infanterie, or AL*) assigned to each infantry division and an observation aéroplane assigned to each AL group. In addition, additional aéroplanes were assigned to provide relief and additional coverage during observation or fire missions. Relief sorties reinforced ongoing fire or observation missions as well as substituting for those aéroplanes already committed. Reconnaissance in these two phases required definitive coverage. French doctrine specified that "When beyond the zone of fortified positions, the Army Corps aeroplanes endeavor to see and to photograph the position of the supporting troops and they observe movement in the rear."[51] Any photographs taken by the escadrilles were interpreted by the various services at the landing ground site.

CA escadrilles accomplished aerial and photographic reconnaissance for the CA as well as registration for any special batteries such as *batteries de position* (batteries left in quiet sectors without motor transport or escadrille support) or batteries placed at the disposal of the CA. The escadrille supporting the divisions provided *avion de réglage* support for divisional artillery, contact patrol, and reconnaissance and photography. Salmson 2A2 escadrilles working with heavy artillery batteries accomplished reg-

---

[47] Pétain, "Notice about Maps and Special Plans," 5, Conger Papers, Box 2, USAMHI; *Aerial Observation for Artillery*, 8.

[48] "Notes on the French System of Intelligence," 10, TNA, PRO: WO 198/983.

[49] *Study and Use of Aerial Photographs*, 15 January 1918, sec. I, 31–32, NARA, RG 120, Box 819.

[50] Maxel, "Instructions on the Intelligence Service," Conger Papers, Box 2, USAMHI.

[51] "Aeronautics," June 1921, 23, NARA, RG 120, Box 819.

istration only missions.[52] The size of a French escadrille in the war varied, but an ideal complement was ten aéroplanes.[53] In 1918, RAF reporting on French Corps Aviation showed at least 45 aéroplanes assigned throughout a typical CA echelon. Within the CA, a nominal count of 10 aéroplanes comprised a CA-subordinate escadrille with the specific responsibility of acquiring either aerial observation or photographic reconnaissance. Additionally, the escadrille would provide registration for any special batteries assigned to the CA. Finally, the escadrille would support its division with additional reconnaissance. For every two divisions that were organic to the CA, an additional escadrille with a nominal count of 10 aéroplanes provided immediate support. When additional divisions were added to the CA, each acquired its own escadrille complement of 10 aéroplanes. An artillery-spotting escadrille with 15 aéroplanes was also assigned for every AL regiment. This unit would only accomplish registration for the batteries.[54]

The French employed armée escadrilles for aerial observation and photographic reconnaissance, air raids, and pursuit. Orders for reconnaissance sorties and air raids were drafted by the 2e Bureau des Armée and signed off by the armée chef d'état-major. For operations in support of the CA, the CA chef d'état-major approved reconnaissance missions generated by the 2e Bureau.[55]

Effective communication required for timely reconnaissance and analysis was integral to the French landing ground operation. An array of telephonic communications connected the CA service aéronautique to the various headquarters in the sector. If telephones failed, the operation had access to TSF and aerial message bags dropped from available aeroplanes. The French kept horses at advanced landing grounds so that the observer could immediately ride off and make his report to Headquarters.[56] The French maintained a procedure for tasking escadrilles for aerial reconnaissance and photographic missions. The 2e Bureau determined from the 3e Corps, SRA, S. R. Aéronautique, and other units what information was required to meet their objectives. The 2e Bureau forwarded its reconnaissance plan to the respective commander of the armée or CA service aéronautique. Mission priorities were then determined and photographic assignment took place. The French photographic observer assigning the mission was responsible for knowing the exact targets and region requiring aerial photographic coverage. The observer had to know the special purpose that the photograph served so that the mission planning best served the scale and final layout of the master Plan Directeur. Furnished with this information, the French observer carefully prepared the reconnaissance, and coordinated with the chef, SPAé, to ensure the correct camera with the correct focal length and magazine was installed and operating. The observer then worked with the pilot on flight patterns required to accomplish the mission.[57]

Since the strategic intelligence obtained by the armée service aéronautique was considered less perishable than that supplied by the CA service aéronautique, the French did not always commit to having an intelligence office at the landing ground. An officer of the armée service aéronautique staff, whenever possible the "Operations" officer, was assigned the duty to check intelligence obtained by reconnaissance and to forward it to the 2e Bureau. In case of time-sensitive situations requiring immediate information, the officer was considered the appropriate person to get the information to those responsible in a timely manner. Photographs taken on reconnaissance missions were immediately developed and proofs distributed as soon as possible. The armée service aéronautique not only sent a preliminary report (or print) of intelligence obtained but also thoroughly examined the sources of information and produced a Daily Summary of Intelligence

---

[52] Sewell, "Notes … on French Corps Aviation," TNA, PRO: AIR 1/475/15/312/201.

[53] Author discussion with Dr. James Davilla.

[54] Squadron strength reflects an average count; no definitive number of aéroplanes was assigned to French escadrilles despite those indicated in the report. Sewell, "Notes … on French Corps Aviation," TNA, PRO: AIR 1/475/15/312/201.

[55] "Notes on the French System of Intelligence," 7, TNA, PRO: WO 198/983.

[56] Sewell, "Notes … on French Corps Aviation," TNA, PRO: AIR 1/475/15/312/201.

[57] "Lecture on Aerial Photography," 25 April 1923, NASM A30.2/36.

illustrated by sketches giving deductions drawn from the information gathered during the day. The armée service aéronautique also assisted SRA with aerial photographic interpretation to update battery index cards.[58]

The 2e Bureau of the armée service aéronautique sent a copy of all photographs acquired from the reconnaissance sorties to the respective armée or 2e Bureau des CA, SRA, and to the group assembling the Plan Directeur. The interpretation conducted at the escadrille included the analysis of the aerial observer. Each photograph was reviewed and used to modify and annotate the current interpretation as required. The chief of the 2e Bureau tactical assistant and officer in charge of photographic interpretation made the final interpretation. High-interest items found from the photographs were circled in red ink.[59] At the CA, drawings were made of changes and improvements in the trench system and reproduced for issue to the staff and to various units in the CA. Copies of all photographs and drawings were sent to the higher echelon armée staffs for further verification and study in the 2e Bureau, and also for use by the Canevas de Tir for keeping Plan Directeur maps up to date.[60] The French also employed the *Bureau de Cartographie* to add all special information on the battle maps. Special information included detailed and confidential information relative to the location of German batteries, minenwerfer, machine guns, ammunition and supply dumps, means of transportation and communication, dugouts, rest camps, railheads, hospitals, and dressing stations.[61]

The entire intelligence process made a marked impression on those who witnessed it first-hand. One French aviator recalled, "The reading and interpretation of the photographs has to be done immediately, for it is of the greatest importance that the information given by the photographs be obtained quickly."[62] The work

routine embodied a philosophical perspective on the fighting life in general. "All the work in a photographic reconnaissance should be done on the same day the reconnaissance is made. The officer should take no rest until everything is finished and the prints sent off, for example, by motorcyclists. It is not uncommon for photographic officers to go several nights without sleeping. What difference does it make? They know the importance of their work and should perform their duties with devotion. When rain comes (and it comes often in France) they will rest."[63] At the CA echelon, French escadrille photographic work was centralized by the SPAé Photographic Officer. He was assisted by observers and was responsible for the development, printing, interpretation and distribution. During a battle, the CA service aéronautique commander attached one of his staff officers to the headquarters of the respective CA to assist in providing the information in a timely manner.[64] Escadrille members were encouraged to participate at daily meetings conducted at the landing ground. It fell on the 2e Bureau to coordinate the inputs from all in attendance.[65] The professional photographic staffs from attending British and American forces had the highest regard for the French process of plotting, translating, and interpreting photographs. Steichen's earliest impressions were forwarded to the Signal Corps Photographic Division: "It is a most excellent system and you may remember it was referred to by Major Campbell as being very much better than the English system."[66] The Americans inherited the French system when they took over a sector at the front.

The French SPAé

French intelligence expanded its presence throughout the force by the continued formation of SPAé to support aerial photographic requirements. The originator of France's SPAé, Capitaine Grout, helped expand the awareness of the forces on the potential of aerial photography

---

[58] "Notes on the French System of Intelligence," 7, TNA, PRO: WO 198/983.

[59] *Study and Use of Aerial Photographs*, 15 January 1918, sec. I, 26, NARA, RG 120, Box 819.

[60] "Memorandum Report of Visit to HQ 1st French Army," Conger Papers, USAMHI.

[61] Zimmerman, "Report on Visit to VIIIth French Army," 1-2, Nolan Papers, USAMHI.

[62] Lieut Michel quoted in Porter, 174.

[63] Lieut Michel quoted in Porter, 175.

[64] Sewell, "Notes … on French Corps Aviation," TNA, PRO: AIR 1/475/15/312/201.

[65] *Study and Use of Aerial Photographs*, 15 January 1918, sec. I, 31-32, NARA, RG 120, Box 819.

[66] 1st Lt Edward Steichen, "Memorandum for Major Decker," 21 December 1917, NASM.

FIGURE 113. **Members of a French photographic laboratory looking at a recently processed photograph.** Source: SHAA.

by generating technical photographic expertise to the commands and units. The continued demand for aerial photography prompted greater emphasis to acquire more photographers and draftsmen. A heavy recruitment for such skills took place, seeking professionals in the art from graduates of a photographic or drawing school and aspiring amateurs. The services rendered by the SPAé des armée were considered so significant that the French commanders made the decision to equip CA escadrilles, escadrilles assigned to divisions, and Heavy, Day Bombardment escadrilles with SPAé.[67] French SPAé became integral to the reconnaissance escadrilles assigned throughout the French armée.[68] In the last year of the war, the French further institutionalized photographic support by assigning photographic officers to both armée and CA headquarters. The photographic officer at the armée echelon coordinated SPAé functions pertinent to that echelon. At CA, the photographic officer directly supervised the SPAé's assigned both directly to the CA and to the infantry divisions that were CA-attached during the course of operations.[69] Key SPAé personnel included the Officer Tactical Photographer who pre-planned the mission with the air crew prior to take off. The Technical Officer was the senior enlisted who ensured the laboratory and other functions were accomplished successfully. This warrant officer was considered the heart of the SPAé, providing the wisdom of years to the younger members of the operation. Other members included draftsmen and specialists in photographic maintenance.[70]

SPAé laboratories were completely equipped to handle the range of tasks for photography, to include loading and downloading photo camera magazines and plate holders, developing and drying plates and prints, recovering various chemical products, and enlarging and projecting prints. The photographic laboratory drawing room was also responsible for marking of photographs after identification; constructing the map of the areas covered; constructing sketches of the reconnaissance; assembling photographs to make a mosaic and mounting of stereoscopic views.[71] Post-mission processing of information from the air crew and cameras was impressive. "Two hours after the Observer photographer has returned to the aviation camp all the pictures he has taken should be sent in all directions, to all departments, regiments, batteries, and the Staffs that need them. In the French Army they make about 80 copies of each picture, and each Observer always brings in 20 to 30 pictures." "It is not uncommon for a squadron photographic section to make 1,000 prints a day; to accomplish this rapid development and printing, each French squadron has a photographic section composed of specifically trained men. Automatic machines develop and print the photographs."[72] Once aerial photographs were processed and interpreted, the French took the photographic proofs and inscribed on the left side of the negative or on a thin sheet of gelatin fixed on the negative a summary of their interpretation.[73] Negatives were filed for ready access. A British visitor commented that "The negatives are all carefully catalogued, being kept in the original plate boxes."[74] In addition to volume, the speed of production and timely reporting were noteworthy. "In some cases, for example with contact patrols, we have to get out our photographic intelligence with the greatest speed. The French photographic service uses a process of developing, printing, and drying which produces one or two prints on paper, completely dried, ten minutes after the photographic airplane has come down."[75] The SPAé also forwarded the necessary photographs to the STCA and the SRA to assist in the final development of the Plan Directeur.[76] As part of their role, the SPAé maintained the necessary cameras for the aeronautical units, to include the standard inventory of 26 cm, 50 cm and 120 cm cameras.[77]

---

[67] "Lecture on Aerial Photography," 25 April 1923, NASM A30.2/36.

[68] "Lecture on Aerial Photography," 25 April 1923, NASM A30.2/36; Carlier, 59.

[69] "Lecture on Aerial Photography," 25 April 1923, NASM A30.2/36.

[70] Carlier, 60-61.

[71] "Lecture on Aerial Photography," 25 April 1923, NASM A30.2/36.

[72] Lieut Michel quoted in Porter, 173-174.

[73] Pouquet, "Working of the Service of Interpretation of Photographs," NARA, RG 120, Box 819.

[74] Gamble, "Photographic Section of the French Flying Corps," TNA, PRO: AIR 1/404/97/1917.

[75] Lieut Michel quoted in Porter, 174.

[76] "Lecture on Aerial Photography," 25 April 1923, NASM A30.2/36.

[77] Pépin, "Lecture on the Study and Interpretation of Aerial Photographs," 1, NASM.

Chapter 9: French Intelligence and Photographic Interpretation

Intelligence distribution was well established by 1916. Photograph distribution was equally prolific. A representative example was the French VIème Armée distribution of coverage. CA escadrille photographs were selected by the commander and distributed by the service aéronautique. Distribution from CA to armée included ten non-interpreted prints to the armée's key staff, to include, 2e Bureau (one print), 3e Bureau (one print), Canevas de Tir (two prints), Artillery (one print), Heavy Long range Artillery (one print), Engineers (one print), commander of the service aéronautique (one print), and *Groupe des Armées du Nord (GAN)* (Group of Northern Armies) (one print). A follow-up distribution of more detailed interpretations was repeated to those offices that required specific attention to detail, to include 2e Bureau (one print), Canevas de Tir (one print), and service aéronautique (one print). Aerial photographs acquired by armée escadrilles had 12 prints generated for the staff and to the Groupe des Armées du Nord. At the CA level, distribution included prints for the staffs of the 2e Bureau, CA, Artillery, and the respective division.[78]

The French armée air park provided rear-echelon logistical support to SPAé. The facility possessed a precision mechanic and a cabinet-maker to repair material and provide inspection of new material. The storehouse was supplied with all photographic material such as plates and paper. SPAé commanders were supplied directly from the armée air park directly under the control of the Assistant Photographic Officer of the Armée.[79]

Photograph distribution also included a broad range of military organizations and schools. The *Service Entrepôt Special d'Aéronautique* No. 2 at Nanterre assembled and classified the respective photographs to facilitate the range of training requirements for the French military. When the United States entered the war, aerial photographs were forwarded to the primary schools at Cornell University and Rochester, NY. In the immediate post-war era, the photographs were used extensively by the various commissions assigned to conduct the peace treaty and to determine the extent of damage in the liberated regions.[80]

The French led all combatants in the First World War in developing an effective reconnaissance mission. In the following years, they emphasized reconnaissance as an equal to the evolving roles of pursuit and bombardment. By the late 1930s the French Air Service was called "Information Aviation," with two primary classes, "Observation Aviation and Reconnaissance Aviation."[81] The intelligence process thus maintained coherence with aviation's capability. Pursuit continued to ensure freedom of action for observation missions. French aviation continued to think defensively, based on the prevailing influence of positional war and its existing fleet of aéroplanes, which were limited in range and strike power.[82] It was the continuation of the defensive mindset of the inter-war years that hindered the ability to ascertain enemy intentions. Innovation in reconnaissance did little to overcome shortfalls in French military strategy in the inter-war period. Even when armed with the capability to acquire information on the enemy, the French military did not meet the challenge of new concepts such as rapid mobility with an appropriate military counter. It resulted in the country's capitulation under the onslaught of the Germans in 1940.

---

[78] "Notes on the French System of Intelligence," 11, TNA, PRO: WO 198/983.

[79] "Lecture on Aerial Photography," 25 April 1923, NASM A30.2/36.

[80] "Lecture on Aerial Photography," 25 April 1923, NASM A30.2/36.

[81] Capt Charles W. Lawrence, "Organization and Assignment of Observation Aviation Observation Airplanes and their Equipment," Air Corps Tactical School, Maxwell Field, Alabama, 1937-38, Air Force Historical Office Archives, IRIS ref. A2810, Maxwell AFB, AL.

[82] Anthony C. Cain, *The Forgotten Air Force: French Air Doctrine in the 1930s* (Washington, DC: Smithsonian Institution Press, 2002), 11.

THE ANALYST
Capitaine **Eugène Marie Edmond Pépin**
(27 June 1887 – 28 April 1988)

Capitaine Eugène Marie Edmond Pépin was one of the greatest pioneers of aerial photographic interpretation in the First World War. His service to France and its allies made aerial photographic interpretation an institution for military operations in the 20th century. He was a man of great diversity and vision, an expert in architectural art, but best remembered as a pioneer in aerial photography and in the application of law to space travel and exploration. Pépin came from an academic background and applied his brilliance toward development of the most important intelligence source of the war. His ability to weave German positional war doctrine and military policy into the interpretation of the aerial photograph advanced the legitimacy of the role of aerial photography as a fundamental tool of intelligence.

Pépin was exposed to the leading edge of intelligence and academe from the start of his military career. While serving compulsory military duty in 1907, he was introduced to new sources of intelligence, including the rapidly evolving science of intercepting wireless telegraphy transmissions. Following this initial period of military service, Pépin pursued a graduate degree at the Sorbonne in legal history and international law. His academic credentials enabled him to become a pioneer in the initial role of international law in defining the limits of aviation. In 1910 he served as secretary to the first international conference on aerial navigation. During this period, Pépin met James Brown Scott, a legal scholar who established the foundation for modern international law. Pépin's network of contacts in this evolving arena reflects his intellectual acumen in understanding the complexities associated with the phenomenon of aviation.[83]

When war broke out in 1914, Pépin was commissioned and assigned to aviation, where his intellectual depth was quickly applied to supporting the expanding role of aerial reconnaissance. The influential Lieutenant Maurice Grout acquired Pépin and had him assigned as Chief of the *IVème Armée* SPAé. This assignment permitted Pépin to establish his expertise in the field of aerial photographic interpretation by providing intelligence support to ongoing French operations. As the war progressed, he soon became responsible for eight French armée SPAé's.[84]

> FIGURE 114. **Pépin Portrait.**
> Source: Pépin Papers, MA&E.

---

[83] Pépin Papers, MA&E, Paris.
[84] Pépin Papers, MA&E, Paris.

FIGURE 115. The French aerial photographic interpreter giants of World War I, Capitaine Jean De Bissy and Lieutenant Eugene Pépin, prior to a sortie in an AR 1. Source: SHAA, 76/1168.

Pépin applied his academic brilliance to refining aerial photographic interpretation and moving it from the realm of novelty to becoming a definitive science. His efforts helped establish French aerial photographic analysis as the intelligence standard among the Allies. His knowledge soon drew the attention and favor of *Général* Pétain, who assigned him to his staff to provide aerial photographic interpretation expertise for campaign planning and to train French officers in aerial photography.[85] He was a brilliant model for introducing intelligence into mainstream military thinking. Among his achievements, he assisted in the development of French policy relating to the application of camouflage. In August 1917, he served as the GQG 2ᵉ *Bureau's* representative to the *Commission Centrale de Camouflage*, where he personally developed the primary instruction manual for French camouflage and aerial photography.[86] He also led the development of the French Armée's aerial photographic interpretation manuals, including *Étude et Exploitation des Photographies Aériennes* and a translation of the U.S. manual, *Study and Use of Aerial Photographs*. Both served as the standard by which aerial photographic interpretation demonstrated its utility as an intelligence medium. His written description provided a comprehensive assessment of the visual configuration of the German battleground network. It remains one of the most extensive and unique first-hand descriptions of warfare at that time.[87]

When the Americans arrived in 1917, Capitaine Pépin was personally assigned by Général Pétain to the newly established French Mission that supported senior AEF staffs with in-depth knowledge on how to conduct modern positional warfare. In September 1917, Pépin became the personal advisor to General Pershing on aerial photographic interpretation. He continued to support Allied planning throughout 1918. During the lead-up to the Meuse-Argonne offensive, he was assigned to the Enemy Works Subdivision of Headquarters First Army, providing comprehensive interpretation of the impending battlefield.[88] When the Meuse-Argonne campaign

---

[85] Pépin Papers, MA&E, Paris.
[86] Dégardin, 22.
[87] "Study and Use of Aerial Photographs," Sec. II, 1.
[88] G-2, 1st Army, AEF to Chief of Staff, 1st Army, AEF, "Report," 53.

commenced, he was a leading analyst supporting American headquarters assessments of threat locations.[89]

At the Armistice, Pépin's expertise was sought to help draft the peace treaty with Germany and its allies. He was reunited with James Brown Scott in the drafting delegation that defined the borders of several new nations. His work in the aeronautical arena continued as well through leading several fora that addressed the evolving role of aerial navigation.[90]

In the inter-war years, Pépin wrote several books describing the culture of the France he knew and loved, including an in-depth review of cathedrals in the Loire River valley. These were a direct reflection of his mastery of aerial photography, covering the terrain in detail, while expounding on the cultural and historical significance of the subject matter. In his work on the cathedral at Chinôn, he not only wrote the book, but also took the photographs.[91]

FIGURE 116. **Pépin in later years.**
Source: Pépin Papers, MA&E.

Pépin was also a leading figure in French international law during the turbulent inter-war period, serving in the French foreign ministry throughout the 1920s. Through his position in the ministry, he became actively involved in Latin American issues. Later, in the 1930s, he extended his interests to Asia, where he served as a legal counselor for the Japanese foreign ministry (*Gaimusha*). In that capacity, he served on the Lytton Commission investigating the disagreement between Japan and China over Manchuria. When World War II commenced, Pépin again served with the French Army as the senior officer in charge of aerial photography. After Germany defeated France, he was retained in the government as a director of the Economy Section, evaluating the consequences of the German occupation on the French economy.[92]

Following World War II, Pépin became a renowned leader in the field of international civil aviation and aviation law. He became general counsel for the French government's aerial transport office and served as general secretary for several international law conferences addressing the role of modern aviation.[93]

In his later years, he served as Director of the Institute of International Air Law at McGill University in Canada. In this capacity, he took on yet another pioneering role in jurisprudence relating to the evolving world of aerospace. His judicial formulation

[89] Pépin Papers, MA&E, Paris.
[90] Pépin Papers, MA&E, Paris.
[91] Eugène Pépin, *Chinôn* (Paris: Henri Laurens, 1924).
[92] Pépin biography in Pépin Papers, MA&E, Paris.
[93] Pépin biography in Pépin Papers, MA&E, Paris.

was seminal in determining the extent of terrestrial boundaries. His analysis uncovered gaps that existed in international regulations governing air traffic. In the age of Sputnik when legal experts in aviation and aerospace law had to come to terms with the technical advances that advanced the exploration of space, Pépin's analysis addressed the new role of satellites revolving around the earth in 90 minutes at an altitude of 300 miles (500 kilometers). As a result of Pépin's leadership, an international body of law recognized the sovereignty of a nation as extending only to the atmospheric space above its territory.[94]

---

[94] Dr. Eugène Pépin, *The Legal Status of the Airspace in the Light of Progress in Aviation and Astronautics* (Montreal: Institute of International Air Law, McGill University, 1957), 1.

BRITISH INTELLIGENCE AND PHOTOGRAPHIC INTERPRETATION

Establishing an Intelligence Legacy

One of the greatest legacies of the First World War was the ability of the French and British to develop parallel, complementary intelligence organizations. The years of conflict helped erode many old differences as dependency increased in order to ensure each Allied partner held up its side of the front line. Both nations were expending their human capital at an exorbitant rate in a long series of offensives with marginal gains. The seemingly endless campaigns prompted the two Allies to consider less costly ways to conduct the war. Greater attention to intelligence not only aided the commander in the conduct of the campaign; it also saved resources. For Great Britain and her Commonwealth Allies, the organized intelligence network that arose from these years of conflict created the primary infrastructure that served their militaries for the remainder of the century.

British intelligence was a well-organized and disciplined formation designed to serve the BEF commander and operations. Like the French, the British viewed aerial photography as an invaluable source to validate information acquired through other means. What differences existed between the two Allies mainly concerned the final product. The British paid greater attention to intelligence summaries to describe what the aerial photograph revealed. Lack of total agreement on the best means to accomplish the intelligence mission is not surprising. They worked together as best as could be expected, but each side had its own views. One British senior, AVM Brooke-Popham, remarked on this in his post-war notes: "I think one sees the difference between these methods in the two services even to-day. The French individually more brilliant but relying on a few star pilots to win the war and constantly failing for want of discipline and organization; the British standing on a firm foundation unmoved by temporary set backs or by drastic reduction, able to face with calmness an indefinite expansion."[1]

The British system of aerial reconnaissance had its American admirers early on in the conflict. Early in 1915, the American attaché to London, Colonel George Squier, reported:

> The presence with the British Army of an aeroplane squadron assigned to each Corps, and in addition a squadron and an aircraft park at GHQ, places in the hands of the Intelligence Service, one of the greatest aids to obtaining information, which as yet has been developed. Aeroplanes are now regularly used, not only for obtaining information concerning the enemy, and his dispatches, but also in cases of a large Army on the move, [where they] are a

---

[1] Air Comm H. R. M. Brooke-Popham, "Personalities of Du Peuty and Trenchard, The War of 1914-1918," RAF Staff College, TNA, PRO: AIR 69/1.

very efficient and ready means of furnishing the Commanding General with the tactical positions of his own troops as well. All reconnaissance reports from aeroplanes are sent immediately to the Intelligence Officer of the different Corps, and generally the aviator reports in person with his report, in order to be interrogated by the Intelligence officer. These reports are forwarded from the different Corps without delay to the Director of the I.D. at GHQ.[2]

Three years after Col Squier filed that assessment and after the Americans had been at war for ten months, AEF seniors attempted to fully understand their Allied counterpart's intelligence process. Liaisons were sent to the various British staffs to review their intelligence process. One observer was Major Henry, AEF G-2 staff, who in the winter of 1918 portrayed the ongoing British intelligence effort:

Before my visit to the British Front I had heard often, as everyone has, many statements of the amount of Intelligence obtained by reconnaissance and aerial photography, and I accepted those statements, as they were made as a matter of course. To what extent Intelligence is thus obtained I do not believe anyone can understand fully who has not seen the actual work of collecting it as it is done by the Squadrons day by day, and the extent to which those whom it concerns depend upon it for the information necessary to enable them to carry on operations. There seems to be no development in the Enemy's system of defenses that is not both quickly observed and photographed. From the front line trenches back through the counterbattery area there are thus made known the location and formation of all trenches, machine gun emplacements, fortified shell holes, tank traps, dumps, trench mortar positions, antiaircraft defenses, artillery pits, wire, dug out positions, roads,

paths, everything in the nature of defensive construction or preparation.... As this Intelligence is collected day by day, changes and new developments in connection with all of these things are quickly shown. In no other way would it be possible to obtain a large amount of intelligence, and probably none of it could otherwise be so accurately and so thoroughly obtained.[3]

The Intelligence Hierarchy

British intelligence was active both in London and with the GHQ in France. The most senior British intelligence offices were in London at the War Office. General Macdonogh led the Directorate of Military Intelligence following the first year of the war when he served as Field-Marshal French's senior intelligence person.[4] Field-Marshal French had the highest regard for Macdonogh despite the altercation at the Battle of First Ypres:

Our intelligence service had been admirably organized, and was working most effectively under the able direction of Brigadier-General Macdonogh. I cannot speak too highly of the skill and ability displayed by this distinguished officer throughout the whole time during which we served together. His service was invaluable; his ingenuity and resource in obtaining and collecting information, his indefatigable brain, and the unfailing versatility and insight with which he sifted every statement and circumstance were beyond all praise. He trained an excellent staff, who valued his leadership, for he had an extraordinary power of getting the most and best work out of every one. His information as to the enemy's movements was remarkably accurate, and placed me throughout in the best

[2] Squier, "Intelligence Services," 16 February 1915, 2, Squier Papers, USAMHI.

[3] Maj David M. Henry, "Report on my Visit to the British Army for the Purpose of Observing the Work of the Intelligence Section of the Royal Flying Corps," 7 March 1918, Conger Papers, USAMHI.

[4] Viscount French, 75.

Chapter 10: British Intelligence and Photographic Interpretation

position to intercept the enemy's probable intentions.[5]

General Macdonogh proved to be one of the most brilliant British generals in the war, conducting an array of intelligence operations against the Germans that gleaned many key strategic intentions. Macdonogh's key intelligence arm, known as the Secret Service, had determined with certitude the date, time, and location of the 1918 Michael offensive. Despite the information, the BEF was not in a position to reinforce those sectors that bore the brunt of the attack. The Channel ports to the north remained the primary concern. Additional troops were thus withheld by the British Prime Minister, Lloyd George, who feared another campaign of attrition, such as had occurred at the debacle of Passchendaele in the Ypres sector the previous fall.[6] On a personal level, Macdonogh had one major shortcoming. He bore the brunt of the senior British military staff's bias as it concerned his religious affiliation. Macdonogh was a recent convert to Catholicism. Key antagonists included Haig and Charteris.[7]

BEF Commander General Haig's intelligence chief, Brigadier-General Charteris, managed intelligence from 1915 to December 1917. Charteris did succeed in institutionalizing aerial photography within the BEF. However, Charteris was less than exemplary in his management of British intelligence at the front. One critique came from General James Marshall-Cornwall, who served on Haig's staff: "I soon discovered that the views held by Charteris, and reported by him to Sir Douglas Haig ... differed widely from the estimates made by the Director of Military Intelligence at War Office...." This view became increasingly negative based on the feeling that Charteris deliberately misled Haig. According to Marshall-Cornwall, Charteris "honestly thought that by suppressing all pessimistic evidence about enemy potential, moral and physical, he was strengthening his chief's determination to win the war."[8] In any event, aerial photography became a fixture in Charteris' ability to tell the story of enemy intentions. The British Prime

FIGURE 117. **The leading British intelligence officer of the First World War was Lieutenant General Sir George Macdonogh. Macdonogh is seen in a post-war photograph with Marechel Foch.** Source: IWM, courtesy Nicholas Watkis.

Minister, Lloyd George, shared Marshall-Cornwall's view: "General Charteris, who was an embodiment of the Military Intelligence which he directed, glowed with victory. For him the news was all good."[9]

Despite the problems associated with Charteris' tenure with the BEF, he institutionalized a more modern Intelligence Corps using new techniques such as an expanded use of radio intercept.[10] Charteris also established the British infrastructure for aerial photography. His initial staff included two regular army officers and three wartime officers, all of whom developed

[5] Viscount French, 92.
[6] Occleshaw, 246-247.
[7] Occleshaw, 347-348.
[8] Marshall-Cornwall quoted in Occleshaw, 325, 326.

[9] Lloyd George quoted in Occleshaw, 331.
[10] "Intelligence Organization and Establishment," 1 November 1917, TNA, PRO: WO 152/262.

skills in the arena of photographic interpretation. The vanguard of British aerial photographic interpretation included Captain Carrol Romer, a barrister (attorney) and surveyor, who devised the first rules for scaling air photographs.[11]

The British Intelligence Architecture

GHQ's intelligence was disseminated through two intelligence products: the Daily Intelligence Summary and the Daily Summary of Information. Both were geared toward providing relevant intelligence to the Commander-in-Chief. GHQ used these reports to support ongoing tactical and strategic planning. Aerial reconnaissance and photographic interpretation reports received at GHQ were also forwarded to General Haig to support his ongoing estimate of the war.[12] At the front, special functions were established to support intelligence processing. For example, the British Commonwealth (Canadian) staff was supported by an aeroplane photo man (a photographic interpreter or photographer) to assist in the generation of its Intelligence Summary.[13] The GHQ also established a special RFC unit to acquire intelligence. Known as the 9th Wing, the organization flew special missions and operated independently of the squadrons in the RFC Brigades. The 9th Wing photographed and reported on key German strategic targets such as aerodromes, railway movements and "special observations."[14]

At GHQ, Section I-a-3 was established to monitor the zone immediately in the rear of the German Army, generating a report on enemy intentions for the Chief of Intelligence. The section collected statements of repatriates, spies, prisoners, army observation reports and aerial photographs. Aerial photographs of the towns and adjacent areas were compiled and made available immediately for review. Train movement was monitored extensively to determine front sustainability.[15] British intelligence also created a

FIGURE 118. **Captain Carrol Romer worked on Brigadier General Charteris' staff and is remembered as one of the first British photographic interpreters.** Source: IWM, courtesy Nicholas Watkis.

network of prisoner interrogation centers. A Prisoner-Examining Officer was appointed at Corps to work with prisoners contained in "cages" where further interrogation of key prisoners was accomplished. Interrogation time averaged ten minutes. Information from prisoners was subsequently collated and disseminated to all parties concerned. A Document Officer was appointed to manage all captured material. Extensive intelligence was acquired from letters, postcards, and printed matter such as orders confiscated during prisoner interrogation.[16]

In 1917, the RFC adopted the Brigade formation to better support the British Army with aviation resources, to include increased aerial photographic coverage. The RFC Brigade comprised an Army and Corps Wing to provide aerial sup-

---

[11] Author discussion with Peter Chasseaud; Watkis, 10.
[12] Henry, "Report on my Visit to the British Army," Conger Papers, Box 2, USAMHI.
[13] Hahn, 129.
[14] Henry, "Report on my Visit to the British Army," Conger Papers, Box 2, USAMHI.
[15] Hubbard, "Report on Trip to British Front," Conger Papers, Box 2, USAMHI.

[16] Stewart, "Report on the Organization and Operation of Intelligence 'A'," Conger Papers, Box 2, USAMHI.

Chapter 10: British Intelligence and Photographic Interpretation

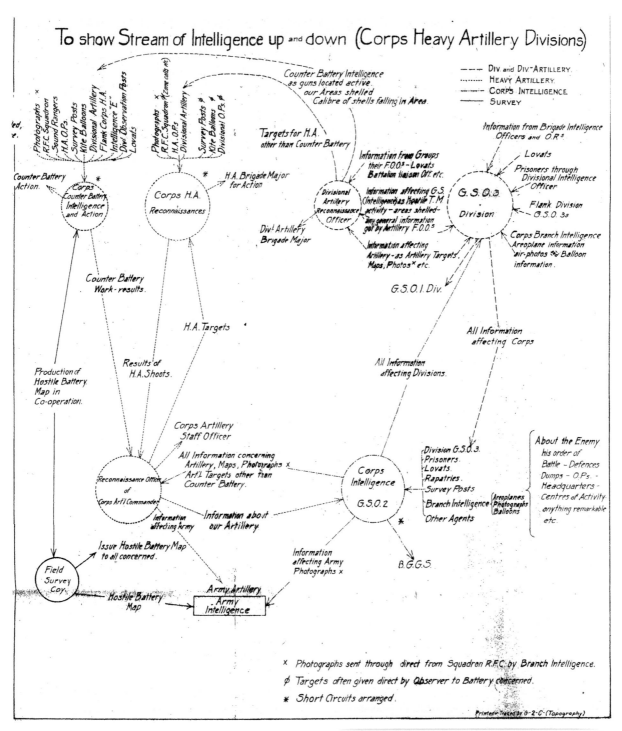

To show Stream of Intelligence up and down (Corps Heavy Artillery Divisions)

FIGURE 119. An AEF visitor's reconstruction of the British Intelligence architecture in support of heavy artillery operations. The amazing detail illustrates a well established information and intelligence flow to support heavy artillery unit targeting. Source: Conger Papers, U.S. Army Military History Institute (USAMHI), Carlisle, PA.

port.[17] Within the Brigade the RFC established the function of Brigade Photographic Officer to overcome the lack of coordination resulting from the variety of policies that proliferated throughout the RFC wings. An additional photographic officer was attached to each wing.[18] Orders for aerial photography were issued by the Brigade to the Army Wing, and a squadron would be tasked

---

[17] Gliddon, 18-19.
[18] "Aerial Photography for Pilots," 4, NASM, A30.2/2.

| | | Brigade H.Q. | | | |
| | | Army Wing | | | |

| Bombing Squadron | | | Reconnaissance Squadron | | |
| | | | Officer Photo | | |

| | | Corps Wing | | | |
| | | Officer Photo | | | |

Squadron	Squadron	Squadron	Squadron	Squadron	Squadron
Squadron Photo	Squadron Photo	Squadron Photo	Squadron Photo	Squadron Photo	*
NCO	NCO	NCO	NCO	NCO	*

* The Sixth squadron did not have a Squadron Photo Officer or NCO assigned.

FIGURE 120. **Royal Flying Corps Brigade Structure.** Sources: Outline derived from "Aerial Photography for Pilots," 4, NASM, A 30.2/2; and "Report on Visit to British Army for Purpose of Studying Branch Intelligence," Conger Papers, Box 2, USAMHI.

to fly the mission. Additional tasking involved special large-scale photographs and long-focus obliques.[19] Brigade Headquarters was also responsible for photographic printing. Once prints arrived at Army or Corps headquarters, the RFC responsibility ceased. The subordinate headquarters continued distribution to the front line trenches.[20] The RFC Brigade, as seen in 1918, showed the expanding influence of aerial photography. Five out of the six squadrons supporting the Corps Wing included photographic personnel, as shown in the above figure.

British Army Wing Squadrons covered the strategic area behind the counterbattery zone and operated as far back of the lines as was practical.[21] Corps Wing Squadrons were limited to the counterbattery zone, extending back a distance of about 2,500 yards from the enemy front-line trenches. The photography covered up to 8,000 yards behind enemy lines.[22] Photo coverage of villages, towns, bomb target dumps, billets, and enemy headquarters required two copies for each addressee on the distribution list.[23] The Branch Intelligence Sections attached to Corps Wing Squadrons generated one copy of all mosaics, one copy of any photograph of particular interest (photographs taken with new cameras or showing new forms of enemy defensive construction using concrete), new fortifications, shell holes, or any other new matter important to successful reading and interpretation of photographs. Additionally, any interesting stereoscopic or oblique coverage was included in the dissemination.[24] Corps and Army commanders placed greatest value on intelligence acquired through the tactically focused Corps Wing Squadrons.[25] It was indicative of the British emphasis on aerial photographic reconnaissance against the Germans that when the sorties were overdue, backup aeroplanes were tasked to complete the work.[26]

[19] "Aerial Photography for Pilots," 5, NASM, A30.2/2.

[20] Laws, "Statement made … to Mr. A. J. Insall," 1924, TNA, PRO: AIR 1/724/91/2.

[21] Henry, "Report on my Visit to the British Army," Conger Papers, Box 2, USAMHI.

[22] "Organization of Intelligence," HQ, British 5th Army, Conger Papers, Box 2, USAMHI.

[23] Henry, "Report on my Visit to the British Army," Conger Papers, Box 2, USAMHI.

[24] Henry, "Report on my Visit to the British Army," Conger Papers, Box 2, USAMHI.

[25] "Organization of Intelligence," HQ, British 5th Army, Conger Papers, Box 2, USAMHI.

[26] Moore-Brabazon, "Photography's Part in the War," TNA, PRO: AIR 1/724/91/2.

Chapter 10: British Intelligence and Photographic Interpretation

Intelligence dissemination to the line became well-orchestrated, especially for the Canadian Commonwealth units that pushed for increased intelligence awareness to better support their personnel. During trench warfare the first duty upon entering a new sector was an immediate reconnaissance in detail of the new defense, to fully understand the sector topography, and make oneself fully cognizant of the general topography of the Brigade front, the disposition of the Brigade front, and the disposition of the units within the Brigade.[27] To assist intelligence awareness within the Brigade, intelligence staffing included one staff captain, twelve observers, one aeroplane photo clerk, two draftsmen and one clerk. They received a mosaic photograph showing the wiring and other features of the German system. They also received photographs of the map showing the German trench system as well as an oblique photograph of the landscape. The mosaic, the photograph of the map, and the landscape photograph were packaged in a way that provided easy handling.[28]

British Commonwealth allies established very effective intelligence networks. The Canadians were cited for their intelligence support to the troops in the front lines. In the Canadian Corps the intelligence officer served as the directing officer and maintained close liaison with the operations officer, maintaining extensive daily interaction. Their desks at headquarters were even configured so that they sat opposite each other.[29]

Key Intelligence Positions

The British intelligence network was well established at the lower echelons. Under the staff title of General Staff Officer (GSO) Intelligence, the organization was configured in numerical order. The senior Intelligence staff member was GSO 1. The GSO 1 was the British Army equivalent to the acknowledged French expert on the sector, the chef d'Cartographie. The British GSO 1 understudy was the GSO 3, responsible for writing the Army's daily summary on artil-

lery activity.[30] GSO 1 addressed enemy losses and related subjects, enemy intentions (prisoners' statements), and captured documents. Analysis included the effect of British air operations and artillery fire, the liaison between enemy infantry and artillery and other similar miscellaneous subjects.[31] British armies developed their own procedures for producing and disseminating intelligence. The British First Army produced an Intelligence Summary and Summary of Information that included intelligence from aerial photographs.[32] The British Second Army was on photograph distribution from their three subordinate army squadrons, four corps squadrons, flank army squadrons and GHQ squadrons. All incoming information was filed according to squadron. The results were posted on the daily map.[33]

At the Somme sector, the British Fifth Army kept a similar structure. The GSO 1 was normally an assigned lieutenant colonel, responsible for maintaining enemy order of battle, maps, and diagrams showing disposition of enemy forces and captured documents. GSO 2 Intelligence Officers were responsible for interpretation of aerial photographs and enemy rear echelon organizations. One GSO 2 worked enemy defenses; the other provided augmentation on the enemy defense function and rear work organizations. The subordinate Corps Branch Intelligence Officer (BIO) personnel comprised an Intelligence Officer, NCO (clerk), orderly, and two draftsmen. The BIO received and consolidated orders for photos, interviewed pilots and observers, prepared a consolidated report, indicated map coordinates on photos, kept a record map showing new work indicated by photos, and distributed aerial photos.[34]

Like the French chef d'Cartographie, the Air Photo Officer served as the senior authority on aerial photography. The Air Photo Officer

[27] Hahn, 87.

[28] Hubbard, "Report on Trip to British Front," 16, Conger Papers, Box 2, USAMHI.

[29] Hubbard, "Report on Trip to British Front," 17, Conger Papers, Box 2, USAMHI.

[30] Stewart, "Report on the Organization and Operation of Intelligence 'A'," Conger Papers, Box 2, USAMHI.

[31] Stewart, "Report on the Organization and Operation of Intelligence 'A'," Conger Papers, Box 2, USAMHI.

[32] Henry, "Report on my Visit to the British Army," Conger Papers, Box 2, USAMHI.

[33] Stewart, "Report on the Organization and Operation of Intelligence 'A'," Conger Papers, Box 2, USAMHI.

[34] "Organization of Intelligence," HQ, British 5th Army, Conger Papers, Box 2, USAMHI.

personally examined all aerial photos relevant to the army sector (roughly 500 per day). This officer's reputation was such that he could locate any photo in the sector without reference to the coordinates. He remained liable at any time to be called on by the GSO 1 for an opinion of the enemy's intentions or to provide a summary of new works. The Air Photo Officer produced a summary of the German defense line, providing detailed descriptions and strength estimates. Select topics of aerial photographic analysis included indications of enemy raids, enemy movement, enemy air activity, and fires and explosions. The Air Photo Officer included his draftsmen in the discussion to prepare the map or target folder.[35] The British First Army employed its Air Photo Officer function to acquire all Army and Corps aerial photographs covering the front. Individual photographs were applied to construct a mosaic for a common reference point. An American visitor in early 1918 observed that they had "thousands of individual photographs, and now they try to paste these photographs together and by rephotographing reduce the many photographs to one."[36]

The British intelligence process was efficient. Every function was designed to perform as effectively as possible, given the capabilities of the organization. Aerial photographic reconnaissance exemplified the efficient network that was established. Squadrons serving the Corps strove to have their initial prints readied a half hour after landing; a secondary issue was dispatched to recipients six hours later. The division had an aeroplane photo man review the photos, record new observations covering German activity and alert the intelligence staff of developments. Comparisons of old and new coverage was a standard process to detect new defenses under construction.[37] One British infantry officer recalled the aeroplane map was a key reference for summarizing patrol work in No-Man's Land. His commanding officer had the patrol retrace their steps on a photograph.[38] They also examined photographs to corroborate information from other sources for the divisional intelligence summary. GSO's validated the summary before dissemination.[39] The aeroplane photo man also served as distribution manager for aerial photos relevant to the division. During interpretation of photos, any items of interest were fed into the intelligence channels through the intelligence officer on-scene.[40]

The Branch Intelligence Officer (BIO)

Within the RFC, the intelligence function evolved quickly. Early on in the war, the central figure for squadron-level intelligence collection and dissemination was the squadron commander. As its role increased, aerial photographic interpretation became the responsibility of the squadron's senior observer. The lack of an intelligence network in place quickly became apparent. The inability to correlate aerial sources of information with other intelligence sources (prisoner interrogations, radio direction) limited the potency of intelligence.[41]

After the Somme experience, the RFC reevaluated its information infrastructure and decided on a new formation. In January 1917, Branch Intelligence Sections included an Intelligence Corps officer, two Field Survey Company draftsmen, a clerk, and an orderly. The Intelligence Corps Officer was now at the squadron headquarters, establishing a stronger acquaintance between intelligence and the air crew. Branch Intelligence Sections were integral to the Corps, with information generated at the squadron being immediately disseminated to Corps for action. The BIO function was established at the Branch Intelligence Section. In early 1918, an American visitor from the AEF G-2 to the British squadrons succinctly summarized BIO responsibilities:

> The first essential for this Officer is that he should be an expert in the reading and interpretation of aeroplane photographs. Unless this is so, he cannot carry on. He must know to whom to send the appropriate items of intel-

---

[35] Stewart, "Report on the Organization and Operation of Intelligence 'A,'" Conger Papers, Box 2, USAMHI.

[36] Hubbard, "Report on Trip to British Front," Conger Papers, Box 2, USAMHI.

[37] Hahn, 119.

[38] Edwin C. Vaughan, *Some Desperate Glory: The World War I Diary of a British Officer* (New York: Simon and Schuster Inc., and Touchstone Books, 1981), 154.

[39] Hahn, 119.

[40] Hahn, 95-96.

[41] Hahn, 258-259.

ligence and must be able to make up his mind which of several items coming in at the same time should be communicated on first. It is imperative that he should keep in close touch with the staffs of all the formations in his Corps and with the Intelligence Staff at Army H.Q. He should get to know these officers personally – also the staffs at Wing and Brigade H.Q. RFC. He should make a point of being hand in glove with the C.C. (squadron commander) of the Squadron to which he is attached – also with all the pilots and observers of that squadron. If he does not do this he will miss a large amount of information which he would be able to collect otherwise. He should endeavor as far as possible to make his office a place where the pilots and observers drop in for a chat about their work (as well as other things); this will prove of great assistance to his efficiency.[42]

The BIO was the ultimate broker for British aerial photography. Despite working at squadron level, the BIO was the primary conduit for aerial photographic intelligence to Corps and Army commanders. American observers highlighted the BIO's responsibility as the ultimate validation point for other intelligence sources.[43] Aerial photograph requests were worked through the BIO in conference with the Squadron Commander. Army units at battalion and higher sent a request to the BIO, who in turn highlighted the area of concern through pin flags on a large-scale map. If the contemplated photography was not excessive, the BIO sent the squadron's flight commander a memo outlining the target request. The squadron commander followed up and detailed additional aeroplanes if the request proved excessive.[44] Following the request for aerial photography, the BIO and squadron commander assigned observers and pilots their missions. The BIO further explained the Corps' intelligence requirements and provided all relevant information such as maps, sketches, and photographs.[45] In addition, the BIO maintained daily contact with Corps Intelligence and the Corps Heavy Artillery intelligence liaison. Frequent interaction reinforced awareness of every requirement, allowing for greater initiative for new observations as well confirming standing requirements.[46] Upon completion of their flight, both pilot and observer reported to the squadron headquarters and the BIO for post-flight interrogation and to deliver the exposed photographic plates. The plates were turned over to the laboratory; in turn, prints and aerial photographic interpretation reports were quickly generated. Extra photograph copies were always maintained. The squadron sent time-sensitive, unwashed and unmarked photos of important targets to the army headquarters as soon as the plates were developed. The early morning shoots arrived at headquarters in the afternoon. Evening shoots arrived later that night.[47]

While the laboratory was producing the prints and photographic interpretation was under way, the air crew filled out a standard form showing what had been accomplished, with significant observations noted. In the British I Corps, the crew personally entered their reports in a blank book with the following format headings: Date; Pilot & Observer; Machine; Report. Second line: Fires; Explosions; Trains; Balloons; Hostile Artillery; Floods; Hostile Aircraft; Miscellaneous. At the end of the day, the information in the book was consolidated and forwarded to the Corps Intelligence Officer. The report of train movements was phoned to Army Branch Intelligence.[48] After the air crew debrief, the BIO telephoned observation and photographic interpreter reports on the average two to three times a day. Aerial photographic prints were disseminated according to established procedures. Rapid dissemination was accomplished by messenger. Less time-sensitive target photographs

[42] "Organization of Intelligence," HQ, British 5th Army, Conger Papers, Box 2, USAMHI.

[43] Henry, "Report on my Visit to the British Army," Conger Papers, Box 2, USAMHI.

[44] Henry, "Report on my Visit to the British Army," Conger Papers, Box 2, USAMHI.

[45] Henry, "Report on my Visit to the British Army," Conger Papers, Box 2, USAMHI; Hahn, 259-260.

[46] Hahn, 261.

[47] "Organization of Intelligence," HQ, British 5th Army, Conger Papers, Box 2, USAMHI; "Summary of Indications of Enemy Preparations for an Offensive in Flanders," Conger Papers, Box 2, USAMHI.

[48] "Organization of Intelligence," HQ, British 5th Army, Conger Papers, Box 2, USAMHI.

were distributed later in the day.[49] Major Henry commented an communications set-up for British dissemination: "One factor that seemed of special importance in the easy and quick distribution of Intelligence and in the working of the whole Intelligence organization was the very extensive and complete telephone system behind the British lines. From any Squadron or from any Headquarters any other place that was wanted could be gotten practically immediately."[50]

The BIOs generated operational reports for their counterparts at the RFC Headquarters Intelligence Section three times a day. The "Situation Wires" were telephoned between eight and nine o'clock in the morning, at one o'clock in the afternoon and after the day's flying. Information to the RFC/RAF included weather conditions, number of artillery adjustments, bombs dropped, photographic plates exposed, enemy aircraft activity, casualties, and other matters affecting the general situation in the Brigade operating area. RFC Headquarters also received copies of all photographs taken during the day. The number of copies forwarded depended upon the nature of the photograph. During active operations, a special messenger delivered high-priority photographs as soon as they were printed.[51] In the evening the Squadron Commander generated a typewritten summary called the Squadron Record Book. The BIO also prepared for Headquarters a "Branch Intelligence Section – Army. Daily Summary." This summary was a compilation of all information in the reports given to him during the day by observers and pilots. The final BIO routine for the day was to keep the situation map updated and the area photographic effort that day outlined. Finally, a summary of significant intelligence was attached to the map.[52]

Within the British RFC and RAF, the Photo Section worked under the direction of the BIO.[53]

Two proofs were prepared from each new plate; date and map coordinates were entered on the back of each in pencil after which the corresponding notations were entered on the plates. As proofs were checked with the record map to determine coordinates, the proofs were examined for new work, with notations indicated on slips clipped to proofs. Such new work was entered on the record map as soon as all proofs had been coordinated. Proofs were distributed to Army, Corps, and other headquarters as required. Requests for additional copies were expected by noon the day following distribution of proofs. The BIO sent off additional copies as he determined the need. The photos were then filed by map sections. A cross-index book was kept to provide ready reference to photos of particular objects (such as dumps, etc.) that were not shown on the maps.[54]

Intelligence manning throughout British forces expanded to meet demand. To support reconnaissance, the British assembled the necessary staff to conduct reporting and interpret aerial photography. Two draftsmen and one clerk were assigned each unit.[55] The British used their draughtsmen to complete the aerial photographic interpretation. In the last year of the conflict a draughtsman was assigned targets based on expertise and he kept up-to-date records and maps of his target.[56] Every squadron in the Corps Wing and two Squadrons in each Army Wing were equipped with a photo section consisting of one noncommissioned officer and twenty men. Estimates at the end of the war showed personnel strength assigned to the Photo Section at 250 Officers and 3,000 of other ranks.[57]

The experience on the front line also shaped the intelligence requirements for the infantry. Initially, the British assigned a small cadre of personnel to accomplish the intelligence work for

[49] Henry, "Report on my Visit to the British Army," Conger Papers, Box 2, USAMHI; Hahn, 259-260.

[50] Henry, "Report on my Visit to the British Army," Conger Papers, Box 2, USAMHI.

[51] Henry, "Report on my Visit to the British Army," Conger Papers, Box 2, USAMHI.

[52] Henry, "Report on my Visit to the British Army," Conger Papers, Box 2, USAMHI"; "Summary of Indications of Enemy Preparations for an Offensive in Flanders," Conger Papers, Box 2, USAMHI.

[53] Henry, "Report on my Visit to the British Army,"

Conger Papers, Box 2, USAMHI.

[54] "Organization of Intelligence," HQ, British 5th Army, Conger Papers, Box 2, USAMHI.

[55] "Organization of Intelligence," HQ, British 5th Army, Conger Papers, Box 2, USAMHI.

[56] "Organization of Intelligence," HQ, British 5th Army, Conger Papers, Box 2, USAMHI.

[57] "Telephone call between Colonel Moore-Brabazon and Capt Wall," 13 November 1918, TNA, PRO: AIR 1/724/91/2; Laws, "Statement made … to Mr. A. J. Insall," TNA, PRO: AIR 1/724/91/2.

the sector. A British battalion initially had one officer assigned responsible for all related functions. By 1918, manning increased to handle the multitude of intelligence requirements. The intelligence staff of a single Canadian Infantry Battalion included an intelligence officer, one scout officer, eight observers, eight snipers, one aeroplane photo interpreter, and draughtsmen.[58] During duty at the front line, the Intelligence Officer kept battalion intelligence maps updated, adjusting as required from intelligence reports. Flank activity was constant and required both monitoring and coordination with counterparts. Knowledge of the enemy at battalion level was frequently coordinated with artillery liaisons, resulting in ongoing target assignments against wire and other obstacles.[59] Observation reporting from elements throughout the battalion sector flowed through the battalion Intelligence Officer. Every square inch of terrain required observation post coverage. Detailed, large-scale maps and aerial vertical and oblique photographs were employed extensively. Aerial oblique photographs proved invaluable, especially when the shot was taken above the observation post location. This gave the same general view and together with the map enabled a very comprehensive study to be made of the ground.[60] The battalion aeroplane photograph man and draughtsman worked directly under the Intelligence Officer. The two personnel assisted the fusion of intelligence by integrating aerial photographic information with the other reports. The division occasionally hosted two-week aerial photography training by the Corps' aerial photography expert with the objective that those in attendance be able to accomplish simple aerial photographic interpretation to serve battalion operations.[61]

At the outbreak of the war the RFC had only one noncommissioned officer and four men assigned for general photographic duties. Aerial photography requirements were not to be established until the following year, resulting in the initial cadre being reassigned for other, more relevant work. An exponential increase in manning occurred as aerial photography gained a foothold and became an integral part of British intelligence. The ground work of photography — photograph development and printing — was initially carried out in squadrons by noncommissioned personnel. The next phase in photographic manning involved establishing Wing Photographic Officer positions. These personnel were drawn from squadrons and assigned photographic functions. The first photographic staff role was primarily experimental in nature. The organization was "elastic and hard-and-fast establishments and systems to a large extent avoided."[62] The demand for photographic experience soon over-tasked the squadrons. Those units not facing increased photographic sorties loaned their photographic personnel to the squadrons experiencing a greater load. RFC squadrons emphasizing photography drew personnel augmentation from those squadrons not presently assigned reconnaissance responsibilities. The mission was to be served at the expense of non-participating squadrons.[63]

When the RFC established the Brigade echelon, intelligence officers were assigned to the subordinate army and corps wing. However, the organization soon had problems in that the absence of a senior photographic officer at the Brigade Headquarters resulted in lack of a central element to deal with the photographic challenges.[64] However, the value of the Photographic Officer function was quickly recognized as more requirements for aerial reconnaissance were established. Soon the function multiplied at all levels, particularly after the RAF was established in 1918. Had the war continued, the transformation of aerial reconnaissance positions under way would have resulted in a Photographic Officer being assigned to each RAF squadron in France.[65]

British Corps intelligence was tactically focused, concerned with front-line activity and recording rear sector activity. It established a systematic process for obtaining aerial photographs of a given area. Initially, the channel of

---

[58] Hahn, 70.
[59] Hahn, 72; 83.
[60] Hahn, 13-14.
[61] Hahn, 82.

[62] Laws, "Statement made … to Mr. A. J. Insall," TNA, PRO: AIR 1/724/91/2
[63] Laws, "Statement made … to Mr. A. J. Insall," TNA, PRO: AIR 1/724/91/2.
[64] Toye, "History of Photography," TNA, PRO: AIR 1/724/91/1.
[65] Toye, "History of Photography," TNA, PRO: AIR 1/724/91/1.

Channels through which air photographs are ordered and distributed.

FIGURE 121. An AEF visitor's portrayal of the RFC aerial photograph dissemination process. Source: Conger Papers, USAMHI.

communications only addressed Corps special requirements. However, liaisons with other collection sources such as the counterbattery office (responsible for flash-spotting) soon led to photographic verification of the ground observations. Corps squadrons began to work with other collection sources, resulting in more refined targeting through aerial observation. The

Chapter 10: British Intelligence and Photographic Interpretation

culmination of the effort was a greater acceptance of aerial photography for validation of other sources.[66] The German artillery activity was continually monitored through ground networks and aerial photography. The British kept situation maps at all echelons labeled with intelligence inputs and sources. The frequency of interaction between the staffs was dependent on the tempo of operations. Daily conferences were held during active operations to keep all offices apprised of the ongoing situation. Attendees included representatives of Field Survey Company, observation groups and sound-ranging sections, representatives from the Balloon Company (working artillery spotting functions recording flashes and movement), Intelligence Officers from Corps Squadrons, Divisional Artillery, and counterbattery offices from adjacent Corps.[67] Timely response to high priority tasking was accomplished by British squadrons in a variety of ways. The first rough print from a negative ("rush copy;" one that was not annotated or washed) was immediately forwarded by dispatch rider from the squadron to the BIO at the Army or Corps Headquarters as an "advance copy." Standard timing for "rush copy" was five hours. A photo of the target at 1000 hours was usually processed, interpreted, disseminated and received by the priority customers by 1500 hours.[68]

Distribution of the initial intelligence product was the responsibility of the aerial unit that collected the intelligence.[69] Once the British Corps received the copy from the squadron, an "advanced copy" of key photographs was printed. The Corps forwarded these to the subordinate division's GSO Intelligence for further examination. The division subsequently provided the division's General Officer Commanding (GOC) relevant photographs containing appropriate remarks. After review by GOC and GSO Intelligence, the photos were properly marked and filed by the Corps Intelligence Office. The division also received secondary distribution to inform the remaining staffs and units. Standard division distribution for a single photograph came to approximately 35 copies.[70] The British Second Army also maintained an Air Photo Section to analyze enemy defenses and rear organizations. Two officers, the Air Photo Officer and 3rd Intelligence Officer, worked on intelligence from aerial photographs. Seven draughtsmen assisted the officers in the interpretation of coverage. Three draughtsmen examined photos over the whole front. The remaining four examined aerial photographs for key targets in an allotted sector of the front. Each of the seven draughtsmen examined photos covering the entire army front, each paying attention to a special subject, such as dumps, airdromes, roads, railways, bridges and hospitals, trench area defenses, and photograph filing.[71] At the British Second Army, BIO personnel were the focus of intelligence-gathering from photographs. They interrogated pilots and observers of photographic squadrons and prepared a chart showing the location of the area covered by the photographs. Once the decision was made as to what prints were to be retained, the photos were filed. A daily summary and the chart of photos taken were distributed to the respective centers. Intelligence concentrated on finding new hangars, sheds, or airdromes. All reports on train movements were forwarded to Army Branch Intelligence and consolidated in the daily summary. Requests for special photos were sent from the Army Intelligence Office through RFC Brigade Headquarters to wing and squadron commanders. There was a standing order that the entire army area, extending from 4,000 to 18,000 yards behind the enemy front line, was to be photographed once each fortnight.[72]

British Photo Sections

The Photo Section configuration was based on demand when the first unit was established in 1915. Manning consisted of one officer, two NCOs, and six men.[73] By 1916, the high demand for photographs overwhelmed the centrally

---

[66] Hahn, 258-259.

[67] Hahn, 261.

[68] Stewart, "Report on the Organization and Operation of Intelligence 'A'," Conger Papers, Box 2, USAMHI.

[69] Henry, "Report on my Visit to the British Army," Conger Papers, Box 2, USAMHI.

[70] Hahn, 118-119

[71] Stewart, "Report on the Organization and Operation of Intelligence 'A'," Conger Papers, Box 2, USAMHI.

[72] Stewart, "Report on the Organization and Operation of Intelligence 'A'," Conger Papers, Box 2, USAMHI.

[73] Campbell, "Notes on Aerial Photography," TNA, PRO: AIR 1/7/6/98/20.

managed wing photo sections, resulting in critical prints and information arriving late. This was especially true for artillery, which required constant updating of photographs to supplement its firing maps. Under the April 1916 reorganization, the foundation producing and disseminating aerial photography was placed at squadron level. The Army Corps staff gave orders directly to the commander of the attached squadron for all photographs within five miles of the Corps front. Beyond this area, photography was the responsibility of the army wing. To speed up the delivery of prints required a small photo section in each corps squadron and in each army reconnaissance squadron.[74] Demands for aerial photographs continued to increase. In February 1917, 40 cameras with lenses were issued to the RFC. Plate production was estimated at 2,400 dozen. Supply started to meet the demand nine months later, when monthly camera production increased over six-fold to 340 cameras, and plate production was up five-fold to 9,600 dozen.[75]

In the last year of the war, logistical support for the Photo Sections was managed by the British Air Ministry in London. Since the Air Ministry focused on strategic issues, wings and squadrons were left with accomplishing most of the analysis. The Air Ministry's Equipment and Personnel Branch did not engage in policy development as it concerned aerial photography. It was, frankly, due to ignorance about the subject. One British memoir of the experience recalled the absence of senior deliberation on aerial photography in a rather sharp tone, "It is strange how the general staff officers fall short in imagination with regard to Air Photography which [was] left without sound and technical advice."[76]

The exponential increase in demand for aerial photographic product during the battle of the Somme overwhelmed the capabilities of photographic equipment resident at the squadrons. One attempt to increase production through half-tone printing failed due to slow production and unsatisfactory results. The demand for large photographs of trench areas required a more sophisticated laboratory. The British AP and SS then offered to assume responsibility for meeting the demand. In October 1916 they established an experimental section at Amiens, equipped with a mechanical photo-printing plant, to produce up to 5,000 whole-plate bromide prints a day. The volume of production was massive. The photographs—including those for intelligence and police purposes—taken or reproduced rose in number from 25,000 in 1916 to 2½ million (whole-plate equivalent) during the first ten months of 1918. The results were so successful that a similar production facility was authorized for each Army. Photographic work extended to panoramas, mosaics, maps, and stereoscopic photographs, as well as reproduction of Graves Registration photographs and police photographs of deserters, escaped prisoners, and spies of both sexes. Also, general outdoor photography for operations, training, and record purposes was accomplished.[77]

British intelligence was well-crafted and reflected a penchant for detail. Contemporary American diagrams of the British intelligence architecture clearly illustrated that the demand on intelligence was pertinent to all echelons. The addition of aerial photography increased awareness of the battleground for British combatants, while it enhanced the credibility of the intelligence. Through aerial photography, intelligence became tangible and clearly visible, and it was measured to an impressive cartographic standard of one yard. With the BIO's establishment at the lowest squadron echelon, British intelligence expertise reinforced the initial intent of aviation to meet the rapidly evolving demands of modern-day combat.

When the marriage of RFC and RNAS resources occurred in 1918, creating the RAF, intelligence operations gained further stature. British aerial reconnaissance was reorganized beyond the tactical realm, building a foundation for strategical analysis that served the expansive British Empire. Each challenge became a catalyst for modern intelligence. The demands of aerial bombardment against the German heart-

---

74 Jones, II, 177.

75 "Provision and Supply," in "Re-Organization of Photographic Activities," TNA, PRO: AIR 2/163.

76 Toye, "History of Photography," TNA, PRO: AIR 1/724/91/1.

77 Edmonds, *1916*, I, 131-132.

FIGURE 122. **J.T.C. Moore-Brabazon made British history as the first citizen to acquire an aero license.** Source: J.T.C. Moore-Brabazon, *The Brabazon Story* (London: William Heinemann, Ltd., 1956).

land prompted greater analysis of cities, ports, and strategic lines of communication. Ongoing military operations in Palestine and Mesopotamia led intelligence operations to address new cultures and frontiers. Such depth proved invaluable to British military operations in the 20th century. The British penchant for detail was manifested on a global scale and established intelligence analytical excellence that went beyond the postwar period to the Second World War. It became the rootstock for the professional intelligence service that exists today.

FIGURE 123. **Moore-Brabazon with "The first pig to fly."** Source: Moore-Brabazon, *The Brabazon Story*.

THE RENAISSANCE MAN
Lieutenant Colonel John Theodore Cuthbert
(J.T.C.) Moore-Brabazon
(8 Feb 1884 – 17 May 1964)

J.T.C. Moore-Brabazon was a true Renaissance man. His aristocratic roots provided a catalyst to adventure, allowing access to opportunities beyond the reach of the average British citizen. Moore-Brabazon took on whatever challenge suited his interests. The genesis of motor-driven technology suited his drive. He took to motor racing with a flourish, winning one of the first races in the history of the sport, the Circuit des Ardennes, in 1907.[78] He expanded his appetite for high-risk adventure to the new phenomenon of aviation, making British aviation history as the first to acquire a British pilot's license.[79] He went on to become the first Englishman to fly an aeroplane

---

[78] Occleshaw, 63.

[79] 2Lt J.T.C. Moore-Brabazon, "For Promotion to Lt. and Refund of £ 75 paid for R.A.C. Certificate," TNA, PRO: WO 339/23903.

Chapter 10: British Intelligence and Photographic Interpretation

(Voisin) in England. His passion for competition led to victory in the first all-English aeroplane race sponsored by the *British Daily Mail*. The event spurred on the birth of the British aeroplane industry. He was a British spokesman for the tenor of the times when he reflected, "I think we were all a little mad, we were all suffering from dreams of such a wonderful future."[80]

Moore-Brabazon possessed an incredible balance of personality and drive. Known as "Brab" to his friends, he "would always be one to tell a story or two."[81] Yet he was passionate to the extreme in achieving the best from his endeavors. Shortly after the outbreak of the war, he enlisted in the RFC and was commissioned a second lieutenant in the Special Reserve.[82] Moore-Brabazon's reputation for taking on new challenges was recognized. His early endeavors with wireless transmissions led to an assignment on the technical side, exemplified by the RFC's No. 9 Squadron. His personality complemented the challenges of the military culture, though he would confess later to being initially petrified to the ways of the military, feigning laryngitis while in command of troops during a march. Thanks to the discrete assistance of the unit's Sergeant-Major, Moore-Brabazon soon learned the basics of command at close quarters.[83] However, his aristocratic background required adjustment to the realities of military decorum. "You will obey your superior officers," the No. 9 Squadron commander once remarked early on. Moore-Brabazon replied, "Superior officer?—senior, if you please, sir."[84]

FIGURE 124. **Photograph of Major Moore-Brabazon.** Source: Nesbit, *Eyes of the RAF.*

Moore-Brabazon found his niche in the rapidly evolving world of aerial reconnaissance. "It suddenly dawned on me that photography from the air was bound to come, and that few could know much about it."[85] The RFC Chief of Staff, Colonel Frederick Sykes, tasked Moore-Brabazon to lead the RFC's development of aerial photography. To gain an appreciation of the technology, he first met with members of the French *Section Technique*, the leading research office in aerial photography on the Allied side.[86] He was soon joined by two other brilliant British experts on photography, C.D.M. Campbell and Victor Laws. The three of them together constituted an impressive collection

[80] Moore-Brabazon, 48.
[81] Coleman, 130.
[82] Moore-Brabazon, 84-86.
[83] Moore-Brabazon, 87.
[84] Moore-Brabazon, 89.
[85] Moore-Brabazon, 92.
[86] Occleshaw, 64.

FIGURE 125. **Lieutenant Colonel Moore-Brabazon, front center, at photo conference.** Source: Gorrell Report, NARA.

of expertise. However, when they arrived at the RFC's No. 1 Wing, Moore-Brabazon remembered, "We were about as welcome as measles."[87] They persevered and created the prototype "A" Type camera. "Six box type cameras were evolved, this being the real R.F.C. camera, and from that moment photography improved a great deal."[88]

Throughout the war, Moore-Brabazon was the catalyst behind British aerial photography's evolution. He led the development of the entire suite of British aerial cameras employed during the war. His intense scientific approach to all challenges led to the resolution of several key issues limiting aerial photography utility, such as designing camera mounts to reduce vibration and using photographic flares for night photography.[89] By the end of the war, he spearheaded the Allies' role in many aerial photographic endeavors, including acquiring optics for cameras, assisting U.S. aerial photography staffs in training and organization and assisting in the ongoing reorganization of aerial photographic interpretation roles at squadron and wings. Reflecting later in life on his accomplishments, he wrote, "As to my own job, I always thought it wonderful that there was never a rounder peg in a rounder hole…. It was an extremely busy and complicated job, but I say without fear of contradiction that at one time I knew more about aerial photography than anyone else in the world. That is a bold claim to make about any subject, but I am perfectly convinced that I am right."[90]

After the war, Moore-Brabazon continued his remarkable career. He led the development of the British aviation community. At the same time, he pursued a successful career in politics. He served as Minister of Transport and later as Minister of Aircraft Production during the Second World War. He was forced to resign in 1942 following the opposition Labour Party's censure over a remark he made in a private forum that the Germans and Russians should exterminate each other. After the war, Moore-Brabazon became an elder statesman, serving in the House of Lords, and remained very active in a broad range of endeavors.[91]

---

[87] Moore-Brabazon, 92.

[88] Moore-Brabazon, "Photography in the RAF."

[89] Occleshaw, 64.

[90] Moore-Brabazon, 96.

[91] "Lord Brabazon of Tara Dies; First Briton to Fly in England; Aviator had Been Early Auto Racer and Minister of Transport for Churchill," Special to the *New York Times*, 18 May 1964. ProQuest Historical Newspapers *The New York Times* (1851- 2001), 29.

Chapter 10: British Intelligence and Photographic Interpretation

CHAPTER 11

AMERICAN EXPEDITIONARY FORCE INTELLIGENCE AND PHOTOGRAPHIC ORGANIZATION

Notwithstanding the horrors of the war, American involvement in the Great War was typecast in dialogue of the day as participating in the "Game." There was a spirit of competition invoked by youthful exuberance. As 2nd Lieutenant Prentiss M. Terry, 91st Aero Squadron BIO, concluded in his manual on intelligence, "the Position [of intelligence] affords you the Opportunity to play a Positive Part in the Game which will help toward Beating the Boche and that is what you are fighting for."[1] Victory meant teamwork and the arriving American forces were the rookies in a well-established game. The U.S. Air Service had to come to terms with obvious shortcomings that came with the nation's overall lack of preparedness for total war. It opted to follow both French and British approaches. The French Plan Directeur and the British BIO served as fundamental building blocks for the Americans' intelligence and aerial photographic interpretation while accommodating the AEF's own needs. The American military culture soon developed an awareness and appreciation of aerial photography's role as an intelligence source supporting military operations. The ultimate benefactor from this experience for the remainder of the century was military intelligence itself.

The Allies voiced serious concerns over America's inadequate preparation six months after entry in the war. One British staff officer's Memorandum to the Air Board conveyed the feeling, "American thoughts and methods do not appear to be at all well understood in this country. At the same time there is so much to be gained from ensuring harmonious action between the two services that it appeared well worth while to ensure if it be possible."[2] The lifeblood of the British and French was ebbing quickly as the war entered the fourth year. Allies and Americans had to quickly come to an understanding on what was required to fight a well-established positional war. "When America declared war on Germany the striking feature was their total unpreparedness in every branch and this was added to in the case of the whole subject of military aeronautics by an absolute lack of knowledge in every department of this subject. This lack of knowledge existed not only among the general public but even with their aviation experts, both Naval and Military."[3]

U.S. military intelligence was also totally incapable of handling the challenges of modern warfare. Most of the state-of-the-art intelligence processes, to include radio intercept, flash- and

---

[1] 2nd Lt Prentiss M. Terry, 91st Aero Squadron, 1st Army, "Notes on Branch Intelligence," 19 August 1918, Gorrell Report, ser. M, r. 44, NARA.

[2] Wing Cdr Seddon, "Report … on Co-Operation between Britain and American Air Services,"13 September 1917, TNA, PRO: AIR 2/35.

[3] Seddon, "Report … on Co-Operation between Britain and American Air Services," TNA, PRO: AIR 2/35.

FIGURE 126. **Lieutenant Colonel George O. Squier served as military attaché to London during the first year of the war. He later assumed command of the U.S. Army Signal Corps.** Source: Maurer Maurer, ed., *The U.S. Air Service in World War I* (Washington, DC: GPO, 1978).

on a tentative intelligence organization based on the British model. The father of U.S. Army Intelligence, Colonel Ralph Van Deman, employed the Military Intelligence (MI) paradigm of both a "positive" and "negative" approach to intelligence. Positive referred to useful information about the enemy, to include intelligence from aerial photographs. Negative intelligence referred to enemy undercover agents to acquire and determine information (in today's parlance counterintelligence).[5] MI-7 became the element within the War Department that handled cartography and to a limited extent aerial photography.[6] The other key figure in American military intelligence was Major General George O. Squier, who established the Aviation Section of the U.S. Army Signal Corps. Squier had been military attaché to London for four years prior to his assignment to the Aviation Section in May 1916. His reporting helped establish awareness of evolving military operations and intelligence processes employed by the British and spurred American military interest in developing similar programs prior to entry into the war. He was later promoted and made Chief Signal Officer in February 1917; he continued in charge of the Aviation Section for most of that year.[7]

As the United States mobilized for war, the U.S. Army Signal Corps became the first branch to create an American aerial photographic program. Officials quickly realized that if the program were to be successfully implemented, they had to defer to the Allies for military aerial photography technology. At first, they commenced a buying spree of any available camera equipment to rectify their supply shortfall. The U.S. Army Signal Corps purchased large quantities of motion picture cameras, hand-held cameras and view cameras. However, these acquisitions did not meet the requirements for aerial photography. The Americans were quickly coming to terms with the realization that they did not yet possess their Allies' three years of wartime ex-

sound-ranging and most important, aerial photography, did not exist within the American Army. What little was known did not carry any weight with the Army hierarchy.[4] Prior to arriving overseas, American military staffs decided

[4] Barnes, "History of Photographic Section #4," 1, Gorrell Report, ser. G, r. 24, NARA.

[5] Roy Talbert, *Negative Intelligence: The Army and the American Left, 1917-1941* (Jackson, MS: University Press of Mississippi, 1991), 20-21.

[6] Maj E. Alexander Powell, *The Army Behind the Army* (New York: Charles Scribner's Sons, 1919), 334.

[7] U.S. War Department, "Report of the Director of Military Aeronautics," in *War Department Annual Reports, 1918* (3 vol., Washington DC: GPO, 1919), I, 1382.

Chapter II: AEF Intelligence and Photographic Organization

perience in aerial photographic reconnaissance. In 1917, the Signal Corps deferred to its Allied counterparts for guidance regarding the standard photographic process and equipment.[8] Likewise, the Americans were forced to acquire maps through any means possible, "begging, borrowing, and perhaps stealing maps of everything from Dieppe to Damascus…. We needed maps for every possible contingency that might confront General Pershing."[9]

Reorganizing the American military to meet the initial demands of mobilization resulted in the Signal Corps becoming the foster parent to the U.S. Air Service. The British and French were quick to recommend that a separate independent air service similar to their air ministries be established to handle the necessary requirements for establishing an effective operating air arm. The recommendations were partially accepted and changes were implemented. Squier continued in the capacity of Chief Signals Officer. A Division of Military Aeronautics was established, with Brigadier General William L. Kenly assigned as Director. Military Aeronautics served as the administrative directorate for aeronautical training, to include developing aerial reconnaissance within the United States.[10]

Despite the U.S. War Department's initial efforts to institutionalize aerial photography, it was the AEF that became the primary proponent for aerial photography in the war. Upon arrival in France, the initial AEF cadre took important steps with the French and British Intelligence authorities, acquiring significant amounts of data based on three years of in-depth analysis and study. The staff commenced careful study of their Allied counterparts' intelligence architecture, establishing observation facilities to monitor ongoing operations. Shortly after arriving in theater, staffs commenced visits to the GQG's 2ᵉ Bureau, IIIᵉᵐᵉ Armée, 11ᵉᵐᵉ CA, and 35ᵉᵐᵉ Division d'infanterie. The Americans then proceeded to the British headquarters and witnessed Ypres

operations with the British Second Army.[11] The Americans were able to follow up on the June 1917 British offensive at Messines Ridge, a battle which was considered by the British to have been the most successful use of intelligence in the war up to that time.[12] Concern with the best way to manage military intelligence also impacted the U.S. Air Service. Discussion evolved over the months into a debate about who was responsible for the intelligence resources. By the spring of 1918, American staff officers were sent out to examine what best suited air intelligence. Major D.M. Henry and Major C.F. Thompson of the U.S. Air Service reviewed both Allies intelligence operations. The decision to process intelligence through a BIO became the preferred option for the staffs.[13]

Both French and British intelligence programs were worth emulating. Their adherence to known intelligence theory and practice had built-in benefits. Active liaison between the French and British intelligence staffs illustrated the value of progressive ideas. In recalling the relations between the newly arriving Americans and the well-experienced French and British staffs, Brigadier General Nolan recalled that the British were "very anxious that they would make us understand how serious all these things were. The French had the same solicitude but they were less tactful in expressing it…. Their attitude was more 'Well, this is the way it is; you can take it or leave it.' The British attitude was 'this is the way it is: for God's sake take it, take our word for it'."[14]

The Americans decided that the key factor in speeding intelligence accommodation to the theater was tied up with geopolitical and ethnic identity. Like the Americans, British forces had to organize intelligence to serve an expeditionary force operating in a foreign country. Also, language was a challenge. The American military assessment that both British and French intelligence

[8] Crowell and Wilson, II, 419-420.

[9] Nolan, "G-2-C, Topography," 3-4, Nolan Papers, USAMHI.

[10] "Report of the Director of Military Aeronautics," in *War Department Annual Reports, 1918*, I, 1382-83.

[11] G-2, GHQ, AEF, to Chief of Staff, "Report," 15 June 1919, NASM.

[12] G-2, GHQ, AEF, to Chief of Staff, "Report," 15 June 1919, NASM.

[13] Alfred E. Bellinger, "Relations of the Air Service with G-2," Gorrell Report, ser. M, r. 41, NARA.

[14] Brig Gen Dennis E. Nolan, "Intelligence," 21, in Nolan Papers, USAMHI.

FIGURE 127. **Two of the greatest advocates of the U.S. aerial reconnaissance role in World War I were Colonel William Mitchell (right) and Lieutenant Colonel Lewis Brereton.** Source: Maurer, ed., *The U.S. Air Service in World War I*

systems accomplished the same results in very much the same manner naturally favored emulation of the more adaptable British system. American military seniors had their own expeditionary challenges. The end result was that U.S. military policy and regulations on intelligence mirrored those of the British. This approach was then suggested to General Pershing and approved.[15] However, intelligence resources such as maps required adaptation to whoever had the supply. The Americans borrowed the French system of designating accurately a given point by numbered coordinates in determining vertical and horizontal grid lines. Such maps proved invaluable when Americans were subsequently assigned to French sectors.[16]

In addition to establishing an intelligence framework relevant to theater operations, the American aviation community had to contend with a flurry of rotations among the senior commanders for aviation. American adjustment to the method of aerial reconnaissance as perfected

by French and British experiences required a pronounced degree of self-initiative. Evolution of the U.S. Air Service in theater was far from a static experience. The first Chief of the U.S. Air Service, Brigadier General Foulois, accompanied the AEF Headquarters when it moved from Paris to Chaumont. A few months later, the entire Air Service staff separated from the AEF Headquarters and established itself at Toul. Along with the geographic separation, ongoing reorganizations caused the American senior aviators to be reassigned. In January 1918, the AEF's 1st Army Corps under the command of Major General Hunter Liggett became the central administrative command for all the American forces on the French front. Colonel Mitchell was appointed as the 1st Army Corps Chief of Air Service. His aerial organization served two masters, the French *VIIIème Armée* (which had tactical control) and Major General Liggett (administrative control). When the first American squadrons arrived in April 1918, they were initially sent to the quiet Toul sector in eastern France. Mitchell, in turn, moved his headquarters to the Toul sector to maintain greater oversight and control.[17] A month later, Pershing appointed Brigadier General Mason M. Patrick Chief of the U.S. Air Service, relieving General Foulois, who was appointed Assistant Chief of Air Service, Zone of Advance (ZOA). Mitchell was placed under Foulois and provided him an opportunity for aviation command as the Brigade Commander, 1st Brigade, Air Service.[18] These changes translated into a greater dependency on Allied experience and policy for the remainder of the war.

U.S. forces had no doctrinal basis for air operations when they arrived in France in 1917; however, by the end of the first year, they had managed to establish a base of understanding of how aerial observation and photographic interpretation worked to support the demands of the forces. Their emphasis remained tactical. Strategic policy evolved in the post-war era.[19] The Americans subscribed to common intelligence

---

[15] G-2, GHQ, AEF, to Chief of Staff, "Report," 15 June 1919, NASM.

[16] Nolan, "G-2-C, Topography," 4, Nolan Papers, USAMHI.

[17] "History of the Air Service," I, Gorrell Report, ser. C, r. 12, NARA; Frank, *American Air Service Observation*, 126.

[18] "History of the Air Service," I, Gorrell Report, ser. C, r. 12, NARA; Frank, *American Air Service Observation*, 127.

[19] James Cooke, *The U.S. Air Service in the Great War, 1917-1919* (Westport, CT: Praeger, 1996), 59-60.

Chapter II: AEF Intelligence and Photographic Organization

practices employed by both the French and the British. The AEF G-2 staff produced on a daily basis its own version of the Plan Directeur, distributing three copies for headquarters.[20] When the American 1st Division arrived in the Toul Sector in January 1918, it was under the control of the French CA, and was required to conform to the practices of a French division within the sector. This included adding a topographic officer and draughtsman to the division to "make hasty drawings, sketches, and diagrams for the General Staff of the Division, study aeroplane photographs of enemy territory, to keep up to date the sector maps showing both Intelligence and Operations Information, to distribute maps, and to collect and forward to the Corps at prescribed intervals the corrections in trenches and other military features for incorporation in new editions of the battle map at Army Headquarters."[21]

The Americans duplicated French techniques for employing army reconnaissance assets for photographic validation of the other intelligence sources. Intelligence manning soon included aerial photographic interpreters to assist in the production of intelligence summaries.[22] As among the Allied counterparts, aerial photography was emphasized as a primary source of intelligence. "The making of aerial photographs of enemy territory is considered one of the most vital functions of the Air Service."[23] At the higher echelons, senior officers relied on the G-2 for advice on aerial photographic reconnaissance. The G-2 subdivision prepared the First Army Summary of Intelligence, providing substantive information on "enemy works, based on the traditional intelligence sources such as prisoner interrogations, validated by aerial photography."[24] In addition, GHQ, AEF, published every midnight a Battle Order map which portrayed the known location of enemy troops in the sector. This was distributed to aero squadrons for review by the air crew

before each sortie.[25] It was testament to the First Army's G-2 office that the airplane photograph office was originally set up "with no clearly defined sphere of operations." By the summer of 1918, the function expanded to assume the responsibility for all information on enemy works, whatever the source.[26]

At lower echelons, the American intelligence process simulated the British style. The hub of American intelligence was embodied in the BIO. The BIO was assigned to the photographic group by the AEF General Staff G-2. Information on the enemy pertaining, directly or indirectly, to aerial operations served as the BIO's primary focus. As it pertained to aerial photographic interpretation, the BIO also had responsibility for assembly, study, interpretation, and distribution. Aerial observer responsibilities included support to the BIO in photographic interpretation.[27] Once the sortie results were explained, the BIO was the responsible officer for updating everyone on new developments. Key actions such as enemy troop movements and transport activity, and facilities such as railroads, dumps and aerodromes, and other targets of interest were covered in the mission report. The "did not observe" comment was just as important as the significant sighting. "The observer must at all time report every thing that he sees, regardless of how unimportant it may seem to him."[28]

In the summer of 1918, the 91st Aero Squadron, the lead U.S. Air Service strategical reconnaissance squadron, published an extensive manual on intelligence for both air crews and intelligence personnel. It represented an impressive effort by the squadron's BIO, 2nd Lt. Prentiss Terry. The manual covered every known facet of the squadron's role in acquiring information, to include procedures for reviewing available intelligence, maps to be reviewed, and a series of self-generated forms designed within the squadron to

[20] G-2, 1st Army, to Chief of Staff, "Account of the Operation," 50, Drum Papers, Box 14, USAMHI.

[21] Nolan, "G-2-C Topography," 7-8, Nolan Papers, USAMHI.

[22] "Historical Account," 57, Drum Papers, USAMHI.

[23] "The Development of Aerial Photography," 12 July 1918, Gorrell Report, ser. G, r. 24, NARA.

[24] G-2, 1st Army, to Chief of Staff, "Account of the Operation," 60, 48, Drum Papers, Box 14, USAMHI.

[25] 1st Lt John Snyder, "'Notes on Reconnaissance,' Lecture given at 2nd A.I.C.," Gorrell Report, ser. J, r. 34, NARA.

[26] G-2, 1st Army, to Chief of Staff, "Account of the Operation,"45, Drum Papers, Box 14, USAMHI.

[27] "Tactical History of Corps Observation: The First Corps Observation Group in the Toul Sector," in Maurer, ed., U.S. Air Service, I, 173.

[28] Snyder, "Notes on Reconnaissance," Gorrell Report, ser J, r. 34, NARA.

include the "Observer's Report" and "Summary of Information Obtained from Photographs." This comprehensive effort provided squadron members with the most detailed understanding of the intelligence process at the squadron level. Terry's manual included the only known illustration of a standardized format for aerial photographic interpretation. The header to the form was a basic description of the function: "That the best results of Photographic study may be obtained some form should be used whereby the information derived from that study may be fully written down and a record kept as to the Photographs upon which the information is found and the map area which covers it."[29] Such efforts did not escape the attention of Capitaine Pépin. He personally reviewed the manuscript to ensure the document captured the essence of intelligence collection and processing[30]

To directly support the American divisions assigned to the front, the AEF acquired topographic expertise from its own 29th Engineers. The personnel were subjected to training in interpretation and restitution of aerial photographs and provided with whatever supplies could be acquired. As more AEF divisions arrived, the supply of engineering expertise from the 29th Engineers was depleted. The solution was to create a mobile training team (in today's parlance) to instruct the division staff on topographic skills prior to proceeding to training in the line under the French.[31] U.S. Air Service photographic reconnaissance tasking came from Army or Corps intelligence offices to the commanding officer of the Observation Group. The Group's operations officer assigned the mission to a squadron and designated the size of the camera to be used. The squadron operations officer then assigned the mission to the observer and the Group's photographic officer. The BIO then commenced preparing the intelligence effort for the mission that started upon receipt of the photographic order.[32] Upon completion of the aerial photographic reconnaissance sortie, the camera was downloaded, plates developed, and prints produced. As one photo laboratory technician recalled the process:

> When dry, the prints were removed from the rack and sorted in sets for each negative and rushed to the Intelligence Department. Here our work ended. The Intelligence Department and General Headquarters worked out the strategy to be pursued and the prints to be distributed to the artillery, infantry, and other departments so operations could be coordinated.[33]

Timely reporting was an indispensable goal. Army squadrons were to produce photographs for the consumer within six hours of the reconnaissance aeroplane's landing.[34] The British baseline for "rush copy" prints remained at five hours, with a photograph of the target taken at 1000 hours being processed, interpreted, disseminated, and received by priority customers at 1500 hours. Communicating the results of the observation sorties began at the landing site. The 1st Corps Observation Group had telephone lines set up to link the Group and Squadron headquarters to the pilot and observer tent on the field. Long-distance lines were maintained with tactical command posts and higher Air Service headquarters. Radio liaison between the Group and all points in the area was established from the radio station. In case of communication failure, the U.S. Air Service advance units at the front also employed pigeons. The Group maintained two pigeon lofts in support of this requirement.[35] The modern world of communications came with its own risks. Reporting to higher headquarters via telephone covered the spectrum of events, to include discussion of operations, intelligence, and developments at other fronts.[36] The American 1st Army G-2 maintained a Radio Intelligence Section not only to monitor enemy radio stations, but

---

[29] This quotation is the only documented format for a WW I aerial photographic interpretation report that the author was able to uncover; to what extent this form was actually used is unknown. Terry, "Notes on Branch Intelligence," Gorrell Report, ser. M, r. 44, NARA.

[30] Pépin Papers, MA&E, Paris.

[31] Nolan, "G-2-C Topography," 8, Nolan Papers, USAMHI.

---

[32] "Photography," Gorrell Report, ser. G, r. 24, NARA.

[33] Note sentence grammar; Dixon, *Diary*, 51.

[34] G-2, 1st Army, to Chief of Staff, "Account of the Operation," 52, Drum Papers, Box 14, USAMHI.

[35] Frank, *American Air Service Observation*, 219.

[36] G-2, 1st Army, to Chief of Staff, "Account of the Operation," 8, Drum Papers, Box 14, USAMHI.

Chapter II: AEF Intelligence and Photographic Organization

to conduct "the policing of our own telephone lines near the front for dangerous conversation which would be overheard by the enemy." Those that violated security were reported to responsible authorities.[37]

America's most notable contribution toward developing aerial reconnaissance and photographic interpretation lay in establishing the entire network for aerial photographic support. At the time war was declared in April 1917, the War Department and the United States Signal Corps were charged with organizing the nation's military for war, to include organization, supply of personnel and materiel, and the greater challenge of training and production. The Signal Corps had major priorities, to include establishing an air service. Aerial photography was too unknown to be relevant for staff consideration. However, thanks to persistent efforts by a core element of photographic experts, the U.S. Signal Corps established the Photographic Division (2 August 1917). Under the lead of the pre-war explorer Major James Barnes, the Signal Corps' Photographic Division commenced a review of existing literature on the subject, to include British intelligence reports and French aviation photographs. Probably the most important figure in the seminal period of American military photography was Barnes' deputy, Edward Steichen. Barnes acknowledged that Steichen was an extremely credible figure in the effort to establish the U.S. military's first efforts with aerial photography. Without Steichen's "aid and advice the Photographic Division might at any time, have gone on the rocks."[38]

The Signal Corps central office faced major challenges as it proceeded to establish aerial photography in the Army. Everything had to be created from scratch. A list of approximately 100 applicants with known photographic experience was compiled and solicitations forwarded for recruitment.[39] Military training camps, photographic laboratories, and a logistical network for photographic supplies had to be established

FIGURE 128. **Major Barnes (right) and Captain Steichen established the Photographic Division of the U.S. Army Signal Corps.** Source: James Barnes, *From Then Till Now: Anecdotal Portraits and Transcript Pages from Memories' Tablets* (New York: D. Appleton-Century Company, 1934).

and personnel trained. Not only did supplies and equipment have to be generated from within the United States, but also the Allied combatants had to allocate already scarce resources. Grooming a new generation of photographic personnel required establishing a curriculum and finding instructors possessing the immediate skills required for aerial photography.[40] All of this occurred during intense competition over priorities in a growing list of urgent requirements generated by the mobilizing Army. Considering the total lack of familiarity among the senior ranks about aerial photography, the accomplishments of this core group were amazing. They stuck to their message throughout, and wisely so. "Nearly nine-tenths of the information for the offensive or defensive" operations in the war were being

---

[37] G-2, 1st Army, to Chief of Staff, "Account of the Operation," 36-37, Drum Papers, Box 14, USAMHI.

[38] Barnes, *From Then Till Now*, 477; Barnes, "History Photographic Section #4," 2-3, Gorrell Report, ser. G, r. 24, NARA; Penelope Niven, *Steichen* (New York: Clarkson Potter Publishers, 1997), 449-450.

[39] Barnes, "History Photographic Section #4," 4.

[40] Niven, 450.

FIGURE 129. **Thanks to the leadership of Barnes and Steichen, Photographic Sections became an integral part of the U.S. Observation Group Aero Squadrons. The 5th Photographic Section supported the 99th Aero Squadron. The unit commander, Lieutenant Sileo, on the left, is with a colleague in front of the photographic van.** Source: USAFA McDermott Library Special Collections (SMS57).

produced by "the work of cameras under trained direction in the air."[41] The Army Signal Corps deserves credit for transitioning America's military to a credible foundation for aerial photography throughout 1917. In November 1917, Barnes and Steichen arrived in theater to establish the Photographic Division for the AEF. They came across an AEF staff already overwhelmed with trying to establish a credible military to aid the Allies. The two officers were left to their own discretion and they faced major challenges in establishing the program in theater. Assistance was limited both from within theater and the home offices. No photographic material arrived from the U.S. until June 1918.[42]

The American cadre established strong links with the Allied aerial photographic pioneers, including the British photographic team of Lieutenant-Colonel Moore-Brabazon, Major Toye, and Major Campbell; and the French Capitaine Pépin and Lieutenant Labussiere.[43] They participated in key conferences regarding photographic standards and training in December 1917. Both British and American photo experts attended a British conference at Blendecques that addressed aerial reconnaissance and photographic interpretation roles with Army and Corps Intelligence. British emphasis on the subject was reflected in the spectrum of attendees: 45 officers represented Aerial Observation, Army and Corps Intelligence, Heavy Artillery, Counter Batteries, Field Survey and Topographical Service attended.[44] A week later, both Barnes and Steichen met with the French at Châlons and adopted the French manual, *Étude et Exploitation des Photographies Aériennes* for AEF aerial photographic training. Despite this critical interaction with the Allies, the AEF senior staff was too overwhelmed by other pressing challenges to pay attention to Barnes and Steichen. Photographic reports were ignored. Despite their frustration, Barnes and Steichen played a significant role serving as the American representatives to several international forums on photography,

[41] Niven, 450-451.
[42] Barnes, "History Photographic Section #4," 11.
[43] Barnes, *From Then Till Now*, 487.
[44] Barnes, "History Photographic Section #4," 13-14.

Chapter 11: AEF Intelligence and Photographic Organization

where discussions addressed standardizing lens and plate size.[45]

The efforts by the Barnes and Steichen advance team proved very successful in the end. They established training facilities and curricula, represented the American position on aerial camera standards, acquired the vanguard of a significant aerial photography team, and initiated the logistical infrastructure necessary to support American efforts toward the end of the war. Their culminating effort was the delineation of responsibilities between the forward-deployed ZOA and the rear echelon support Services of Supply (SOS). It was agreed that the best personnel were to work ZOA operational missions. Their efforts helped prepare the way for establishing the American first Photographic Section, supporting the operations of the newly arrived 1st Aero Squadron in April 1918.[46] The Herculean effort by the photographic vanguard did result in establishing Photographic Sections both in the United States and in-theater with the AEF. The demand for aerial photographic skills continued to increase while resources in-theater remained extremely limited. One Steichen proposal requested photographic elements at ten separate organizations, to include Headquarters, Air Service, headquarters of an army, photographic laboratories with observation and bombardment squadrons, air depots, and the Photographic School at 2nd Aviation Instruction Center (AIC). However, the proposal never took shape due to lack of proper equipment and the need to borrow what could be spared from the Allies. Only two laboratories (No. 1 with the 1st Corps Observation Group at Ourches, and No. 2 with the 91st Aero Squadron at Gondreville) were partially functioning by April 1918.[47]

The Barnes and Steichen photographic team separated in February 1918 to work for different offices in the theater. Barnes was eventually recalled to Washington, DC, to further assist War Department efforts to standardize the Photographic Section. Upon arrival, however, Barnes was reassigned to Rochester, NY, to assume command of the photographic school. Steichen remained in

Europe past the Armistice and became the most knowledgeable U.S. expert on aerial photography.[48] Thanks to the tireless efforts of Barnes and Steichen, the first two U.S. Photographic Sections (Photographic Section 1 and Photographic Section 2) had arrived in theater in April 1918. Unfortunately, the two units arrived without any usable equipment. Extensive efforts by the AEF's Photographic Division had been made to ensure that equipment for the required photographic laboratory would arrive unscathed. The marked crates with the outside label of photographic equipment showed up in England; however, the contents were not the critical photographic equipment required but a collection of 24 long-handled shovels. Nonetheless, the esprit of America's initial Photographic Section cadre was not to be dampened. The personnel proceeded on to France and marched with shovels at their shoulder. The incident was subsequently labeled an effort "to camouflage this important agrandizement [sic] of the forces of the A.E.F."[49]

Lessons Learned—The American Way

As more squadrons proceeded to the front, increased photographic coverage was acquired. The volume of coverage soon exceeded the capability on the ground to process and disseminate the information. At the end of the war, the reviews showed the infrastructure supporting observation was inadequate. Division of responsibility for photography between the Air Service and Intelligence Section was one area that needed attention.[50] Another was effective rear echelon coverage. "In general our back area photographic information was unsatisfactory, owing to the rapidity of our advance and the bad weather, which combined to keep our Squadrons photographing the areas just ahead."[51]

After the Armistice Brigadier General Mitchell issued a "Provisional Manual of Operations of Air Service Units" on 23 December 1918. He was working out of Koblenz, Germany, in the

[45] Barnes, "History Photographic Section #4," 13-14.
[46] Barnes, "History Photographic Section #4," 15-17.
[47] Barnes, "History Photographic Section #4," 21-22.

[48] Barnes, "History Photographic Section #4," 21-22.
[49] Barnes, "History Photographic Section #4," 18.
[50] Steichen, "Aerial Photography," Gorrell Report, ser. G, r. 24, NARA.
[51] G-2, 1st Army, to Chief of Staff, "Account of the Operation," 56-57, Drum Papers, Box 14, USAMHI.

Army of Occupation. His vision for structuring aviation to be more dynamic included a strong reconnaissance arm. His reconnaissance target priorities were "all enemy works, such as dumps, lines of defense in rear of the front lines, concentration points, aviation fields hospitals, and railroad yards." He foresaw that aerial reconnaissance had to focus on the emerging mobile targets that used roads and railroads to accomplish their objective. Mosaics of lines of communication were necessary to provide the mobile battlefield commander with a definitive look at the overall force in motion. Mitchell recognized that the Army had to be intimately involved throughout the reconnaissance process. Priorities were to be levied "as far in advance as possible, [and] the objectives to be photographed, together with the order of their importance."[52] His guidance reemphasized the need for timely and effective aerial reconnaissance and the intelligence that was important for the operation. "During an attack, especially, speed in distribution of the photographs is of the utmost importance, and delivery of the first urgency prints should be made by airplane."[53]

Mitchell's vision was further refined by Lieutenant Colonel William C. Sherman, Chief of Staff of the First Army Air Service. Sherman authored a "Tentative Manual for the Employment of the Air Service" in early 1919, which was subsequently published in April 1919 under the title *Notes on Recent Operations*. Sherman covered aerial reconnaissance and the supporting infrastructure of the photographic laboratory and intelligence.[54] His manuscript emphasized the BIO function and described the basic functions which had become institutionalized during the war.[55] It also illustrated the normal sortie altitudes required for effective reconnaissance; 3,000 meters was mentioned as the usual altitude for aerial photography. A solo aerial photographic plane was capable of operating at higher altitudes (5,000 to 5,500 meters) to accomplish

the mission.[56] Perhaps what was most significant in Sherman's manual were statements that addressed an aerial photographic reconnaissance in transition. Like Mitchell, Sherman addressed a more mobile battlefield that required a more flexible reconnaissance effort. "During stable trench warfare tactical maps are based on data furnished by Corps and Army aerial photographs of the enemy's territory. Photographs during war of movement are of little value in studying the enemy organization but serve to acquaint the Command with details of terrain…. During open warfare photographic missions are only occasional and are requested to clear up map obscurities or most other specific demands for information."[57] In his view, remaining with the traditional aerial reconnaissance process would not effectively serve the changing dynamic of combat.

The most significant U.S. assessment of the evolving role of aerial photographic reconnaissance came from the leader of America's aerial photographic program in theater, Major Steichen. On 26 December 1918, Steichen addressed the entire photographic interpretation issue with his manifesto. (See Appendix 3 for the Steichen Report.) The necessary depth of understanding of photography, he asserted, could not come from the typical military introductory course. The art of the photograph required a complete understanding of the photographic process. Frequently throughout the war, the mistakes made at the squadron level in photographic interpretation were due to ignorance of the process of photography.[58] His declaration was an amazing assessment of the role of photographic intelligence, both in the sense of lessons learned in the war and with respect to its potential in supporting future conflicts. However, his recommendations were to be ignored by AEF seniors. What transpired in the inter-war years was accommodation for observation, but not for photographic intelligence. The latter mission was relegated to the National Guard. Thanks to the National Guard, the aerial photographic experience in the inter-war

---

[52] "Provisional Manual of Operations," Maurer, ed., *U.S. Air Service*, II, 275.

[53] "Provisional Manual of Operations," Maurer, ed., *U.S. Air Service*, II, 270.

[54] "Tentative Manual for the Employment of Air Service," Maurer, ed., *U.S. Air Service*, II, 326.

[55] "Tentative Manual for the Employment of Air Service," Maurer, ed., *U.S. Air Service*, II, 326.

[56] "Tentative Manual for the Employment of Air Service," Maurer, ed., *U.S. Air Service*, II, 342.

[57] "Tentative Manual for the Employment of Air Service," Maurer, ed., *U.S. Air Service*, II, 342.

[58] Steichen, "Aerial Photography," Gorrell Report, ser. G, r. 24, NARA.

period was successfully maintained. One Illinois Guard unit in an exercise was able to photograph the front lines and deliver to the battlefield commander the wet print in eight minutes.[59] When the United States entered the Second World War, the experience base was limited at best, lacking the wisdom embodied in Steichen's vision.

The American role in intelligence within the Great War demonstrated rapid assimilation to the mission once the commitment was made. The transition to a more effective program was greatly aided by the assistance from British and French staffs to the fledgling American elements. What best exemplifies the marshalling of American resources to the task at hand was the creation, training, and eventual mobilization of Photographic Sections to support aerial reconnaissance. When the Armistice arrived, not only did the Americans have 21 Photographic Sections in theater, but more were on the way. Such a commitment reinforced the Americans' determination to contribute to both aerial reconnaissance and intelligence.

---

[59] Maurer Maurer, *Aviation in the U.S. Army 1919-1938* (Washington, DC: Office of Air Force History, 1987), 430.

THE ARTIST
Major Edward Jean Steichen
(27 March 1879–25 March 1973)

If anyone exemplified the best in aerial photography in World War I, it was the photographic master Edward Jean Steichen. Passion, intensity and drive were his trademarks. His daughter described him as an artist who "liked things to look the way they look. Show things as they are."[60] He applied his genius for photography toward military applications and became the most articulate spokesman on the medium throughout America's tenure in the conflict.[61]

FIGURE 130. Edward Steichen is holding a German-made aerial camera while posing in front of a Breguet 14 B2 aerial bombardment aeroplane. Source: Steichen Photo Collection, New York, NY.

The Steichen family emigrated from Luxembourg to the United States when Steichen was eighteen years old. Three years later, Steichen returned to Europe to study painting in Paris. While there, he met the great photographer of the time, Alfred Stieglitz, who was in the forefront of getting photography recognized as art. Steiglitz recognized Steichen's talent and potential, and he strongly encouraged his pursuit of photography.[62] When the war commenced, Steichen was living in northern France. As the Germans advanced on the Marne River, Steichen cabled a contact in New York City to determine the best course of action at that precarious moment. "Advise strategic retreat" was the prompt reply. He departed just before the German Army arrived.[63]

When the United States entered the war in 1917, Steichen—at age 38—was eight years over the age limit set by the U.S. Air Service. However, due to his reputation as a photographer, he was commissioned a first lieutenant and assigned to the branch responsible for photography, the Signal Corps.[64] His proud mother commented, "The United States government has one of the great creative artists of the world now training young men to go over the top with cameras instead of guns."[65]

---

[60] Steichen's daughter, Dr. Mary Steichen Calderone, was a noted physician and co-founder of the Sex Information and Education Council of the United States. Dr. Mary Steichen Calderone, 29 May 1986, New York City, Telephone Interview, NASM.

[61] Goddard, 20.

[62] Robert E. Hood, *12 at War, Great Photographers Under Fire* (New York: G.P. Putnam's Sons, 1967), 71-72.

[63] The book is paginated by photographs rather than text. Edward Steichen, A *Life in Photography* (Garden City, NY: Doubleday & Company, Inc, 1981), chap. 5.

[64] Niven, 448.

[65] Niven, 448.

Chapter II: AEF Intelligence and Photographic Organization

FIGURE 131. Major Victor Laws and Captain Steichen together — two aerial photographic giants of the 1st World War. Source: Gorrell Report, NARA.

Aerial photography's foundation was well established long before Steichen entered the ranks. In the summer of 1917, he met the RFC photographic pioneer Major C.D.M. Campbell, while Campbell was campaigning for support of aerial photography in Washington, D.C. Campbell quickly filled Steichen with enthusiasm for aerial photography's potential.[66] Steichen soon teamed with the big game hunter photographer, James Barnes, to initiate an aerial photography program for the U.S. Army. He said of Barnes that "All he knew about photography was whatever he had learned on a hunting safari when he made a motion picture of wild animals."[67] However, outranking Steichen, Barnes became the voice of aerial photography for the Signal Corps. Nonetheless, Barnes recognized that Steichen was the true expert in the field of photography, who served as the linchpin for achieving success in any role that the AEF had in store for aerial photography.[68]

Both men left for France in October 1917 with Major Barnes continuing his leadership of the Photographic Section and Steichen serving as technical advisor for aerial photography. They set up an office in Paris, trying to make a difference in the rigid thinking about aerial reconnaissance, while reminding themselves that "the whole photographic situation for the overseas Air Service" was an entirely new phenomenon.[69] Over the following months, the Allied staffs quickly recognized Steichen's expertise. Among aerial photographic veterans such as Campbell, Steichen's reputation advanced. He wrote Barnes that Steichen was "the finest master of photographs technique in the world."[70]

When Barnes transferred back to the United States, Steichen assumed overall responsibility for the AEF's photographic operation. It was challenging work, but Steichen excelled, showing strong managerial ability, skill in coordination, and the capability to handle personnel and materiel.[71] Additionally, he excelled as a photographer. He learned to appreciate the camera's ability to render great detail. His photographic art became sharp and clear, providing the image quality that the war demanded in aerial photographs.[72] This quality became a hallmark of his art in later years and reflected

---

[66] Steichen, xx.
[67] Steichen, chap. 5.
[68] Steichen, chap. 5; Barnes, 477.
[69] Niven, 457.
[70] "Major Campbell Letter to Major Barnes," 30 January 1918, NASM.
[71] Steichen, chap. 5; Hood, 71-72; NASM, Notes on Steichen's Military Personnel File.
[72] Steichen, chap. 5; Hood, 74-75.

his personality. On occasion during the war, Steichen had joked that anyone turning in a fuzzy photograph would be court-martialed.[73]

In late July 1918, Steichen met one of the greatest influences of his military career, Brigadier General Billy Mitchell. Both men were vigorous, energetic, and driven in pursuit of improving aviation's role in warfare. In addition, Steichen personified the aviator that matched Mitchell's standards. In Mitchell, Steichen found a senior military mentor, while Mitchell had in Steichen his aerial photographic expert. Their relationship continued beyond the Armistice.[74]

Steichen summarized his approach to his work by recalling on the night of the Armistice, "I had never been conscious of anything but the job we had to do: photograph enemy territory and enemy actions, record enemy movements and gun emplacements, pinpoint targets for our own artillery." For Steichen the challenges went beyond combat itself. "We had had to improvise all along the way with inadequate equipment and materials and inadequately trained personnel. But the photographs we made provided information that, conveyed to our artillery, enabled them to destroy their targets and kill."[75]

In the postwar era, Lieutenant Colonel Steichen supported military aerial photography until his Reserve retirement in 1924. He returned to his photographic art and became a noted celebrity. His photography increasingly demonstrated attention to detail, reflecting the demands imposed on aerial photography. World War II brought him back to action. In the fall of 1941, at the age of sixty-two, Steichen attempted to enlist in the Army Air Corps, but he was turned down due to his age: "When I arrived, the officer in charge took down my name and address politely, but when he came to the year of my birth, 1879, he put down his pen with an air of finality and told me he was sorry, but I was beyond the age limit for induction into active service."[76]

After Pearl Harbor, he was offered a commission in the Navy Reserves as a lieutenant commander. "I almost crawled through the telephone wire with eagerness," he later wrote.[77] He was assigned to organize a team of photographers to record naval air activities. He was aboard the U.S.S. Lexington aircraft carrier in 1943 and at the battle of Iwo Jima in 1945. At war's end, Steichen concluded his illustrious military career as a Navy Captain in charge of all naval combat photography.[78] Toward the end of his life, he mused on his distinguished military career, saying, "I've spent over six years of my life in uniform. That's quite an indictment of civilization…War is a monstrous piece of human stupidity. And I can't look at it any other way."[79]

---

[73] Christopher Phillips, *Steichen at War* (New York: H.N. Abrams, 1981), 1.
[74] Steichen, chap. 5; Niven, 463.
[75] Steichen, chap. 5.
[76] Steichen, chap. 12.
[77] Steichen, chap. 12.
[78] Hood, 76-77.
[79] Hood, 76-77.

AN INTERPRETATION METHODOLOGY FOR THE FRONT LINES

Obstacles to our Progress

Four years of intense combat shaped positional war into a well-established pattern. Photographic signatures sketched from film demanded thousands of man-hours of labor under brutal conditions. To describe the battleground verbally from these products required an understanding of what each signature entailed. A summary perspective was provided for arriving American aviators in 1918 prior to their exposure to the operational realities in flying over the front:

> It has been the plan of the German staff, when it is their intention to put up a prolonged and stubborn resistance, to organize at least two positions, one in the rear of the other, and in the neighborhood of one or two kilometers apart, and under certain circumstances, these distances may be considerably increased. Positions in the front line are as if it were suspended on a succession of organized strong points, these strong points constituting a stabilizing influence on the whole line. Between the first and second line there are shelters for the reserves of the sectors, centers of distribution of supplies, and a large number of field or short range guns.[1]

Years of photo-based analysis reinvigorated the role of intelligence in positional war. The interpreter served as overseer, monitoring all activity for intelligence value. The breadth and depth of aerial coverage of enemy territory created a wealth of material to ascertain enemy intentions.[2] The aerial photograph assumed the role of military standard for inquiry, providing a basis for determining detectable change in the zone of combat. The entire landscape was scrutinized for any changes in configuration. The photographic interpreter became as sensitive to the policy of the Germans as much as the actual German combatant. Any distinctive signature was carefully noted, quickly followed by indications of intention disseminated to the commander.[3] The descriptions that came forth from interpreting the photographic print established a new means to express military thinking, one that helped shape the military culture of modern warfare.

Trenches

When the 1914 war of maneuver stalemated at the river Aisne and Ypres, the military science of positional war commenced. No-Man's Land became the sobriquet for frontal terrain transformed through an intensity of destruction never witnessed up to that time. The French pioneer of

---

[1] "Aerial Photography for Pilots," NASM, A30.2/2.

[2] Pépin, "Lecture on the Study and Interpretation of Aerial Photographs," 4-5, NASM.
[3] *Study and Use of Aerial Photographs*, 15 January 1918, sec. II, 4, NARA, RG 120, Box 819.

aerial photographic interpretation, Capitaine Jean De Bissy, remarked in his first assessment of aerial observation a year after that first trench was dug that "Trenches are obstacles to our progress."[4] The initial trench configuration was based on terrain. Spadework produced "broken lines … adapted to the ground as well as possible."[5] Each defensive point represented a "small salient," carefully constructed to ensure a continual defensive perimeter reinforced by flanking detachments.[6]

"Obstinate defense" became a standard term to describe German intentions. "When the enemy intends to make an obstinate defense he organizes at least two positions, one behind the other."[7] Positional war's initial defensive configuration comprised a basic design of two principal lines of resistance, lines that linked the North Sea to the Swiss border. Throughout the German trench network, it appeared they wanted permanence and expected to stay in one place for a long time. The French had no intention of establishing a permanent defensive network to keep the Germans eternally at bay. Their conflict required retaking their sovereign territory and driving the Germans back to their homeland. On the Allied side, the underlying assumption of all construction was that they expected to move forward at any moment.[8] The German front lines of 1915 that faced French and British forces comprised several lines of trenches with the closest trench facing No-Man's Land serving as the real line of resistance. The prototypical trench network that first year of positional warfare comprised a frontline firing trench reinforced by a second trench at a distance of 100 to 400 meters to as much as 1 to 2 kilometers separation.[9] The initial German defensive works comprised two to three successive lines, spaced to limit the lethality of the heavy artillery barrage. The trench configuration was also designed to complicate enemy artillery firing patterns by forcing the gun crew to have to re-

adjust when it fired at another target. The second trench line paid particular attention to the terrain, frequently employing the rear slope for additional cover.[10] The number of trenches increased to accommodate the flow of infantry between the first trench and the second and third trenches of the front line position. Since trenches were configured to the terrain, they appeared irregular in shape and form on the aerial photograph. Such irregularity also ensured protection from flanking enfilade fire.[11]

The aerial photograph usually portrayed the trench as a black line, further identified by turnouts in the line called traverses and firebays. The traverse was designed to limit the threat posed by enfilade fire to the trench passageway. Both appeared as dark to light lines that varied with the direction of light. Identifying trench design required a variety of elaborate and intriguing descriptions, to include "Greek," the broken line, the indented line and the sinuous line.[12] On slopes facing the Allied lines, communication trenches became serpentine.[13] Sometimes loops in the trench were established at intervals to afford free passage of troops coming in and going out.[14] The primary trench design analyzed from photography showed the main thoroughfare employing a large traverse every 30 meters. Traverses

---

[4] *Illustrations to Accompany Captain De Bissy's Notes*, xx.
[5] *Bulletin of the Aerial Photography Department in the Field*, 8.
[6] *Bulletin of the Aerial Photography Department in the Field*, 8.
[7] *Bulletin of the Aerial Photography Department in the Field*, 8.
[8] Porter, 195-196.
[9] *Bulletin of the Aerial Photography Department in the Field*, 8.

---

[10] *Illustrations to Accompany Captain De Bissy's Notes*, 3.
[11] *Notes on the Interpretation of Aeroplane Photographs*, March 1917 (S.S. 550), 9; "Aerial Photography for Pilots," 24, NASM, A30.2/2.
[12] *Study and Use of Aerial Photographs*, 15 January 1918, sec. II, 8, NARA, RG 120, Box 819.
[13] *Bulletin of the Aerial Photography Department in the Field*, 16.
[14] *Illustrations to Accompany Captain De Bissy's Notes*, 3.

DIAGRAM SHOWING GERMAN DEFENSIVE SYSTEM.

Cantonment

Practice trenches

Riding school

Troops resting (10-16 Km.)

Camp

Riding school

Minor track

RAILHEAD

Stream

Watering place

RAILWAY LINE (Normal gauge)

Main track

NARROW GAUGE RAILWAY

Bivouac

B⁴

B⁴

B⁴

Bivouac

REFILLING POINT

Bivouac

2ᴺᴰ LINE OF DEFENCE

Anti Aircraft Battery

Artillery track

Bivouac

Bivouac

Reserves for the sector
(1 Bt. in underground shelters)

Observation post

4-6 Km.

4ᵗʰ line

Redoubt

Communication trench prepared for defence

3ʳᵈ line

Principal communication trench

Observ. post

2ⁿᵈ line

Observation post

150 M.

1ˢᵗ line

SUPPLIES

Limit of sector

1ˢᵗ LINE OF DEFENCE

Regimental Sector (2 Battalions)

a. Recesses for snipers
b. Sentry shelters protected against explosions
c. Large shelters (heated rooms, quarters for the commander and the men, dressing station).
d. Communication trench.

FIGURE 133. The French designation for trench designs. Source: *Étude et Exploitation des Photographies Aériennes.*

FIGURE 134. The first trench facing No-Man's Land was referred to as the firing trench. The schematic illustrates the details of the trench network to include the communication and circulation trench. Source: *Bulletin du Service de la Photographie Aérienne aux Armées* (Paris: Imprimirie Nationale, 1916.)

in sectors with reduced manning were usually spaced 15 to 20 meters apart. Photographic analysis determined that a typical traverse measured two to four meters wide at their top, with a length of eight to ten meters. In very exposed positions, traverse length was reduced to four to five meters. In places exposed to flanking fire, special recesses for sharpshooters and machine gunners were included. Trench formation was defined by shadows from the two to four meter-wide piles of earth and sandbags piled on facing both front and rear.[15] The other feature of the trench was those "dependencies" otherwise known as trench commodities to promote sanitary living conditions. The signature for cesspools and latrines was a small rectangular hole at the end of the small trench (boyau).[16]

Determining the center of resistance and most frequented traffic routes was a priority for aerial reconnaissance.[17] Central to analysis was determining the key avenue in the trenches, commonly known as the communication trench (boyau de communication). It was this main thoroughfare that linked front-line fire trenches to the rear sectors. This configuration let the infantry maneuver safely within the trench labyrinth to defend against attack and create an expeditious route for reinforcement. The genesis for the communication trench came from limitations in trench design. The forward firing trench was dug deep and narrow to provide the best protection. However, the combatants soon learned that this design complicated the infantry's ability to circulate. To avoid having to enlarge the trench and improve force mobility from within, a series of smaller circulation trenches were organized

---

[15] *Study and Use of Aerial Photographs*, 15 January 1918, sec. II, 6, NARA, RG 120, Box 819; "Interpretation of Aerial Photography," 3, NASM, A30.2/28; Porter, 197; Hahn, 22.

[16] *Study and Use of Aerial Photographs*, 15 January 1918, sec. II, 6, NARA, RG 120, Box 819; "Interpretation of Aerial Photography," 3, NASM, A30.2/28; Porter, 197; Hahn, 22.

---

[17] "Aerial Photography for Pilots," 22, NASM, A30.2/2.

along the main firing trench.[18] The configuration of the communication trench length varied with the terrain. It averaged two meters in depth and extended over one and a half kilometers in distance. Traffic density played a major role in the design. The communication trench was generally broad and straight to accommodate urgent reinforcment of the firing trench against the enemy attack.[19]

As the war continued, the front line transitioned from a trench containing the main infantry elements to a select cadre of sentinels, scouts, and observers. Shell holes and holes dug out by sharpshooters became the priority for analysis. Activity from patrols and secondary defense activity became detectable. Trench improvements provided visual clues that the adversary was intending to reinforce the present location rather than proceed to gain new ground.[20] Lack of activity also helped gauge the value of the terrain. Sometimes deep recesses were found in old trenches that had broken down during prolonged periods of bad weather, suggesting the trench declined in defensive priority. An additional signature was any absence of shadows in the trench line which suggested the sector contained either dummy or incomplete trenches.[21] When taking up a new position, the Germans designed trenches based on natural strong points. The network prepared for defense had been first backed up with a series of fire trenches to support additional operations. These "centers of resistance" comprised several fortified areas. At least two but more often three successive positions or systems of defense were prepared. Trench lines linked strong points such as villages, farms or woods in the forward area.[22] Villages were especially attractive when the houses had cellars. These obstacles helped the defenders hold against an attack long enough

to allow reinforcements to augment the sector. Machine guns and minenwerfer were added to complicate the enemy's ability to gain ground.[23] German labels helped clarify the trench configuration. The very front line was termed "fire position" or "observation position" followed by the cover position. Support and reserve positions occupied the rear sector.[24]

The trench firing pattern included firing notches and sniper's posts. To the photographic interpreter, these appeared as T-shaped appendages to the main trench. Firing trenches were distinguished from all other trenches by the presence of fire steps and loopholes for the gunners. The aerial photograph portrayed fire steps as tiny black notches having the appearance of sawteeth. Lookout holes in the trench network were usually located in a smaller adjacent covered trench. A splinter-proof shelter was usually observed nearby.[25] In the rear trenches, the Germans configured the arrangement to ensure effective cross-fire and flanking fire toward the front sector or between the prepared elements of the trench itself.[26]

As the German infantry proceeded to the front lines, each echelon occupied its assigned sector. Divisions divided into brigades and regiments at predetermined points in the line. At the lowest echelon of company and platoon, each unit proceeded to its own predetermined quarters in the trenches.[27] Sectors were linked by several communication trenches, which decreased in number as the distance increased away from the front line.[28] Analysis of sector and unit echelon alignment commenced once a network of communication trenches was determined. Deployment activity, reinforcement routes, and centers of resistance were the subject of investigation. To help rationalize the sector layout, the interpreter

---

[18] *Bulletin of the Aerial Photography Department in the Field*, 7; Porter, 83-84.

[19] "Interpretation of Aerial Photography," 3, NASM, A30.2/28.

[20] Pépin, "Lecture on the Study and Interpretation of Aerial Photographs," 1, 10 December 1917, NASM; *Study and Use of Aerial Photographs*, 15 January 1918, NARA, RG 120, Box 819; Hahn, 190.

[21] *Study and Use of Aerial Photographs*, 15 January 1918, sec. II, 20, NARA, RG 120, Box 819.

[22] *Notes on the Interpretation of Aeroplane Photographs*, March 1917 (S.S. 550), 9, and February 1918 (S.S. 631), 4-5.

[23] Porter, 195-196.

[24] Porter, 83-84.

[25] *Bulletin of the Aerial Photography Department in the Field*, 11-16; *Illustrations to Accompany Captain De Bissy's Notes*, 3; "Aerial Photography for Pilots," 24, NASM, A30.2/2.

[26] Pépin, "Lecture on the Study and Interpretation of Aerial Photographs," 4-6, NASM.

[27] Porter, 190.

[28] *Notes on the Interpretation of Aeroplane Photographs*, March 1917 (S.S. 550), 9, and February 1918 (S.S. 631), 4-5.

FIGURE 135. Each sector was intensely scrutinized to determine which sections of the trench showed any signs of activity. Analysis focused on the important centers of resistance against Allied operations. Source: *Étude et Exploitation des Photographies Aériennes.*

assumed the role of the enemy sector commander. The most important lines of communication were described by level of activity, purpose, and possible unit assignment.[29] The approximate sector boundary was determined by where tracks terminated. Natural divisions between sectors were sometimes created from topographical features, such as canals, rivers, main roads, or railway lines. It was generally expected that a regimental

---

[29] *Study and Use of Aerial Photographs*, 15 January 1918, sec. II, 20, NARA, RG 120, Box 819.

Chapter 12: An Interpretation Methodology of the Front Lines

boundary would occur between each set of three battalion sectors.[30]

Life within this environment settled into a well-established routine. Soldiers assumed a nocturnal existence to avoid detection from the enemy front-line observation and overhead aerial reconnaissance. Sentries manned the parapet using a periscope to observe signs of activity and alert snipers of possible targets. The remainder of the infantry stayed under cover. The three lines, firing, support, and reserve, appeared deserted during the daylight hours. Observable activity commenced in the evening. Firing trenches served as the springboard for work parties. The communication trench became the major lifeline of the trench network and replenished all the adjoining sectors. When conflict resumed, the setting was transformed. An alarm sounded and the ground

shook with a constellation of artillery fire, very lights (flares) and signal rockets. At sunrise, the garrison stood to arms and repeated the cycle.[31]

Reporting trench activity from photographs reflected a standard format. The most detailed descriptions were included in intelligence summaries published at the higher headquarters, such as the following:

> Photos of October 1st show that little work has been done on the enemy withdrawal position around CHAMPIGNEULLES. The prisoner's statement

---

[30] Each sector was compared to a human hand and arm, with the main arteries running down the arm and feeding the spread fingers through the smaller veins which lead to the fingertips and return. *Notes on the Interpretation of Aeroplane Photographs*, March 1917 (S.S. 550), 9.

[31] Edmonds, *1916*, I, 157-158.

FIGURE 137. **Trenches in 1917 showed greater construction activity along the line.** Source: *Étude et Exploitation des Photographies Aériennes.*

appearing in our Summary of October 1, that new trenches had been built filling in the gap southeast of CHAMPIGNEULLES, between 295.4-287.1 and 297.6-286.5, is disproved by these photos, as are also his other statements regarding new trenches. A new trench about four hundred meters long follows the counter slope of a hill at 296.5-283.1, running along the north edge of some woods one kilometer southeast of MARQ. Other photographs of October 1st serve to strengthen the belief that the enemy is intending to make a strong resistance on the position which he at present occupies along the ridges which run north of and parallel to the EXERMONT stream between GESNES and EXERMONT. Photo-

graphs were taken on reconnaissance crossing this line at two points – in the region of the town of EXERMONT and at a point between the RUISSEAU du GOUFFRE and the Bois de la MORINE. In the first region a new trench is seen running from the point 300.4-281.1 due east to the point 301.6-281.1, the latter point being about 300 meters directly north of the town of EXERMONT. Elements of a communicating trench approach this line from the north and give further evidence of the intention of the enemy to hold and consolidate this position.[32]

A French Vème Army Bulletin of 9 July 1918 reported with less detail: "Aeroplane Photographs, July 7, 1918, 7th Army Corps: The photographs of this reconnaissance show the line of defense bordering the dirt road Licy-Hutevesnes is occupied."[33]

---

[32] G-2, 1st Army, "Summary of Intelligence," 2 October 1918, NARA, RG 120, Box 3370.
[33] G-2, 1st Army Corps, "Summary of Intelligence," 9 July 1918, Drum Papers, Box 14, USAMHI.

Chapter 12: An Interpretation Methodology of the Front Lines

Saps (Sapes d'Attaque)

One primary indication that an attack was being readied was the discovery of a sap (derived from the French term, *Sapes d'Attaque*). Saps were below-grade excavations or tunnels constructed to provide the offensive with jump-off trenches immediately preceding the charge. Their presence signaled to the aerial photographic interpreter that an attack was possible within one to two days. Saps offered another benefit to the attacker by providing an advance line to configure a new firing trench. Saps were designed to rapidly link together and form a new front line. The interpreter checked for sap construction by regularly examining thin threadlike paths from the front line trench to listening posts. Earthen spoil was removed to the rear areas as covertly as possible to decrease evidence of ongoing sap construction. Sap design had several descriptive labels to include curved (most common), serpentine, and indented.[34]

Fortified Shell holes

Fortified shell holes evolved from the devastation on the battleground. Like the sap, shell holes supported front line operations while at the same time providing additional protection. The Germans found it economical to align shell holes to produce a new front line. General Haig commented on the new defensive configuration in his 28 August 1917 diary entry:

> Trenchard reported on the work of the Flying Corps. Our photographs now show distinctly the "shell holes" which the enemy has formed into "strong points." The paths made by men walking in the rear of those occupied first got our attention. After a more careful examination of the photo, it was seen that the system of defence was exactly on the lines directed in General Sixt von Arnim's pamphlet on "The Construction of Defensive Positions.[35]

[34] Other sap descriptions varied with the source, to include winding, sawtooth, and "cronolated." "Aerial Photography for Pilots," 26, NASM, A30.2/2; *Bulletin of the Aerial Photography Department in the Field*, 1918, 25-26; Hahn, 188.

[35] Haig's 28 August 1917 diary quoted in Occleshaw, 67.

FIGURE 138. **French manual shows the standard dimensions of a sap structure.** Source: *Bulletin du Service de la Photographie Aérienne aux Armées.*

The aerial photographic interpreter searched for evidence of an occupied shell hole by examining the adjacent areas for footpaths. The fortified shell hole was normally singled out from the rest of the craters in the area since it portrayed a darker appearance. Any excess earth spoil was usually thrown into an adjacent unused shell hole. A fortified shell hole was selected for its proximity to a well-drained area and passage to a common shelter. Camouflage was added to provide additional cover.[36] An American 1st Army Corps intelligence summary during the 8 July 1918 battle near Belleau Wood illustrated the significance of potential enemy resistance from fortified shell holes. "July 6 to July 7, 1918. Oblique photos from French squadron taken July 5, 1918, show position of fragmentary 1st line German position from Bois de la Brigade de Marine to Vaux. Co-ord. 76.5-

[36] *Study and Use of Aerial Photographs*, 15 January 1918, sec. II, 8, NARA, RG 120, Box 819; "Interpretation of Aerial Photography," 4, NASM, A30.2/28; *Notes on the Interpretation of Aeroplane Photographs*, February 1918 (S. S. 631), 8; Hahn, 30-31.

FIGURE 139. Saps were constructed from the main trench to serve as a jump-off point for troops. Note the sap extending into No Man's Land. Source: Illustrations, S.S. 550a.

62.5 to 80.2-59.2 Occupied pits, pits probably occupied, paths and shallow trenches."[37]

Shelters

From the beginning of the conflict, harsh conditions dictated an immediate need for shelter (French: *abris*; British, American: dugout) to provide some measure of cover from lethal munitions as well as to allow refuge for the infantry during its deployment to the front. Allied shelter construction remained rudimentary as a reminder to themselves that positional war on French and Bel-

[37] G-2, 1st Army Corps, "Summary of Intelligence," 9 July 1918, Drum Papers, USAMHI.

gian territory was temporary. German construction was more refined, reflecting an elegance that suggested permanence for the occupying forces.[38] The routine for the first year of positional war had infantry units responsible for the defense of the trenches conduct their normal routine during the day in shelter, either in the actual first line (those troops immediately responsible for defense) or farther in the rear (reserves) at a distance from the trenches varying 800 to 2,000 yards (one to two kilometers).[39] Whereas in the latter half of the war, the most important shelters were found in the second and third line trenches.[40] In the first year of the war, the Germans constructed a variety of protective shelters: splinter-proof, surface, underground shelters, and covered trenches. Splinter-proof shelters were dispersed among the trenches to limit the risk from direct hits. The excessive moisture of the front line soil forced the inhabitants to build their shelter to a standard that included a double layer of roofing beams with at least a meter of earth thrown on top of the roof. These shelters did not extend above the parapet to any noticeable degree so as to provide protection against small projectiles. Splinter-proof shelters proved very difficult to locate by aerial photography. The search would focus on an area 12 to 15 meters to the rear of the firing trench or communication trench being served. Sometimes an abnormal amount of rubbish in front of the firing trench provided an indication that a shelter was nearby. Deep underground shelters were built from the many hard limestone caves that existed in northern France. These proved necessary to withstand the pounding from heavy artillery. As the network approached the rear sector, the normal shelter configuration consisted of covered trenches.[41]

A typical shelter followed basic characteristics. Shelter dimensions normally equated to the size necessary to house garrison strength for the area. A standard estimate of personnel assigned to

A. Saps pushed out and trenches dug to hold raiding and covering parties

B. Tracks of patrols sent out from opposing line to reconnoitre work.

FIGURE 140. **Line drawing of the sector shows the progression of sap construction.** Illustrations, Source: S.S. 550.

a shelter equated to two groups of nine men (one noncommissioned officer and eight men each). Any observed construction activity helped lead to the discovery of shelter entrances. One logical place for an entrance was the corner of a traverse to help ensure maximum protection from incoming shell fire. Whenever a shelter was discovered from aerial photography, the interpreter would further examine the area for any signs of tunneling. Ventilation shafts, small tunnels, and rectangular openings were sought after to gauge the shelter's total accessibility to the main trench. Communications in the vicinity led to the PC that controlled the forces in the area.[42] Oblique coverage contributed immensely to understanding the potential dimensions.[43] Those shelters to the rear

[38] Pépin, "Lecture on the Study and Interpretation of Aerial Photographs," 5, NASM.

[39] *Illustrations to Accompany Captain De Bissy's Notes.*

[40] *Illustrations to Accompany Captain De Bissy's Notes.*

[41] *Bulletin of the Aerial Photography Department in the Field*, 27-35; "Interpretation of Aerial Photography," 3, NASM, A30.2/28; Brooks, in White, 104; "Aerial Photography for Pilots," 25-26, NASM, A30.2/2; Pépin, "Lecture on the Study and Interpretation of Aerial Photographs," 5, NASM; "Aerial Photography for Pilots" 25-26, NASM, A30.2/2.

[42] *Bulletin of the Aerial Photography Department in the Field*, 27-35; "Interpretation of Aerial Photography," 3, NASM, A30.2/28; Brooks, in White, 104; "Aerial Photography for Pilots," 25-26, NASM, A30.2/2; Pépin, "Lecture on the Study and Interpretation of Aerial Photographs," 5, NASM.

[43] Porter, 202.

were more dispersed along existing transportation networks.[44]

The most famous shelters in the war were the Stollen, constructed by the Germans for safely holding troops and advanced weapons and used to great effect before the commencement of the Verdun campaign in 1916. The walls of the average Stollen shelter were estimated to be 1.50 meters by 2 meters, with the construction reaching to a depth of 15 to 20 meters beneath the surface. French intelligence identified four Stollen shelters in the Verdun complex: Hangstollen, Fabienstollen, Gluckaufstollen, and Kuchenstollen. The Verdun experience reminded the aerial photographic interpreter that underground facilities such as Stollen could have disastrous consequences on operations and required constant surveillance and analysis.[45]

Shelters proved a lucrative target for artillery fire. Besides discovering the actual shelter location, the interpreter would also determine the shelter's ability to withstand bombardment. Once the calculations were complete, the information was relayed to the artillery planner for consideration. A scale of four degrees of resistance, from a simple shelter to cavernous dwellings, was then posted on the Plan Directeur to alert the artillery to the destructive power needed.[46]

Barbed Wire

Barbed wire was one of the most pervasive obstacles to confront the infantry. It was applied row upon row in a broad swath. As an obstacle, barbed wire helped define the traverse of No-Man's Land. It was considered an auxiliary defense (défenses accessoires), designed to reinforce the trench network. Barbed wire also strengthened defenses for lookout posts, bases of resistance, and battery emplacements. Later, fortified shell holes, villages, hedges, and ditches were observed with barbed wire belts. Barbed wire was not arrayed in parallel to the fire trenches. Instead, it reinforced the trench

flanks from a broad attack line of advancing infantry. German trench design after 1916 complicated the layout. They established a network of barbed wire compartments. From an aerial photograph, the compartment assumed a triangle-shaped geometric form, 6 to 10 meters thick and connected by cross entanglements. The design was spaced throughout to limit destruction from hostile artillery and other weapons. Since most barbed wire belts were constructed at night, the following day's aerial coverage would be examined for signs of foot tracks along either side of the belt.[47]

Planning operations in No-Man's Land required a precise knowledge of barbed wire locations and design. This shaped the strategy and tactics of forces that were advancing in an offensive or conducting a trench raid. The battalion at the front was responsible for accomplishing required analysis of the front sector. Its observation routine determined any change in status, describing nature and condition of the wire in the sector while at the same time updating any reference map. Most intelligence on barbed wire was obtained through prisoner interrogations. Aerial reconnaissance and photographic interpretation validated the reports and reinforced final planning. Once the planning had been accomplished, artillery was then called upon to clear what wire obstacles lay in front of the battalion. Firing 20,000 artillery rounds on a fifty-mile front was the standard that artillery used to reduce the wire obstacle. An incomplete barrage only heightened the lethality for Allied troops on the offensive. Enemy machine guns could rapidly deploy to locations to cover gaps in the wire created from the barrage. When the Germans finalized the Seigfried Stellung, wire covered the area in front to an average width of 10 meters and over one meter in height.[48] Barbed wire bands at the front were not continuous. Operational planning required openings to allow movement

---

[44] Notes on the Interpretation of Aeroplane Photographs, March 1917 (S.S. 550), 9.

[45] Pépin Papers, MA&E, Paris.

[46] Pouquet, "Working of the Service of Interpretation of Photographs," NARA, RG 120, Box 819.

[47] Bulletin of the Aerial Photography Department in the Field, 36-41; "Interpretation of Aerial Photography," 4, NASM, A30.2/28; Pépin, "Lecture on the Study and Interpretation of Aerial Photographs," 1, NASM; Notes on the Interpretation of Aeroplane Photographs, February 1918 (S.S. 631), 5; Hahn, 22-23; "Aerial Photography for Pilots," 26, NASM, A30.2/2.

[48] Hahn, 73; Porter, 192-193.

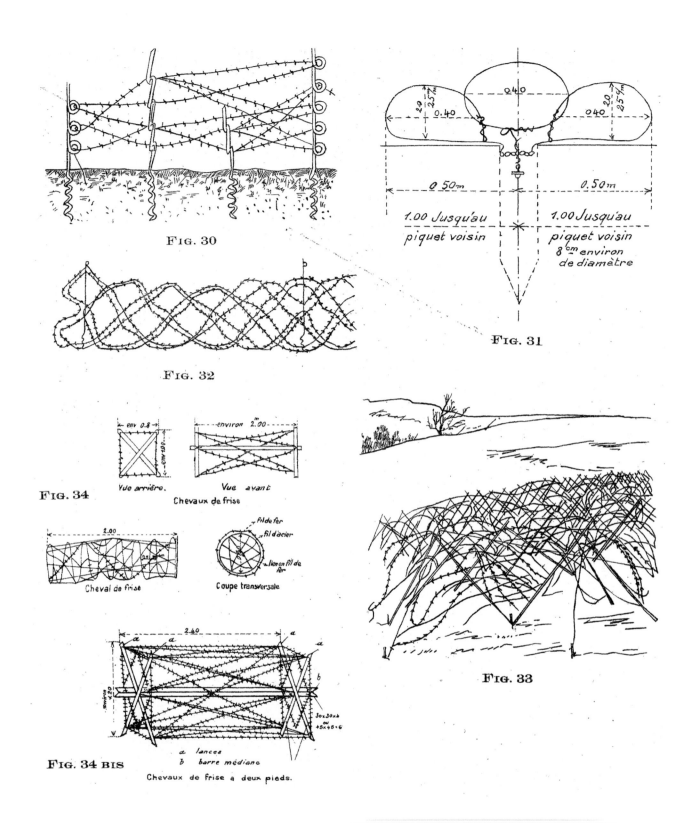

FIG. 30

FIG. 31

FIG. 32

FIG. 34

Vue arrière.

Vue avant

Chevaux de frise

Cheval de frise

Coupe transversale

FIG. 33

FIG. 34 BIS

a   lances
b   barre médiane

Chevaux de frise a deux pieds.

of sentinels out into No-Man's Land. A wire entanglement called a *chevaux de frise* or knife rest (a wooden or metal frame on which wire is fastened) was constructed to obstruct any passage. Additional obstacles included abatis (felled trees), branches and *trous de loup* (pits). When sentinels and patrols ventured out, they

FIGURE 141. **French manual shows the various barbed wire configurations.**
Source: *Bulletin du Service de la Photographie Aérienne aux Armées.*

FIGURE 142. **The vast array of barbed wire produced a geometric design on the battlefield.** Source: *Étude et Exploitation des Photographies Aériennes.*

followed a zig-zag route through the defenses. Such routes were easily detected on an aerial photograph.[49]

Visually detecting barbed wire on the front line was not simple because the wire presented a variety of signatures. Aerial photographs portrayed the bands as a dark ribbon, light gray to almost black depending on the newness of the wire and the contrast of the color with the texture of the ground. When the wire was laid down it provided a visible sheen that was easily detected. Over time barbed wire tarnished and blended in with the terrain. This caused the interpreter to analyze the history of coverage of the area to determine the width of the bands. Vertical coverage was not effective in determining the extent of the wire. A better glimpse of the barbed wire belts came from oblique coverage. The variety of barbed wire also contributed to the degree of difficulty of analysis. Concertina wire proved a challenge to detect. In winter,

analysis was simplified as snow and frost highlighted the bands.[50] The following is an American intelligence assessment that mentioned a wire entanglement in the battle sector: "Information obtained from 1st Corps photographs taken July 30, 1918: Wire entanglement from Foret de Nesles at 195.4-277.7 W. across RR. Pits possibly occupied near edge of woods just E. of road, at 196.8-276.1."[51]

---

[49] *Bulletin of the Aerial Photography Department in the Field*, 36-41; "Interpretation of Aerial Photography," 4, NASM, A30.2/28; Pépin, "Lecture on the Study and Interpretation of Aerial Photographs," 1, NASM.

[50] *Bulletin of the Aerial Photography Department in the Field*, 36-41; "Interpretation of Aerial Photography," 4, NASM, A30.2/28; Pépin, "Lecture on the Study and Interpretation of Aerial Photographs," 1, NASM; *Notes on the Interpretation of Aeroplane Photographs*, February 1918 (S.S. 631), 5.

[51] G-2, 1st Army Corps, "Summary of Intelligence," 9 July 1918, Drum Papers, USAMHI.

Ancienne

voie

ferrée

2   Région de Berthenicourt   17.7.17.. 2600ᵐ. F:50

Light Railways

Smaller, accessible light railways (tramways) were a feature of the vast trench network that helped the interpreter better understand sector operations. Light railways were the logistical lifeblood of the trenches. The German forward railway systems were constantly being constructed or altered, especially during active operations. A single track built on an ungraded bed could be constructed at the rate of 8 to 16 kilometers in a 24-hour period. The load capability was based on the gauge of the track. Standard gauge track signified a heavy freight load that delivered larger quantities of troops and supplies. Smaller light railways extended the service to the front lines, supporting both infantry and artillery requirements. By the end of the war there were thousands of miles of light rail operating at the front.[52]

The light railway systems fell out into three groups: the more common 1.00 m and 0.80 m

FIGURE 143. **Companion line drawing reveals details of the elaborate configuration.** Source: *Étude et Exploitation des Photographies Aériennes.*

gauge; 0.60 m gauge; and 0.40 m gauge. 1.00 m and 0.80 m lines existed here before the war. As a general rule, new 1.00 gauge was built only where lines of that gauge already existed, and where the use of a different standard caused needless transshipment. The 1.00 m track held a high priority for logistic sustainability. For example, during the battle of Verdun the Germans used the 1.00 m tracks to move up their heavy artillery (420 mm howitzers) to assist their offensive. The 0.60 m and 0.40 m gauge (also known as the trench tramway) came into existence at the beginning of trench warfare. Rail of 0.60 m tracks was extended to the very front lines, serving the logistic needs of all major trench networks. Further analysis of the tracks helped distinguish them from paths in the area. Rail lines formed regular curves, generally following roads

---

[52] Porter, 209.

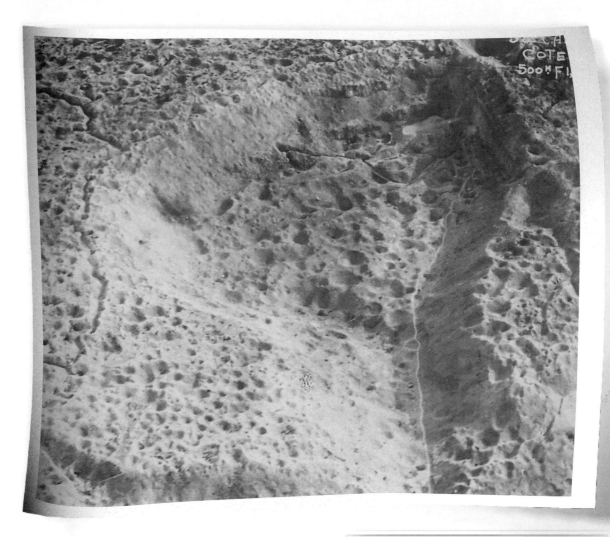

along the valleys or contours. These two narrow gauge tracks were only found in the forward areas. The starting point generally was a railway station. The 0.40 m gauge, restricted to the more forward trench tramways where mechanical traction was rarely used, showed as a fine line on aerial photographs.[53]

Light railways were distinguished on aerial photographs by a visible straight track leading into the trench network. Once among the trenches, sharper curves were observed. The German forward railway system was altered continuously to meet logistical requirements of the moment, especially during active operations. Tracks were removed as soon as they were no longer needed, and were used again to construct a new line. Photographic interpretation focused on signs of deterioration and disuse. The mark of the track re-

FIGURE 144. **Mineshafts were ideal for providing safe haven for troops in the front sector. Geologic formations provided an additional barrier against artillery fire.** Source: *Étude et Exploitation des Photographies Aériennes.*

mained for some time after the rails had been removed. Aerial photographs could detect additional activity from footprints of men walking between the rails.[54] A 1st Army AEF intelligence summary discusses light railway activity in the following report: "Photographs of the region to the north of this show a new narrow gauge railroad running in a general southeasterly direction from about 302.5-282.5, to 303.3-281.7. These

---

[53] *Notes on the Interpretation of Aeroplane Photographs,* March 1917 (S.S. 550), 7, and February 1918 (S.S. 631), 7; Pépin, "Lecture on the Study and Interpretation of Aerial Photographs," 10, NASM.

[54] *Notes on the Interpretation of Aeroplane Photographs,* March 1917 (S.S. 550), 8, and February 1918 (S.S. 631), 7; "Interpretation of Aerial Photography," 5, NASM, A30.2/28; "Aerial Photography for Pilots," 30, NASM, A30.2/2; Hahn, 28-29.

Entrée du tunnel

Déblais

Voie d'évacuation

Vaste carrière

Piste

two points are in the vicinity of military camps and it is probable that the railroad serves not only as a communication between these camps, but also to supply the new trench system."[55]

Tracks and Trails

The central focus of photographic analysis of enemy activity during the war involved the study of tracks and trails, the main thoroughfares of the front. During battle, tracks and trails helped determine whether new trenches, shell holes, and other defenses were occupied. Footpaths provided the greatest insight into what the enemy accomplished on a daily basis. Photographic interpretation manuals continually stressed this feature.[56] The most important purpose for analyzing trails was to spot activity such as working parties

FIGURE 145. **The companion line drawing highlights how the complex entrance was connected to a railroad network.** Source: *Étude et Exploitation des Photographies Aériennes.*

that correlated directly to the state of readiness of a given sector.[57] The interpreter could distinguish a well-trodden pathway by gauging the volume of activity on a respective trail as well as determining which routes were ignored. Tracks and trails also led the interpreter to key features within the sector such as dump locations, battery positions, headquarters, gaps through the wire, patrol paths and critical enemy observation posts. Tracks and trails also helped determine traffic patterns within

---

[55] G-2, 1st Army Corps, "Summary of Intelligence," 9 July 1918, Drum Papers, USAMHI.

[56] *Notes on the Interpretation of Aeroplane Photographs,* March 1917 (S.S. 550), 8, and February 1918 (S.S. 631), 6.

[57] "Interpretation of Aerial Photography," NASM, A30.2/28; Porter, 190.

a village, leading the interpreter to enemy operational centers and advanced listening posts.[58]

Infantry movement within fire and communication trenches was continually analyzed. Patterns of activity constituted targets worthy of disruption.[59] Footpaths monitored from aerial photographs could not only gauge the level of activity in a sector, but also provided the analyst with an ability to determine sector boundaries, an invaluable insight when planning the battle. Infantry regiments and battalions used an assigned line to accomplish their respective sustainability requirements. Oblique coverage provided the best photographic angle for determining the principal lines of traffic. The aerial photographic interpreter had to refine his knowledge of the front line infrastructure both by identifying the primary and secondary lines and eliminating those tracks that no longer supported operations.[60]

[58] *Notes on the Interpretation of Aeroplane Photographs*, March 1917 (S.S. 550), 8, and February 1918 (S.S. 631), 6-7; "Interpretation of Aerial Photography," NASM, A30.2/28.

[59] *Illustrations to Accompany Captain De Bissy's Notes*, 2.

[60] *Illustrations to Accompany Captain De Bissy's Notes*, 1-2; Hahn, 27-28.

FIGURE 146. In-depth study of the disarray of No-Man's Land revealed tracks and a light rail (tram) line in the front sector. Illustrations, Source: S.S. 550a.

Soil

Aerial photography maintained constant surveillance of any new construction in a sector. Trench improvement, saps extending forward into No-Man's Land, or further excavation for shelters were examined on each photograph. In positional warfare, each change noted on the aerial photograph became a gauge of the volume of soil brought to the surface. An abnormal level of earth material correlated to the extensive activity required for digging deep or expansive shelters. Such activity was normally found near the primary communication trenches to shelter support elements or reserves. During the first year of combat, analysis showed the amount of earth removed from the trench correlated to the required width and depth for a communication trench as well as highlighting a certain sector's weapons

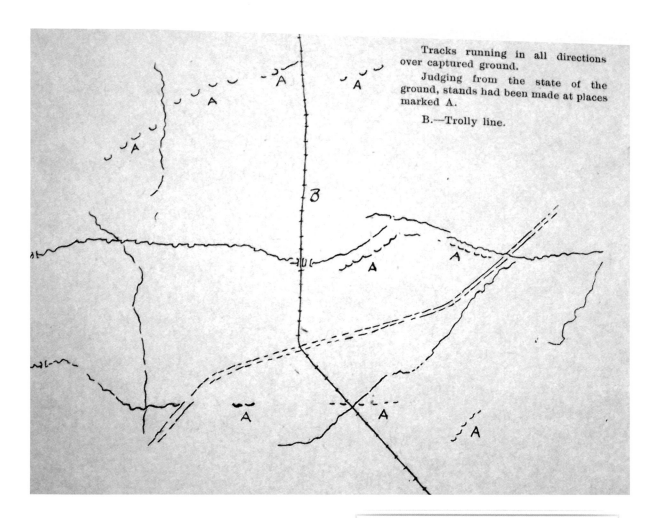

Tracks running in all directions over captured ground.

Judging from the state of the ground, stands had been made at places marked A.

B.—Trolly line.

FIGURE 147. Companion line drawing highlights selected details of the front sector. Source: Illustrations, S.S. 550a.

and ammunition depots.[61] Spotting excavated earth prompted ground observation to increase inspection of a given area. Once the decision was made on the extent of the underground activity, the location became an artillery target.[62]

It became a fact of life for all combatants that the aerial photograph detected even the slightest disturbance of the topsoil. The greatest aid came from the first images, providing a standard by which change could be measured.[63] The Germans soon modified their field procedures to cover the evidence. Working parties followed instructions to distribute the earth from excavations all over the landscape.[64] Light railways proved invaluable in redistributing the soil. Soil excavation analysis proved challenging since

detection of new soil was a simple database maintenance function rather than a discovery of major construction.[65] Front line mining operations were a notable feature of positional warfare with excavations penetrating as deep as the terrain allowed. The presence of large amounts of soil excavation became a signature. To compensate for the large volume, the soil was frequently put in sandbags to be taken to the rear and discarded.[66] German successes at Verdun, attributed to the use of Stollen, gave the Allies concern for the remainder of the war. Stereoscopic coverage was continually desired. In the

---

[61] *Notes on the Interpretation of Aeroplane Photographs* March 1917 (S.S. 550), 9, and February 1918 (S.S. 631), 4.

[62] *Illustrations to Accompany Captain De Bissy's Notes,* 1; *Study and Use of Aerial Photographs,* 15 January 1918, NARA, RG 120, Box 819; Hahn, 22; 72-73.

[63] Hahn, 23.

[64] Porter, 201.

[65] Hahn, 24.

[66] Hahn, 73; *Notes on the Interpretation of Aeroplane Photographs,* March 1917 (S.S. 550), 9, and February 1918 (S.S. 631), 5.

FIGURE 148. **Snow provided outstanding detail for aerial photographic interpretation.** Source: *Étude et Exploitation des Photographies Aériennes.*

FIGURE 149. **The companion line drawing clarified the extent of both German and French trench lines.** Source: *Étude et Exploitation des Photographies Aériennes.*

absence of good coverage, the demand for prisoner interrogations increased.[67]

Knowledge of geological formations impacted the thinking of operational planners. The war clearly demonstrated that protection against modern, high-power artillery could not be guaranteed by surface structures, no matter how strong the construction. Adequate defense against artillery was possible only by the excavation of deep works protected by undisturbed

earth or rock. Geology governed the time allotted to construct the defense. Geological analysis assumed an important role toward the later stages of the conflict. The experiences on the Western Front prompted greater attention toward terrain analysis and the geological make-up of the battleground. After receiving orders to construct the appropriate defensive position, the engineer in charge reviewed the topographical conditions within the zone, determining to what extent ex-

---

[67] *Study and Use of Aerial Photographs*, 15 January 1918, sec. II, 11, NARA, RG 120, Box 819.

Chapter 12: An Interpretation Methodology of the Front Lines

cavation was possible.[68] Positional war focused on determining a lethality opportunity-cost for every man-made object below the surface. The commander now had to understand the geologic make-up at the front in order to assume the correct defensive posture.[69]

Snow

The climate of Northern France created a harsh environment for combatants in the winter season. For aerial photographic interpretation, the climate was a boon to analysis. Photographs taken immediately after snowfall provided breakthroughs in discovering the extent of activity. Black and white marks became the interpreter's standard for gauging the extent of recent activity. Wire, ditches, occupied shelters, and camouflage stood out with clear contrast. Artillery was equally at risk, leaving a distinct black blast mark with every round fired.[70]

Bereitschaft (German Reserves in Readiness)

German reserves in readiness (*Bereitschaft*) remained an ongoing concern for the Allied planner and for intelligence. *Beireitschaft* reinforcements helped sustain German positions. Trench network design ensured communication trenches were interspersed with shelters for rapid movement of rear-echelon-based reserves to any endangered sector. Bereitschaft movement was further supported through a network of rail centers that accommodated rapid transfer of personnel from other sectors as necessary. Supply depots were positioned to further reinforce any troop movement with weapons and materials. Beyond aerial coverage, prisoner interrogations proved invaluable for determining the extent of Bereitschaft in a given sector.[71]

Machine Guns

Machine guns were the most sought-after target for aerial photographic analysis. Artillery was an equally ominous threat, but it could be detected through the variety of collection resources besides aerial photographic intelligence, to include flash and sound-ranging, balloon observation, and ground observation. German weapons manuals attested to the machine gun's value, as reported in a 2nd Army assessment:

In General. All kinds of machine guns isolated or combined at close or medium range, are an absolute success, if backsight and good observation of cone of fire are correct. Any attack will break down under the flanking fire of cleverly placed machine guns of any kind, served by resolute men.

In action around shell holes and in fights for strong points. Great morale effect of high machine gun sweeping fire in connection with Artillery. Preparation and while flanking positions. Cones of fire keep crews of trenches and strong points down. Especially adapted for repelling counter-attacks. Therefore machine guns of all kinds are to be employed on the front lines. Machine guns of the defense in strong points are to be taken generally only by storm troops with hand grenades, smoke bombs, flame throwers and strungout hand grenades by flank or rear attack.[72]

The machine gun was a different type of threat. Its compact size and outstanding maneuverability resulted in a greater lethality being applied anywhere along the front. Machine guns could survive a blistering barrage while contained deep below in a shelter, resurface, and quickly commence fire against the oncoming adversary. It was a redundant threat of great consequence. If one machine gun team was destroyed, another surfaced and continued the mission.[73]

---

[68] Brooks, in White, 99-100.

[69] Brooks, in White, 98-99; Hahn, 73; *Notes on the Interpretation of Aeroplane Photographs*, March 1917 (S. S. 550), 9.

[70] *Notes on the Interpretation of Aeroplane Photographs*, February 1918 (S.S. 631), 9.

[71] Pépin, "Lecture on the Study and Interpretation of Aerial Photographs," NASM; *Notes on the Interpretation of Aeroplane Photographs*, February 1918 (S.S. 631), 10.

[72] G-2, 2nd Army, "Effectiveness of Different Weapons," 25 October 1918, NARA, RG 120, Box 10.

[73] "Aerial Photography for Pilots," 27, NASM, A30.2/2.

A. *Typical strong point*
B. *Assembly trenches*
C. *First line not held in strength*
D. *Liberal supply of communication trenches to facilitate the speedy passage of the garrison at A to any threatened point*

FIGURE 150. **British aerial photograph showing front lines, assembly trenches, and reserves in readiness known by the Germans as the Bereitschaft.** Source: Illustrations, S.S. 550a.

FIGURE 151. **Companion line drawing highlights the Bereitschaft assembly area.** Source: Illustrations, S.S. 550.

Aerial reconnaissance and photographic interpretation emphasized annihilating the machine gun as the highest priority. In the subsequent published manuals, the emphasis was clear. "The discovery of machine guns is of the utmost importance. It is essential that, in case of our attacking, every hostile gun should be destroyed by our bombardment. A single one remaining intact may be the cause of very heavy casualties."[74] Logical steps were taken to understand all facets of the machine gun's role and apply a methodology for detection and follow-up elimination through artillery targeting. In the first year of positional warfare, the German machine gun emplacements were only prepared when the trenches were occupied. Given that a field of fire for a machine gun was generally 400 or 500 yards, the weapons were emplaced to cover one line of trenches. Machine guns were placed farther to the rear if the slope of the terrain or shelter from houses with cellars were available to provide more cover.[75]

The experiences of 1915 taught the French that the Germans maintained their machine guns in completely isolated shelters at a considerable distance from the trenches. This was done as a deterrent to the threat posed by artillery. The shelter was made as innocuous as possible. Excavated earth was carried away. The machine gun crew was provided with several days rations to sustain itself in place without detection by footpath. When possible, additional cover was

---

[74] *Illustrations to Accompany Captain De Bissy's Notes*, 3.

[75] *Illustrations to Accompany Captain De Bissy's Notes*, 3-4.

Chapter 12: An Interpretation Methodology of the Front Lines

ROAD

GOMMECOURT WOOD

PROBABLY M·G· EMPLT
NOT YET CAMOUFLAGED

E 28 0

PROBABLY "M·G·"
SQUARE LOOPHOLES WITH A
SCREEN OR PROTECTION
BETWEEN THEM.

SAP AT E28b.38·24

provided by tree branches.[76] A review of captured German documents dated September 1916 revealed to the photographic interpreters that at least fifty percent of the machine guns were moved to rear echelons, observed in the second or the preferred third-line trench. The emplacements were selected to "have a very wide field of fire or can at the very least flank the position."[77] With each photo examined, special attention focused on any abnormal configuration of the trench line. Any traverse configuration that departed from normal size, shape or angle was scrutinized. Oblique coverage provided another angle to ascertain anomalies for further scrutiny.[78] Covered emplacements became passé by the last year of combat; by then, mobility of the guns held a priority to sustain the defensive

FIGURE 152. A superb oblique shot of the German lines at Grommecourt in 1917. The interpreter was able to assess possible locations for machine gun nests along the forward trench. Source: Illustrations, S.S. 550a.

and increase survival. Only the quiet sections of the front retained a configuration that included fixed emplacements.[79]

Locating machine guns was a difficult intelligence task, fraught with frustration for all concerned. Analysis of both aerial coverage of the front and of the policies cited from captured German documents focused on any available means to predict machine gun locations within

[76] *Illustrations to Accompany Captain De Bissy's Notes*, 3.
[77] Pépin, "Lecture on the Study and Interpretation of Aerial Photographs," 6, NASM.
[78] *Notes on the Interpretation of Aeroplane Photographs*, March 1917 (S.S. 550), 5.

[79] *Notes on the Interpretation of Aeroplane Photographs*, February 1918 (S.S. 631), 5.

Chapter 12: An Interpretation Methodology of the Front Lines

the sector. Despite the effort to accurately predict machine gun locations in a given sector, the totality of the analysis did not successfully deter the threat. The French photographic interpreter pioneer, Capitaine De Bissy, remarked on this challenge: "One is therefore compelled to give up almost entirely any attempt to discover the exact position of a machine gun from a photograph, but after examining the photograph, if one cannot say definitely there is a machine gun at such and such a point, one can say, if there is a machine gun in this sector, it is almost certainly at such and such a point." [80] As a rule, machine guns were found in the vicinity of communication trenches, allowing for rapid retreat to the second line. They sometimes were emplaced between traverses to increase protection from enfilade fire. The interval between the traverses included only the shelter for the machine gun, its ammunition and the machine gunners.

By 1917 the objective of locating machine guns via aerial photographic interpretation was deemed nearly impossible. The manuals of that time reflected the frustration: "the search for machine guns is more and more difficult."[81] At the commencement of combat, the machine guns were retrieved from shelters and placed at designated locations within the trench network. Interpretation methodology continually emphasized an extensive knowledge of the terrain. However, it was a knowledge based not on the map that comprised the Plan Directeur, but rather on stereoscopic photographs. Wire entanglements served as a guide to the intervals and the obstacles to be swept by machine guns.[82] In 1917, the focus for discovering machine guns shifted to the rear trenches that flanked the primary sector. Recognition features on the photograph included niches, observed indentations on the trench line; salients where the machine gun was a few yards to the rear; shelters that appeared to be strongly defended (calling upon stereoscopic coverage to reveal any spoil); and loopholes at a certain distance from the trench and within easy reach of

a communication trench. Since the machine gun reinforced the flank, any associations with that role were also emphasized during the examination of the photograph.[83]

In the last year, as the fixed emplacements became rare, unique armor and turret configurations sometimes appeared at the head of a long winding sap running from a firing trench and surrounded by wire entanglements. Like the rest, these bunker-type guns were constructed with a view to affording flanking fire.[84] Potential signatures for analysis included "V"-shaped marks in the forward edge of a parapet to permit the traverse of the gun. At the back of the "V" a small dark spot similar to a shelter entrance provided a possible signature. What emplacements were left took the form of a square tray or concrete platform that varied in appearance with the sun angle, showing up as a white mark with a dark edge or as a comparatively dark square.[85] Attention to all sources of intelligence was required to locate and destroy "these murderous weapons." Prisoner interrogation concentrated on specific details that covered location, training, and doctrine. Ground observation focused on location and direction of fire. However, the majority of machine guns were discovered by deduction from all available evidence.[86] Once a position was determined, it was highlighted on the Plan Directeur map.[87] The following 1st Army Intelligence summary revealed a host of machine gun emplacements in a given sector:

Study of photographs taken Sept. 2.

M.G. emplacements: 67.98-36.90; 67.90-36.86; 68.03-37.03.

New wire at 69.05-37.20 with M.G. emplacement in corner of M.G. emplacement at 68.80-36.88. Tr. Du Cri evidently used considerably at night for reliefs, rations, etc.

[80] *Illustrations to Accompany Captain De Bissy's Notes,* 3-4.

[81] *Study and Use of Aerial Photographs,* 15 January 1918, sec. II, 5, NARA, RG 120, Box 819.

[82] *Study and Use of Aerial Photographs,* 15 January 1918, sec. II, 5, NARA, RG 120, Box 819.

[83] Pépin, "Lecture on the Study and Interpretation of Aerial Photographs," 1, NASM; *Notes on the Interpretation of Aeroplane Photographs,* March 1917 (S.S. 550), 5.

[84] "Aerial Photography for Pilots," 27, NASM, A30.2/2.

[85] Hahn, 25; "Interpretation of Aerial Photography," NASM, A30.2/28.

[86] Porter, 203.

[87] *Illustrations to Accompany Captain De Bissy's Notes,* 4.

Path, much used, running N. from edge of woods parallel to Boyau des Releves, along E. edge of quarries with camouflage erected along E. side. Probable quarry entrance at 73.92-38.24 and 73.92-38.28.

Covered. M.G. emplacement at 69.6-36.7. 2 M.G. emplacements at 68.80-36.86.[88]

Minenwerfer (Trench Mortar)

Another lethal weapon in the World War I arsenal was the minenwerfer, providing the front lines with continual fire at short range. The following German description of minenwerfer emphasized their flexible firepower:

> In General. The field grenade fire, in close range high angle fire (up to 1300 m.) is mainly effective against living targets. Supports Artillery during the preparatory bombardment, often even after the beginning of the attack. Effective fire with rapidity up to 20 rounds a minute.

> In action around shell holes and in fights for strong points. In action against Infantry (Riflemen). As a consequence of great mobility especially adapted for the quick breaking up of enemy resistance in combat for positions and strong points. Accompanying Stormtroops and storm Infantry, firing from flat trajectory carriage, effective against living targets, also against prone riflemen at ranges up to 1,000 m. It replaces Field-Artillery — the Ammunition supply requires special attention.[89]

Light minenwerfers were encased within an armored compartment or casemate, having a photographic signature of a whitish or grayish blot representing the hole of the tube. These holes were either round or square and their depth was determined by examining the shade created within the tube.[90] A typical minenwerfer firing pit was akin to a sap along the communication trench. Medium-caliber minenwerfer were sometimes identified in shelters that had the roof removed. Larger minenwerfer were adjacent to supply lines for easier access to munitions stockpiles.[91] Another approach to discovering minenwerfer locations was through a simple formula developed by the British. Because the weapon was only as effective as its range, minenwerfer emplacements were identified within the trench network by following a line drawn parallel to the British front line at a distance of about 500 yards to 700 yards. German observation posts were usually linked to the minenwerfer squad to determine the effect of fire.[92] One challenge to interpreting minenwerfer positions was the similarity to the latrine position. One was often mistaken for the other. Care was taken when searching for minenwerfer to determine the purpose of the adjacent sap. The sap leading to the minenwerfer was irregularly constructed in a zigzag pattern while that to the latrines was generally a straight path.[93]

Chemical Munitions

Despite an ability to detect chemical munitions through aerial photography, intelligence collection was never able to preempt chemical employment. The aerial reconnaissance search for chemical warfare continued throughout the war. In the final months of the war, the Allies' Supreme War Council alluded to the possibility of finding enemy gas projector positions through aerial reconnaissance.[94] It remained a priority intelligence target.[95] The combatants' anxiety over chemical munitions is evident in the 17 June 1918 correspondence of the U.S.

---

[88] G-2, 1st Army Corps, "Summary of Intelligence," 2 September 1918, Drum Papers, USAMHI.

[89] "G-2, 2nd Army, "Effectiveness of Different Weapons," NARA, RG 120, Box 10.

[90] *Bulletin of the Aerial Photography Department in the Field*, 48-51.

[91] Pépin, "Lecture on the Study and Interpretation of Aerial Photographs," 5, NASM; Porter, 205; "Interpretation of Aerial Photography," 6, NASM, A30.2/28; Hahn, 26.

[92] *Notes on the Interpretation of Aeroplane Photographs*, March 1917 (S.S. 550), 6, and February 1918 (S.S. 631), 6.

[93] "Aerial Photography for Pilots," 27-28, NASM, A30.2/2; Hahn, 26.

[94] Supreme War Council, Inter-Allied Aviation Committee, "Draft Minutes of the 1st Session … held in the Council Chamber, Versailles," 9 May 1918, TNA, PRO: AIR 1/2299/209/77/29.

[95] Research for this book did not turn up any aerial reconnaissance or photographic interpretation reports to fulfill this intelligence requirement despite its high priority.

2nd Division staff during fighting in the Belleau Wood sector. As the hotly contested battle ensued, a request went out to verify any chemical munitions projector emplacements in the area.[96] Hand-to-hand fighting was gruesome. Chemical weapons made the battlefield experience even more hideous.

Tactical coverage of the Western Front gave new meaning to the role of intelligence. Thanks to the stabilized front line, the aerial photographic interpreter could hone skills and provide the commander with as precise a depiction of the battlefield as visually possible. Such precision was best described by the ability of the interpreter to detect individual footpaths along the trench network. Intense scrutiny forced tactical operations to avoid detection through the cover of darkness or by working underground.

The Western Front did not end with the third line of trenches. The tactical sector of the front line gained its strength from the strategical rear echelon. A new array of targets and weapons challenged intelligence to define the Western Front in terms of sustainability. The strategical arena further impelled the evolution of aerial reconnaissance and photographic interpretation. The array of targets in the rear echelon proved a challenge as combatants constantly sought a breakthrough and a return to battlefield mobility.

[96] 2nd Division Memorandum, "Orders for Gas Defense," 17 June 1918, in U.S. Army, Office of Military History, *United States Army in the World War, 1917-1919, Military Operations of the American Expeditionary Forces* (17 vols., Washington, DC: GPO, 1948; reprint, Washington, DC: U.S. Army Center for Military History, 1988-92), IV, 500.

STRATEGICAL TARGETS IN THE REAR ECHELON

apitaine Paul-Lewis Weiller recognized that strategical targets were important for the commanders' understanding of the total battlefield. When his Weiller Grouping converted to aerial reconnaissance of targets well beyond the front, they institutionalized an intelligence process that remains to the present day. Weiller was supported by an elite team of strategical aerial photographic interpreter analysts that specialized in a certain sector. Each day the sector's key targets were examined for any changes.[1] Strategical analysis determined the enemy's ability to sustain a major operation, going beyond the immediate front sectors to cover an "objective at a great distance" followed by the ability to "ascertain the damage done."[2] Despite the emphasis at the time, the term "strategical" did not become embedded in the military jargon of the later 20th century. It reflected the terminology of the era, with a more succinct "strategic" taking precedence in the postwar era. For the combatant of the Great War, the strategical rear echelon covered a broad range of very important targets to include rail networks, depots/dumps, long-range artillery batteries, aerodromes and landing ground, ports, industries, and population centers.[3]

Rail Networks

Strategic sustainability was accomplished through an extensive array of rail networks. Intelligence priorities included determining the extent of activity from the amount of rolling stock in the yards or nearby supply depots (dumps) so as to ascertain if activity was normal or abnormal.[4] Both tactical and strategical analysis required assessment of enemy operations through close study of railways and trench tramways. Besides the normal gauge lines, which were mostly built before the war, the Germans made extensive use of the light railway system in the occupied portions of France and Belgium. They constructed new tracks near the front on a large scale. Personnel, stores, and materiel were brought up by side tracks and branch lines, which ran to nearly all important points and villages in the front line system. The battery groups and single heavy batteries were almost entirely supplied by this method. Supply depots were located at the breaks of gauge as well as at various points along the tracks. Railroad stations had unloading platforms for transferring supplies to the narrower tracks and switches. Each division employed a central supply station to support the reinforcement. The depots from overhead appeared as large squares or rectangles separated by alleys and garageways. Depots supporting food ration supplies showed extensive pedestrian

---

[1] Christienne and Lissarague, 181.

[2] Estienne, "Army Photographic Reconnaissance as it Should Be," 5, NASM, A30.2/34.

[3] G-2, 1st Army, to Chief of Staff, "Account of the Operation," 45-47, Drum Papers, Box 14, USAMHI; Henry, "Report on my Visit to the British Army," Conger Papers, Box 2, USAMHI.

[4] Snyder, "Notes on Aerial Reconnaissance," 2, Gorrell Report, ser. J, r. 34, NARA.

FIGURE 154. **Strategical reconnaissance continually monitored railroad activity for indications of increased support to the front sector.** Source: Library of Congress, Mitchell Papers.

and vehicle activity.[5] Train movements were a high priority target for aerial observation and intelligence reporting. This was reflected in the British policy that mandated lower-echelon squadrons supporting Corps sectors to report on train movements as quickly as possible to higher-echelon Army Branch Intelligence. The reports were consolidated with information from adjacent armies into the daily summary.[6] Here is an example of strategical reconnaissance reporting of activity at a German-controlled railroad station.

> Photos of September 14th taken at 11 hours show the following: The more northerly of the two large stations at PAGNY-sur-MOSELLE has been completely destroyed. No especial destruction is shown among the tracks, nor in the material dump on the platform, which is larger than usual. The big central building (machine shop) in the MONTIGNY station at METZ has been hit, and a big slice cut off from its southwestern corner. The tracks in front were also hit and a few cars have been wiped out.[7]

---

[5] *Notes on the Interpretation of Aeroplane Photographs*, March 1917 (S.S. 550), 7-8, and February 1918 (S.S. 631), 7; Pépin, "Lecture on the Study and Interpretation of Aerial Photographs," 9, NASM; *Study and Use of Aerial Photographs*, 15 January 1918, sec. II, 37, NARA, RG 120, Box 819; "Aerial Photography for Pilots," 30, NASM, A30.2/2.

[6] Stewart, "Report on the Organization and Operation of Intelligence 'A'," Conger Papers, Box 2, USAMHI.

[7] G-2, 1st Army, "Summary of Intelligence," 14 September 1918, Drum Papers, USAMHI.

Chapter 13: Strategical Targets in the Rear Echelon

Depots/Dumps

Positional war's insatiable demand for supplies created an extensive infrastructure of depots/dumps. The needs of infantry and artillery dominated the inventory of goods delivered forward. In supply dumps less precarious materiel was stored without attention to any particular arrangement. Camouflage was applied when available. Volatile goods demanded greater attention. Projectiles were stored in pits separated by thick splinter-proof earth shields designed to limit the effects of a partial explosion. Explosive powder charges were spaced at intervals under cover in smaller protected shelters.[8]

Photographic interpreters searched narrow gauge railway networks to collocate any corresponding depot. Analysis showed points of convergence along the routes, tracks, and railways of narrow and normal gauge as well as parallel road networks required for movement of the munitions.[9] Large munitions depots were generally situated at railheads or convenient rail systems. Smaller depots in the vicinity of reserve trenches were quite common, generally taking the form of open dugouts for projectiles with separate accommodations for explosives.[10] The volatile nature of munitions storage required necessary precautions to avoid fratricide from an inadvertent explosion. The arrangement became a typical signature for large munitions depots. RNAS reporting of large coastal artillery reflected the standard: "Numerous wooden huts separated by a considerable distance from one another, and surrounded by earth ramparts in order to localize the effects of a possible explosion are placed alongside the road or railway...."[11] The following is an American intelligence summary concerning depots and dumps:

The ammunition dumps of Bois du CHAPELET and the one north of CHAM-BLEY show no change since September 2nd. These dumps were reported burning two days ago. The ammunition dump south of MARS-la-TOUR shows no change since September 2nd, and that of St. JEAN les BUZY no change since May 19th. The materiel dumps at the last two towns show no change since September 2nd and July 19th respectively. The indications in this area do not suggest any withdrawal by the enemy beyond the Hindenburg Line.[12]

Heavy Artillery of Great Power

One of the highest priority strategical targets of the Great War was the long-range artillery, classified by the French as the Heavy Artillery of Great Power (*artillerie lourde à grande puissance* [ALGP]). The most notorious, the 210 mm naval gun, with a range of 132 kilometers (82 miles), was a strategical threat and a weapon of terror against the French people.[13] As a long-range weapon the gun provided a random strategical threat to population centers by creating havoc. Paris, Dunkirk, Châlons, and Nancy became the victims of the German long-range terror weapons. Such weapons acquired the sobriquet of the city that they targeted (i.e., Paris Gun). The 210 mm was derived from worn-out 380 mm (known as the Long Max) railroad guns.[14] The 380 mm gun was equally impressive. It alone weighed 154 tons. Set on a cradle weighing 26 tons, the gun carriage was massive. The entire emplacement weighed 400 tons, rotating on 96 eight-inch steel roller balls.[15] The numbers of this type of artillery were not substantial enough to contribute to any advance or success at the front. The 380 mm gun had a distinctive signature for the photographic interpreter. A branch of normal gauge railroad supported the weapon system, providing the ammunition required. Should the

---

[8] *Study and Use of Aerial Photographs*, 15 January 1918, sec. I, 24, NARA, RG 120, Box 819; Hahn, 35-36.

[9] *Study and Use of Aerial Photographs*, 15 January 1918, sec. II, 6-7, NARA, RG 120, Box 819.

[10] "Aerial Photography for Pilots," 30, NASM, A30.2/2; Hahn, 35-36.

[11] 5th Group, RAF, "Result of Aerial Photography by the R.N.A.S. in 1917," 13 February 1918, TNA PRO: AIR 1/93/15/9/240.

[12] G-2, 1st Army, "Summary of Intelligence," 2 September 1918, Nolan Papers, USAMHI.

[13] Ian Hogg, *The Guns, 1914-18* (New York: Ballantine Books, Inc., 1971), 141.

[14] Hogg, 137.

[15] Henry W. Miller, *The Paris Gun: The Bombardment of Paris by the German Long Range Guns and the Great German Offensives of 1918* (New York: Jonathan Cape & Harrison Smith. 1930), 200-203.

FIGURE 155. A 380 mm gun photographed in the woods, to the upper right of the frame. Note the craters from Allied counter artillery. Source: *Étude et Exploitation des Photographies Aériennes*.

gun be moved, the rail network was available to accomplish the task. Constant surveillance of the railway network was maintained to identify the weapon before it was put into action. Its setup took substantial time. The entire complex was positioned in woods and extensively camouflaged. This was, except for the visible gun barrel, typical of heavy batteries. The larger the gun, the more camouflage was employed. The blast of the gun was so great that it often killed some of the vegetation in the vicinity, which became an additional signature for finding the weapon system. The gun was mounted on a concrete platform about 20 to 25 meters in diameter and protected by a shield. Before the gun was fired, it was contained within a rectangular hangar to conceal its construction. The gun complex was surrounded by shelters and supplied through established logistical networks.[16]

To complicate Allied intelligence efforts to locate the 380 mm gun, the Germans collocated up to thirty batteries of various calibers in the region. As the gun fired, a simultaneous barrage by all the units occurred, masking the gun's actual firing location and complicating any observation from flash and sound-ranging units, captive balloons or aerial observation. The most lucrative sources of information came from aerial photography of the sector or from radiogoniometric detection of the gun batteries' supporting radio units.[17]

The photographic interpreter developed lists of signatures to identify a specific German gun type. Besides the 380 mm, the Germans had a variety of large artillery pieces that were identified by proximity to rail networks and the gun carriage. The 21 cm and 24 cm resided on a platform at the bottom of a trench of 12 by 16 meters

---

[16] *Bulletin of the Aerial Photography Department in the Field*, 63-64; Pépin, "Lecture on the Study and Interpretation of Aerial Photographs," 8, NARA; "Aerial Photography for Pilots," 29, NASM, A30.2/2.

[17] Hogg, 141.

and about 1.25 meters in depth, bordered by two sections of parallel railways. The 355 mm cannon used an analogous disposition with larger trench dimension of 15 by 17 by 3 meters. The 28 cm and 305 mm cannon were used almost exclusively on the seacoast and mounted on massive foundations of concrete. 305 mm and some 420 mm mortars were transported over roads by tractors. The long cannon of 21 cm and 24 cm and the long-range 420 mm mortars (16,000 meters range approximately) fired from trucks or platforms; 28 cm, 305 mm, and 355 mm cannon fired from a platform connected by a railway. The photographic interpreter kept in mind when searching for these weapons that dummy emplacements and artillery also were located within the area to complicate the targeting.[18]

Aerodromes and Landing Grounds

Among the most significant targets throughout the war were aerodromes and landing grounds. The definition of both overlapped to cover the area where aviation assets were maintained and operated.[19] Intelligence priorities addressed the increase in number of aeroplanes and their location. Unoccupied aerodromes were considered as important as those being used. This was credited to German aviation's ability to maneuver and operate around the region. As one lecture to air crews put it, "The German aviation is marvelously mobile."[20] Key to the interpretation was identification of the aeroplanes and the type of hangars that provided protection and maintenance.[21] As signified by "Landing Ground," the original airfields

FIGURE 156. **Aerial coverage of Marville landing ground. Please see Figure 157 for detail.** Source: Aviation: Data on German Air Service, NARA, RG 120, Box 5778.

[18] Miller, *The Paris Gun*, 200-203.

[19] *Notes on the Interpretation of Aeroplane Photographs*, February 1918 (S.S. 631), 10.

[20] Snyder, "Notes on Reconnaissance," 3, Gorrell Report, ser. J, r. 34, NARA.

[21] *Notes on the Interpretation of Aeroplane Photographs*, February 1918 (S.S. 631), 10.

MARVILLE AIRDROME N°30
COORDINATES-332.2,-298.1
AUGUST 28.1918
SCALE 1:20,000
MARVILLE SHEET

FIGURE 157. 1/20,000 scale map shows the aerodrome hangars in relation to the aerial photograph of the landing ground. Source: Aviation: Data on German Air Service, NARA, RG 120, Box 5778.

were temporary facilities that exemplified the mobile nature of aerial operations. Many airfields included smaller canvas hangars collocated near houses that served as billeting facilities.[22]

Aerial photographic analysis established a routine for assessing aerodrome operations. If observed activity indicated new construction of aerodromes or hangars at existing fields, the German "probably intends to make some move on the ground" and allow for aviation to "conceal his preparedness."[23] The first step in developing the landing ground was to construct small canvas hangars followed as quickly as possible by sheds to provide a more permanent configuration. As new hangars were built, a corresponding decrease in the rear echelon aerodromes was observed.[24] Aerial photography also verified the type, locations, and numbers of aeroplanes at the field. One aero-

drome feature visible on aerial photography was the Landing "T," a signaling device used to alert the pilot to the wind direction.[25] Over time the Landing "T" was replaced by smoke from a well-placed and controlled fire. The Allies learned from prisoner interrogations that German air crews preferred a less conspicuous symbol at the airfield since even ground observation could detect the smoke originating from the field.[26]

The shape of aerodrome hangars varied with the type of aeroplane. Small canvas hangars accommodating two scouts or one two-seater machine appeared semi-circular in shape and of

---

[22] Hahn, 36; "Aerial Photography for Pilots," 31, NASM, A30.2/2.

[23] Snyder, "Notes on Reconnaissance," 3, Gorrell Report, ser. J, r. 34, NARA.

[24] "Summary of Indications of Enemy Preparations for an Offensive in Flanders," Conger Papers, Box 2, USAMHI.

---

[25] *Aerial Observation for Artillery*, 49.

[26] *Notes on the Interpretation of Aeroplane Photographs*, February 1918 (S.S. 631), 10.

FIGURE 158. **Intelligence document derived from aerial photograph from escadrille Nieuport 38 showing the key targets in the Chatelet-sur-Retourne sector.** Source: Pépin Papers, MA&E.

a light color. The smaller pursuit planes used rectangular-shaped dark sheds. Twin-engined bombers had large canvas hangars for protection. The rectangular "bessonneaux"-type hangar provided cover for several aeroplanes. Aircraft parks accomplishing extensive maintenance usually had large wooden hangars or lattice girder structures.[27]

The British published extensive information on aerodrome location and activity primarily based on aerial photographic confirmation. A "Weekly list of Hostile Aerodromes on the British Front" described aerodromes of interest to the respective sector. British reporting covered the numbers of observed sheds and hangars at each aerodrome. Additional data on aerodromes came from prisoner interrogations, agents, and repatriated citizens.[28] Whenever an aerodrome was discovered, the Branch Intelligence Section generated six copies of all aerial photographs covering the target. For previously discovered aerodromes, they generated four copies.[29] The Americans also produced their own weekly assessment of aerodrome status.[30]

---

[27] *Notes on the Interpretation of Aeroplane Photographs,* February 1918 (S.S. 631), 10; Pépin, "Lecture on the Study and Interpretation of Aerial Photographs," 11, NARA.

[28] "Index to Periodical Summaries of Aeronautical Information," TNA, PRO: AIR 1/2124/207/74/3.

[29] Henry, "Report on my Visit to the British Army," Conger Papers, Box 2, USAMHI.

[30] Author discussion with Steven Suddaby.

FIGURE 160. **The line drawing illustrates the munitions lines to the artillery.** Source: *Étude et Exploitation des Photographies Aériennes.*

FIGURE 159. **Coastal artillery emplacements based on the Battery Hindenburg model were closely examined by French and British naval analysts for direction of fire. Battery Tirpitz was especially important, for the guns were aimed toward the vital port city of Dunkirk.** Source: *Étude et Exploitation des Photographies Aériennes.*

French intelligence established a targeting plan that required all German aerodromes be identified and photographed. Target value was based on the number of tents and hangars identified on the aerial photograph. The French established six regions for German airfield analysis: the Somme, Oise, Reims, Meuse, Moselle, and the region south of Strasbourg. Other 2ᵉ Bureau branches studied the entire German Air Force, focusing on order of battle based on aéroplane type, German aerial daytime tactics, night signaling operations and the use of ground beacons for aéroplane routes. A 2ᵉ Bureau liaison from GQG was assigned to each French bombardment group to brief the air crews on any updates and to forward information gleaned from the bombardment sortie.[31]

An American intelligence summary illustrates key features of a targeted enemy aerodrome: "Photos of September 15 show two planes on the east field and four on the west field at BATILLY. Both of these airdromes have hitherto been reported as unoccupied. Many trucks

---

[31] Martel, 269.

appear on the field, probably indicating that air squadrons are moving in from vacated airdromes nearer the front."[32]

Along the coastline, seaplane bases were a priority target for RNAS and French Navy aerial reconnaissance. During the 1916 time frame, only one German seaplane base existed on the Belgian coast. German seaplanes soon proliferated, accomplishing pursuit, torpedo, aerial bombardment, and reconnaissance missions. RNAS summary analysis reflected the increased sightings of seaplanes: "Reconnaissances have enabled us to ascertain that the enemy in 1917 used his seaplanes for scouting over the sea, without needing to use his land machines."[33]

Ports, Industries, Population Centers

Intelligence monitored the German threat against the vital sealanes connecting France and Great Britain. Aerial coverage of the entire coastline from the Dutch border to Calais was acquired by British and French maritime aviation. Target descriptions covered submarine shelters; naval order of battle to include destroyers, torpedo boats, and submarines; ports; large artillery batteries in defense of the ports; and associated aeroplanes and seaplanes.[34] The primary means of photographing these targets was by seaplanes using hand-held cameras.

RNAS analysis of submarine shelters along the coast showed six bases, two each at Bruges, Ostend, and Zeebrugge. Aerial photography confirmed the use of floating docks to repair the submarines. This high-value target was constantly scrutinized through all available intelligence. The RNAS report related that "Different reconnaissances made in 1917 show that there were in the ports on the Belgian coast and at Bruges at least 15 submarines at anchor or on the stocks, without counting those that were submerged at sea or in the shelters."[35]

Aerial photographic analysis supported naval order of battle assessments and port activity. French reporting accomplished on 21 November 1916 showed extensive activity: "enemy boats alongside the Quay, T.B.'s [torpedo boats] under steam, moving trains, rows of trucks, new railway lines, new buildings, numerous dugouts, smoke, etc."[36] When the port at Ostend was struck by aerial bombardment in June 1917, destroyers and torpedo boats diverted to Bruges.[37] Aerial photographic analysis covering the vital Zeebrugge Mole was constant. Coverage pinpointed the location of minefields and confirmed the access channels. Additional trenches and barbed wire along the shore showed the extent of German efforts to protect against possible amphibious landings.[38]

FIGURE 161. **The success of the Zeebrugge raid was verified by aerial photographic coverage.** Source: Barrie Pitt, *Zeebrugge* (New York: Ballantine Books, 1959).

[32] G-2, 1st Army Corps, "Summary of Intelligence," 15 September 1918, Drum Papers, USAMHI.

[33] 5th Group, RAF, "Result of Aerial Photography," 13 February 1918, TNA PRO: AIR 1/93/15/9/240.

[34] 5th Group, RAF, "Result of Aerial Photography," 13 February 1918, TNA PRO: AIR 1/93/15/9/240.

[35] 5th Group, RAF, "Result of Aerial Photography," 13 February 1918, TNA PRO: AIR 1/93/15/9/240.

[36] "Study by Corporal Mallet of the R.N.A.S. Photographs Nos. 527 to 540, Reconnaissance of November 21st 1916," in "Photographic Studies" III (January-September 1918), TNA, PRO: AIR 1/82/15/9/204.

[37] 5th Group, RAF, "Result of Aerial Photography," 13 February 1918, TNA PRO: AIR 1/93/15/9/240.

[38] 5th Group, RAF, "Result of Aerial Photography," 13 February 1918, TNA PRO: AIR 1/93/15/9/240.

German long-range naval artillery was always an intelligence priority. French and British naval analysts shared aerial photos to better determine the threat posed by the German weapons. One study by a French aerial photographic interpreter using RNAS coverage provided an in-depth assessment of Battery Hindenberg on the Belgian coast. Aerial photography provided descriptions of the guns' rotation and operating configuration, to include measurements of the gun battery spacing, found to be approximately 35 meters apart. Intelligence on the battery acquired from a deserter gave analysts an approximate size of the gun barrels (280 mm; about 11 inches). Gun rotation was estimated to be 165°, with the zone of fire "confined to the sea."[39] Subsequent RNAS reporting in 1917 described ongoing construction of "batteries of large caliber" to have deep emplacements and concrete shelters for ammunition and the gun crew. The distance between the guns was increased with the large-caliber gun batteries divided into two groups of two guns. Around several batteries trench works provided additional defense against an infantry attack.[40]

In April 1917 RNAS photographed Ghent and Antwerp four times at an altitude of 20,000 feet. They subsequently photographed Ostend, Bruges, and Zeebrugge using a "big camera." RNAS reports said the sequence of coverage "helped understand certain works in connection with naval and submarine warfare." Subsequent coverage helped British analysts understand construction under way on coastal artillery, aerodromes, antiaircraft batteries, and munitions depots. Strategical analysis benefited when RNAS merged with RFC to become the RAF. Now experts from both services could apply their analytical skills to ongoing activities along the coast as well as establish precedent for subsequent strategical targets.[41] When the Royal Navy con-

FIGURE 162 (OPPOSITE PAGE).
Detailed aerial coverage of the largest German city on the Rhine taken by RAF No. 55 Squadron. Source: Pépin Papers, MA&E.

ducted its historic raid on the German naval base at Zeebrugge, Belgium, on 22-23 April 1918, the process of in-depth strategical aerial photographic analysis was in place.[42]

Antiaircraft Artillery

Antiaircraft artillery was originally designed as an anti-balloon weapon against the prevailing dirigible threat prior to the start of the war. Formations of antiaircraft batteries were integral to the front line and the strategic rear. The initial photographic signature in 1915 was a round pit with the pivot in the center (identified by its circular platform) which allowed the antiaircraft gun to fire in every direction.[43] From the beginning of 1917, the Germans employed small-caliber (2 cm, 33 mm, 3.5 cm) antiaircraft cannon to defend against low-altitude raids on the front line trenches.[44] The circular pattern was retained throughout the war and was easy to recognize. The normal configuration was two, three, or four guns per battery. The breastworks for the guns were constructed in several formations throughout the defended area to allow for rapid transfer of the weapons to established positions.[45] Antiaircraft gun emplacements did not necessarily signify their operational status, since the guns left no blast marks upon the ground.[46]

RNAS analysis of antiaircraft artillery along the coastline showed various signatures. Antiaircraft weapons were in place to protect the large-caliber artillery that threatened Allied naval operations, and to protect the munitions

[39] "Study by Corporal Mallet of the R.N.A.S. Photographs," TNA, PRO: AIR 1/82/15/9/204.

[40] 5th Group, RAF, "Result of Aerial Photography," 13 February 1918, TNA PRO: AIR 1/93/15/9/240.

[41] The "big camera" was most likely the 47" (119.38 cm) lens aircraft camera. The newly arrived DH 4 had an operational ceiling of 20,000 feet and most likely flew the sorties for this historic coverage. 5th Group, RAF, "Result of Aerial Photography," 13 February 1918, TNA PRO: AIR 1/93/15/9/240.

[42] A. J. Jackson, *De Havilland Aircraft Since 1909* (London: Putnam & Company, Ltd., 1962), 56.

[43] *Illustrations to Accompany Captain De Bissy's Notes*, 1.

[44] *Study and Use of Aerial Photographs*, 15 January 1918, sec. III, 3-4, NARA, RG 120, Box 819.

[45] Pépin, "Lecture on the Study and Interpretation of Aerial Photographs," 8, NASM.

[46] "Aerial Photography for Pilots," 28, A 30.2/2.

depots and aerodromes in the vicinity. Reports highlighted a signature for the antiaircraft artillery emplacement that suggested a strategic plan for aerial defense: "The tendency has been not to place antiaircraft batteries close to the objective it is desired to protect, but at a certain distance from them."[47]

Targets in the German Heartland

The French prioritized German industrial complexes as the primary target regions. Four primary target areas, Mannheim-Ludwigshafen, Mainz, Köln, and Saar-Lorraine-Luxembourg, were selected. Of the four, the French decided that the closest target area, Saar-Lorraine-Luxembourg, was their primary objective for strategical aerial bombardment. Their goal was to create material damage to German industry. The impact on German citizen morale was not a priority to the French.[48] They did attempt aerial bombardment against German civilian targets in retaliation for German attacks on French cities.[49] The British considered morale a secondary "bonus" effect.[50] By October 1917, the French had narrowed their assessment of strategical bombardment effects to isolation, or what they termed "internal blockade." Isolation made it difficult for the Germans to move critical raw materials for their war effort. The important Metz-Luxembourg rail links were a focus of much strategical bombardment.[51]

Had the war continued beyond the 11 November 1918 Armistice, the Allies were prepared to conduct a more aggressive strategic bombing campaign against targets deep within the German heartland. British long-range aerial reconnaissance conducted by No. 55 Squadron covered many German cities, to include Frankfurt, Trier, and Köln.[52] A unique strategic targeting opportunity arose when the Austro-Hungarian Empire fell on 8 November 1918. The Allies planned to use bombardment aeroplanes flying out of Prague to strike key German cities, to include Berlin, Munich, Leipzig, Nürnberg, Frankfurt an der Oder, and Breslau. The British planned to fly long-range Handley-Page bomber missions against Berlin. The Armistice curtailed further effort.[53]

The strategical targeting legacy defined aerial reconnaissance for the remainder of the 20th century. Sustainability governed many decisions on the Western Front. Military planners sought any knowledge that could describe the German ability to conduct an offensive or defend against an Allied thrust. The preponderance of intelligence information remained in tactical summaries. The seeds of strategical analysis lay in determining the strategic makeup of the rear echelon. The ability to wreak havoc against vulnerable population centers from rear echelons carried a new message that modern warfare was total war.

---

[47] 5th Group, RAF, "Result of Aerial Photography," 13 February 1918, TNA PRO: AIR 1/93/15/9/240.
[48] Williams, 4.
[49] Author discussion with Dr. James Davilla.
[50] Williams, 28.
[51] Williams, 56.

[52] Pépin Papers, MA&E, Paris.
[53] The editor's note in Martel, 238, describes the planning for bombing German and Austro-Hungarian cities.

Chapter 13: Strategical Targets in the Rear Echelon

ARTILLERY ORGANIZATIONS

Artillery, the "King of Battle," ruled throughout positional war, determining the limits of conventional lethality. Artillery focused on trench destruction and wire cutting prior to the infantry's advance. It also served as the primary means of disrupting enemy communications and countering the adversary's own artillery potential through the process of counterbattery. Calculating the numbers of artillery pieces in a given sector was a priority for ongoing analysis throughout the war. Any discernable changes bore a direct correlation to enemy intentions.[1] Artillery batteries were located along the entire front. An American estimate at the time showed the Germans alone had one field gun for every 19 yards of front, a light field howitzer for every 57 yards, a heavy field howitzer and a 6-inch gun for every 128 yards, a medium siege howitzer for every 256 yards, and a heavy siege gun for every 512 yards.[2] German statements about artillery's role illustrated the offensive focus: "Main object is to help the Infantry break quickly through the enemy strong points, to keep the attack going even in the face of strong enemy resistance, and to increase the element of surprise."[3]

Not only did artillery serve as the primary means for destruction, it also was an important source for delivering chemical munitions. A captured German field directive confirmed German employment of gas shells for neutralization fire against allied batteries.

> The general appreciation of the value of the gas shell has now risen very much, as is proved by the high demands. Although the proper recognition of the useful nature of gas-shell bombardments is very gratifying, the general principle of economy has in this case to be considered, to a special degree, as the supplies are limited. It is therefore of special importance to have a sufficient amount of gas shell in the battery positions, in order at the right moment, when the enemy is starting attacks on a larger scale, to neutralize the enemy's artillery and thus, at the same time, nip the enemy's infantry attack in the bud. Small harassing bombardments are to be confined to special cases.[4]

Locating Enemy Artillery

Aerial observation placed a high priority on locating enemy artillery in a timely fashion so that acquired data could help achieve accurate counterbattery fire. When a major offensive was planned, aerial observation was airborne and on-scene to assist the first lethal rounds.[5] Artillery operations were continuous, regardless of weather

---

[1] Hahn, 187; Porter, 191.
[2] Porter, 209.
[3] G-2, 2nd Army, "Effectiveness of Different Weapons," NARA, RG 120, Box 10.

[4] *Artillery Operations of the Ninth British Corps at Messines*, 23-24.
[5] *Aerial Observation for Artillery*, 10.

FIGURE 163. **Extensive analysis within the city limits reveals a detailed layout of German artillery concealed by buildings.** Source: Illustrations, S.S. 550a.

FIGURE 164. **The line drawing shows the extent of cover applied by artillery in a congested area.** Source: Illustrations, S.S. 550a.

or darkness. A steady flow of information on enemy artillery was the daily standard. If the flow was disrupted for any reason, the squadron commander was held responsible for informing the artillery battery.[6] Guidance to aerial reconnaissance was part of the planning process. When the British IX Corps during the Messines offensive promoted the need for annihilation of key targets, the planning showed accurate fire was critical:

The bombardment will be carried out not with the view of total destruction of the enemy's trench system but in order to destroy machine gun emplacements, strong points, headquarters, and other selected points—by the destruction of which the enemy defensive system will be thoroughly disorganized. The further object of the bombardment, in addition to killing as many of the enemy as possible, is to thoroughly demoralize and starve out the troops holding the trenches. This will be accomplished by barraging continuously day and night the enemy communications and lines of approach and by shelling his billets and dumps.[7]

---

[6] *Artillery Operations of the Ninth British Corps at Messines,* 32-33.

[7] *Artillery Operations of the Ninth British Corps at Messines,* 28.

FIGURE 165 (TOP). **The search for artillery batteries was assisted by the black blast marks in the snow.** Source: *Étude et Exploitation des Photographies Aériennes.*

FIGURE 166 (BOTTOM). **The line drawing shows the battery configuration.** Source: *Étude et Exploitation des Photographies Aériennes.*

5. **Région de Somme-Py** _ 25.2.17 _ 2.000ᵐ _ F:50 .

The photographic interpreter was in an ideal position to track enemy artillery tactics and employment. Early in the war, épaulements (emplacements) provided sheltered protection for the guns and the support wagons. The photographic signature showed an alignment of four to six emplacements.[8] By 1917, the emplacements were abandoned to increase artillery survivability through mobility.[9] Enemy lines of approach and known intersections were targeted when precise reconnaissance data were lacking. When the artillery resorted to mobile operations, especially in the last few months of combat, batteries generally fired in the open without protection for guns or personnel. Under these circumstances natural features were utilized to the fullest extent to escape photographic detection.[10] The interpreter scrutinized tracks, where a sudden stop or modification to the track suggested a nearby battery position.[11] Once the artillery was discovered and coordinates

FIGURE 167. German antiaircraft artillery was set on a circular platform to allow fire in every direction. Source: George P. Neumann, *Die Deutschen Luftstreitkraste im Weltkriege* (Berlin, 1920).

determined, the perishable intelligence report had to be forwarded as quickly as possible.[12]

Topography not only shaped the battlefield but the role of artillery. Northern France's topography included numerous quarries, villages, hedges, and closely wooded terrain. Houses were particularly favored for providing artillery batteries with cover and potential camouflage.[13] A primary signature for detection was the blast mark. The force of the shock wave created visible erosion on the surface that was discernable on the

---

[8] *Illustrations to Accompany Captain De Bissy's Notes,* 1; "Aerial Photography for Pilots," 28, NASM, A30.2/2; *Bulletin of the Aerial Photography Department in the Field,* 58-62.

[9] *Study and Use of Aerial Photographs,* 15 January 1918, sec. I, 16, NARA, RG 120, Box 819.

[10] Hahn, 33-34.

[11] *Illustrations to Accompany Captain De Bissy's Notes,* 2.

---

[12] Bailey, 60.

[13] *Notes on the Interpretation of Aeroplane Photographs,* March 1917 (S.S. 550), 6-7, and February 1918 (S.S. 631), 8-9.

FIGURE 168. **The interpreter's world was complicated by the use of dummy batteries.** Source: Illustrations, S.S. 550a.

FIGURE 169. **The line drawing depicts the dummy configuration.** Source: Illustrations, S.S. 550a.

print as white score.[14] To avoid blast marks being discovered, the battery sought cover from any place that could assist in obscuring their position, to include forests, houses, hedges, orchards, and ditches.[15] The hilly terrain of Northern France complemented artillery tactics. As artillery was put into position, the Germans sought a reverse slope slightly behind the crest of a ridge to cover artillery operations from ground observation and ballon observateur.[16] Such tactics were put at risk by áeroplanes.

Targeting Artillery

Intelligence support to artillery targeting was continual. Flash-spotting and sound-ranging operated day and night, whenever conditions permitted. Intelligence garnered from prisoner interrogation was only as good as the source.[17] Aerial reconnaissance offered a timely and definitive source of information for serving artillery needs. "The best means of obtaining information is by photography, for the interpretation of aerial photographs affords information which would not be noted by an observer during a reconnaissance."[18]

---

[14] *Bulletin of the Aerial Photography Department in the Field*, 66.

[15] "Interpretation of Aerial Photography," NASM, A30.2/28.

[16] Bailey, 59.

[17] "Interpretation of Aerial Photography," 2, NASM, A30.2/28.

[18] *Aerial Observation for Artillery*, 7; *Bulletin of the Aerial Photography Department in the Field*, 65.

FIGURE 170. **In the absence of the companion line drawing, annotations were effective at showing the location and strength of the artillery battery.** Source: USAFA McDermott Library Special Collections (SMS57).

Chapter 14: Artillery Organizations

The French applied a triangulation methodology to direct counterbattery fire. Using aerial photography, the enemy battery location was associated with prominent landmarks on the map. The convergence of the triangulated lines became the targeted area.[19]

Aerial coverage provided a sense of assurance to artillery staffs. With it they possessed information that clearly defined their target sets, to include observation posts, dimensions of the artillery battery area, and trafficability. To their delight, the coverage also provided them with an image of ongoing activity that included ground traces, railroad terminal points, and telephone lines.[20] A dynamic liaison between the photographic interpreter and artillery unit was strongly encouraged for the mutual benefit of understanding each others craft and to help the battery understand its vulnerability to the adversary's aerial camera. The interpreter gained a better appreciation of the realities that confronted artillery in the field.[21] Despite emphasis on using all available intelligence culminating in the aerial photograph, the French photographic interpreter Capitaine Pépin reminded all that "in most cases photography alone will remain powerless."[22]

The British took extensive measures to manage the stream of information available on enemy artillery. In 1915, the British established a special topographic group known as the Compilation Section to monitor and track enemy artillery. Officers assigned to the function were sometimes flooded on a daily basis with over 100 aerial photographs covering known and possible enemy battery locations.[23] A year later at the Somme, the British established the counterbattery staff officer (CBSO) function to coordinate reporting from the battery and the squadrons to verify success of ongoing targeting.[24] The CBSOs also focused on rapidly changing German artillery tactics.[25] The CBSO managed the Counterbattery Office function which accumulated information on hostile batteries operating in a given sector. A detailed battery database was established, containing known battery history, location, all ongoing and subsequent activity, allied counterbattery activity against the battery, and the latest available aerial photograph. The Counterbattery database proved very successful, eliminating waste and effectively managing British artillery employment. Accurate reporting on artillery batteries was reported by the observers to meet the following scale: "A" accuracy signified that the observer could distinguish the separate pits of the battery under observation; "B" Accuracy could distinguish the front and flank of the battery; and "C" Accuracy only provided an approximate position of the battery. A British Counterbattery Zone map was created paralleling the Plan Directeur for function, with updates reprinted and distributed to all concerned.[26]

Artillery ruled supreme within the confines of positional war. It was the most lethal and effective means by which a commander could clearly annihilate the enemy. Instrumental toward achieving this objective was a well-established liaison network in place throughout the front, reinforced by an array of available communications. Through this elaborate and extensive network, aerial observation and the intelligence from photographic interpretation were effectively distributed. Such a network enabled the transfer of information to the right weapons system.

[19] "Aerial Photography for Pilots," 22, NASM, A30.2/2.

[20] Study and Use of Aerial Photographs, 15 January 1918, sec. III, 24, NARA, RG 120, Box 819.

[21] Study and Use of Aerial Photographs, 15 January 1918, sec. I, 27, NARA, RG 120, Box 819.

[22] Study and Use of Aerial Photographs, 15 January 1918, sec. III, 3-4, NARA, RG 120, Box 819.

[23] Innes, 49.

[24] Mead, 100-101; Innes, 69.

[25] Innes, 69.

[26] Hahn, 262-263.

CHAPTER 15
COMMAND LIAISONS AND COORDINATION OF ARTILLERY

Early into positional war, military seniors learned that a successful campaign required effective information management through a well-established communication and liaison infrastructure. This infrastructure eventually encompassed the entire breadth and depth of the front on both sides. It was linked throughout the trench networks and integrated with artillery. Despite the recognition of the aerial photograph as the primary intelligence source, analyzing command and control photography was recognized as incomplete. *Étude et Exploitation des Photographies Aériennes* reminded the practitioners that:

> It is not possible to reconstitute the whole organization of the liaisons of a sector by the mere study of the photographs."[1] Since the established targeting methodology was based on the nightly construction of the Plan Directeur and Firing Map, the photograph also validated sources that were distinct and separately equal from photography. All contributed to the intelligence process known at the time as the "Means of Investigation of the Enemy.[2]

The primary source of collection against German communication networks was accomplished through radio intercepts. Despite radio's infancy at the start of the war, it quickly became integral to the conduct of operations. Both sides employed a host of alternative communication sources to ensure awareness of events under way and assist in decision making for operating in the sector. From the start of the war a network of radiogoniometric intercept units was established to monitor enemy transmissions. During the war's first battles, signals intelligence revealed critical information on command location and enemy intentions. Triangulated radiogoniometric intercepts of radio emissions helped pinpoint critical nodes in the command and control network that comprised the Command Post. An added benefit from intercept was identification of units and construction of the enemy force's order of battle. This was essential in positional war's assessment of enemy capabilities.[3]

It was through liaison that information flowed throughout the front. Liaison represented the human-in-the-loop role of information transference among the combatants. French discussion conveyed the critical need for effective liaison:

> The purpose of liaison is to enable the Command to keep itself constantly informed of the situation of the Units

---

[1] Study and Use of Aerial Photographs, 15 January 1918, sec. III, 17, NARA, RG 120, Box 819.

[2] Pépin, "Lecture on the Study and Interpretation of Aerial Photographs," 11, NASM.

[3] *Study and Use of Aerial Photographs*, 15 January 1918, sec. II, 16-17, NARA, RG 120, Box 819.

under its orders and to supply it with the elements of its decisions, secure, between adjacent Units and among various arms, the transmission of orders, requests, reports, information and in a general manner, of all necessary communications in order to obtain the convergence of efforts, and in particular the intimate co-operation of the infantry and artillery.[4]

Besides radio, both sides employed a variety of methods to communicate. Transmissions between key points such as headquarters and artillery batteries were primarily accomplished through telephone and telegraph.[5] Portable searchlights communicated with aérostats using prearranged signals. Rockets (fireworks) were used as signals to order artillery barrage fire. Audio alarms available through bugles, hand sirens (hand-operated klaxons) and oxygen sirens

FIGURE 171. **Post of command buildings did not follow an established design pattern. This German PC was overrun by the Americans at the Meuse-Argonne.** Source: USAFA McDermott Library Special Collections (SMS57).

(compressed air klaxons), provided an additional means of communication.[6]

Post of Command (PC)

PCs (the British term was Command Post) served as the commander's domain, the decision point for the respective zone of action. It served as a center for total awareness of events occurring throughout the sector and maintaining an air of permanence with liaisons to cover any event, any time. Ground observers attached to a particular PC signaled enemy preparations, reporting changes through TPS. The PC staff received observation reports and combined the substance

---

[4] "A Study of the Organization of the French Army," 91, NARA, RG 120, Box 819.

[5] "A Study of the Organization of the French Army," 91, NARA, RG 120, Box 819.

[6] "A Study of the Organization of the French Army," 94-95, NARA, RG 120, Box 819.

Chapter 15: Command Liaisons and Coordination of Artillery

FIGURE 172. **View from a British observation post on the Somme. Observation posts provided the closest, yet most hazardous, view of the battle.** Source: IWM via Nicholas Watkis.

with the other sources, to include aerial photographic interpretation.[7] PCs were normally in close proximity to artillery batteries, yet sufficiently spaced to avoid destruction in case the battery was shelled.[8] There was no visual standard for PC shelter construction on either side of the front. It varied from concrete to log cabin.[9] As the information hub for the given sector, the PC's location was critical, requiring accessibility for the combatants within the sector, yet secure from enemy fire. It was the aerial photographic interpreter's challenge to understand the network as well as be an expert on the surrounding terrain to determine the PC's location.[10]

In the second half of the war, the front transformed from active defense to a posture of continuous situation awareness. The main defensive

line shifted from the front-line firing trench to the rear trenches. The function of the forward trench transformed into "listening units" (also referred to as listening posts) linked to the respective PC of the sector.[11] They were observed as small excavations either under or just behind the first belt of wire. Listening units became an integral design feature of the formidable Seigfried Stellung, reinforced by collocated machine guns, making their discovery a priority target.[12]

German observation posts served as the focal point for determining the enemy situation. Normally the post was constructed of concrete. It

[7] "A Study of the Organization of the French Army," 92-93, NARA, RG 120, Box 819.

[8] "Interpretation of Aerial Photography," 5, NASM, A30.2/28.

[9] "Interpretation of Aerial Photography," 5, NASM, A30.2/28.

[10] "A Study of the Organization of the French Army," 92-93, NARA, RG 120, Box 819.

[11] "Aerial Photography for Pilots," 31, NASM, A30.2/2; "Interpretation of Aerial Photography," 4, NASM, A30.2/28.

[12] Hahn, 26-27.

FIGURE 173. **The detail derived from the photograph was a testament to the skill of the interpreter. The cable line helped determine the command and control network in the given sector.** Source: Illustrations, S.S. 550a.

in height.[13] The towers (also called pylons) were detected by the shadow of the support poles.[14] Aerial reconnaissance was continually searching for tracks or saps leading to enemy observation posts. Stereoscopic coverage was ideal, for it gave clarity to any footpaths in the vicinity.[15] It was standard for both sides that observers had to be able to enter and leave their observation post unobserved day or night to avoid detection from aerial observation.[16]

Communication Networks

There were three primary targets for identifying German telephone communication networks: buried cables (cable trenches), telephone aerial lines, and visual signaling.[17] As was recalled in a post-war summary, "Telephones form the nervous system of the trenches."[18] Telephone line networks were invaluable aids in finding headquarters, or locating a telephone central contained within a shelter, camouflaged batteries, observation posts, and important centers or any significant location where enemy execution orders were disseminated.[19]

At the beginning of the war, both sides realized that they needed more communication links to enable commanders to conduct critical conversations with key elements engaged in battle. Command and control were first employed to ac-

appeared to be rising just above the ground surface. Loopholes and periscopes provided access for visual sighting. German observation posts were constructed apart from the trenches, employing concrete shelters for protection. Other posts were near the entrance of a dugout/ mine gallery shelter. These facilities employed wooded areas and terrain features to further mask the construction. Observation posts were a challenge to detect, due to the entrances being "camouflaged with care." When the terrain permitted, certain artillery observation posts were placed in front and in the vicinity of the batteries which they served. Observation posts on elevated ground served either the PC or artillery. The more distant observation posts in the rear echelon were noted for the construction, generally wooden or metallic towers 20 to 30 meters

[13] Hahn, 8.

[14] Pépin, "Lecture on the Study and Interpretation of Aerial Photographs," 11, NASM.

[15] "Interpretation of Aerial Photography," NASM, A30.2/28; Pépin, "Lecture on the Study and Interpretation of Aerial Photographs," 11, NASM.

[16] Hahn, 8.

[17] "Interpretation of Aerial Photography," 5, NASM, A30.2/28.

[18] Georges Blanchon quoted in Porter, 209-210.

[19] Pépin, "Lecture on the Study and Interpretation of Aerial Photographs," 11, NASM; Jones, II, 177-178.

quire answers to urgent questions relative to the ongoing operation. Over time, communication links extended to all elements both at command centers and to key organizations established throughout the sector. After the front stabilized during positional war, the requirement for greater and more effective communications between the PC and the artillery battery lasted throughout the remainder of the war. Artillery fire control became so refined that each group or battery was linked through a variety of means to ground and aerial observation stations.[20]

Most telephone lines were buried across the front. Artillery barrages frequently broke the cable, requiring constant excavation to repair the damage. A temporary solution was to lay the telephone lines on the surface. Cable trenches containing underground cable lines for telephones converged toward locations where either visible or concealed shelters existed. They maintained a comparatively straight course and narrow construction and had the appearance of either a covered sub-aqueduct (a white path slightly in relief) or an uncovered channel (the earth being thrown out only on one side or alternating on both sides). The description for the pathway was described in one manual as having a somewhat "woolly" appearance.[21] Photographic analysis required frequent monitoring since the ground signature faded over time. It was an important part of the daily photographic interpretation routine to mark both buried cables and telephone aerial lines when freshly dug before the traces disappeared.[22] Cable trenches were generally visible on aerial photographs by the appearance of long straight narrow light marks similar to trails. They conveyed an appearance of either covered channels or an uncovered ditch with the earth thrown up on both sides. Open cable ducts appeared as straight white lines with ragged borders, and a dark line in the center. The convergence of these lines toward a given point provided a significant signature of either a very important headquarters

FIGURE 174. **The line drawing makes an interesting assessment of "H.Q. betrayed by buried cable."** Source: Illustrations, S.S. 550a.

or a telephone central. In the latter case, most of the cable trenches radiated toward the front.[23]

Aerial (air) lines continued the communication feed outside of the trench area.[24] The connecting telephone aerial lines appeared as a series of regular white dots from the displaced earth created from the poles set to hold the wire. The white dots were not the poles themselves, but the disturbed earth from digging postholes. Foot tracks

---

[20] "A Study of the Organization of the French Army," 4-5, NARA, RG 120, Box 819.

[21] "Interpretation of Aerial Photography," 5, NASM, A30.2/28.

[22] "Interpretation of Aerial Photography," 5, NASM, A30.2/28.

[23] "Aerial Photography for Pilots," 30, NASM, A30.2/2.

[24] "Interpretation of Aerial Photography," 5, NASM, A30.2/28.

from work crews walking from pole to pole were visible. The interpretation sometimes benefited from shadows cast by the poles.[25]

German policy, as revealed by captured documents, provided further insight into the positions of telephone junctions. A 23 June 1917 OHL document ordered units to camouflage the surface lines and put the junction at a distance of about one-half kilometer from the PC. Photographic interpreters found the search for PCs along the Western Front to be less challenging a target. The facility was strongly protected, employing various communication links—telephone, radio, and footpaths for runners. The primary signal intelligence role, radiogoniometric analysis, was employed extensively and integrated with the photographic coverage to confirm the location.[26] The search for survivable communications within the front sector led to employment of TPS ground telegraph lines. Conductivity of the terrain (illustrated on geological maps) was a factor in the employment of the ground path. Despite being susceptible to intercept, TPS was a great improvement for communicating within the front lines at an extended distance.[27]

The final means of communication was through visual signaling stations employing two variations of searchlights (signal lamps). Searchlight posts were installed for visual signaling and normally located at higher elevations in the rear of the sector. Searchlight locations were supported by a network of saps.[28] Searchlights were capable of signaling up to 15 miles during the day and 45 miles at night. Smaller searchlights were effective from 3 to 12 miles during the day and 6 to 30 miles at night. The use of visual signaling was largely dependent on the nature of the ground. Sometimes the unit resorted to modifying the immediate terrain to support

the receptivity of the signal. Such modifications showed up quite plainly in a photograph, especially through wooded terrain.[29] The notches in the soil created a "luminous pencil of lights."[30]

Communications and Artillery

The ensemble of German batteries within a division sector was divided into regiment-size units designated as a Close Combat group (i.e., the field artillery and sometimes a few heavy [short-range] batteries under command of the Division) and group of Distant Combat (heavy and especially long-range artillery serving the German Regimental Foot Artillery staff). The Germans further subdivided their artillery into corresponding battalions of dismounted artillery and field artillery. It was difficult to align observed batteries to a particular unit because German artillery sometimes intermingled. Aerial photographic analysis could not delimit the German artillery table of organization. However, the composite of PCs, observation posts, artillery tracks, telephone links uniting the various batteries, and support infrastructure provided a fairly good estimate of the artillery configuration within the given sector.[31]

On the Allied side, the French saw communication as effective only "if it is in intimate liaison with the Infantry on behalf of which it works."[32] The liaison network became the essential link for all echelons. The commander viewed liaison as integral to understanding the artillery's program, emplacement and coverage of fire, the extent of munitions to be expended by the artillery unit, proportion of shells with each battery, battery movements, and priority of information required for the artillery operation. In turn, artillery looked to the liaison to alert them to the Infantry's planned maneuver, prepared signals, and the future locations for the advancing PCs. The liaison was required to thoroughly know the sector from a study of the Plan Directeur, relief

[25] Hahn, 29-30; *Study and Use of Aerial Photographs*, 15 January 1918, NARA, RG 120, Box 819; "Interpretation of Aerial Photography," 5, NASM, A30.2/28; "Aerial Photography for Pilots," 30, NASM, A30.2/2; *Notes on the Interpretation of Aeroplane Photographs*, March 1917 (S.S. 550), 8, and February 1918 (S.S. 631), 7.

[26] "Aerial Photography for Pilots," 30, NASM, A30.2/2.

[27] W. E. Pitman, "American Geologists at War: World War I," in Underwood and Guth, 43.

[28] "Aerial Photography for Pilots," 31, NASM, A30.2/2.

[29] "Interpretation of Aerial Photography," 5, NASM, A30.2/28.

[30] *Study and Use of Aerial Photographs*, 15 January 1918, sec. II, 17, NARA, RG 120, Box 819.

[31] "A Study of the Organization of the French Army," 97, NARA, RG 120, Box 819.

[32] "A Study of the Organization of the French Army," 97, NARA, RG 120, Box 819.

Chapter 15: Command Liaisons and Coordination of Artillery

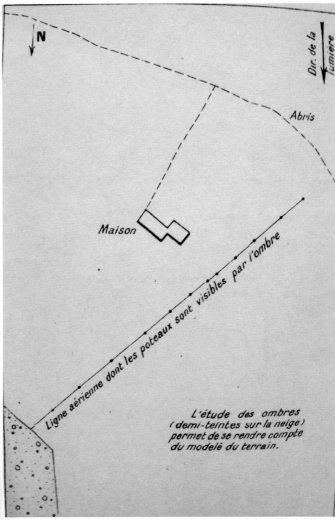

Abris

Maison

Ligne aérienne dont les poteaux sont visibles par l'ombre

Dir. de la lumiere

L'étude des ombres
(demi-teintes sur la neige)
permet de se rendre compte
du modelé du terrain.

FIGURE 175. **The aerial lines provided communication connectivity in a degraded trench network.** Source: *Étude et Exploitation des Photographies Aériennes.*

FIGURE 176. **The line drawing illustrates the aerial line network.** Source: *Étude et Exploitation des Photographies Aériennes.*

models, and aerial photographs. Liaisons communicated with the artillery through the telephone, backed up by visual signals and carrier pigeons. As for electronic connectivity, two telephone circuits were maintained, one by the artillery and one by the infantry.[33]

In the evolution of conflict, command and control exemplify the ability of a military force to manage the battlefield in times of chaos and the "fog of war." The lessons of the Great War

showed that effective communication links were of supreme importance for gauging an adversary's ability to continue the battle. In the years when positional war dominated the battle, command and control applied a host of new technologies such as radio and TPS to better manage application of force. Technology provided the commander with an ability to reach the entire battleground directly from the rear echelon. Aerial photography's role in this transformation contributed to, but did not dominate, knowledge of enemy command and control. Instead, it provided an additional source that reinforced the decision maker's understanding of the battle under way.

---

[33] "A Study of the Organization of the French Army," 99, NARA, RG 120, Box 819.

Chapter 15: Command Liaisons and Coordination of Artillery

PART THREE:
CHALLENGES THAT SHAPED AERIAL RECONNAISSANCE AND PHOTOGRAPHIC INTERPRETATION

CHAPTER 16
DURING THE BATTLE

The reputation of aerial reconnaissance as a difference-maker on the battlefield was burnished by the recollection of a participant. Moore-Brabazon described a serious situation where last-minute reconnaissance had delivered the impending attack from possible catastrophe:

> On a subsequent occasion, at another part of the Front, an attack had been planned to take place at dawn but the last photograph taken on the previous day revealed on examination a new position which proved to be a strong nest of machine guns. Had this not been discovered by photography, undoubtedly the attack would have been held up. As it was, orders were sent out to postpone the attack until the artillery had been brought to bear on the position. During the bombardment, photographs were taken to show how completely it had been destroyed and the attack was then opened with complete success.[1]

The ultimate test of aerial photography was its role in support of the offensive. The French experience at Fort Douaumont on 22 May 1916 demonstrated aerial photography's influence on commanders, even at the eleventh hour. Real-time access to information came with the air crew's ability to arrive at the landing ground, download the camera and photographic plates, develop them in the mobile laboratory, and quickly interpret the images. Tactical coverage provided a sense of assurance prior to commencing the battle.

Preparing Against an Enemy Offensive

Aerial reconnaissance reinforced Allied readiness preparations. In positional war the upper hand was achieved if defenses were ready to counter any attack. Surprise strengthened the chance for success in the campaigns. Reaction time was often the determinant of whether forces could withstand the destruction imposed. French doctrine emphasized that:

> At the moment of the enemy attack, the missions were identical to the French offensive. The uncertainty of the hour of attack complicated reconnaissance employment to effectively cover enemy actions exactly at the moment desired. This required the reconnaissance forces to maintain a greater vigilance and generate sorties with minimal delay. Reporting on the exact situation at the end of the day and in the morning remained a necessary requirement.[2]

---

[1] Moore-Brabazon, "Photography's Part in the War," TNA, PRO: AIR 1/724/91/2.

[2] "Aeronautics," June 1921, 24-25, NARA, RG 120, Box 819.

The photographic interpreter applied principles of timeliness, depth of understanding, accuracy, and application. First and foremost, the interpreter had to ensure timely interpretation immediately after each aerial reconnaissance sortie. Intelligence was perishable and required that a sense of urgency be adopted throughout the entire process. The interpreter prepared for the battle by studying the battleground's key features.

FIGURE 177. **Constant analysis of the battleground helped determine what shell holes were occupied.** Source: *Étude et Exploitation des Photographies Aériennes.*

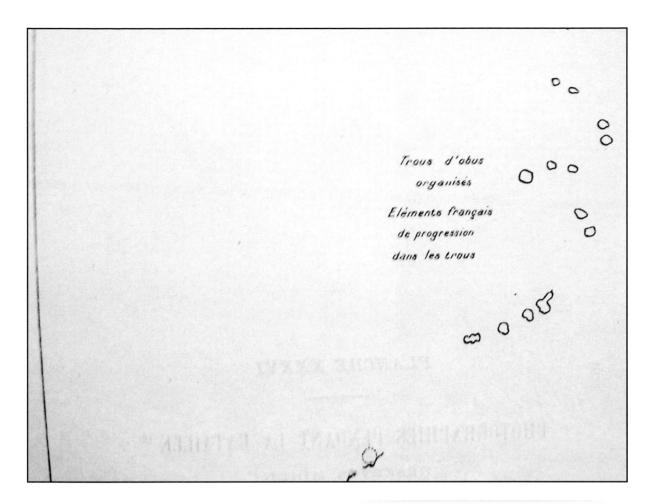

Trous d'obus
organisés

Eléments français
de progression
dans les trous

Any inaccurate interpretation not only increased the risk to the air crew acquiring the photographs but also to the infantry defending the front.[3]

The first indications of an enemy attack were ascertained from coverage of the rear areas. The signatures were observed in this sequence:

- (a) The reenforcement of antiaircraft defenses.
- (b) The construction of new routes of railways, normal and narrow track, and camps, and the like.
- (c) The appearance of new battery emplacements.
- (d) The appearance of new works for infantry shelters, communications, minenwerfer emplacements.
- (e) The contraction of sectors.

An additional striking feature of the impending enemy campaign was the discovery of a num-

FIGURE 178. An associated line drawing points out the advancing French troops on a Flanders battleground in October 1917. Source: *Étude et Exploitation des Photographies Aériennes.*

ber of Red Cross signs on the roofs of buildings. It became apparent that the enemy's medical arrangements were on a far more elaborate scale than the standard required for the normal allotment of divisions occupying the front line.[4] German field hospitals marked with a red cross appeared as early as a month prior to commencement of the operation.[5] Here is an example of an intelligence report on a hospital in the battle area: "2 new red-cross signs are seen W. of the Bois

---

[3] Pouquet, "Working of the Service of Interpretation of Photographs," NARA, RG 120, Box 819.

[4] "Summary of Indications of Enemy Preparations for an Offensive in Flanders," Conger Papers, Box 2, USAMHI.

[5] *Study and Use of Aerial Photographs*, 15 January 1918, sec. II, 12, NARA, RG 120, Box 819.

Gerard (66.5-40.8), not far from the 17 centimeter naval gun lately reported active."[6]

German aerial activity increased markedly prior to an upcoming battle, to reconnoiter the battle lines and refine last-minute planning.[7] Aerial support to the offensive required that aerodromes be located as close to the front as possible. The last visible signature of the forward-deployed aerodrome was hangars under construction. Canvas structures were first established, followed by larger and more permanent sheds. This process allowed the aerodrome to provide immediate cover as necessary, evolving to more permanent structures as the battle proceeded. It also freed up the supply of canvas to establish new forward aerodromes as the forces advanced.[8]

The orchestration of balloons along the front also added to indications of enemy intentions. The saying, "When the balloon goes up," be-

FIGURE 179. **When troops witnessed aerial observation balloons being inflated and launched, it alerted them to the possibility of an impending attack. Hence, the aphorism, "When the balloon goes up."** Source: USAFA McDermott Library Special Collections (SMS57).

came a part of the soldier's vernacular, reflecting the anticipated firestorm unleashed following the event.[9] Aerial observation from Allied aeroplanes and balloons monitored enemy balloons to determine if they were in ascension or on the ground. Locations and status were provided to Allied aerial pursuit or artillery for targeting. Occasionally, the Germans moved balloons around the sector to confuse Allied assessments of enemy aerial observation locations. One such deceptive operation attached a partially raised balloon to a motor vehicle driving from point to point.[10]

---

[6] G-2, 1st Army Corps, "Summary of Intelligence," Drum Papers, USAMHI.

[7] Hahn, 188.

[8] "Summary of Indications of Enemy Preparations for an Offensive in Flanders," Conger Papers, Box 2, USAMHI.

[9] Cooke, 24-25.

[10] Snyder, "Notes on Reconnaissance," 5, Gorrell Report, ser. r. 34, NARA.

Chapter 16: During the Battle

Distinct indications such as a sudden increase in artillery activity prompted the worst feeling that an attack was imminent. Additional barbed wire at key locations signified a shift in the enemy's priority for defenses, encouraging further intelligence analysis to support follow-on targeting by artillery. New configurations within the trench network such as construction of new saps, traverses, or shelters meant the offensive had to contend with new obstacles. Improvements observed within the German communication trenches suggested greater ability to move troops from the rear echelons to key forward sectors. New saps constructed forward of the first trench and hastily linked up provided additional protection for the advance guard in last-minute maneuvers. Finally, commanders and staffs closely watched for any change in the logistical infrastructure. A rapid increase in the number of light railways sent a signal that the trench was being readied for protracted operations.[11]

Analysis for ongoing battle planning had to be "pushed in depth" to the rear echelons of the sector. The search for staging areas, areas for potential counterattacks, camps, communication flows, observation centers, and artillery configurations always remained an ongoing concern. Such information was critical in the final hours prior to the Allied advance. Whenever preparedness activity was detected the aerial observer conducted rapid calculations. Any column of troops in the rear echelons was analyzed for unit size, location, time, and direction. A simple formula used by aerial observers to prepare the intelligence staffs for subsequent analysis showed a column of squads with four men abreast equaled two men per meter in length or 2,000 men per 1,000 meters. Likewise, a column of two men abreast equated to 1,000 men per 1,000 meters.[12]

The Allies Advance

The dynamic environment of the attack made it necessary to take frequent photographs at the

FIGURE 180. **A U.S. captive balloon on station.** Source: USAFA McDermott Library Special Collections (SMS57).

last minute, prompting the French to equate the experience to "hasty organizations." As intelligence received aerial photography in the closing minutes prior to the H-Hour attack, the aerial photographic interpreter quickly studied the planned battleground for any last-minute changes. Since time was of the essence, the interpreter reviewed plate negatives instead of waiting for prints to be developed.[13] The final preparation called for exact determination of whether or not the enemy trench was occupied. Early morning aerial reconnaissance was conducted with longer focal length cameras to acquire enough large-scale photographs to confirm enemy soldiers in place within the trench lines. Actual signs of occupation included tracks of supply, personal relief, and activity at PC locations. Enemy rear echelon areas were monitored for last-minute activity.[14]

The Germans disciplined themselves to employ as few trails as possible to limit any evidence of activity, since the trench lines were constantly

---

[11] *Notes on the Interpretation of Aeroplane Photographs,* March 1917 (S.S. 550), 9-10, and February 1918 (S.S. 631), 11.

[12] Snyder, "Notes on Reconnaissance," 2, Gorrell Report, ser. J, r. 34, NARA.

[13] *Study and Use of Aerial Photographs,* 15 January 1918, sec. III, 23, NARA, RG 120, Box 819.

[14] *Study and Use of Aerial Photographs,* 15 January 1918, sec. II, 22-23, NARA, RG 120, Box 819.

FIGURE 181. **German aerodrome collocated with hospital complex (note red cross symbol on the roof). Hospital sightings alerted intelligence to a possible enemy buildup of operations.** Source: Aviation: Data on German Air Service, NARA, RG 120, Box 5778.

reviewed. When Allied artillery commenced its barrages, aerial observers photographed the entrances to communication trenches or to temporary shelters to assist assessments of whether or not the shelter was still serviceable. Such analysis also aided in estimating casualties.[15]

As the Allied attack proceeded forward in an offensive, aerial reconnaissance focused on reevaluating the enemy areas for new firing areas, footpaths, storage, and new locations.[16] Detecting any signs of potential counterattack remained an immediate priority. The trails were constantly monitored for the footpaths that could lead the analyst to new headquarters and reserve areas.[17] Oblique photographs of the front lines were highly favored prior to the actual offensive for analyzing ongoing activity and finding additional enemy shelters with reinforcements. When the H-Hour for launching the attack drew near, an exhaustive series of photographs, maps, and plans were made and issued confidentially to commanding officers.[18]

As the battle commenced, intelligence and planning staffs concentrated on locating new artillery targets.[19] They were confronted with a chaotic situation. Massive artillery barrages cut up the ground, obliterating trenches. Sometimes a new trench evolved from a line of fortified shell holes.[20] Locating and destroying machine guns was a priority during an attack.

[15] Pépin, "Lecture on the Study and Interpretation of Aerial Photographs," 12, NASM; Porter, 193-194.

[16] Pépin, "Lecture on the Study and Interpretation of Aerial Photographs," 11, NASM.

[17] Pépin, "Lecture on the Study and Interpretation of Aerial Photographs," 12, NASM.

[18] Porter, 122.

[19] "Instructions on the Employment of Aerial Observation in Liaison with Artillery," in Maurer, ed., *U.S. Air Service*, II, 182.

[20] *Notes on the Interpretation of Aeroplane Photographs*, March 1917 (S.S. 550), 9-10, February 1918 (S.S. 631), 11.

FIGURE 182. **Continuous bombardment of the front line added to the drama of witnessing the ongoing battle through the lens and the photograph.**
Source: Pépin Papers, MA&E.

Machine guns were found outside of trenches to conduct flanking fire against the advancing infantry. The photographic interpreter looked for a small white or black dot in a shell hole suggesting the location of weapons. Stereoscopic coverage was ideal. Not only did it provide more detail; it gave the photographic interpreter the best tool to conduct the necessary terrain analysis for the commander.[21] Seeking active artillery batteries was an additional priority for the interpreter throughout the battle.[22] Warning of counterattacks required an ongoing, thorough examination of shelters. Throughout the battle any discernable tracks leading to the battleground were examined for new enemy approaches.[23]

As an Allied division moved forward into the battleground, it was assigned a route of march and a zone of action. Aeroplanes reconnoitered this zone and transmitted information by projectors (aerial searchlights), signal lights, dropped messages, or radio. Reception centers were established successively along the planned route of the advance to ensure continuous reception. Information centers were collocated at the landing ground, employing an array of communication means through telephone, radio, carrier pigeons, additional aeroplanes and automobiles.[24]

Photographic interpretation during the time of the offensive included the first use of battle damage assessment (BDA; French term was Register of Destructions). This time-sensitive function was accomplished without delay. It involved special analysis of the plate or negative at the earliest possible moment (normally 15 or 20

---

[21] Pépin, "Lecture on the Study and Interpretation of Aerial Photographs," 12-13, NASM.

[22] *Notes on the Interpretation of Aeroplane Photographs*, March 1917 (S.S. 550), 9-10, and February 1918 (S.S. 631), 11.

[23] Coleman, "Interpretation of Aerial Photographs," 1921, 4, NARA, RG 120, Box 819.

[24] *Aerial Observation for Artillery*, 10-11.

FIGURE 183. **The worn battleground at Moronvilliers showed extensive destruction. Interpretation required detailed analysis of each shell hole.** Source: *Étude et Exploitation des Photographies Aériennes.*

minutes after the return of the aeroplane). Register of Destructions located the parts destroyed, breaches made in the barbed-wire fences, areas which were hit but not demolished, and untouched areas. This study compared successive conditions of the target area from both direct analysis and the study of new shadows. The French process was to provide a simple multicolored sketch or diagram (solid blue representing an untouched target area, red hatching representing a semi-demolished area, and solid red a completely destroyed target area). The sketch was forwarded immediately to the GQG and lower-echelon headquarters so they could make prompt use of the information. A limited number of prints was produced for the headquarters and artillery to verify sketches and other battle infor-

mation. The photographs served the effectiveness of fire function by providing information about fire adjustments and destruction of strategic targets (batteries, railway stations, etc.).[25]

French artillery employed its SRA to focus on relevant targets being struck during the barrage. The database was a series of battery index cards containing relevant information to help the observers "follow" the targets.[26] SRA coordination with artillery extended to recommending the caliber of the round to either destroy or render ineffective any potential remaining threat, such as concrete shelters uncovered by earth shifting from the bombardment. The information provided to both artillery and infantry at the final moment prior to H-Hour was a critical facet of barrage analysis. An exact and complete map of the destroyed targets compiled from aerial photographic analysis was perceived as the best means to convey to the infantry commander what obsta-

---

[25] Pépin, "Lecture on the Study and Interpretation of Aerial Photographs," 13, NASM; "Aerial Photography for Pilots," 22, NASM, A30.2/2.

[26] *Study and Use of Aerial Photographs*, 15 January 1918, sec. III, 23, NARA, RG 120, Box 819.

Chapter 16: During the Battle

Cette vue oblique complète la photo 1 ci-dessus,
quoiqu'elle soit antérieure de huit jours.

Les trous d'obus organisés se voient ici très nettement.

Trous d'obus organisés

Amorce de tranchée

Première ligne française

2. Région de Moronvilliers.- 16.6.17.- 700ᵐ F: 120

FIGURE 184. The line drawing described the remnants of combat capability in the area. Source: *Étude et Exploitation des Photographies Aériennes.*

cles could be in the way when the advance commenced.[27] To assist the counterbattery fire, each French division employed a 75 mm battery in reserve. The battery was readied to quickly respond with a barrage should intelligence indicate a German counterattack was under way.[28] The French had an experienced aérostier assigned to the staff to assist in planning. Constant communication was an asset for balloon observers, particularly through telephonic contact.[29]

Plan Directeur maps issued at the commencement of the battle required constant updates to confirm subsequent artillery targets. The French described its purpose: "The Plan Directeur map of destruction which is made out daily during an offensive, will give at once the result of our fire of counter-preparation and of the enemy's fire of destruction."[30] The Plan Directeur provided the location of the Allied advance as well as an update of enemy defenses.[31] Along with the standard information portrayed on the Plan Directeur, the SRA contributed detailed information about the smallest caliber required to destroy the target.[32]

---

[27] *Study and Use of Aerial Photographs*, 15 January 1918, sec. III, 23, NARA, RG 120, Box 819.

[28] "Notes on the French System of Intelligence," 5, TNA, PRO: WO 198/983.

[29] *Aerial Observation for Artillery*, 11.

[30] "Aeronautics," June 1921, NARA, RG 120, Box 819, 24-25.

[31] "Notes on the French System of Intelligence," 9, TNA, PRO: WO 198/983.

[32] "Notes on the French System of Intelligence," 9, TNA, PRO: WO 198/983.

FIGURE 185 (OPPOSITE PAGE). A
detailed croquis de intelligence map
shows the extensive German trench network in the Moronvilliers sector north
of Soissons. Source: Map Library, Library of
Congress.

Prior to the battle, the landing ground was organized to accommodate the entire communications network. When possible, the division commander generally had his artillery commander with him, moving successively from one information center to another as the offensive moved forward. The division artillery commander used the information center to communicate with escadrilles working with the division to task infantry contact patrols. Aeroplanes designated for such duty (in theory one allotted per division) reported to the information center of the division, either from the air via radio or after landing, to find which battalion they were to work with and the objectives. Once assigned, the battalion placed the identification panels to complete the communication with the aeroplanes.[33]

Determining exact aeroplane objectives and assignment of duties was very important for planning roles during the battle. Auxiliary landing fields were designated near the division information center or in areas where effective communication was ensured. The division artillery commander kept in close contact with aerial observation, sending instructions through an auxiliary landing field. Artillery observers served as liaisons between the artillery staff and the air crew, meeting and coordinating with the air crew upon landing.[34] Intelligence offices at CA were notified as soon as possible. Visual reconnaissance reports were telephoned in and followed up with a written report. Photographs were developed as soon as the aeroplane landed. Two hours later the prints were dropped by courier

aeroplanes to the CA battle headquarters (two prints, one of them for the artillery); at each divisional battle headquarters (two prints, one of them for the artillery); armée headquarters (two prints, one of them for the artillery). Simultaneously, the 2e Bureau (the British source refers to the equivalent BIO) and the CA GCTA (British source refers to the Corps Topographical Section) commenced interpreting the photographs. A few hours later the annotated prints were forwarded on to the required distribution centers. The Topographical Section simultaneously revised the battle maps with the photographs. This provided commanders and infantry with a more specific understanding of the terrain and supplemented existing information on the German positions.[35] More detailed analysis from aerial photography was generated by a daily report; a sketch map showed the results of the day's observations, and a sketch map for the artillery showed batteries observed in action. These reports and sketch maps were submitted for final review at the "daily reunion" of the 2e Bureau.[36]

The French emphasized timely delivery of developed prints to support the ongoing battle planning. However, the prints were initially produced without the accompanying detailed interpretation. Armée and CA headquarters received the initial distribution. The remaining prints were sent with the report (when coming from a CA escadrille) or in the course of the evening (when coming from an armée escadrille). Additional prints required for ongoing analysis were sent as quickly as possible. Interpreted prints were usually the last to arrive for distribution.[37]

---

[35] "Notes on the French System of Intelligence," 4, TNA, PRO: WO 198/983.

[36] "Notes on the French System of Intelligence," 4-5, TNA, PRO: WO 198/983.

[37] "Notes on the French System of Intelligence," 11, TNA, PRO: WO 198/983.

---

[33] *Aerial Observation for Artillery*, 10-11.

[34] *Aerial Observation for Artillery*, 11.

FIGURE 186. **Cornillet was a key battleground during the Nivelle spring offensive of March 1917. The photograph shows a partially destroyed German front line trench still in use.**
Source: *Étude et Exploitation des Photographies Aériennes.*

Tr. réparée - Entrées d'abris visibles.
Une tranchée de soutien a été construite.
Preuve d'occupation par les pistes.

N

premiière ligne allemande

Dix de la lumière

4. 10 Maî

The End of the Battle

At the end of the battle, aerial photography assisted in determining the exact position of the new battle lines. Photographic confirmation of panel flags and smoking Ruggieri pots placed along the forward edge of the battle line provided an understanding of the new sector area. The panels were clearly seen by the photographs, even with a short-focus 26 cm camera. Aerial photographic interpreters annotated any coverage showing the infantry advance as "historical documents of great value."[38]

The classic signs of occupation were loopholes for firing, organized shell holes, obstacles

in the trenches (boyau(s)), outlines of trenches, rifle pits, tracks, and frequently the men themselves. Photographic signatures of the advance included tracks from the Allied side ending at shell holes or fragments of trenches, obstacles remaining in the trenches, refitted enemy trenches for Allied use (niches in the fortifications [*parados*] or in shell holes), and the direction in which the earth was thrown. In times of Allied advances the Germans dug a hasty line to reinforce their defensive positions. Traverses

---

[38] Pépin, "Lecture on the Study and Interpretation of Aerial Photographs," 14, NASM.

were reversed to accommodate new strongpoints and movement of machine guns and minenwerfer. Terrain examination was key to analysis of the new battle line. In-depth stereoscopic analysis determined potential machine gun emplacements, and kept in mind new alignments for flanking fire. Minenwerfer and *granatenwerfer* (grenade launcher) were also discovered in new shell holes. Small paths were detected to the new locations. It was hoped that the verification of the Allied advance justified the offensive. Such activity was accomplished a few hours after an attack or shortly thereafter the following day. Large-scale photographs were produced and extensive analysis was accomplished with the magnifying glass. The photographs became the new adjudicators for terrain arrangement and the emplacement of the lines. As soon as the study was accomplished the photographs were distributed to produce map updates with new trench lines.[39] Ongoing analysis continued between the aerial photographic interpreter and the intelligence staff. The 2[e] Bureau remained responsible for disseminating intelligence updates through intelligence summaries and directives based on new targets or techniques discovered.[40]

Full-scale battles in the war were moments of great intensity; but they were not the norm. Quiet sectors covered most of the Western Front. When battle commenced, it was usually the culmination of a highly planned operation within a particular sector. Timely and critical battle decisions required accurate data. Despite the reliance on aerial photography in this war, it was clearly limited in its ability to define activity in motion. RFC speed tests conducted prior to the Battle of the Somme reflected an urgency to acquire aerial photography for the commander to make the correct decision to influence the battle. Timely and accurate coverage remained a worthy goal for every aerial observation unit. However, aerial coverage as a tactical asset in battle was limited. Strategical coverage of the rear echelon held greater sway in determining ultimate success. Understanding the adversary's ability to sustain the ongoing battle became a focus of intelligence. As such, in the post-war environment aerial photography better served strategical analysis than the combatant.

---

[39] Pouquet, "Working of the Service of Interpretation of Photographs," NARA, RG 120, Box 819.

[40] Pouquet, "Working of the Service of Interpretation of Photographs," NARA, RG 120, Box 819.

Chapter 16: During the Battle

STUDY OF BATTLEFIELD DESTRUCTIONS

French interpreters considered the "study of destructions" a continuation of battle analysis. Imposing harm on the enemy was accomplished through two primary means: artillery and aerial bombardment. Success was gauged by the degree of damage inflicted on the enemy. Aéroplane and ballon observateur served as the primary sources for determining destruction; yet both were limited in scope. An exact appreciation of the extent of destruction required ancillary information from sources such as prisoner interrogations. Destruction provided Allied commanders and planners with a degree of confidence that they could take the war to the enemy, be it artillery fired into the trench or aerial bombardment of the heartland. Annihilation created an appearance of progress on the battlefield.

Destruction at the Front

The annihilation created by massive artillery barrages during the war transformed the entire region. The axiom of artillery was that "sufficient fire could destroy any trench."[1] In many sectors along the front the destruction was so massive that a history of coverage was essential to determine the transformation. Coverage acquired after an artillery barrage was subjected to a standardized routine of analysis. Again, the first priority was placed on locating the most lethal weapons such as machine guns. Once an un-

derstanding of the immediate threat was accomplished, the trench network was examined to ascertain the flow of personnel and supplies reinforcing and sustaining the battle. This required a complete assessment of the shelters needed to maintain an existence in the forward area.[2] Gauging the value of a particular trench network meant determining the effort under way to rebuild. Analysis included searching for signs of activity, new footpaths, and any visible materials that supported the defense.[3] A study then followed on what occurred at the time that the photograph was taken. The final step was to produce a standard template so that all participants could quickly assimilate the acquired information. In the case of French photographic interpretation, the information was arrayed on the 1/5,000 map to provide as much detail as possible.[4] Particular works being reconstructed after destruction or preserved in spite of the bombardment received special attention for analysis.[5]

Analysis of the entire trench network produced a standard methodology of destruction. The target in the forward sector was assumed destroyed when its defensive value was reduced to that of connected shell holes. The

---

[1] Porter, 192.

[2] Pouquet, "Working of the Service of Interpretation of Photographs," NARA, RG 120, Box 819.

[3] Porter, 192.

[4] Pouquet, "Working of the Service of Interpretation of Photographs," NARA, RG 120, Box 819.

[5] Pouquet, "Working of the Service of Interpretation of Photographs," NARA, RG 120, Box 819.

FIGURE 188. **Signs of any life in the former town of Bixschoote are not apparent on this aerial photograph.** Source: *Étude et Exploitation des Photographies Aériennes.*

trench was seriously damaged when it no longer could maintain the role that it was designed to accomplish.[6] Functional trench works were examined for trafficability and utility. The extent of demolition was measured in the soldier's ability to exist within. The trench was considered operational if shelter was still available.[7] One French master of photographic interpretation, *Sous-lieutenant* Pouquet, provided his own methodology:

> A trench provided with large deep shelters is heavily damaged when half the shelters are unusable and when half the garrison is obliged to wait in the trench. An ordinary trench without shelter is seriously handicapped when it has been hit every 20 meters. A boyau is seriously affected when a continuous and sheltered traffic becomes impossible, for instance, when it is cut for 20 meters every 100 meters.[8]

FIGURE 188. **Signs of any life in the former town of Bixschoote are not apparent on this aerial photograph.** Source: *Étude et Exploitation des Photographies Aériennes.*

An artillery battery was considered demolished when guns, casements, dugouts, and the other targets in the area were destroyed.[9] It was harder to gauge the extent of damage to auxiliary defense such as barbed wire belts or concertina wire. Surmising the extent of the layout following heavy shelling was even more difficult.[10] Analytical estimates on building and damage destruction considered structure composition, to include earth emplacement, masonry, cellars, and walls. Height of the rubble was derived from the length of the projected shadow.[11]

---

[6] *Study and Use of Aerial Photographs*, 15 January 1918, sec. III, 25, NARA, RG 120, Box 819.

[7] Porter, 192.

[8] Pouquet, "Working of the Service of Interpretation of Photographs," NARA, RG 120, Box 819.

[9] Porter, 192.

[10] Hahn, 23.

[11] Pouquet, "Working of the Service of Interpretation of Photographs," NARA, RG 120, Box 819.

Restes d'un village

Passerelle

Dir d Tumi

combat

de

fin

en

française

ligne

Première

P"

P

A

T

P.C. probable

P'

A.A' _ Déblais nettement rejetés du coté de l'ennemi.
P.P:P" _ Petites pistes allant vers l'arrière.
T _ Amorce de traverse

FIGURE 189. **This companion line drawing, rotated 90° clockwise, shows what little remains of the community.** Source: *Étude et Exploitation des Photographies Aériennes.*

The human toll from destruction was not easily discerned from aerial reconnaissance reporting. An examination of the hospitals in the area offered one perspective of annihilation. In the adjacent graveyard the interpreter could estimate the casualties from the number of crosses.[12]

Artillery and aerial bombardment strikes against road networks near the front and in the rear echelons provided an indication of enemy priorities for resupply and movement of forces. New routes were created as Allied harassing fire limited the effectiveness of routes, requiring ongoing map and aeroplane photograph study by the photographic interpreter to determine alternative routes. New tracks verified that the Germans were still operating in the sector and the

---

[12] *Study and Use of Aerial Photographs*, 15 January 1918, sec. II, 12, NARA, RG 120, Box 819.

FIGURE 190. **Extensive intelligence annotations have been applied to the AEF's map of St. Mihiel.** Source: Map Library, Library of Congress.

intended Allied destruction was incomplete.[13] The Germans put a higher priority on repair and construction activity of road networks than on improvements to light railways. Piles of road gradient ("extensive dumping") were observed along the roads to provide ready-made rapid repair against harassing Allied fire. The Germans built railheads to accommodate rapid transfer of personnel and equipment to narrow gauge rail. When Allied artillery destroyed the facilities, interpreters detected alternative railheads being constructed to maintain a steady logistical flow. Once movement was reestablished, sightings of new and larger stockpiles became noticeable. When the supply dumps were built, signs of ammunition stockpiles became readily apparent. The identification of enemy priorities on the front and rear echelons guided interpreters to determine sector readiness for follow-on offensive operations.[14]

Targets were classified either as temporarily out of action or completely destroyed. Analysis involved coordination with other experts to ascertain the degree of annihilation. The French had the artillery liaison assigned to the 2ᵉ Bureau confirm the caliber of the fired round to gauge the impact crater. The photographic interpreter correlated the calculations with stereo and oblique coverage to calculate the amount of soil unearthed from the barrage. Once the coordinated analysis was completed, the results were forwarded to the artillery unit to adjust fire as required. If the level of destruction was determined to be inadequate for the job, subsequent photographic analysis was conducted to ascertain if the

---

[13] Hahn, 28.
[14] "Summary of Indications of Enemy Preparations for an Offensive in Flanders," Conger Papers, Box 2, USAMHI.

Chapter 17: Study of Battlefield Destructions

artillery employed was of the wrong caliber or experiencing imperfections.[15]

The final step in the French daily assessment of destruction was, that night, to modify the Plan Directeur for commanders' review. Photographic coverage in the morning and evenings provided the necessary material to gauge the extent of destruction.[16] The photographic interpreter marked every observed strike and transferred the information to the Plan Directeur (1/5,000 scale) via an agreed-to color scheme of marks.[17] Once completed, commanders and staff prepared for the next advance.

Aerial Bombardment

Strikes beyond the reach of conventional artillery were the domain of aerial bombardment aeroplanes. These extended well beyond the corps' sector limit of 10 kilometers (10 miles for British). Not only did aerial bombardment pro-

FIGURE 191. **Oblique photograph by Edward Steichen of the town of Vaux (near Chateau Thierry). Each building was analyzed for any threat that could hide within the destruction.** Source: McDermott Library, USAF Academy, Dwight Collection.

vide a capability to destroy targets in the strategic rear echelon; it also served the Allies as the only force capable of taking the fight directly to the German heartland. Destruction by aerial bombardment was limited due to the aeroplane's inability to carry major ordnance payloads. Technology in aerial bomb construction was still in its infancy throughout the war. Accuracy was disputable, relying on the technique of the pilot dropping the bomb at the right place and time. Steichen assessed aerial photography's role in bombardment: "Vertical photographs made by the day bombing squadrons occasionally present

---

[15] Porter, 192.

[16] "Aeronautics," June 1921, 22-23, NARA, RG 120, Box 819.

[17] Pouquet, "Working of the Service of Interpretation of Photographs," NARA, RG 120, Box 819.

a spectacular and dramatic interest in addition to their value as a record of the bomb raid."[18]

GQG's Aviation Militaire complemented its aerial bombardment campaign with extensive aerial photography and analysis before and after raids.[19] The coverage not only confirmed the results of bombardment; it also established detailed maps of the bombardment routes. Rail stations and airfields remained a priority photographic target throughout the campaign.[20] Upon return, the aerial photographs of rear areas were examined by the 2[e] Bureau for indications of activity and change in the target area. Any differences were marked on the 1/20,000 Plan Directeur with information embellished by written notes.[21] An RFC staff visit to a French aerial bombardment escadrille concluded the French chose aerial tar-

gets that were either a munitions factory or an important railway junction and station.[22]

In 1917, GQG's Aviation Militaire initiated "a very remarkable photographic service" that emphasized photographic aéroplanes' accompanying bombardment aéroplanes on bombing missions.[23] *Groupes de Bombardement* started acquiring intelligence officers and established intelligence facilities at the bombardment escadrilles. Targeting objectives and aerial photographs of the bombing routes were provided to the air crews to assist in their long-range planning. Aerial photographic interpretation analyzed enemy defenses from aerodromes or antiaircraft artillery detected along the planned bombing

---

[18] Steichen, "American Aerial Photography at the Front," 1, NASM, A30.2/24.

[19] Capt I.W. Learmont, R.F.C., "Report ... of a Visit to the French Bombardment Group at Malzeville," TNA, PRO: AIR 1/475/15/312/201.

[20] Martel, 161.

[21] "Memorandum Report of Visit to HQ 1st French Army," Conger Papers, USAMHI.

[22] Learmont, "Report ... of a Visit to the French Bombardment Group," TNA, PRO: AIR 1/475/15/312/201.

[23] Martel, 161.

INTELLIGENCE MAP - VAUX
AMERICAN 2d DIVISION
TRACED FROM AERIAL PHOTOGRAPHS DATED 6-16 JUNE 1918
29 JUNE 1918

Bois de la ROCHE

THIN WOODS

THICK WOODS

REMARKS
HOUSES BUILT OF HARD FLINTY STONE
AVERAGE THICKNESS OF WALLS 45 cm
AVERAGE THICKNESS OF GARDEN WALLS 40 cm
AVERAGE HEIGHT OF GARDEN WALLS 190 cm
" " HOUSES 14-18 m
NUMBER OF HOUSES 92
NUMBER OF INHABITANTS 250

METZ

PARIS WIDTH 22 m

REMARKS
INFORMATION OBTAINED FROM
INHABITANTS OF VAUX
25 JUNE 1918

MAP No 44   0   100   200   300 M

LEGEND

1 BARRICADE OR CAMOUFLAGE
2 ENTRANCE TO La ROCHE (THE ROCK) CAVE
  THICKNESS OF ROCK 4 m SIZE OF CAVE
  5 m WIDE 10 M LONG 4 m HIGH
3 MAISON La ROCHE SURROUNDED BY WALLS
  THICKNESS 2-5 m STRONG HOUSE
4 RAILROAD STATION
5 ENTRANCE TO BROOK TUNNEL
6 OPENING IN BROOK TUNNEL

7 MAISON DEBOIS (WINE MERCHANT) GOOD
  BIG CELLAR STRONG HOUSE
8 MACHINE GUN NEST
9 EXIT OF BROOK TUNNEL
10 Mme PLUEN (SOLID CONSTRUCTION)
11 M. DE LA VENCY
12 MAISON GERENDET (STRONG HOUSE)
13 MAISON LEROY
14 • CELLARS

FIGURE 193. **AEF G2 personnel compiled even more details on Vaux using both aerial photography and intelligence information from the inhabitants.** Source: U.S. Army, Office of Military History, *United States Army in the World War* (Washington, DC: GPO, 1948).

routes. The air crews applied this to flight planning to determine appropriate defensive measures enroute to and returning from the target area.[24] The French commenced post-strike aerial photographic missions to determine bombing results, forwarding the assessments to commanders for determining results and strength of German defenses, and improving on subsequent sortie procedures. An additional benefit from aerial photographic coverage was rendering "the greatest service, notably by permitting the unmasking of the adversary's systems of camouflage."[25]

The British also paid attention to aerial photography in the conduct of their aerial bombardment campaign. Pictures of various kinds, maps,

sketches, descriptions, and all relevant information on targets were maintained in target folders. Strategic reconnaissance included the examination of all photographs for information relating to bomb targets and for the locations of aerodromes reported but not verified by photographs.[26] Their squadrons' aeroplanes were equipped for both bombardment and aerial photography. A leading strategic unit, No. 55 Squadron, conducted extensive long-range operations against the German heartland, including coverage of Köln, Coblenz, and Mainz.[27] The squadron's war diary described aerial photography's role with the bombardment sorties. The majority of aerial photographic sorties were unsuccessful. The diary simply stated, "It was impossible to take any photographs." However, no explanation for the deficiency was provided.[28] Bombardment results did not escape the attention of Intelligence at GHQ. One very successful aerial bombardment raid and companion photographic mission in April 1917 was highlighted by Brigadier-General Charteris with: "Seventeen aerodromes, dumps, and railways bombed, eight tons of bombs dropped, 1700 photographs taken."[29]

American aerial bombardment training at the Flying Officers School at St. Maixent emphasized aerial photography from the start. The photographic aeroplane was either in the lead of the bombardment formation or right behind in the No. 2 or 3 position. Lectures by the Headquarters, Air Service, Photograph Department to air crews recommended that a lightweight automatic film camera be employed for taking photos of the bombardment.[30] Exposure to aerial photography was not to create photographic experts, but "rather to give the students practical knowledge of aerial photography that will enable them to carry out intelligently any photographic mission that may be assigned them." Air crews were reminded that aerial photography was necessary

---

[24] Martel, 161.

[25] Martel, 161.

---

[26] Henry, "Report on My Visit to the British Army," 10, Conger Papers, Box 2, USAMHI.

[27] Pépin Papers, MA&E, Paris.

[28] "Detailed Raid Report, Capt. A. Gray, Commanding RFC No. 55 Squadron, 11 December 1917," in Williams, 105.

[29] Morris, 75.

[30] The type of camera was not identified; it probably referred to a simple hand-held camera available on the market. "Development of Aerial Photography," Gorrell Report, ser. J, r. 34, NARA.

FIGURE 194. Detailed 1/5000 map of Vaux used by 26th Division prior to advancing on the village. Aerial photography such as Steichen's provided clues as to the disposition of enemy forces in the area. Source: Massachusetts National Guard Museum.

to "bring back accurate and durable records of enemy activity behind his lines and to record the results of our own artillery and aircraft activities." The discussion emphasized that the camera was the "best observer there can be."[31]

An aerial bombardment aeroplane's ability to conduct strategic strikes against the enemy heartland was dependent on the airframe and engine

limitations.[32] French aerial reconnaissance went beyond the range of aerial bombardment sorties. In the course of the war, the French accomplished the longest known Allied aerial reconnaissance to Friedrichshafen and Essen (approximately 600 kilometers).[33] Before the war concluded, the French strategic bombardment was conducted by groupe d'armées (army groups [GA]) and armées with the understanding that aerial photographic reconnaissance was integral to the mission. In the northern sector, the Aviation Militaire serving IVème Armée controlled short-range missions. Armée-level escadrilles conducted photographic reconnaissance. The longer and more complicated missions, such as night missions, were planned by the Aviation Militaire serving the French groupe d'armées du nord (Army Group North [GAN]). It was specifically stated in the planning that long-range bombing operations ordered by GAN were to include aerial photographic reconnaissance. French Breguet bombers subsequently began targeting key railroad stations and enemy aerodromes. Guidance for their missions stipulated bombing in groups, maintaining a defensive posture in formation, avoiding any attacks on cities, and taking aerial photographs. Strategical targets in the German heartland included factories at Péchelbronn, Rothweil, and Oberndorf.[34]

Proponents of aerial bombardment in the final year of the conflict became the strongest advocates of aerial photography. American bombardment units were reminded that aerial photography validated their efforts. "In fact, next to bombing, it will be their most important work."[35] The purpose of aerial photography cited in training for bombardment units was to bring back accurate and durable records of enemy activity from behind the lines and to record the results of artillery and aircraft activities. The senior leadership looked to aerial photographs to prove the value of their bombing squadrons:

---

[31] "Report on Day Bombardment Training," Gorrell Report, ser. J, r. 35, NARA.

[32] George K. Williams, *Biplanes and Bombsights: British Bombing in World War I* (Maxwell AFB, AL: Air University Press), 4

[33] Estienne, "Army Photographic Reconnaissance as it Should Be," 5, NASM, A30.2/34.

[34] Martel, 161.

[35] "Report on Day Bombardment Training," Gorrell Report, ser. J, r. 35, NARA.

A Squadron may go out, drop its bombs with excellent results, and do a considerable amount of destruction, but if on returning it has no photographic record of the destruction done, the exact extent and amount of it, it can hardly be expected to receive credit for what it did. Obviously, it is to the interest of the pilots and observers concerned to perfect themselves in aerial photography.[36]

Bombardment units recognized the limitations of the human observers, who were looking for enemy aircraft, flustered by antiaircraft fire, and unable to see the details that an aerial camera provided. Photographic Officers assigned to the unit continually stressed the necessity of obtaining good photographic results so that the squadron received credit for a successful raid.[37]

Aerial photography's role in a bombing raid was described at the Air Bombardment School:

FIGURE 195. **During a British aerial bombardment mission against Mannheim in September 1918, a DH 9A from No. 110 Squadron was photographed below.** Source: Sir Robin Rowell photo in Liddle, *The Airman's War* .

Having gained altitude and crossed the lines, the pilot of the photographic aeroplane soon approached the objective. The photographs were taken to verify the bomb bursts on the specific target area. If the photographic aeroplane led the formation or flew the No. 2 or 3 position, the aerial photographic pilot throttled down and waited twenty or thirty seconds before the observer exposed any plates. If the aerial photographic aeroplane flew back in the formation, the observer took photographs as soon as he was over the target and continued to do so as rapidly as possible until the target had passed from his sight (and simultaneously kept an

[36] "Report on Day Bombardment Training," Gorrell Report, ser. J, r. 35, NARA.

[37] "Report on Day Bombardment Training," Gorrell Report, ser. J, r. 35, NARA.

FIGURE 196. **British aerial bombardment under way by a DH 4 flight. The aerial photograph captures a high-risk moment for the formation as a bomb is dropped precariously near a lower-flying member of the formation.** Source: SHAT.

to such bursts, the better results will they get."[38]

Aerial photography did not stop with target destruction analysis. The return leg of the bombardment mission included aerial photography of additional areas requiring coverage. The "camera machines" were withdrawn from the formation after the bomb run to cover the next target area. In case of enemy fighter attack, the observer fired a prearranged flare, alerting the others in the formation to quickly regroup and help defend against the attack. After the threat disappeared, the formation proceeded back to base as quickly as possible. "It must be realized that it is of more importance for the machines to return home with what information they have than to try to secure all their photographs and not reach home."[39] Any sighting of "superior enemy planes" before reaching the target required the photographic machines to return home without engaging the enemy. "Pilots and observers of bombing, photographic and reconnaissance machines should realize that it is tactically wrong for them to seek combat with enemy planes, and that it is more to their credit to return with reliable information regarding enemy activity, having successfully dropped their bombs, than it is to return with no information but with a report of several enemy aircraft shot down in flames in the course of combat."[40]

The study of destructions remains one of the most important functions for intelligence, assuming the role of "a veritable map of fire on which the shots may be counted, located, the effect appreciated and distinguished by comparison with previous documents, previous shots whose role has in general been nil, recent hits alone being effectual for the preparation of an attack."[41] Analysis of destruction was a discipline in itself. Its role in the strategic war was among the earliest justifications for aviation's potential in warfare, for it helped gauge the level

eye out for enemy aircraft). The aerial photographic aeroplane flew a rather erratic course to counter the threat from antiaircraft fire. This procedure was understood but contradicted the dictum that such missions were to be flown straight and level to acquire the photographs. There was also the possibility that the plates would fog up due to the antiaircraft bursts. However, that was considered unusual. "In fact, the less attention observers pay

[38] "Report on Day Bombardment Training," Gorrell Report, ser. J, r. 35, NARA.
[39] "Report on Day Bombardment Training," Gorrell Report, ser. J, r. 35, NARA.
[40] "Report on Day Bombardment Training," Gorrell Report, ser. J, r. 35, NARA.
[41] Pouquet, "Working of the Service of Interpretation of Photographs," NARA, RG 120, Box 819.

BOMB DROPPING   RESULT OF BOMB HIT

FIGURE 197. Aerial bombardment operations strongly encouraged aerial photographic verification of the strike location. The camera was considered the "best observer there can be."
Source: U.S. National Air and Space Museum, Garber Facility Archives

FIGURE 198. **The AEF's 9th Photographic Section arrived just before the Armistice. Its assignment to the 2nd Aerial Bombardment Group illustrated the growing role of aerial photography within the operational units. Note two 50 cm cameras and one 26 cm (Grand Champ) camera in their operational inventory.** Source: Gorrell Report, NARA.

and effectiveness of destruction by the artillery. Destruction analysis supporting aerial bombardment in the Great War measured the success of strategic strikes against the enemy heartland. The intelligence discipline's study of destructions evolved into Battle Damage Assessment (BDA) that has aided analysis throughout the remaining wars of the 20th and 21st centuries.

CAMOUFLAGE AND DECEPTION

A Duel of Intellect

Positional war forced participants into a game of hide-and-seek. On an intellectual plane it involved two distinct adversaries. One was a technician by training, determining any change through interpretations of minute differences on a film base. The other was an artist, using the battlefield terrain as a canvas. Their war became a struggle to shape perception. The combatants fought a war that required cover from the trained aerial photographic eye and mind, while injecting opportunities for distortion into the daily routine.[1] One officer noted, "In a more general way, remember that camouflage is intended in the absence of complete invisibility to render powerless enemy observation on earth, aerial or photographic, and must be conducted with extreme caution."[2]

To the participants, "it was an interesting game."[3] Despite the pervasive theme that the camera does not lie, the art of camouflage was applied to undermine aerial photographic interpretation. Unreliable interpretation was to be avoided, for it created uncertainty that gave advantage to the enemy.[4] "The enemy, who is fully aware of the importance of the aerial photographs, will do everything in his power to make the study of film difficult. Skillful camouflage of organizations in large numbers and fake works are all means which permit the enemy to mislead our investigation."[5]

Throughout the war, the battle of minds adhered to the dictum, "The eye only sees what it knows."[6] Survival using or evading the "Eye" required that armies "work smarter" and differently. It created a new art form, transforming the landscape to mask intentions. Aerial photographic interpretation developed its methodology through deductive reasoning gleaned from the aerial photograph, backed by the interpreter's knowledge of the battlefield. Both aerial photographic interpreter and combatant required knowledge of the technical and scenic possibilities of camouflage, applying ever-changing techniques to this part of warfare. "Art" was applied like a painter or sculptor who appreciates the part played by light, shadow, and tone.[7] The French adopted this theme in their assessment of camouflage in 1918. "To conceal oneself is now an art—an art all the

---

[1] Solomon, 2-3.

[2] "A Study of the Organization of the French Army," 26, NARA, RG 120, Box 819.

[3] Barnes, *From Then Till Now*, 495.

[4] A.T. Fuller, "Mysteries of Camouflage," *Army and Navy Register* (16 August 1919): 222-223.

[5] *Study and Use of Aerial Photographs*, 15 January 1918, sec. I, 3, NARA, RG 120, Box 819.

[6] Sir Joshua Reynolds in Solomon, 53.

[7] Solomon, vii; Carlier, 144-161.

FIGURE 199. **The self-portrait of Andre Mahr, a member of the French camoufleur unit, suggests the Cubist influence on modern-day camouflage.** Source: Graffin, *Carnets de Guerre.*

Chapter 18: Camouflage and Deception

FIGURE 200. **The French camou-fleurs adopted the chameleon as their insignia.** Source: Image by Ian Sumner, *The French Army 1914-18* (London: Osprey Publishing Ltd., 1995).

more difficult now that the means of observation are being constantly perfected."[8]

Camouflage practitioners were masters of the art of illusion. As early as February 1915, the French assembled a camouflage section from specialists at each command echelon to build dummy tree trunks or mannequin-like men and horses.[9] The camouflage discipline soon included talent from the art world. One French artist, Lucien-Victor Guirand de Scévola, was acquired from the artillery branch to which he was assigned and given the challenge to expand the camouflage program.[10] In 1914, as a telephone operator in the Pont-à-Mousson sector, he observed how vulnerable weapons and ordnance were at the front. To counter that vulnerability, de Scévola led development of a camouflage cover—a net splashed with earthen colors in a disjointed, "cubist" manner. Shortly after the

battle of the Marne, Guirand de Scévola communicated with both Général Joffre and President Raymond Poincaré about his discovery, leading to the first *section de camouflage* for the French Armée. Armed with this expertise, the Armée began to systematically develop camouflage for its soldiers and equipment. De Scévola's artistic experience included the newly developed Cubist technique, established by Picasso around 1907. He described his approach: "In order to totally deform objects, I employed the means Cubists used to represent them—later this permitted me, without giving reasons, to hire in my [camouflage] section some painters, who, because of their special vision, had an aptitude for denaturing any kind of form whatsoever."[11] By 1918, the French camouflage section employed three thousand camoufleurs, to include another well-known French artist, André Dunoyer de Segonzac.[12] By the end of the war, de Segonzac served as chief of the French IIIème Armée's camouflage section and was awarded the Croix de Guerre.[13] The unit was designated *La section des caméléons*. The camoufleurs had the distinction of carrying an insignia emblazoned with a chameleon.[14]

In December 1915, the British military staff selected a camouflage enthusiast, Solomon J. Solomon, Royal Artillery, to work with the French and learn from their experiences. Solomon proceeded to establish the first British detachment to develop camouflage techniques.[15] He sought out skilled artists, trained in designing imitations of nature within the "world of the photograph." The discipline required an understanding of the military art.[16] Art became a military tool to counter aerial observation, creating a new class of "war babies," camouflage, and aerial photographic interpretation.[17]

[8] American Mission with the Commanding General, Allied Forces of Occupation, Mainz, Germany, Part XXXVIII, "Camouflage," Sec 2, July 1921, 9-11, NARA, RG 120, Box 819.

[9] Edmonds, *1916*, I, 82-83.

[10] Edmonds, *1916*, I, 82-83.

[11] Stephen Kern, *The Culture of Time and Space 1880-1918* (Cambridge, MA: Harvard University Press, 1983), 303; André Mare and Laurence Graffin, *Carnets de Guerre, 1914-1918* (Paris: Herscher, 1996), 46.

[12] Kern, 303.

[13] Anne Distel, *Dunoyer de Segonzac* (New York: Crown Publishers, 1980), 93.

[14] André Mare was another known artist who was a *camoufleur*. He later served as an instructor of camouflage with the British and Italians. Mare and Graffin, 46; Kern, 303.

[15] Edmonds, *1916*, I, 82-83.

[16] Solomon, 53.

[17] Solomon, vii.

BB 387.0 - 245.9 6Ac 11Photo Sec BS+S NW

FIGURE 201. The "impression of life" was exemplified by decoys. Two tanks, British heavy and French Renault, were constructed to convey presence of armor in a given sector. Source: Gorrell Report, NARA.

Military camouflage practitioners paralleled the art world. Camouflage influenced perception through shape, aspect, shadow and relief, regularity, and color and its relative values. Camouflage artists avoided geometrical shapes that revealed a false environment.[18] Camouflage required attention to shadow, highlighting the face of the object or a neighboring object. It used shadow and light to determine the object's value, as "in the language of the painter."[19] Abnormal shadows gave away early attempts at camouflage and were avoided. They sought color harmony with the surrounding objects.[20] Color served as another indicator of camouflage, including analysis of the spectral composition of incident light, the state of the surface of the colored matter, observation distance and direction.[21] These practitioners of the art of camouflage directed that it be "less as a question of painting than as a question of sculpture, i.e. treat it by reliefs rather than by colors."[22] Behind the science of the camouflage art, aerial photography became the discriminator, reproducing the distinct spectral compositions beyond what the trained eye could determine.[23] In his post-war reflection on camouflage art, Solomon summarized the thinking of the military practitioner:

Even when art may be used to effect surprise it is doing no worse, but practically the same thing as the general who is pitting his brain against his opponents. That is known by the name of strategy or tactics. It is clear then, that the art which merely replaces the defensive or offensive concealment which nature in earlier wars afforded the needs to be developed to a high pitch of efficiency; for the side which neglects it will be unduly exposed to the onslaughts of an adversary who

---

[18] "Camouflage," Sec 2, July 1921, 24, NARA, RG 120, Box 819.

[19] "Camouflage," Sec 2, July 1921, 12-13, NARA, RG 120, Box 819.

[20] "Camouflage," Sec 2, July 1921, 25, NARA, RG 120, Box 819.

[21] "Camouflage," Sec 2, July 1921, 17-19, NARA, RG 120, Box 819.

[22] "Camouflage," Sec 2, July 1921, 23, NARA, RG 120, Box 819.

[23] "Camouflage," Sec 2, July 1921, 20, NARA, RG 120, Box 819.

Tools to Counter Camouflage

With art as a baseline, the aerial photograph became the discriminator, validating the ability of camouflage to provide adequate cover. Not only was the aerial photograph employed against the Germans' use of camouflage, it substantiated Allied camouflage throughout the war. Photographs were taken vertically and obliquely, in varied light, different sun angles, and at various aeroplane altitudes to simulate the enemy observer. Prior to a military operation, French planners tasked aerial reconnaissance escadrilles to photograph sectors in order to evaluate the infantry or artillery unit's ability to mask any identifiable signature.[25]

Aerial photographic equipment employed against camouflage included various panchromatic plates and color filters. The problem for the aerial photographer was differentiating colors at a level beyond the limits of human eyesight. The color-filter lens resolved the hues of the spectrum into their parts and imparted a definite and characteristic shading on the photographic plate, disclosing a spot of impure color. Foliage green, for example, resembled red; the camouflage remained green or turned black on the print. This assisted the interpreter in determining real from artificial foliage. A plate susceptible to green was employed to show differences between green grass and foliage. Camouflage blurred on the image.[26]

The most successful means of defeating ongoing camouflage was to exploit the history of coverage of a given sector. The aerial photographic archive complemented the battle-planning process.[27] The interpreter could trace changes at given points in time thanks to a collection of aerial photographic coverage of the same location. The archived collection sometimes detected construction activity in progress. History of coverage allowed the interpreter to detect new works and extent of destruction, as well as explaining enemy intentions. However, once the camouflage was in place, it became difficult to interpret what was underneath.[28]

Optics facilitated aerial photographic analysis of camouflage and deception. The most sought after coverage was stereoscopic, the dual optics providing a three-dimensional portrayal of the terrain. The stereoscope endowed the photographic interpreter with perspective and depth, a capability that could sometimes penetrate German efforts to camouflage vital installations. The stereoscope became the necessary instrument for discerning badly camouflaged works or evidence of "too much" debris.[29]

Despite access to tools, the interpreter's inevitable shortfall in accurately detecting camouflage and deception was due to ignorance of enemy intentions. The Germans established the function of "security officer" as a constant reminder to enforce rigid observance of the camouflage discipline. Some were attached with balloon units to monitor their own lines for discrepancies.[30] Another challenge was operational ignorance about the basics of aerial observation and photography. Few laymen knew how to look at an aerial photograph. Airmen had the reputation of never looking at a photograph with a magnifying glass. The British camouflage expert Solomon later remarked, "How they could expect to find incriminating clues, unaided, passes comprehension. There was ever the same incredulity right up to the end, in spite of the illuminating fact that bombing airmen were warned not to confuse an Earl's Court city with its real counterpart on the Rhine put up by camoufleurs to fog them."[31]

The Institution of Military Camouflage

The best way to combat ignorance was to educate the combatants on camouflage construction

---

[24] Solomon, 51.

[25] "Camouflage," Sec 2, July 1921, 27, NARA, RG 120, Box 819.

[26] Porter, 175-176; Barnes, *From Then Till Now*, 495; Ives, 244.

[27] "Camouflage," Sec 2, July 1921, 27, NARA, RG 120, Box 819.

[28] "Interpretation of Aerial Photography," 1, NASM, A30.2/28.

[29] Hanson, 15.

[30] Fuller, 222-223.

[31] Solomon, 48.

and application techniques by revealing the secrets behind application of camouflage and easing the layman's confusion about the detection process. Camouflage was defined as "The art of deceiving the Intelligence service of the Enemy." The target was the enemy intelligence service, which was "responsible for discovering and appreciating the facts as to our movements and intentions; therefore it is that service which it must be our first object to deceive."[32] Systematic camouflage included a positive and negative approach. Negative camouflage concealed the true facts from the enemy's intelligence service by preventing its members from discerning the important organizations, to include concealment of an intended attack by monitoring for saps, trenches, loopholes for observation and firing, machine gun emplacements, shelters, accessory defenses, and "fitted up shell holes."[33] The other technique was to create "the impression of life."[34] By imitating reality they created positive camouflage, suggesting that an attack was to take place where no attack was intended, demonstrating the existence of troops, trenches, batteries, and the like, in locations that held no such things. The prevailing attitude was to engage "in the deepest mystery."[35]

All combatants took necessary precautions against aerial or ground observation. Given the stasis of the battlefield, the combatants had to adapt to life under constant scrutiny. Integral to success was the discipline required to avoid detection by constantly applying positive and negative camouflage techniques. Despite extensive camouflage efforts, the simple carelessness of a single soldier could lead to detection.[36] The French manual on trench fortifications commented, "The first requisite of all fortifications is to provide cover." Soldiers were directed to keep traffic to a minimum and to mask shiny objects on clothing and weapons. Creature comforts were further minimized by suppressing smoke emissions and fire at night. That meant "invis-

ibility." Specifically, "the trench should be as invisible as possible to observers on the ground or in the air."[37]

A camouflaged trench appeared on an aerial photograph as a slight blur, either lighter or darker than the surroundings, caused by insufficient or too much shadow in the texture of the material used.[38] Within the trench, positive and negative camouflage could be applied. In the construction of observation posts, soil could be deposited so that it appeared as trench improvement. Debris from large excavations could go into sandbags dumped at a dummy emplacement or location of little consequence should it draw fire.[39] A good camouflage maxim was "Make your dummies at the same time or before your real positions."[40] Instead of the normal 2-meter depth, a dummy trench could be established with as little as 40 to 50 centimeters of depth. An aerial photographic study of shadows served as the only way to ascertain the true depth.[41] Protruding saps were difficult to hide from aerial photography due to their trace on the landscape. Again, depth was determined through stereoscopic analysis of aerial photographs. Trench camouflage concentrated on covering fire-steps, observer loopholes, and shelter entrances. Machine gun emplacements were "practically impossible to discern" on the aerial photograph. Ironically, camouflage led to suspicion about an emplacement. "An excess of precautions can be injurious."[42] History of coverage remained the best approach to counter any development or changes within trench networks.[43]

Various techniques were created to challenge photographic interpretation. "Umbrella camouflage" employed netting on posts with can-

[32] Supreme War Council, Draft Minutes, 9 May 1918, TNA, PRO: AIR 1/2299/209/77/29.

[33] Supreme War Council, Draft Minutes, 9 May 1918, TNA, PRO: AIR 1/2299/209/77/29.

[34] "Camouflage," Sec 2, July 1921, 76, NARA, RG 120, Box 819.

[35] Fuller, 222-223; Supreme War, Draft Minutes, 9 May 1918, TNA, PRO: AIR 1/2299/209/77/29.

[36] Fuller, 222-223.

[37] "Notes on Field Fortifications for the Use of Troops of All Arms," in *Trench Fortifications, 1914-1918: A Reference Manual* (London: The Imperial War Museum, and Nashville, TN: The Battery Press, Inc., 1998), 16-17.

[38] "Interpretation of Aerial Photography," 3, NASM, A30.2/28.

[39] Hahn, 10.

[40] Solomon, 8.

[41] *Study and Use of Aerial Photographs*, Section II, 20; "Interpretation of Aerial Photography," 1, NASM, A30.2/28.

[42] "Camouflage," Sec 2, July 1921, 50-51, NARA, RG 120, Box 819.

[43] *Notes on the Interpretation of Aeroplane Photographs*, February 1918 (S.S. 631), 3.

vas strips attached. The umbrella covered large objects like ammunition dumps and spoil from mines.[44] Fishnets were placed on wires to confuse analysis of trench defenses after a heavy bombardment.[45] A deceptive color scheme for buildings and roofs was developed. Scrim, a material used for curtains or upholstery lining, disguised buildings by altering the outline, shadows, and coloring. The British modified a house used as a corps headquarters to look like a ruin from aerial observation.[46] Decoys were another component to deception. For example, false ammunition dumps were created with camouflage to serve as a false lure to the observer. The real dump might be in the connecting cellars of a ruined and demolished village, or in the excavated embankment of an abandoned railway.[47] Constructing dummy field hospitals was suggested by planners in the last year of the conflict, but was rejected as a violation of the Geneva Convention.[48]

Camouflage was not confined to individual equipment. It expanded over the course of the war to cover large areas of the terrain network. Roads were screened to thwart enemy observation. The first attempts used canvas sheets painted to represent an aerial portrayal of the ground. Heavy to erect and difficult to maintain in position, on the suggestion of Solomon the canvas was replaced by lighter and more manageable material such as old fish nets or wire netting, garnished with tufts of painted or dyed fibers from African palms. In 1916, prior to the Somme offensive, British engineers wove thousands of rolls of wire netting with the fiber. In the course of time all British artillery batteries were equipped with the fiber covers. As the demand increased and the supply became inadequate, less flammable canvas strips were substituted for the cover.[49] Major George Patton, AEF, provided a brief description of road camouflage in a letter to his wife in May 1918. "The Maj. and I left here at 7:30 and went by motor to within about 1,500 yds of the front line. Most of the way the road was screened with camouflage.

FIGURE 202. **Netting covers a light rail (tramway) in the front sector.** Source: Gorrell Report, NARA.

Sacking about 12 feet high on Frames it keeps the enemy from seeing what is on the road so he can not fire on it."[50]

The art of camouflaging artillery was considered a vital element of artilleryship, "a knowledge of which is of as high importance for the battery commander as the preparation and conduct of in-direct fire, the knowledge of battery transport, or of any other of the basic principles of his education." [51] Artillery operations and camouflage were intertwined. Camouflage concealed the battery position, communications, and observation posts. It also helped direct enemy artillery toward a false battery. [52] Some artillery units disguised their gun positions by preparing several emplacements for each battery of four guns. The guns fired from one position for a time and then moved, generally at night, to another. This pattern was repeated between various positions. To complicate enemy detection, small detachments

[44] Edmonds, *1916*, I, 84.

[45] Fuller, 222-223.

[46] Edmonds, *1916*, I, 84.

[47] Barnes, *From Then Till Now*, 495.

[48] Supreme War Council File, Draft Minutes, 9 May 1918, TNA, PRO: AIR 1/2299/209/77/29.

[49] Edmonds, *1916*, I, 84.

[50] Martin Blumenson, *The Patton Papers, 1885-1940* (2 vols., Boston: Houghton Mifflin Company, 1972), II, 582.

[51] Guidance provided to U.S. aviators through a member of the Belgian Artillery. Capt F. T. Colby and Capt Cushing-Donnell, "Notes on Artillery Camouflage and its Employment," HQ AEF, October 1917, Jefferson Hayes Davis Papers, McDermott Library, USAFA, SMS 57.

[52] Colby and Cushing-Donnell, "Notes on Artillery Camoflauge," Davis Papers, USAFA.

at the vacated emplacements fired off flares resembling the muzzle flashes of guns while at the same instant the real guns fired from another position. A combination of stereoscopic and ordinary photographs countered the deception by determining the blast marks from the artillery discharge.[53] Elaborately camouflaged artillery was often detected with ease when the concealed object cast a noticeable shadow. History of coverage of a given location helped detect any attempt to add artificial cover.[54] The French configured their artillery camouflage to the phase of the operation. During the active movement of maneuver, camouflage was not a priority. However, when the battery was established for fire, an appropriate cover was applied.[55] It was indicative of a commander's attention to camouflage that the forces were reminded to take appropriate measures. Such was the case during the Allied summer offensive in 1918, when Général Vincent, artillery commander of the 38ème CA, alerted both

subordinate American and French artillery commanders of concerns over appropriate camouflage for operations. Vincent reminded the commanders to have their batteries photographed through aerial reconnaissance regularly to "perfect the camouflage." Reinforcing the policy was the directive that the first aerial photographs were to be "rushed" to the commanders of division and heavy artillery.[56] Artillery camouflage attempted to avoid the repetition of the battery signature. The geometric form of the employed battery required covering any discernable angles where the camouflage joined the soil. That required attention to what the shadow revealed. Tracks were

---

[53] Hanson, 17-18.

[54] Pépin, "Lecture on the Study and Interpretation of Aerial Photographs," 7, NASM; *Notes on the Interpretation of Aeroplane Photographs*, February 1918 (S.S. 631), 9.

[55] "Camouflage," Sec 2, July 1921, 62-63, NARA, RG 120, Box 819.

[56] Général Vincent Memorandum to Artillery Commander of U.S. 3rd Division, Divisional Artillery Commander of French 39th Division, and Heavy Artillery Commander of the 38th Army Corps, "Necessity for Battery Camouflage," in *United States Army in the World War, 1917-1919*, III, 590.

conspicuous, requiring the unit to lay down turf in irregular fashion. The best camouflage for tracks was "obtained by discipline."[57]

Artillery employed dummy configurations, notable for overcompensated features, providing the aerial photographic interpreter with conspicuous blast contours and artificial tracks. Additional tricks included smoke from false hutments to suggest life in the area. An operational technique to reinforce the site's deception was to quickly maneuver artillery into the dummy emplacement at night. Rounds fired gave the impression that the location contained an active unit.[58] Unoccupied emplacements served as false batteries. One German document instructed that four emplacements should be constructed: a forward, a spare forward, a withdrawal, and a spare withdrawal emplacement. The battery could maneuver between those locations, conveying an environment of non-activity.[59]

Camouflage and deception activities included planning to mask various signatures from enemy observation. Cooperation among the planning staffs was essential. Elaborate precautions for moving troops by road or rail during the night were useless "if the construction of large and obvious dumps" and "new hutments, aerodromes and Field hospitals are springing up like mushrooms long before an attack is to take place."[60] In the rear echelon areas, dummy aerodromes and aeroplanes were a positive technique employed to confuse order of battle analysis.[61] By 1917, it was obvious that all facets of aviation were vulnerable to observation and aerial bombardment. The French began camouflaging their áeroplanes that October. Colonel E. S. Gorrell, in a memo to the chief of the U.S. Signal Corps, mentioned the transformation: "Within the last three weeks there has taken place a great

FIGURE 204. **Camouflage netting over field artillery was designed to disrupt the value of enemy aerial photography.** Source: USAFA McDermott Library Special Collections (SMS57).

change in the method of doping French airplanes. All the French airplanes are now being doped a sort of silver gray color underneath … the sides and tops are camouflaged in a somewhat similar method as the camouflage of the Bessonneau hangars."[62]

Despite the attempt to institutionalize camouflage, natural settings aided and confused combatants. Aerial photography during spring and summer had to break through the leaves and natural cover. However, interpreters considered camouflage with fresh branches and undergrowth a simple matter to discern.[63] Cultural practices of the region also complicated analysis. In late 1914, an RFC aviator circulated a memo describing the lessons learned from observation in Northern Europe. Mistakes in identifying objects on the ground held potential risk for correctly determining the true force disposition. Rows of straw shelters used by farmers for drying tobacco or an indigenous herb were erroneously reported as enemy bivouacs. Additionally, some farmers' practice of piling beet or

[57] "Camouflage," Sec 2, July 1921, 54-57, NARA, RG 120, Box 819.
[58] "Camouflage," Sec 2, July 1921, 76, NARA, RG 120, Box 819.
[59] "Interpretation of Aerial Photography," 6, NASM, A30.2/28; "Aerial Photography for Pilots," 29, NASM, A30.2/2.
[60] Supreme War Council, Draft Minutes, 9 May 1918, TNA, PRO: AIR 1/2299/209/77/29.
[61] Frank, *American Air Service Observation*, 394; "Instructions on the Employment of Aerial Observation," in Maurer, ed., *U.S. Air Service*, II, 182.

[62] Col E. S. Gorrell, 26 October 1917 Memorandum, quoted in Toelle, 67.
[63] *Notes on the Interpretation of Aeroplane Photographs*, March 1917 (S.S. 550), 6, and February 1918 (S.S. 631), 8.

Chapter 18: Camouflage and Deception

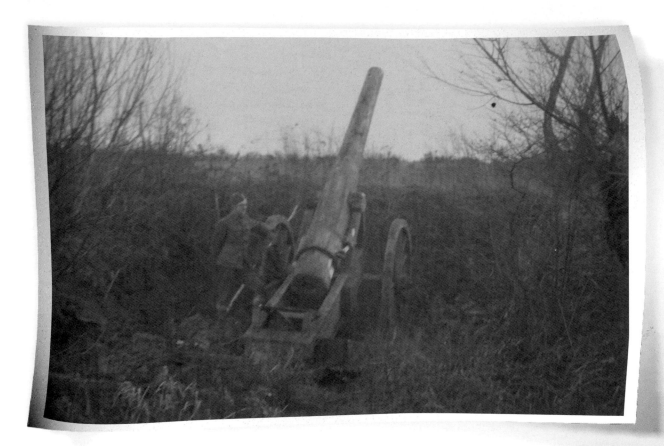

turnip roots contributed to the misleading image of trenches where none existed.[64]

Camouflage in Conflict

Both sides paid extensive attention to camouflage and deception, yet with mixed results. Ironically, the British had demonstrated a propensity early on to use the technique, but apprehension and ignorance among the senior staff slowed the rigorous application of the art. In 1912, the British Army conducted maneuvers with aeroplanes, providing aerial observation for the first time. One British division was so successful in hiding itself that the press labeled it "The Lost Division." Lieutenant General Sir James Grierson, commanding the maneuver, when asked by King George V how he accomplished the feat, replied, "The men put their waterproof sheets over their heads and made noises like mushrooms." In reality, the troops acquired camouflage material from tree branches, while straw and waterproof sheets covered guns and other essential items. They took the extra step to

[64] Lieut I. M. Bonham-Carter, "Notes," 1 November 1914, TNA, PRO: AIR 1/834/204/5/240.

FIGURE 205. **Combatants on the Western Front complicated the photographic interpreter's analysis by creating fake artillery pieces. The artillery being examined was a German decoy.** Source: Gorrell Report, NARA.

blend in by bivouacking close to hedges, walls, houses, and woods.[65]

Camouflage and deception remained a constant requirement for the combatants. By March 1915 French aerial observation reports emphasized that German artillery batteries had commenced taking evasive action and hiding from the ongoing Allied aerial reconnaissance.[66] "Keep everything low" was a camouflage instruction found on a German prisoner.[67] Ernst Jünger, a future Sturmtruppen commander, echoed the precautions taken by the infantry: "On account of the danger from aircraft we had to keep our-

[65] Edmonds, *1916*, I, 82.
[66] Weiller in de Brunoff, 64.
[67] Solomon, 22.

selves close in the over-crowded place."[68] By the final year, operational emphasis on the issue was clearly discernable. One German instruction emphasized:

> Concealment from airplane observation is more important than all other considerations in the choice of a location for an encampment. Carefully conceal beaten paths, trample down no paths thru grain and clover. Columns should leave established roads under cover. Do not park vehicles in rows, but individually under trees or carefully concealed, never on the street. Keep at least ten meters inside the edge of the woods. It is the permanent duty of officers of General Headquarters, of balloon and aviation officers, to see to the carrying out of these orders.[69]

The Germans became expert in simulating rail and road movements to confuse aerial observation and intelligence analysis. They marched back and forth on the same roads, employing a team of men on bicycles with smoke-producing devices to imitate clouds of dust on sheltered roads. Smoke-emitting automobiles were placed on railroads to simulate rail activity. The deception increased as aerial observation was forced to fly at higher altitudes.[70]

Four years of positional war clearly confirmed the proposition that surprise was critical to successful conduct of the campaign. The Germans masterfully developed underground facilities and applied them in major operations.[71] Their most notable success was staging their 1916 advance attack in the Stollen underground facilities at Verdun. By 1917, German camouflage included construction of passages between shell holes. The excavated earth was thrown into neighboring holes or spread on the ground. Tunneled dugouts were designed to appear like shell holes so that aerial observation could not determine an entrance.[72] In the final year, the most brilliant accomplishment was the strategic masking of the German forces staging in the Somme region prior to the Michael offensive.[73] The Germans successfully coordinated their deception operations. The French proved inflexible in effectively applying their cryptological and radio intercept strengths to deceive and counter the German buildup. One French général, reflecting on the inadequacy of the French approach to camouflage and deception goals, summarized the effect: "camouflage … is an anachronism."[74]

The British oversimplified German intentions prior to the March 1918 Michael offensive, based on over-dependence on order-of-battle information. This misperception helped the Germans' overall deception campaign. David French recounts the British conviction that the Michael Offensive was against the Channel ports, causing them to move an extra division and twenty batteries to reinforce the British Second Army guarding the coast.[75] British offensive doctrine and strategy chose to ignore to these lessons. By 1917, British policy had concluded that preparing for a large offensive was impossible to hide from the Germans. British military strategists determined that the best approach toward fighting the war was to overwhelm the Germans with a superior force. This doctrine failed in the Cambrai offensive that took place that November. The subsequent disaster from Michael showed acute Allied vulnerabilities in misjudging the German strategic camouflage program and the latter's ability to mislead estimates of German force strength and intentions. Such a shortfall was almost fatal

---

[68] Ernst Jünger, *Storm of Steel: From the Diary of a German Storm-Troop Officer on the Western Front* (trans., London: Chatto & Windus, 1929; reprint New York: Howard Fertig, 1996), 16-17.

[69] Von Kathen, "Memorandum for Encampments," in HQ 26th Division, "Intelligence Bulletin," 26 July 1918," NARA, RG 120, Box 1.

[70] Supreme War Council, Draft Minutes, 9 May 1918, TNA, PRO: AIR 1/2299/209/77/29.

[71] Solomon, 39.

[72] "Intelligence Summary," 19 August 1918, TNA, PRO: AIR 1/2124/207/74/3.

[73] Porch, 113.

[74] Radio intercept units had to be on guard when subjected to an absence of enemy communications reflecting either a change in the command and control of a particular sector or a deceptive cover for an impending operation. Général Ribadeau Dumas, quoted in Porch, 113, n. 84 and n. 543.

[75] David French in Dockrill and French, 79-83.

SPARAPPELHOEK.

for the Allies.[76] Partial blame can be pinned on a less rigorous application of preventive measures through aerial reconnaissance. The Supreme War Council in the spring of 1918 concluded, "The failure to make the necessary photographic tests is the only explanation of much bad camouflage work which has been done in the past." If Allied camouflage was to succeed, it required greater coordination between the camouflage and aerial photographic interpreter. As late as May 1918, the Inter-Allied Aviation Committee meeting at Versailles to plan the strategic campaign for the

FIGURE 206. German dummy aeroplanes in line were intended to confuse air order-of-battle analysts. Source: Solomon J. Solomon, *Strategic Camouflage* (New York: E.P. Dutton and Company, 1920).

coming year cited camouflage as an area requiring more emphasis.[77]

Art remained in conflict with tradition. For example, French operational and tactical systems were too inflexible to take advantage of camouflage developments that supported German attack methods. By 1918, the French command

---

[76] The RFC also maintained an aggressive offensive strategy that would have overlooked signs for the buildup while engaging tactical targets. Author discussion with James Streckfuss; David French in Dockrill and French, 79-83.

[77] "Supreme War Council File," Draft Minutes, 9 May 1918, TNA, PRO: AIR 1/2299/209/77/29.

had not developed techniques equal to German camouflage and deception. "It must be admitted that our military education has not been developed in this direction before the present events, the very idea of concealment being distasteful to our character."[78]

Allied commanders preparing for the final offensives prior to the Armistice did consider camouflage and deception. However, the experience did not always meet expectations. The innovative American aviator, Brigadier General Mitchell, personally took measures to complicate German analysis prior to the September 1918 St. Mihiel offensive, ordering aerial units in the sector to construct fake hangars and aeroplanes at various locations close to the impending battleground. In the days before the offensive, fabricated aeroplanes were moved around the airfield suggesting minimal activity at the location. While this charade was exercised, real aeroplanes arrived at the forward aerodromes prior to dawn's light. The camouflaged hangars were replaced overnight by functioning hangars of similar dimensions. For the most part, the effort was successful. However, it only takes one mistake and the operation can be compromised. In Mitchell's case, one aero squadron made the critical mistake of arriving in broad daylight and commencing aerial reconnaissance of the strategic rear echelons near Metz. Their increased aerial activity alerted German intelligence to the impending operation.[79]

Making camouflage and deception integral to success in positional war required extensive resources. When the Americans arrived in the war, a U.S. Camouflage Corps was established. Its average monthly consumption was an illustrative example of commitment to the art. In order to provide camouflage cover for the American sector, approximately 4,328,000 square yards of burlap; 200,000 gallons of paint; 7,700 fish nets; 50,000 pounds of wire; and 2,160,000 square yards of poultry netting were required to conceal both trenches and artillery battery emplacements. A single square mile of the front line was estimated to contain approximately 900 miles of barbed wire; 6,000,000 sandbags; 1,000,000 cubic feet of timber; and 36,000 square feet of corrugated iron.[80] Had the conflict continued into 1919, the Americans could have been the de facto leader of the Allies for applying camouflage to their operations, thanks to their industrial might. An American intelligence assessment indicated the presence of German camouflage: "Study of Photographs taken Sept. 15, 1918. Camouflage work at C.5.16-0.40, and new trench work at C.5.17-C-45."[81]

The genesis of deceiving the enemy in modern warfare covered all facets of intelligence and information acquisition. Trench warfare created the right environment for testing the limits of perception, for the combatant was trapped in a stationary world. The inability to maneuver outside of the aerial reconnaissance and photographic interpretation sphere of influence complicated the operational reality of combatants accustomed to maneuvering at will. The camouflage and deception challenge extended beyond the visual to other sensory arenas such as communication. The war also demonstrated the adversary's ability to intercept and create false transmissions despite advances in radio technology. The ability of the combatant to operate in a world clouded by misperception required discipline and an unfailing belief that daily operations and procedures could be conducted in a way that ultimately ensured success.

---

[78] "Camouflage," Sec 2, July 1921, 7, NARA, RG 120, Box 819.

[79] Brig Gen William Mitchell, *Memoirs of World War I: From Start to Finish of Our Greatest War* (New York: Random House, 1960), 242-243.

[80] Fuller, 222-223; Porter, 178.

[81] G-2, 1st Army Corps, "Summary of Intelligence," 15 September 1918, Drum Papers, USAMHI.

CHAPTER 19
ARRANGING AERIAL RECONNAISSANCE

The Plattsburg Manual, a popular army training manual employed by U.S. forces at the time, illustrated American leaders' confidence in the role of aerial reconnaissance:

Airplanes will move far out, perhaps hundreds of miles, in front of our most advanced cavalry for the purpose of gathering information on large bodies of the enemy's forces. This is called Strategical Reconnaissance. Other airplanes do more local scouting. They go but comparatively short distances from the firing line for the purpose of determining the location of trenches, supports, reserves, artillery positions, etc. This is called tactical reconnaissance. They give their artillery commanders information as to where their projectiles are falling. During siege operations (as in Europe, where some trenches have remained in about the same place for long periods), photographers go up in airplanes each morning and photograph the enemy's trench lines. Blueprints are made of these lines. By comparing these with the lines of the previous day it is easy to determine the changes that have been made during the night. Other airplanes are detailed for the purpose of combat. They pre-

vent opposing airplanes from gathering information.[1]

The manual's summary of aviation highlighted the obvious: aviation's role was aerial observation. Any mention of combat came from the last line, and even that reflected the information-gathering function. The companion *French Manual on Trench Warfare* made it clear that, "In stationary trench warfare, observation is continuous as in combat…. The aeroplane and balloon are employed to obtain information [observations, photographs]."[2] The French were the most aggressive in applying aerial observation to positional warfare. Their specialized system for the observation squadrons emphasized photography, infantry liaison, and adjustment of artillery fire.[3] They led in acquisition, integration, and analysis of aerial photography. In the early stages of the war they recognized that aviation "furnished nevertheless very valuable intelligence, but this intelligence lacked the indisputable confirmation which photography affords."[4]

[1] Capt O. O. Ellis and Capt E. B. Garey, *The Plattsburg Manual: A Manual for Military Training* (New York: The Century Co., 1917), 213.

[2] *French Manual on Trench Warfare, 1917-1918: A Reference Manual*, French General Staff, reprint of *Manual of the Chief of Platoon of Infantry*, 1918 (London: The Imperial War Museum and Nashville, TN: The Battery Press, Inc. 2002), 234.

[3] Office of the Chief of Air Service, "Recommendations, Command, Equipment, Organization," Gorrell Report, ser. C, r. 12, NARA.

[4] "Aeronautics," June 1921, 1, NARA, RG 120, Box 819.

Voices from the aviation community of this era made it clear that the reconnaissance mission was the most important mission. One of the aviation pioneers for the U.S. Air Service, Lieutenant Colonel Lewis H. Brereton, remarked: "The basis of all war-time aviation is the observation air service…. The air service observation is the most important intelligence agent of an army…. Information regarding his [the enemy's] intentions … is derived largely from aerial photography."[5] Such a feeling was echoed by the American aerial fighter legend, Captain Edward "Eddie" Rickenbacker, who summarized his views on aviation at the time with, "In fact, I believe this function of 'seeing for the army' is the most important one that belongs to the aviation arm in warfare. Bombing, patrolling, and bringing down enemy airplanes are but trivial compared to the vast importance of knowing the exact positions of the enemy's forces and 'looking before you leap'."[6] This attitude permeated the ranks. One poignant comment was written by a leader within the U.S. Air Service ranks, Major Philip Roosevelt, concerning the death of his aviator cousin Quentin (President Theodore Roosevelt's son): "If Quentin has given his life we know that he gave it with a high heart in the performance of duty of prime importance, for the photographs which were obtained played no small part in enabling one French army to know with some precision the nature of the attack which sixteen hours later was launched against it."[7]

Aeroplanes were clearly recognized as a valuable asset as the war progressed, yet military commanders defined their purpose in traditional terms, applying their unique capabilities to existing military operations. The aeroplane's ability to roam the battlefield and beyond was a definite asset for both tactical and strategic operations. In early 1915, U.S. attaché Colonel Squier wrote: "For strategic and tactical reconnaissances the aeroplane is at present simply indispensable. In the present form of trench warfare the aeroplane is used to watch, sketch and plot the development of the enemy's trenches day by day, and in most cases it is the only method of keeping informed of the progress of their preparations."[8] Besides observing the trenches on a daily basis, aerial reconnaissance covered the immediate battle area to locate and examine gun emplacements, reserves, and railheads, chiefly to satisfy the corps or divisional commanders with timely information of the immediate threat. The longer-range strategic reconnaissance extended beyond the realm of the immediate tactical battleground to the adversary's ability to sustain combat operations. It provided insight into enemy intentions.[9]

The link to tactical and strategic levels was via tasking based on visual parameters.[10] By the end of November 1914, the British were describing an aviation organization that allotted the area of operations to the wings for "reconnoitering and offensive duties for the units in that area."[11] From this early stage, aerial reconnaissance was determined by the command echelon ordering the mission: "Normally, strategic reconnaissance will be ordered from RFC Headquarters and only tactical reconnaissance be required by Corps Commanders."[12] Missions assigned as "tactical work" were assigned by the command echelon requiring information within its sector. However, the early taskings to the RFC also showed a strategic emphasis with "Special attention to be paid to rolling stock at all stations…."[13] In the opening phases of combat, tactical reconnaissance required further explanation. Timeliness was essential: "the nearer the landing ground can be to Artillery H.Q. the better."[14] As positional war evolved, so did the

---

[5] Lt Col Brereton quoted in Knappen, 199-200.

[6] Capt Eddie Rickenbacker, *Fighting the Flying Circus* (New York: Fredrick A. Stokes Co., [c1919]; reprint, Chicago: R.R. Donnelley & Sons Company, 1997), 158.

[7] Philip to Quentin's brother Theodore, Jr., 16 July 1918, quoted in Bert Frandsen, *Hat in the Ring: The Birth of American Air Power in the Great War* (Washington, DC: Smithsonian Books, 2003), 176-177. In WW II, Theodore, Jr., led a unit at Utah beach on D-Day and was awarded the Medal of Honor.

[8] Squier to War Department, 26 February 1915, quoted by James J. Cooke, *The U.S. Air Service in the Great War, 1917-1919* (Westport, Connecticut: Praeger, 1996), 15.

[9] Jones, II, 80.

[10] *Aerial Observation for Artillery*, 8.

[11] "Memorandum on New Organization of the Royal Flying Corps," 29 November 1914, TNA, PRO: AIR 1/751/204/4/8.

[12] "Memorandum on New Organization of the Royal Flying Corps," 29 November 1914, TNA, PRO: AIR 1/751/204/4/8.

[13] HQ, RFC, "Orders for Reconnaissance," 24 October to 28 November 1914," TNA, PRO: AIR 1/751/204/4/8.

[14] "Organisation of RFC BEF December 1914," TNA, PRO: AIR 1/751/204/4/8.

Chapter 19: Arranging Aerial Reconnaissance

Ballon captif type R

x x'
ℓ ρ̄'ρ̈"
y y'
m
n
Nacelle avant
Forward Basket
Nacelle arrière
Rear Basket
Nacelle unique
Single Basket

VUE D'ENSEMBLE — GENERAL VIEW

FIGURE 207. **A detailed representation of the captif ballon of World War I.** Source: *Instruction sur le Ballon Captif Allonge Type R* (Washington, DC: Government Printing Office, 1918).

ability to slice the airspace into zones of responsibility. The analysis, acquisition, and transmission of information became institutionalized.

If aerial reconnaissance was to be of value to the combatant, it required acceptance by infantry and artillery arms. "For infantry, order is above rapidity," was a prevailing mindset that provided a baseline for thinking.[15] Whatever was to be accomplished by aviation ultimately had to benefit the fighting soldier. Doctrine conveyed through French training manuals clearly showed aérostats and aéroplanes as subordinate

to the respective armée or CA. To meet the needs of the commander, aerial reconnaissance coverage was in three categories. First, aérostats provided the general observation and observation of fire against objectives visible from that vantage point. The limits of ground observation were employed to define this category. Second, views not accessible due to terrain obstructions were to be acquired through the aéroplane. Finally, aéroplanes were longer-range resources, useful beyond the visual spectrum of the captif ballon and ground observation. The Service Aéronautique commander serving armée or CA artillery objectives assigned duties to aérostat and aéroplanes as required.[16]

Balloon Observation/Ballon Observateur Parameters

Balloon observation (ballon observateur) was the prized resource for artillery, providing artillery spotting for precision fire against targets

---

[15] French doctrine quoted in Porter, 126.

[16] *Aerial Observation for Artillery*, 9.

FIGURE 208. **French aérostiers preparing for an ascent. Note the moving picture camera.** Source: Gorrell Report, NARA.

out of the limits of ground observation. Aérostat/captif ballons were regarded as elevated ground observing posts (other descriptions include a high terrestrial observation station) with extended range of vision.[17] Areas not visually accessible by the aérostat/balloon were covered by aeroplane. Aérostat/captif ballon observation depended on the altitude of the balloon, the range, the atmospheric conditions, and the terrain. Rules governing French aérostat/captif ballon employment stated they were to ascend no closer than 5 kilometers from the front.[18] Two observers could ascend to 1,200 meters while a single observer could reach 1,600 to 1,800 meters. When terrain obstructed the view, the aérostat/captif ballon commander prepared a visibility sketch for each point of ascension and forwarded it to his headquarters command and the artillery commander.[19] Balloon observation target assignment came from headquarters, artillery units, and Service Aéronautique reporting.[20] The French also directed division-assigned captif ballons through

direct telephonic contact to the division PC.[21] One advantage of ballon observation over the aéroplane was instant telephone connection to the artillery unit, providing communication for rapid targeting.[22] In 1917, French captif ballon companies increased their connectivity to operations. They were equipped with a radio receiver to enable them to receive aéroplane TSF transmissions flying in their area of responsibility. Aerial observation became further enhanced with aérostat and aéroplane working together against targets in the sector.[23]

When the Americans established their aerial reconnaissance, they followed the lead of the French and British in aligning their balloon units

---

[17] *Study and Use of Aerial Photographs*, Sec. I, 41.
[18] Christienne and Lissarague, 70.
[19] *Aerial Observation for Artillery*, 6-7.
[20] *Aerial Observation for Artillery*, 9.

[21] "A Study of the Organization of the French Army," 105, NARA, RG 120, Box 819.
[22] Cooke, 24-25.
[23] Christienne and Lissarague, 73.

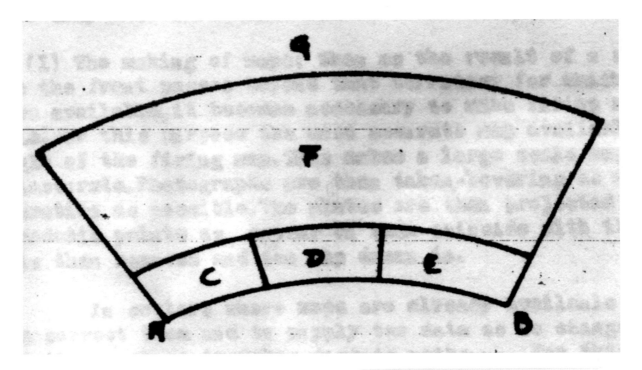

to the army echelon requiring support. American balloons assigned at the army echelon were attached to a "Balloon Group." The balloons were then reallocated to serve the needs of the lower echelons. The Americans assigned their most reliable observers to support the corps sector to ensure the most accurate direction of fire for medium-caliber guns. Balloons supporting the division helped regulate divisional artillery fire as well as provide surveillance and liaison for the infantry divisions. The number of assigned balloons usually corresponded directly to the number of divisions in the army corps. Balloon reporting covered those targets within the visual range of the platform, to include enemy infantry and artillery activity, enemy aeronautical activity, movements on road and rail, and sightings of explosions.[24] Aerial photography from captive balloon platforms was considered but the lack of photo sections precluded it becoming an integral component of the force. The U.S. Air Service policy established that if photographic officers desired oblique coverage from balloons they were allowed a balloon ascent. Once acquired, the prints were processed by the photo section and not the balloon unit.[25]

> **FIGURE 209.** The sectors are clearly defined in this diagram from a U.S. Air Service training aid. A-B represents the front line. C,D,E are the division assigned sectors. F is the CA or Corps sector. Finally, the Army strategical sector is G.
> Source: Gorrell Report, NARA.

Aeroplane Tactical Reconnaissance

Tactical reconnaissance extended the limits of captive balloon coverage as it covered both corps and division sectors. In keeping with its span of control, the division sector contained the smallest area of coverage. The Divisional Observation Squadron worked close to the front lines, providing direct support to the respective division. The squadron reconnoitered only the areas opposite its division's sector to a limit of 5 kilometers.[26] The French CA Service Aéronautique and the equivalent U.S. Army Corps Observation were limited to less than 10 kilometers from the front line (the British operated their corps squadrons out to 10 miles). In practice, aéroplanes assigned to armée escadrilles were allowed to reconnoiter within the CA zone as required without

---

[24] "Commanding Officers of Balloon Groups and Balloon Companies," 4 October 1918, 1st Army, Gorrell Report, ser. F, r. 22, NARA.

[25] "Balloon Section Report," 31 December 1918, Historical, 36, Gorrell Report, ser. F, r. 23, NARA.

[26] Snyder, "Notes on Reconnaissance," Gorrell Report, ser. J, r. 34, NARA.

prior approval.[27] Army Corps Observation zone of action corresponded to the Army corps' artillery range.[28]

The British "Corps Wing" accomplished the more intimate work of tactical reconnaissance to include aerial photography, artillery spotting, and patrolling near the line. This allowed the supported British army to employ dedicated aerial resources to tactical missions. The formation of wings foreshadowed further decentralization aimed at preserving the identity of the Corps, while at the same time distributing its operating units among the various commands of the Army.[29] The Corps Wing contained up to four squadrons and all were equipped for aerial photography, operating from landing grounds close to the headquarters of the Army corps. The number of squadrons varied with the requirements of the Army's assigned sector. As a general rule, the Army squadrons' landing field was farther back from the front line while corps squadrons were in close proximity to corps headquarters. These corps squadrons conducted their sortie operations at an altitude of 8,000 to 12,000 feet, employing an 8- or 10-inch focal length lens, with a 20-inch lens used for "special occasions."[30]

Strategical Reconnaissance

Strategical reconnaissance accomplished visual and photographic reconnaissance over the front of the entire Army to a depth of 50 kilometers behind the front lines. It was the domain of escadrilles and squadrons assigned to the respective army.[31] Strategical reconnaissance gave an "idea of the occupation of suspected regions and of the extent of zones of containment."[32] Strategical reconnaissance missions accomplished strategic scouting of the rear echelon and determined potential threats to the front lines from long-range artillery and aeroplanes. Order-of-battle analysis was conducted through strategic reconnaissance. Once that was determined, the potential for offensive operations or withdrawal was analyzed. The French recognized that strategic intelligence collection required a fusion of all sources and "cannot be perceived in one single glance."[33] Aviation complemented intelligence analysis at the headquarters level. Reconnaissance groups accomplished this through day and night reconnaissance with day reconnaissance being dependent on aerial photography.[34]

A leading French advocate for strategical aerial reconnaissance was Paul-Lewis Weiller. He found that coverage acquired from a rigorous flying schedule over the rear echelon provided successful intelligence on German intentions in a given sector. The best formation, Weiller reasoned, was a group of large-scale reconnaissance flights committed to photograph the rear echelons to a depth of 100 kilometers as frequently as conditions permitted. The Breguet 14 A2 aéroplane excelled under this strategy. It was rugged and could perform well against enemy pursuit aeroplanes. The combination of Weiller Group aerial coverage and 2e Bureau intelligence analysis proved to French commanders such as Général Foch that it was possible to estimate as far as one month in advance where the Germans were planning to attack or abandon a sector. Prior to this the burden of intelligence estimates was on prisoner interrogations, which yielded vital information only hours before the impending operation. Foch became the strongest advocate of strategical reconnaissance. He launched real as well as simulated counterattacks based on the Weiller Group's key maps. Most importantly for the conduct of the campaign, Foch directed maximum effort against those sectors that were identified through strategical reconnaissance to be abandoned. The enemy in the last months of the war became victim to the Foch strategy, a strategy reinforced by in-depth strategical reconnaissance.[35]

---

[27] "Notes on the French System of Intelligence," 7, TNA, PRO: WO 198/983.

[28] "Aeronautics," June 1921, 21, NARA, RG 120, Box 819; Snyder, "Notes on Reconnaissance," Gorrell Report, ser J, r. 34, NARA.

[29] Gliddon, 18-19.

[30] *Aerial Photography*, Air Publication 838, TNA, PRO: AIR 10/853.

[31] 1st Lt John Snyder, "Notes on the Relative Importance of Information to be Obtained by Observers When on a Visual Reconnaissance," Gorrell Report, ser. J, r. 34, NARA.

[32] "Aeronautics," June 1921, 17, NARA, RG 120, Box 819.

[33] "Aeronautics," June 1921, 17, NARA, RG 120, Box 819.

[34] "Aeronautics," June 1921, 17, NARA, RG 120, Box 819.

[35] Christienne and Lissarague, 183.

Chapter 19: Arranging Aerial Reconnaissance

The Army Wing focused on strategical reconnaissance, bombing, and aerial photography. This echelon fielded suitable aircraft to accomplish these missions. Additional missions included pursuit and aerial superiority.[36] The Corps Wing worked the tactical requirements of the corps assigned within that particular army. The British assigned two squadrons equipped for photographic work at each Army Wing. Aerial photography was accomplished by the Army Wing serving the Army staff. The final number of squadrons varied according to local requirements. The essential and basic functions of army and corps remained distinct. However, an army squadron might be called

[36] Gliddon, 18-19.

FIGURE 210. **Thanks to the key map showing the Weiller Group strategical reconnaissance effort, analysts had a better idea of the level of activity in rear echelons.** Source: de Brunoff, ed., *L'Aeronatique.*

upon to do work normally falling to the corps squadrons. One army squadron was equipped for photography. As the war progressed, the British intended to have every squadron equipped for aerial photography.[37] Since army squadrons

[37] Gliddon, 18-19.

FIGURE 211. French emphasis on faster and higher-flying aerial reconnaissance led to employment of the existing pursuit inventory for reconnaissance. The 50 cm aerial camera behind the cockpit allowed the single-seat pursuit fighter to perform aerial reconnaissance. Source: SHAA, 87.2859.

were intended to fly at higher altitudes (12,000 to 18,000 feet), the aeroplanes were configured for cameras with 20-inch focal length lenses.[38]

The heavy attrition of photographic reconnaissance sorties prompted the French to reconfigure single-seat pursuit fighters such as the Nieuport 17, Spad VII, and Spad XIII to photographic reconnaissance roles. Formation flying ending in dramatic dogfights continued to take a toll on reconnaissance assets. The independence of the single-seat fighter was an intriguing feature that aerial strategists figured would benefit aerial photography. However, photographic collection demanded straight and level flight, increasing the vulnerability of the fighter/reconnaissance aéroplane.[39] The French continued applying this capability to their long-range reconnaissance missions in support of armée objectives. Their pursuit aéroplanes were configured with a semi-automatic camera operated by the pilot through a Bowden cable. These sorties acquired high-altitude aerial photographs (4,000 to 6,000 meters) and oblique coverage.[40] One escadrille, SPA 49, was recognized for flying as far as 200 kilometers behind enemy lines, taking 6,000 photographs during September 1918 alone.[41]

Organizing the Aerial Force

Organizing aerial observation to accomplish expanding missions helped establish and refine the French escadrille and British squadron. Better control of aéroplane resources required assigning similar type aéroplanes together. The aviation mix changed to homogeneous units for more

---

[38] *Aerial Photography*, Air Publication 838, TNA, PRO: AIR 10/853.

[39] Nesbit, 42-43.

[40] Carlier, 30-31; "Final Tactical Report of Chief of Air Service," Maurer, ed., *U.S. Air Service*, I, 226-227.

[41] Davila and Soltan, 503.

Chapter 19: Arranging Aerial Reconnaissance

FIGURE 212. **Photo of SPAD XII used for high-speed reconnaissance. Note the word PHOTO applied to the fuselage. The figure to the far right is Charles Nungesser, the great French ace.** Source: Renaud via James Davilla.

effective maintenance. The French escadrille was commanded by an aéroplane pilot capitaine. Escadrille personnel normally included 10 pilots, 8 observers, and 3 machine gunners in addition to officers and men entrusted with the maintenance of flying materiel, rolling stock, radio telegraphy, and armament.[42] Additionally, the aéroplane could serve a diversity of roles, be it aerial observation, pursuit, or bombardment. Modification came with new requirements. French long-range reconnaissance gravitated to multi-engine aéroplanes to acquire strategic information well beyond the front lines.[43] The French also made a significant change in supporting heavy artillery targeting. Elite reconnaissance air crews were assigned to Artillerie Lourde (AL) escadrilles to detect and photograph significant targets. AL escadrilles were numerically designated within the range of 201 through 228. The aerial reconnaissance specialists were experts, forwarding essential information to longer-range heavy artillery units capable of delivering more lethal firepower.[44]

As the demand increased for more aerial photographic coverage, the burden impacted the entire Allied aerial configuration and stretched available resources. For example, AL escadrilles supporting CA artillery were exempt from assignment to other duties.[45] More aéroplanes and air crews were needed to meet the demand. By the end of the war, the French modified their aerial reconnaissance force along the lines of capability. A long-range reconnaissance group consisted of one escadrille of Spad single-seaters (10 Spad VII or 10 Spad XIII) for fast reconnaissance, one Breguet escadrille (10 Breguet 14s), and one night Voisin escadrille (10 Voisin bombers) for night reconnaissance. Additionally, the armée possessed an aviation group for

---

[42] "Aeronautics," June 1921, 19, NARA, RG 120, Box 819.

[43] "Aeronautics," June 1921, 10-11, NARA, RG 120, Box 819.

[44] This was also known as *Section Artillerie Lourde* (SAL); Toelle, 2; Hodeir, 115.

[45] "Aeronautics," June 1921, 10-11, NARA, RG 120, Box 819.

FIGURE 213. **A telling hint at the possibilities for aerial reconnaissance by the fighter pursuit force. The U.S. Air Service's is fabled 94th Aero Squadron acquired a SPAD XIII configured with an aerial camera compartment.** Source: USA-FA McDermott Library Special Collections (SMS57).

long-range reconnaissance consisting of one escadrille of Spad single-seaters (10 aéroplanes), one Breguet escadrille (10 aéroplanes), and one night Voisin escadrille (10 aéroplanes).[46] The RFC determined that to effectively meet the demands levied on aviation required increasing the squadron size from 12 to 18. Soon the British GHQ envisioned a force comprising two squadrons of two-seater fighter reconnaissance machines, two long-distance reconnaissance machines of 8 hours fuel capacity, one squadron of single-seat fighters, and 6 bomb-dropping squadrons.[47] U.S. Air Service aero squadrons assigned to aerial observation roles in 1918 also had 18 aeroplanes assigned. The daily schedule had two flights of six aeroplanes accomplishing aerial reconnaissance. During active operations all flights were operational.[48]

As the war entered its third year of combat, the British recognized that the aeronautical forces needed to be more effectively integrated with the army to support ongoing operations. The RFC was subsequently reorganized to include brigade-level formations that were attached to the respective army at the front. Similarly, the RFC Brigade placed the headquarters within the vicinity of the army it served. These brigade-level units, commanded by a brigadier general, directed both corps- and wing-level resources specifically to support an assigned British army sector. An RFC Brigade controlled a total of 108 aeroplanes, with its headquarters located near the headquarters of the army it was supporting, approximately 14 miles behind the front line. Within this force, the Brigade could allocate aeroplanes either to the army or the subordinate corps.[49]

The Evolving Strategy of Formation Flying

The aerial campaign was changing by 1916. The traditional array of aeroplane sorties eventually confronted an increase in aerial combatants, causing the mission to become dependent on formation flying. Discussion of the aerial campaign at that time reflected the growing numbers involved in accomplishing the mission. "All reconnaissance, ordinary patrol, and bomb raids are now done by numbers of machines varying from three for line patrol, to bomb raids of as many as 20 machines, i.e., all work is done in formation."[50] Aerial observation became extremely vulnerable to the evolving German pursuit aeroplanes in 1916. Major-General Trenchard, RFC, observed that, "Information can no longer be obtained by dispatching single machines on reconnaissance duties. The information has now to be fought for, and it is necessary for reconnaissance to consist of at least 5 machines flying in formation."[51] The evolving aerial landscape indicated clearly that, if aerial observation was to survive, it required the increased firepower offered by additional observation planes configured for aerial combat or pursuit aeroplanes. The attacking Ger-

---

[46] The actual *escadrille* aéroplane inventory varied throughout the war. Author discussion with Dr. James Davilla; "Aeronautics," June 1921, 10-11, NARA, RG 120, Box 819.

[47] "Proposals for a Long Distance Machine," TNA, PRO: AIR 2/16.

[48] 1st Lt Elmer R. Haslett, "Bulletin of Information Air Service American Expeditionary Forces. Notes on the Duties of the Operations Officer of an Observation Squadron or Group," Jefferson Hayes Davis Papers, McDermott Library, USAFA, SMS 57.

[49] Gliddon, 18-19; Riggs, "Report on Visit to British Army for Purpose of Studying Branch Intelligence," Conger Papers, USAMHI; Lamberton, 11.

[50] "Central Flying School," TNA, PRO: AIR 1/1625/204/89/7.

[51] "Proposals for a Fighting Machine," TNA, PRO: AIR 2/16.

Chapter 19: Arranging Aerial Reconnaissance

man fighter scouts used "guerrilla tactics, hanging on the flanks and rear of the formation, ready to cut off stragglers, or attacking from several directions simultaneously...."[52] There was safety in numbers, no matter what the mission. As one British aviation lecturer in 1916 commented, "On reconnaissance a straggling machine will probably be attacked by superior numbers, though the formation itself will be left alone. If a pilot therefore finds that he cannot keep up and is certain to be left behind, he should turn back at his own discretion. This applies only to reconnaissance."[53] When the Americans commenced aerial observation, they adopted the standard of two protection planes flying with a single aerial photographic plane.[54]

Techniques in formation flying were refined each year. By 1916, British instruction paid attention to the role of flight leader, working the rendezvous, flying at a reasonable speed that all could maintain, and keeping the rest of the aeroplanes in the same direction. The flight leader was distinguished by streamers attached to the wings. The formation circled the landing ground until the flight leader was satisfied that all aeroplanes were ready to proceed. While in formation for reconnaissance, pilots were advised that hostile aircraft should not be attacked unless "a good opportunity offers."[55] Aerial photographic formations settled on a triangle design, with the three aeroplanes in the lead carrying aerial cameras. This allowed for the rear three aeroplanes to provide cover while the aeroplanes carrying cameras could concentrate on the photographic mission at hand, "knowing that their tails are being protected." The scouts were there to provide defensive protection since the primary objective was to obtain the required photographs.[56]

FIGURE 214. The evolution of formation flying emphasized protection of aerial reconnaissance. A British training manual portrays two FE 2b formations. Source: TNA, PRO: AIR 1/1625/204/89/7.

Air superiority became a more dominant objective as the war progressed. By the conclusion of the conflict, attention to improving combat potential surpassed what aerial observation had accomplished. As one discussion on the subject toward the end of the conflict surmised, "Air superiority ensures you two things: a screen for your own movements and a knowledge of the enemy's. Such knowledge eventually leads to but one conclusion, the ultimate superiority in arms of the aerially superior forces."[57]

---

[52] British GHQ, France, "Fighting in the Air," February 1918, in Jones, 102.

[53] "Notes on Air Fighting from Royal Flying Corps," September-December 1916, TNA, PRO: AIR 1/1625/204/89/7.

[54] "Final Report of Chief of Air Service," Maurer, ed., *U.S. Air Service*, I, 181; Frank, *American Air Service Observation*, 222-223.

[55] "Notes on Air Fighting from Royal Flying Corps," TNA, PRO: AIR 1/1625/204/89/7.

[56] "Notes on Air Fighting from Royal Flying Corps," TNA, PRO: AIR 1/1625/204/89/7.

[57] "Aerial Photography for Pilots," 1, NASM, A30.2/2.

Aerial photographic formations retained the basic configuration to the end of the conflict. American guidance on photographic missions recommended the triangular formation, with the plane with the camera being in front and the other two, spread on either side, slightly behind and above, giving protection to the camera man with their machine guns. Pursuit support to photographic missions was retained throughout the war, and sortie planning was favorably inclined to include pursuit resources in the formation.[58] Ironically, a formation of several aeroplanes providing protection for the aerial photographic aeroplane caused so much attention that it often led to an attack by enemy formations. Several aerial observation teams finally preferred to go alone on these missions, trusting to the pilot to spot any "Huns," and feeling that if they were attacked it was easier to take care of themselves than to keep in a formation and fight a pitched battle.[59] Inevitably, the issue of what constituted the best use of reconnaissance resources in this precarious environment led to the genesis of aerial reconnaissance performed by "a fast machine capable of flying at a great altitude."[60] Such consideration carried on long after the war. It would become the standard for the Second World War and subsequent Cold War missions.

Defending the Reconnaissance

Aerial warfare revolved around escort duty for reconnaissance. For some it was a monotonous experience. The 1916 diary of Canadian Lieutenant John Brophy portrayed the routine where the bait was the "camera machine": "I was on escort duty to FEs who were going over to take pictures. I stuck just above the camera machine and followed him around. As we came to the lines we saw four huns, who made off when they saw us coming for them. Flew about while the FEs took pictures." Brophy commented a few days later, "Went out again at 11 to escort FEs who were taking photographs. The FE arrived late and in the meantime four of us were tearing up and down the whole Somme front looking for him. Dropped four bombs on Le Transloy for old time's sake and finally found FE after

FIGURE 215. **The German 88 mm antiaircraft gun was a formidable threat in two world wars. "Archie" was a continual threat throughout the war, prompting aerial reconnaissance to operate at extremely high altitudes.** Source: Neumann, *Die Deutschen Luftstreitkraste.*

dodging archies for over an hour. Sat above the FE while he toured about."[61]

The demand on aviation resources to protect aerial reconnaissance soon prompted designers to suggest changes in reconnaissance aeroplanes. The reconnaissance mission required that the aerial observer pay attention to manipulating the camera over watching out for threats. It was comparatively easy for an enemy patrol of pursuit planes to come within striking distance before the observer was aware of its approach. The greatest advantage an enemy pursuit plane had in the attack on the observation plane was surprise. Even with other planes in formation spotting an incoming attack, the inability to effectively communicate with the aerial photography aeroplane made the mission difficult. Sometimes the only indication of danger was machine gun fire. By the end of the war, aerial reconnaissance turned to improving the

---

[58] Gilchrist, 127.
[59] Hart, 37.
[60] "Fighting in the Air," Jones, 102.

[61] Lieut John Brophy, Diary, in Brereton Greenhous, ed., *A Rattle of Pebbles: The First World War Diaries of Two Canadian Airmen* (Ottawa: Canadian Government Publishing Centre, 1987), 35.

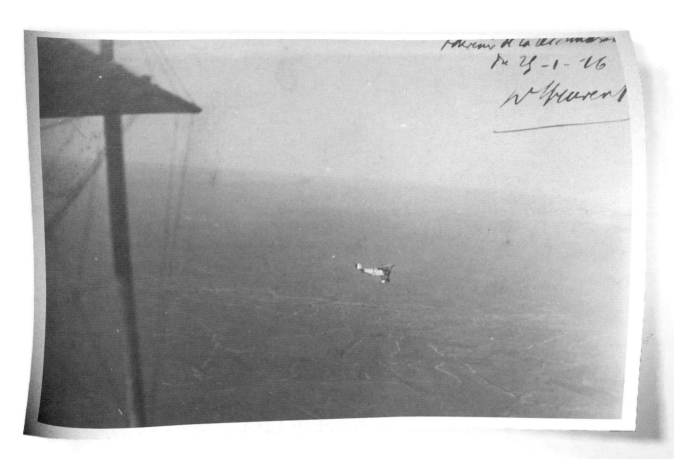

FIGURE 216. **Friends in the area protecting aerial reconnaissance contributed to the evolution of the air superiority role in aerial combat. A Nieuport 17 pursuit fighter is seen here on patrol with an aerial reconnaissance aeroplane.** Source: Pépin Papers, MA&E.

camera mechanics so they operated automatically. The first semi-automatic cameras such as the French De Ram and the British "LB" Type were attempts to free the air crew from totally concentrating on the camera and taking the photograph.[62] The pilot assumed responsibility for taking the photographs while the observer both looked out for enemy fighters and conducted visual observations to supplement the information derived from the photographs.[63]

Aeroplane evolution paralleled armament, employing weapons of greater firepower and versatility. The prevailing view throughout the conflict was that reconnaissance aircraft should emphasize collection over protection. However, after the first year of combat, protection was a part of aircraft design. By 1916, mounted, synchronized machine guns allowed aircraft to engage in a frontal attack. The observer also became an aerial gunner. Despite such efforts to improve armament, aerial reconnaissance aeroplanes were vulnerable to the single-seat pursuit fighter to the very end of the war.[64]

The other threat that prompted aviation to ascend to higher altitudes in order to accomplish the mission was from ground antiaircraft weapons. At the outset of the war, before the accuracy and range of antiaircraft guns increased, observation planes flew at lower altitudes and took satisfactory aerial photographs with rudimentary equipment. However, antiaircraft became more effective, forcing the planes to fly higher. It culminated in many improvements in the aeroplane, motor, and air crew flying gear.[65] The tendency of aerial reconnaissance

[62] Lindstrom, "Photographic Missions," Gorrell Report, ser. N, r. 53, NARA.

[63] "Development of Aerial Photography," Gorrell Report, ser. J, r. 34, NARA.

[64] Author discussion with Dr. James Davilla.

[65] Crowell and Wilson, II, 418; Powell, 294.

to fly a standard straight line course at a constant altitude gave anti-aircraft, referred to by British pilots as "Archie," as perfect a target as they could desire.[66] The name "Archie" is said to have originated from the character of the bad boy Archibald in the comedy of "Mamma's Boy," produced in London in 1915. The catch line of the comedy was an ineffectual shot followed by the reply, "Now, Archibald!"[67] One aviator recommended a gentle slideslip to a lower altitude as an effective way of getting away from Archie's dangerous fire.[68]

Modes of Communication

It took extensive cooperation between aerial resources and the traditional combat arms to develop the missions that defined aerial observation for the war. The first months of positional warfare honed the requirement. Communication accelerated observation's role during the first year of combat more than camera systems. The one-

FIGURE 217. The evolution of aerial reconnaissance in the final year of the war created a formidable fighting machine. The Breguet 14 A2 was well-armed fore and aft. It lent a new meaning to the label "PHOTO." Source: Gorrell Report, NARA.

way radio Morse key transmission from aircraft to artillery battery became a fixture for the entire war. Not only did it provide observation depth beyond balloon range, it provided greater mobility to the artillery in selecting targets. Two-way communication was achieved by patterns of cloth strips laid out by ground units to be seen by the aircraft. Most communications were to artillery batteries to provide definitive updates on the impacts.[69] Communication improved in both range and effectiveness over the years. By 1917, challenges caused by communication fratricide and jamming from German radio intercept units were countered by development of a "clapper break" that allowed the Morse key pitch to vary with

---

[66] Hart, 36-37; 1st Lt John Snyder, "Notes on Army Observation," Gorrell Report, ser. J, r. 34, NARA; Watkis, 12-13.

[67] Porter, 96-97.

[68] Lindstrom, "Photographic Missions," Gorrell Report, ser. N, r. 53, NARA.

[69] Lamberton, 9-11; Barnes, *From Then Till Now*, 426.

Chapter 19: Arranging Aerial Reconnaissance

each aircraft. The British Sterling radio transmitter was the primary unit employed, providing a range of 8-10 miles, sufficient for supporting corps-level operations. The transmitting aircraft extended a 120-foot aerial from the fuselage to conduct the artillery support mission. By the end of the conflict, radio transmissions extended well over the strategic sector, providing communication up to 70-80 miles to the ground receiver.[70] In 1915, a new pattern of ground-strip for communication in the form of an arrow was developed. The ground signal was displayed by battalion headquarters when the advance was held up by enemy resistance. The arrow gave the direction, and bars were added, each symbolizing two hundred yards that the obstacle was distant from the arrow. The British historian, Sir James Edmonds, considers this the first established organization for air-ground cooperation.[71]

Communication between the observation aeroplane and ground receiver was state-of-the-art for the time. The aeroplane transmitted via radio/ radio telephone, projector, messages (or photographs) dropped in bags, or by signal light. The ground receiver responded by displaying white cloth panels (that highlighted certain objectives gained), smoke signals, radio/radio telephone, or lamp. The Allies used a simple code, spelling out letters in Morse that were sent by a signaling panel—a shutter of lathes like a Venetian blind, exhibiting white on one side and dark green on the other. The observer reported location, designated objectives, and results of fire. They were supplied with special lithographed maps for marking the positions of the Allied and enemy troops. Radio was the main communication link for artillery spotting, used for urgent information on position of friendly troops, requests for fire, extension of fire, and the like. The Allied infantry communicated with the aviators by setting off flares within the trenches so as not to attract further attention from the enemy. The advanced troops received signals from the aerial observers by message bag, lamp, Klaxon horn, and/or white Very light (flare pistol).[72] Very lights generally comprised four signals: "where are you?"; "understood"; "counterattack"; and "organizations I am flying over are unoccupied by enemy." The signal lights were fired above the German lines so that the lights fell in front of the troops.[73] As a general rule, visual signals were repeated and panel signals left in position until the aeroplane replied, "Understood," preferably by light signal.[74] The use of the Very pistol had its drawbacks for the air crew. A member of the Royal Artillery, Lieutenant Colonel Neil Fraser-Tyler, flew with the RFC over enemy lines to gain a better appreciation of the artillery spotting mission. He described a memorable moment when they attempted to signal to the batteries. "On firing coloured lights from a Very pistol the battery engaged pre-arranged targets, but it was a squally day of thunderstorms and hail, making observation very difficult. The Hun antiaircraft guns always get very fussy when a plane starts firing lights; apparently they think it is a signal for something desperate to happen."[75]

Missions

Aerial observation functioned in the capacity of special missions covering the spectrum of operations. Significant roles included artillery spotting, infantry contact, aerial photographic and long-distance reconnaissance, reconnaissance of particular zones or localities, and exercises. All special missions required extensive preparation with the ground liaison. The group or squadron operations officer preplanned the mission and named the air crew in advance.[76]

Artillery spotting remained the priority for aeroplane aerial observation throughout the war. Since it accomplished sightings beyond the visual range of aérostats/balloons, the aeroplane assumed the most important role. Aerial reconnaissance developed techniques that helped gauge potential destruction of the battery emplacement area. Active and inactive gun

[70] Lamberton, 193.

[71] Edmonds, *1915*, II, 142-143.

[72] Edmonds, *1916*, I, 89; *Aerial Observation for Artillery*, 2; "A Study of the Organization of the French Army," 101-102, NARA, RG 120, Box 819.

[73] Sewell, "Notes … on French Corps Aviation," TNA, PRO: AIR 1/475/15/312/201.

[74] "A Study of the Organization of the French Army," 103, NARA, RG 120, Box 819.

[75] Neil Fraser-Tytler, *With Lancashire Lads and Field Guns in France, 1915-1918* (Manchester, UK: J. Heywood, 1922), 65-66.

[76] "Final Report of Chief of Air Service," Maurer, ed., *U.S. Air Service*, I, 178.

positions were determined through direct observation of guns firing. The seasons were employed to reinforce the estimate. During the winter observers learned that dark smudges in fresh snow marked recent firing. Even hidden artillery could be revealed by this and associated trails. The ideal time frame for artillery reconnaissance was at dusk when the flash could be detected.[77] *Avion de réglage* also constituted another mission in support of artillery. Aerial photographs were taken in advance by a designated artillery unit to determine accuracy of fire.[78] One recollection of the British process for artillery spotting involved No. 3 Squadron, Royal Australian Air Force:

> After takeoff, the RE 8 would wait for the Battery to lay out a giant white linoleum-formed letter "L" on the ground to signify the Battery was ready to commence firing. The RE 8'd then cruise at about 85 miles per hour toward the target area and, using the Standard Sterling Transmitter in the RE 8 with its 120-foot-long trailing aerial, they'd key, in Morse Code, the letter "G" to let the battery know they could let "go" with their salvo. On the ground, near each Battery location, a Wireless Operator would receive the RE 8s signal on his crystal detector receiver using a "cat's whisker" tuner, headphones and an aerial pole about 30 feet high. Incidentally, the "cat's whisker" had to be continually retuned to the point on the crystal which gave the best signal reception because, as the shoot progressed, the receiver would be constantly jolted by the concussion of the Battery's guns and the enemy's counter-bombardment. Nevertheless, the RE 8's signals, relayed to the Battery, would start each salvo and the RE 8's job was to note where each salvo fell in relation to the clock-face on the photograph and to then signal the Battery with the clock-code-letter designating the distance the salvo fell short of the target. Of course, the Battery would keep correcting its aim, al-

ways trying to hit the target, while the RE 8 would continue to fly in large circles between the Battery and the target to report changing circumstances.[79]

Infantry contact patrols provided an overview of the situation at a given sector at a given time, especially during an attack. This was difficult because of the hostile environment. Observations included indications of fresh digging or newly taken positions.[80] The infantry contact patrol closely followed the movements of the attacking force and transmitted the results by the quickest means available. The attacking infantry informed the infantry contact patrol with banners or rockets. The infantry contact patrol relayed the information to the headquarters by radio or message drop. Upon landing, the infantry contact patrol made an immediate telephone report to the CA battle headquarters and the divisional headquarters.[81] The French allocated one infantry contact aéroplane (*avion d'accompagnement de l'infanterie*) per division to accomplish the mission. While flying over the given sector, the infantry contact aéroplane was responsible for observing the signals of the PC and transmitting to the général commanding the division. Additional roles included transmitting orders of the division's commanding general to the infantry as well as providing information quickly to the Artillery Command. These division subordinate aéroplanes were to fly above the advanced elements at an altitude not to exceed 1,200 meters or below 500 meters.[82] The infantry

---

[77] "Aerial Photography for Pilots," 13, NASM, A30.2/2.
[78] Porter, 169.

[79] Neil L. Smith, *History of 3 Squadron, AFC, RAAF*, URL: <http://www.3squadron.org.au/history.htm>, accessed 10 January 2005.
[80] "Aerial Photography for Pilots," 13, NASM, A30.2/2.
[81] *Aerial Observation for Artillery*, 11.
[82] "A Study of the Organization of the French Army," 101, NARA, RG 120, Box 819.

PLANE TO P.C.

Code	Meaning
ART	Artillery
AVI	Enemy aviator
BAV	Bat.against avia.
BCA	Anti tank battery
BTA	Battery in action
BTO	Battery occupied
CAV	Cavalry
COV	Convoy
DIR	Direction(Followed by name of local'y)
DRO	Right at
EST	East of
FDF	Barbed wire
FRO	Front(Followed by number of meters)
GAU	Left at
IFC	Infantry in column
IFD	Infantry deployed
IFR	Infantry massed
IDI	Here available aeroplane
NOR	North of
OUS	West of
PRF	Depth(Followed by a number)
QUE	Rear at
RAS	Nothing to report
REG	Request for orders
RLV	Relieve me
SUD	South of
TAM	Friendly troops
TCF	Railroad train
TET	Head at
TRA	Trenches
VRV	Coming to rel.you

P.C. TO PLANE BY PANEL

Signal	Panel
P.C. of Battalion	◀
P.C. of Regiment	◖
P.C. of Brig.or Div.	●
Objective reached	— ◀ —
Request barrage	◀⌐
Request fire for attack preparation	◀‖
Friendly field art. fires on us	◀—
Friendly heavy art. fires on us	◀⊏
We are ready to attack	▮◀▮
Will not be ready to attack at fixed time	▮◀—
We wish to advance lengthen fire	◀—
Replacement of small arm ammunition	◀+
Replacement of hand grenades	◆▷
Message understood	◀▬

SERVICE SIGNALS

Signal	Morse	Code
Ready to rec	- - - - - -	BR
End of mess.	- - - - -	AR
Understood	- - - -	SN
Wait	- - -	AS
Repeat	- -	UD
Separation	-	DA

BY T.C.F.

Signal	Code
- - - -	QT
- - -	O
- - - - -	CE
- - -	S
- - - -	V
- -	I
- - - - - -	GW
- - - -	H
- - - - -	Y
- - - - -	Q
- - - - -	SN

ALPHABET

Letter	Morse
A	.-
B	-...
C	-.-.
Ch	----
D	-..
E	.
F	..-.
G	--.
H	....
I	..
J	.---
K	-.-
L	.-..
M	--
N	-.
O	---
P	.--.
Q	--.-
R	.-.
S	...
T	-
U	..-
V	...-
W	.--
X	-..-
Y	-.--
Z	--..

NUMBERS

Number	Symbol
1	I
2	⌐
3	III
4	IV
5	V
6	VI
7	L
8	LI
9	IX
0	X

PLANE TO P.C.

Code	Meaning
01	First piece
02	Second piece
03	Third piece
04	Fourth piece
05	By piece
06	Is battery ready
07	Has battery fired
08	Can't see proj'tr
09	Aim on me
11	Can't see panels
12	Datum point
13	Verify fire
14	Fire from the right
15	Precision fire
16	By salvo
17	By salvo by two pcs
18	Fire from the left
19	How many guns fire
21	Impossible observe
22	Range irregular
23	Could not observe
24	Deflec'n irregular
25	Will observe as req
26	H.E.Shell
27	Lost
28	Cease firing
29	Result accompl'd
31	Fr.shells fall'g or
32	Continue the fire
33	To much distrib'n
34	Shrapnel,time fire
35	Z.F.I cease observ
36	To much concent'n
37	By battery volleys
38	Continuous fire,I cease regular obs'n
39	Repeat

P.C. TO PLANE BY PANEL

Signal	Panel	Signal	Panel
Observe for group	◣	Fire by piece	▮▮
Request adjustment	■—	Fire by salvo	▮▮▮
Observe fire on Tar (Foll'd by coordin)	■K	Amelioration	▮▮
Adjust on Target you just indicated	—■—	Fire in series of 24 rounds	▮⊓
First battery ready	▮▮	Continue fire for effect	■-I-
Second bat'ry ready	_▮▮	Verify fire	I▮▮
Third battery ready	=▮▮	Enemy attacks. By prev.agreement	■△
Wait a few minutes	▮- - -	No further need of you	■⌐
Bat.not ready,delay at least 10 minutes	⊥	Hostile aeroplane near you	Y
Battery has fired	▮⌐	Fire for precision	—■—
Wireless O.K.but si confused.REPEAT	▮▮	Zone fire	—■=
Can't hear you, fire not adjusted	◣	Attention	⌐↯
Understood. Message received	◣	Understood Unable to reply	↯
No	▮▮—▮		
Continue to adjust	▮—		■—

SERVICE

Signal	Code
Fire 3 dashes	
Right 2(I)	- - - -
Left 2(m)	- - - -
Short 2(h)	- - - -
Over (ch)	
Def.correct (Z)	
Range cor. 2(n)close	
Target (b)	
Change targ 2(k)close	
Error 10 dots	- - - - - - - - - -
Will land (bv)	- - - -
Air burst (f)	

contact mission provided some of the best information on locations of friendly troops as well as
enemy movements.[83]

Infantry contact was one of the most demanding of missions, requiring the air crew to
fly the aeroplane at dangerously low altitudes. Lt.
Katcher, an AEF Air Service observer before the
start of the Meuse-Argonne offensive, reflected
on the infantry contact mission:

> An observer to be successful, must
> bring up to the minute the informa-
> tion he has obtained before leaving
> the airdrome. He will get this by flying
> over our batteries' zone, before visit-
> ing the advanced infantry and observ-
> ing attentively the aerial activity, the
> artillery battle, the grenade fights, etc.
> When he has grasped the situation and
> sees a relative calm, he will then come
> over the infantry and ask for the line.
> And, even then, he cannot always see
> bayonet fighting during the course of
> which the infantry cannot display their
> panels, therefore, causing his mission
> to be unsuccessful. To keep the com-
> mand well informed as to the situation
> of our advanced line is the first and
> most important duty for the observer
> of an infantry contact plane; the diffi-
> culties that he will have to overcome
> to be successful do not permit those in
> command to expect him to give regu-
> larly other information or have him un-
> dertake different missions. However,
> after the location of the advanced line
> has been reported, or, in open warfare,
> if the troops are advancing rapidly, the
> observer may render other services, a
> few of which follow given in order of
> importance.[84]

Post-war reflections on the impact of infantry contact emphasized that success required

FIGURE 219. **A ground panel signal
is laid out for the infantry contact aeroplane.** Source: Maurer, ed.,*The U.S. Air Service in World War I.*

commitment by both the aviator and the infantry
combatant. During the Meuse-Argonne advance,
U.S. Air Service support to the First American
Army's 5th Corps was unable to find the front line
due to lack of panel markings being displayed by
the infantry. Panels were never detected while
the attack proceeded. During lulls in the battle,
markings were misleading due to panels being
spread out well behind the actual front. Infantry
contact was most successful when the air crews
flew down to 300 meters and actually spotted the
brown uniforms of the advancing American infantry. The Germans' blue-green uniforms were
cited by the air crews as having a superior blend-
ing quality that proved more difficult to spot,
even at such low altitudes. The best solution for
determining the front line was to locate friendly
troops at a given point and fly vertically over the
length of the line while the observer marked the
position. The confirmed reference point helped
orient the observation to other friendly pockets
of infantry in the advance.[85]

---

[83] Edmonds, *1918*, I, 169.

[84] Philip Katcher, "Bulletin of Information Air Service
American Expeditionary Forces, Notes for Divisional Staffs,
Commanding Officers and Aerial Observers on Work of
Infantry Contact Airplanes," 24 September 1918, Katcher
Papers, USAMHI.

[85] 2nd Lt Joseph E. Eaton, "Methods in Observation
Practiced with Fifth Corps First American Army on the
Fronts, St. Mihiel Sector, September 12 to 16, 1918
Argonne-Meuse Sector, September 12 to November 11,
1918," *Air Service Information Circular* 2, No. 115 (20
September 1920): 4-5, Jefferson Hayes Davis Papers,
McDermott Library, USAFA, SMS 57.

The U.S. Air Service had a different term for infantry contact. Known as the "cavalry reconnaissance patrol," American observation aeroplanes flew at altitudes to accomplish closer observation of the terrain immediately in front of the advancing Allied infantry, locating the position of machine gun nests, strongpoints, and all other hostile defenses likely to retard the progress of the attack. Information was transmitted to the immediate front line troops by dropped written messages. The infantry was kept informed at short intervals of time of all developments in the area immediately ahead and was given information of great value in aiding its advance. This negated the time constraints of aerial photographic interpretation, but did not supplement the verifiable process that went with the analysis.[86] In addition to reconnaissance, the U.S. Air Service observation planes were sometimes called upon during the low altitude sorties to drop newspapers and cigarettes to the advancing troops at the front lines.[87]

The Daily Schedule

The aerial domain added a new dimension for the intelligence section. A sector designated as an area of interest was usually covered daily by the observer aircraft. An aerial photographic sortie occurred about every three to five days, depending on the aerial photographic collection requirements of the intelligence staff.[88] To gain the maximum benefit from each sortie, reconnaissance sought to surprise or discover an exposed enemy as well as provide the ideal sun angle for acquiring shadow on the aerial photograph. The ambient light aided the photographic interpreter in the analysis of the photo print by accentuating features and shadow. One post-war summation showed daily operating hours for aerial photography occurred between 0800 and 1600 hours in midsummer, 1000 and 1400 hours during the spring and autumn, and 1130 and 1230 hours during the limited hours of winter.[89] When the season permitted, routine sorties fell

between 0900 and 1200 hours, 1400 and 1700 hours, and a final flight shortly before sundown.[90] A prevailing opinion on the time for reconnaissance was provided by one French aviator: "The whole sector to which the aerial photo section has been assigned should be photographed daily; sometimes it is even worth while to do this twice daily, morning and evening; the pictures should be developed very quickly."[91]

Weather permitting, aerial reconnaissance sorties began before sunrise. Normally, about 45 minutes to an hour before daybreak the aéroplane took off to a desired altitude and flew back over the enemy's line in order to be over the rear echelon areas at the break of day.[92] The ultimate goal was to acquire coverage at any time under any conditions. A French aviator commented, "We must be thoroughly convinced of this principle; photographs must be taken at all hours and in all kinds of weather."[93] The reality was that there were collection limitations. Most challenging was the ability to fly under austere weather conditions. The sortie would be flown at very low altitudes (100 meters or less) when the ceiling was between 200 and 300 meters. This took the enemy by surprise, gaining information or inflicting damage before quickly ascending to the cover of the cloud bank. Another advantage gained in flying during inclement weather was enemy chase "did not have to be reckoned with on these missions."[94] One British general summed it up: "The war has taught us to laugh at weather."[95]

Aerial observation's established routine became a liability. Thanks to the enemy maneuvering primarily under cover of darkness, aerial observation was forced to accomplish night reconnaissance to support commanders with updates on enemy activity. Observers on the early morning sortie often saw extensive movement

---

[86] "Final Tactical Report of Chief of Air Service," Maurer, ed., *U.S. Air Service*, I, 254.

[87] "Combat Activities of Army Group Air Service during November 1-2, 1918," Gorrell Report, ser. C, r. 12, NARA.

[88] Cooke, 59-60.

[89] "Tentative Manual for the Employment of Air Service," Maurer, ed., *U.S. Air Service*, II, 342.

[90] Frank, *American Air Service Observation*, 220.

[91] Lieut Michel quoted in Porter, 173.

[92] Snyder, "Notes on the Relative Importance of Information," Gorrell Report, ser. J, r. 34, NARA.

[93] Lieut Michel in Porter, 175.

[94] Eaton, "Methods in Observation Practiced with Fifth Corps First American Army," *Air Service Information Circular*, 2, No. 115 (20 September 1920): 4-5, Davis Papers, McDermott Library, USAFA, SMS 57.

[95] Major-General and Air Vice-Marshal Sir Williamsefton Brancker, quoted in Porter, 175.

across the sector.[96] Prior to the first signs of daybreak or the onset of night, aerial observation capitalized on the commencement or closure of activity.[97] Evening reconnaissance was conducted for the sole purpose of spotting active hostile batteries. The flash from the guns was clearly observed in the hours of dusk. The sorties took off approximately one hour before dark and flew at an altitude of 2,000 meters inside friendly lines. The missions gave excellent results. Not only could the location be ascertained, but the caliber of the artillery piece could be determined by the frequency of fire. The last vestige of daylight allowed the aeroplane to return to the landing ground. In the absence of the light, the field would employ flares for the returning air crew.[98]

Night reconnaissance involved ascertaining the amount of light available to conduct aerial observation. The four types of night flying were considered bright moonlight, half moon, quarter moon, and dark starlight. During bright moonlight sorties, the pilots were told to fly below 2,000 feet "or under to be able to observe the type of movement." Lectures on the mission described troops or transport observed on the road in these conditions as "dim patches." Parachute flares were employed to light up a quarter-of-a-mile-square area. Dropped from an average altitude of 1,800 feet, the flare burned for about four minutes.[99] Night aerial photography tests using flares were undertaken by the British right up to the Armistice.[100]

Night reconnaissance required strict operator discipline, with the French selecting their best air crews to accomplish the mission. The focus was on rail traffic, activity in the industrial centers, and aerodromes. Traffic density had to be addressed, with the possibility of over 100 aéroplanes operating simultaneously in a particular region. Each unit was required to establish clearly defined air routes and altitudes to avoid potential collisions.[101]

Night operations ensured ongoing reconnaissance of rail and road activity to determine the extent of reinforcement. French aviation soon gravitated toward night operations for aerial bombardment. In 1915, bombardment escadrilles collected information while on the sortie. Upon return, any relevant observations were collated and forwarded to the 2ᵉ Bureau staff.[102] Such activity gained importance as the Germans employed cover of darkness to mask their major operations. By 1918 it was endemic. In July a German general mandated "Large troop movements and marches incidental to a change of billets will, as a rule, only take place at night. When troops on the march are taken by surprise at night by parachute flare dropped by a hostile airplane they will stop immediately and not move."[103] Allied night reconnaissance paid off in the final months. French escadrilles specifically set up for night reconnaissance were recognized by Général Pétain for their continued efforts. American aviation soon created its own night reconnaissance flights. Prior to termination of hostilities, the 9th Aero Squadron became the sole American squadron assigned with night reconnaissance responsibilities.[104]

Photography Ascendant Over the Aerial Observer

In the final summer of the conflict, the U.S. Air Service through its Office of the Director of Military Aeronautics provided lectures to newly arriving aviators on the benefits of aerial photography over observers. The discussion was to the point. Human frailties did not measure up to the power of technology. One report observed:

> Let us consider point by point the advantages possessed by the lens and

[96] Frank, *American Air Service Observation*, 234; Snyder, "Notes on the Relative Importance of Information," Gorrell Report, ser. J, r. 34, NARA.

[97] Frank, 234; Snyder, "Notes on the Relative Importance of Information," Gorrell Report, ser. J, r. 34, NARA.

[98] Eaton, "Methods in Observation Practiced with Fifth Corps First American Army," *Air Service Information Circular*, 2, No. 115 (20 September 1920): 15, Davis Papers, McDermott Library, USAFA, SMS 57.

[99] "Notes on Night Reconnaissance and Bombing," July 1918, Gorrell Report, ser. J, r. 35, NARA.

[100] Lt Col J. T. C. Moore-Brabazon, "Night Photography," 1 November 1918, TNA, PRO: AIR 1/1118/204/5/2041.

[101] Martel, 282.

[102] Capitaine Faure, "Instruction Relative aux Bombardments par Avions," quoted in Fischer, 103.

[103] Brig Gen von Sauberzweig, "Summary of Air Transportation," quoted in Fischer, 105.

[104] Fischer, 106-107.

the plate over the eye and the memory. It covers a given subject in a thorough manner far more perfectly than the eye, which is disturbed by many causes within and without, seeing as it does only one thing at a time, while the lens sees all at once with perfect impartiality. It eliminates any element of imagination, for the lens is neither dramatic nor poetic and sees things as they are. The lens can cover a territory or wider in scope, and in a shorter time, than the eye and the brain and memory could cover even under the most ideal conditions; and its whole maze of detail being grasped and recorded simultaneously.[105]

Aviators recognized their limitations. One RFC pilot, Lt. C.D. Smart, wrote in his diary, "Taking photographs is a poor game. It is highly dangerous and it doesn't give one a chance of telling any fairy tales."[106]

The camera was clearly the victor in aerial observation:

The camera has been adapted to act as an interpreter extraordinary.... The camera, therefore, has the advantage of a calm and keen perception and a perfect memory, to say nothing at all about the speed with which it gathers and records all in view with positive finality that leaves no question of a doubt. Possessing these extraordinary powers of perception, together with the power of retaining and recording matter gathered, it, therefore, constitutes an asset which is invaluable to the director of any military operations, whether they be contemplated on a large or on a small-scale. The pilot and observer, therefore, should realize this and feel that, in the camera, they have the best aid to the proper discharge of

their duties, without which their reconnaissance, no matter how diligently and courageously performed, would be minimized or even nullified.[107]

French post-war analysis of aviation gives a synopsis of the observer. Observation had peaked in 1916. By 1918, aviation was an integral part of the battle, preceding the infantry, breaking counterattacks, and pursuing a retreating enemy. The visual role provided by the aerial observer was still critical, but it did not compare to photographic technology. The verdict was clear: observation as an integral part of aerial reconnaissance did not emphasize the human observer in the loop. Observation was not advancing as an integral part of combat in the last year of the war. The quality of the observation force could not equal the advances in photography.[108] Three years of war refined the photographic process so that the intelligence contribution to daily operations was a standard fixture of daily life. The front lines were well monitored throughout. Both sides maintained extensive photographic coverage. French analysis revealed disappointment that "observation aeronautics did not yield the results which it gave in 1916. For this we may attribute as the principal reason the decline in the value of observers."[109]

The British *Notes on Observation from Aeroplanes* in February 1918 reviewed the prevailing attitude among the forces toward aerial observation. Ignorance of the mission was still prevalent among the "officers of other arms." In hopes of eliminating any doubts, British aerial observers emphasized key points about their occupation. "Fighting upon the ground is conducted upon one plane. Aerial fighting is complicated by a third dimension."[110] The discussion emphasized the challenges involved in artillery spotting. "It must be remembered that the artillery machine is heavily laden, but has poor speed and climb relatively with fighting machines, and that its attention is concentrated upon work on

[105] "Aerial Photography for Pilots," 3, NASM, A30.2/2.

[106] C.D. Smart, "The Front Cockpit: The Diary of Lt. C.D. Smart, No. 5 Sqdn, RFC," *Cross and Cockade, Journal of the Society of World War I Aero Historians* 10, No. 1 (Spring 1969): 15.

[107] "Aerial Photography for Pilots," 2-3, NASM, A30.2/2.

[108] "Aeronautics," June 1921, 5-6, NARA, RG 120, Box 819.

[109] "Aeronautics," June 1921, 5-6, NARA, RG 120, Box 819.

[110] "Notes on Observation from Aeroplanes," TNA, PRO: AIR 10/193.

the ground."[111] In conclusion, the publication reemphasized what had hitherto been the common belief about the aerial reconnaissance role: "Aeroplanes cannot do the work of cavalry."[112]

Mobile Warfare

In 1918, when positional war gravitated to mobile operations, the demand for higher-altitude coverage transitioned to a demand for coverage from lower altitudes. Short-focus lenses and wider viewing angles, required for quick reconnaissance to identify newer terrain features facing the advancing forces, now dominated the information battlefield.[113] During this time, the French increased their information networks to ensure that vital reports reached the mobile combatants. American post-war discussion described how the information was processed as forces advanced:

> During movements, each large unit, generally the division, is assigned a route of march and a zone of action. Airplanes reconnoiter this zone and transmit information by projectors, signal lights, dropped messages, or radio to information centers. These are established successively along the route so as to secure continuous reception. Information centers are in communication with the landing field of the airplanes by visual signals, telephone, radio, carrier pigeons, airplanes, or automobiles. An officer of the Air Service of the army corps or division reconnoiters if possible a suitable landing field near the information center. The necessary sentinels are assigned to it and communications organized. The division commander generally has his artillery commander with him, and moves successively from one information center to another as the movement continues.[114]

The architecture had come full circle. The landing zone techniques that applied in 1914 became policy in the final advance of 1918.

It is a testament to aerial reconnaissance that it met the initial skepticism of a well-entrenched military establishment with conclusive results, results that brought combat arms on "speaking" terms with intelligence. Four core missions resulted from the aerial reconnaissance legacy. First, artillery spotting ensured effective targeting for the most destructive weapon in the inventory. Second, visual reconnaissance ensured the most effective employment of weapons at the commander's disposal. Third, the aerial photograph proved to be the most effective technology for confirming both strategic and tactical assessments of the battlefield. Finally, greater liaison between the air arm and ground forces created the infantry contact mission that both accelerated awareness of enemy vital areas and improved targeting. The four core missions were supplanted by two additional tasks, tasks that soon became the lasting legacy of aviation of the time. Aerial combat took precedence over aerial reconnaissance. Preventing the adversary's access to the "higher ground" as well as protecting one's own reconnaissance ability to acquire information became the new objectives of aviation. Aerial superiority became the final outcome of this relationship, as armed forces sought total dominance of the sky.[115]

---

[111] "Notes on Observation from Aeroplanes," TNA, PRO: AIR 10/193.
[112] "Notes on Observation from Aeroplanes," TNA, PRO: AIR 10/193.
[113] Ives, 61; Barnes, *From Then Till Now*, 485.

[114] "Final Report of Chief of Air Service," Maurer, ed., *U.S. Air Service*, I, 183.
[115] Mead, 62-63; Lamberton, 10.

Chapter 19: Arranging Aerial Reconnaissance

THE SPECTRUM OF TECHNOLOGY

Aerial photography as an intelligence source changed the very nature of the Great War's battleground. Access to aerial reconnaissance information governed many decisions on the Western Front. Camera technology—the apparatus, film and photographic plate medium, and techniques associated with acquiring and developing an image—was in place before the war and remained consistent throughout. The magnitude of aerial photography's role did not immediately alter the science of photography. Charles Gamble, the RNAS leader on aerial photography, noted in his post-war reflections that the application of photography in a combat environment was an unsurprising key to success:

> It would be difficult to find any form of energy either visible or invisible capable of influencing the sensitive material whose effects had not been registered by the camera. The problem then that presented itself to the pioneers in war aerial photography was simply a problem in photography and the proof of this lies in the fact that having stated it to be a practicable thing they proceeded without any more ado to put the belief into practice.[1]

The Critical Component

The heart of camera technology was the lens, the most critical component governing the aerial camera's ability to image the target. The lens determined the aerial reconnaissance altitude and the required ground track. Intelligence and information gleaned from aerial photography was at the mercy of lens quality,[2] and lenses in quantity were needed to meet increasing demands for aerial reconnaissance coverage.[3] Many issues complicated the lens problem: a lack of standardization among the Allies, limitations caused by airframes, and probably most important, a serious shortage of raw material to make high-quality optics. The lack of a standardized lens for Allied aerial photography was serious, since the many variations in commercially produced lenses forced the use of inconsistent, makeshift cameras. When aerial photography gained a foothold in British military operations, the Ministry resorted to advertising for and paying premium prices for many critical photographic components, especially lenses.[4] Limitations imposed by aeroplane designers determined camera size and specifications. British aeroplane designers built "stop-gap" lenses configured to the aeroplane designer's specification and space available.[5] Moore-Brabazon reflected on trying

---

[1] Gamble, "Technical Aspects of British Aerial Photography," TNA, PRO: AIR 1/2397/267/7.

[2] Ives, 61.

[3] Ives, 44; Barnes, *From Then Till Now*, 485.

[4] Moore-Brabazon, "Photography's Part in the War," TNA, PRO: AIR 1/724/91/2.

[5] Ives, 45.

to work through the restrictions on camera design in relation to aeroplane specifications, noting that "The lesson that sticks out from these difficulties is that a great machine having one small part missing throws the whole scheme out of gear. Every part has to be planned and allowed for beforehand if disaster is to be avoided."[6] The final restraints on camera technology were the lack of raw materials and the industrial processing of the lens itself. In 1914, only two manufacturers in the world made the heavy crown barium glass necessary for building high-speed, high-power lenses. Germany's Carl Zeiss firm (located in Jena) and France's Parra-Mantois factory were the world's leading manufacturers of high-quality optics. Parra-Mantois became the de facto sole supply source of heavy crown barium glass for the Allies.[7]

Other French firms produced a lesser-quality glass, to include Hermagis, Lacour-Berthiot, and Krauss. What little they produced was sufficient only to meet the demands of Aviation Militaire.[8] The British had no rival manufacturer. Their only link to Parra-Mantois was that they were the source of high-grade coal required for achieving the temperatures necessary to fire the glass.[9] Once the aerial camera was produced in early 1915, the British War Ministry staff attempted to gain access to a reliable source of lenses. British attempts to acquire lenses from the French Lacour-Berthiot firm were unsuccessful due to lack of available stock. The French Service Géographique strictly controlled its indigenous lens output and made it clear to the British that they were unable to supply lenses in a reasonable time owing to the lack of glass.[10] Facing a serious "glass problem,"[11] the British staff resorted to extraordinary measures, visiting every second-hand lens dealer in Paris. It was of little use, for the quality of what remained was very poor.[12] As the war progressed, the optical supply worsened for the British. British optical glass

FIGURE 220 (OPPOSITE PAGE). A remarkable admission of a critical resource deficit in time of warfare. Like the British in 1915, the Americans faced a critical lens shortage in 1917, culminating in a call for lenses from the public through popular publications such as the *National Geographic.* Source: *National Geographic,* January 1918.

manufacturing remained practically non-existent until 1918.[13]

The British military made the case with the optical branch of the British Ministry of Munitions that a shortage of high-quality optical glass handicapped ongoing aerial reconnaissance. The Ministry subsequently announced a "compulsory return of lenses from the public" to serve RFC purposes and commenced to work closely with British industry to solve the optical glass shortage. They became acutely aware that wartime demands far exceeded contributions from the British public. Advertisements were inserted in trade and other papers for lenses of 8- to 12-inch focal length. People owning such lenses flocked into the Air Ministry to offer their lenses for use in the field. Despite such support, an industrial surge to produce high-quality glass remained the only solution to achieve and maintain an allowable level of critical optics necessary to support the ongoing British aerial reconnaissance effort. They reached this goal only in the final months of the war.[14]

All the Allied participants felt the strain. In post-war analysis of the crisis, former U.S. Photographic Section staff officer Captain Herbert Ives commented on the impact on the Allied aerial reconnaissance effort:

It is important that the historical aspect of this matter be well understood by the student of aerial photographic

---

[6] Moore-Brabazon, *The Brabazon Story*, 101.

[7] Ives, 44; Barnes, *From Then Till Now*, 485.

[8] Gamble, "Photographic Section of the French Flying Corps," TNA, PRO: AIR 1/404/97/1917.

[9] Moore-Brabazon, *The Brabazon Story*, 100-101.

[10] Gamble, "Photographic Section of the French Flying Corps," TNA, PRO: AIR 1/404/97/1917.

[11] Ives, 45.

[12] Gamble, "Photographic Section of the French Flying Corps," TNA, PRO: AIR 1/404/97/1917.

[13] Moore-Brabazon, "Photography's Part in the War," TNA, PRO: AIR 1/724/91/2.

[14] Moore-Brabazon, "Photography's Part in the War," TNA, PRO: AIR 1/724/91/2; Toye, "History of Photography," TNA, PRO: AIR 1/724/91/1.

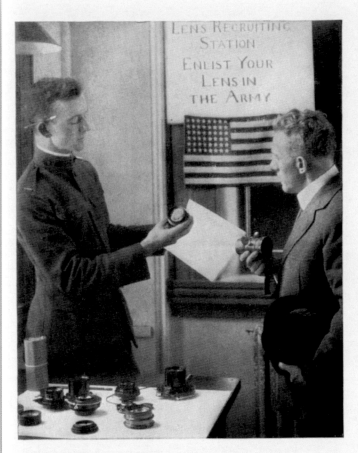

Enlist Your Lens in the Air Service

IF you have a powerful photographic lens, put it to work for our men "over there;" let it disclose from the skies of France hidden machine-gun nests waiting to spread death among advancing American troops; let it save hundreds of American lives from being snuffed out in the trenches by shells from concealed batteries. An official report calls the situation "critical," brooking no delay.

What is especially desired at the present time are lenses of from 7 inches to 24 inches focal length and with speeds of from F 3.5 to F 7.7. Practically all lenses of this type will be purchased as soon as they can be found. The following are some of the foreign makes wanted: Carl Zeiss Tessars, Bausch & Lomb Tessars, Voigtlander Heliar, Euryplan, Cooke, Goerz, Bush, Ross, Ross-Zeiss, Krauss, Krauss-Zeiss, Steinheil-Isostigmar, Rodenstock. In addition, matched pairs of stereoscopic lenses, with speeds of F 4.5, focal lengths of 4½, 5, 5½, 6, 6½, and 7 inches, are needed.

If you are in doubt as to the value of your lens, ask the nearest photographer.

Remember that you can probably replace your Anastigmat lenses with others just as serviceable for you but not adaptable for the army. If you have a lens such as your army needs, send at once its description and the price you think fair to

SIGNAL EQUIPMENT No. 33
WASHINGTON, D. C.

This page contributed to the U. S. Army by the National Geographic Society methods, for the use of these odd-lot lenses reacted on the whole design of aerial cameras and on the methods of aerial photography, particularly in England and the United States. Almost without exception the available lenses were of short focus, considered from the aerial photographic standpoint; that is, they lay between eight and twelve inches. This set a limit to the size of the airplane camera, quite irrespective of the demands made by the nature of the photographic problem. Lenses of these focal lengths produced images which, for the usual heights of flying, were generally considered too small, and which were, therefore, almost always subsequently enlarged. Such was the English practice, which was followed in the aerial training of aerial photographers in America, where exactly similar conditions held at the start with respect to available lenses. French glass and lens manufacturers did succeed in supplying lenses of longer focus (50 centimeters), in numbers sufficient for their own service, although never with any certainty for their allies.

The French, therefore, almost from the start, built their cameras with lenses of long focus, and made contact prints from their negatives.[15]

The British solved the demand for a longer lens (20-inch; 50.8 cm) using a variety of sources. Moore-Brabazon reported: "[W]hile we were waiting for the first British production, 50 cm. lenses were captured from the enemy almost every day for 3 weeks. This saved the situation by

---

[15] Ives, 45.

Comparable Allied Aerial Camera Measurements—Lens Length

British Standard	French Metric
4 inches	10.2 cm
6 inches	15.2 cm
6 1/4 inches	15.9 cm
7 inches	17.8 cm
8 inches	20.3 cm
9.8 inches	25 cm
10 inches	25.4 cm
10.2 inches	26 cm
10 1/2 inches	26.7 cm
12 inches	30.5 cm
14 inches	35.4 cm
15 inches	38 cm
19.7 inches	50 cm
20 inches	50.8 cm
20.4 inches	52 cm
27 inches	68.6 cm
47 inches	119.4 cm
47.2 inches	120 cm
72 inches	183 cm

giving us the very lenses we required most."[16] Every lens was employed. The British even developed the "B" Type camera—at their repair depots in France—using recycled lenses of downed German reconnaissance aircraft.[17] The lack of lens materials constrained British employment of cameras, adding to the frustration of maintaining aerial reconnaissance operations. "We never knew from day to day where we were going to get our next lenses, and the situation often became tense—indeed it was at times heartbreaking."[18] Another post-war review of the situation by one

FIGURE 222. **Allied lenses were of differing focal lengths, to meet varying publication capabilities and needs.** Source: Author analysis.

[16] Moore-Brabazon, "Photography's Part in the War," TNA, PRO: AIR 1/724/91/2.
[17] Toye, "History of Photography," TNA, PRO: AIR 1/724/91/1.
[18] Moore-Brabazon, *The Brabazon Story*, 101.

of Moore-Brabazon's counterparts, Major Toye, recalled, "Looking back on the glass situation, it is remarkable how quickly the prejudices and difficulties with regard to the production of high class optical glass were overcome, although at the time the progress seemed to be maddeningly slow."[19] It was soon evident that French lenses, as well as French glass, had to be a shared resource. In the summer of 1917, the issue was addressed by the highest French authorities and the Inter-Allied board. Under the direction and guidance of the French *Service Géographique, Section Optique*, lens production was soon increased and the output placed on an allocation basis satisfactory to Aviation Militaire demands.[20]

The increased demand for higher-quality optics directly correlated to the need for intelligence on the battleground. Intelligence analysts insisted on detail, demanding at a minimum 20-inch lenses.[21] Longer focal length resulted directly in more detailed photographs as well as increased air crew protection. In the first three years of the conflict, improvements in air defense forced observation planes to ascend from an initial operational altitude of three to four thousand feet to 15,000 to 18,000 feet and higher.[22] The evolving aerial observation mission required greater numbers of longer lenses such as the French 120 cm.

Lenses were a critical component for all combatants, but particularly for the Allies. American photographic experts learned of the lens supply crisis when they arrived in theater in late 1917. 1st Lt. Steichen notified the Signal Corps' Photographic Division in December that the French Service Géographique, Section Optique, was the "central and absolute authority having control of all optical glass questions for the French Government." Steichen concluded, "Their word is final on all such matters and, as you can see, vague." He advocated that the ultimate solution to the glass situation "lies in the production of glass in America."[23]

This was not a trivial issue for the U.S. Air Service. Colonel Raynal C. Bolling, the lead for advising both AEF and the War Department on critical challenges facing the U.S. war effort, personally kept Brigadier General Foulois, Chief of Air Service, updated on the lens problem. In a 22 January 1918 memorandum, Bolling discussed the Service Géographique's position and the need for accepting some independent action. The Parra-Mantois domination of heavy crown barium glass, plus the inability of British and American efforts to manufacture the required amount, was of serious concern. Bolling mentioned that Parra-Mantois' production was wholly inadequate to meet the combined needs of France, England, and the United States. Consideration was given to Parra-Mantois's profitability from increased production of the glass ("undoubtedly a precarious and unprofitable business"). The firm was concerned by the cost of setting up new production, and of creating a huge surplus when the war ended and demand subsided. Bolling even considered working out a deal to guarantee profitability for Parra-Mantois after the war. The Service Géographique insisted on the universal adoption of French lenses. At the time, speculation was that the British production authorities were undecided. Bolling concluded that the problem of adequate negotiation rested with the Service Géographique staff. "The French Service Géographique are entirely unwilling to entertain this suggestion, but speaking frankly, their attitude not only in this but in some other matters has not indicated to us sufficient openness of mind and spirit of give and take to make us ready to recommend simple acceptance of their decision." Bolling concluded that although he had led the U.S. effort up to that time on the issue, it was time to have a more senior person working within the Committee on French-American relations to come to an agreeable conclusion.[24] In the interim, the British established a capability and commenced their own glass production suitable for aerial cameras.

The Americans' advance aerial photograph team was quickly caught up in the controversy.

[19] Toye, "History of Photography," TNA, PRO: AIR 1/724/91/1.

[20] "Final Report of Chief of Air Service," Maurer, ed., *U.S. Air Service*, I, 151.

[21] Moore-Brabazon, "Photography in the RAF," TNA, PRO: AIR 1/724/91/1.

[22] Ives, 61; Barnes, *From Then Till Now*, 485.

[23] Steichen, "Memorandum for Major Decker," NASM.

[24] Col Raynal C. Bolling, "Memorandum, Subject: 'Situation Regarding Glass for Air Service Photographic Lenses'," 22 January 1918, Gorrell Report, ser. G, r. 24, NARA.

Major James Barnes, pioneer photographic interpreter, commented:

> The entire Allied Air Photography is dependent on the glass output of the firm of Parra-Mantois and this is controlled by the *Service Géographique*. Captain Laronde insisted that everything possible had been done that increased the output of the Parra-Mantois firm. He did not give any proof to substantiate this and our information leads us to believe the contrary. He decided that the only method of increasing production was by adopting one type of lens.... Captain Laronde's argument in favor of adopting French lenses as the desired type of lens is that these lenses are a safer manufacturing proposition, as smaller glass melts are needed. This is more of a laboratory than a military point of view.[25]

Barnes added, "American opinion favors lenses now made in England, as they are generally better and fifty per cent faster, consequently giving more day and longer hours for taking air photographs."[26] He noted that the American supply of lenses sufficed only for three more months. The shortage coincided with the operational employment of America's first observation squadron to support operations in the front. A solution was required as soon as possible. Major Campbell responded to Barnes on 30 January 1918, revealing that British demands were being simplified, suggesting they were going to rely on their own resources to meet the requirement for high-grade lenses.[27] Barnes expressed his growing frustration when he wrote Moore-Brabazon on 17 February 1918 that "The French are trying to get out of making any delivery of not only glass but I believe of the lenses they have contracted to deliver. They are exactly three months behind now and have not delivered any at all since the 29th of November."[28]

Major Toye wrote Barnes that the British had solved the glass problem to their satisfaction. They decided to ask for lenses only, not glass. He also mentioned that Campbell "has gone under" from overwork. The standing up of the RAF at that time was also consuming a lot of time.[29] The staffs worked feverishly to resolve the issue, which was elevated to the ministerial level. Brigadier General Foulois received word from the AEF staff on 26 March 1918, updating him on the precarious state of camera optics: "The lens and glass situation with the A.E.F. is at present in a most crucial state. In spite of all attempts to arrive at some definite understanding with the French Government, nothing yet has been accomplished." Confusion was being created by myriad offices sending different cables on the situation. A diplomatic crisis had evolved to the point that "it is in desperate need of solution."[30]

AEF staff recommended that General Pershing send Steichen to represent the Air Service and work with the Director of the Technical Section in dealing with the French on the lens issue.[31] At the subsequent Conference on the Glass Situation held on 25 April 1918, the American staff leader, Major Gros, took notes that the British required 120 cm lenses. A production rate of 62 lenses per month was required. The French estimated monthly production of 200 of the 26 cm, 145 of the 50 cm and 17 of the 120 cm lenses for 1918. At that time, the British representative mentioned they only had 12 of the 50 cm lenses in the entire British Army. Captain Steichen placed the U.S. need at a minimum of 50 of the 50 cm lenses. The French responded that the only way to distribute lenses was based on the

---

[25] Maj James Barnes, "Conference on the Optical Glass and Aviation Lens Situation," 25 January 1918, NASM.

[26] Barnes, "Conference on the Optical Glass and Aviation Lens Situation," NASM.

[27] Campbell, Letter to Maj James Barnes, 30 January 1918, NASM.

[28] Maj James Barnes, "Photographic Matters," 17 February 1918, NASM.

[29] Maj E. G. Toye, Letter to Maj James Barnes, 23 February 1918, NASM.

[30] "Appointment of Officer to Represent Air Service and U.S. Gov't. in Glass and Lens Negotiation," 26 March 1918, NASM.

[31] "Appointment of Officer to Represent Air Service," NASM.

number of infantry divisions at the front.[32] The 26th Division was the only American unit serving at the front during this time. By August 1918, the Americans had 12 divisions on the front line. Steichen strongly appealed for the French to immediately provide the British with the number of lenses required to allow them to catch up. The French representative insisted upon not drawing on the reserve stock of lenses, "which he states are kept for a possible rainy day."[33] That remark drew the following comment from Captain Steichen: "lenses would be much better stocked at the front, where they can be used, than kept in reserve at the *Service Géographique*."[34] Discussion ensued about the word "stock." The conference ended with the agreement that the allocation of 50 cm lenses be: French (55), British (55) American (11).[35] The French agreed to provide the vital, heavy crown barium glass, and the lenses for both countries were to be made in England, in accordance with a British formula, which accelerated the final assembly of the lens.[36] The final allocation for this critical resource was made in April 1918.[37] Lieutenant-Colonel J. T. C. Moore-Brabazon described subsequent discussions in June 1918 at an Inter-Allied Conference on Photography. He observed that the French Parra-Mantois firm remained the only Allied industrial center that could produce raw glass of the quality required for photographic lenses.[38]

The solution to the lens shortage crisis came in the final year of the war. British glass manufacturers commenced a major effort to produce optical glass equal to the German standard. Moore-Brabazon recalled:

This was a challenge to the British manufacturer who at once took it up. Lenses were soon being sent in for test and amongst the first was the Cook Avair by Taylor Taylor & Hobson. I think their second effort proved to be equal to the best German Zeiss that we could procure. The tests were made from a height of 9000 feet in Cameras fitted with two lenses side by side photographing exactly the same object, the Zeiss on the one side and the Avair on the other. The tests were very encouraging. Then came the question of production. No serious delay was experienced. Following the Avair came the Ross Express and the Ross Airo both wonderful lenses and soon we had more lenses than Cameras to put them in. As time went on there came a demand for lenses of longer focal length, namely 20." This was at once taken up with the manufacturers who worked hard and again triumphed. They produced lenses with wonderful covering power and very fast. Large numbers of these were at once put on order and we were soon well ahead of our requirements.[39]

Plate versus Film

One legacy of WWI aerial photographic reconnaissance, the photographic plate, has fallen into obscurity. The photographic plate medium by which the image was captured consisted of glass with a silver bromide emulsion on one side. Plates were packed with the emulsion side facing each other and were separated by cardboard.[40] Film technology existed, but problems with cameras and the film itself precluded it from becoming the primary image base. The film option was tried out early in the conflict by Lieutenant Grout and Lieutenant Pépin, whose 300 photos acquired from a 6 cm x 200 meter film strip covered the Verdun sector using the Douhet-Zollinger camera. This camera proved too difficult to handle

---

[32] Maj Edmond Gros, "Notes ... on Conference on Glass Situation Held at the Bureau of Monsieur Ganne," 25 April 1918, NASM; "Official Report of the Conference Held at the Office of the Under Secretary of State of the Presidency of the Council," 25 April 1918, Gorrell Report, ser. G, r. 24, NARA.

[33] Gros, "Conference on Glass Situation," NASM; "Official Report of the Conference," 25 April 1918," Gorrell Report, ser. G, r. 24, NARA.

[34] Gros, "Conference on Glass Situation," NASM.

[35] Gros, "Conference on Glass Situation," NASM.

[36] Barnes, *From Then Till Now*, 487.

[37] Barnes, *From Then Till Now*, 487-488; "Official Report; Cession of Optical Instruments to the American and English Governments," Gorrell Report, ser. G, r. 22, NARA.

[38] Lt Col J. T. C. Moore-Brabazon, "Report on ... Visit to the Conference Held in Paris," 16 June 1918, NASM.

[39] Moore-Brabazon, "Photography's Part in the War," TNA, PRO: AIR 1/724/91/2.

[40] "Plates and Development of Plates," Steere Papers, USAMHI.

and its short lens limited the operational altitude for acquiring readable coverage.[41]

The British also experimented with film in a combat environment. As the war entered the second year, they developed a film camera, the Aero Camera or "F" Type camera. The Russians used this camera on the Eastern Front to support their cartographic production. The "F" Type camera was designed to take a continuous series of pictures on a roll of film 5 inches wide and 25-50 feet in length. A 50-foot roll provided coverage for 120 exposures. The "F" Type camera was uniquely configured for flight, being positioned on a bomb rack. The automatic camera was driven by air pressure from a small four-bladed propeller. Every 300 propeller revolutions triggered the camera to take a photograph, providing a continuous stream of coverage.[42] Despite experimentation with this medium, the Allies stayed with plates. Film also had its difficulties due to electrical discharges that disturbed the emulsion in cold and dry environments such as those found in the upper atmosphere.[43]

The true champion of film for aerial photography throughout the war was George Eastman, chairman of the Eastman Kodak Company of Rochester, New York. From the start, Eastman monitored development of the aerial camera, occasionally meeting with the British on the subject. In 1915, he observed that "The military and naval authorities are taking considerable interest in photography for aerial observation…. Experiments have been going on lately at the military flying grounds in the use of automatic photography on airplanes."[44] The war provided Eastman with an outstanding opportunity to develop and promote an aerial film camera. He aggressively promoted his automatic camera, reminding everyone that plates were not as effective as his film:

FIGURE 223. **A glass photographic plate showing detail in good light.** Source: SHAT.

We are especially devoting ourselves to aerial photographic work, and have already devised special emulsions and apparatus for the purpose, some of which are very promising. Among other things we have an automatic film camera which will make fifty exposures, six inches square, in succession, which are equal to anything that can be taken singly with glass plates…. The Allies are using plates almost exclusively, because they have been unable to get the photographic results required on films. This is partly because they have been trying to use the ordinary camera films, which are quite unsuitable for the work. They also have been unable to handle the films mechanically.[45]

---

[41] Dégardin, in *Vues d'en Haut*, 20-21; Pépin Papers, MA&E, Paris; Carlier,18

[42] Toye, "History of Photography, TNA, PRO: AIR 1/724/91/1.

[43] Carl W. Ackerman, *George Eastman* (Boston: Houghton Mifflin Company, 1930), 296; Crowell and Wilson, II, 422-423; Powell, 294-295.

[44] Ackerman, 289.

[45] Ackerman, 299.

Kodak's subsidiary, Folmer & Schwing, came through with a state-of-the-art aerial film camera. It was radically different from anything that had been seen in Europe up to that time. The aerial film automatic camera, known as the "K" type, carried film capable of 100 exposures (18 x 24 cm) per loading. The 40-pound "K" was light for aerial cameras. The film rolls were easy to handle and light (4 pounds). The most novel and ingenious feature of the "K" camera, the "vacuum back," held film flat. The filmstrip passed over a flat perforated sheet behind which a partial vacuum was created by suction from a Venturi tube extending outside the body of the aeroplane. It was driven either by a wind turbine of adjustable aperture or, in warplanes, by electric current from the heating and lighting circuit. The "K" camera allowed the observer to start the machinery going and regulate its speed according to the rate of travel of the aeroplane. The final result was a series of pictures that formed a continuous mosaic photograph of the aeroplane's ground track.[46] Eastman persisted in making the design available for government inspection. He told Secretary of War Newton Baker that "Mr. Folmer will at once proceed with the construction of experimental models of cameras to be submitted to you, and we will place blueprints of the drawings of these models at your disposal to enable you to obtain tenders for their construction from other firms as well as ourselves."[47] The "K" camera design was a winner, and the U.S. War Department promptly adopted it, but it never saw combat.[48] The problem for Kodak and the film camera was that the Allies favored plates. When the AEF arrived in theater, it quickly accepted what was available and did not debate the issue. Despite this setback, Kodak continued to refine its aerial film camera. Its persistence paid off in the long run. Film became the mainstay for American aerial photography shortly after the war.[49] Eastman championed the "K" camera throughout the war. In a letter to the War Department, he remarked:

We have tried the camera out twice in the air at the field of the Curtiss Company near Buffalo and it worked perfectly from the start, and the second trial was made only for the purpose of correcting the focus of the lens. It operates very simply, using the air pressure generated by the plane itself. The pictures are sharp and in every way satisfactory. The speed at which the exposures can be made is variable and the starting and stopping of the camera and the speed regulation is done with one lever so that the instrument is a one-man affair, to be operated by the aviator, which is a very important thing considering the lives it will save. The film has a special emulsion which overcomes all the objections you have noted. The reloading of the camera can be very easily done in the air, but in that case it would probably have to be done by an observer.[50]

Aerial plate cameras had mixed reviews throughout the war. Vibration was always a concern. Instructors cautioned that the observer not touch the plane while taking pictures. The magazine was difficult to operate and required sensitive handling. That the plates were glass also contributed to their limitations.[51] One combat veteran observer still advocated plates, commenting on film's limitations:

It is a curious thing that films can't be used in the air with any consistent success. The center of a film photograph is almost invariably out of focus. The aerial photo covers so much ground that a film is never flat enough and apparently can't be stretched flat enough, to preserve the focus. Britain and France discovered this after unwearying investigation and a constant succession of failures, and America was wise enough, for once, to profit by somebody else's experience. Since aerial photographs are worthless unless they are clear and

[46] Crowell and Wilson, II, 422-423; Powell, 294-295; Ives, 144; Carlier, 36.

[47] Ackerman, 296.

[48] Crowell and Wilson, II, 422-423; Powell, 294-295.

[49] Crowell and Wilson, II, 420; Powell, 294.

[50] George Eastman quoted in Ackerman, 302.

[51] Gill and Hibben, "Preparation of Photographic Missions," Gorrell Report, ser. J, r. 34, NARA.

full of detail, the question of bulk and weight was also set aside and plate cameras were universally adopted. This meant a lot of extra work to ensure success, for the photographic observer had to shift every plate through the magazine at least once before the aircraft left the ground to ensure the plates fit.[52]

The Component Contribution

The Allies at the Western Front stayed with plates for the duration of the war. Despite their shortcomings, and in part because they were already in use and a familiar item, the British and French stayed with plates. Americans followed suit as the dependent newcomer. Film was on the cusp of acceptance, coming into its own immediately after the war.

Aerial photography's technological challenges went beyond the camera. In northern Europe lighting posed a challenge most of the year. The atmospheric conditions made photographing a target a formidable obstacle. As the threat from pursuit aeroplanes and air defense artillery forced photographic missions to operate at higher altitudes, the issue of haze became a more urgent concern. Above a certain height—varying depending on the haze—a normal lens could not image the target. After extensive research the solution was found to be in the use of special color filters containing a yellow cast, which obscured the bluish light characteristic of haze. Filters of new materials specially adapted to aeroplane use were made available as a result of study.[53] The rule of thumb was "the greater the density of haze the deeper the filter should be."[54] When the view was almost clear and no filter was used, photographic results were found to be flat. Filters cut through the haze of northern Europe, but not through cloudbanks. Weather still ruled the success of the mission.[55] By war's end, panchromatic plates were in use. One British observer recalled: "In our day, the sensitive material was at best orthochromatic, such as the Wellington Anti-Screen plate of honored memory, of a speed not more than 300 H&D. We generally used an X2 yellow lens-filter, fitted as a disc of gelatine between the lens-components, when the light was good."[56]

Filters also conferred a critical tactical and strategic advantage to intelligence. The panchromatic plates and filtration of light through the color filters helped identify enemy attempts at camouflage. The aerial photographic interpreter had to differentiate between colors that ordinarily looked alike but were actually of different color composition. A color-filter lens was developed that separated the hues of the spectrum into their parts and imparted to each a definite and characteristic shading in the photographic plate, disclosing a spot of impure color. Those areas that were camouflaged came out blurred on the image.[57] The filters complicated the ongoing strategy of positional war: Units such as artillery depended on camouflage to increase firing battery survival; the photographic image, refined through the filter, increased the uncertainty of preparing the battlefield.

Technology Transfer

French and British photographic experts expected the arriving American forces to come to the battleground appropriately equipped to conduct aerial photographic reconnaissance. The Americans were recognized as leaders with film. However, such expertise did not serve the well-established French and British aerial photographic infrastructure. Instead, for the remainder of the war, both had the additional burden of supplying Americans with critical photographic resources.[58] As a result, each ally tried to establish the priorities for production and development. One senior AEF staff officer told colleagues that the French were trying to influence the direction of the talks on the sensitive issue of simplifying lens construction. The chief of the Service Géographique wrote a letter to the GQG to prevail upon the Americans and the other Allies to reduce the size of the plates, thus simplifying the

---

[52] Porter, 171.
[53] Crowell and Wilson, II, 425; Porter, 175.
[54] Aerial Photography, Air Publication 838, TNA, PRO: AIR 10/853.
[55] Porter, 175-176.

[56] Insall, 158.
[57] Porter, 175-176; Barnes, From Then Till Now, 495; Ives, 244.
[58] Crowell and Wilson, II, 419-420.

fabrication of the lenses. The American officer wrote, "To my mind this reads like the man who tried to persuade himself to cut off his nose so that he would not have to wash it."[59] The suggestion did not carry; lens standards remained as they were.

The Allies moved sometimes reluctantly toward a standard approach to photographic practices. Photographic instruction in the United States followed British techniques. The Americans followed French practices when they flew aeroplanes of British design. Further adding to the complicated scenario, the Americans configured their British-built aeroplanes with French cameras.[60] A more rigid structure had to be imposed. The Americans gained agreement from the British and French to standardize aerial photographic plate size and lens size. Since French

FIGURE 224. The French were the first to develop a mobile photographic facility. The laboratory was self-contained and transported on the back of a French Camion (truck). Source: SHAA.

and British plate sizes varied, not only did it represent a challenge in dimensions, it also consumed valuable time to achieve a standard. If the French used British photographs or maps, a photographic enlargement was required. Likewise, a reduction was necessary if the British used French images. The lack of standardization increased the time spent on handling the different size plates rather than in accomplishing the analysis. By 1918, all agreed to a format of 18 x 24 cm. Additional standards included a 50 cm lens and British dimensions for camera cone and

---

[59] Lt Col E. S. Gorrell, "Memorandum for Colonel Dunwoody," 21 December 1917, Gorrell Report, ser. G, r. 24, NARA.

[60] Crowell and Wilson, II, 419; Ives, 45-46.

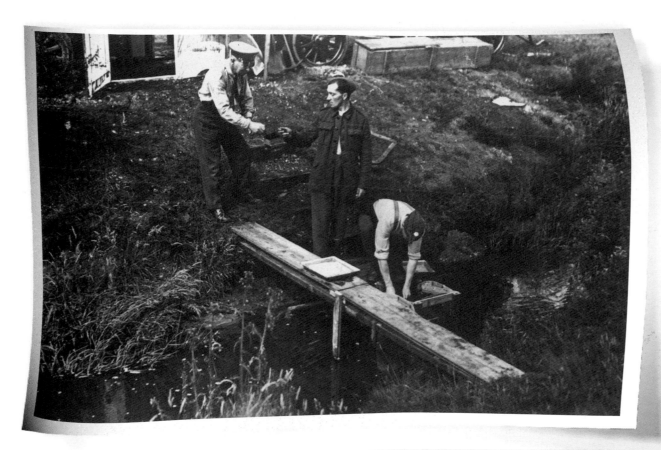

FIGURE 225. "We never had running water." Developing aerial photographs in the mobile laboratories took advantage of whatever the terrain provided. Source: Courtesy of Michael Mockford and the Medmenham Collection, Chicksands, UK.

attachments.[61] Steichen remarked in a memo to the Signal Corps Photographic Division that the standards impacted the British more because their cameras had to be enlarged to handle the new photographic plate size.[62] All things considered, the French had made the greatest effort during the war to provide photographic resources. U.S. Photographic Section records show that five per cent of materials came from England, eight per cent came from the United States, and the remaining eighty-seven per cent from French supply stocks. Not a single American-made negative or photograph was at the Front prior to the signing of the Armistice.[63] The first train of American plates and paper was en route between Paris and Columbey-les-Belles on 11 November.[64]

The technology exchange throughout the war reflected a strong camaraderie among the experts. However, warm relationships were not as prevalent among the military in general. Moore-

Brabazon, for example, amiably resolved a technical question with peers, but suffered the political consequences: "[I]n photography nobody could help me—nobody else knew anything about it." He went to the French technical experts at the *Section Technique* in Versailles. The discussions were totally open and promoted a sharing of techniques and capabilities. However, upon return, Moore-Brabazon was "soundly told off" by Brigadier-General Trenchard for making the trip to Paris. About two weeks later, Trenchard was present at an inspection conducted by the French on one of the British squadrons. To his delight, the French had asked Trenchard for permission to "copy one of our gadgets in photography" for use in their own machines. Trenchard was magnanimous and agreed. However, he was totally ignorant as to what the "gadget" could do

---

[61] Barnes, *From Then Till Now*, 487.
[62] Steichen, "Memorandum for Major Decker," NASM.
[63] Steichen, "Aerial Photography," Gorrell Report, ser. G, r. 24; Toulmin, 317-319.
[64] Steichen, "Aerial Photography," Gorrell Report, ser. G, r. 24; Toulmin, 317-319.

or where it came from. Moore-Brabazon, when approached, revealed that not only was the device of French design, but he had received Section Technique permission for incorporating it into the British camera system: "I cannot tell you how delighted the General was to think that within a fortnight of my visit to Paris the French were asking our permission to use something they had invented themselves!"[65]

Inter-Allied conferences became the best medium for Allied photo experts to reach compromise on technical issues. The breadth of exchange on photographic research was almost breathtaking. At a conference one month before the Armistice, as reported by Steichen, "The British representative submitted a report of their experiment with night photography, and showed sample prints made. These photographs are the first concrete results in night photography that have come to the attention of the Allied Photo Services. It was decided that all information of this nature should be promptly distributed among the Allies."[66] In early November 1918, Moore-Brabazon described efforts up to that time in developing the Photographic Flare to illuminate railway stations and to determine enemy activity. The flare was designed to enable photographs to be taken by night from a height of 1,000 to 2,000 feet. The flare was dropped from the 20-lb bomb carrier and timed to explode at a height of 400 to 500 feet above the surface. The effective part of the flash lasted about 1/100th of a second. The photographic plate was kept exposed during the whole of the flash. The successful tests occurred the last month of the war at the RAF's Armament Experimental Station, in Orfordness.[67]

Another interesting insight into ongoing photographic research conducted by the Italians was discussed at the October 1918 conference. Italian research on the photographic spectrum had discovered a unique application. Colonel Tardivo, Photographic Section, Italian Army, described the theory of infrared photography for submarine detection and signaling, but no written data were furnished.[68] Aerial photography was quickly heading toward a new frontier.

Aerial Photographic Ground Support Technologies

Post-war popular publications discussing the lessons of World War I entertained their readers with elaborate descriptions of behind-the-scenes processes that contributed to the Allied victory. One source described with great imagination what aerial photographs revealed about enemy intentions. The key technology behind the entire process was the magnifying optics employed by the aerial photographic interpreter, to include the basic magnifying glass for single-frame shots and the more elaborate and highly-prized stereoscope. Without the ability to see and interpret detail through stereoscopic analysis, aerial photographic interpretation would have been severely handicapped. The stereoscopic legacy remains an important component of imagery analysis, even if it does not live up to its literary reputation as "the deadliest weapon of the war."[69]

Intelligence analysis at the landing ground was possible due to the photographic laboratory technology supporting the effort. Once the aerial photographic plates were in the photo laboratory, the tank method called for plates to remain in the developer until they just began to fog. Too long a period in the developer created flatness on the surface of the negative, contributing to a lack of contrast. The prints were dried in alcohol. For time-sensitive coverage of targets of high value, the French were able to produce prints thirty minutes after the plane had landed. The normal development time was two hours.[70]

Mobility was integral to SPAé, Photo Section operations. Each Ally had its own variant of camion, lorry, and truck. Photographic processing mobility increased intelligence value by shortening acquisition, processing, and interpre-

---

[65] Moore-Brabazon, *The Brabazon* Story, 96-97.

[66] Lt Col Edward Steichen, "Report of Inter-Allied Photographic Meeting," 17 October 1918, Gorrell Report, ser. G, r. 24, NARA.

[67] Lt Col J. F. C. Moore-Brabazon, "R.A.F. Night Photography," TNA, PRO: AIR 1/2395/255/1.

[68] Steichen, "Report of Inter-Allied Photographic Meeting," Gorrell Report, ser. G, r. 24, NARA.

[69] Hanson, 15.

[70] Gamble, "Photographic Section of the French Flying Corps," TNA, PRO: AIR 1/404/97/1917.

FIGURE 226. **Interior view of mobile lab shows space allotted to interpretation and filing.** Source: Gorrell Report, NARA.

tation time.[71] The basic model required two men to drive and maintain the lorry, charge batteries, and help in the dark room as needed. Four personnel mixed chemicals, developed, washed prints, fixed, enlarged, dried, trimmed, and handled photos and negatives. NCOs were responsible for all the work done in the lorry. They assisted the indexing, numbering, filing of plates, prints, and other tasks. The NCOs also kept a tally on all stores and ensured stock was maintained. The officer ensured the collection of photographs was kept safe and available on request. The photos were catalogued by map squares. The officer also instructed observers on the camera and its use.[72] However, it was a flexible operation. "Even in the most unfavorable of circumstances, the lorry can be drawn up near a house of some description where a table and chair can be placed at his disposal upon which the work of identifying the photos, and getting them ready for issue can be carried out."[73] The only environ-

mental addition was access to a water source. One photo lab man remembered: "Water was the most essential, but the scarcest of our needs, and had to be trucked in G.I. cans from the rivers, which sometimes were several kilometers away. We never had running water."[74]

The basic mobile photographic laboratory was compact in design. British specifications resulted in a cramped environment that all photo processing and interpretation personnel had to endure. "The Dark Room Lorry was to be 12 feet long by 6 feet 6 inches in width. It was divided into five compartments: small store, officers' desk, enlarging and printing room, dark room for papers and dark room for plates. The dark room was initially envisioned for 6 men or more

---

[71] Toye, "History of Photography," TNA, PRO: AIR 1/724/91/1.

[72] Campbell, "Notes on Aerial Photography," TNA, PRO: AIR 1/7/6/98/20.

[73] "2nd Lt Kippel, OIC Photographic Section, 1st Wing, R.F.C.," 14 June 1915, TNA, PRO: AIR 1/2151/209/3/244.

[74] Dixon, *Diary*, 50.

Longueur: 5.ᵐ∞

Écran d'agrandissement   Refend   Lanterne d'agrandissement

Chambre noire   Chambre de travail à la lumière

Porte de séparation
étanche à la lumière

Réservoir
d'eau propre   Porte d'entrée

FIGURE 227. **The French also employed a photographic trailer. The line drawing shows the layout of work spaces.** Source: de Brunoff, ed., *L'Aeronautique*.

to work in if necessary with a place for the OIC to write and watch his stores."[75] French laboratories possessed additional support equipment. The Photographic Camion consisted of a tractor, laboratory trailer which could accommodate eight personnel, and a generator to provide power for the laboratory. A wooden portable laboratory known as a Photographic Cabin (*baraque*) accommodated larger production requirements.[76] An entourage of Photographic Camions could be assembled to support an operation on demand. As one French officer recalled, "In the sectors of attack, several sections are brought together and assigned to a large photographic barracks where the automatic machines are installed."[77]

When the AEF set up operations in-theater, the Americans worked with what was available and also commenced development of an American version of the mobile laboratory. Their mobile photographic truck contained all the equipment necessary to rapidly produce prints in the field. The truck body was equipped with a dynamo for furnishing the electrical current required for lights and drying fans. Each unit

contained an acetylene generator for emergency use if the electrical apparatus should break. The mobile dark room carried on the trailer of each unit was equipped with tanks, enlarging camera, printing boxes, and other necessary apparatus. Some 75 complete units were built in the United States and shipped overseas.[78]

Technological questions held center stage as procedures were worked out for efficient aerial reconnaissance. Deliberation went on among the Allies to find the best techniques to process and analyze photography. Perhaps even more important was the allocation of critical resources such as the high-quality glass used in making camera lenses and determining the extent to which each ally should commit to sharing trade secrets. The arrival of the Americans to the theater only increased the urgency of working out how to share limited resources. This situation

[75] Lt Col J. T. C. Moore-Brabazon, "OIC Photos in the Field," 21 June 1915, TNA, PRO: AIR 1/2151/209/3/244.
[76] Carlier, 65.
[77] Lieut Michel quoted in Porter, 174.

[78] Crowell and Wilson, II, 425-426; Powell, 296-297.

Chapter 20: The Spectrum of Technology

was emblematic of the times; a fair allocation of scarce resources had to be established amongst the Allies to ensure each member could carry on with the war.

FIGURE 228. **Accommodations for photographic processing and interpretation were increased by the fixed Photographic Baraque (Cabin).** Source: de Brunoff, ed., *L'Aeronautique.*

CHAPTER 21
OPERATIONAL AERIAL CAMERAS

amera design and photography evolved steadily for seventy years prior to the war. By war's start, photography was limited only by the imagination of the viewer. It offered a tremendous outlet for both the professional and the novice, because of its ability to capture the moment. Buyers enjoyed a selection of cameras from the Kodak hand-held to elaborate movie equipment. However, camera systems that had been developed, such as aerial mapping cameras, were far too heavy for serious consideration by aeroplane designers. As aerial observation gained value with military forces, efforts were made to develop cameras that could effectively photograph the battleground, with refinements to improve both reliability and ease of handling in a severe combat environment. Technology transformation occurred, not in the science of optics, but in the ability to stabilize the airframe and manipulate the photo plates so that a series of photographs could be acquired while maintaining constant vigilance against a rapidly growing anti-aircraft threat.

Taking a photo with an aerial camera comprised three steps: set the shutter, release the shutter, and change the plate. Aerial plate-camera design covered four principal parts: box, lens, shutter, and plate holder. The box was light but strong enough to support the mechanisms required to take the photographs. The inside of the box was black to prevent any unnecessary reflection on the plate. The lens was the critical component and was made of high-quality glass.[1] Aerial cameras required the shutter to acquire a calculated amount of light for the photographic image while moving at a certain speed. Some of the aerial cameras used at this time were manually operated, creating a distorted image of the ground. Another challenge to aerial cameras was vibration from the aeroplane motor, which forced the use of a shutter speed of 1/125 of a second or less.[2] The plate holder or magazine contained a metal device known as the septum that held both unexposed and exposed plates. From these basic components, camera design evolved to handle the rigors of flight.[3]

The Aerial Camera Inventory

Shortly after war was declared, the camera-aware public rushed to offer the combatants suggestions on its use in the conflict. In Britain, military staffs received novel ideas concerning the art of the photographically possible. One memorable offer came from the noted American explorer and photographer of the African continent, James Barnes, who later launched America's photo effort for the U.S. Signal Corps in 1917. In

---

[1] "General Lecture on Cameras," Steers Papers, USAMHI; Campbell, "Notes on Aerial Photography," TNA, PRO: AIR 1/7/6/98/20.

[2] Author discussion with Alf Pyner.

[3] "General Lecture on Cameras," Steers Papers, USAMHI; Campbell, "Notes on Aerial Photography," TNA, PRO: AIR 1/7/6/98/20.

August 1914, Barnes had just arrived in Britain as the forces were mobilizing. Having just extensively employed an array of still and movie cameras to record his latest sojourn, he was quick to point out to a British military senior at Westminster Town Hall the value of photographic reconnaissance, emphasizing that much of the military information on which an army could act, either on the defensive or on the offensive, came from the air. The only way one could achieve accuracy in this endeavor was by using a recording "flying eye"—the camera. Barnes and his explorer colleague together offered plans for a portable photographic laboratory—a motor lorry, fitted up with dark room, drying frames, in fact, everything necessary for the development of negatives taken automatically on continuous film. The prints also were to be made in the field in the shortest period of time. The novel Barnes proposal included a "guarantee to show to any general officer or the Intelligence Department a moving picture on the screen, of the country traversed by any air scout within an hour after descent from flight of inspection."[4] The resulting response was brief but gracious. The immediate priorities of mobilizing forces and deploying to the combat areas were too overwhelming for the British to take advantage of the offer. Barnes had his chance to apply his photographic prowess later in the war when he established the U.S. Army's Photographic Division.

Aerial photography in the first year of fighting was accomplished with hand-held cameras. British and French efforts prior to the outbreak of the war were experimental. The early cameras were not well-suited for aerial observation. One hand-held camera that received considerable attention from the early British aviators was the Pan-Ross, a Goerz-Anshutz camera type used by press photographers.[5] When the RFC set out for France in August 1914, five "Penros" hand-held cameras were listed on the equipment inventory list, fitted with 6-inch Panocentric lenses.[6] Af-

ter the adoption of the original scheme of taking aerial photographs with the Pan-Ross camera, the unexpected occurred. The bellows on the camera was misshapen from the airstream and the focus became permanently disturbed.[7] Despite these shortcomings, hand-held cameras performed as well as early machine-mounted configurations.

The vast majority of cameras in the First World War were non-automatic. The ideal was the automatic camera, allowing the air crew to concentrate on defending themselves while flying the sortie. When automatic camera operations finally became reality the last year of the conflict, the responsibility of taking photographs shifted to the pilot, allowing the observer to take additional photographs with a more portable hand-held camera as well as conduct defensive operations. The combination increased the coverage and provided supplementary information that aided the photographic interpretation process.[8] Some single-seater fighter aircraft were also configured with rudimentary controls to operate a semi-automatic camera; however, the mechanism was found to be unstable and unreliable.[9]

The aerial camera of this era was categorized by the method of operation and the sensitive material (plates versus film) employed. Plates were the standard, despite the fact that film was equally effective. There were three types of plate aerial cameras: non-automatic, semi-automatic, and automatic.[10] World War I aerial cameras were mostly fixed-focus box styles configured for plates. The average plate size varied with nationality. British cameras used a smaller 4 x 5 inch. French frames were larger at 18 cm x 24 cm. The French 18 x 24 cm plates produced contact prints for which the British had to accomplish an additional step in the development process using an enlarging camera to produce larger 6½ x 8½ inch prints from the 4 x 5-inch negative. In all British aerial fixed-focus cameras the lenses were inter-

---

[4] Barnes, *From Then Till Now*, 424-425.

[5] The name of the camera varied with the source; Penros, Pan-Rose, and Pan-Ross were mentioned. See Appendix B for a list of all cameras of this type as Pan-Ross. Gamble, "Technical Aspects of British Aerial Photography," TNA, PRO: AIR 1/2397/267/7; Author discussion with Alf Pyner.

[6] 6 in. equals 15.24 cm. Gamble, "Technical Aspects of British Aerial Photography," TNA, PRO: AIR 1/2397/267/7.

[7] "Aerial Photography for Pilots," 21 August 1918, A30.2/2.

[8] "Development of Aerial Photography," Gorrell Report, ser. J, r. 24, NARA.

[9] "Aerial Photography for Pilots," 21 August 1918, NASM, A30.2/2.

[10] Ives, 43, 102.

changeable so that either a short- or long-focus lens could be fitted to suit the requirements of the mission. Shorter lenses were used for broad coverage or for supporting map production. Long-lens cameras produced the large-scale photographs that helped analysts interpret targets.[11] Nomenclature for aerial cameras varied with each country. In 1918, both the French and the British took the step to label their cameras with an alphanumeric designation. French cameras were listed with an "F." The British separated their cameras by medium and function. Plate cameras received a "P" prefix, film cameras were labeled as "F," and gun cameras carried a "G" moniker.[12]

French Research on Aerial Cameras

The French government had long recognized the military value of photography. At Versailles, their Section Technique laboratory examined a broad array of technologies for military applications to include aerial photography. Section Technique successfully developed camera systems that served as the core of French aerial photographic reconnaissance for most of the war and into the immediate post-war period. The designs were consistent, with the aerial camera body configured to a pyramid shape and built of aluminum. The French established their nomenclature process for aerial cameras based on focal length such as the 26 cm, 50 cm, or 120 cm. Later in the war, a standard nomenclature was developed such as F-1 for the 26 cm camera. It was a tribute to the success of Section Technique that a post-war military assessment considered development of the aerial camera (photographic equipment in order to take vertical photographs) of equal importance with other key military-related technologies such as the "wireless telegraphic sending apparatus, machine guns firing by synchronization through the propeller, machine guns in the rear turret, and bomb-throwing gear with shells in the wings."[13] Also instrumental in aerial camera design were the Gaumont and Duran firms,

which provided the key components for camera assembly.[14]

Early French aerial photography was not solely the domain of French technology. The Douhet-Zollinger camera provided the initial breakthrough for French aerial photography of the front opposite the French IVème Armée sector in March 1915. The Douhet-Zollinger was built about 1913 in Turin, Italy, under the direction of Commandant Douhet and an engineer named Zollinger. The French acquired a prototype for testing when war was declared. The Douhet-Zollinger was one of the few operational automatic film cameras in the war. The camera body was aluminum, configured with a Tessar-Zeiss optical lens set to a focal length of 10 cm. The shutter speed was set at 1/100 a second. This German lens was not available to the Allies after the start of the war. The film was 6 cm by 20 meters, providing continuous coverage for 300 photographs. The film was perforated along the edge, driven through the camera by means of sprockets. This automatic camera was replaced by the more sturdy plate cameras such as the 26 cm. The automatic function was not reevaluated until the final year of the conflict.[15]

The British Prototype "A" Type Camera

The British initiative in developing aerial photography was spawned by both their own aviators and introduction to the ongoing efforts by the French. It became apparent to RFC pioneers, Lt. Pretyman and Lt. Darley, that handheld cameras yielded limited results. Moore-Brabazon later recalled, "We were then asked to produce the same results [as the French]. Handicapped as we were for apparatus, etc., work was commenced with the five existing cameras which were very soon reduced to two owing to losses due to enemy action and cameras becoming unserviceable."[16] We "were sent home to design and make a camera; this was done about February 1915. Six box-type cameras were

---

[11] "Notes on Aerial Photography," Part II, Baghdad, 1918, TNA, PRO: AIR 10/1001.
[12] Nesbit, 51.
[13] "Aeronautics," June 1921, 3, NARA, RG 120, Box 819.

[14] "Aerial Photography for Pilots," 21 August 1918, NASM, A30.2/2.
[15] Carlier, 26-28.
[16] Moore-Brabazon, "Photography's Part in the War," TNA, PRO: AIR 1/724/91/2.

FIGURE 229. **The first "A" Type British camera was difficult to handle, requiring up to 11 distinct steps for the first exposure. It was subsequently modified to take 18 successive photographs by means of a changing apparatus.** Source: Roy Nesbit, *Eyes of the RAF*.

evolved, this being the real R.F.C. camera, and from that moment photography improved a good deal."[17] Moore-Brabazon and C.D.M. Campbell returned to England to commence camera development. Moore-Brabazon recalled, "We started with a bellows camera—that is, a camera which pulls out—and you can imagine what a bellows camera would be like in an aeroplane."[18] "It was at once realized that we had to design a camera specially for this work so the personnel then in the field consulted together and produced ideas which were conveyed home to Messrs. Thornton-Pickard who in a very short time produced what was known as the 'A' Type camera."[19] In February 1915, Mr. Richard Hesketh, secretary of the Thornton-Pickard Photographic Manufacturing Company, Ltd., met with Moore-Brabazon and Campbell and talked about British aerial reconnaissance basics, yet being sensitive to not violate the prevailing security laws. The discussion led to what was required to configure an effective aerial camera. It became the genesis behind the first RFC aerial camera, the "A" Type camera. All significant issues were addressed, to include protecting the fabric focal-plane shutter from pressure or air suction and the position of the two handling straps.[20] Campbell, a photographic expert prior to the war, knew which technical barriers had to be crossed to develop a functional aerial camera. On 16 January 1915, he outlined the requirements:

Simplicity and strength are of primary importance. The apparatus comprised the lens, camera, shutter, and a method to change plates. The lens at present used on the Aeroplex camera is the Telecentric by Ross of 12-inch

---

[17] Moore-Brabazon, "Photography in the RAF," TNA, PRO: AIR 1/724/91/1.

[18] Moore-Brabazon, *The Brabazon Story*, 94.

[19] Moore-Brabazon, "Photography's Part in the War," TNA, PRO: AIR 1/724/91/2.

[20] Insall, 73.

equivalent focus, and has a back focal length of 6¼ inches. Optically, this lens gives fair definition of full aperture. Assuming 6,000 feet to be the lowest an aeroplane can fly over the enemy lines with comparative safety. This served as the height taken as a standard on which size of image was based. The lens gave a scale of 1 mile to 10.6 inches. Pictures were made to have a scale of one mile to 21.2 inches, or 1/3,000 roughly. The scale for trench work is too big and the small area made identification difficult. The team showed the images of varying size taken from one standpoint, concluding that a focal length of 8 inches would serve as the happy medium.[21]

Campbell also calculated that a photograph taken from approximately 6,600 feet equated to a ready-made 1/10,000 scale map, ideal for restitution.[22] Hesketh immediately followed up, sending a telegram to the Thornton-Pickard staff on the criteria behind the camera design. Mr. Thornton-Pickard, chairman of the firm, met with Hesketh upon arrival and further defined the camera's criteria. When Moore-Brabazon met Thornton-Pickard a few days later, he was handed a completed camera.[23] The "A" Type camera was shaped like a conical box and constructed to withstand major vibration from the aeroplane. It comprised a folding-type configuration that included a bellows. The lens was fixed in distance from the plate, an idea promoted by Campbell whereby the aerial camera focus was set at infinity. This served as the standard for the remainder of the war.[24] The first "A" Type camera was not easy to handle. The first exposure required eleven distinct operations followed by ten distinct operations for each subsequent exposure.[25] Under the leadership of Campbell, the

"A" Type camera was modified to take 18 successive photographs by means of a changing apparatus.[26] The ongoing effort to streamline the photographic process continued throughout the war. What was important for British aerial operations was that the camera provided an important platform for imaging the battle area. As the initial challenges were discovered and solved, the "A" Type prototype had served its fundamental purpose. An aerial camera could support critical operational planning. Once the final modifications were made, the prototype was rushed to France and flown over the German lines on 2 March 1915. The first 4 x 5 inch plate was exposed above the village of Fauquissart by an observer of No. 3 Squadron. Prints were made and personally briefed to the General Staff. The first aerial camera designed to military specifications

FIGURE 230. **Exterior view of the "A" Type camera.** Source: Nesbit, *Eyes of the RAF.*

---

[21] Campbell, "Notes on Aerial Photography," TNA, PRO: AIR 1/7/6/98/20.

[22] Campbell, "Notes on Aerial Photography," TNA, PRO: AIR 1/7/6/98/20.

[23] Insall, 153-154.

[24] Camera lenses set for infinity allow for photography at a distance; Campbell, "Notes on Aerial Photography," TNA, PRO: AIR 1/7/6/98/20.

[25] Jones, II, 89-90; Watkis, 9; Babington-Smith, 10; Mead, 66; Gamble, "Technical Aspects of British Aerial Photography," TNA, PRO: AIR 1/2397/267/7.

[26] Toye, "History of Photography," 27, TNA, PRO: AIR 1/724/91/1.

FIGURE 231. **The second operational British aerial camera, the "C" Type, was similar in appearance to the "A" Type, but possessed a semi-automatic device for changing plates.** Source: Courtesy of Michael Mockford and the Medmenham Collection.

was born. The RFC now possessed the technology and the organization required for operational aerial photographic reconnaissance.[27]

Growing interest in the "A" Type at both the War Office and the RFC showed that the Moore-Brabazon camera "has been found quite satisfactory. The 1st Wing reported that the Camera had quite fulfilled expectations, and that the Squadrons ... are delighted with it."[28] The only early complaint was that slides carrying plates were apt to break rather easily. The "A" Type prototype became a source for modifying aerial cameras to better handle the challenges of flight. The "A" Type was operated by the observer, who gripped the camera through straps or brass handles and leaned over the side of the aeroplane to take photographs. Unfortunately for the observer, the process of taking a

photograph was very complicated, particularly in the harsh environment of open cockpit flying.[29] One observer recalled his experience with the "A" Type camera: "On my first jaunt, taking pictures of a certain trench-line in the vicinity of Thiepval, I nearly lost my balance as I leant over the side with my two gauntleted hands firmly clamped in the weighty affair's straps. My safety-belt was lying idle on the floor of my nacelle, and I was reaching out to avoid a landing wire that was in my field of fire."[30] Later that summer, the British design team developed the "C" Type camera, a semi-automatic plate-changing mechanism to assist the air crew's handling of the camera during flight.[31] Along with the camera design, steps were taken toward institutionalizing the supply depot necessary to accommodate the demand for aerial camera supplies and component parts. A Photographic Supply unit was created within Britain's Military Aeronautics Branch of the War Office. This office was responsible for the dispatch of cameras and photographic stores to France and to the other theaters. It was not a smooth operation. Eventually, the Directorship of Aircraft Equipment (DAE) was formed to purchase cameras and deliver the required goods to the photographic officer making the request. Post-war discussion mentioned the process had problems and bookkeeping was "dreadful."[32]

Stabilizing the Aerial Camera

After the first fixed mounting of the camera in the summer of 1915, for the next six months coverage was marred by camera vibrations. The primary British photographic aeroplane of the time, the BE 2c, suffered from extensive vibration to the outside mounting that resulted in blurred coverage. Tests were accomplished to determine a solution to the vibration caused by the propeller draught. The ideal place for the camera was determined to be internal and behind the pilot. The resulting designs for aerial photographic planes in-

[27] Jones, II, 89-90; Watkis, 9; Gamble, "Technical Aspects of British Aerial Photography," TNA, PRO: AIR 1/2397/267/7.

[28] Capt Cuddell, Asst Dir of Mil Aeronautics, 3 March 1915, War Office, TNA, PRO: AIR 1/2151/209/3/244.

[29] "Photography in the RAF," TNA, PRO: AIR 1/724/91/1.

[30] Insall, 155.

[31] Jones, II, 89-90; Gamble, "Technical Aspects of British Aerial Photography," TNA, PRO: AIR 1/2397/267/7.

[32] Toye, "History of Photography," 17-18, TNA, PRO: AIR 1/724/91/1.

corporated these findings.[33] Research by C.D.M. Campbell led to a successful design for strapping the "A" Type camera firmly to the side of the fuselage with leather straps and a wooden frame. This not only reduced vibration, a constant source of failed aerial photographs; it also increased the verticality of the photograph for restitution.[34] In his post-war notes, AVM Brooke-Popham credited RFC NCO pilot Scholefield as the first to fix the camera rigidly to the aeroplane fuselage and take photos from that configuration.[35]

Camera stabilization represented one of the successes in aerial photography during the conflict. Early attempts at photography through a hole in the cockpit floor used a variety of measures to steady the camera for each exposure. Great care had to be taken in the manipulation of the camera so that it did not interfere with the control wires. Additionally, aerial photography had to contend with the vibration of the aeroplane motor and air flow which caused serious problems when the tiny metal screws of the camera system became loose, causing the camera lens to drop out.[36] The French advocated that the camera be held between the knees whenever possible. They recognized that the body was the best shock and vibration absorber for the aerial camera. Another unique shock-absorbing mechanism was four tennis balls configured within the suspension. However, this did not support the camera effectively when the aircraft landed. In the latter part of the war aerial cameras were mounted on a suspension framework cushioned with foam rubber.[37]

---

[33] Lt Col C. J. Burch, "Notes on Report Dealing with Camera Vibration," 8 February 1916, TNA, PRO: AIR 1/724/91/2.

[34] Toye, "History of Photography," TNA, PRO: AIR 1/724/91/1.

[35] Air Vice Marshal H. R. M. Brooke-Popham, "The War of 1914-18," TNA, PRO: AIR 69/1.

[36] Porter, 161.

[37] Gamble, "Photographic Section of the French Flying Corps"; Labussière, in de Brunoff, 178; "Aerial Photography for Pilots," 21 August 1918, NASM, A30.2/2.

Once aloft, the size of the camera determined if the observer could take photographs outside or within the cockpit. Internal camera operations varied with the camera and the airframe. An American journalist, Ralph Pulitzer, described the operating space of a Caudron G.4 during one sortie in August 1915:

> In the floor of the little cockpit, right in front of my feet, was a little glass window through which I could watch the ground passing directly (though some thousand feet) underneath. Just behind this window, in the floor under my feet, was a little metal trap-door. By straddling my feet I could open this, for the purpose of either taking vertical photographs or of dropping bombs.[38]

British Aerial Cameras

The British inventory of cameras reflected an aggressive application of technological improvements over the course of the war. Moore-Brabazon, Campbell, and Laws continued to be the design team for British aerial cameras.[39] The prototype hand-held "A" Type camera was replaced in the latter half of 1915 by Thornton-Pickard's "C" Type camera. The "A" Type had a tendency to distort the image due to the angle at which the aerial observer held the camera. The "C" Type became the first aerial camera designed to be strapped to the outside of the aeroplane fuselage to produce better quality vertical photographs.[40] The "C" Type, employing the body and plates of the "A" Type camera, could acquire more aerial photographs and use a longer lens.[41] It was fitted with a semi-automatic device for changing plates from one full magazine. Eighteen unexposed plates were placed in the position above the focal plane aperture. For each exposure, a handle at the top of the camera changed the camera plates. During the exposure period the slide projected into a compartment on the opposite side of the camera from the receiv-

FIGURE 233. **The third operational British aerial camera, the "E" Type, sported a sturdy metal frame.** Source: Courtesy of Michael Mockford and the Medmenham Collection.

ing magazine. The cycle continued until the 18 plates were exposed.[42] The "C" Type remained the standard RFC aerial camera until the spring of 1917. Its greatest shortcoming: the wooden construction could expand and contract at different altitudes and temperatures, sometimes causing the lens to be thrown out of focus.[43] Some of the remaining "A" Type cameras were modified with the "C" Type plate changer. This variant was known as the "D" Type camera.[44]

---

[38] Ralph Pulitzer, *Over the Front in an Aeroplane and Scenes inside the French and Flemish Trenches* (New York and London: Harper & Brothers Publishers, 1915), 4.

[39] Nesbit, 35.

[40] Moore-Brabazon, "Photography's Part in the War," TNA, PRO: AIR 1/724/91/2.

[41] Nesbit, 35.

[42] Toye, "History of Photography," TNA, PRO: AIR 1/724/91/1.

[43] Moore-Brabazon, "Photography's Part in the War," TNA, PRO: AIR 1/724/91/2; Toye, "History of Photography," TNA, PRO: AIR 1/724/91/1; Ives, 109-110.

[44] Author discussion with Alf Pyner.

Chapter 21: Operational Aerial Cameras

PRS 2A0

FIGURE 234. The "B" Type was designed in the British Repair Depots. It was primarily used for oblique shots and was unique in using captured German aerial camera lenses. Courtesy of David Humphrey, Photographic Museum at RAF Cosford.

882 2
PRS 2A0

The U.S. Army adopted a "C" Type variant for training. The American-made "C" Type was produced by the Folmer and Schwing Division of Eastman Kodak Company and employed an 8½-inch lens that imaged the standard 4 x 5 inch plates. Like the original British design, each "C" Type camera was equipped with two gravity-loading magazines with a total capacity of 18 plates.[45] Both the "C" Type and follow-on "E" Type served as the primary camera types for training the British and Americans.[46]

The "E" Type camera was developed in the fall of 1916. It was the first British all-metal vertical aerial photography camera.[47] It differed from the "C" Type in being constructed of metal that included a flap over the lens, eliminating the sliding screen. An added capping shutter covered the focal plane shutter during resetting. Remote control was accomplished by cords (called the Bowden Brake Cable) attached to the plate-changing machine. Its most significant improvement, an adjustable lens focus, allowed broad or detailed focus with an 8 to 10½-inch lens.[48] Both "C" Type and "E" Type cameras had one major design flaw. They were never built for plates larger than 4 x 5 inches or for lenses of more than a 12-inch focus.[49]

During the Somme campaign of 1916, the demand for aerial photography prompted the British to come up with a unique camera, incorporating German aerial camera components. This "B" Type camera with a simple aluminum cone design was manufactured at the British Repair Depots.[50] The "B" Type camera was primarily used for oblique photographs.[51] What made it

---

[45] "Report on Day Bombardment Training," Gorrell Report ser. J, r. 35, NARA.

[46] Ives, 43; Crowell and Wilson, II, 420.

[47] "E" Type Camera," RAF Museum, London.

[48] Toye, "History of Photography," TNA, PRO: AIR 1/724/91/1; Ives, 109-110; Moore-Brabazon, "Photography's Part in the War," TNA, PRO: AIR 1/724/91/2; Nesbit, 35.

[49] Ives, 43-45.

[50] "B" Type camera labels covered several variants. One was originally a cinematic movie camera. The variant developed at Repair Depots was sometimes referred to as the "EB" Type camera. Toye, "History of Photography," TNA, PRO: AIR 1/724/91/1; author discussion with Alf Pyner.

[51] Nesbit, 35.

unique was that the critical lens component was acquired from captured German aeroplanes.[52] British intelligence assessed that most German aeroplanes were configured to handle aerial photographic reconnaissance and any lenses acquired from captured or downed aeroplanes were a lucrative find.[53] The German Zeiss or Goerz lenses were "superior to anything made in England."[54] The "B" Type lens length was 20 inches, much longer than any produced at that time by British manufacturers.[55] Not only did the Germans have a variety of lenses (10 in., 14 in., 20 in., 27 in.) and plate size (9 cm x 12 cm; 12 cm x 18 cm), but their cameras were well designed for the reconnaissance mission.[56] Another feature of the "B"

[52] Toye, "History of Photography," TNA, PRO: AIR 1/724/91/1.

[53] Nesbit, 35.

[54] Gen H. R. M. Brooke-Popham, "General Notes of German Aeroplanes," TNA, PRO: AIR 1/7/6/98/20.

[55] Toye, "History of Photography," TNA, PRO: AIR 1/724/91/1.

[56] Brooke-Popham, "General Notes of German Aeroplanes," TNA, PRO: AIR 1/7/6/98/20.

FIGURE 236. **The 47" frame camera was one of the longest lens cameras used by the British in the war.** Source: RAF Museum, London.

Type included a larger 6½ x 8½ inch plate, compared to the standard British 4 x 5 inches.[57] An additional feature was that exposures were taken remotely by means of a Bowden cable.[58] A further testament to the value of German optics was the urgency with which they were sought after by both sides throughout the war.[59]

The demand for more detailed photographs by intelligence personnel led to longer, 20-inch lenses.[60] The British produced a long-lens variant in 1916 known as the 47-inch camera. It was designed to specifications similar to the French 120 cm and configured to the front of pusher aeroplanes like the FE 2b.[61] Moore-Brabazon recalled that the British acquired obliques for planning tank attacks using a camera with a 72-inch focal length. As he described the configuration, the extremely long lens was "a remarkable feat."[62]

The 1916 Somme experience demonstrated to the British that large quantities of photographs were needed to assist both infantry and artillery in achieving their operational objectives. Later that year while at Training Brigade, the innovative photographic genius, Victor Laws, developed the "L" Type aerial camera.[63] Produced in greater numbers than any other line of British aerial cameras, the semi-automatic "L" Type camera improved on the "E" Type camera and became the most successful British aerial camera of the war. The semi-automatic arrangement of the plate changer made it possible for the pilot to operate the camera and freed the air crew to defend their machine against any attacker. The photo plate magazine was made of metal and accommodated twenty-four plates.[64] Like the previous "C" Type and "E" Type, the British continued to produce the standard 8½-inch lens for

the "L" Type camera configured for the 4 x 5 inch plate.[65]

Lieutenant Colonel Moore-Brabazon reflected on the transition to the "L" Type: "Improvement on cameras was again effected by the use of the wind vane, rendering the changing of the plates purely an automatic affair, the Pilot having but to release the shutter."[66] The automatic mechanism changed the plate and set the shutter after each exposure. An air velocity of over 50 miles per hour caused the cycle of camera operations to be accomplished within 10 seconds.[67] When the "L" Type was set to automatic, a locking device was put in place to keep the camera trigger from activating until the camera

FIGURE 237. **The best British aerial camera of the war, the "L" Type.** Source: Gorrell Report, NARA.

[57] Nesbit, 35.

[58] Toye, "History of Photography," TNA, PRO: AIR 1/724/91/1.

[59] Nesbit, 35.

[60] Moore-Brabazon, "Photography in the RAF," TNA, PRO: AIR 1/724/91/1.

[61] Photo of a 47-inch (119.38 cm) lens camera shows a moniker of "B.E.3" on the housing, RAF Museum, London.

[62] Moore-Brabazon, *The Brabazon* Story, 104.

[63] Nesbit, 40.

[64] Moore-Brabazon, "Photography's Part in the War," TNA, PRO: AIR 1/724/91/2; "Report on Day Bombardment Training," Gorrell Report ser. J, r. 35, NARA.

[65] Moore-Brabazon, "Photography in the RAF," TNA, PRO: AIR 1/724/91/1.

[66] Moore-Brabazon, "Photography in the RAF," TNA, PRO: AIR 1/724/91/1.

[67] Toye, "History of Photography," TNA, PRO: AIR 1/724/91/1; Ives, 109-110.

was reset.[68] However, biases existed among the air crew. The semi-automatic feature was usually disregarded in favor of hand operation. The air crew did not trust the propeller (wind vane) designed to operate the camera, regarding it as another part that could fail. "L" Type camera drawbacks included the upper magazine that could not be closed or removed until all the plates had passed through, as well as a gravity feed plate-changing mechanism that tended to jam while the aeroplane was flying. British observers compen-

sated for the jams by turning the propeller backward or sometimes just shaking or "thumping" the camera.[69] Jamming the magazine was also the fault of the operator, not the camera. A photo lab man remembered, "The magazines on the other cameras would jam once in awhile when the observer, in his excitement, would operate the pump change too rapidly and not allow the plate enough time for the springs to elevate it enough to move into the back position."[70] The "L" Type was the first aerial camera produced in the United States under contract. Steichen recalled, "The only aerial cameras received from the U.S.A., which could be utilized in France were a small number of type L of British design, of American manu-

---

[68] Nesbit, 42.

[69] Ives, 117-120.
[70] Dixon, *Diary*, 50.

facture. This camera showed some minor improvement from the L type of British manufacture. The few we had were used with good results at various training centers, but were not used at the front."[71] The American equivalent employed a 24-plate configuration rather than the British 18-plate standard.[72] It was favorably received by aerial units requiring aerial photography support. The U.S. Air Service's Bombardment unit tried out various cameras (26 cm; 50 cm; "L" Type) and came to the conclusion that the British camera, both on account of its focal length and of the facility with which it was installed in the planes, provided the best configuration for bombardment coverage. The rail surrounding the observer cockpit was also too high to permit holding the "L" Type over the edge. The bombardment unit used six of the "L" Type cameras as an experiment.[73]

The British "LB" Type was a modification of the "L" Type, designed by both Laws and Moore-Brabazon to supply the simplest, quickest, and most certain means of obtaining instantaneous photographs from an aeroplane in motion. The "LB" Type was similar in principle to the "L" Type camera, but the mechanism was simplified. The chief difference was an easily removed self-capping focal plane shutter, which could be replaced without disturbing the other parts of the mechanism.[74] The greatest advantages over the "L" Type were the possibility of using lenses of any focal length from 4 to 20 inches and having a detachable shutter.[75] After the war the "LB" Type was designated the P7 camera.[76]

The final British camera to see service in the war was the "B.M." Type camera. It was becoming apparent in 1917 that, with the increasing altitude required for safe coverage from enemy pursuit aircraft and improving air defenses, British designs incorporating a 10-inch lens and enlarged

print from a 4 x 5 inch frame were insufficient to accomplish the mission. The "B.M." Type camera was developed to overcome this difficulty by employing a larger plate and a 20-inch lens. In the final year of the war, because the inter-Allied

FIGURE 240. The "LB" Type semi-automatic camera had interchangeable lenses. The camera as shown features a 20" lens. Source: Courtesy of Nesbit, *Eyes of the RAF.*

FIGURE 241. The "BM" Type was the largest aerial camera employed by the British in the war. This camera is contained within the fuselage of a Bristol Fighter. Source: Courtesy of Nesbit, *Eyes of the RAF.*

---

[71] The American version of the "L" Type camera is sometimes referred to as the "LA" Type camera. Steichen, "Aerial Photography," Gorrell Report, ser. G, r. 24, NARA.

[72] Ives, 87, 102; Crowell and Wilson, II, 421.

[73] W. O. Farnsworth, "Photographic Officer Zone of Advance," 20 December 1918, Gorrell Report, ser. A, r. 2, NARA.

[74] Toye, "History of Photography," TNA, PRO: AIR 1/724/91/1; Nesbit, 42.

[75] Moore-Brabazon, "Photography's Part in the War," TNA, PRO: AIR 1/724/91/2.

[76] Nesbit, 51.

commission recommended a common photographic format that provided British aerial photographic interpreters with a more convenient medium, the size of the plate was changed after the manufacture of the first two models to the standardized Allied 18 x 24 cm format.[77] The "B.M." Type was the largest and final camera type introduced by the British in the war. It was metal, including the magazines, and each magazine held twelve plates of 18 x 24 cm. The "B.M." Type camera was enormous, weighing in at 82 pounds (competing with the 90-pound French De Ram). It served a variety of reconnaissance requirements with the ability to interchange four lens cones (7 in., 10 in., 14 in., 20 in.). The "B.M." Type mechanism operated under the same mechanical principles that powered the "LB" Type. A wooden propeller was carried in a propeller bracket fixed on the side of the aeroplane. Power was conveyed to the camera from the propeller through a flexible shaft in a casing attached by bayonet couplings. The shutter release was triggered by a Bowden cable.[78]

Early handheld cameras like the Pan-Ross were replaced by more sophisticated equipment. The "A" Type hand-held camera served British reconnaissance for most of the war. This durable system acquired necessary coverage from a sortie.[79] Later in the war, the British would develop the P14 hand-held camera to replace the "A" Type. The metal P14 was fitted with a 10-inch lens. It provided the aerial observer with a more rugged and less complicated photo camera

FIGURE 243. **The "P" Type camera was the most popular of the British hand-held cameras. Here a RNAS officer demonstrates holding the camera.** Source: Ives, *Airplane Photography.*

---

[77] Steichen, "Memorandum for Major Decker," NASM.
[78] Toye, "History of Photography," TNA, PRO: AIR 1/724/91/1.

---

[79] Author discussions with Nicholas Watkis and Michael Mockford.

did not exist. The British prototype "A" Type cameras were employed for the remainder of the war wherever a requirement existed for aerial photography. British aerial cameras supported Allied forces on the battlegrounds beyond the Western Front, to include Gallipoli, Italy, Macedonia, Palestine, and Mesopotamia. Each deployment of aerial photographic cameras came with a companion entourage of photographic interpreters and laboratories. The only difference in the entire operation was the interpreters' knowledge of the terrain and culture of the region.[84]

for the remainder of the war.[80] Another RNAS aerial camera was produced by the Houghton-Butcher company and called the P18.[81] Hand-held cameras were essential for RNAS seaplane operations locating submarines or photographing German targets on the coast. The seaplane could not accommodate an outside attachment for vertical shots. Subsequent RNAS photography was primarily accomplished with hand-held cameras shooting at an oblique angle. RNAS hand-held cameras constituted a variety of modifications and lens lengths (6 to 15 inches).[82] The Americans brought with them an array of "private cameras" to acquire short-focus aerial photographs. This lessened their dependency on the Allies, particularly in covering the normal field of view that lenses such as the 26 cm offered.[83]

Since aerial cameras were a critical resource in the conduct of every campaign, the idea of an expiration date for an older aerial camera system

FIGURE 245. **American soldier examining a 26 cm de Foyer, the first French production line aerial camera.** Source: Gorrell Report, NARA.

[80] Nesbit, 51.

[81] Author discussion with Alf Pyner.

[82] Toye, "History of Photography," TNA, PRO: AIR 1/724/91/1.

[83] Steichen comment at conference at the Office of the Under Secretary of State of the Presidency of the Council, 25 April 1918, Gorrell Report, ser. G, r. 24, NARA; "Cession of Optical Instruments to the American and British Government," 4, Gorrell Report, ser. G, r. 24, NARA.

[84] Author discussions with Nicholas Watkis and Michael Mockford.

French Aerial Camera Inventory

French cameras were configured for the mission. The 26 cm (F-1) hand-held camera was the oldest camera variant used by the French, ideal for acquiring broad area photographic coverage. The 26 cm was produced by the De Maria Lapierre firm with components such as the shutter provided by other industries such as Kopcic. The magazine held twelve 13 x 18 cm photographic plates.[85] The 26 cm proved ideal for aerial mapping and provided the French with their first aerial surveys of the battleground. Subsequent roles for the 26 cm included artillery observation and fire control. By the end of war, the 26 cm provided the means to test the quality of Allied camouflage. The broad area of coverage also served infantry contact (infantry aeroplane) missions that located the advance line of troops during combat operations.[86] De Maria Lapierre's 26 cm required the operator to point the lens upward after the exposure. The plate was changed by pulling the inner body of the magazine out and then back into the camera framework. The operator

FIGURE 246. **Aiming the 26 cm de Foyer for a shoot, here demonstrated by the aerial observer.** Source: Gorrell Report, NARA.

FIGURE 247. **Three photographs showing the various configurations of the 50 cm within a fuselage. The unique tennis ball suspension at the top of the camera was complemented by the spring suspension at the bottom.** Source: Gorrell Report, NARA.

then set the shutter. The final step was to point the camera at the target and expose the next plate by a gentle pull on the exposing lever.[87] When the

---

[85] Gill and Hibben, "Preparation of Photographic Missions," Gorrell Report, ser. J, r. 34, NARA; Carlier, 23.
[86] "Lecture on Aerial Photography," 25 April 1923, NASM A30.2/36.
[87] Ives, 43; 89.

Chapter 21: Operational Aerial Cameras

FIGURE 248. **The 50 cm fit snugly in back of the SPAD VII cockpit.** Source: SHAA, 87.2856

FIGURE 249. **The 26 cm Grand Champ provided larger contact frame aerial photographs than its 26 cm de Foyer predecessor. A Breguet 14 A2 aerial observer demonstrates the aiming technique.** Source: SHAA.

U.S. Air Service's Bombardment unit tested the 26 cm camera, its members expressed frustration over the fact that it took up too much room in the observer's cockpit when trying to invert it to change the plates.[88] When the French modified their cameras to the larger 18 x 24 cm camera plates, the process was simplified, requiring each exposed plate simply to be pulled out after each shot.[89]

Once broad area coverage was acquired by the 26 cm, a subsequent aerial photographic reconnaissance sortie employed the 50 cm (nomenclature F-2; also designated 52 cm) to acquire more detailed coverage of the terrain. The F-2 went operational in 1916.[90] Operating the 50 cm required pulling the drawer out of the magazine after each exposure. The French design had the magazine on the top of the camera, a handling challenge to observers when it was attached to the gun turret rail.[91] Like the 26 cm, the 50 cm employed the standard 13 x 18 cm plate. Gaumont produced the twelve-plate magazine. Later the French reconfigured the 50 cm to a larger photo plate of 18 x 24 cm. The working area of the plate was reduced to 17 x 23 cm to compensate for the 0.5 cm edge.[92]

In 1917, the French upgraded their 26 cm (F-1) with another 26 cm hand-held camera known as the *Grand Champ* (nomenclature F-3; also known as 25 cm). It covered a broad area for mapping reconnaissance, employing a larger photographic plate of 18 x 24 cm. This larger plate

---

[88] W. O. Farnsworth, "Photographic Officer Zone of Advance," 20 December 1918, Gorrell Report, ser. A, r. 2, NARA.

[89] Ives, 99.

[90] Labussière, in de Brunoff, 184; Ives, 43; Carlier, 22-25; Gill and Hibben, "Preparation of Photographic Missions," Gorrell Report, ser. J, r. 34, NARA.

[91] Hart, 36-37.

[92] Gill and Hibben, "Preparation of Photographic Missions," Gorrell Report, ser. J, r. 34, NARA; Carlier, 22-25

FIGURE 250. **Photograph shows 120cm camera size in comparison to a member of the AEF photo section.** Source: Ives, *Airplane Photography.*

size remained the standard for French reconnaissance for several years after the Armistice.[93]

Finally, the 120 cm (F-4), also designated the 1.20 meter, photographed particular points or a limited sector in order to secure a definite piece of information. The 120 cm camera was long, sometimes protruding as much as two feet below the standard Maurice Farman or Caudron fuselage. If the 120 cm was not streamlined in configuration, the aeroplanes could lose up to 20 horsepower. The use of this camera was limited to good weather due to the small lens opening.[94] The public media labeled the 120 cm the "vest pocket" camera.[95] The 120 cm was built by the Gaumont firm. The photograph magazine carried twelve larger-format 18 x 24 cm plates.[96]

The majority of cameras used by the Americans in 1918 were of French design, and they appreciated the simplicity of the process. One AEF staff member remarked that "the camera is a simple metal box fitted with a 20 inch lens and focal plane shutter; the plates are carried in magazines with a capacity of 12 plates."[97] By the end of 1917, the French were producing 25 aerial cameras a month for the American forces en route to the theater. Practically all aerial photographs taken by the Americans were 18 x 24 cm format.[98] Simplicity governed the American attitude toward aerial cameras.

FIGURE 251. **A classic pairing of a 120 cm camera with an MF11 aircraft.** Source: 877/092 SHAA.

---

[93] "Lecture on Aerial Photography," 25 April 1923, NASM A30.2/36.

[94] "Lecture on Aerial Photography," 25 April 1923, NASM A30.2/36; "Nomenclature Chart," Gorrell Report, ser. F, r. 22, NARA.

[95] "The Camera at the Front: Why the Military Authorities Have Use for Their Own Cameras but None for the Enemy's," *Scientific American* (24 November 1917): 380, 390.

[96] Gamble, "Photographic Section of the French Flying Corps"; Carlier, 25.

[97] 20 in. equals 50.8 cm. Steichen, "Memorandum for Major Decker," NASM.

[98] Steichen, "Memorandum for Major Decker," NASM.

Advocates of greater technological advance for photography appeared among all the Allies. One French observer commented:

Aerial cameras may be automatics, semi-automatics, etc. Automatic cameras are proper for one-seaters, for the Pilot cannot let go of his controls to take the photographs, but they are not needed on airplanes with two seats. The best thing on two-seaters is a good plate camera such as the French and English use. Automatic cameras have complicated, fragile mechanisms, which get out of order easily, and in France, where the temperature is often very low in the air, we run the risk of having the oil in the mechanism freeze and the machine refuse to work at all; besides the operator cannot tell during the flight whether or not his camera is working, and this causes a great deal of trouble. For this reason we should positively not use an automatic camera on an airplane with two seats. Such course would have bad points and no good points at all.[99]

The "De Ram" Semi-Automatic Camera

In support of automatic cameras, Steichen spoke for many when he declared, "During a mission over the lines the operation of this camera took up all the attention of the observer. From the beginning of our experience, it was clear that an automatic camera was not only desirable, but would eventually become a necessity." Allied efforts to build an automatic camera resulted in several unsatisfactory prototypes. In the last month of the war the Americans fielded and operated 15 semi-automatic cameras over the lines.[100]

The development and deployment of an automatic camera was a dominant concern as the Americans established their presence. They found something close to what they were looking for in the French-built De Ram camera,

FIGURE 252. **The largest semi-automatic Allied camera of the war was the De Ram.** Source: André-H. Carlier, *La Photographie Aérienne pendent la Guerre* (Paris: Libraire Delegrave, 1921).

named for the inventor, Lieutenant G. de Ram of the French Aviation Militaire. The semi-automatic camera allowed the pilot and observer to concentrate on defending themselves while the camera took sequential photographs. A prototype of this camera was designed by the end of the war.[101] The De Ram came to the attention of AEF senior staff members in July 1917. It was a large, heavy camera mounted in the fuselage of an airplane and operated by either the pilot or the observer. The camera weighed approximately 90 pounds when loaded with the maximum stock of 50 plates,[102] an enormous quantity for the time. The large format plate (18 x 24 cm) assisted the photographic interpreter. Operating the De Ram appeared to be a simple process. An

---

[99] Lieut Michel quoted in Porter, 172.
[100] Steichen, "American Aerial Photography at the Front," 3, NASM, A30.2/24.

[101] Ives, 129.
[102] Capt Proctor, "Training Section, Photographic Branch Memorandum for Major Sullivan, Subject: 'Situation De Ram Camera'," Gorrell Report, ser. G, r. 24, NARA.

exposure was created after the operator pressed the release, resulting in the plate changing and the shutter being set automatically for the next exposure.[103] Preparing the camera before and after flying the mission required extra maintenance, since the entire camera assembly, instead of only the lens cone, was removed from the aircraft.[104] De Ram first met with failure when his prototype was rejected by the French government. His disappointment was short-lived. The Americans were impressed.

In November 1917, Colonel E. S. Gorrell of the AEF staff contacted the senior U.S. pho-

FIGURE 253. **Assembling a semi-automatic De Ram aerial camera in the factory.** Source: Gorrell Collection, NARA.

tographic experts in theater, Major Barnes and Capt Steichen, to review the De Ram. Gorrell was sold on the prototype he saw and wanted the experts to confirm his impressions. Barnes and Steichen subsequently visited the De Ram workshop and provided positive reports on its configuration and operation. The De Ram contained a changing box with a capacity of fifty 18 x 24 cm plates. The plate movement was controlled by a propeller or helix connected with the machine by a tube. The advantages of the De Ram were

---

[103] "Final Report of Chief of Air Service," Maurer, ed., *U.S. Air Service*, I, 402; Crowell and Wilson, II, 422; Ives, 116, Carlier, 30-31.
[104] Ives, 123.

that its movement could be exactly controlled by a pilot or observer. Barnes reported that the De Ram's principal defect was weight and post-mission processing. The camera had to be removed from the fuselage and taken to the dark room to be opened.[105] Besides the rotary magazine of 50 plates (changing box), the De Ram was configured with interchangeable objective cones for the French focus standard of 26 cm, 50 cm, and 120 cm.[106]

Leading photographic experts had the highest hopes for the De Ram. Steichen commented, "if the De Ram Camera works out satisfactorily as a building proposition, it will very likely be adopted by the allied armies as the Standard Camera."[107] Steichen's praise was exuberant:

These cameras were ingenious instruments invented by Lieutenant De Ram and were built under his supervision in a small shop near Paris. The camera works entirely automatically; it can be set for any given interval of exposure and simply requires to be started when the airplane reaches the region to be photographed. It has a capacity for 50 exposures. In spite of the fact that this machine was new in principle and that these first cameras could scarcely have been considered final or complete, results were produced that were not only valuable in themselves, but pointed the way to new and hitherto impossible accomplishments in aerial photography."[108]

Unfortunately for the prevailing single-engine reconnaissance aéroplanes, De Ram's fit only in the Salmson A2.[109]

The American acquisition process involved several layers of government. A model of the De Ram was sent to the United States for evaluation, where it gained acceptance. Manufacturing rights to produce the De Ram were acquired. American requirements stipulated that it be semi-automatic so that the observer or pilot only had to release the shutter at will and a fresh plate would "always" be in place.[110] Delivery time was scheduled for November 1918. At the time of the Armistice, 200 De Ram Cameras were approaching completion.[111] The discussions revolving around the value of the De Ram lasted throughout the last year of the war. In a June 1918 memo from an inter-Allied conference, the British delegation leader, Moore-Brabazon, expressed concern over the American infatuation with the De Ram. "The Americans seemed to be gambling on a supply of De Ram Cameras as their big type Camera, but they want to be helped out later by a supply of B.M.'s [British semi-automatic aerial camera] if we could see our way to supply our own needs and have an excess."[112] As the war neared the Armistice, Moore-Brabazon reversed his opinion, expressing the hope that the Americans could produce enough cameras to fulfill British requirements as well.[113]

In the end, only a few French-produced De Ram cameras ever saw combat.[114] The De Ram camera received its baptism of fire in the Argonne offensive. During one reconnaissance mission, seven German fighters attacked two Salmson A2's flown by Americans. One of the aéroplanes was equipped with a De Ram automatic and the other with a hand-operated camera. The Americans shot down two of the fighters and drove off the remainder without interference to their own photographic work. The De Ram camera had successfully and automatically accomplished the

---

[105] Maj James Barnes, "Memo to Lieut-Colonel Dunwoody, Subject: 'De Ram Camera'," 29 November 1917, Gorrell Report, ser. G, r. 24, NARA; Toulmin, 320.

[106] "Lecture on Aerial Photography," 25 April 1923, NASM A30.2/36; Carlier, 31-32.

[107] Steichen, "Memorandum for Major Decker," NASM.

[108] Steichen, "American Aerial Photography at the Front," 3, NASM, A30.2/24.

[109] Steichen, "American Aerial Photography at the Front," 3, NASM, A30.2/24.

[110] "Final Report of Chief of Air Service," Maurer, ed., *U.S. Air Service*, I, 402; Crowell and Wilson, II, 422.

[111] Steichen, "Aerial Photography," Gorrell Report, ser. G, r. 24, NARA; Crowell and Wilson, II, 422.

[112] Lt Col J. T. C. Moore-Brabazon, "Report on ... Visit to the Conference Held in Paris," 16 June 1918, NASM.

[113] Steichen, "Aerial Photography," Gorrell Report, ser. G, r. 24, NARA; Crowell, II, 422.

[114] Steichen, "Aerial Photography," Gorrell Report, ser. G, r. 24, NARA; "Final Report of Chief of Air Service," Maurer, ed., *U.S. Air Service*, I, 402; Crowell and Wilson, II, 422.

photography required.[115] The De Ram gave the air crews a taste of the aerial photographic future. Now the observer could increase his survivability by focusing on the enemy threat and operating the Lewis gun.[116]

There are conflicting accounts of the De Ram's performance. A postwar account of aerial support to the First American Army stated that "A French automatic (De Ram) camera gave better results than those hand operated, furnishing

FIGURE 254. **An exceptional photograph showing an aero squadron's entire camera inventory. From left to right: the De Ram, four 50 cm, 26 cm Grand Champ, and the 26 cm de Foyer.** Source: USAFA McDermott Library Special Collections (SMS57).

over 70 per cent of the later photographs taken on the Fifth Corps front."[117]

---

[115] Steichen, "American Aerial Photography at the Front," 3, NASM, A30.2/24; "Final Report of Chief of Air Service," Maurer, ed., *U.S. Air Service*, I, 154.

[116] Niven, 458.

[117] Eaton, "Methods in Observation Practiced with Fifth Corps First American Army," *Air Service Information Circular*, 2, No. 115 (20 September 1920): 16, Davis Papers, McDermott Library, USAFA, SMS 57.

Not all memories of the De Ram were that positive. The 1st Army Observation Group was not impressed, declaring the camera unreliable. The cameras were mounted and tested in September 1918. The De Ram's worked fairly well at first. However, when assigned to operational missions, the cameras continually jammed or the plates were either unexposed or unevenly exposed.[118] This feeling was echoed at squadron level. One photographic laboratory workman with the 88th Aero Squadron remembered: "We also had a French-made De Ram camera assigned to us. It held fifty 8 x 10 inch glass plates. When one was exposed it was placed in the back, and the next plate came into position for the next exposure. It had a tendency to jam easily, so we did not use it much."[119]

Allied cameras in World War I reflected profound ingenuity in the design of rugged and reliable systems necessary to accomplish a difficult mission. Despite the challenges, aerial camera design was simplified to operate within the constraints of plate configuration. The French designs of 26 cm, 50 cm, and 120 cm showed the greatest consistency, partly because they were retained for almost the entire war. The British penchant for improving the technology resulted in the well-thought-of "L" Type camera that produced most of the photographs in the final year of the conflict. Attention to semi-automatic and automatic aerial cameras made clear that aerial reconnaissance needed to balance mission accomplishment with the ability to defend. Interestingly, film did not catch on despite the successful employment of the Douhet-Zollinger in early 1915. Had the war continued, film would have made its debut thanks to the persistence of George Eastman and his influence on the Americans. That was to be the case in the postwar era, as aerial photography transitioned to automated film systems.

---

[118] "Final Report of Chief of Air Service," Maurer, ed., *U.S. Air Service*, I, 278-279.
[119] Dixon, *Diary*, 50.

CHAPTER 22
AERIAL RECONNAISSANCE PLATFORMS AND THEIR CONFIGURATION

Aeroplane design during the war transitioned from a frail airframe to a configuration that redefined the role of aerial reconnaissance. As aerial observation missions expanded to serve increasing demand for information and aerial photographs, aircraft design similarly improved. Each successive year demonstrated the need to improve on the ability to engage and defeat the enemy. It emphasized more effective fighting machines with greater firepower and airframes designed to take the stresses of rapid maneuver. The early years showed that non-maneuvering aerial observation platforms were easy prey. However, aerial maneuver did not support successful photography. An interim solution became aerial supremacy through formations. However, such formations drew the attention of enemy pursuit aircraft and anti-aircraft batteries. The solution lay in advancing aircraft design to meet the demands of combat and the reconnaissance mission. The next evolution was to ascend to higher altitudes to escape both the anti-aircraft firing envelope and the limits of enemy pursuit fighters. To stay up with changes in the wartime environment, reconnaissance aircraft had to evolve to survive.

Aeronautical technology received feedback during all facets of the war. Human limitations in visual acuity required aerial observation to operate more slowly and in low-flying aerial platforms. Operating above an altitude of 1,000 meters stretched the ability of the air crew to see activity. It also challenged the early designs, for climbing to that observation level took over 15 minutes. The optimum pusher aeroplane with its unlimited range of observation ("veritable balcony") had to give way to a more rugged and survivable tractor aeroplane. Aeroplanes and aerial photography evolved simultaneously, and the needs tended to merge. Instead of a separate primitive aircraft and an inadequate camera, the needs of the war forced rapid development of aircraft specifically designed to facilitate photography, using cameras specifically designed to work on aircraft.

Critical to aeroplane design for the Great War was the attention paid to the existing camera configuration required for successful aerial photography. The lack of long lenses in the British and American optics inventory resulted in camera frames of limited dimensions. British and American aeroplane designers therefore developed a corrupted and limited view of what constituted the necessary dimensions for an aerial camera. Americans employing French aéroplanes and adopting French aerial reconnaissance practices enjoyed the benefits of longer focal length cameras such as the 50 cm and 120 cm embedded internally. For most of the war the British had to rely on smaller cameras attached to the outside of airframes.[1]

Aerial reconnaissance planes serving in World War I covered the spectrum of capability from some of the best aircraft of the era to some of the worst. The ten most notable aerial observation aeroplanes to serve the Allies on the Western Front are described in the following sections.

---

[1] Ives, 46.

Blériot XI

The Blériot XI aeroplane is best remembered for the first flight across the English Channel in 1909. It served a successful role as an acceptable airframe for many European nations' introduction to military aviation, to include France and Great Britain. Blériot XI's fulfilled an important purpose; they helped define the basics of flight and the role of aerial reconnaissance, to include aerial observation, artillery spotting, and a platform for taking photographs with hand-held cameras. Blériot XI aerial observation roles were conducted at low altitudes and slow airspeed. The primary threat was the carbine, either from infantry on the ground or rudimentary attempts by German adversaries in the equally slow-flying Tauben. Blériot XI observation was complicated due to the wide wingspan directly under the forward cockpit where the observer sat. After 1914, the Blériot XI served the Allies as a basic trainer.

The Blériot XI Characteristics[2]	
Crew:	1 or 2 dependent on variant
Average Maximum Airspeed:	*100 km/h*; 62.1 mph (single-seat); *120 km/h*; 74.5 mph (two-seat)
Climb to *1,000 meters:*	12 minutes
Ceiling:	*1,520 meters*; 5,000 feet
Endurance:	3 hours (single-seat); 3½ hours (two-seat)
Aerial Camera:	Hand-held

FIGURE 255. **The Bleriot XI Parasol has a modification to improve the aircrew's view without the wing obstruction.** Source: SHAA B87.3513.

[2] Davilla and Soltan, 54-61; Bruce, *Aeroplanes of the Royal Flying Corps (Military Wing),* 128-132; Lamberton, 70-71, 216-217; Kenneth Munson, *Bombers: Patrol and Reconnaissance Aircraft, 1914-1919* (New York: Macmillan Publishing Co., Inc., 1968), 97.

Blériot Experimental (BE) 2a – 2f

The most recognizable British aerial observation aircraft for the first three years of the war was the ubiquitous BE 2. It arrived with the first BEF expedition to France in August 1914 and remained in later reconnaissance variants until 1917. Stability and safety were the driving requirements behind the BE 2's initial pre-war design, and stability would be retained for the rest of its tenure. It suffered from a broad range of critical vulnerabilities, to include low-powered engines and an inherent inability to outmaneuver any threat.[3] As an aerial reconnaissance platform, the BE 2 performed as well as could be expected. The observer sat in the front seat surrounded by a "cage" of struts, wires, and engine that severely limited what little defensive firepower the aircraft had.[4] The BE 2 was the pioneer platform for development of the British "A" Type camera and carried the majority of subsequent types for the remainder of its tenure. Despite an incredible service record of providing aerial observation for British forces, the memories of the BE 2 aircraft by the pilots that flew it were not flattering. It was an understatement when a 1914 British report on the plane stated that the BE 2b's "are not liked by all pilots."[5] In retrospect, as one aerial observer who flew BE 2s surmised: "The BE 2c aeroplanes were designed for drudgery, and carried weapons for self-defense—like old ladies never without their parasols."[6]

FIGURE 256. **A common sight for most of the war, the BE 2c acquired most of the RFC's aerial photography until replaced by the more survivable DH 4, Bristol Fighter, and RE 8.** Source: Courtesy of Michael Mockford and the Medmenham Collection.

FIGURE 257. **An early model of a BE 2c from the RFC No. 6 Squadron.** Source: Courtesy of Aaron Weaver.

---

[3] Watkis, 13, Munson, 134, Nesbit, 30.
[4] Munson, 14-15; Lamberton, 48.
[5] Douglas, "Notes on Equipment of Units of RFC with BEF," TNA, PRO: AIR 1/836/204/5/268.
[6] Insall, 80.

The BE 2a to 2f Characteristics[7]	
Crew:	2
Average Maximum Airspeed:	BE 2c: *115*; 72 mph; BE 2d: *141.6 km/h*; 88 mph; BE 2e: *144.8 km/h*; 90 mph
Climb to *1,060 meters*; 3,500 feet (BE 2c):	6 minutes, 30 seconds
Climb to *1,520 meters*; 5,000 feet (BE 2d):	24 minutes
Climb to *1,830 meters*; 6,000 feet (BE 2e):	20 minutes, 30 seconds
Climb to *1,980 meters*; 6,500 feet (BE 2c):	20 minutes
Climb to *3,050 meters*; 10,000 feet:	BE 2c: 45 minutes, 15 seconds; BE 2d: 82 minutes, 50 seconds; BE 2e: 53 minutes
Ceiling:	BE 2c: *3810 meters*; 12,500 ft; BE 2d: *3660 meters*; 12,000 ft; BE 2e: *2740 meters*; 9,000 ft
Endurance:	BE 2c: 3¼ hours; BE 2d: 5½ hours; BE: 4 hours
Aerial Camera:	Hand-held; "A" Type, "B" Type, "C" Type, "E" Type, "L" Type

FIGURE 258. **Later production model of the BE 2c. Note the observer cockpit under the wing with the Lewis gun over the pilot's cockpit.** Source: Courtesy of Aaron Weaver.

[7] Bruce, *Aeroplanes of the Royal Flying Corps (Military Wing)*, 344-370; Lamberton, 46-51, 214-215; Munson, 129-132.

Maurice Farman (MF) 11

Another pre-war design aeroplane with extensive service for the first half of the war was the MF 11. The MF 11 was a pusher biplane with a raised nacelle serving as a fuselage. The wide-open front design was superb for aerial reconnaissance. However, the observer sat in the back and manned the machine gun in early models. Later, the seating was reversed to provide better observation.[8] When the MF 11 was assigned to photograph with the 120 cm camera, a steel tube frame was installed to hold the camera in place at the front of the nacelle.[9] The MF 11 could climb very quickly and land at a short distance, making it a favorable tactical aerial observation platform in the first years of the war. However, airframe construction contained several design flaws when even the slightest shock could damage the landing gear and the nacelle.[10] The MF 11 was known by the British pilots as the "Shorthorn" in relation to the companion MF 7 "Longhorn" that had pronounced outriggers protruding from the front of the plane to support its forward elevators.[11]

The MF 11 Characteristics[12]	
Crew:	2
Average Maximum Airspeed:	*118 km/h*; 73 mph (MF 11); *116 km/h*; 72 mph (Shorthorn)
Climb to *2,000 meters*; 6,560 feet:	22 minutes
Climb to *910 meters*; 3,000 feet:	15 minutes
Climb to *1,980 meters*; 6,500 feet;	21 minutes
Ceiling:	*3,810 meters*; 12,500 feet
Endurance:	3 hours (MF 11); 3¾ hours (Shorthorn)
Aerial Camera:	(FR) (MF 11) Hand-held, 26 cm, 50 cm, 120 cm; (UK) (Shorthorn) Hand-held, "A" Type, "B" Type, "C" Type.

FIGURE 259. **Remarkably clear photograph of the MF 11 from the rear quadrant showing the operating position of the 120 cm camera in proximity to the aircrew.** Source: SHAA 77/096.

[8] Nesbit, 12.

[9] Collection S.H.D., 377/094, SHAA.

[10] Martel, 77-78.

[11] Bruce, *Aeroplanes of the Royal Flying Corps (Military Wing)*, 242.

[12] Davilla and Soltan, 222-232; Bruce, *Aeroplanes of the Royal Flying Corps (Military Wing)*, 241-246; Lamberton, 86-87, 218-219.

Caudron G.4

If there were a design that could be equated with aerial reconnaissance for the first half of the war, it would be the Caudron G.4. It was one of the best second generation allied reconnaissance aeroplanes, entering into operational service in August 1915. The Caudron G.4's predecessor, the Caudron G.3, had helped define roles for aerial reconnaissance.[13] The follow-on Caudron G.4 possessed greater potential, designed with a second engine that increased the range and loiter time (5 hours), and it gave the aerial observer an unobstructed forward view. One pilot recalled, "The G.4 was more satisfactory, even though it was slower. It was more reliable. You could maneuver it at will and loop it and it would never go into a spin. It was about as safe as an aircraft can be, as far as flying performance is concerned."[14] In 1916, Caudron G.4 aéroplanes gave significant support to the French armées at Verdun, accomplishing aerial reconnaissance and avion de réglage missions. Additional Caudron G.4 escadrilles were assigned to support French AL.[15] The British also produced Caudron G.4's under license, primarily supporting RNAS coastal patrol.[16]

The G4 Characteristics[17]	
Crew:	2
Average Maximum Airspeed:	*130 km/h*; 81 mph (sea level); *125 km/h;* 78 mph (2,000 m; 6560 feet)
Climb to *1,980 meters*; 6,500 feet:	17 minutes
Climb to *2,990 meters*; 9,800 feet:	33 minutes
Ceiling:	*4,300 meters*; 14,100 feet
Endurance:	5 hours
Aerial Camera:	(FR) Hand-held, 26 cm, 50 cm, 120 cm, 26 cm (Grand Champ); (UK) RNAS: Hand-held

---

[13] Jon Guttman, *Caudron G.3* (Berkhamsted, UK: Albatros Productions, Ltd., 2002), 5.

[14] Peter Kilduff, "Kenneth P. Littauer: From the Lafayette Flying Corps to the 88th Aero Squadron," *Journal of the Society of World War I Aero Historians* 13, No. 1 (Spring 1972): 25.

[15] Guttman, 9-10.

[16] Munson, 147.

[17] Davilla and Soltan, 222-232; Bruce, *Aeroplanes of the Royal Flying Corps (Military Wing)*, 241-246; Lamberton, 86-87, 218-219.

FIGURE 260. **The Caudron line of aerial reconnaissance aeroplanes was the mainstay of French aerial photography in the first half of the war.** Source: SHAA, B88.1218.

FIGURE 261. **The combination of the stable G4 aeroplane with a long lens 120 cm camera provided some of the most detailed aerial photographs in the war.** Source: SHAA, photo in Christienne and Lissarague, *A History of French Military Aviation.*

Farman Experimental (FE) 2b

The British Royal Aircraft Factory FE 2b was initially used as a reconnaissance aircraft, evolving to other missions, to include night bombardment. The observer had an excellent view, sitting far forward in the nacelle directly in front of the pilot. The FE 2b was one of the first aeroplanes to carry an aerial camera inside the nacelle.[18] The FE 2b did engage in aerial combat, being equal to a Fokker Eindecker in aerial maneuver and credited for ending the "Fokker Scourge" over the Somme battlefield.[19] Such capabilities gave the FE 2b reconnaissance aircraft the reputation that it could fly extended sorties over the front, with an objective "to bring back its information as quickly as possible without incurring casualties."[20]

The FE 2 Characteristics[21]	
Crew:	2
Average Maximum Airspeed:	*147.2 km/h*; 91.5 mph (sea level); *130 km/h*; 81 mph (*1,980 meters*; 6,500 ft)
Climb to *910 meters*; 3,000 feet:	7 minutes 24 seconds
Climb to *3,050 meters*; 10,000 feet:	39 minutes 44 seconds
Ceiling:	*3,350 meters*; 11,000 feet
Endurance:	3 hours
Aerial Camera:	"A" Type; "C" Type; "E" Type: "L" Type; 53

FIGURE 262. **The FE 2b was the first British aeroplane to carry a camera internal to the fuselage. However, cameras such as the "C" Type provided coverage while strapped to the outside.** Source: Courtesy of Nesbit, *Eyes of the RAF.*

---

[18] Bruce, *Aeroplanes of the Royal Flying Corps (Military Wing)*, 406-407.
[19] "Notes on Air Fighting from Royal Flying Corps," TNA, PRO: AIR 1/1625/204/89/7.
[20] "Notes on Air Fighting from Royal Flying Corps," TNA, PRO: AIR 1/1625/204/89/7.
[21] Bruce, *Aeroplanes of the Royal Flying Corps (Military Wing)*, 403-418; Lamberton, 63, 214-215.

Chapter 22: Aerial Reconnaissance Platforms and Their Configuration

FIGURE 263 (ABOVE). **Aerial operations over the front by an FE 2b.** Source: Illustrations, S.S. 550a.

FIGURE 264 (BELOW). **One of the last pusher aerial reconnaissance aeroplanes, the FE 2b also served as a fighter and aerial bombardment aeroplane.** Source: Gorrell Report, NARA.

Sopwith 1½ Strutter

The Sopwith 1½ Strutter served British (RFC and RNAS), French, and U.S. squadrons from 1916 to 1918. It acquired its name from the arrangement of the upper wing center section W-strut supports. It was first delivered to the RFC in early 1916.[22] It had the distinction of being the first true tractor pull configuration two-seat fighter with an efficient synchronized forward-firing armament (Vickers gun) to see service in the war.[23] The Sopwith 1½ Strutter's long range made it the inevitable choice for distant reconnaissance flights, participating in the significant campaigns of the Somme, Arras, Messines, and Ypres.[24] The 1½ Strutter's modest £842 per airframe price tag appealed to the Allies— this aircraft was significantly better and less expensive than the BE 2 series.[25] The RNAS was the first to receive the Sopwith 1½ Strutter and initially assigned it to offensive patrols and fighter escort for French bombardment aeroplanes. The RNAS eventually employed the aeroplane to accomplish aerial reconnaissance of the coastal region. The French were very impressed with the Sopwith 1½ Strutter for its reconnaissance and bombardment capabilities. They subsequently acquired the license from the British and built 4,200 Sopwith 1½ Strutter airframes, calling their version the Sopwith 1 A2.[26] When the Americans operated at the Front between May and July 1918, several units (88th, 90th, 99th Aero Squadrons) flew the Sopwith 1½ Strutter in reconnaissance sorties over quiet sectors.[27]

The Sopwith 1½ Strutter Characteristics[28]	
Crew:	2
Average Maximum Airspeed:	*167 km/h*; 104 mph (sea level); *160 km/h*; 100 mph (*1,980 meters*; 6,500 ft)
Climb to *1,980 meters*; 6,500 feet:	12 minutes, 40 seconds
Climb to *3,050 meters*; 10,000 feet:	17 minutes 50 seconds
Ceiling:	*3,350 meters*; 11,000 feet (15,500 feet)
Endurance:	4 hours
Aerial Camera:	(UK) "A," "C" Type, "E" Type, "P" Type; (FR) 26 cm, 50 cm, 120 cm; (U.S.) 26 cm, 50 cm, 120 cm, "L" Type

---

[22] Peter Cooksley, *Sopwith Fighters in Action* (Carrollton, TX: Squadron/Signal Publications, Inc., 1991), 14.

[23] J. M. Bruce, *War Planes of the First World War, Fighters, Great Britain* (2 vols., Garden City, NY: Doubleday and Company, Inc., 1968), II, 115-117; Munson, 135.

[24] Bruce, *War Planes of the First World War, Fighters*, II, 115-117.

[25] "Price-List of Various British Airframes and Engines," in Jones, Appendices, 155-156.

[26] Davilla and Soltan, 466.

[27] Bruce, *War Planes of the First World War, Fighters*, II, 121.

[28] J. M. Bruce, *The Sopwith 1½ Strutter* (London: Profile Publications, 1967); Bruce, *Aeroplanes of the Royal Flying Corps (Military Wing)*, 499-509; Davilla and Soltan, 465-473; Christienne and Lissarague, 107; Munson, 58; Lamberton, 58-59, 216-217.

FIGURE 265. The British-designed Sopwith 1½ Strutter accomplished a wide variety of functions to include aerial reconnaissance, aerial bombardment, and RNAS submarine-spotting missions. Source: Courtesy of Nesbit, *Eyes of the RAF*.

FIGURE 267. The French produced the Sopwith 1 A2 (the French nomenclature for the Sopwith 1½ Strutter) under license. Aerial photography was a primary mission for this aeroplane. Source: SHAA.

FIGURE 266. The French 50 cm easily fit within the Sopwith 1½ Strutter. Source: Gorrell Report, NARA.

Reconnaissance Experimental (RE) 8

The RE 8, the most widely used British 2-seater on the Western Front, accomplished the majority of British artillery spotting, contact patrol, and aerial photography for the last eighteen months of the war. One former BE 2e pilot commented on the RE 8, "This machine has an adjustable tail plane for varying the speed and climbing powers. It can be moved in the air by means of a wheel and is a most fatal gadget if used at the wrong time… I cannot say that I like the machine. It is much too heavy and cumbersome, more like flying a steam roller than an aeroplane. Still, they do 105 m.p.h., which is quite an advantage over the old B.E. 2e."[29] Known as the "Harry Tate" from the name of a swivel-mustachioed music hall comedian (and its closeness to sounding like RE 8), this aeroplane was a stalwart member of the RFC/RAF.[30] The cameras were configured internally forward of the observer's cockpit. Designed to replace the BE 2, 4,099 RE 8 aeroplanes were produced during the war. Its worst moment was at Arras in April 1917, when on one day six RE 8's of No. 59 Squadron were shot down by von Richthofen's Jasta 11 of the elite Jadstaffel. Despite such setbacks, the RE 8 performed admirably in artillery spotting and aerial photography supporting British offensives at Messines, Ypres, and Cambrai. A single RE 8 (A4397) accomplished an impressive 147 sorties over the Western Front, logging 440 hours and 35 minutes of flying time.[31] By the end of the war, fifteen RE 8 squadrons operated on the Western Front.[32]

The RE 8 Characteristics[33]	
Crew:	2
Average Maximum Airspeed:	*157 km/h*; 98 mph (*1,980 meters*; 6,500 ft); *148.8 km/h*; 92.5 mph (*3,050 meters*; 10,000 ft)
Climb to *1,980 meters*; 6,500 feet:	21 minutes
Climb to *3,050 meters*; 10,000 feet:	39 minutes 50 seconds
Ceiling:	*3,350 meters*; 11,000 feet
Endurance:	4 hours 15 minutes
Aerial Camera:	"A" Type, "E" Type, "L" Type, "LB" Type, "P" Type

---

[29] Smart, "The Front Cockpit: The Diary of Lt. C.D. Smart, No. 5 Squadron, RFC," 17.

[30] Lamberton, 56.

[31] Lamberton, 56.

[32] Munson, 134.

[33] Bruce, *Aeroplanes of the Royal Flying Corps (Military Wing)*, 458-464; Munson, 57; Lamberton, 56-58, 214-215.

FIGURE 268. **Early line drawing of an RE 8. Note the compact British aerial camera under the pilot's cockpit.** Source: J.M. Bruce Collection.

FIGURE 269. **The RE 8 withstood punishment from enemy pursuit aircraft and anti-aircraft weapons.** Source: via Colin Owers.

FIGURE 270 (Right). **This RE 8 survived a strike by an artillery shell during a sortie over the front.** Source: via Colin Owers.

Breguet 14 A2

The Breguet 14 A2 was one of the finest aéroplanes to see service in the war and post-war era. It was a remarkably rugged airframe, built of duralumin oxy-welded joints (claimed to be the first aircraft built of that type) that could take damage and allow the aircraft to carry enough firepower to inflict its own damage.[34] The legacy of the Breguet 14 was primarily the aerial bombardment function that the Breguet 14 B2 bombardment version assumed and carried on with distinction. The companion Breguet 14 A2 assumed many reconnaissance roles, both tactical and strategic. Eventually, it replaced most of the French AL escadrilles supporting heavy artillery targeting. The Breguet 14 A2's ability to combine a rugged and defendable airframe with an impressive operating ceiling (7,600 meters) made it one of the most formidable aerial reconnaissance platforms of the war.

The Breguet 14 A2 Characteristics	
Crew:	2
Average Maximum Airspeed:	*157 km/h*; 98 mph (*1,980 meters*; 6,500 ft); *150 km/h*; 93 mph (*3,050 meters*; 10,000 ft)
Climb to *1,980 meters*; 6,500 feet:	21 minutes
Climb to *3,050 meters*; 10,000 feet:	39 minutes 50 seconds
Ceiling:	*3,350 meters*; 11,000 feet
Endurance:	4 hours 15 minutes
Aerial Camera:	"A" Type, "E" Type, "L" Type, "LB" Type, "P" Type

---

[34] Bruce and Noel, 6.
[35] Davilla and Soltan, 101-125; Munson, 65, 144; Lamberton, 72, 216-217.

FIGURE 272. **An interior view of the Breguet 14 A2 airframe illustrates the very limited operating space for the aerial observer.** Source: Gorrell Report, NARA.

FIGURE 271 (OPPOSITE PAGE). **A side view of the Breguet 14 A2 without windows on the fuselage. The bombardment Breguet 14 B2 did have windows.** Source: Gorrell Report, NARA.

FIGURE 273. **An early Breguet 14 A2 fuselage frame with a 50 mm camera in place. Note the duralumin tubing that imparted extra strength to the airframe.** Source: Gorrell Report, NARA.

Airco De Havilland (DH) 4

The Airco DH 4 was one of the most versatile aeroplanes designed and built during the war. It was a powerful airplane for the time, both in power plant and armament. Aerial photographic reconnaissance was accomplished through internally-mounted cameras. The DH 4's airframe interior was large enough to handle the standard line of both British and French plate cameras.[36] This was the first time that a British-designed aeroplane could accommodate the state-of-the-art cameras internal to the fuselage, a critical improvement of British aerial reconnaissance design.[37] The pilot was underneath the top wing and separated from the observer by an 85-gallon gas tank. Communication between the two crew members required the use of sign language.[38] Despite the air crew communication challenge, this multi-purpose aeroplane provided both British and American forces with a sturdy aerial platform capable of flying long-range sorties deep into German territory at high altitude.[39] DH 4 capabilities prompted the RNAS to plan a long-range (14-hour sortie) reconnaissance against Northern Germany, but the sortie was never accomplished.[40] American units flew the DH 4 powered by the American-built Liberty 12 engine (a subject of great pride for American aviation forces), with the following characteristics:

FIGURE 274 (ABOVE). **A DH 4 aerial observer receives the 26 cm camera from the photographic officer.** Source: Gorrell Report, NARA.

FIGURE 275 (ABOVE RIGHT). **The cramped conditions of the observer's compartment complicated taking oblique photographs from within the fuselage.** Source: Gorrell Report, NARA.

FIGURE 276 (RIGHT). **The British-designed DH 4 was capable of operating the heaviest Allied aerial camera, the semi-automatic De Ram.** Source: Gorrell Report, NARA.

---

[36] Steichen, "American Aerial Photography at the Front," 3, NASM, A30.2/24.

[37] Ives, 46.

[38] Smart, 21.

[39] Colin Owers, *De Havilland Aircraft of World War I*, Vol. I, *D.H.1 –D.H.4* (Boulder, CO: Flying Machine Press, 2001); J. M. Bruce, *The de Havilland D.H.4* (London: Profile Publications, 1965); J. M. Bruce, *The American D.H.4* (London: Profile Publications, 1966); Bruce, *Aeroplanes of the Royal Flying Corps (Military Wing)*, 276-280; Lamberton, 36; Munson, 138.

[40] Owers, 17.

The Airco De Havilland (DH) 4 Characteristics[41]	
Crew:	2
Average Maximum Airspeed:	(Eagle VIII power plant) *202 km/h*; 126 mph (*4,570 meters*; 15,000 ft); (Liberty 12 power plant) *193 km/h*; 120 mph (*4,570 meters*; 15,000 ft)
Climb to *1,830 meters*; 6,000 feet (Eagle VIII power plant):	4 minutes 50 seconds
Climb to *3,050 meters*; 10,000 feet (Eagle VIII power plant):	9 minutes
Climb to *4,270 meters*; 14,000 feet (Eagle VIII power plant):	14 minutes 45 seconds
Climb to *5,490 meters*; 18,000 feet (Eagle VIII power plant):	23 minutes 30 seconds
Climb to *1,980 meters*; 6,500 feet (Liberty 12 power plant):	8 minutes 30 seconds
Climb to *3,050 meters*; 10,000 feet (Liberty 12 power plant):	14 minutes 48 seconds
Climb to *4,570 meters*; 15,000 feet (Liberty 12 power plant):	33 minutes 42 seconds
Ceiling:	(Eagle VIII power plant) *6,700 meters*; 22,000 feet; (Liberty 12 power plant) *6,100 meters*; 20,000 feet
Endurance:	3¾ hours
Camera:	(GB) "L" Type, "LB" Type, "BM" Type, "P" Type; (U.S.) "L" Type, "LB" Type, 26 cm Grand Champ, 50 cm, 120 cm

FIGURE 277. **The versatile DH 4 carried a variety of British and French aerial cameras. The major shortfall in the design — the distance between air crew members — made communication difficult.** Source: Gorrell Report, NARA.

---

[41] Bruce, *Aeroplanes of the Royal Flying Corps (Military Wing)*, 49-61; Smart, 29; Lamberton, 214-215; Munson, 137-139.

Salmson 2A2

The Salmson 2A2 served extensively on the Western Front with the Aviation Militaire and the U.S. Air Service. The camera was mounted through a trap door in the floor of the rear cockpit. The Salmson 2A2 was the only single-engine aerial reconnaissance aéroplane to carry the semi-automatic De Ram camera. The De Ram's 90 pounds and bulk were too much for other single-engine platforms. The observer acquired additional oblique coverage by mounting a smaller camera (i.e., 26 cm Grand Champ) on the gun turret rail in place of twin-Lewis guns.[42] The Salmson 2A2 was a dynamic aéroplane with good performance and handling characteristics that favored the air crews. When it became operational in late 1917, the Salmson 2A2 provided the Aviation Militaire with a reconnaissance aéroplane that could compete with German advances in aeroplane design. Its only design flaw was similar to the British counterpart, the DH 4. The distance between the pilot and observer caused communication challenges, especially during intense combat.[43] One U.S. aviator, Lt. W.P. Erwin of the 1st Aero Squadron, destroyed eight enemy aircraft using only the front gun of the Salmson 2A2.[44]

The number of airframes committed to aerial observation throughout the war far exceeded any other purpose. As they evolved, not only did they fly at higher altitudes to compensate for the increasing threat of antiaircraft guns and pursuit fighters; they were more effective, faster photographic platforms. With the evolution of the more sophisticated automatic cameras, aeronautical design had to compensate for the increased weight and provide maneuverability against potential threats. Such was the case with the Salmson 2A2, one of the finest aéroplanes to see combat in the war.

The Salmson 2A2 Characteristics[45]	
Crew:	2
Average Maximum Airspeed:	*188 km/h*; 116.8 mph (sea level); *181 km/h*; 112 mph (*3,000 meters*; 9,840 feet)
Climb to *2,000 meters*; 6,560 feet:	7 minutes, 17 seconds
Climb to *4,000 meters*; 13,120 feet:	17 minutes, 20 seconds
Climb to *5,000 meters*; 16,400 feet:	27 minutes, 30 seconds
Ceiling:	*6,250 meters*; 20,500 feet
Endurance:	3 hours
Camera:	(FR) 26 cm (Grand Champ), 50 cm, 120 cm; (U.S.) 26 cm (Grand Champ), 50 cm, 120 cm, De Ram

[42] Colin A. Owers, John S. Guttman, and James J. Davilla, *Salmson Aircraft of World War I* (Boulder, CO: Flying Machine Press, 2001), 15; Munson 142-143.

[43] Owers and others, 1.

[44] Munson, 143.

[45] Davilla and Soltan, 439-446; Munson, 63; Lamberton, 218-219.

FIGURE 278. **This Salmson 2 A2 was assigned to the AEF's 1st Aero Squadron.** Source: McDermott Library, USAFA, SMS 57.

FIGURE 279. **The Salmson 2 A2 was a superb aerial reconnaissance aeroplane, flown by both French escadrilles and American aero squadrons.** Source: Gorrell Report, NARA.

FIGURE 280. **An aerial view of the Salmson 2 A2 with camouflaged surface.** Source: via Colin Owers.

PART FOUR:
The Enduring Professional Legacy

CHAPTER 23
TRAINING THE FIRST GENERATION OF AERIAL PHOTOGRAPHIC INTERPRETERS

Initiation

"Cadet Goddard, you're a photographer." "Well, not really sir. I am an artist." "But you take pictures. You own a camera." "I suppose so, sir." "We're establishing an officers training school for aerial photographers. We need the right kind of people in it." "It is a vitally new important field in fighting a war. The training course is three months, and you'll be a commissioned officer before most of your fellow cadets finish their pilot training." "Well that's fine, sir, but I joined the air service to be an aviator." "And I promise you, you will … some day. But right now we need aerial photographers more than we need pilots."[1]

This rocky introduction to aerial photographic interpretation created a lasting memory for Brigadier General George W. Goddard, a leading American figure in the first half century of photographic reconnaissance. The rush to acquire expertise to meet the demands of the war effort meant shaping a cadre in the photographic interpretation ranks from those possessing an immediate and recognizable background in photography. The call went out early on all sides for people who knew what a camera was,

what was required to process the film base, and what the picture represented. Very quickly, what was a hobby became a cornerstone of intelligence gathering, and the foundation was laid for imagery analysis. From hand-held cameras and "happy snaps" came a new profession within intelligence, and many of the techniques and methods in use a century later were developed in the Great War by this first generation of aerial photographers and analysts.

A French post-war aeronautics assessment succinctly stated, "We may say it was as the fighting went on that this science was evolved and developed."[2] The evolution of aeronautics bred the foundation for 20th century reconnaissance—both a science and an art form. The new aerial photographic mission challenged the armed forces, particularly in the acquisition and development of human resources to support the mission. The criteria behind personnel selection, training, and organization of flying forces developed into an educational system on a scale much larger and more diverse than anyone anticipated. No nation had, up to the outbreak of the war, ever trained an aviator sufficiently to meet the demands of aerial warfare. The knowledge gap extended to every component of the aerial platform including radio communication, photography, aircraft maintenance, and the other specialized

---

[1] Goddard, 7-8.

[2] "Aeronautics," June 1921, 1, NARA, RG 120, Box 819.

skills.[3] Each nation went through similar trial and error. All participants from the recruits to commanders had to come to terms with the aerial platform in their own way. What worked over time was extensive interaction between the traditional arms of artillery and infantry and the new force of aviators and photographic interpreters.[4] The military institution needed a training regimen that ensured aerial photographic interpretation was equal to the challenges at hand and that established a level of credibility with the combatants. The first years of the conflict put a burden on everyone developing the proper training regimen. By the time the Americans entered the conflict, the value of aerial photography was clear and the training plans were well established.[5]

The Empirical Baseline—Lessons Learned from the French and British

Photographic interpretation came into its own after a year and a half of war. The leading photographic interpreters of France and Great Britain were called in to author the manuals that served as the baseline for photographic interpretation in the 20th century, validating the idea that aerial photograph was a vital commodity. In late 1915, Capitaine Grout, the SPAé (Photo Section) pioneer, was reassigned to establish the complete course curriculum for training and certi-

fying qualified personnel for SPAé.[6] On March 1916 he established the Photographic school at Chalais-Meudon and subsequently moved it to Plessis-Belleville. The school focused on learning the process of restitution and supporting Plan Directeur development. Besides interpretation, the students learned the art of developing mosaics from vertical and panoramic photographs and of analyzing stereo photographs.[7]

The British preceded the French by half a year with their School of Photography, Mapping, and Reconnaissance (also called the RFC School of Photography) at Farnborough in September 1915. The British photographic pioneer, Sergeant-Major Laws, took the initiative to stand up the operation.[8] While working with Moore-Brabazon and Campbell, Laws had avoided a commission for financial reasons. As a Sergeant-Major, Laws made more money than an incoming lieutenant, and he could avoid the bills that came with officers' mess membership. In November 1915, Laws accepted a commission in the RFC and became commandant of the newly created RFC School of Photography at Farnborough.[9] Four months after standing up the school, Farnborough produced five officers and 42 NCOs trained in aerial photography. Their training was equal, if not superior, to the overseas wings, which had access to recent aerial photography. A parallel effort with wing photographic officers to train pilots and observers in aerial photography was not as successful. A contemporary report revealed it "still leaves much to be desired."[10] By the autumn of 1916, training was not keeping up with the demand for photographic expertise. Aerial photographic training within the RFC had been entrusted to

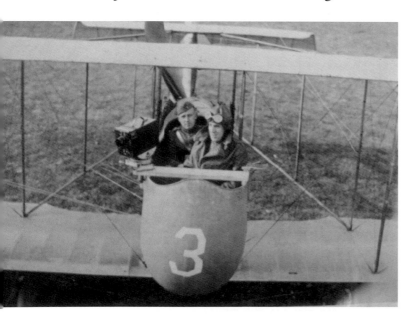

FIGURE 281. **Basics in aerial reconnaissance were taught to aviators such as this American air crew on a British MF 11. A handheld camera is mounted forward.** Source: James Davilla, MA23874.

---

[3] Frank, *American Air Service Observation*, 145.

[4] "Tactical History of Corps Observation," Maurer, ed., *U.S. Air Service*, I, 182-183.

[5] Goddard, 8.

[6] Maurice Marie Eugène Grout personnel records, SHAA.

[7] Hodeir, 116; Labussière in de Brunoff, 184; Carlier, 19.

[8] Watkis, 11; Toye, "History of Photography," TNA, PRO: AIR 1/724/91/1.

[9] Nesbit, 35.

[10] Campbell, "Progress of Photography," TNA, PRO: AIR 1/724/91/2.

Moore-Brabazon, but the responsibility required an administrative ability to organize training objectives. At the same time, photographic supply problems also were building, resulting in increased friction between the BEF and the War Office. The problems were solved by assignment of additional personnel to the photo staff.[11] The RFC also increased awareness of aerial photography by establishing an Officer Training Brigade to train personnel at the Wings.[12]

The RFC School of Photography was initially housed in "two large disused plane packing-cases." Attendance at the school soon numbered in the hundreds and developed into an up-to-date scientific institution, equipped with every modern device and latest appliance. In the model darkrooms every candidate for acceptance as an RFC photographer first had to pass a test to determine his suitability for the work. He received a month's practical intensive training, with attention paid to the process of development and enlargement of negatives by artificial light. Much importance was attached to timely production of the enlargements, "for the fate of a battle often depended upon the promptness with which large-scale copies of a vital subject could be supplied the Intelligence Staff."[13]

At the RFC School of Photography, the student received training in the principles of color photography, lantern-slide making, the production of stereoscopic mosaic photographs, the rapid drying and finishing of prints, map reading and plotting, and other relevant subjects. Upon completion of the course work, the airman photographer was reassigned to a Service Squadron overseas and served a Photo Section working in support of an RFC Reconnaissance Flight.[14]

The British complemented their aerial photography training with an Intelligence School at Harrow, providing a comprehensive understanding of the German military order of battle. Another school was located at the Horse Guards in London.[15] For the novice in the intelligence arena, the school provided a good foundation on the organization of the German military. By 1918, Americans started attending and found the course on intelligence good, but too focused on learning the organization of the British army. One recalled that subject was "minutely taught for two weeks."[16] One student wrote Lt Col Conger, AEF Assistant G-2, "The course is good and planned entirely to fit the students for 'fighting intelligence.' Excellent lectures on all subjects and the aerial photography, which we have just started, promises much."[17]

Key to learning were the manuals, describing both the concept of positional warfare and fundamentals of aerial photography. The *Reference Manual of British Trench Warfare 1917-1918* commented on battlefield preparation including reconnaissance:

> Success in an attack on a line of trenches depends on the training of the troops and on the thoroughness of the preparations made. Units in occupation of a system of trenches must always consider their line and the enemy's defenses from the point of view of attack. Constant observation and patrolling will be required to add to the information available. The ground between the opposing front lines must be accurately reconnoitered so that no unsuspected obstacles, such as sunken wire or ditches, may hold up an assault. Every effort must be made to locate machine gun emplacements or strong points in the enemy's line, so as to be able to assist the artillery in the bombardment of the hostile defenses. The whole of the enemy's system of defenses over which the assault is to go must be made familiar to all ranks. A great deal of information is available from the excellent trench maps compiled from aeroplane

[11] Toye, "History of Photography," TNA, PRO: AIR 1/724/91/1.

[12] Toye, "History of Photography," TNA, PRO: AIR 1/724/91/1.

[13] Middleton, III, 119-120.

[14] Middleton, III, 119-120.

[15] Royall Tyler, G-2, HQ AEF, "Letter to Col Nolan," 7 March 1918, Conger Papers, Box 2, USAMHI.

[16] 1st Lt John Stewart, "Report," 4 October 1918, Conger Papers, Box 2, USAMHI.

[17] "Correspondence," 23 March 1918, Conger Papers, Box 2, USAMHI.

photographs and a study of the photographs themselves.[18]

The manual also mentioned one of the best techniques for learning about aerial photography: "The use of a magic lantern to throw aeroplane photographs on a screen has been found of great value."[19]

Training or familiarization on aerial photography was also conducted at the front, even for senior members of the British Army. One recollection from Lieutenant Thomas McKenny Hughes, a British Army intelligence officer with aerial photographic experience, put British training into perspective. He was assigned as an instructor of "Interpretation of aeroplane photographs." A memorable class included the visit of a senior officer:

> After a bit of business getting the light to work, I got under way with my celebrated lantern exhibition and was getting along quite nicely when the door behind the screen opened and the Corps Commander and the BGGS [Brigadier-General, General Staff] shuffled in, tripped over the electric light wire, put the light out and fused the arc light. The Corps Commander then fell over a chair and I felt it was time to pull up a blind, which I did. He then told me to carry on as if he wasn't there, which was difficult as we should have a light working if he hadn't been there. However, it eventually got going again and I continued.[20]

Hughes was an experienced aerial observer. He accomplished several aerial photographic missions in his time at the front. Finally, in February 1918, Hughes went on a "shoot" and was shot down and killed while taking oblique photographs in the vicinity of Bailleul.[21]

FIGURE 282. **Lieutenant McKenny Hughes studying aerial photographs prior to a mission.** Source: IWM, courtesy of Nicholas Watkis.

Introducing Aerial Photographic Reconnaissance—The American Way

The American experience provided a concise overview of how aerial photography entered into the military mainstream of the early 20th century. The Americans employed the best aerial photographic methods of the British and French, and proceeded to implement a program to employ photographic talent.[22] Instruction covered three separate categories of students: observers to operate the cameras in the air, intelligence officers on the ground to interpret them, and technicians to aid in developing, printing, and enlarging photographs and keeping the equipment in serviceable condition.[23]

The war engendered a sense of urgency throughout the U.S. military to produce a credible fighting force and achieve victory. The greatest demand for specialization rested with the Air Service. At the start of the war there was no real experience in handling airplanes that were already combat ready. American instructors did not exist. The existing schools in the United States were technically unprepared to meet the demands.

---

[18] *British Trench Warfare*, 64.
[19] *British Trench Warfare*, 64.
[20] Brown, 136.
[21] Brown, 153.

[22] Barnes, *From Then Till Now*, 488.
[23] Frank, *American Air Service Observation*, 160.

America looked to the Allies to assist them. The initial vanguard to develop the Air Service training program included then-Major William Mitchell and Captain Joseph Carberry. Carberry commenced an orientation with French Flying Schools to gain an appreciation of what had to be established to serve the immediate needs of the Allies. The orientation quickly revealed that the United States had to establish training programs in France to acquire true operational experience and become a more credible fighting force. Carberry was designated in July 1917 as Officer in Charge of Instruction under the general supervision of Colonel Mitchell, Aviation Officer of the AEF. In September, the Instruction Department was established with Carberry as Chief and Major Davenport Johnson as Assistant Chief. The initial staff included Private 1st Class Douglas Campbell, soon to be commissioned and destined to be the first American aviator "ace."[24]

In December 1917, Brigadier General Foulois assumed direction of the U.S. Air Service. Three schools were established to work aviation requirements. In a reorganization on 30 April 1918, the Training Section established an Intelligence Division to complement the existing training under way for pursuit, bombardment, and observation. 1st Lt. L.A. Smith was appointed the first chief, and his duties included:

> A collection of all information from activities in the Zone of Advance and of all technical information such as would be of interest in the training of Aviation Personnel. The preparation and edition of the Weekly Training Bulletin, a bulletin of information of value to the Training Schools and training students, and a proper distribution of such bulletins. A general supervision of Intelligence Organizations at the Aviation Training Schools, to ensure proper dissemination of all Air Service information published and distributed to the schools.[25]

Along with the photographic discipline, there was a requirement to master the intelligence discipline. Visits with the Allies provided a definitive sounding board for the American novices. Training an efficient cadre took time. At the Canadian Corps Headquarters, Canadian intelligence officers recommended that Americans acquire older men for intelligence work. The Canadians stated from experience that it took a man accustomed to responsibility and with a broad general knowledge of military affairs. The American intelligence function was primarily manned with young and inexperienced officers. Inexperience in warfare had been a serious handicap for the infantry, only slowly being hardened to the realities of the ongoing struggle. The Americans in general were already at a disadvantage coming into the struggle at the fourth year of the conflict. Whatever lessons could be learned had to be acquired quickly. The combatants most likely paid little attention to the newly acquired, youthful intelligence staff.[26]

Aerial Observation

It was obvious to the AEF command at Chaumont that the French regarded air observation as essential, especially on a battlefield dominated by artillery. The AEF got its aerial observer manpower from the ranks of the ground forces of the AEF, with the focus on artillery officers well grounded in the requirements of artillery targeting. The observer, or the "second man" in the plane, did not have to be a qualified pilot. In the summer of 1917 the AEF sought volunteers, but subsequently resorted to detailing artillery and infantry officers to aerial observation. Leaning on the French experience resulted in the AEF's adopting French concepts. Pershing had French manuals for liaison between air and artillery translated into English and distributed to AEF Air Service trainers and observers. He also encouraged the War Department to accept and teach French tactical and operational concepts.[27]

Efforts to train an effective observation force met with challenges from the start. Aerial

---

[24] "History of the Training Section, Air Service, A.E.F.," Gorrell Report, ser. J, r. 34, NARA.
[25] "History of the Training Section," Gorrell Report, ser. J, r. 34, NARA.

[26] Hubbard, "Memorandum for Col Nolan," 29 December 1917, Conger Papers, Box 2, USAMHI.
[27] Cooke, 22-23.

were available.[29] By the time the Americans arrived in theater, the Allies had transformed aerial observation and photographic interpretation into an art and science. Both French and British were magnanimous in providing whatever material was required.[30] However, training objectives were incomplete. It was assumed that both the aerial squadrons and the photographic laboratories would experience parallel training objectives and proceed to the Western Front at the same time. However, this was not the case, for training in photographic science took longer to master.[31]

For many American aerial observers, the Air Service Observation School at Post Field, Fort Sill, Oklahoma, was their first entry into the aerial observation arena. The course of training generally under the heading of "Theory" covered 19 hours of Artillery Contact, 6.5 hours of Visual Reconnaissance, 23.5 hours of Photography, and 25 hours of Infantry and Cavalry Contact. Under the heading of "Practice," training covered approximately 6 hours of Artillery Adjustment,

FIGURE 283. **Aerial observers in training learning how to orient a map to the terrain.** Source: *National Geographic,* January 1918.

FIGURE 284. **U.S. aerial observers receiving in-depth training using French aerial cameras such as the 26 cm.** Source: Gorrell Report, NARA.

observers trained in the United States arrived in France "with most indefinite ideas regarding the principles involved in the performance of actual aerial missions over the lines. In some instances they had been taught obsolete methods."[28] Cooperation among the Allies was essential for gauging the success of the effort. French instructors gave photographic training to the pilots and observers at the AEF training centers. A great shortage of instructors was constantly felt, because no American officers of experience

---

[28] "History of the Training Section," Gorrell Report, ser. J, r. 34, NARA.

[29] Harry A. Toulmin, Jr., *Air Service, American Expeditionary Force, 1918* (New York: D. Van Nostrand Company, 1927), 320.

[30] "Final Report of Chief of Air Service," Maurer, ed., *U.S. Air Service,* I, 154.

[31] Barnes, *From Then Till Now,* 483.

5 hours of Visual Reconnaissance, and 1 hour of Aerial Photography.[32] Subsequent training in France was more realistic. One French instructor, Lieutenant Ledy, devoted much time to aerial photography, to include basics in interpretation. Lieutenant Gilchrist recalled: "We learned that newly dug dirt photographs different from other dirt, that tracks reveal all sorts of things, such as gun positions although the guns themselves are hidden, that shadows tell the time of day."[33] The fully trained observer had to send and receive eight words a minute by telegraph code, make 12 good aerial photographs on 18 assigned locations, locate and direct artillery fire against enemy batteries, and conduct a pre-arranged shoot without error.[34] The most enduring lessons came with combat experience.

Despite recognition of the importance of observation among the aviation community, the quality of the observer force was always an issue with the field army units, the intelligence staffs, and among the air crews themselves. This was especially true for the AEF Air Service in the final days. The rush to meet manning requirements resulted in lower training standards. Lt. John Snyder, an aerial observer who served in the 91st Aero Squadron, wrote an editorial that the squadrons were being filled up to full strength with pilots and observers who had just completed "a very meager training consisting of: Observations as seen from a class-room, and rushed through to be sent to the front."[35] His comments were amazingly frank, going beyond the standard lecture and describing in detail the concern that his colleagues were not on top of their "game." His nine months of combat experience as an observer gave him more time than most American air crews engaged in the final year of combat. [36]

FIGURE 285. A leader in U.S. aerial reconnaissance was Lieutenant John Snyder. Veteran of the 91st Aero Squadron, he would become an authority on aerial observation. His lessons are the most definitive explanation of air crew roles during the war. Source: Gorrell Report, NARA.

As the war entered the final weeks, shifts in training were implemented to meet the demand. By November 1918, more attention to night reconnaissance was called on as the campaign became more mobile. Aerial observation was forced to develop methods to track night troop movements. Navigation was emphasized more in the curriculum. However, after the Armistice, the AEF discontinued training and transferred the functions to rear echelon staffs. Organized training on photography in the closing weeks did not materialize. The value of aerial photography in a mobile battlefield was becoming questionable.[37]

[32] 1st Lt Theodore J. Lindoff, "Photographic Mission," Lindoff Papers, USAMHI.

[33] Gilchrist, 48.

[34] Frank, *American Air Service Observation*, 154; Arthur Sweetser, *The American Air Service: A Record of Its Problems, Its Difficulties, Its Failures, and Its Final Achievements* (New York: D. Appleton and Co., 1919), 116-117.

[35] Snyder, "Notes on Army Observation," Gorrell Report, ser. J, r. 34, NARA.

[36] Snyder, "Notes on Army Observation," Gorrell Report, ser. J, r. 34, NARA.

[37] "History of the Training Section," Gorrell Report, ser. J, r. 34.

Establishing an American Photographic Training Program

The effort required to establish a credible aerial photographic interpretation capability was Herculean in scope. Upon the entry of the United States in the conflict, the Signal Corps still held authority over the role of aircraft. All units were burdened with organization standup, supply, material, personnel, training (both aerial and interpretation), and production. Aerial observation was a "small side issue."[38] Training of pilots and observers in photography at Air Service installations was usually entrusted to the French. However, establishing Photographic Sections put the burden on indigenous resources within the United States.[39] Fortunately for the Americans, they possessed a wealth of photographic talent throughout the nation, particularly from industry.

The first requirement was to assemble an initial cadre for aerial observation, aerial pho-

tographic interpretation, and the photographic laboratory. Once the staffs of the Signal Corps recognized this, the call went out across the nation for those with photographic experience. All Army posts and recruiting centers were requested to have their commanders provide the Signal Corps' Photographic Division with a list of such enlisted men claiming to have photographic training of any sort. The recruitment phase was even supported through ads and articles in local papers.[40] Manning shortfalls remained a constant challenge for the headquarters staff. Even as troops arrived in theater, there was a constant review of any available talent to meet the envisioned demand. Enlisted personnel already in the AEF were screened to acquire a cadre of experienced labor. Talent was soon identified from among the volunteers and assigned to build the program.[41] Orchestrating the training from headquarters was equally challenging. Establishing a Photographic Division to monitor ongoing developments required inputs from sources never previously considered. Ingenuity became the order of the day. The first priority was establishing laboratories at the schools where it was assumed the photographic training would take place. Though the preexisting training centers in theater at Issoudun, Tours, and Amanty continued, many of the new instruction centers were not functioning until the end of February 1918, just in time for handling the arriving masses serving the AEF.[42] The British and French had regular schools to instruct their officers. The British school was at St. Omer, location of the British Headquarters. Americans attended these courses until their own service set up a course designed to support AEF missions.[43] For the members of U.S. Photographic Section No. 5, their memories of the time reflected an unbelievable opportunity to join the photo ranks:

> "The Air Service needs men with photographic experience" appearing in our daily papers caught the eye of not only thousands of professional photographers but of many others of all walks of life, professions and occupations, who

FIGURE 286. The first U.S. school was established at Langley Field in Virginia. Schools at Cornell and Rochester would shortly take over the operation. Trainees learned to operate a mobile photographic laboratory complete with camouflage coverage. Source: USAMHI.

---

[38] Barnes, *From Then Till Now*, 475-476.
[39] Frank, 204.

[40] Barnes, *From Then Till Now*, 477.
[41] Barnes, *From Then Till Now*, 488.
[42] Barnes, *From Then Till Now*, 488.
[43] Barnes, *From Then Till Now*, 495.

had at one time or another done some kind of photographic work, at a time when they were seriously considering what branch of the service they were most fitted for to serve their country.[44]

Accounts of the wonderful work accomplished in aerial photography, the prospect of early service in France, and the excitement of flying over the trenches caught the immediate attention of the recruits. This was further reinforced by the assurance of early promotions and commissions that prompted hundreds to offer their services at once. The prevailing initial expectations of duty were a few weeks of training in the States and then transfer across the water to photograph the maneuvers of the Kaiser's army. Selectees went to one of three new schools for Aerial Photography: Cornell University or Rochester, both in New York, or Langley Field, Virginia, where they were simultaneously instructed in the principles of aerial photography and the art of becoming a soldier. The first American school of aerial photography was opened at Langley Field on 19 October 1917. The school had one camera, of foreign make, and was pleased if 50 percent of the pictures taken at 6,000 feet turned out well.[45] Developers and printers were trained at Rochester, and 680 graduated by 30 June 1918. The officers' school at Cornell University taught map compilation and interpretation. In-theater training was also offered at photographic "huts" at the flying fields.[46] After completing the work of those schools, some of the men were sent to various aviation fields for practice and official work while others continued to do "Squads-Right" until they received overseas orders.[47]

When the United States declared war on Germany, George Eastman of Eastman Kodak informed Secretary of War Baker, "We offer use of any of our experts in an advisory capacity.... We shall be glad to provide school accommodations and instructors for training men for the photographic work of the Aviation Section here

FIGURE 287. The Cornell University photographic school maintained an up-to-date aerial photographic map of the entire Western Front. Source: USAMHI.

in Rochester.... We will also select some of our younger specialists and recommend them to you for service with the photographic division of the Aviation Section here and abroad."[48] The offer was appreciated but nothing was done for

FIGURE 288. Capitaine Carlier was one of the leading aerial photographic instructors at the Cornell University photographic school. Source: USAMHI.

[44] "History of Photographic Section #5, Air Service, U.S.A.," 1918, Gorrell Report, ser. G, r. 24, NARA.
[45] Porter, 166
[46] "Report of the Director of Military Aeronautics," I, 1388.
[47] "History of Photographic Section #5.
[48] George Eastman quoted in Ackerman, 296.

FIGURE 289. **Major James Barnes would leave the AEF and in July 1918 assume command of the U.S. Aerial Photography School at Rochester, New York.** Source: USAMHI.

photographic work, and have already devised special emulsions and apparatus for the purpose, some of which are very promising.[49]

On 10 January 1918, nearly seven months after Eastman first offered to assist the Signal Corps in the establishment of its Rochester School of Aerial Photography, the War Department asked Eastman to restate his proposal, which he did in explicit detail:

> We offer, without rental, for a period not exceeding six months from the 1st of February, 1918, the use of the third story of our restaurant building No. 28, known as the Assembly Hall, for barracks…. The Government will have to feed its force of men but we offer the use of our kitchen, which has a capacity for feeding two thousand people at a time…. We are prepared to draw on our staff for any assistance you may need. We can loan you a certain number of specialists to assist in the instruction and to give lectures, etc., both from our scientific staff and from those sections of our employees who have to deal with the teaching of photography, a considerable number of our men being engaged in the instruction of photographers throughout the country. We would be glad to loan without charge the services of such of these men as you may require until you can replace them by men trained in the school.[50]

several months. The War Department initially declined Eastman Kodak's offer to establish the school. Eastman wrote Dr. Richard C. Maclaurin, president of the Massachusetts Institute of Technology:

> We offered to establish a photographic school for aviators here and furnish the equipment and materials. The reason the Government gave for turning down our offer was that it could not send men away from camps for instruction. Of course we have facilities here that could not be obtained elsewhere, and we believe that we could teach the men much more effectively than could be done anywhere else, as we would have a staff of instructors such as they could not possibly get together in any other place…. We are especially devoting ourselves to aerial

The War Department made a concerted effort to channel more intelligence personnel through aerial photographic training. The requirement for commercial or amateur photographic experience was now met by completion of a three- to six-month training program. Special instruction was necessary to explain the basics behind Army photographic work, even when the work covered simple darkroom procedures or retouching.[51] Major Barnes, one of the driving forces

---

[49] George Eastman quoted in Ackerman, 298.
[50] George Eastman quoted in Ackerman, 304-305.
[51] Porter, 171.

behind the U.S. military's initial commitment to aerial photography in addition to Steichen, eventually commanded the school at Rochester in the summer of 1918. He agreed that the caliber of the officers and enlisted at the Rochester school was very impressive. The enlisted men were, in the main, "of a very high order of intelligence."[52] Barnes commanded about 3,000 men during his tenure. They possessed an esprit de corps that Barnes had never seen equaled. This was reflected in the post-war after-action reports. The American Photographic Sections were judged excellent and their training received from Rochester was rated highly satisfactory.[53] A few students who demonstrated a greater ability and intelligence for the discipline were sent to Cornell University for further training and commissioning as Photographic Intelligence Officers.[54]

By June 1918, an overall training center in theater was approved to provide organizational orientation for incoming units and personnel. A baseline was critical to help all participants understand the mix of nationalities, echelons, new technologies, and intelligence priorities that affected aerial photography. The school opened in August, and with each passing month more aerial photographic-experienced personnel arrived in-theater.[55] The public media were excited about the photography training architecture. The *Scientific Monthly* reported in April 1918:

> Plans have been completed for the great enlargement of facilities for training and equipping the aerial photographic force for photographing the German trenches from the skies and keeping up to the last-minute the large composite picture of the whole German front…. Aerial photography has greatly developed during the war. During the single month of September, British official reports stated that 15,837 aerial photographs were taken by the British alone. No new trench

can be dug, no new communication system opened up, no new batteries placed but the ever-present and infallible camera above records it for the examination of the staff below. So piercing has been the work that camouflage has been developed as a protection, thus forcing aerial photography to even greater ingenuity. Every sector of the front is divided into plots about half a mile square, each one numbered and entrusted to a squad of photographers, who become fully familiar with it. As fast as the photographs are made, they are developed, printed, reduced, or enlarged to a standard scale, and then fitted into their place on the large composite photograph of the sector.[56]

Allied cooperation was critical to developing U.S. aerial photographic interpretation training both in Europe and America. When the United States entered the war in April 1917, Great Britain and France sent many personnel to America to aid in organizing the forces, particularly the Air Service and auxiliary units such as photographic interpretation. At first, it was an exercise in futility. Many handpicked Allied liaisons initially wandered around Washington with practically nothing to do. They approached the designated action officers such as Major Barnes and imparted wisdom on subjects that were still vague, but recognizable for their potential value. Self-study assisted the standup. Available literature and textbooks became the seed corn for the institution. Soon, heretofore untouched Intelligence Department files of British reports were scrutinized. The French Mission provided aerial photographs that served as the foundation for subsequent training.[57]

American efforts to initiate aerial photographic training proceeded with the help of experienced allies. Barnes requested that the War Department seek immediate British support. The British came through with a superb duo of experts. Three weeks after the Barnes request, the British aerial photographic pioneer Major C.D.M. Campbell, aided by Sergeant-Major

---

[52] Barnes, *From Then Till Now*, 500.
[53] "Final Report of Chief of Air Service," Maurer, ed., *U.S. Air Service*, I, 151.
[54] Porter, 171. Ackerman, 306.
[55] Barnes, "History Photographic Section #4," 25, Gorrell Report, ser. G, r. 24, NARA.

[56] *Scientific Monthly*, April 1918, quoted in Ackerman, 306.
[57] Barnes, *From Then Till Now*, 476.

Haslitt, arrived in Washington. Campbell's coming was a godsend, for his reputation was already legendary among people in the aerial reconnaissance field. The tour in the United States was meant to prolong his already illustrious service, for Campbell was slowly dying of consumption (tuberculosis). His assignment was perceived as a means to lighten his load from three intense years at the British Air Ministry. He came armed with extensive supplies relevant to setting up the photographic training program. Samples of all the British cameras in use, lantern slides for several sets of lectures, and the complete photographic equipment of an air squadron, from plates and paper to all the chemical materials required, became the nucleus of training. Campbell also brought the Campbell Photographic Gun which, instead of shooting bullets, recorded on a film the precision of aerial gunners.[58] Campbell's efforts were extensive and a great help to the newly established American program. He toured the training centers, gave extensive lectures, and showed movies and air pictures portraying the German lines and back areas. An old Standard training plane that included an attached English camera was used to demonstrate the photographic configuration. To top off each occasion, training was accompanied by tea served to the attendees.[59]

Aided by Campbell's reputation, Barnes and Steichen demonstrated to senior leadership the amazing potential of aerial photography. Campbell was a persuasive influence, using his entourage of equipment and the Standard training plane to deliver a photograph to a general on the ground barely fifteen minutes after it was made in the air, instantly demonstrating the potential of gaining incredible information from aerial photography.[60] Sadly, the barnstorming tour did little for Campbell's failing heath. He was ordered home to England that spring and died on 3 September 1918. Major Campbell is still remembered as the godfather of American aerial photography training. His depth of knowledge was such that even brilliant members of the photographic community such as Steichen were willing apprentices.[61]

The Schoolhouse

The Americans quickly and successfully established viable training centers to meet the demand for aerial photography and interpretation. Schools at Cornell University and the Eastman-Kodak plant were established within a few weeks. Cornell opened on 9 January 1918.[62] Goddard remembered that the first forty students to arrive constituted the first class. At Schoellkopf Hill, classrooms accommodated sinks, tables, and partitions for the photographic laboratory, darkroom, and classroom facilities. This effort coincided with the arrival of the British and French instructors.[63] As a result of its rapid establishment, the school soon consumed the necessary chemicals and lenses required. The school had to resort to advertising in newspapers and mailing to all photographic studios to buy available lenses.[64] Goddard recalled that the art of aerial photographic interpretation required a careful eye and a quick mind. However, the students considered it a "pretty tame business." What was more exciting was the possibility of flying and taking the photos themselves.[65]

It took a significant level of effort to establish a bona fide school that took into account the latest photography of the Western Front. The Cornell school maintained an up-to-date map of the entire battle area from the English Channel to the Swiss border. The coverage was located on a long, high wall in the classroom. The details covered not only the first, second, and third German trench systems and No-Man's Land, but the entire network of English, American, and French trench systems. The entire front was covered and current photographs taken by French, British, and American photographic units were forwarded to the schools every two weeks. Each day the students interpreted the various pictures with the assistance of the French and British instructors familiar with the particular areas along the battle lines. The students then revised the map with updates.[66]

[58] Barnes, *From Then Till Now*, 279.
[59] Barnes, *From Then Till Now*, 482.
[60] Niven, 452.
[61] Niven, 461.

[62] Frank, *American Air Service Observation*, 160.
[63] Goddard, 8.
[64] Barnes, *From Then Till Now*, 482.
[65] Goddard, 10.
[66] Goddard, 8.

Both Campbell and Haslitt served at Cornell. Their depth of knowledge was critical to getting the American novices adjusted to the rigor of aerial photographic interpretation.[67] Goddard remembered Haslitt as "a tough little banty rooster, all spit and polish, who had served over the lines in France as an aerial photographer. He knew his business but he was highly critical of what he considered our deplorable lack of discipline and slovenly unmilitary dress."[68] Barnes recalled Haslitt "could click his heals more loudly and give a snappier salute than any other noncommissioned officer in the service."[69] His passion for the art was complemented by words of wisdom: "Once the bloomin' sun goes down and it gets dark, armies are blind as bats. Neither one knows what the other's up to till the blinkin' light's turned on again."[70]

At Cornell, French instructors presented an equally passionate view of the photographic art. Lieutenant André-H. Carlier was physically and mentally the opposite of Haslitt. Carlier gained an early reputation for brilliance as the deputy to Capitaine Grout in establishing the French SPAé. After the war, Carlier produced *La Photographie Aérienne Pendant la Guerre*, the single most detailed assessment of World War I aerial photography and interpretation. His passion for the aerial photographic art rivaled that of Campbell and Haslitt. The only thing that was important was getting the photograph, even if it meant forsaking military discipline to achieve the objective. Haslitt and Carlier engaged in roaring arguments over their respective approaches, the result being a continuous contest for doctrinal dominance on the relative merits of British and French photographic methods and achievements over enemy territory.[71]

Besides classroom instruction, the training included operations with aircraft. At Rochester's nearby Baker Field, aerial photographs were taken by one of the three photographic aircraft assigned to the school. The film was quickly downloaded, rushed by motorcycle to the mobile laboratory, and delivered to the final judge (the mayor of Rochester) within 30 minutes of landing. Barnes expressed wonder at the ability of the students to perform this task so well. "To see laboratory workers dry a negative by pouring alcohol on it, ignite it without injuring its clearness in the slightest way, and then to see them do the same thing with the photographic prints was an exhibition of skill that was astonishing."[72] Rochester's curriculum included Copying Camera, Contact Explanation, Photographic Unit Configuration, Maps, Mosaic Maps, Plates, and Development of Plates.[73] Life was disciplined according to the standards of the day. However, it had an air of community. The school published its own newspaper, *The Airscout's Snapshot*, providing a glimpse into daily life. Major Barnes became the commander at Rochester, succeeding Captain Charles F. Betz as commandant of the United States Army School of Aerial Photography at Kodak Park on 31 July 1918. Barnes, the original member of the U.S. Photo Service, served in this capacity for the rest of the war.[74]

Grout's RFC counterpart, F.C. Victor Laws, remained a photographic leader for his entire career in the RAF. In September 1916, Laws was reassigned to the Training Brigade where he not only designed the "L" Type aerial camera, but also acquired his aviator's wings.[75] In December 1917, he took Moore-Brabazon's place as Senior Photographic Officer at GHQ and remained in that capacity for the remainder of the war. Moore-Brabazon left to manage photographic requirements at the War Office in London.[76] Laws continued to serve in uniform for another 25 years until the close of World War II, retiring as an RAF Group Captain. At the end of the Second World War, Laws employed his vast photographic experience to establish a company that photographed the finish line at greyhound and horse racing tracks.[77]

---

[67] Barnes, *From Then Till Now*, 279.
[68] Goddard, 8-9.
[69] Barnes, From Then Till Now, 279.
[70] Sgt-Maj Haslitt quoted in Goddard, 26.
[71] Goddard, 8-9.

[72] Barnes, *From Then Till Now*, 500-501.
[73] *The Airscout's Snapshot*, 28 August 1918, Steere Papers, USAMHI.
[74] *The Airscout's Snapshot*, 28 August 1918, Steere Papers, USAMHI.
[75] Nesbit, 41.
[76] Nesbit, 43.
[77] Moore-Brabazon, 103.

In retrospect, the Allied aerial photographic training regimen was an unqualified success. The United States alone generated 25 Photographic Sections and their full complement of aerial photographic interpreters, photographic laboratory officers, and staffs to provide an overwhelming depth to the ongoing requirement for intelligence and aerial photography. Had the war continued into the next year, American energy toward establishing a broad range of trained aerial photographic talent would have surpassed the well-established resources of France and Great Britain. Yet, as quickly as it became an integral part of the expanding Allied force structure, the aerial photographic talent would subsequently disappear as the forces drew down and returned to civilian life.

CHAPTER 24

THE HUMAN EXPERIENCE BEHIND AERIAL RECONNAISSANCE

The "Office"

"Reconnaissance work is not spectacular."[1] It involved a sortie that could last for up to three hours at a time, with interruptions at any time from atmospheric conditions or incidents of combat.[2] Aerial observation missions were not glamorous. One British aviator compared aerial reconnaissance to a routine office job, taking the daily train to and from work and waiting while the board sat in debate over the profit and loss account.[3] Another view reflected the frustration of the experience: "Photography again. I am getting thoroughly fed up with this job. It is a most difficult and dangerous job a pilot can get."[4] Commentary on the observer role was equally descriptive:

> I soon found that the main function of an observer, during the training period of an R.F.C. pusher aircraft squadron in this country, was to act as ballast. His

FIGURE 290. **The aerial observer, the unsung hero of the Great War.** Source: SHAA.

---

[1] Jones, II, 82.
[2] "Instructions on the Employment of Aerial Observation," in Maurer, ed., *U.S. Air Service*, II, 182.
[3] Jones, II, 82.
[4] Smart, "The Front Cockpit: The Diary of Lt. C.D. Smart, No. 5 Squadron, RFC," 23.

other duties included the very simple one of starting the rotary monster, bearing the illogical name Gnome, imprisoned in its cage behind the pilot, on every occasion of a forced landing beyond the reach of the aerodrome staff, plus that of accepting full responsibility for any error in navigation on the part of the helmsman.[5]

To be fair to the veterans of the discipline, not all reminiscence on the aerial observer role was negative. One British aerial observer reflected on the reward of accomplishing an aerial observation mission: "There was something hugely satisfying, however, in both these pursuits…. To go over the lines and look vertically down on the enemy's most treasured and private property, and to know that you had it in your power to bring about its destruction or capture, that was in truth a job worth doing."[6] Whatever the view of the practitioner, aerial observation was critical for acquiring the intelligence necessary to conduct the campaign.

Opinion varied on what made the ideal observer. One declared that the assignment demanded "a steady, philosophical, and physically tough type. In vertical map-making he needed all these qualities, for despite shaking from Archie bursts he had to fly an undeviated course, exposing plates at finely calculated intervals so that they would overlap precisely to form a mosaic."[7] One post-war British assessment described the person behind the camera as "a man in a state of stress and in the strained condition which ensues from any operation he may be called upon to perform in the course of a flight … so that it may become to him almost an automatic action."[8] A successful observer had to develop the knack for both observing and remembering the aerial view, for he was liable for whatever was seen or not seen. Background experience in the military arts was necessary: "The observer had to be a trained tactical officer, because in reconnaissance of this nature, an untrained person cannot interpret the military significance of what he sees."[9] Demands went beyond the physiological challenges of operating in an often cold, wet, icy, windy, open cockpit while someone is trying to kill him. The observer had to possess a mental discipline that demanded a precise concentration on what was observed: "He must withstand the temptation to make conjectures, or to think that he has seen something when he is not absolutely certain of the fact, since an error in observing, or an inaccuracy in reporting may lead to false conclusions and cause infinite harm."[10] Succinctly put: "The vital duty of the observer was to know exactly what his objectives were and how to get it on the plate."[11]

The initial criterion for becoming an aerial observer was rudimentary at best. One of the British RFC pioneers was William "Sholto" Douglas, an observer in the British No. 2 Squadron, who described his initial introduction to aerial observation: "The various observers in the squadron were canvassed with a view to finding out whether any of them knew anything about photography. I had had a camera as a boy, and had taken, developed and printed some very amateurish photographs. On the strength of this, I was appointed the squadron's official air photographer."[12] Douglas learned first-hand that the observer function required innovation to ensure success. Flying observer in the BE 2a, Douglas took the bold step of cutting an oblong rectangular hole in the bottom of his cockpit and pushed the camera through the hole to take a snapshot. "It did not occur to us to fix the camera in the floor of the cockpit; but in any case this would have been impossible, as the camera was of the folding type with bellows."[13]

The observer had to know how to operate the camera and determine at what intervals aerial photographs were to be taken to ensure effective overlap. Once over the target, the observer "was

---

[5] Gliddon, 44.

[6] Insall, 155-156.

[7] Morris, 102-103.

[8] Gamble, "Technical Aspects of British Aerial Photography," TNA, PRO: AIR 1/2397/267/7.

[9] "Military Aviation," Maurer, ed., *U.S. Air Service*, II, 49.

[10] Turner, 198-199.

[11] Porter, 165.

[12] See Chap. 23 for a similar experience with Goddard. W. "Sholto" Douglas, "Notes on First Steps in Air Photography on the Western Front, January to March 1915," TNA, PRO: AIR 69/2.

[13] Douglas, "First Steps in Air Photography," TNA, PRO: AIR 69/2.

FIGURE 291. Radial lines painted on the side of a 1st Aero Squadron Salmson 2 A2 assisted the aerial observer in the shoot. The angle of the lines corresponded to the vertical angle of the lens of the aerial camera. The time it took to fly between the marks served as an estimate for the coverage acquired by the photo plate. Source: via Colin Owers.

on his hands and knees in the 'office' looking down through the little glass plate in the floor, releasing the shutter, changing the plates and counting out the seconds between exposures."[14] Douglas remembered: "This procedure was not too easy in the cramped space available, especially as the weather was cold and [a] bulky flying kit a necessity. Each plate had to be changed by hand, and I spoilt many plates by clumsy handling with frozen fingers."[15] Taking a successful

photograph required tremendous patience and agility on the part of the observer. Pointing a camera through the floor was difficult because "one could not see the ground at all," except through the camera's aperture.[16] Later designs allowed the observer to sight through a pinhole, releasing the shutter just as the target centered.[17] What instruments that existed within the aeroplane were needed to fly the plane. One aero squadron ground crew recalled the cockpit display: "A tachometer, oil pressure gauge, altimeter, air speed indicator, and a compass were about all they had. There was no gasoline gauge, and gas consumption was measured by time and the R.P.M. of the motor, which added up to approximately two and one half hours to a tankful."[18]

Later aeroplane designs included features to assist in the "shoot." Two radial lines were painted on the outside of the fuselage in an area convenient to the observer's visual reference.

---

[14] Hart, 43.

[15] Douglas, "First Steps in Air Photography," TNA, PRO: AIR 69/2; Jones, II, 89.

[16] Douglas, "Notes on Equipment of Units of RFC with BEF," 27 September 1914, TNA, PRO: AIR 1/836/204/5/268.

[17] Porter, 160.

[18] Dixon, Diary, 50.

FIGURE 292. **Oblique photographs were improved when an aerial camera such as the 26 cm was attached to the gun rail.** Source: via Colin Owers.

The angle of the lines corresponded to the vertical angle of the lens of the particular camera on board. This configuration allowed a reference for adjusting the camera at any altitude. Sighting took place along the first line toward a designated reference point. Once the aeroplane passed the reference point, the observer either commenced counting or activated a stopwatch to gauge when the second line passed. The flight time between the marks served as an estimate of the area covered by one photo plate. Dividing the time by two provided the proper time between exposures to allow for a 50 percent overlap.[19]

On the reconnaissance mission the observer not only maintained the camera but annotated a mapping board and notebook to retain information and the location of the print. These notes were invaluable both to the observer and to the aerial photographic interpreter.[20] Observers had to learn the art of acquiring oblique photographs either through reconfiguring the French 26 cm camera on the aerial gunner's machine gun turret rail or through use of a hand-held camera such as the British "P" Type camera. One American observer recalled the challenges in using the aerial camera for oblique photographs:

We experienced a great deal of difficulty in our attempts to take oblique photographs. Our first attempt to suspend the camera was on the inside of the fuselage but this proved to be very unsatisfactory, in as much as the oil from the motor could not be properly guarded against causing the lens to become dirty and fogging the plates. With this method of suspension great difficulty was experienced in securing a sufficiently small angle with the horizontal. The photos did not give the proper perspective after several attempts at getting a suspension to fit the machine gun turret [rail] so the photos were taken over the side where the observer could see what he was shooting. This later arrangement gave excellent results after a yoke had been made which absorbed all vibrations from the plane. However, besides being very hazardous to fly at very low altitudes over the enemy lines with this suspension instead of the machine guns it was also very difficult to manipulate due to the blast of the propeller coming full on to the camera, making it extremely difficult to swing the camera toward the side. In changing magazines difficulty was also encountered with the shutter of the cameras.[21]

One aeroplane was kept ready for any short-range reconnaissance missions. Once the observer was notified of his assignment, he received instructions from the operations officer on the details of terrain, type of information desired, tactical situation, and communications data. Following that initial brief, the observer then conferred with his pilot.[22] Prior to mission takeoff, the observer consulted with the intelligence staff on the target area. Those observers detailed to aerial photographic reconnaissance missions carefully studied the maps of the territory to be photographed, looked at previously taken photographs, and completed a thorough analysis of the ground to be covered, to include any important points associated with the mission.

[19] Snyder, "Notes on Army Observation," Gorrell Report, ser. J, r. 34, NARA.

[20] "Aerial Photography for Pilots," 12, NASM, A30.2/2

[21] Lindstrom, "Photographic Missions," Gorrell Report, ser. N, r. 53, NARA.

[22] Frank, *American Air Service Observation*, 220-221.

While the observer completed his final preparations, the squadron photographic officer assured the mounting of the camera and accessories in the airplane designated for the flight. The photographic officer also made sure that the observers using cameras knew how many photographs they were to take and how many plates they required in the magazines. Observers were told to expose all the plates: "This is a rule, the importance of which cannot be over-emphasized."[23]

The aerial observer in the first year of conflict developed techniques for tracking the path of the aeroplane over the designated target area. The observer would direct the pilot to fly toward a prominent landmark. Getting to the exact point sometimes required the observer to lean over the side of the fuselage, signaling to the pilot from time to time with his hand so that the course would be exactly as required for the photographic shoot. One early technique required the aircraft to fly from the landmark toward one of the cardinal points of the compass. Once over the landmark the observer commenced shooting the camera and marking the spot on tracing paper covering the map contained within the cockpit. The steps would aid the subsequent interpretation and restitution.[24]

Upon return, the observer taking the aerial photographs assisted the intelligence staff in identifying the plates for development and interpretation. The mission was not complete until the interpretation report was completed.[25] The veteran American observer, Lt. John Snyder, reaffirmed that aerial observation reporting, with or without benefit of the camera, required:

> ...the observer to make out his report immediately upon his return from a mission regardless of whether it is of a positive or negative nature, for it is just as important to get negative reports as it is the positive ones, but when an ob-

server does make negative reports he must be sure that the report is accurate.... The observer must at all times report every thing that he sees, regardless of how unimportant it may seem to him. It may verify some other observer's report or some report that the staff received from agents.[26]

In the case of bombardment missions, observers were strongly encouraged to expose all plates taken over the target to acquire as much information as possible from the sortie.[27] Each observer had his routine prior to takeoff. Lt. Snyder shared his techniques with new students to the theater:

> After getting into the plane and before starting on the mission, I make a very careful examination of the camera and see that it functions properly. I always remove the magazine from the camera, wind up the curtain then releasing it to see that it works properly, and then put the magazine back and work the drawer at least once to see that it does not bind. As for the setting of the lens

FIGURE 293. **The exposed photo plates are delivered to the Photographic Section for development and interpretation.** Source: Gorrell Report, NARA.

[23] "Tactical History of Corps Observation," Maurer, ed., U.S. Air Service, I, 181; "Report on Day Bombardment Training," Gorrell Report, ser. J, r. 35, NARA.

[24] Squier, "Map Room and Printing Room," Squier Papers, USAMHI.

[25] "Tactical History of Corps Observation," Maurer, ed., U.S. Air Service, I, 181; Frank, *American Air Service Observation*, 222-223.

[26] Snyder, "Notes on Reconnaissance," Gorrell Report, ser. J, r. 34, NARA.

[27] "Report on Day Bombardment Training," Gorrell Report, ser. J, r. 35, NARA.

and the curtain aperture, that must be left to the photographers who are specialists in that line…. When taking off I always hold the camera with my hands, keeping it free from the wires, and keep the extra magazines between my feet so as to prevent them from falling over or bouncing, which would result in the breaking of plates.[28]

The amount of time in a mission allotted for aerial observation was limited and required the observer's total concentration. Lt. Snyder related that it took about one hour to gain the altitude necessary to work Army observation missions. Once at cruising altitude, the air crew adapted to their "office" environment and began "to feel at home" while in the air: "After attaining the desired altitude and before crossing the lines I again

FIGURE 294. **Lieutenant Snyder is handed the readied 50 cm camera from the squadron's Photographic Officer for installation prior to takeoff.** Source: Gorrell Report, NARA.

try the shutter so that in case it would have been affected by either the cold or the vibration, we would not have to risk our lives unnecessarily, but would turn back and get another camera."[29]

There were clearly differences in opinion among the Allies as to the appropriate role for the pilot when it came to aerial observation. One British observer remarked: "In French Corps Squadrons, the pilot is generally a mere chauf-

---

[28] Snyder, "Notes on Army Observation," Gorrell Report, ser. J, r. 34, NARA.

[29] Snyder, "Notes on Army Observation," Gorrell Report, ser. J, r. 34, NARA.

Chapter 24: The Human Experience Behind Aerial Reconnaissance

feur."[30] Despite the British notice of their French counterparts' role, the pilot was an integral part of the aerial observation mission. The pilot had to know the elements, to include direction of the wind, so that he could make proper corrections for drift, altitude, and speed of the aeroplane. He also had to keep to a carefully prescribed straight and level course, a process that required tremendous discipline, precision, and steady nerves.[31] To achieve mission success required the pilot be a top performer, possessing great skill and a sense of orientation.[32]

The French took extensive measures to assign some of their best personnel to aerial reconnaissance. Each French escadrille included a photographic section composed of specially trained men.[33] Many recollections spoke of the discipline required to be a successful reconnaissance aviator. One pilot recalled:

> Flying a photo machine is the most difficult and "brainy" flying of all. The conditions are such that it demands the most of a Pilot, while it is of such importance that the enemy spares no expense or trouble to bring him down. His machine is always the objective of all enemy chase machines who can reach him, and a target for the antiaircraft batteries, for he has to fly a straight and even course, always. He cannot vary his line of flight to avoid the inferno of antiaircraft shells that are belching forth from dozens of guns. The only time a Pilot on photo mission will leave his course is when the enemy machines attack him, and then he fights on the defensive. If he can drive off the attacking enemy planes, he sticks to his aerial post and continues his mission. Nothing matters to him except those pictures which must be taken and delivered to the home station behind the lines.[34]

FIGURE 295. **Upon return, Lieutenant Snyder hands off the exposed plate magazine to the motorcycle dispatch.** Source: Gorrell Report, NARA.

Flying well served the mission, and helped to escape the enemy. The view from the infantry on the ground provided a combatant's perspective of the danger and fascination of aeronautics. One British officer recalled after observing aerial combat: "A daring Boche chaser pursues one of our observer planes. Clever diving alone saves our man who gets away within 100 feet of the ground."[35] A standard aerial photographic sortie involved the observer sighting the ground track and assisting the pilot in flying to a recognized point. The pilot flew as straight and level a course as possible to achieve a true vertical shot, necessary for the photographic interpreter's analysis or the construction of the mosaic. Maintaining straight and level flight was generally determined by the pilot's own sense of balance or from applications of mechanical nature, such as improvised instruments showing water levels or plumb lines. Acquiring straight and level coverage was the exception rather than the rule due to

[30] Sewell, "Notes ... on French Corps Aviation," TNA, PRO: AIR 1/475/15/312/201.

[31] Hart, 43.

[32] "Aerial Photography for Pilots," 9, NASM, A30.2/2.

[33] Lieut Michel quoted in Porter, 174.

[34] Unknown source quoted in Porter, 225.

[35] 2nd Lieut Frank Warren quoted in Brown, *Imperial War Museum Book of 1918*, 17.

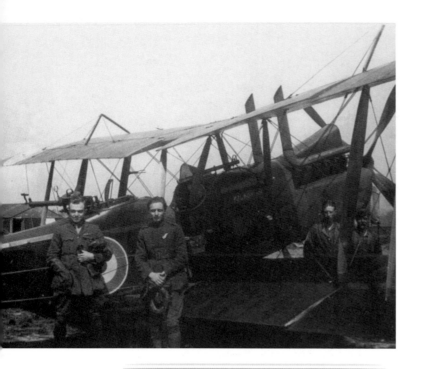

observer alone.[39] The public portrait of both pilot and observer mirrored the general public awe associated with aviation: "You will be astonished to learn that the average age of R.F.C. pilots doing reconnaissance work is twenty and of observers twenty-two. It requires young blood and muscle to stand the strain, risk and excitement of this branch of the air service. That results so far have more than justified expectations, is a tribute to the skill and bravery of these youngsters."[40]

Esprit de Corps

The popular image of aviation in World War I was the pursuit pilot. Without doubt his exploits were incredible feats of daring to face the adversary alone in a hostile environment with no safety net other than airmanship skills. The pursuit pilot received the limelight throughout the war and long afterward. However, the majority of aviation during the conflict served the ground combatant through aerial observation. It was perhaps the most perilous of all aerial missions because the observer had to accomplish a number of important functions and

hazards posed by hostile aeroplanes, antiaircraft, and weather.[36] The RFC RE 8 pilot, Lt Smart, reflected on the reconnaissance mission after one sortie, "Photography is a good job when you don't get hurt."[37]

Aerial observation demanded teamwork among the crew, creating a "feeling of homogeneity." Ideally, they worked to achieve synchronized reactions, judgments, and decisions. The pilot was to follow the observer's directions promptly. The parlance of the day equated the relationship to the pilot being "married" to his observer.[38] Despite the close relationship, pilots did not consider themselves "observation pilots." Among American aero squadrons, the crews preferred that the term "observation" apply to the

FIGURE 297. **The survival of the aerial reconnaissance air crew was always in question. Here a French Morane-Saulnier T escadrille attends a mass with an aeroplane altar.** Source: SHAA, B80.36.

---

[36] "Aerial Photography for Pilots," 9, NASM, A30.2/2
[37] Smart, "The Front Cockpit: The Diary of Lt. C.D. Smart, No. 5 Squadron, RFC," 20.
[38] "Aerial Photography for Pilots," 9, NASM, A30.2/2; Porter, 221.

---

[39] Porter, 218.
[40] Henry Bruno, "The Eyes in the Air," *Popular Science Monthly* (1918): 511.

defend himself at the same time. It was nearly impossible to do both when tucked inside the cockpit taking photos.[41] The American observer Lieutenant Percival Hart spoke for his counterparts on coming to terms with the dangers associated with the aerial reconnaissance mission: "The definite nature of these missions left nothing to the observer's imagination—he had to bring back photographs of exact positions regardless of whether or not he thought it was entirely safe to do so. As time went on this work was entrusted mainly to the most experienced and daring teams."[42] Such flying established its own sense of honor. Reflections of the time suggested the aerial reconnaissance crew were of the "do or die" order. The flight was there to acquire "snaps," even if it resulted in sacrifice.[43]

For the British aviator, such an attitude extended from the military culture. Colonel Squiers observed on 20 April 1915:

> No name is ever made known in connection with any feat however important. I was told that on the day of our arrival Sir John French had asked the commander of the Flying Corps to tell him who had performed a particularly clever bit of work, and he was reminded of the rule of the organization and withdrew the question. They are so modest that I could not get any of them to admit that they have command of the air, although one hears it everywhere else both in the army and in England.[44]

The priority in aerial reconnaissance, according to one American flying with the French prior to the United States coming into the war, was "to get back to headquarters with the information you have gained. If you are attacked and see no chance of successfully fighting off the enemy, it is your business to run."[45] Confronting the German aviation threat was a subject of de-

FIGURE 298. **The RFC counterpart is a church service for the FE 2b squadron with the cockpit serving as a pulpit.** Source: IWM, Joubert de la Ferté, *The Forgotten Ones.*

bate among the experienced. One French instructor at the Second Artillery Observation School at Camp de Souge conveyed the sentiment of aerial observation survival against an aggressive enemy: "You are young, you are eager; you all want to be aces, shooting down the Boche. But you are not fighters, you are observers. You fight when you must, but your job is to bring back information. That is what we are training you for. We French have had terrible losses. We conserve our men. If possible avoid conflict. Your planes will be slower, less maneuverable. Do not hesitate to run."[46] Many Americans had their own view on how to take on the fight, and criticism was evident. Snyder commented that the "majority of French aviators would look for enemy aircraft nine-tenths of the time and look at the ground the remainder of the time."[47]

[41] Hart, 37.
[42] Hart, 37.
[43] Middleton, III, 117; Porter, 9.
[44] Squier, "Map Room and Printing Room," Squier Papers, USAMHI.
[45] Carroll D. Winslow, *With the French Flying Corps* (New York: Charles Scribner's Sons, 1917), 183.

[46] Unknown source quoted in Gilchrist, 48-49.
[47] Snyder, "Notes on Army Observation," Gorrell Report, ser. J, r. 34, NARA.

FIGURE 299. **Flying aerial sorties on a regular basis gave the aerial observation crew the confidence of knowing the sector throughly.** Source: *Étude et Exploitation des Photographies Aériennes.*

Collecting Information

Collecting information was the purpose of aerial reconnaissance. The entire mission revolved around details, be they the memory of the air crew or the information gleaned from the analysis of the photographs. Preparation required an ongoing review of target materials, normally defined by the coordinate location.[48] British aerial observers established a reporting format to account for observations noted on the sortie. Colonel Squier, the American attaché, reported in Febru-

ary 1915 that the form contained instructions for "observers," and on the back they were to fill out the report in the aeroplane and produce duplicate copies in the field.[49] This was later changed to an Objective Card describing each target, particularly enemy artillery batteries.[50] One U.S. Air Service squadron, the 91st Aero Squadron, was aggressive in its approach to understanding significant targets associated with each sortie. The crews had to be familiar with the key targets of the sector, to include enemy-held towns, supply dumps, and aerodromes. The squadron drilled the members through a rigorous study of aerial photographs posted on the cards, with the names of the various places shown under each. The displayed photographs were studied for several days, after which the captions were removed and the towns, dumps, and airfields memorized. The training resulted in higher-quality reconnaissance. Both pilot and observer knew what to look for. Their routes were covered more accurately and the crew returned with valuable reports.[51]

Once aloft, crew members described the terrain. One such description portrayed by Lieutenant Cecil Lewis in his memoir, *Sagittarius Rising*, provided an aerial perspective that reflected a hint of ennui. After an initial introduction flying ten hours over the front, Lewis was handed his first real job to "photograph the enemy second-line trenches." He reflected on the reconnaissance mission:

> The lines, from the air, had none of the significance they had from the ground, mainly because all the contours were non-existent. The local undulations, valleys, ravines, ditches, hillsides, which gave advantage to one side or the other, were flattened out. All you saw was two more or less parallel sets of trenches, clearer in some places than in others according to the color of the earth thrown up in making them. These faced each other across the barren strip of no-man's land, and

[48] *Aerial Observation for Artillery*, 8.

[49] Squier, "Intelligence Services," Squier Papers, USAMHI.

[50] *Aerial Observation for Artillery*, 8.

[51] "History of the 91st Aero Squadron," in Frank, *American Air Service Observation*, 233.

behind them started a complicated network of communication trenches, second-line trenches, and more communication trenches, and then the third-line trenches. The network was more complex at the important positions along the line; but everywhere it was irregular, following the lie of the ground, opening up to a wide mesh at one place, closing up, compact and formidable, at another. As positions were consolidated more trenches were dug, and later, when I came to know my section of the line as well as the palm of my hand, I could tell at a glance what fresh digging had been done since my last patrol.[52]

Another reflection on an important observation was written by A.J. Insall, a British aerial observer, in his post-war memoir:

One afternoon, when I was looking down on to a part of the German line below Gommecourt, after spending some twenty minutes photographing a stretch of reserve trench asked for by Third Army, I suddenly became aware of a line of closely grouped whitish dots in a part of the same trench-line a little to the south of the section we had just passed over. The dots were so minute that they were only just distinguishable from the 9,000 feet at which we were flying. I thought for a moment that they might be pit-props, but dismissed the idea as soon as I had made a more careful examination through my field glasses and had noted the typically sound condition of the trench and the bunching of the dots. There was, to my mind, little doubt that these were troops, their helmets catching the light. So I got my pilot to describe a slow S turn, and reloaded my camera. It was the last plate in the box, and I took my time over it. Later that evening our Wing Photographic Officer rang through to congratulate me on this one negative, which, according to him, made the others I had taken that afternoon look rather indifferent. As he was an experienced Fleet Street man and not usually inclined to issue compliments, I was thrilled. The prints he had made from it apparently showed a concentration of troops quite clearly, and a day or two later a note appeared in the official news bulletin that read: On the southern part of our line, aerial reconnaissance reported a local concentration of the enemy to the north of Beumont-Hamel, which our artillery dispersed.[53]

Even Lewis described a sense of accomplishment upon returning from one aerial reconnaissance sortie. In conversation with his sergeant-gunner after a hair-raising sortie, he related:

The sergeant came up. "Are you all right, sir?" "Fine! And you?" "Quite, thank you, sir." "I thought he'd got us with that second burst." "Always turn, sir, as soon as a machine attacks. It can't get its sights on you so easy. And it has to allow for the traverse…. If you'll phone the squadron, sir, and order out a tender and a repair squad, I'll dismount the camera and get a guard put over the machine. You got all the photos, didn't you, sir?" "Yes, Twenty-two in all." "The corps will be pleased. They wanted them badly."[54]

The Photographic Laboratory

The photographic laboratory was an extension of the aerial observation aeroplane. If the camera was not just right or if the laboratory did not have the right chemical mix to produce the necessary prints for a diverse array of customers, the aerial photographic reconnaissance mission was a failure. The responsibilities that came with the function of Photographic Officer impacted the air crew in many ways. He was ultimately responsible for the camera equipment and supervised installation and extraction of cameras

---

[52] Cecil Lewis. *Sagittarius Rising [Reminiscences of Flying in the Great War]* (London: Peter Davies, 1936; reprint, London: The Folio Society, 1998), 43-44.

[53] Insall, 155-156.
[54] Lewis, 48.

FIGURE 300. American photographic section maintenance personnel work on both the French-designed De Ram semi-automatic camera and the British-designed "L" Type camera. Source: Gorrell Report, NARA.

and plates from the aeroplane. Only the Photographic Officer could designate who could touch the camera. The observer was required to operate the camera only over the target area.[55] However, the observer was not exempt from malfunction. As one veteran commented: "The worst mistake was to be unaware that the camera was not working."[56] The Photographic Officer also governed the laboratory manned by 30 lab specialists, filling functions ranging from supply, draughtsman, maintenance, print specialists and motorcycle riders.[57] Such responsibilities were not taken lightly. Lieutenant Smart of the 135th Aero Squadron recalled a harrowing mission photographing Nonsard to Thiacourt. While returning from the mission his crew fought off four Fokker DVII's and two Pfalz D III's. They were lucky and managed to escape and land safely. They then discovered that the Photo Officer, responsible for installing the camera, had neglected to take the protection

cover off the lens. "He had to buy drinks for the squadron that night and from then on, that cap was checked twice before takeoff."[58]

Memories of the role the photographic laboratory played in the aerial reconnaissance process are murky. One illuminating source came from the diary of Sergeant Eric E. Dixon in his privately published memoir of his photographic laboratory experiences in the U.S. Air Service. His recollections reflect a sense of pride that came with the photographic laboratory's ability to contribute to the fight. Sgt. Dixon described the routine supporting the 1st Aero Squadron: "Camera and loaded magazines were always ready for

---

[55] "Notes on Branch Intelligence," 91st Aero Squadron, 1 November 1918, 21, Gorrell Report, ser. M, r. 40, NARA; "Final Report of Chief of Air Service," Maurer, ed., *U.S. Air Service*, I, 173; Porter, 170.

[56] Porter, 165.

[57] Terry, "Notes on Branch Intelligence," Gorrell Report, ser. M, r. 40, NARA; "Final Report of Chief of Air Service," Maurer, ed., *U.S. Air Service*, I, 173; Porter, 170.

[58] Smart, 43.

Chapter 24: The Human Experience Behind Aerial Reconnaissance

instant action. When a mission was scheduled, Perkins took the cameras and magazines to the planes in a truck and installed them as needed."[59] The cameras were loaded and downloaded by the photographic lab crew. Those working in aerial photography soon developed an elite role:

> The field men were much envied, as they got at first hand all the thrilling reports brought back by the Observers and Pilots, and to see the planes come in bullet riddled and tattered. After a time the cameras were kept in a tent on the field, which also served as the camp barbershop. However, the magazines had to be carried back and forth the mile to the field, and one might occasionally see the field men trudging along with five magazines hung on a pole, suspended between them and carrying one in each hand, thereby making one trip.[60]

The photographic laboratory included the entire range of photographic processing. A negative lab mixed the chemicals and processed the negatives. Lab personnel loaded the plates into the camera magazines. Other lab functions included printing, developing, and print drying. Prints were developed on a printing machine. Developers sometimes had twenty prints in the tray at the same time. Immediately after the aeroplane landed, the camera magazines were quickly brought to the negative lab for processing.[61] Timely photo processing involved putting the exposed plates in a bath of chemical developer. Once the plates had been coated with the chemicals, they were dipped in a "short stop dip" to neutralize the chemicals before the final step of placing in a fixing bath. The plate negatives were placed on a "light box" for viewing. Restitution was applied in determining the area covered by the photograph. Once that was accomplished the area was outlined on the map. The plate negative was assigned an identification number with pertinent data (number, date, altitude) along the lower edge. A complete set of prints was then printed, developed, fixed, rinsed, and the excess water was "squeegeed" off." Getting the prints ready for intelligence analysis was the next step. A five-man crew worked one printing machine. Several men were necessary in this operation to keep up with the workload. The printing, developing, and fixing was accomplished under the haze of an orange light.[62]

The laboratory was important to the success of the observation squadron. As such, the culture of the squadron soon recognized the role played by each laboratory member. One BE-2 pilot, Lt. C.D. Smart, marveled at the efficiency of his photo section counterparts: "Wonderful the way photography is worked in the R.F.C. Within a [sic] hour and a half of reaching the ground, I had a complete set of the 18 photographs, all pinned together in the form of a map, put into my hands. I consider this fairly quick work."[63] As Sergeant Dixon recalled, "The photo unit had one redeeming feature; that was we were excused from all drills, guard duty, and K.P. On days we were working we could also go to the head of the chow line, much to the envy of all others."[64] Such perks were earned through hard work:

> The print lab was a very busy place. Everyone, including myself, worked like galley slaves and kept at it until the last print was delivered to Intelligence. Sometimes our work would cover only three or four hours of darkroom work, but it usually was much more. Once we worked 36 hours straight, with hardly time to eat. Food was brought in and we grabbed a bite when we could and really turned out the work. We usually ran one or two print crews, but when our personnel was increased, we used three. We used a bromide paper, which was very fast and exposure went from a flash to several seconds. At times a printer could turn out 250 prints an hour.... Despite the long and hard work, there were fond memories of some of the laboratory crew. The use

---

[59] Dixon, Diary, 51.

[60] "History of Photographic Section #2, Air Service, U.S.A.," 1918, Gorrell Report, ser. G, r. 24, NARA.

[61] Dixon, Diary, 49-50.

[62] Dixon, *Diary*, 51.

[63] Smart, "The Front Cockpit: The Diary of Lt. C.D. Smart, No. 5 Squadron, RFC," 8.

[64] Dixon, *Diary*, 53.

of alcohol to dry the prints had its moments. Not all the alcohol burned, and the men working the rack sometimes got a mild jag on from inhaling the fumes. One man we called "Gee" who ordinarily was a bit on the sour side would loosen up, get real happy, sing songs, and even dance a jig.[65]

The prevailing attitude was to get the job done to meet the expectations of the commanders and operators. The work revolved around the weather. French recollections reflected a common theme; the work got done no matter the situation. One French officer observed:

All the work in a photographic reconnaissance should be done on the same day the reconnaissance is made. The officer should take no rest until everything is finished and the prints sent off, for example, by motorcyclists. It is not uncommon for photographic officers to go several nights without sleeping. What difference does it make? They know the importance of their work and should perform their duties with devotion. When rain comes (and it comes often in France) they will rest.[66]

Based on the operations group records, weather controlled the schedule. However, the French realized that photographic reconnaissance was necessary regardless of what the climate offered. "We must be thoroughly convinced of this principle; photographs must be taken at all hours and in all kinds of weather."[67] Weather constantly challenged successful aerial observation throughout the war. When navigating a shoot, air crew commonly had to repeat the process when coming in contact with a thick bank of clouds.[68] Steichen commented on the meteorological challenge with "The ground photographer chooses his weather; the General Staff chooses the aerial photographer's weather."[69] The weather conditions during both the Argonne and St. Mihiel operations were exceptionally poor. The most favorable days were crammed with photographic activity, and even days with barely enough light to produce the faintest trace of an image on the photographic plate had to be "photo days."

Getting the product out remained a challenge throughout the war. Post-war American staff commentary reflected the ongoing distribution of prints and intelligence needed improvement: "The current distribution of photos has interfered greatly with the regular running of the office."[70] Despite the emphasis on timeliness, aerial photographs from army aero squadrons often did not arrive at the corps until the next day. One post-war assessment groused about staff wasting time awaiting the arrival of the photographs. Once received, it was a "laborious task" sorting and distributing the materials to other offices and line units. Shift work was not a solution. As a result, staffs worked through the night, caught up on what little sleep they could, and then waited for the next round of aerial photographs and interpretation reports. Solutions focused on establishing large photographic processing and distribution centers such as the British AP and SS. Had the war continued, the discussions would have become reality.[71]

---

[65] Dixon, *w*, 52.
[66] Lieut Michel quoted in Porter, 175.
[67] Lieut Michel quoted in Porter, 175.

[68] Squier, "Map Room and Printing Room," Squier Papers, USAMHI.
[69] Steichen, "American Aerial Photography at the Front," 2, NASM, A30.2/24.
[70] G-2, 1st Army, to Chief of Staff, "Account of the Operation," 67, Drum Papers, Box 14, USAMHI.
[71] G-2, 1st Army, to Chief of Staff, "Account of the Operation," 67, Drum Papers, Box 14, USAMHI.

Chapter 24: The Human Experience Behind Aerial Reconnaissance

THE INTRIGUE OF AERIAL PHOTOGRAPHIC INTERPRETERS

In his post-war memoir describing the challenges of the aerial photographic interpreter, James Barnes captured with a vivid imagination the essence of what the aerial photographic interpreter accomplished.

The reading and interpretation of airplane photographs demands a peculiar mind—the type of mind that would work out chess problems or, nowadays, cross-word puzzles, perhaps. To the uninitiated a photograph of a line of entrenchments and myriad shell holes might mean very little, but to the puzzle solver, working over a clear photograph, with a magnifying glass, those shadows and lines and suggested slopes and rises mean much. They tell a story. Often his imagination is set on fire by some puzzling little thing, the reason for which he cannot quite discover; and then, all at once, he has it! Those funny, little dots are iron fence posts with strong wires strung along them. The men who went to that big shell hole left no trace of a path, for they reached their hidden machine gun emplacement by walking along the lower wire as a sailor would use the foot rope on the yard of a sailing vessel. That well-traversed path some hundred yards away, leading to another rounded pit in lower ground is deliberate deception; there are no guns there.

The battle between the camera and camouflage was on. It was like a poker game with aces up the sleeve.[1]

For Barnes and his colleagues, the most critical link in the aerial photographic process was the human imagination needed to discern the activity and intentions of the enemy. Despite the acknowledged importance of the function, little information remains on individual interpreters, other than a few romanticized accounts in a few articles of the popular media. The lasting legacy is of aviators and aeronautical platforms engaged in combat. The roll call of those interpreting the photographs and performing analysis, so eloquently portrayed by Barnes, faded into anonymity as the years passed.

Public Awareness of Aerial Photographic Interpretation

A captivating sidelight of the aerial reconnaissance and photographic interpretation experience was the public's perception, shaped by popular journals, of a process steeped in the intrigue of intelligence and the mysteries associated with that medium. An air of drama and suspense was portrayed in the 24 November 1917 *Scientific American* article, "The Camera at the Front." The lead paragraph introduced a new dimension of warfare:

---

[1] Barnes, 494-495.

That peaceful-looking camera which we use on Sundays for snapping pictures of our friends and of pretty views, becomes a deadly instrument when it is brought into the military world. It may be the means whereby invaluable fortifications can be quickly destroyed; it may give away important ideas or inventions to the enemy; it may betray the location of important batteries and doom them to early destruction; and it may result in heavy loss of life to troops whose position is divulged by the black-and-white markings of a photographic plate or film. At any rate, the camera in the war zone is no longer a peaceful instrument; it is many times deadlier than its equivalent weight of high explosive.[2]

Discussion of aerial photographic interpretation lent an air of suspense:

These negatives, or contact prints made from them, by some route or another make their way to spy headquarters, and there they are enlarged and studied by specialists trained in "reading" photographs. These specialists we are told, can glean a tremendous amount of information from what appeared to the layman to be a most uninteresting and valueless print. And when such informations are properly collated and distributed to the various military departments where they can do the most good — and the most harm to the opponent — the deadliness of the camera begins to dawn on us.[3]

In July 1918, the *Scientific American*, under the byline, "The Weekly Journal of Practical Information," added to the appeal with a cover article titled, "The Photographic Eye and Memory of the Military Airman." Again, an air of drama was unfolded in the opening paragraph:

It is difficult to conceive of a photographic plate that holds the fate of hundreds of thousands of men, batteries of guns, and possibly the decision of a great battle, in its thin coating of emulsion. Yet there are numerous such plates made every day by intrepid airmen, which, after being developed in less than fifteen minutes after reaching the ground and then flashed on the stereopticon screen in the presence of skilled photograph readers and officers, sign the death warrant of numerous soldiers and the order for the destruction and extensive military works and equipment, so to speak.[4]

Such mystery continued for several years. Adding to the intrigue was a series of articles published in *Popular Mechanics* by Douglass Reid, entitled "The Eye Behind the Lines."[5] In the series Reid dramatically described the power of: "The stereoscope, which has even been called by those well qualified to judge, 'the deadliest weapon of the war,' and the application of the stereoscopic principle to photographs taken with ordinary cameras."[6] In 1919 Reid elaborated:

In a picture of a village 15 miles behind the lines, the photographic officer notes buildings that instantly betray themselves as barracks. Definite trails, that only soldiers living in them could make, lead to them. Near by is a villa, further on a town. He sees that the place is a railroad center and a division point. The villa he scans closely. Hard by it is a faint irregular circle on the grass. This was made, he reasons, by horses being led about by orderlies so that they may cool off gradually while their riders are inside. The riders have come for information. The villa is a headquarters. Aside from machine gun officers, majors are the lowest of

---

[2] "Camera at the Front," *Scientific American* (24 November 1917): 380.

[3] "Camera at the Front," *Scientific American* (24 November 1917): 380.

[4] "The Photographic Eye and Memory of the Military Airman," in *Scientific American* (27 July 1918), 61.

[5] Douglass Reid, "The Eye Behind the Lines," *Popular Mechanics* (March-May 1919).

[6] Hanson, 15.

Chapter 25: The Intrigue of Aerial Photographic Interpreters

foot soldiers that are mounted. Hence the man to whom the majors come for orders must be a colonel or better.

Now behind the villa, the detective spies a larger and more regular circle on the grass. This, he deducts, is made by orderlies exercising horses daily, according to routine. The officer in the villa has a private stable of horses for himself and staff. Now he knows an all-important fact: the German is either a brigadier or major general.

Next he discovers practice trenches and machine gun pits on the outskirts of the town: an infantry organization. Then he finds still another circle made by horses, a circle just large enough for one troop of cavalry to use in practicing. This tells him that the officer in the villa is a major general, since no brigadier in the German army boasts a troop of cavalry.

He scans this last circle more closely. Its shape informs him that the troop is composed of lancers rather than saber men, since it is round, whereas the circles of saber men riding in practice are in the shape of a figure "8." Lancers drill, thrusting from the right-hand side only, their horses being trained to step so that weight of both man and beast will be thrown into the blow, thus weaving in and out in a figure eight.

Discovering this, the detective turns over in his mind the names and organizations of the various German major generals. Only one has a troop of lancers attached. Major General von A.

This, then, is he.

What is he planning?

The photographic officer bends over the system of trenches which the enemy infantrymen have created for practice. This is a replica of some little sector of the Allied lines which the Germans

are going to attack. They have photographed it, worked it out carefully and duplicated it exactly, in order that their men in the hour of the attack may be perfectly familiar with their objective.

Our detective calls for a map of the Allied lines within a radius of 50 miles. Experience has told him that the Germans will not be planning to attack farther away than that. He goes over this map carefully, and finally finds a plan of trenches in such and such a sector of the French lines, 30 miles south, let us say, that he is safe in concluding is the particular sector the enemy is going to attack.

Again he bends over the picture. The Germans have not completed their work. He knows that they will practice two weeks after their completion and then occupy a day and a night transferring to the place of the battle. So with a final scrutiny of the number of machine gun practice pits he writes out a report to the army commanding officer informing him that Major General von A. with so many thousand infantrymen will attack such and such a sector on such and such a day, employing a certain number of machine gunners, and that in the meantime bombers can find Major General von A. at this certain spot. His report is positive — the aerial detective can be relied upon.

The following day the photographic officer sends another camera man to hover over Major General von A. and make another picture, and each day thereafter the same thing, so that when at last the German officer leads his men to the objective, not only is he met and defeated, but his entire record is hanging on the wall where it may be used as a key to his way of preparing, his habits and his weaknesses, against the next time he sallies forth.[7]

---

[7] Reid, quoted in Hanson, 8-10.

FIGURE 301. French interpreters intently deduce the meaning of the battlefield landscape. Source: SHAA, photo in Christienne and Lissarague, *A History of French Military Aviation.*

Reality for public consumption, as it concerned aerial photographic interpretation, was introduced in the 1920s by Capitaine Carlier and Major Harold E. Porter. Carlier, one of the first French photographic interpreters, instructed the first American photographic interpreters at Cornell University in 1918, and wrote the most detailed assessment of photographic interpretation in *La Photographie Aérienne pendant la Guerre.* Probably the best discussion of photographic interpretation outside of the manuals of the war came from Harold Porter's *Aerial Observation.* Porter's work provided the most extensive look into aerial reconnaissance, covering the challenges of aerial observers during the sortie, the culture of the aviation community at large, and the contribution of the photographic interpreter.

The French Legacy

Perhaps the most passionate and erudite description of the role of intelligence was provided by Pépin within the confines of his manual on photographic interpretation: "The study of an aerial photograph must be confided to specialists and that these specialists must surround themelves with the largest possible number of means of control and of verifications."[8] The interpreter had to be precise in his analysis, using logical order to ascertain what was observed, yet being sensitive "of our imagination and verify our facts as often as possible."[9] When Pépin prepared to instruct the newly arriving American interpreters, he remarked: "To study these various documents one must have a very thorough training, a liking for minute research and some aptitude."[10] The French approach to aerial photographic interpretation demanded intellectual rigor in the analysis. "The reading of the photos may induce certain officers to make deductions. The plain information must however always be transmitted, in order to enable the check to be made by a specialist of photograph interpretation."[11] Pépin concluded:

> To summarize, the minute study of aerial photographs is based solely upon a close examination of forms, trails, shadow and relief, and upon a comparison of successive photos. The interpretation requires good sense, method, and a certain knowledge of German theories and practice. I hope that the many and varied photographs will develop the confidence of every one in aerial photography which when thoroughly exploited, enables us to penetrate into the life and even the intentions of the enemy; and in the calmest times as well as the most active, to follow the destructive work of our Artillery and to register the victorious advance of our Infantry.[12]

Pépin's counterpart, Sous-lieutenant Pouquet, emphasized the need for the interpreter to be engaged with the various elements of aerial observation throughout the cycle of reconnaissance:

> It is obvious that the interpreter should keep in constant liaison with the observers of escadrilles, who may aid him

---

[8] *Study and Use of Aerial Photographs*, Section I, 4.

[9] *Study and Use of Aerial Photographs*, Section I, 34.

[10] Pépin, "Lecture on the Study and Interpretation of Aerial Photographs," 2, NASM.

[11] *Study and Use of Aerial Photographs*, Section I, 39.

[12] Pépin, "Lecture on the Study and Interpretation of Aerial Photographs," 14, NASM.

Chapter 25: The Intrigue of Aerial Photographic Interpreters

in the study of photographs of their respective sectors, but it appears to me indispensable that the latter should have a room for meetings, study and files, that is absolutely distinct from that of the interpreter, who in moments of extreme activity can only rely on himself."[13] He concluded that such endeavor required the ability to concentrate at great lengths in a proper environment:

Before entering into the detailed explanation of works corresponding to these three periods, I shall add a word on the installation as regards material which it appears to me, should be furnished to the person entrusted with the interpretation of the photos. His work must be at the same time accurate and speedy; it requires more reflection than decision; that is to say, order and quiet are necessary. As a consequence, we shall reserve to the interpreter an office where he can shut himself in at his wish; this office may be small, but well lighted (if possible on two sides). His files are absolutely private.[14]

French attention to the discipline was distinctly recalled by those visitors seeing the spaces where the intelligence staff worked. One impression left on the mind of the RAF visitor to a reconnaissance escadrille was of space and lucidity: "Large light rooms containing every conceivable map, order plan and photograph and separate telephone cabins for the use of artillery observers—equally spacious offices for the Photographic Officer, his "interpreters" and draughtsmen." Also noted was the esteem granted the senior in charge: "The Corps Aviation Commander is the source of all wisdom and all orders and information come from him."[15] The discipline assumed structure as the war concluded. One checklist summarized what was essential for the successful interpreter:

Excellent eyesight

Knowledge of enemy documents, especially those relative to fortification

Be very attentive and most conscientious

Know how to interpret and assemble information from all sources

Have a wide experience in reading photographs

Finally, have a large supply of patience[16]

A British Interpretation

The British view of the aerial photographic interpreter paralleled that of the French. The detective ability of a "Sherlock Holmes" was alluded to in one post-war analysis. Paying attention to "Minute, almost imperceptible details, overlooked by the amateur, conveyed to the trained eye a wealth of meaning."[17] Jones summarized the scope of interpretation: "Experience in the reading of air photographs had shown that they might be made to reveal considerably more than the positions of trenches and strong points."[18] The British camoufleur, Solomon Solomon, further described the function in basic photographic terms: "The photographer's picture is made by the sun; he makes no personal effort to reproduce or analyze. The sun reproduces for him. His main concerns are purely mechanical, not analytical as are those of the artist, who knows what is meant by the perspective of shadows, and will see where there are other abnormalities besides those for which he has been asked to look, and would see after careful study what escapes the photographer."[19]

An illuminating description of the British photographic interpreter experience was provided by an AEF staff member, Captain Stanford, visiting Headquarters, British Fifth Army, to gain an understanding of its intelligence organization:

[13] Pouquet, "Working of the Service of Interpretation of Photographs," NARA, RG 120, Box 819.

[14] Pouquet, "Working of the Service of Interpretation of Photographs," NARA, RG 120, Box 819.

[15] Sewell, "Notes … on French Corps Aviation," TNA, PRO: AIR 1/475/15/312/201.

[16] "Lecture on Aerial Photography," 25 April 1923, NASM A30.2/36.

[17] Middleton, III, 122.

[18] Jones, II, 177.

[19] Solomon, 53.

He must study and get to know thoroughly the enemy lines opposite his Corps front; this is absolutely essential if he is to get through his work in good time and keep his office routine running smoothly. He should read all Intelligence Summaries – and especially reports from the line [patrol reports and reports on raids]; these will be of help to him in interpreting his photographs.[20]

A competent and trusted photographic interpreter had to transcend the experience of the combatant:

He should have experience of trench life and so get to know what the man in the trench wants to know, and wants to have in the way of photographs. He ought to periodically to go round the units of his Corps – at any rate as far as Brigade H.Q. (both Infantry and Artillery) and see that the photographs are getting properly circulated to the right people. In this way he can make himself useful in helping to solve difficulties of interpretation which may have arisen in the lower formations.[21]

Captain Stanford's observations of British Intelligence illuminated an important feature of the relationship between the intelligence staff and the aviator: "He should endeavor as far as possible to make his office a place where the pilots and observers drop in for a chat about their work (as well as other things); this will prove of great assistance to his efficiency."[22] Interpersonal skills were critical for effective information dissemination to staff personnel: "It is imperative that he should keep in close touch with the staffs of all the formations in his Corps and with the Intelligence Staff at Army H.Q. He should get to know these officers personally—also the staffs at Wing and Brigade H.Q. R.F.C.

He should make a point of being hand in glove with the C.C. of the Squadron to which he is attached—also with all the pilots and observers of that squadron. If he does not do this he will miss a large amount of information which he would be able to collect otherwise."[23] Such a relationship was further reinforced by the British observer, A.J. Insall, in his recollection of one memorable intelligence officer serving with the 12th (Army) Wing Headquarters:

The Wing Photographic Officer was an extraordinary character. I knew him as well as one got to know anyone with whom one had practically daily contact, and he was always welcome in our mess, as incidentally, were the other members of that Command's staff, including the Commander himself, like our own C.O. an Irishman. The Wing Photographic Officer's name was 2nd Lt. E. W. J. Payne. To his friends—and they were legion—he was always known as "Agony." He smoked like a chimney, and, no matter who you happened to be, sooner or later when he was around he would lunge forward, a fistful of "yellow perils" thrust out at you, and you would be bidden uncompromisingly to "Ave a gasper, cock!"[24]

An American Perspective

American views of the art echoed those of their Allied counterparts. The veteran aerial observer, Harold Porter, described the interpreter:

The interpreter, above all, must have a very lively mental vision. He should be imaginative, not as a writer of fiction is imaginative, but rather as a reader of it ought to be. That is, he ought always to be wondering about the outcome, and trying to guess it before he has finished with the story. He must know just how any given object on the ground will look when seen from above. He must have learned his business from

---

[20] Capt Stanford, "Summary of the Qualifications of a Branch Intelligence Officer," 15 February 1918, in "Organization of Intelligence," HQ, British 5th Army, Conger Papers, Box 2, USAMHI.
[21] Stanford, "Summary of the Qualifications," Conger Papers, Box 2, USAMHI.
[22] Stanford, "Summary of the Qualifications," Conger Papers, Box 2, USAMHI.

[23] Stanford, "Summary of the Qualifications," Conger Papers, Box 2, USAMHI.
[24] Insall, 156-157.

the ground up, and then with equal thoroughness from the air down. He must put himself in the enemy's frame of mind, and know how the enemy applies himself to the arduous duty of thinking. He must know, by constant study, every inch of the country which has been and is to be photographed, so that he won't be misled by the absence of contours from the photographs.[25]

Steichen provided a more thoughtful perspective. "There has been a tendency to wrap the technique of aerial photography in a veil of secrecy and mystery. This attitude may have been useful in stimulating curiosity, but there comes a time when such a pose seriously interferes with the free development of a new process."[26] Steichen remained sensitive to the fact that not all understood aerial photography. "It is but fair to note the following remark by a colonel of the infantry: 'They sent me some of that stuff (referring to aerial photographs), but I couldn't make anything out of them'."[27] Steichen proceeded to provide his perspective on interpretation:

The value and meaning of aerial photography has been definitely and conclusively established, and the success with which aerial photographs can be exploited is measured by the natural and trained ability of those concerned with their study and interpretation. The aerial photograph is in itself harmless and valueless. It enters into the category of "instruments of war" when it has disclosed the information written on the surface of the print. The average vertical aerial photographic print is upon first acquaintance as uninteresting and unimpressive a picture as can be imagined. Without considerable experience and study it is more difficult to read than a map, for it badly

represents nature from an angle we do not know.[28]

A photographic interpreter had no distinct advantage being French, British, or American, for none showed any particularly greater wisdom than the other. All had the necessary expertise to discern details from a photographic print. What made the ultimate difference was the way information was channeled to the customer. Once the decision had been made based on the interpretation evidence, the reconnaissance mission was complete. One assessment of the needs of interpreters in a culture of aviators concluded, "He should not be too young."[29] The average age for American aviators was 20; for the experienced and more mature interpreters it was 21.

The Routine

Photographic interpretation was hard work. Intelligence had to be timely and in quantity to have value. Photographic intelligence was slave to the laboratory process that required the same environment, regardless of the climate. Sgt. Dixon's memories of photographic development included how intelligence worked with the prints. "The first set of prints was rushed to the Intelligence Department [G-2] where they were looked over and a decision made on how many prints were wanted from each negative. The number could vary from under ten to 150 or even 200 or more."[30] After the war, Major Steichen discussed the photographic interpreter's challenges with his brother-in-law, the noted 20th century author Carl Sandburg. Steichen "sympathized with the sturdy lads who almost suffocated in the little pup-tent darkrooms, cellars and dugouts used in field service," while they "developed the art of reading lines, shadows, blurs, camouflage in the finished prints of the day's duty."[31] At the battle of Château-Thierry in June 1918, one American photo section was cited for working six straight days and nights in an improvised laboratory and interpretation room within a tent modified

[25] Porter, 183.
[26] Steichen, "American Aerial Photography at the Front," 2, NASM, A30.2/24.
[27] Steichen, "American Aerial Photography at the Front," 1, NASM, A30.2/24.

[28] Steichen, "American Aerial Photography at the Front," 1, NASM, A30.2/24.
[29] Stanford, "Summary of the Qualifications," Conger Papers, Box 2, USAMHI.
[30] Dixon, *Diary*, 51.
[31] Niven, 460.

FIGURE 302. **Public awareness of aerial reconnaissance through the media gave an ideal view of both the impact on the decision maker and the intrigue behind the analysis.** Source: *Scientific American*, 26 January 1918.

Chapter 25: The Intrigue of Aerial Photographic Interpreters

with tar paper and opaque curtains. They were remembered for performing "as bravely and as doggedly as any organization which ever took the field."[32]

There was a philosophical air to recollections covering the demands of interpretation. In a historical summary of one of the first U.S. Photo Sections (Section No. 1), the emphasis of hard work throughout the campaign was evident:

> At two A.M., one hasn't the "pep," the energy, that one had at 8 A.M., the previous morning. But the work must go on, the war cannot wait. In a few hours, men standing in grave conference at headquarters; men standing beside cannon and gun limbers; men looking eagerly at the enemy from the front line trenches — will be waiting anxiously for these photographs. For these prints, that disclose and reveal all of Fritz's secrets; that tell where he is strong and ready for attack, where he is weak and demoralized, where he

FIGURE 303. A tribute to the Photographic Sections of the Great War. The 4th Photographic Section reveals the secret weapon behind the Allied victory. Thanks to their photographic expertise, a larger-than-life 50 cm camera is on display with the Section's personnel. Source: USAFA McDermott Library Special Collections (SMS57).

has many cannon, where he has few, and exactly where each and everyone is located. Tomorrow, "they" will need these prints in order to continue the attack. So tonight, as many another night, we in the lab go on with the work. Other men pour over maps and plans locating the enemy's positions, his batteries, his headquarters, his supply dumps, his telegraph and telephone lines, his innermost, hidden secrets. Still other men walk innumerable miles around and around and around the giant drying frame that dry these prints in several seconds. Still others sort them, number

---

[32] Porter, 174.

them, count them, wrap them, ready to be delivered to "them" at the appointed time.... Such is our lab in the long stretches of twenty, thirty hours' work that the war demands.[33]

The attitude of the photo sections mirrored Steichen, their staff leader. Steichen later told friends of wartime experiences, working long hours with little sleep (on the seat of a car), thinking the entire time of "how to spot the enemy's positions, how to knock hell out of the opposition and tear the living guts out of him."[34]

The Matter of Interpretation and Exploitation

The guidance contained within the array of published material described the discipline itself. Both French and British manuals constituted the primary source describing aerial photographic interpretation. The intellectuals of

the discipline, such as de Bissy, Pépin, Pouquet, Moore-Brabazon, Campbell, and Solomon, made it clear in these documents that the ability to fight a modern war revolved around the ability to interpret photographs. Pépin summarized the prevailing attitude and reinforced the purpose of interpretation:

Aerial photography constitutes at the present time the principal source of information concerning the enemy. It enables us to study his organization as a whole and in detail and oftentimes even to predict his plans. Nevertheless this study of photographs will be advantageously supplemented, checked and often borne out by other sources of information (terrestrial and aerial observation, reports from patrols, in-

[33] Friedmann, "History of Photographic Section #1, Air Service," U.S.A. 1918.

[34] Carl Sandburg remembered Steichen's descriptions of his wartime experiences; Sandberg's wife, Lilian Steichen Sandburg, was Steichen's younger sister, Niven, 461.

formation obtained by questioning prisoners, observation of flashes from the enemy guns, direction of reports from hostile fire, etc.). But, in case of slightly different information or data, the photograph will almost always settle the discrepancy. Hence, all those who collect data, check them or utilize them, must be able to read and interpret the aerial photographs which are furnished them in various forms by the Aerial Photography Section.[35]

Aerial photography created a new military intelligentsia. It was an intense science, requiring each participant to focus on the material. Manuals reminded the practitioners to "Concentrate your whole mind on the particular objects which you are seeking. Do not let your attention wander to subsidiary objectives. Follow every traverse and detail with a pointer in regular and logical order, but be careful not to mark the photograph."[36]

Shortly after the Armistice, as the Allied armies settled into the Rhineland to begin the occupation, staffs began an intellectual debate on the best way to continue the discipline. Steichen's memorandum, "Aerial Photography, The Matter of Interpretation and Exploitation," stated that increased awareness of the technology behind photography was the best solution. He made clear that an intellectual position was best established through experience, not academic research via texts:

> The best French and British interpreters have insisted that the essential requisite for the training of interpreters is that they shall know modern warfare, either from having had experience at the front or from having made extended study of the actual ground on reconquered territory. The mistakes that are made by a student in interpretation whose knowledge has been gained entirely from the study of

FIGURE 305. **After the Armistice, three great aerial photographic pioneers, Major Laws, Major Steichen, and Lieut-Colonel Moore-Brabazon, share a lighthearted moment.** Source: Moore-Brabazon, *The Brabazon Story.*

books and pictures are flagrant; a few hours spent on the battlefield studying the ground and organizations in connection with aerial photographs previously made, are of more value than any amount of classroom work.[37]

Steichen argued that intellectual depth was integral to the aerial photographic reconnaissance mission. Of particular interest was his identifying to the French as the model for this discipline:

> The interpretation of photographs is in no sense an exact science, but is largely a matter of astute deductions, and men picked for this work must have qualifications that will make it possible for them to develop along such lines. The Intelligence Section was not only charged with the interpretation of photographs, but also with ordering them to be made. With the exception of one or two cases the Branch Intelligence Officers know absolutely nothing about photography

---

[35] Pépin, "Lecture on the Study and Interpretation of Aerial Photographs," 7, NASM.

[36] *Notes on the Interpretation of Aeroplane Photographs*, March 1917 (S.S. 550), 5, and February 1918 (S.S. 631), 3.

[37] Steichen, "Aerial Photography," Gorrell Report, ser. G, r. 24, NARA.

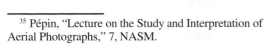

or its possibilities and consequently were not able to judge as to what could be done or what was desirable. It is believed that the Photographic Interpreter should have a very thorough knowledge of photography. Frequent cases have been noted where an interpreter who knew nothing about photography mistook imperfections in the photographic plate or print for things recorded by the camera. Numerous British officers have stated that the French get more value out of their photographs than the British do. From observation this is also our opinion, and while recognizing certain racial characteristics in the French that particularly fit them for meticulous and keen work of this kind, the fact that in the French service the interpretation and all matters pertaining to aerial photography rests in the hands of the French Air Service is chiefly responsible for this superiority.[38]

Steichen's articulation of the science critiqued the existing order:

The organization planned by the Intelligence Section to handle this work was inadequate, and gradually more and more of the work supposed to be done by the Branch Intelligence Officer and his staff of draftsmen fell upon the shoulders of the draftsmen attached to our Photographic Sections, and the better qualified B.I.O.'s were quick to realize the value of these photographic men and wisely made use of it. The extemporized Photographic Section at Ligny-en-Barrois, which did most of this photographic printing, also, with the help of a French officer, did a major part of the interpretation of the oblique photographs that were sent out, as the Intelligence Personnel was insufficient in number to do the work. Furthermore, this division of the work entails a great deal of unnecessary du-

plication, as, for instance, in the packing for distribution of prints to their ultimate destination.[39]

Steichen's solution was both occupational and "racial." "Our recommendation would be that the officer charged with interpretation of photographs at an Observation Group, be a Photographic Officer belonging to the Photographic Section of the Air Service: this would be along the lines of the French Organization.[40]

Steichen's attempt to realign established aerial photographic interpretation from the intelligence staff to the aerial photographic expert did not gain the attention of any senior officer within the AEF or Allied counterparts. In postwar thinking, his position met opposition from other members of the new military intelligentsia. Notably, Solomon, the leading British expert on camouflage, dissented. He countered Steichen's position with a descriptive summary. Such advocacy was "as logical as requesting a compositor to translate and annotate an abstruse work, because he set up the type for its printing."[41] Postwar, aerial photographic technology continued improving through the use of film cameras. However, the practice of aerial photographic interpretation waned throughout the Allied forces. By the mid-1920s it was a lost art.

The human experience behind aerial reconnaissance and photographic interpretation clearly showed how a cadre of courageous, hardworking, and intelligent people could directly influence a well-established military culture. The ability to accomplish aerial observation, one of the most dangerous assignments of the war, on a daily basis in all kinds of harsh and lethal conditions was testament to the aviators. The expectations that came with the assignment to not only understand aviation well enough to survive a variety of situations, but also be learned enough to establish the intelligence baseline for the war, had created a different breed of combatant. Evolution did not stop at the landing ground. A new

---

[38] Steichen, "Aerial Photography," Gorrell Report, ser. G, r. 24, NARA.

[39] The French officer was Capt. Pépin. Steichen, "Aerial Photography," Gorrell Report, ser. G, r. 24, NARA.
[40] Steichen, "Aerial Photography," Gorrell Report, ser. G, r. 24, NARA.
[41] Solomon, 53.

Chapter 25: The Intrigue of Aerial Photographic Interpreters

breed of experts defined the technology of photography in terms of production, dissemination, and interpretation. The latter determined the ultimate value of aerial reconnaissance. All efforts by aviation to accomplish the reconnaissance were held in check until the interpretative analysis was successfully accomplished. In his immediate post-war review, Steichen wrote that greater expertise in the photographic medium could have improved the process of interpretation. In the post-war implementation, the emphasis was on improving the technology of the aircraft, with little interest in refining and developing the intelligence aspects of flight.

With the decline in the 1920s, and further neglect in the Depression era of the 1930s, the photographic medium experienced little advancement beyond the greater use of film. Not until the start of another war would the need resurface for skilled aerial photography professionals.

FIGURE 306. A permanent legacy of how aerial photographic interpretation was accomplished exists in the manuals of instruction and the tools that were employed. One such tool, the Schweissguth stereoscope, was a mainstay for French and American interpretation operations. The stereoscope acquired the popular press's hyperbolic characterization as "The Deadliest Weapon of the War." Source: Ives, *Airplane Photography*.

INTELLIGENCE AND MODERN WARFARE

The Military Intelligence Response to the Static Battlefield

Rapid troop movement in the first weeks of World War I quickly degenerated into static trench warfare. As a result of this strategic siege spanning an entire continent, combatants became entrapped in a stationary battle of seemingly interminable duration, were continuously monitored by new technologies, and forced to suffer from a vast inventory of powerful new weapons. Among these was the new discipline of aerial reconnaissance using human observers and, increasingly as the war progressed, aerial cameras to oversee the battlefield. Contemporary accounts paid tribute to the effective use of aeroplanes to direct artillery fire. One eloquent and fatalistic German soldier fighting at Chauffour Ravine during the battle at Verdun in late June 1916 put it best: "A silent enemy flyer pursued the individual wanderer, and French artillery shells accompanied his path. To run, stand still or lay down, it was all the same."[42]

Aerial reconnaissance quickly emerged during the early phases of the Great War as a significant information-gathering device that tapped into new sources of combat knowledge about the enemy, giving field commanders and strategic planners unprecedented insights into enemy dispositions, capabilities and, by extrapolation, battlefield intentions. However reluctantly, commanders, faced with the conundrum that traditional military doctrine failed to achieve breakthroughs and only yielded large casualty lists, turned to new means to achieve tactical and strategical advantages over their enemies, especially aerial reconnaissance and signals intelligence. The increasing accuracy and timeliness of intelligence from these sources gave commanders new confidence in their ability to plan effectively. Consequently, by the time the United States entered the war in 1917, American combatants quickly learned from the experiences of their Allied counterparts that "under the conditions of modern warfare, no army can long exist without using every possible means of gathering information; and of all these means aerial photographs present probably the best medium."[43]

Command-level willingness to adapt to the emergence of new technology-driven information sources also altered conventional battle planning by making intelligence a major contributor. This new emphasis on intelligence as a planning factor also drove the evolution of intelligence to achieve unprecedented levels of precision and timeliness. On the one hand, artillery targeting rapidly matured to take advantage of the overhead perspective, both to identify

---

[42] Unidentified source, quoted by Höfl (translation by Thomas Gudmestad).

[43] Hibben, "Interpretation of Aerial Photography," Gorrell Report, ser. J, r. 34, NARA.

lucrative targets and to assess damage inflicted on the enemy. The French Plan Directeur and British Firing Maps provided an extremely detailed analysis of enemy positions. On the other hand, intelligence reports were transmitted by every conventional means to speed their dissemination to the command element for planning purposes and to the front lines for execution of those plans. Dissemination devices ranged from the traditional use of carrier pigeons and fireworks to electronic communications networks throughout the trench systems. This insured effective liaison, coordination, and information sharing among the Allies. In addition, the needs of the three largest Allied armies, spread from the English Channel to the Alps, drove the first-ever attempt to mass-produce intelligence. All of these transformations created a new way of thinking about and applying intelligence to campaign planning. As a result, the Great War became the first information and intelligence war.

Challenges to Military Intelligence Effectiveness

Intelligence cannot win battles or wars on its own, but only contributes to the operational planning and execution process. Allied commanders had not initially embraced either photographic or signals intelligence with confidence. That confidence grew only with the ability of these disciplines to provide usable, accurate, and timely insights about the enemy. However, as significant battlefield success never materialized, military seniors expressed their exasperation that even aerial photography did not result in substantial progress. For example, as the battle of the Somme raged, the BEF's senior intelligence officer, Brigadier-General John Charteris, relayed to the senior British intelligence officer at the War Ministry, General Macdonogh, that "Airplanes as a battle means of information have failed us."[44] This contemporary opinion reinforces a pervading illusion that intelligence could be a panacea for wartime success based on its accuracy and apparent completeness. It also reflects a misunderstanding of the limited role of intelligence in the command decision-making process,

one which could not consistently overcome traditionalist military doctrine, such as the value of frontal assaults. In addition, such an opinion did not recognize that World War I intelligence often fixated on assessing the enemy order of battle to extrapolate (often inaccurately) the depth of enemy strength.[45] Allied commanders, however, maintained their confidence in aerial photographic intelligence until the autumn of 1918 when the war returned to a mobile battleground. It was then that Great War military planning, reinforced by aerial reconnaissance and photographic interpretation, fell victim to the rapidly evolving front line.

Creating a perception of certainty was an underlying theme behind intelligence generated during the war. Aerial photography fashioned reality in the front line. It overcame many enemy denial and deception efforts, especially their extensive use of camouflage, through the use of rapidly evolving and creative photographic interpretation skills. Camouflage techniques and the war of illusion represented a marriage of warriors and the intelligentsia of the art world and provide a fascinating glimpse into the cognitive processes of modern war. Both sides conducted psychological war based on the perceived reality of the photograph: paint, canvas, and netting were the weapons of the camoufleur and stereoscopes the weapon of the imagery interpreters. What reconnaissance could not overcome was any enemy retreat underground and any nighttime movement, except through traces left as tell-tale indicators visible in daylight. Nevertheless, aerial reconnaissance and photographic interpretation remained the ultimate arbiter for perceiving the threat and making sense of enemy operations.

Military Intelligence Interaction with the Outside World

Public eagerness for information shaped the image of what aerial reconnaissance and photographic interpretation accomplished in the Great War. The entire landscape of the war was brought directly to the home front of all combatants through the lens of the aerial camera. Magazines such as *Scientific American, Popular*

---

[44] Charteris to Gen Macdonogh, 28 July 1916, TNA, PRO: WO 158/897.

[45] David French makes this point in "Failures of Intelligence" in Dockerill and French. David French, 79-83.

Science Monthly, and the *Army and Navy Register* brought the mysteries of aerial reconnaissance and camouflage to public notice. Aerial photography conveyed the extent of damage to population centers and cultural symbols, such as churches, with vivid clarity. To a limited extent, the public accepted the mystique and hyperbole of the photographic interpreter penetrating the image, seeing through the camouflage and detecting targets for infantry and artillery response. The label "the deadliest weapon of the war" applied to the simple stereoscope brought an overwrought, popular slant to an otherwise obscure craft. Intense public interest in the tools of intelligence continues to the present day.

The growing demand for ever larger volumes of aerial photographs pressured Allied air services and industry to produce cameras with optical lenses with sufficient resolution necessary for interpretation and cartographic purposes. The military partnership with industry made the military war effort increasingly dependent on the civilian production infrastructure. At one point, the shortage of high-quality glass for camera optics created a crisis. The French managed to meet their objectives, thanks to a limited, higher-quality, pre-war optics industrial base. The British optics industry, however, could not meet the demand from its own infrastructure, which prompted a plea to the public at large to turn in whatever personal camera lenses they had available. Moreover, the Allies began forcing German reconnaissance aeroplanes to land behind Allied lines in order to capture their lenses for use in their own camera systems. The optics crisis also directly affected British aeroplane design. By 1917 wider fuselage frames were necessary to mount the new internal camera bays. In the last year of the war, the British conducted ministry-level negotiations with the French to acquire additional lenses and also commenced production of their own higher-quality optics for a new series of state-of-the-art aerial cameras. At the time of the Armistice, such military-industry partnerships clearly demonstrated that aerial photography had made an impact well beyond the analysis of aerial photography to derive military intelligence. It alerted the nations to new vulnerabilities arising from lack of an industrial infrastructure—vulnerabilities that created additional dependencies on Allied relations.

Allied Intelligence Relationships

Beyond the impact of technology itself, the Great War defined how modern states shared intelligence. The Anglo-French relationship was unique. Each nation supported and cooperated with the other while continually suspecting each other's intentions. From the beginning, both shared technical lessons that advanced knowledge of the principles, practice, and potential of aerial reconnaissance, which led to an intelligence revolution. When the Americans arrived in 1917, not only did they benefit from the joint experience of three years of warfare, they also adopted the entire process for generating intelligence on the battlefield. French-American relations were especially critical, and French techniques, handbooks, manuals, and technical information provided the standard by which American aviation operated. American intelligence seniors opted for British intelligence methods based on staff visits to Allied headquarters, and adopted the British position of BIO at each squadron. However, the close relationship of Americans with their French aviator and photographic interpreter counterparts at the unit working level overcame the preferences of those senior officers. Even at the headquarters of the American Expeditionary Forces, General Pershing's senior intelligence advisor was Eugène Pépin, the foremost French aerial photographic interpretation officer of the entire war, who had been personally selected for the position by Général Pétain. Consequently, the aerial reconnaissance and photographic techniques used in the St. Mihiel and Meuse-Argonne campaigns had a distinctly French flavor. Interestingly, the extent of the French-American intelligence connection has been almost universally overlooked in the near-century since the end of the Great War. The Anglo-American bias likely predominated because of common language and cultural ties.

Wartime Accomplishments of Aerial Reconnaissance and Photographic Interpretation

The accomplishments and ultimate shortcomings of aerial reconnaissance and photographic interpretation in the Great War were eloquently captured by the legendary British photographic interpreter, Constance Babington-Smith, in her World War II memoir:

> By the time of the Armistice, photographic intelligence had proved itself, and was recognized as the indispensable eye of a modern army. But largely because of the technical limitations of the day—the performance and range of the aircraft and the scope of the cameras—it had become essentially regarded as tactical in value. After the war, the concept became 'frozen stiff' in the thinking of the staff colleges of the world.[46]

Aerial reconnaissance and photographic interpretation profoundly influenced the conduct of the war, which saw the emergence of aerial photographic and signals intelligence as the primary information-gathering tools of the battlefield alongside less well-known techniques like acoustic intelligence. These supplemented the traditional but still important collection of intelligence from prisoners, deserters, spies, reconnaissance patrols, captured documents, and the direct observation of the battlefield by field commanders. The war required accurate information to reinforce artillery's ability to deliver destruction. The urgency of the early campaigns prompted critical thinking from a cadre of artillery-trained experts to help define how information could best be applied to targeting. A military intelligentsia of key individuals involved in the Great War arose to meet that need, including a pantheon of visionaries such as Grout, de Bissy, Pépin, Weiller, Moore-Brabazon, Campbell, Lewis, Laws, and Steichen, all of whom created a credible and important role for wartime aerial reconnaissance and photographic interpretation. All made significant breakthroughs that either advanced information's role in achieving successful military operations, defining aerial platforms as reconnaissance vehicles, or improving the aerial photograph to become the definitive intelligence source. Their leadership made an indelible mark on all sectors of the front.

Postwar Decline in the Status of Aerial Photographic Reconnaissance

Change came slowly to labor-intensive aspects of aerial reconnaissance and photographic interpretation techniques after the Armistice. Aircraft technology, on the other hand, advanced steadily over the next 20 years. Camera and film technology also advanced, with film replacing photographic plates as the storage medium and automatic film cameras becoming the mainstays of aerial reconnaissance for the remainder of the century. The weak link, as seen in post-war aerial reconnaissance doctrine, was the human in the loop, the aerial observer. With the downgrading of the aerial observer position, single-seat aerial reconnaissance platforms capable of flying at higher altitudes and at faster speeds became the preferred mode of aerial photographic collection.

Despite the intelligence lessons to be learned from the war and especially the final campaigns, most Allied ground commanders continued to insist that aviation's role was limited to cooperating with ground troops by providing tactical reconnaissance. American commanders, in particular, held to the traditional position that battlefield success relied solely on the ability of the infantry to drive back the enemy and conquer territory. The veteran aerial observer, Harold Porter, echoed this attitude in his comprehensive 1921 analysis of aerial observation by quoting Pershing, who had declared during the war that it was necessary to "utilize all the auxiliary fighting arms in helping the infantry to get forward to the objective of his attack, which is the enemy's line, and in that aviation plays a very large part that requires a very careful and close training in time of peace with the infantryman who carries a gun. You must protect him from attack by the enemy's aviation and from observation in order

---

[46] Babington-Smith, 9-10.

to save him from being the object of the enemy's artillery destruction."[47]

The debate over the role of aerial reconnaissance and photographic interpretation continued during the post-war era. Senior American commanders had to come to terms with how the emerging Air Service could conform to traditional roles more effectively. The controversy concerning Brigadier General Mitchell did not alter the establishment's dogma, although recognition of aerial reconnaissance and photographic interpretation's potential in modern battle did not disappear from the thinking of senior commanders. They clearly treasured what aviation had provided—superior information gained from aerial reconnaissance created a decisive advantage. When Air Service and later Air Corps officers argued for more control of aviation resources to fulfill that potential, Army commanders were not tolerant of such innovation, especially coupled with Air Corps demand for strategic bombing. Despite the recognition that American aerial reconnaissance and photographic interpretation equated to modern battlefield success, little progress was made in the interwar period toward defining their role for the next war.[48]

The French quickly put their aerial reconnaissance and photographic interpretation techniques and processes under a veil of secrecy. The strategical advances made by the Weiller Grouping and associated photographic interpretation had strongly influenced French military leadership. On 11 November 1918, Maréchal Foch concluded his presentation of the Legion of Honor to Capitaine Paul-Louis Weiller for his aerial reconnaissance accomplishments over the entire war with the admonition to keep this method of reconnaissance secret in order "to preserve for France the considerable lead it had then attained over the rest of the world in the conduct of the war."[49] Simultaneously, French post-war military doctrine espoused a greater role for aerial reconnaissance, with emphasis on increasing national technological advances in film cameras. Unfortunately, the prestige of national-level endorsement did not translate into effective operational art. Aerial reconnaissance and analysis suffered fatal flaws during the German Sitzkrieg of 1939, followed by the Blitzkrieg and the rapid capitulation of France in 1940.

British attention to aerial reconnaissance settled onto a plateau in the interwar years despite the ringing endorsement of Field-Marshal Haig in his post-war writings. For example, as early as 1923 the RAF Director of Training, Air Commodore T. C. R. Higgins, expressed concern because "The question has arisen concerning the interpreting or extracting information from aeroplane photographs. It appears to run some risk of becoming a lost art, and one that requires very considerable practice."[50] His correspondent, Air Commodore H. R. M. Brooke-Popham, noted increasing concern about the status of the Branch Intelligence Sections at flying squadrons, and he concluded, "I am very glad that this question is being taken up again and I think it is most important. Otherwise, the Army will quite forget that we can take photographs."[51] The issue had developed over the commitment of resources, especially what was required to train the next generation of aerial photographic interpreters. As a shared responsibility between the Royal Army and the RAF, joint training remained in jeopardy because of competing priorities.

Legacies

The most enduring legacy of the Great War is that it was the first information and intelligence war, and it established abiding principles and expectations that underlie all subsequent intelligence operations. Aerial reconnaissance and photographic interpretation have held the rapt attention of national and combat leaders during

---

[47] Acceptance of new weapons such as the tank remained equally problematic. The prevailing post-war thinking of the American military showed cavalry still had an important role to play in 20th century warfare. Armor would have to wait. It was indicative that the leading practitioner of American armored combat in WWII, George Patton, saw the handwriting on the wall and returned to postings in the cavalry in the early 1920s. Like the tank, information warfare had its time in the limelight at a later date in the 20th century. General Pershing, quoted in Porter, 18-19.

[48] Author's discussions with Dr. David Mets.

[49] Foch quoted in Christienne, 184.

[50] Air Commodore T. C. R. Higgins to Air Commodore H. R. M. Brooke-Popham, 28 February 1923, in "Instruction Regarding Interpretation of Aerial Photographs," TNA, PRO: AIR 2/277.

[51] Brooke-Popham, to Higgins, 8 March 1923, TNA, PRO: AIR 2/277.

and since the 20th century. These information sources demonstrated the extent to which intelligence could influence command-level planning and operations. Interestingly, despite the great efforts put into developing cameras for employment on aerial platforms, not one new photographic principle was discovered and applied during the war. Aerial photography made a difference, rather, in providing accurate, current, and insightful intelligence — in describing battle scenes, assessing effects from artillery barrages, facilitating terrain analysis, uncovering camouflage and deception, and enabling the ultimate post-battle assessment of the "period of destruction."

The initiative of the aerial reconnaissance pioneers achieved more than simply marrying contemporary intelligence needs to available technologies. They also established the foundations of modern intelligence.

Since the Great War, many of the practices of aerial reconnaissance and much of the architecture supporting photographic interpretation have undergone rapid change and adaptation to new technologies and new wartime requirements. Tactical reconnaissance by today's unmanned aerial vehicles, for example, abides by many of the standards employed by early 20th century manned aeroplanes. Modern strategic reconnaissance continues the Great War strategical goal of examining the defense and industrial infrastructure within enemy borders. Modern spacecraft-borne imagery is directly linked to the pioneering efforts of the early aviators, interpreters, and all their colleagues.

Nowhere has this entire evolutionary development based on World War I principles been more successfully demonstrated than in the first Gulf War in 1991 when space-borne imagery provided Allied commanders with the intelligence that enabled the famous "end run" around the flank of the Iraqi positions. The seemingly unchanging principles behind this field of endeavor underlie the operational processes that remain to this day. Ironically, repeating experience demonstrates that military intelligence, and the information that is shared, remains a perishable commodity.

APPENDIX A
WORLD WAR I AERIAL RECONNAISSANCE PLATFORMS

Abbreviations
(FR)   France
(GB)   Great Britain
(US)   United States
Abbreviations for aeroplane models, such as BE (for Bleriot Experimental), are the most commonly used designations.

YEAR	AEROPLANE	TYPE	CAMERA
1914	**FRENCH DESIGN**		
1914	Bleriot (BL) XI (FR)	Reconnaissance	Hand Held
1914	Bleriot XI (GB)	Reconnaissance	Pan-Ross Hand Held
1914	Bleriot XI Artillerie (FR)	Reconnaissance	Hand Held
1914	Bleriot Parasol (GB)	Reconnaissance	Pan-Ross Hand Held
1914	Breguet AG 4 (FR)	Reconnaissance	Hand Held
1914	Caudron G 3 (FR)	Reconnaissance	Hand Held
1914	Deperdussin (FR)	Reconnaissance	Hand Held
1914	Henri Farman (HF) 20 (FR)	Reconnaissance	Hand Held
1914	Henri Farman F.20 "Longhorn" (GB)	Reconnaissance	Hand Held
1914	Maurice Farman (MF) 7 (FR)	Reconnaissance	Hand Held
1914	Maurice Farman MF 11 (FR)	Reconnaissance	Hand Held
1914	Maurice Farman "Shorthorn" (GB)	Reconnaissance	Hand Held
1914	Maurice Farman S.7 (GB)	Reconnaissance	Hand Held
1914	Morane-Saulnier (MS) Type L (FR)	Reconnaissance	Hand Held
1914	Morane-Saulnier Type L (GB)	Reconnaissance	Pan-Ross Hand Held
1914	REP N (FR)	Reconnaissance	Hand Held
1914	Voisin 3 (FR)	Reconnaissance	Hand Held

YEAR	AEROPLANE	TYPE	CAMERA
	BRITISH DESIGN		
1914	Avro 504 (GB)	Reconnaissance	Pan-Ross Hand Held
1914	Bleriot Experimental (BE) 2a; BE 2b (GB)	Reconnaissance	Pan-Ross Hand Held, Aeroplex Hand Held
1914	BE 8 (GB)	Reconnaissance	Hand Held
1914	Reconnaissance Experimental (RE) 1 (GB)	Reconnaissance	Hand Held
1914	RE 5 (GB)	Reconnaissance	Hand Held
1914	Wight Pusher Seaplane (GB)	Reconnaissance	Hand Held
1915	**FRENCH DESIGN**		
1915	Bleriot XI (GB)	Reconnaissance	Aeroplex Hand Held
1915	Caudron G3 (FR)	Reconnaissance; Army Cooperation	26 cm
1915	Caudron G3 (GB)	Corps Machine for Artillery Work	"A" Type
1915	Caudron G4 (FR)	Reconnaissance; Army Cooperation	26 cm; 50 cm; 120 cm
1915	Caudron G4 (GB)	Reconnaissance	"A" Type, Hand Held
1915	Farman F.40 (FR)	Reconnaissance; Army Cooperation	26 cm; 50 cm; 120 cm
1915	Henri Farman HF 20 (FR)	Reconnaissance; Army Cooperation	26 cm
1915	Henri Farman "Longhorn" (BR)	Corps Machine for Artillery Work	"A" Type
1915	Maurice Farman MF 7 (FR)	Reconnaissance; Army Cooperation	26 cm
1915	Maurice Farman MF 11 (FR)	Reconnaissance; Army Cooperation	26 cm; 50 cm; 120 cm
1915	Maurice Farman "Shorthorn" (GB)	Corps Machine for Artillery Work	"A" Type; "C" Type
1915	Morane Saulnier Type L (GB)	Reconnaissance; Army Cooperation	"A" Type; "C" Type
1915	Nieuport 10 (FR)	Reconnaissance; Army Cooperation	26 cm; 50 cm
1915	Nieuport 12 (FR) (GB)	Two-Seat Fighter-Reconnaissance	"A" Type; "C" Type
1915	Voisin 5 (FR)	Reconnaissance, Artillery Registration	Douhet-Zollinger; 26 cm

YEAR	AEROPLANE	TYPE	CAMERA
	BRITISH DESIGN		
1915	BE 2a; BE 2b; BE 2c (GB)	Corps Machine for Artillery Work	Aeroplex Hand Held; "A" Type; "C" Type
1915	Fighting Experimental (FE) 2a (GB)	Two-Seat Fighter-Reconnaissance	"A" Type; "C" Type
1915	RE 1 (GB)	Corps Machine for Artillery Work	"A" Type
1915	RE 5 (GB)	Corps Machine for Artillery Work	"A" Type; "C" Type
1915	RE 7 (GB)	Corps Machine for Artillery Work	"A" Type; "C" Type
1915	Sopwith "Baby" Floatplane (GB)	Float Seaplane	"A" Type; Hand Held
1915	Vickers Fighting Biplane (FB) 5 (GB)	Two-Seat Fighter-Reconnaissance	"A" Type; "C" Type
	FRANCO-BRITISH DESIGN		
1915	Franco-British Aviation Flying Boat (FR)	Float Seaplane	26 cm
1915	Franco-British Aviation Flying Boat (GB)	Float Seaplane	"A" Type
1916	**FRENCH DESIGN**		
1916	Caudron G3 (FR)	Reconnaissance; Army Cooperation	26 cm; 50 cm; 120 cm
1916	Caudron G3 (GB)	Corps Machine for Artillery Work	"A" Type
1916	Caudron G4 (FR)	Reconnaissance; Army Cooperation	26 cm; 50 cm; 120 cm
1916	Caudron G4 (GB)	Reconnaissance	"A" Type
1916	Caudron G6 (FR)	Long-Range Reconnaissance	26 cm; 50 cm; 120 cm
1916	Farman F.40 (FR)	Reconnaissance; Army Cooperation	26 cm; 50 cm; 120 cm
1916	Farman F.40-A2 (FR)	Reconnaissance; Army Cooperation	26 cm; 50 cm; 120 cm
1916	Letord 1 A3 (FR)	Reconnaissance; Army Cooperation	26 cm; 50 cm; 120 cm
1916	Maurice Farman MF 11(FR)	Reconnaissance; Army Cooperation	26 cm; 50 cm; 120 cm

YEAR	AEROPLANE	TYPE	CAMERA
1916	Maurice Farman "Shorthorn" (GB)	Corps Machine for Artillery Work	"A" Type, "C" Type, "E" Type
1916	Morane-Saulnier BB (GB)	Corps Machine for Artillery Work	"A" Type, "C" Type
1916	Morane-Saulnier T (FR)	Long-Range Reconnaissance	26 cm; 50 cm; 120 cm
1916	Nieuport 12 (FR)	Reconnaissance	26 cm
1916	Nieuport 12 (GB)	Two-Seat Fighter-Reconnaissance	"A" Type, "C" Type
1916	R.4 (FR)	Long-Range Reconnaissance	26 cm; 50 cm; 120 cm
1916	Salmson-Moineau (SM) 1 (FR)	Long-Range Reconnaissance	26 cm; 50 cm; 120 cm
1917	Tellier T.3 (FR)	Flying Boat	Hand Held; 26 cm 'Grand Champ'
1916	Voisin 5 (FR)	Reconnaissance; Artillery Registration	26 cm; 50 cm; 120 cm

BRITISH DESIGN

YEAR	AEROPLANE	TYPE	CAMERA
1916	BE 2c; BE 2d; BE 2e (GB)	Corps Machine for Artillery Work	"A" Type; "C" Type; "E" Type
1916	FE 2b; FE 2c; FE 2d (GB)	Two-Seat Fighter-Reconnaissance	"A" Type; "C" Type; "E" Type
1916	Martinsyde G.100 (Elephant) (GB)	Corps Machine for Artillery Work	"A" Type; "C" Type; "E" Type
1916	RE 7 (GB)	Corps Machine for Artillery Work	"A" Type; "C" Type; "WA" Type
1916	RE 8 (GB)	Corps Machine for Artillery Work	"A" Type; "C" Type
1916	Short 184 (GB)	Float Seaplane	"A" Type; Hand Held
1916	Sopwith 1½ Strutter (GB)	Two-Seat Fighter-Reconnaissance	"A" Type; "C" Type;"E" Type
1916	Sopwith 1 A2 (FR)	Reconnaissance; Army Cooperation	26 cm; 50 cm; 120 cm

FRANCO-BRITISH DESIGN

YEAR	AEROPLANE	TYPE	CAMERA
1916	Franco-British Aviation Flying Boat (GB)	Float Seaplane	"A" Type; Hand Held
1916	Franco-British Aviation Flying Boat (FR)	Float Seaplane	26 cm

Appendix A

YEAR	AEROPLANE	TYPE	CAMERA
	UNITED STATES DESIGN		
1916	Curtiss H12 (GB)	Flying Boat	Houghton-Butcher Naval Camera; "A" Type
1917	**FRENCH DESIGN**		
1917	AR 1 A2 (FR)	Reconnaissance; Army Cooperation	26 cm 'Grand Champ'; 50 cm; 120 cm
1917	AR 2 A2 (FR)	Reconnaissance; Army Cooperation	26 cm 'Grand Champ'; 50 cm; 120 cm
1917	Breguet 14 A2 (FR)	Reconnaissance; Army Cooperation	26 cm 'Grand Champ'; 50 cm 120 cm
1917	Caudron G 4 A2 (FR)	Corps Machine for Artillery Work	26 cm 'Grand Champ'; 50 cm; 120 cm
1917	Caudron G 6 (FR)	Long-Range Reconnaissance	26 cm 'Grand Champ'; 50 cm; 120 cm
1917	F.40 series (FR)	Reconnaissance; Army Cooperation	26 cm 'Grand Champ'; 50 cm; 120 cm
1917	Letord 1/2/4/5 (FR)	Reconnaissance; Army Cooperation	26 cm 'Grand Champ'; 50 cm; 120 cm
1917	Maurice Farman M.F. 11 (FR)	Reconnaissance; Army Cooperation	26 cm 'Grand Champ'; 50 cm; 120 cm
1917	Morane-Saulnier P (FR)	Reconnaissance; Army Cooperation	26 cm 'Grand Champ'
1917	Morane-Saulnier T (FR)	Reconnaissance; Army Cooperation	26 cm 'Grand Champ'; 50 cm; 120 cm
1917	R.4 (FR)	Long-Range Reconnaissance	26 cm 'Grand Champ'; 50 cm; 120 cm
1917	Salmson S.M.1 (FR)	Reconnaissance; Army Cooperation	26 cm 'Grand Champ'; 50 cm; 120 cm
1917	SPAD VII (FR)	Single-Seat Fighter	26 cm 'Grand Champ'; 50 cm
1917	SPAD VII (US)	Single-Seat Fighter	"C" Type
1917	SPAD XI A2 (FR)	Reconnaissance; Army Cooperation	26 cm 'Grand Champ'; 50 cm
1917	Voisin 7 (FR)	Army Cooperation	26 cm 'Grand Champ'; 50 cm

YEAR	AEROPLANE	TYPE	CAMERA
		BRITISH DESIGN	
1917	Airco De Havilland (DH 4) (GB)	Two-Seat Fighter-Reconnaissance;	"L" Type; "P" Type
		Short Distance Day Bomber	"L" Type; "P" Type
1917	Armstrong Whitworth F.K.8 (GB)	Corps Machine for Artillery Work	"L" Type; "P" Type
1917	BE 2d; BE 2e, BE 2f; BE 2g (GB)	Corps Machine for Artillery Work	"A" Type; "E" Type; "L" Type; "P" Type
1917	BE 12a (GB)	Corps Machine for Artillery Work	"L" Type; "LB" Type
1917	Bristol F.2B (GB)	Two-Seat Fighter-Reconnaissance;	"L" Type; "P" Type
		Corps Machine for Artillery Work	"L" Type; "P" Type
1917	FE 2d (GB)	Corps Machine for Artillery Work	"E" Type; "L" Type; "P" Type
1917	Felixstowe F.2A (GB)	Large Flying Boat	Houghton-Butcher Naval Camera; "A" Type; "P" Type
1917	Fclixstowe F.3 (GB)	Large Flying Boat	Houghton-Butcher Naval Camera; "A" Type; "P" Type
1917	RE 8 (GB)	Corps Machine for Artillery Work	"L" Type; "LB" Type
1917	Short 184 (GB)	Float Seaplane	"A" Type; "P" Type
1917	Sopwith 1½ Strutter (GB)	Two-Seat Fighter-Reconnaissance	"C" Type;"E" Type; "P" Type
1917	Sopwith 1 A2 (FR)	Reconnaissance; Army Cooperation	26 cm 'Grand Champ'; 50 cm; 120 cm
1917	Sopwith Torpedo Plane (GB)	Torpedo Aeroplane	"A" Type; "P" Type
1917	Wight (GB)	Float Seaplane	"A" Type; "P" Type
		UNITED STATES DESIGN	
1917	Curtiss H 12 (GB)	Flying Boat	Houghton-Butcher Naval Camera; "A" Type; "P" Type

YEAR	AEROPLANE	TYPE	CAMERA
1918	**FRENCH DESIGN**		
1918	AR 1 A2 (FR)	Reconnaissance; Army Cooperation	26 cm 'Grand Champ'; 50 cm; 120 cm
1918	AR 1 (US)	Reconnaissance/ Photographic	26 cm; 50 cm; "Short Focus Cameras"
1918	AR 2 A2 (FR)	Reconnaissance; Army Cooperation	26 cm 'Grand Champ'; 50 cm; 120 cm
1918	AR 1 (US)	Reconnaissance/ Photographic	26 cm; 50 cm; "Short Focus Cameras"
1918	Breguet 14 A2 (FR)	Reconnaissance; Army Cooperation	26 cm 'Grand Champ'; 50 cm; 120 cm; De Ram
1918	Breguet 14 A2 (US)	Reconnaissance/ Photographic	26 cm 'Grand Champ; 50 cm; 120 cm; "Short Focus Cameras"
1917	Caudron G6 (FR)	Long-Range Reconnaissance	26 cm 'Grand Champ'; 50 cm; 120 cm
1918	Caudron R11 (FR)	Reconnaissance; Army Cooperation	26 cm 'Grand Champ'; 50 cm; 120 cm
		Long-Range Reconnaissance	26 cm 'Grand Champ'; 50 cm; 120 cm
1918	Georges-Levy 40 HB2 (FR)	Flying Boat	26 cm 'Grand Champ'; Hand Held
1918	Salmson 2 A2 (FR)	Reconnaissance; Army Cooperation	26 cm; 50 cm; 120 cm; De Ram
1918	Salmson 2 A2 (US)	Reconnaissance/ Photographic	26 cm; 50 cm; 120 cm; De Ram
1918	SPAD VII (FR)	Single-Seat Fighter	26 cm 'Grand Champ'; 50 cm
1918	SPAD XI A2 (FR)	Reconnaissance; Army Cooperation	26 cm 'Grand Champ'; 50 cm; 120 cm
1918	SPAD XI (US)	Reconnaissance/ Photographic	26 cm 'Grand Champ'; 50 cm
1918	SPAD XIII (FR)	Single-Seat Fighter	26 cm 'Grand Champ'; 50 cm
1918	SPAD XVI A2 (FR)	Reconnaissance; Army Cooperation	26 cm 'Grand Champ'; 50 cm
1918	SPAD XVI (US)	Reconnaissance/ Photographic	26 cm 'Grand Champ'; 50 cm
1918	Tellier T.3 (FR)	Flying Boat	Hand Held; 26 cm 'Grand Champ'

YEAR	AEROPLANE	TYPE	CAMERA
1918	Voisin 10 (FR)	Night Reconnaissance	26 cm 'Grand Champ'
	BRITISH DESIGN		
1918	Armstrong Whitworth FK 8 (GB)	Corps Machine for Artillery Work	"L" Type; "LB" Type; "P" Type
1918	BE 2d; BE 2e; BE 2f; BE 2g (GB)	Corps Machine for Artillery Work	"L" Type; "LB" Type; "P" Type
1918	Bristol F.2B (GB)	Two-Seat Fighter-Reconnaissance;	"L" Type; "LB" Type; "BM" Type; "P" Type
		Corps Machine for Artillery Work	"L" Type; "P" Type
1918	DH 4 (GB)	Two-Seat Fighter-Reconnaissance	"L" Type; "LB" Type; "BM" Type; "P" Type
		Short Distance Day Bomber	"L" Type; "P" Type
1918	DH 4 (US)	Two-Seat Fighter-Reconnaissance	"L" Type; 26 cm; 50 cm; 120 cm; De Ram
		Short Distance Day Bomber	"L" Type; "Short Focus Cameras"
1918	Airco De Havilland DH 9 (GB)	Two-Seat Fighter-Reconnaissance	"L" Type; "LB" Type; "BM" Type; "P" Type
		Short Distance Day Bomber	"L" Type; "LB" Type; "BM" Type; "P" Type
1918	Airco De Havilland DH 9a (GB)	Two-Seat Fighter-Reconnaissance	"L" Type; "P" Type
1918	H.12 (GB)	Large Flying Boat	Houghton-Butcher Naval Camera; "P" Type
1918	Felixstowe F.2A (GB)	Large Flying Boat	Houghton-Butcher Naval Camera; "P" Type
1918	Felixstowe F.3 (GB)	Large Flying Boat	Houghton-Butcher Naval Camera; "P" Type
1918	RE 8 (GB)	Corps Machine for Artillery Work	"L" Type; "LB" Type; "BM" Type; "P" Type
1918	Sopwith 1 A2 (FR)	Reconnaissance; Army Cooperation	26 cm 'Grand Champ'; 50 cm; 120 cm
1918	Sopwith 1½ Strutter (US)	Reconnaissance/ Photographic	26 cm 'Grand Champ'; 50 cm

YEAR	AEROPLANE	TYPE	CAMERA
1918	Sopwith Torpedo Plane (GB)	Torpedo Aeroplane	Houghton-Butcher Naval Camera; "P" Type
1918	Short 184 (GB)	Float Seaplane	Houghton-Butcher Naval Camera; "P" Type
1918	Wight (GB)	Float Seaplane	Houghton-Butcher Naval Camera; "P" Type

Sources for Appendix A

"Re-Organisation of Photographic Activities," TNA: PRO AIR 2/163

"Eyes of the RAF, A History of Photo-Reconnaissance"

"French Aircraft of the First World War"

The Aeroplanes of the Royal Flying Corps (Military Wing)

Gorrell Report, National Archives, RG 120

APPENDIX B
WORLD WAR I ALLIED AERIAL CAMERAS

CAMERA NOMENCLATURE	NATIONALITY	TIME FRAME	MANUFACTURER	LENS FOCAL LENGTH	MAGAZINE	PLATE SIZE
"Pan-Ross"	Great Britain	1914	Pan-Ross	6"	12 plates	5 x 4 inch
DOUHET–ZOLLINGER	France	1915	Douhet-Zollinger	10 cm	Film	6 cm x 20 m
"A" Type	Great Britain	1915-1917	Thornton-Pickard	8 1/4", 10"	Plate (Mackenzie-Wishart)	5 x 4 inch
26 cm de foyer	France	1915-1918	De Maria; Gaumont	26 cm	Gaumont (12-plate magazine)	13 x 18 cm
MODEL F-1 CAMERA	United States	1918		26 cm		
"C" Type	Great Britain	1915-1917	Thornton-Pickard	8 1/2", 12", 17"	18 Plates	5 x 4 inch
"WA" Type	Great Britain	1916-1917	British RFC Repair Depot	7", 8", 10", 14"; (Wide Angle)	Plates	8 1/2 x 6 1/2 inch
"B" Type	Great Britain	1916	British RFC Repair Depot	Captured German 10", 14" 20", 27" Lenses	Plates	8 1/2 x 6 1/2 inch
				British 20", 47"	Plates	
"E" Type	Great Britain	1916-1917	Thornton-Pickard	8 1/2", 10"	36-plate magazine	5 x 4 inch
"EB" Type	Great Britain	1916-1917	Thornton-Pickard	20"	36-plate magazine	
47"	Great Britain	1916-1917		47"	Plate	5 x 4 inch
50 cm	France	1916-1918	De Maria, Gaumont	50 cm; 52 cm	Gaumont (12-plate magazine)	18 x 24 cm
MODEL F-2 CAMERA	United States	1918		50 cm; 52 cm	Gaumont (12-plate magazine)	18 x 24 cm
26 cm 'Grand Champ'	France	1917-1918	De Maria	26 cm (Wide Angle)	Gaumont (12-plate magazine)	10 x 24 cm
MODEL F-3 CAMERA	United States	1918		26 cm		
120 cm	France	1916-1918	De Maria	120 cm	Gaumont (12-plate magazine)	18 x 24 cm
MODEL F-4 CAMERA	United States	1918		120 cm		
"F" Type	Great Britain	1916	Thornton-Pickard	8"	5 x 4 inch on 25 or 50 foot spools	50 feet provided 120 exposures
"L" Type	Great Britain	1917-1918	Williamson Brothers	6", 8 1/2", 10", 20"	18-plate magazine	5 x 4 inch
	United States	1918	Eastman Kodak Co.			
"LB" Type	Great Britain	1917-1918	Williamson Brothers	4", 5", 8", 12", 20"	18-plate magazine	5 x 4 inch
"BM" Type	Great Britain	1917-1918	Williamson Brothers	7", 8", 10" 14" 20", 36"	12- or 18-plate magazine	18 x 24 cm; 8 1/2 x 6 1/2 inch
MODEL DR-1 CAMERA	France	1918	De Ram	50 cm	50-plate magazine	18 x 24 cm
MODEL DR-2 CAMERA	France	1918	De Ram	26 cm	50-plate magazine	18 x 24 cm
MODEL DR-3 CAMERA	France	1918	De Ram	50 cm	50-plate magazine	18 x 24 cm

CAMERA NOMENCLATURE	NATIONALITY	TIMEFRAME	MANUFACTURER	LENS FOCAL LENGTH	MAGAZINE	PLATE SIZE
MODEL DR-4 CAMERA	United States	1918	De Ram; Burke and James Instrument Co.	50 cm	50-plate magazine	18 x 24 cm
Houghton-Butcher	Great Britain	1917	Houghton-Butcher	10"	Plate	5 x 4 inch; 4 x 7 inch
"P" Type; Type Pl4	Great Britain	1917-1918	H. Munro	10"	Plate	5 x 4 inch
Type 18	Great Britain	1918	Houghton-Butcher	6", 8", 10"	Plate	18 x 24 cm
"Private Cameras"	United States	1918	Eastman Kodak and others	Short Focus Cameras	Film	
"K" CAMERA	United States	1918	Eastman Kodak	12", 20", 40"	Film	18 x 24 cm
MODEL G.E.M. CAMERA	United States	1918	Groom, Elliot & Mottlau Co.	8 1/2", 12"	36 exposures	6 x 6 inch film
"LA" CAMERA	United States	1918	Eastman Kodak	8 1/2", 10"	24-plate magazine	5 x 4 inch

Sources for Appendix B:

Alf Pyner, Air Cameras R.A.F. and U.S.A.A.F. 1915-1945

David Parry, Descriptions of Aerial Reconnaissance Cameras Used, or Evaluated for use by the Royal Flying Corps and Royal Air Force

Photographic Museum at RAF Cosford – Circa 2003 – POC Dave Humphrey

Maurice de Brunoff, 1914-1918, L'Aeronautique Pendant la Guerre Mondiale

Toye, "History of Photography"

"Cession of Optical Instruments to the American and British Government," 4, Gorrell Report, Series G, Roll 24

Author discussions with Alf Pyner

APPENDIX C
STEICHEN MEMO[1]

HEADQUARTERS AIR SERVICE, S.O.S., A.E.F.,
OFFICE OF C.A.S.
PHOTOGRAPHIC SECTION

December 26th 1918.

PART I

AERIAL PHOTOGRAPHY.

The Matter of Interpretation and Exploitation.

The importance and value of aerial photography in warfare has been clearly demonstrated to our army during the last few months of military activities.

This has been made clear in spite of the fact that photography was certainly not used as fully or as intelligently as it could have been. The following reasons are given:

(a) Lack of knowledge in the army at large as to the value of photography and its uses.

(b) Lack of competent and trained personnel for the interpretation and exploitation of photographs.

(c) Division of responsibility for photography between the Air Service and Intelligence Section.

In reference to (a) it would seem advisable that all field officers have a certain knowledge of aerial photography and the role it plays in modern warfare. They should be given illustrated lectures on what photography can do in the way of aiding them, and they should all have a summary knowledge of the interpretation of photographs. It is further recommended that popular lectures be given to field troops, this chiefly to acquaint them as to how the enemy can see, by means of aerial photography, just what they are doing, even miles behind the lines. By illustrated lectures or pamphlets they can be shown that carelessness in making paths at the front, or of allowing camouflage to deteriorate etc., they are endangering their lives as well as the success of their operations. It would be well for every soldier to know that the enemy observation planes flying high overhead are a much more dangerous enemy to them than those that come with bombs or harass them by machine-gun fire.

In reference to (b) and (c) the Photographic Section in America gave considerable attention to the interpretation of photographs in training its photographic officers and photographic laboratory men. As a matter of fact there were a number of men in the Photographic Section who, as a result of this training, were better qualified to be entrusted with the responsibility of interpreting photographs than were some of the Branch Intelligence Officers working with the observation groups. It is quite obvious that the interpretation of photographs is, from a military point of view, the most important phase of the work, and

---

[1] Source: Gorrell Report, NARA.

too much stress cannot be laid on choosing and training the right men to do the same. The best French and British interpreters have insisted that the essential requisite for the training of interpreters is that they shall know modern warfare, either from having had experience at the front or from having made extended study of the actual ground on reconquered territory. The mistakes that are made by a student in interpretation whose knowledge has been gained entirely from the study of books and pictures are flagrant, a few hours spent on the battlefield studying the ground and organizations in connection with aerial photographs previously made, are of more value than any amount of class room work. The interpretation of photographs is in no sense an exact science, but is largely a matter of astute deductions, and men picked for this work must have qualifications that will make it possible for them to develop along such lines. The Intelligence Section was not only charged with the interpretation of photographs, but also with ordering them to be made. With the exception of one or two cases the Branch Intelligence Officers knew absolutely nothing about photography or its possibilities and consequently were not able to judge as to what could be done or what was desirable. It is believed that the Photographic Interpreter should have a very thorough knowledge of photography. Frequent cases have been noted and where an interpreter who knew nothing about photography mistook imperfections in the photographic plate or print for things recorded by the camera. Numerous British officers have stated that the French get more value out of their photographs than the British do. From observation this is also our opinion, and while recognizing certain racial characteristics in the French that particularly fit them for meticulous and keen work of this kind, the fact that in the French service the interpretation and all matters pertaining to aerial photography rests in the hands of the French Air Service is chiefly responsible for this superiority. The organization planned by the Intelligence Section to handle this work was inadequate, and gradually more and more of the work supposed to be done by the Branch Intelligence Officer and his staff of draftsmen fell upon the shoulders of the draftsmen attached to our Photographic Sections, and the better qualified B.I.O's were quick to realize the value of these photographic men and wisely made use of it. In a similar way the Intelligence Section planned to take over the mass reproduction of all photographs, the making of assemblages, and the exploitation of the information contained in the photographs for training purposes. As a matter of fact very little work in exploiting photographs for field training was done by the Intelligence Section. It is reported that the mass photographic printing they planned to do for the St. Mihiel offensive was very unsatisfactory because of slow production, and some of the pictures did not arrive until two days after the attack. In the first Argonne offensive this work of mass printing was turned over to the Photographic Section, all the printing required was done promptly and in due time under very difficult conditions. The extemporized Photographic Section at Ligny-en-Barrois, which did most of this photographic printing, also, with the help of a French officer, did a major part of the interpretation of the oblique photographs that were sent out, as the Intelligence Personnel was insufficient in number to do the work. Furthermore, this division of the work entails a great deal of unnecessary duplication, as, for instance, in the packing for distribution of prints to their ultimate destination. Our recommendation would be that the officer charged with interpretation of photographs at an Observation Group, be a Photographic Officer belonging to the Photographic Section of the Air Service: this would be along the lines of the French Organization.

With aerial photography clearly understood and an organization adequate to exploit same, this Photographic Officer becomes a very important figure in the Air Service. He is chosen first for his special and natural aptitude, such as keenness, imagination, tact, astuteness and personality. It is desirable that he shall have had previous photographic experience and under any conditions that he take the full course in photo laboratory work. He should also receive the training currently given to an observer and be on a flying status, as it is desirable that this officer make occasional flights over the enemy lines. In this way he will become personally acquainted with his sector and have a better understanding of conditions. He will also in this manner develop the Air Service point of view and will more fully understand his observers and be able to intelligently advise them, as well as secure information from them. He must have the photographic point of view so that he may know just how much he can get out of the laboratory. This will further make the whole Photo Section a more vital working force as it will stimulate the whole section and keep up their interest which is always important where such quantities of work must be speedily turned out. With the aid of the observers and the Photo Section he will interpret the photographs and properly record them. With the aid of the observers and the Photo Section he will interpret the photographs and properly record them. From this point onward the photographic material properly belongs within the domain of the Intelligence Section, so that this Photographic Officer in reality acts as a liaison between the Air Service and the Intelligence Section. This Photographic Officer should not command or administer the Photo Section proper, but simply direct this work. The administration and laboratory work should be entrusted to a subordinate officer. This Photographic Information Officer should be responsible for the photographs but not for the photography. He should be in a position to know both what is wanted and what can be accomplished. Up to the present photography has been a commodity without enough customers, and each army needs officers qualified to drum up trade and to show the army what they can get and how they can use it.

The Photographic Section was rarely asked to make assemblages except for office ornaments. Stereoscopic prints were only occasionally called for. Not once was a large assemblage requested of an entire sector. Initiative in these direction [sic] on the part of the Photographic Sections was discouraged and there was a general atmosphere concerning these things which suggested that it was none of our affair and did not conform to Army Intelligence Regulations.

The fact an adequate supply of proper material and sufficient personnel was at last beginning to arrive from America placed us in a position to undertake new things. The following is cited as an instance: A number of specialists, stereoscopic printers had been trained at the Photo School, 2nd A.I.C., with a view to assigning them to the various Photo Sections at the front. All photo missions could then have been sent out in stereo-prints as well as the usual single prints. This would have materially increased the work of the Photo Section in the field. The experiment was successful, and in a short time this would have become a general practice, and the value of the photographs to those studying them would have been very materially increased.

In this connection it is noted that we recommended the adoption of our Richard stereoscope to the Intelligence Section. This was done and the instruments were secured by their Supply Service, but, to the best of our information they were never issued to the Branch Intelligence Officers and the Photographic Sections were consequently never called upon to make the stereopositives required for use in these instruments. It was on the strength of this failure that the Photographic Section took the initiative and decided to force the stereographs on the market instead of waiting for the request.

In addition to having a Photographic Information Officer with each Photo Section at a Corps Observation Group, a Chief Photographic Information Officer should similarly be attached to the Air Service Army Headquarters Staff. It would be the duty of this officer to co-ordinate the work of the Corps Group officers and hold the army negative and print files. All negatives from Corps Sections to be sent to the Army Section at the end of two weeks so as to relieve the Corps Section of the task of making the reprints required. This reprinting in a Corps Group during periods of great activity unnecessarily complicates their work. This Army Photo Officer would also receive first copies of all prints from the Corps Sections. He will therefore be acquainted with the work of the army and can furnish adjoining armies with any data of interest to them.

In this case he also forms the liaison for photographic information matters between the Air Service and G-2. His office would also furnish a center from which photographic material could be drawn for training purpose at the flying schools. He would also have at his disposal an army base laboratory plant for making reproductions, assemblies, copies and enlargements for general distribution throughout the army. This base laboratory plant to be operated by a regular Photographic Section.

Not having had a Photographic Officer at Army Headquarters, except during the last few weeks of the war has often made the co-ordination very difficult, and it has necessitated the writer's personally taking charge of photographic operations during active periods.

E.STEICHEN

Major, A.S.

BIBLIOGRAPHY

ARCHIVAL AND MANUSCRIPT SOURCES

AIR UNIVERSITY LIBRARY, MAXWELL AIR FORCE BASE, ALABAMA

Chester, Einar W., Captain. "The Development and Use of Air Forces from January 1, 1916, to the End of the War." The Army Infantry School, Fort Benning, GA. Company Officers' Course, 1925–26.

—. "Fundamental Principles for the Employment of the Air Services." Army War College. Command Course No. 3, 1925–26.

Lawrence, Charles W., Captain. "Organization and Assignment of Observation Aviation Observation Airplanes and their Equipment." Air Corps Tactical School, Maxwell Field, AL, 1937–38. Air Force Historical Office Archives, IRIS ref. A2810.

LIBRARY OF CONGRESS, WASHINGTON, DC

Brigadier General William Mitchell Papers, Manuscripts Division

"Depots de Munitions Ennemis, Woevre et Hauts de Meuse."

Diary, 21 April 1917.

"Gares Ennemies, en Face du Front de la II-Armée."

George Goddard Papers, Manuscripts Division

Telephone Interview with Dr. Mary Calderone, Daughter of Edward Steichen, 29 May 1986, New York City.

W.B. Prince Collection, Diary, Map Library

MUSÉE DE L'AIR ET DE L'ESPACE, LE BOURGET, FRANCE

Eugène Pépin Papers.

NATIONAL AIR AND SPACE MUSEUM, WASHINGTON, DC

"Aerial Photography for Pilots," 21 August 1918. A30.2/2.

"Appointment of Officer to Represent Air Service and U.S. Gov't. in Glass and Lens Negotiation," 26 March 1918.

Assistant Chief of Staff for Intelligence, General Headquarters, American Expeditionary Forces. "Report" to Chief of Staff, American Expeditionary Forces, 15 June 1919.

Barnes, James, Major. "Conference on the Optical Glass and Aviation Lens Situation," 25 January 1918.

—. Letter to Colonel Van Horn. Subject: "Conference on the Optical Glass and Aviation Lens Situation," 25 January 1918.

—. Letter to Major J. T. C. Moore-Brabazon. Subject: "Photographic Matter," 17 February 1918.

—. "Photographic Matters," 17 February 1918.

Campbell, C. D. M., Major. "Letter to [Major James] Barnes," 30 January 1918.

Estienne, Lieutenant. "Army Photographic Reconnaissance as It Should Be," 29 March 1923. A30.2/34.

Gros, Edmond, Major. "Notes by Major Gros on Conference on Glass Situation Held at the Bureau of Monsieur Ganne," 25 April 1918.

"Interpretation of Aerial Photography." I.S. 282 (EDA). 30.2/28.

"Lecture on Aerial Photography, Centre d'Etudes de l'Aeronautique," 25 April 1923. A30.2/36.

Letter to Colonel J. G. Morrow, O.I.C. Photographic Section. Subject: "Photographic Cameras," 9 May 1918.

Moore-Brabazon, J. T. C., Major. "Letter to [Major] Barnes," 12 February 1918.

—, Lieutenant-Colonel. Report of "Moore-Brabazon's Visit to the Conference, Held in Paris, on the 16th June, 1918."

"On the Study of German Organizations by Means of Aerial Photographs. Sapping Works." A30.2/17.

Pépin, Eugène, Lieutenant. "A Lecture on the Study and Interpretation of Aerial Photographs," 10 December 1917. War Department, Office of the Chief Signal Officer, Information Section—Air Division, Washington, DC, Stencil No. 682.

Steichen, Edward J. "American Aerial Photography at the Front."

—, Army Personnel File.

—, Captain. Letter to Major Barnes. Subject: "Optical Glass Situation," 6 March 1918.

—, First Lieutenant. "Memorandum for Major Decker, Photographic Division, Signals Corps, Washington D.C.," 21 December 1917.

"Tactical History of Corps Observation A.E.F." *Air Service Information Circular* 1, No. 75 (12 June 1920).

Toye, E. G., Major. "Letter to [Major James] Barnes," 23 February 1918.

United States Army. Air Service, Chief Photographic Officer. Letter to Chief of the Air Service. Subject: "Appointment of Officer to Represent Air Service and U.S. Gov't in Glass and Lens Negotiation," 16 March 1918.

United States. War Department, Office of the Director of Military Aeronautics. "Aerial Photography for Pilots, Study in Detail of the Part that Photography Plays in the Present War, Lecture on Aerial Photography for Pilots," 21 August 1918. A30.2/2.

—. *Aerial Photography in Modern Warfare*. 19 April 1920. A30.2.

NATIONAL ARCHIVES AND RECORDS ADMINISTRATION, WASHINGTON, DC

Gorrell Report

Microfilm citation: *Gorrell's History of the American Expeditionary Forces Air Service, 1917–1919.* Washington, DC: National Archives and Records Service, 1974. 58 microfilm reels.

"Balloon Section Report," 31 December 1918. Gorrell Report, Series F, Roll 23.

"Balloon Training." Gorrell Report, Series F, Roll 23.

Barnes, James, Major. "History of Photographic Section #4, Air Service, U.S.A., 1918." Gorrell Report, Series G, Roll 24.

—. "Memo to Lieut-Colonel Dunwoody, Subject: 'De Ram Camera'," 29 November 1917. Gorrell Report, Series G, Roll 24.

Bellinger, Alfred E. "Relations of the Air Service with G-2." Gorrell Report, Series M, Roll 41.

Bolling, Raynal C., Colonel. Memorandum, Subject: "Situation regarding Glass for Air Service Photographic Lenses," 22 January 1918. Gorrell Report, Series G, Roll 24.

"Combat Activities of Army Group Air Service during November 1–2, 1918." Gorrell Report, Series C, Roll 12.

"Commanding Officers of [1st Army] Balloon Groups and Balloon Companies," 4 October 1918. Gorrell Report, Series F, Roll 22.

"The Development of Aerial Photography. Treatise by Photo Department, 12 Jul 1918, HQ, A.S., S.O.S." Gorrell Report, Series G, Roll 24, NARA.

Farnsworth, W. O. "Photographic Officer Zone of Advance," 20 December 1918. Gorrell Report, Series A, Roll 2.

First Army Corps. General Staff, Second Section. "Distribution of Photographs Made by the Aviation Section of the Corps," 11 August 1918. Gorrell Report, Series C, Roll 12.

—. Headquarters, Office of Chief of Air Service. "Report of Operations, for April 20, 1918." Gorrell Report, Series C, Roll 12.

Friedmann, Martin E., Corporal. "History of Photographic Section #1, Air Service, U.S.A., 1918." Gorrell Report, Series G, Roll 24.

Gill, G. W., Lieutenant, and First Lieutenant Thomas E. Hibben. "The Preparation of Photographic Missions. Notes from Lectures of the Photographic Department," Observers School, 2nd Aviation Instruction Center. Gorrell Report, Series J, Roll 34.

Gorrell, E. S., Lieutenant Colonel. "Memorandum for Colonel Dunwoody," 21 December 1917. Gorrell Report, Series G, Roll 24.

Hibben, Thomas E., First Lieutenant. "The Importance of Aerial Photographs in Intelligence." Lecture given at 2nd A.I.C. Gorrell Report, Series J, Roll 34.

—. 49th Infantry Att. A. S. "Interpretation of Aerial Photography." Gorrell Report, Series J, Roll 34.

—. "Topography. Lecture delivered at the Second Aviation Instruction Center." Gorrell Report, Series J, Roll 34.

"History of Photographic Section #2, Air Service, U.S.A.," 1918. Gorrell Report, Series G, Roll 24.

"History of Photographic Section #5, Air Service, U.S.A.," 1918. Gorrell Report, Series G, Roll 24.

"History of the Air Service." Gorrell Report, Series C, Roll 12.

"History of the Training Section, Air Service, A.E.F." Gorrell Report, Series J, Roll 34.

Lindstrom, G. T. "Photographic Missions." Gorrell Report, Series N, Roll 53.

"Nomenclature Chart." Gorrell Report, Series F, Roll 22.

"Notes on Branch Intelligence," 91st Aero Squadron. Issued by Second Section, General Staff, American Expeditionary Forces, 1 November 1918. Gorrell Report, Series M, Roll 40.

Office of the Chief of Air Service. "Recommendations, Command, Equipment, Organization." Gorrell Report, Series C, Roll 12.

"Official Report: Cession of Optical Instruments to the American and English Governments." Gorrell Report, Series G, Roll 24.

"Official Report of the Conference held at the Office of the Under Secretary of State of the Presidency of the Council." 25 April 1918. Gorrell Report, Series G, Roll 24.

"Photography." Gorrell Report, Series G, Roll 24.

Proctor, Captain. "Training Section. Photographic Branch Memorandum for Major Sullivan, Subject: 'Situation on De Ram Camera'." Gorrell Report, Series G, Roll 24.

"Report on Day Bombardment Training." Flying Officers School, St. Maixent. Gorrell Report Series J, Roll 35.

Snyder, John, First Lieutenant. "Notes on Army Observation." Gorrell Report, Series J, Roll 34.

—. "'Notes on Reconnaissance,' Lecture given at 2nd A.I.C." Gorrell Report, Series J, Roll 34.

—. "Notes on the Relative Importance of Information to be Obtained by Observers When on a Visual Reconnaissance." Gorrell Report, Series J, Roll 34.

Steichen, Edward, Lieutenant Colonel. "Aerial Photography: The Matter of Interpretation and Exploitation," 26 December 1918. Gorrell Report, Series G, Roll 24.

—. "Report of Inter-Allied Photographic Meeting," 17 October 1918. Gorrell Report, Series G, Roll 24.

"Table of Information for Taking Aerial Photographs." Gorrell Report, Series G, Roll 24.

Terry, Prentiss M., Second Lieutenant, 91st Aero Squadron. "Notes on Branch Intelligence," 19 August 1918. Gorrell Report, Series M, Roll 44.

Third Army Corps. Headquarters, Office of Chief of Air Service. "Operations Report for November 5, 1918." Gorrell Report, Series C, Roll 12.

Record Group 120

Air Service. American Expeditionary Forces. *History of the Air Services.*

    Series C. *Tactical Units.* 14 Volumes.

    Series E. *Squadron Histories.* 26 Volumes.

    Series G. *Photographic Section.* 4 Volumes.

    Series N. *Duplicates of all First Army Material.* 23 Volumes.

American Mission with the Commanding General, Allied Forces of Occupation, Mainz, Germany. "A Study of the Organization of the French Army Showing its Development as a Result of the Lessons of the World War and Comprising Notes on Equipment and Tactical Doctrine Developed in the French Army, 1914–1921." Prepared by Colonel Le Vert Coleman. Box 819.
Part XXXVII. "Aeronautics." Section 3. June 1921.
Part XXXVIII. "Camouflage." Section 2. July 1921.
Part XL. "Infantry: Its Organization, Its Equipment, and Its Present and Future Use Based on the Lessons of the War." 1921.
    Section 5. Publication on its Employment, Liaisons. 1921.
Part XLIII. "Interpretation of Aerial Photographs." November 1921.

Assistant Chief of Staff for Intelligence, First Army. "Summary of Intelligence." 2 October 1918. Box 3370.

Aviation: Bates on German Air Service. Box 5778.

First Army Historical Files. Box 22.

"Interpretation of Aerial Photographs." Prepared by Colonel LeVert Coleman, November 1921. Box 819.

Pouquet, Sous Lieutenant. "Working of the Service of Interpretation of Photographs in an Offensive Sector (Conference by Sub/Lieutenant Pouquet)." Box 819.

Second Army, Headquarters, General Staff, Second Section. "Effectiveness of Different Weapons against Each Other." *Supplement to Summary of Intelligence*, No. 14, 25 October 1918. Translation of German Document. Box 10.

Study and Utilization of Aerial Photographs. Translation from the French edition of 15 January 1918. Headquarters American Expeditionary Forces, France. July 1918. Box 6202.

26th Division. "Intelligence Bulletin," 26 July 1918." Box 1.

26th Division, 103rd Regiment. "Map of Vaux."

Von Kathen. "Memorandum for Encampments." In Headquarters, 26th Division, "Intelligence Bulletin," 26 July 1918." Box 1.

NATIONAL ARCHIVES – PUBLIC RECORDS OFFICE, LONDON

Air Ministry Record (AIR)

AIR 1/7/6/98/20. Captain C. D. M. Campbell. "Notes on Aerial Photography."

AIR 1/7/6/98/20. Captain C. D. M. Campbell. "Report of Photographic Section, R.F.C."

AIR 1/7/6/98/20. General H. R. M. Brooke-Popham. "General Notes on German Aeroplanes."

AIR 1/7/6/98/20. "Packet of Photographic Reproductions (RNAS),"12 December 1918.

AIR 1/7/6/98/20. "Report on Aeronautical Matters in Foreign Countries for 1913."

AIR 1/7/6/98/20. 2nd Lieut V. F. Bryce, Photographic Officer, 1st Brigade, BEF. "Report," 1 June 1916.

AIR 1/82/15/9/204. "Study by Corporal Mallet of the R.N.A.S. Photographs Nos. 527 to 540, Reconnaissance of November 21st 1916." In Photographic Studies III (January – September 1918).

AIR 1/93/15/9/240. 5th Group, R.A.F. "Result of Aerial Photography by the R.N.A.S. in 1917," 13 February 1918.

AIR 1/123/15/40/144. "Notes on Captive Balloons for Use in Land Warfare."

AIR 1/127/15/40/147. Lieutenant Colonel C. C. Marindin. "Conference Notes," 23 July 1915.

AIR 1/138/15/40/287. "Camera Vibration."

AIR 1/404/97/1917. Lieutenant Charles W. Gamble. "Photographic Section of the French Flying Corps."

AIR 1/404/97/1917. Lieutenant Charles W. Gamble. "Visits to Manufacturers."

AIR 1/475/15/312/201. Major J. P. C. Sewell, R.A.F. "Notes … French Corps Aviation," August 1918.

AIR 1/475/15/312/201. Captain I. W. Learmont, R.F.C. "Report … of a Visit to the French Bombardment Group at Malzeville."

AIR 1/724/91/1. Captain C. D. M. Campbell, R.F.C. "Progress of Photography in Royal Flying Corps at Home, to 31st December, 1915," 22 January 1916.

AIR 1/724/91/1, 87/7298. "The General Officer Commanding, 6th Brigade, Royal Flying Corps. Memorandum. Signed by C. C. Marindin, Lieut-Colonel," 3 February 1916.

AIR 1/724/91/1. Major E. G. Toye. "History of Photography (being a General History of Air Photography, Its Cameras, Lens, etc.) …, 1914–1918."

AIR 1/724/91/2. "Aerial Photography. Statement made by Squadron Leader F. C. V. Laws to Mr. A. J. Insall," 3 June 1924.

AIR 1/724/91/2. Lieutenant Colonel C. J. Burch. "Notes on Report Dealing with Camera Vibration," 8 February 1916.

AIR 1/724/91/2. Lieutenant Colonel J. T. C. Moore-Brabazon. "Photography in the R.A.F. 1914–1918."

AIR 1/724/91/2. "Squadron Leader F. C. V. Laws, O.B.E., to G.O.C., Advanced Operations," 18 November 1918.

AIR 1/724/91/2. Lieutenant Colonel J. T. C. Moore-Brabazon. "Photography's Part in the War."

AIR 1/724/91/2. "Telephone Call between Colonel [J. T. C.] Moore-Brabazon and Capt Wall," 13 November 1918.

AIR 1/751/204/4/8. Headquarters, R.F.C. "Orders for Reconnaissance from 24th Oct. 1914 to 28th Nov. 1914."

AIR 1/751/204/4/8. "Memorandum of New Organization of the Royal Flying Corps," 29 November 1914.

AIR 1/751/204/4/8. "Organization of the Royal Flying Corps, British Expeditionary Force," December 1914."

AIR 1/ 834/204/5/240. Captain D. S. Lewis. "Procedure of Ranging." 25 January 1915.

AIR 1/834/204/5/240. "H.Q. R.F.C., G 165/1. Officer Commanding No. 9 Squadron," 15 January 1915.

AIR 1/834/204/5/240. Lieutenant I. M. Bonham-Carter, R.F.C. "Notes," 1 November 1914.

AIR 1/836/204/5/268. "Notes on Equipment of Units of RFC with BEF," 27 September 1914.

AIR 1/836/204/5/268. "Photography from Aeroplanes," 20 December 1914.

AIR 1/1118/204/5/2041. Colonel J. T. C. Moore-Brabazon. "Night Photography," 1 November 1918.

AIR 1/1139/204/5/2305. Report of "Visits to Paris of Gen. [H. R. M.] Brooke-Popham & Gen [Hugh] Trenchard, Feb 1916 – July 1917."

AIR 1/1211/204/5/2627. "Instructions Regarding the Co-Operation of Aeroplanes with Other Arms."

AIR 1/1625/204/9/7. "Central Flying School."

AIR 1/1625/204/89/7. "Notes on Air Fighting from Royal Flying Corps, Sept 1916 – December 1916."

AIR 1/2124/207/74/3. "Index to Periodical Summaries of Aeronautical Information."

AIR 1/2124/207/74/3. "Intelligence Summary,"19 August 1918.

AIR 1/2124/207/74/3. "Protection of Artillery Positions from Air Observation." Captured German document.

AIR 1/2151/209/3/240. Brigadier General W.S. Brancker, R.A. and RFC. "Aerial Defence of Paris. Notes."

AIR 1/2151/209/3/244. "Capt. Cuddell, Assistant Director of Military Aeronautics, 3 Mar 1915, War Office, London, S.W."

AIR 1/2151/209/3/244. Lieutenant J. T. C. Moore-Brabazon. "OIC Photos in the Field," 21 June 1915.

AIR 1/2151/209/3/244. "Photographic Lorries."

AIR 1/2299/209/77/29. Supreme War Council. "Draft Minutes of the 1st Session of the Versailles Inter-Allied Aviation Committee held in the Council Chamber, Versailles on 9th May, 1918, at 10.0 a.m."

AIR 1/2395/255/1. Lieutenant Colonel J. F. C. Moore-Brabazon. "R.A.F. Night Photography."

AIR 1/2395/255/1. Squadron Leader C. C. Darley. "Notes on Photography in No. 3 Squadron, Royal Flying Corps. December 1914 – End of February 1915."

AIR 1/2397/267/7. Charles W. Gamble. "The Technical Aspects of British Aerial Photography during the War 1914–1918."

AIR 2/16. "Letter from Col. E. F. D., R.F.C., 28/2. Enclo. 1A., 'Proposals for a Long Distance Machine'."

AIR 2/35. Wing Commander Seddon. "Report … on Co-Operation between Britain and American Air Services," 13 September 1917.

AIR 2/36. Flight Commander Mitchell. "Report on Photography and Recommendations," 31 January 1917.

AIR 2/39. "Extracts from Official French Manual on Photographic Reconnaissance," 20 August 1925. Translated.

AIR 2/163. "Re-Organisation of Photographic Activities," 24 January 1917.

AIR 2/277. Air Commodore T. C. R. Higgins. Memorandum to Air Officer Commanding, Inland Area, R.A.F., Course: "Interpretation of Air Photographs."

AIR 2/277. "Instruction Regarding Interpretation of Aerial Photographs," 2 February 1923.

AIR 2/277. War Office Memorandum to Secretary of the Air Ministry, 13 May 1925.

AIR 10/61. "Characteristics of the Ground and Landmarks in the Enemy Lines Opposite the British Front from the Sea to St Quentin."

AIR 10/853. "Aerial Photography." Air Publication 838.

AIR 10/5521. "Illustrated Hand-Book for R.A.F. Intelligence Officers Employed on Interpretation of Air Photographs. December 1940."

AIR 10/1001. "Notes on Aerial Photography. Part II. The Interpretation of Aeroplane Photographs in Mesopotamia."

AIR 1/2151/209/3/244. "2nd Lt Kippel, OIC Photographic Section 1st Wing, R.F.C.," 14 June 1915.

AIR 20/705. "Papers Collected by Air Vice Marshal Sir W. G. H. Salmond, Period 1916–1922."

AIR 69/1. Air Vice Marshal H. R. M. Brooke-Popham. "The War of 1914–1918." RAF Staff College.

AIR 69/1. "Personalities of [Colonel] Du Peuty [French Air Service] and [General Hugh] Trenchard," in "The War of 1914–1918." RAF Staff College.

AIR 69/2. W. "Sholto" Douglas. "Notes on First Steps in Air Photography on the Western Front, January to March 1915."

AIR 75/131. "Air Reconnaissance in Open Warfare. The Story of Two Incidents in the Advance to the Aisne, Sept. 1914." Official Papers of Sir John Slesser.

War Office Papers (WO)

WO 158. "Intelligence Corps Organization and Establishment." 1 November 1917.

WO 158/48. "Conference at Dury at 11.0 p.m., Sunday, March 24th, 1918."

WO 158/897. "Brig-Gen John Charteris to Gen Macdonough, War Ministry (London), General Headquarters," 28 July 1916.

WO 158/983. "Notes on the French System of Intelligence during the Battle of the Somme," 23 September 1916.

WO 158/898. "General Macdonogh, February 1917."

WO 297/61. "German System of Squaring Maps."

WO 339/23903. "2Lt J. T. C. Moore-Brabazon, R.F.C. (S.R.), 'For Promotion to Lt. and Refund of £75 for R.A.C. Certificate'."

ROYAL AIR FORCE MUSEUM, LONDON, UNITED KINGDOM

Year 1916. 47" Lens Aircraft Camera.

Year 1918. Hand Held Oblique Aircraft Camera Type P 14.

SERVICE HISTORIQUE DE L'ARMÉE DE L'AIR (SHAA), VINCENNES, FRANCE

Bellenger, Lieutenant Colonel Georges. Letter to François Baban, 6 February 1954.

Collection S.H.D., 377/094.

"Cours de Perfectionnement (Décembre 1916 – Janvier 1917)." A 278. d. 4.

de Bissy, Jean, Capitaine. "Note Concernant l'Interpretation Methodiqie de Photographies Aériennes," 19 November 1915.

Grand Quartier Général Défenses et Différents Points du Territoire, Artillerie Lourde, Services (Septembre 1914 – Novembre 1919). Dossier 7, Service de Photographie Aérienne (23 Octobre 1914–14 Avril 1919). A.19.

Grout, Maurice Marie Eugène, Lieutenant. Personnel Records.

Manouevres du 6ème Corps d'Armée. Flight Log, 18 September 1911.

"Organisation et Administration des Unités." A.20.

Pouchet, Sous Lieutenant. "Conference du SLT Pouquet sur le Fonctionnement du Service d'Interpretation des Photographies dans un Secteur Offensif faite au G.D.E., le 27 December 1916." A 278. d. 4.

Rapport du Capitaine du Genis Saconney, au Sujet des Experiences de Cerfs-Volants Effectuées Avec Nacelle Lestrée à bout de Cable. 21 February 1910.

SERVICE HISTORIQUE DE L'ARMÉE DE TERRE (SHAT), VINCENNES, FRANCE

Extrait du Plan Directeur, S.T.C.A., 6ème Armée. "Carte d'activité de l'Artillerie ennemie du 1er au 15 Juin 1917."

—. "Carte des Renseignements Recueillis sur l'Ennemie dans la Zône du C.A." [1917].

S.595. Bois Alberick. SP. III Armée. C. 28D 052/653.

U. S. AIR FORCE ACADEMY, McDERMOTT LIBRARY, COLORADO SPRINGS, COLORADO

Jefferson Hayes Davis Papers

Colby, F. T., Captain, and Captain Cushing-Donnell. "Notes on Artillery Camouflage and Its Employment." Headquarters, American Expeditionary Forces, France, October, 1917. SMS 57.

Eaton, Joseph E., 2nd Lieutenant. "Methods in Observation Practiced with Fifth Corps First American Army on the Fronts, St. Mihiel Sector, September 12 to 16, 1918 Argonne-Meuse Sector, September 12 to November 11, 1918." *Air Service Information Circular* 2, no. 115 (20 September 1920). SMS 57.

Haslett, Elmer R., First Lieutenant. "Bulletin of Information Air Service American Expeditionary Forces. Notes on the Duties of the Operations Officer of an Observation Squadron or Group." SMS 57.

"Liaison for All Arms." General Headquarters, American Expeditionary Forces, France. June 1918. SMS 57.

"Notes for Observers and Pilots in Army Corps Aviation Squadrons." SMS 57.

U.S. ARMY MILITARY HISTORY INSTITUTE, CARLISLE, PENNSYLVANIA

Arthur L. Conger Papers

"Channels through which Air Photographs are Ordered and Distributed."

"Correspondence," 23 March 1918. Box 2.

"Example of Summary Indications of Enemy Preparations for an Offensive in Flanders (from Air Photographs)," September 1918.

Frank, Coleman D., First Lieutenant. "Report of a Visit to VIIIth Army Headquarters to Attend the Interrogatory of Prisoners Taken in the Coup de Main on the Lorraine Sector," 20 February 1918.

Henry, Daniel M., Major. "Report on My Visit to the British Army for the Purpose of Observing the Work of the Intelligence Section of the Royal Flying Corps," 18-29 September 1918.

Hubbard, S. T., Jr., Captain. "Memorandum for Col. Nolan," 29 December 1917. Box 2.

—. "Memorandum for Col. Nolan, Subject: 'Report on Trip to British Front,' 3 January 1917 [i.e., 1918]."

"Instructions on the Functions of the Corps Intelligence Service."

Maxel, Général, Vth Army Staff, 2nd Bureau. "Instructions on the Intelligence Service in the Divisions," 16 January 1917.

"Organization of Intelligence, H.Q. British 5th Army."

Pétain, Henri, Général. "French General Staff and 3rd Bureau No. 1077/3. Notice about Maps and Special Plans to Be Drawn by the Armies." Box 2.

Riggs, Kerr T., Major. "Memorandum to Chief Intelligence 'A,' 14 February 1918, Subject: 'Memorandum Report of Visit to Headquarters 1st French Army'."

—. "Report on Visit to British Army for Purpose of Studying Branch Intelligence."

"Scale of Issue of Periodical Publications."

Stanford, Captain. "Capt Stanford's Summary of the Qualifications of a Branch Intelligence Officer," 15 February 1918, in "Organization of Intelligence," H.Q. British 5th Army. Box 2.

Stewart, John L., First Lieutenant. "The Organization and Operation of Intelligence 'A' at the British II Army." September 1918.

—. "1st Lt John Stewart Report." 4 October 1918. Box 2.

"Summary of Indications of Enemy Preparations for an Offensive in Flanders (from Air Photographs) together with a Note on the System of Collecting and Disseminating the Information." Prepared by Air Photo Officer, II British Army, July 1918.

"To Show Stream of Intelligence Up and Down (Corps Heavy Artillery Divisions)."

Tyler, Royall. Headquarters, American Expeditionary Forces, Office of the Assistant Chief of Staff for Intelligence. "Letter to Col Nolan." 7 March 1918. Box 2.

Dennis E. Nolan Papers

Assistant Chief of Staff for Intelligence, 1st Army Corps. "Summary of Intelligence."

"Codes & Ciphers."

"G-2-C, Topography."

"Intelligence."

Zimmerman, Arthur A. "Report on Visit to VIIIth French Army, February 22 to March 2, 1918," 7 March 1918.

George O. Squier Papers

Squier, George O., Colonel. "The Flying Corps, April 20, 1915."

—. "Intelligence Services of the British Army in the Field, February 16, 1915."

—. "The Map Room and Printing Room, April 20, 1915."

Hugh Drum Papers

Assistant Chief of Staff for Intelligence to Chief of Staff, 1st Army, American Expeditionary Forces. "Account of the Operation from the Standpoint of Enemy Works." Box 14.

"Historical Account."

Philip Katcher Papers

Katcher, Philip. "Bulletin of Information Air Service American Expeditionary Forces, Notes for Divisional Staffs, Commanding Officers and Aerial Observers on Work of Infantry Contact Airplanes," 24 September 1918.

Theodore J. Lindoff Papers

Lindoff, Theodore J., First Lieutenant. "Photographic Missions."

William J. Steere Papers

The Airscout's Snapshot, 28 August 1918.

"General Lecture on Cameras."

"Plates and Development of Plates."

CONTEMPORARY SOURCES, MEMOIRS, AUTOBIOGRAPHIES, ETC.

Ackerman, Carl W. *George Eastman*. Boston: Houghton Mifflin Company, 1930.

L'Aéronautique pendant la Guerre Mondiale, 1914–1918. Edited by Maurice de Brunoff. Paris: M. de Brunoff, 1919.

Aerial Observation for Artillery, Based on the French Edition of December 29, 1917. [Washington, DC: Government Printing Office], May 1918.

Artillery Operations of the Ninth British Corps at Messines, June, 1917. Edited at the U.S. Army War College. Washington, DC: Government Printing Office, 1917.

Bagley, James W. *The Use of the Panoramic Camera in Topographic Surveying*. Washington, DC: Government Printing Office, 1917.

Baring, Maurice. *Flying Corps Headquarters: 1914–1918*. London: William Heinemann, 1930; reprint, London: Buchan & Enright, 1985. Reprint of R.F.C. H.Q., 1914–1918. London: G. Bell and Sons, 1920.

Barnes, James. *From Then Till Now: Anecdotal Portraits and Transcript Pages from Memory's Tablets*. New York: D. Appleton-Century Company, 1934.

Bethell, H. A., Colonel. *Modern Artillery in the Field*. London: Macmillan and Co., Ltd., 1911.

Blumenson, Martin, editor. *The Patton Papers 1885–1940*. 2 volumes. Boston: Houghton Mifflin Company, 1972.

Brooks, Alfred H. "The Use of Geology on the Western Front." In United States Geological Survey. Professional Papers. *Shorter Contributions to General Geology, 1920*. Washington, DC: Government Printing Office, 1921.

Brown, Malcom, editor. *The Imperial War Museum Book of the First World War: A Great Conflict Recalled in Previously Unpublished Letters, Diaries, Documents, and Memoirs*. London: Sidgwick & Jackson, 1991.

Bruno, Henry. "The Eyes in the Air." *Popular Science Monthly* (1918): 508-511.

Bulletin du Service de la Photographie Aérienne Aux Armées, 7 January 1916. Paris: Imprimerie Nationale, 1916.

Bulletin of the Aerial Photography Department in the Field. Washington, DC: Government Printing Office, 1918.

"The Camera at the Front: Why the Military Authorities Have Use for their Own Cameras but None for the Enemy's." *Scientific American* (24 November 1917): 380, 390.

Carlier, Andre H. *La Photographie Aérienne Pendant la Guerre*. Paris: Librairie Delagrave, 1921.

Charteris, John. *At G.H.Q.* London: Cassell and Company, 1931.

Coleman, Frederic. *With Cavalry in 1915: The British Trooper in the Trench Line*. Toronto: William Briggs, 1916.

Crowell, Benedict and Robert Forrest Wilson. *The Armies of Industry: Our Nation's Manufacture of Munitions for a World in Arms, 1917–1918. Illustrated with Photographs from the Collections of the War and Navy Departments*. 2 volumes. New Haven, CT: Yale University Press, 1921.

De Bissy, J. de Lannoy, Captain. *Illustrations to Accompany Captain De Bissy's Notes Regarding the Interpretation of Aeroplane Photographs (Ia/1311)*. Translated. N.p., n.d.

— *Notes Regarding the Interpretation of Aeroplane Photographs (Ia/1311)*. Translated. N.p., n.d.

—, Commandant. "Les Photographies Aériennes et leur Étude au Point de Vue Militaire." *Revue Militaire Française* 12 (April–June 1924): 257-277.

Dixon, Eric E. *Diary of Eric E. Dixon, Whippany, N.J., U.S.A.: An American Citizen*. Whippany, NJ: n.p., n.d. Copy in Eric E. Dixon Papers, U.S. Army Military History Institute, Carlisle, Pennsylvania.

Douglas, Shotto, Marshal of the Royal Air Force, Lord Douglas of Kirtleside. *Years of Combat* [Autobiography]. London: Collins, 1963.

Duval, Jacques. *L'Armée de L'Air*. Paris: L'Édition Française Illustrée, 1918.

Edmonds, James E., Brigadier-General, [General Editor]. *Military Operations, France and Belgium, 1914*. Compiled by Brigadier-General James E. Edmonds. 3rd revised edition. 2 volumes. London: Macmillan and Co., Ltd., 1933; reprint, London: Imperial War Museum and Nashville, TN: Battery Press, 1995–96.

—. *Military Operations, France and Belgium, 1915*. Compiled by Brigadier-General James E. Edmonds and Captain G. C. Wynne. London: Macmillan and Co., Ltd., 1927–28; reprint, London: Imperial War Museum and Nashville, TN: Battery Press, 1995.

—. *Military Operations, France and Belgium, 1916*. Compiled by Brigadier-General James E. Edmonds and Captain Wilfrid Miles. 2 volumes. London: Macmillan and Co., Ltd., 1932–38; reprint, London: Imperial War Museum and Nashville, TN: Battery Press, 1993–95.

—. *Military Operations, France and Belgium, 1917*. Compiled by Brigadier-General James E. Edmonds, Captain Cyril Falls, and Captain Wilfrid Miles. 3 volumes. London: Macmillan and Co., Ltd., 1940–48; reprint, London: Imperial War Museum and Nashville, TN: Battery Press, 1991.

—. *Military Operations, France and Belgium, 1918*. Compiled by Brigadier-General James E. Edmonds and Lieutenant-Colonel R. Maxwell Hyslop. 5 volumes. London: Macmillan and Co., Ltd., 1935–47; reprint, London: Imperial War Museum and Nashville, TN: Battery Press, 1993–94.

Ellis, O. O., Captain, and Captain E. B. Garey. *The Plattsburg Manual: A Handbook for Military Training*. New York: The Century Co., 1917.

Flicke, Wilhelm F. *War Secrets in the Ether*. Edited by Sheila Carlisle. 2 volumes. Laguna Hills, CA: Aegean Park Press, 1977. Original typescript translation of *Kriegsgehemeinisse im Aether* by the National Security Agency, 1953, is located at National Archives and Records Administration, Record Group 38, Records of the Office of the Chief of Naval Operations (Records of the Naval Security Group), Box 16.

Frances, General Headquarters. Armies of the North and Northeast. *Bulletin of the Aerial Photography Department in the Field*. Washington, DC: Government Printing Office, 1918.

—; General Headquarters. Armies of the North and Northeast. *Study and Exploitation of Aerial Photographs*. Translated and Issued by the Division of Military Aeronautics, U.S. Army. Washington: Government Printing Office, July 1918. Copy in U.S. Army Military History Institute.

—; General Headquarters. Armies of the North and Northeast. *Study and Use of Aerial Photography*. November 1921. Copy in Part XLIII, Section 5, in American Mission with the Commanding General, Allied Forces of Occupation, Mainz, Germany, "A Study of the Organization of the French Army." National Archives and Records Administration, Record Group 120, Box 819.

—. Grand Quartier Général des Armées du Nord et du Nord-Est. État-Major. *Bulletin du Service de la Photographie Aerienne aux Armées*. Paris: Imprimerie Nationale, 7 January 1916.

—. Grand Quartier Général des Armées du Nord et du Nord-Est. État-Major. *Notes sur l'Interprétation des Photographies Aériennes*. Paris: Imprimerie Nationale, 30 December 1916.

—. Grand Quartier Général des Armées du Nord et du Nord-Est. État-Major. *Étude et Exploitation des Photographies Aériennes*. Paris: Imprimerie Nationale, 1918.

Fraser-Tytler, Neil. *With Lancashire Lads and Field Guns in France, 1915–1918*. UK: John Heywood, 1922.

French, Field-Marshal Viscount French of Ypres. *1914*. Boston: Houghton Mifflin Company. 1919.

French Manual on Trench Warfare, 1917–1918: A Reference Manual, French General Staff. Reprint of translation of *Manual of the Chief of Platoon of Infantry*, 1918. London: The Imperial War Museum and Nashville, TN: The Battery Press, Inc., 2002.

Fuller, Alvan Tufts. "Mysteries of Camouflage." *Army and Navy Register* (16 August 1919): 222-223.

Gilchrist, John W. Stuart. *An Aerial Observer in World War I*. Richmond, VA: Privately printed, 1966.

Gleichen, A. E. W. Edward, Count, editor. *Chronology of the Great War, 1914–1918*. 3 volumes. London: Ministry of Information, 1918–20; reprint, 3 volumes in 1. London: Greenhill Books, 2000.

Goddard, George W., Brigadier General. *Overview: A Life-Long Adventure in Aerial Photography*. Garden City, NY: Doubleday & Company, 1969.

Goussot, C. M., Lieutenant. *Précis de Photographie Aérienne*. Paris: Librairie Aéronautique, 1923.

Gouvieux, Marc. *Notes d'un Officier Observateur en Avion*. Paris: Pierre Lafitte, 1916.

Graffin, Laurence. *Carnets de Guerre, 1914–1918*. Paris: Herscher, 1996.

Grahame-White, Claude. *The Aeroplane in War*. London: T. Werner Laurie, 1912.

Great Britain. General Staff (Intelligence). General Headquarters. *Notes on the Interpretation of Aeroplane Photographs*. 1st edition (S.S. 445). France: Army Printing and Stationery Services, November 1916.

—. Illustrations to Accompany Notes on the Interpretation of Aeroplane Photographs. 1st edition (S.S. 445a). France: Army Printing and Stationery Services, November 1916.

—. *Notes on the Interpretation of Aeroplane Photographs*. 2nd edition (S.S. 550). France: Army Printing and Stationery Services, March 1917. Copy in Combined Arms Research Library, Fort Leavenworth, KS.

—. Illustrations to Accompany Notes on the Interpretation of Aeroplane Photographs. 2nd edition (S.S. 550a). France: Army Printing and Stationery Services, March 1917. Copy in Combined Arms Research Library, Fort Leavenworth, KS.

—. *Notes on the Interpretation of Aeroplane Photographs*. 3rd edition (S.S. 631). France: Army Printing and Stationery Services, February 1918. Copy in National Air and Space Museum Archives, A30.2/29. Reprint, edited by Captain Einar W. Chester, U.S. Army Division of Military Aeronautics. Washington, DC: Government Printing Office, 1918.

—. *Illustrations to Accompany Notes on the Interpretation of Aeroplane Photographs*. 3rd edition (S.S. 631a). France: Army Printing and Stationery Services, February 1918. Copy in Princeton University Library, Princeton, NJ.

Greenhous, Brereton, editor. *A Rattle of Pebbles: The First World War Diaries of Two Canadian Airmen*. Ottawa: Canadian Government Publishing Centre, 1987.

Grinnell-Milne, Duncan. *Wind in the Wires*. New York: Ace Publishing Corporation, 1968.

Hahn, J. E., Major. *The Intelligence Service within the Canadian Corps*. Toronto: The Macmillan Company of Canada, 1930.

Haig, Sir Douglas. *Sir Douglas Haig's Despatches*. Edited by Lieutenant Colonel J. H. Boraston. London: J. M. Dent & Sons, Ltd., and New York: E. P. Dutton & Co., 1920.

Hanson, Joseph M., Major, editor. *The World War through the Telebinocular: A Visualized, Vitalized History of the Greatest Conflict of All the* Ages. 5th edition. Meadville, PA: Keystone View Company, 1928.

Haslett, Elmer. *Luck on the Wing: Thirteen Stories of a Sky Spy*. New York: E. P. Dutton & Company. 1920.

Henderson, David, Brigadier General. *The Art of Reconnaissance*. 3rd edition. London: John Murray, 1914.

The History of the 6th Garde Infantry Regiment. n.p., 1931.

Höfl, Colonel. *The History of the Royal Bavarian 20th Infantry Regiment, "Prinz Franz."* Munich: n.p., 1929.

Innes, John R. *Flash Spotters and Sound Rangers: How They Lived, Worked and Fought in the Great War*. London: George Allen & Unwin, Ltd., 1935; reprint, Trowbridge, Wiltshire, UK: Redwood Books, Ltd., 1997.

Insall, A. J. *Observer: Memoirs of the R.F.C., 1915–1918*. London: William Kimber, 1970.

Instruction sur le Ballon Captif Allonge Type R. Washington, DC: Government Printing Office, 1918.

Ives, Herbert E. *Airplane Photography*. Philadelphia: J.B. Lippincott Company, 1920.

Jauneaud, Marcel, Commandant. *L'Aviation Militaire et la Guerre Aérienne*. Paris: Ernest Flammarion, 1923.

Johnson, Douglas Wilson. *Topography and Strategy in the War*. New York: Henry Holt and Company, 1917.

—. *Battlefields of the World War, Western and Southern Fronts: A Study in Military Geography*. New York: Oxford University Press, 1921.

Joubert de la Ferte, Sir Philip, Air Chief Marshal. *The Fated Sky, An Autobiography*. London: Hutchinson & Co., 1952.

Jünger, Ernst. *The Storm of Steel: From the Diary of a German Storm-Troop Officer on the Western Front*. Translated by Basil Creighton. London: Chatto and Windus, 1929; reprint, New York: Howard Fertig, 1996.

Kluck, Alexander von, General. *The March on Paris and the Battle of the Marne 1914*. London: Edward Arnold, 1920.

Knappen, Theodore M. *Wings of War: An Account of the Important Contribution of the United States to Aircraft Invention, Engineering, Development and Production during the World War.* London and New York: G. P. Putnam's Sons, 1920.

Le Goffic, Charles. *Général Foch at the Marne: An Account of the Fighting in and near the Marshes of Saint-Gond*. New York: E. P. Dutton and Company, 1918.

Lewis, Cecil. *Sagittarius Rising [Reminiscences of Flying in the Great War]*. London: Peter Davies, 1936; reprint, London: The Folio Society. 1998.

Liddell Hart, Basil H. *Foch: The Man of Orleans*. Boston: Little, Brown, and Company, 1932.

"Lord Brabazon of Tara Dies; First Briton to Fly in England; Aviator had Been Early Auto Racer and Minister of Transport for Churchill," Special to the *New York Times*, May 18, 1964. ProQuest Historical Newspapers, *The New York Times* (1851– 2001).

Ludendorff, Erich von, Quartermaster General of the German Army. *Ludendorff's Own Story, August 1914– November 1918: The Great War from the Siege of Liege to the Signing of the Armistice as Viewed from the Grand Headquarters of the German Army*. 2 volumes. New York: Harper & Brothers Publishers, 1919.

Martel, René. *L'Aviation Française de Bombardment (des Origines au 11 Novembre 1918)*. Paris: Paul Hartmann, 1939.

Maurer, Maurer, editor. *The U.S. Air Service in World War I*. 4 volumes. Washington, DC: Government Printing Office, 1978.

Maxwell, W. N. *A Psychological Retrospect of the Great War*. New York: The MacMillan Company, 1923.

The Means of Communication between Aeroplanes and the Ground. Edited at the Army War College. Washington: Government Printing Office, 1917.

Middleton, Edgar. *The Great War in the Air*. 4 volumes. London: The Waverley Book Co., Ltd., 1920.

Miller, Leonard. *The Chronicles of 55 Squadron, R.F.C. and R.A.F.* London: Unwin Brothers, Ltd., 1919.

Mitchell, William. *Memoirs of World War I: From Start to Finish of Our Greatest War*. New York: Random House, 1960.

Moore-Brabazon, J. T. C., Lord. *The Brabazon Story*. London: William Heinemann, Ltd., 1956.

Neumann, Georg Paul. *Die Deutschen Luftstreitkraste im Weltkriege*. Berlin: Ernst Seigfried Mittler und Sohn, 1920.

Notes on Anti-Aircraft Guns. Compiled at the Army War College from the Latest Available Information. April, 1917. Washington: Government Printing Office, 1917.

Pépin, Eugène. *Chinôn*. Paris: Henri Laurens, 1924.

Pétain, Henri Philippe, Marshal of France. *Verdun*. New York: The Dial Press, 1930.

"The Photographic Eye and Memory of the Military Airman." *Scientific American* (27 July 1918): 61, 76.

Porter, Harold E. *Aerial Observation: The Airplane Observer, The Balloon Observer, and the Army Corps Pilot*. New York: Harper & Brother Publishers, 1921.

Powell, E. Alexander, Major. *The Army behind the Army*. New York: Charles Scribner's Sons, 1919.

Pulitzer, Ralph. *Over the Front in an Aeroplane and Scenes Inside the French and Flemish Trenches*. New York and London: Harper & Brothers Publishers, 1915.

Raleigh, Sir Walter A., and H. A. Jones, *The War in the Air, Being the Story of the Part Played in the Great War by the Royal Air Force*. 6 volumes and appendices. Oxford: The Clarendon Press, 1922–37; reprint, London: The Imperial War Museum and Nashville, TN: The Battery Press, 1998.

Rickenbacker, Edward V., Captain. *Fighting the Flying Circus*. New York: Frederick A. Stokes Co., [1919]; reprint Chicago: R. R. Donnelley & Sons Company, 1997.

Smart, C.D. "The Front Cockpit: The Diary of Lt. C.D. Smart, No. 5 Sqdn., RFC." *Cross and Cockade, Journal of the Society of World War I Aero Historians* 10, No. 1 (Spring 1969): 1-33.

Smart, Lawrence L., First Lieutenant. *The Hawks that Guided the Guns*. N.p.: Privately printed, 1968.

Smith, Neil Leybourne. *History of 3 Squadron, AFC, RAAF*. URL: <http://www.3squadron.org.au/history.htm>. Accessed 10 January 2005.

Solomon, Solomon J. *Strategic Camouflage*. New York: E. P. Dutton and Company, 1920.

Squier, George O. *Aeronautics in the United States at the Signing of the Armistice*. [New York?: n.p., 1919].

Steichen, Edward. *A Life in Photography. Published in Collaboration with the Museum of Modern Art*. Garden City, NY: Doubleday & Company, Inc., 1963.

Study and Utilization of Aerial Photographs. Paris: Imprimerie Nationale, July 1918. Translated. Headquarters American Expeditionary Forces, France, July 1918. Copy in National Archives and Records Administration, Record Group 120, Box 6202.

Sweetser, Arthur. *The American Air Service: A Record of Its Problems, Its Difficulties, Its Failures, and Its Final Achievements*. New York: D. Appleton and Co., 1919.

Toulmin, Henry A., Jr. *Air Service, American Expeditionary Force, 1918*. New York: D. Van Nostrand Company, 1927.

Turner, Charles C. Major. *The Struggle in the Air, 1914–1918*. New York: Longmans, Green & Co., and London: Edward Arnold, 1919.

Tytler, Neil Fraser. *With Lancashire Lads and Field Guns in France, 1915–1918*. Edited by F. N. Baker. Manchester, UK: John Heywood, 1922.

Underwood, James R., and Guth, Peter L., editors. *Military Geology in War and Peace*. Boulder, CO: The Geological Society of America, Inc., 1998.

United Kingdom. War Office. General Staff. *British Trench Warfare, 1917–1918: A Reference Manual*. [London?]: n.p., 1918. Reprinted, London: Imperial War Museum, and Nashville, TN: The Battery Press, Inc., 1997.

United States Army. Office of Military History. *United States Army in the World War, 1917–1919*. 17 volumes. Washington, DC: Government Printing Office, 1948; reprint, Washington, DC: U.S. Army Center for Military History, 1988–92.

United States War Department. "Report of the Director of Military Aeronautics," 3 November 1918. *Annual Report of the Secretary of War for the Fiscal Year 1918*. 2 volumes. Washington, DC: Government Printing Office, 1918. I, 1381–1390.

Utilization and Role of Artillery Aviators in Trench Warfare. Washington, DC: Government Printing Office, 1917.

Vaughan, Edwin C. *Some Desperate Glory: The World War I Diary of a British Officer*. New York: Simon and Schuster, Inc., and Touchstone Books, 1981.

Warran, John W., Captain. *Cooperation of Division Aviation with the Field Artillery*. Maxwell Field, AL: Air Corps Tactical School, 6 April 1938.

White, D. editor. *Shorter Contributions to General Geology, 1920*. Washington, DC: Government Printing Office, 1921.

Willcox, Cornelis De Witt. *A French-English Military Technical Dictionary*. Washington, DC: Government Printing Office, 1917.

Winslow, Carroll D. *With the French Flying Corps*. New York: Charles Scribner's Sons, 1917.

Woglom, Gilbert T. *Parakites*. New York: G. P. Putnam's Sons, 1896.

Wood, Eric Fisher. *The Note-Book of an Intelligence Officer*. New York: Century Co., 1917.

SECONDARY SOURCES

Asbrey, Robert B. *The German High Command at War: Hindenburg and Ludendorff Conduct World War I.* New York: William Morrow and Company, 1991.

Asprey, Robert B. *The First Battle of the Marne.* Philadelphia, PA: J. B. Lippincott Company, 1962.

Babington-Smith, Constance. *Air Spy: The Story of Photo Intelligence in World War II.* New York: Ballantine Books, 1957.

Bailey, J. B. A. *Field Artillery and Firepower.* Oxford, UK: The Military Press, 1989.

Beckett, Ian F. W. *The First World War: The Essential Guide to Sources in the UK National Archives.* Kew, Surrey, UK: Public Record Office, 2002.

Bickers, Richard Townshend. *The First Great Air War.* London: Hodder & Stoughton, 1988.

Blond, Georges. *The Marne.* Harrisburg, PA: The Stackpole Company, 1965.

Bowen, Ezra. *Knights of the Air.* Alexandria, VA: Time-Life Books. 1980.

Brayer, Elizabeth. *George Eastman, A Biography.* Baltimore: The Johns Hopkins University Press, 1996.

The British Army and Signals Intelligence during the First World War. Edited by John Ferris. Wolfeboro Falls, NH: Alan Sutton Publishing, Inc., 1992.

British Trench Warfare, 1917-1918: A Reference Manual, General Staff, War Office, reprint, London: The Imperial War Museum and Nashville, TN: The Battery Press, Inc. 1997.

Brown, Malcom. *The Imperial War Museum Book of 1918, Year of Victory.* London: Sidgwick & Jackson, 1998.

—. *The Imperial War Museum Book of the Western Front.* London: Sidgwick & Jackson, 1993.

Bruce, J. M. *The Aeroplanes of the Royal Flying Corps (Military Wing).* London: Putnam, 1982.

—. *The American D.H.4.* London: Profile Publications, 1966.

—. *The de Havilland D.H.4.* London: Profile Publications, 1965.

—. *The Sopwith 1½ Strutter.* London: Profile Publications, 1967.

—. *War Planes of the First World War, Fighters, Great Britain.* 2 volumes. Garden City, NY: Doubleday and Company, Inc., 1968.

— and Jean Noel. *The Breguet 14.* Leatherhead, Surrey, UK: Profile Publications, 1967.

Cain, Anthony C. *The Forgotten Air Force: French Air Doctrine in the 1930s.* Washington, DC: Smithsonian Institution Press, 2002.

Chamier, J. A. *The Birth of the Royal Air Force.* London: Sir Issac Pitman & Sons, Ltd., 1943.

Charteris, John. *Haig.* London: Cassell and Company, 1930.

Chasseaud, Peter. *Artillery's Astrologers: A History of British Survey and Mapping on the Western Front 1914–1918.* Lewes, UK: Mapbooks, 1999.

—. "British Western Front Mapping 1914–18, Summary of Geodetic Situation with Reference to the Operations Maps Actually in Use in 1918." In *The Imperial War Museum Trench Map Archives CD-ROM.* London: The Naval & Military Press and The Imperial War Museum, 2000.

—. *Topography at Armageddon: A British Trench Map Atlas of the Western Front, 1914–1918.* Lewes, UK: Mapbooks, 1991.

Christienne, Charles and Pierre Lissarague. *A History of French Military Aviation.* Washington, DC: Smithsonian Institution Press, 1986.

Cooke, James. *The U.S. Air Service in the Great War, 1917–1919.* Westport, CT: Praeger. 1996.

Cooksley, Peter. *Sopwith Fighters in Action.* Carrollton, TX: Squadron/Signal Publications, Inc., 1991.

Crary, Jonathan. *Techniques of the Observer: On Vision and Modernity in the Nineteenth Century.* Cambridge, MA: Massachusetts Institute of Technology Press, 1991.

Davilla, James J., and Arthur M. Soltan. *French Aircraft of the First World War.* Boulder, CO: Flying Machine Press, 1997.

Distel, Anne. *Dunoyer de Segonzac*. New York: Crown Publishers, 1980.

Dockrill, Michael, and David French. *Strategy and Intelligence: British Policy during the First World War*. London: The Hambledon Press, 1996.

Farrar-Hockley, Anthony. *Death of an Army*. London: Arthur Barker, Ltd., 1967.

Ferris, John. "The British Army and Signals Intelligence in the Field during the First World War." *Intelligence and National Security* 3, No. 4 (October 1988): 23-48.

Fischer, William E., Jr. *The Development of Military Night Aviation to 1919*. Maxwell AFB, AL: Air University Press, 1998.

Frandsen, Bert. *Hat in the Ring: The Birth of American Air Power in the Great War*. Washington, DC: Smithsonian Books, 2003.

Frank, Sam Hager. *American Air Service Observation in World War I*. Doctoral Dissertation. Gainesville, FL: University of Florida, 1961.

Frankel, Lory, editor. *Steichen at War*. New York: Harry N. Abrams, 1981.

French, David. "Failures of Intelligence: The Retreat to the Hindenburg Line and the March 1918 Offensive." In *Strategy and Intelligence, British Policy during the First World War*. Michael Dockrill and David French, editors. London: The Hambledon Press, 1996.

Gardner, Nikolas. *Trial by Fire: Command and the British Expeditionary Force in 1914*. Westport, CT: Praeger, 2003.

Gill, Bob. "Over the Front in a Balloon Observer's Gondola," *Cross and Cockade, Journal of the League of World War 1 Aviation Historians* 20, No. 1 (Spring 2005): 4-17.

Gliddon, Gerald. *The Battle of the Somme*. Phoenix Mill, UK: Sutton Publishing, 1987.

Guttman, Jon. *Caudron G.3*. Berkhamsted, Hertfordshire, UK: Albatros Productions, Ltd., 2002.

Hodeir, Marcellin. "La Photographie Aérienne: 'de la Marne à la Somme,' 1914–1916." *Revue Historique des Armées*, no. 2 (1996): 97-108.

—. "Une Integration Difficile: La Photographie Aérienne comme Élément de Renseignement et de Cartographie Militaire (1890–1919)." Conference: "Le Terrain du Militaire: Perceptions et Representations." Château de Vincennes, France, 11-12 September 2002.

Hood, Robert E. *12 at War, Great Photographers Under Fire*. New York: G.P. Putnam's Sons. 1967.

Hogg, Ian V. *The Guns, 1914–18*. New York: Ballantine Books, 1971.

Jackson, A. J. *De Havilland Aircraft since 1909*. London: Pitnam, 1978.

Jenbrau, Hélène and Eugène Pépin. *The Glory of the Loire*. New York: Viking Press, 1971.

Joubert de la Ferte, Sir Philip, Air Chief Marshal. *The Forgotten Ones: The Story of the Ground Crews*. London: Hutchinson & Co., 1961.

Judge, Arthur W. *Stereoscopic Photography: Its Application to Science, Industry and Education*. London: Chapman & Hall, Ltd., 1950.

Kahn, David. *The Codebreakers: The Story of Secret Writing*. New York: The Macmillan Company, 1967.

Kennett, Lee. *The First Air War, 1914–1918*. New York: The Free Press, 1991.

Kern, Stephen. *The Culture of Time and Space 1880–1918*. Cambridge, MA: Harvard University Press, 1983.

Kilduff, Peter. "Kenneth P. Littauer: From the Lafayette Flying Corps to the 88th Aero Squadron." *Cross and Cockade, Journal of the League of World War I Aero Historians* 13, No. 1 (Spring 1972): 22-45.

Lamberton, W. M. *Reconnaissance & Bomber Aircraft of the 1914–1918 War*. Edited by E. F. Cheesman. Letchworth, UK: Harleyford Publications Ltd., 1962.

Liddle, Peter H. *The Airman's War, 1914–18*. Poole, UK: Blandford Press, 1987.

Macdonald, Lyn. *1914: The Days of Hope*. New York: Atheneum, 1987.

—. *To the Last Man: Spring 1918*. New York: Carroll & Graf Publishers, Inc., 1999.

Martel, Francis. *Pétain: Verdun to Vichy*. New York: E. P. Dutton & Company, Inc., 1943.

Mason, David. *Verdun*. Gloucestershire, UK: The Windrush Press. 2000.

Maurer, Maurer. *Aviation in the U.S. Army 1919–1938*. Washington, DC: Office of Air Force History, 1987.

Mead, Peter. *The Eye in the Air: History of Air Observation and Reconnaissance for the Army, 1785–1945.* London: Her Majesty's Stationery Office, 1986.

Michelin Road Atlas France. 9th edition. London: Paul Hamlyn, 1996.

Middleton, Edgar. *The Great War in the Air.* 4 Volumes. London: The Waverley Book Co., Ltd. 1920.

Miller, Henry W. *The Paris Gun: The Bombardment of Paris by the German Long Range Guns and the Great German Offensives of 1918.* New York: Jonathan Cape & Harrison Smith, 1930.

Morgan, William A. "Invasion on the Ether: Radio Intelligence at the Battle of St. Mihiel, September 1918." *Military Affairs* 51, No. 2 (April 1987): 57-61.

Morris, Alan. *Bloody April.* London: Jarrolds Publishers, 1967.

Morrow, John H., Jr. *The Great War in the Air: Military Aviation from 1909 to 1921.* Washington, DC, and London: Smithsonian Institution Press, 1993.

Munson, Kenneth. *Aircraft of World War I.* London: Ian Allan, 1968.

—. *Bombers: Patrol and Reconnaissance Aircraft, 1914–1919.* New York: Macmillan Publishing Co., Inc., 1968.

Neiberg, Michael S. *Fighting the Great War: A Global History.* Cambridge, MA: Harvard University Press, 2005.

Nesbit, Roy C. *Eyes of the RAF, A History of Photo-Reconnaissance.* Phoenix Mill, UK: Alan Sutton Publishing, Ltd., 1996.

Niven, Penelope. *Steichen.* New York: Clarkson Potter/Publishers, 1997.

Occleshaw, Michael. *Armour Against Fate: British Military Intelligence in the First World War.* London: Columbus Books, 1989.

O'Connor, Mike. *Airfields and Airmen, Ypres.* London: Leo Cooper, 2001.

Oldham, Peter. *The Hindenburg Line.* London: Leo Cooper, 2001.

Owers, Colin. *De Havilland Aircraft of World War I.* Volume I: *D.H.1 – D.H. 4.* Boulder, CO: Flying Machines Press, 2001.

—, Jon S. Guttman, and James J. Davilla. *Salmson Aircraft of World War I.* Boulder, CO: Flying Machine Press, 2001.

Parry, David. "Descriptions of Aerial Reconnaissance Cameras Used, or Evaluated for Use by the Royal Flying Corps and Royal Air Force." In *Aerial Archeology E-Mail Newsletter,* 2003.

Pépin, Eugène, Dr. *History of the International Institute of Space Law of the International Astronautical Federation (1958–1982).* New York: American Institute of Aeronautics and Astronautics, Inc., 1982.

—. *The Legal Status of the Airspace in the Light of Progress in Aviation and Astronautics.* Montreal: Institute of International Air Law, McGill University, 1957.

Phillips, Christopher. *Steichen at War.* New York: H.N. Abrams. 1981.

Pitt, Barrie. *Zeebrugge.* New York: Ballantine Books, 1959.

Porch, Douglas. *The French Secret Services, From the Dreyfus Affair to the Gulf War.* New York: Farrar, Straus and Giroux, 1995.

Pyner, Alf. *Air Cameras R.A.F. & U.S.A.A.F., 1915–1945.* Crouch, UK: Privately published, 1988.

Showalter, Dennis E. *Tannenberg: Clash of Empires.* Hamden, CT: Archon Books, 1991.

Skelton, M. L. "Major H.D. Harvey-Kelly, Commanding Officer, No. 19 Squadron." *Cross and Cockade, Journal of the League of World War 1 Aero Historians* 16, No. 4 (Winter 1975): 375.

Sumner, Ian. *The French Army, 1914–18.* London: Osprey Publishing, 1995.

Talbert, Roy, Jr. *Negative Intelligence: The Army and the American Left, 1917–1941.* Jackson, MS: University Press of Mississippi, 1991.

Tanks & Weapons of World War I. Edited by Bernard Fitzsimons. New York: Beekman House. 1973.

Terraine, John. *Mons: The Retreat to Victory.* New York: The Macmillan Company, 1960.

Toelle, Alan D. *Breguet 14.* Berkhamsted, UK: Albatros Productions, Ltd., 2003.

Trench Fortifications, 1914–1918: A Reference Manual. London: The Imperial War Museum, and Nashville, TN: The Battery Press, Inc. 1998.

Tuchman, Barbara W. *The Guns of August.* New York: Bantam Book, 1976.

Underwood, James R., and Peter L. Guth. *Military Geology in War and Peace.* Boulder, CO: The Geological Society of America, Inc., 1998.

Vaughan, Edwin C. *Some Desperate Glory: The World War I Diary of a British Officer.* New York: Simon and Schuster Inc., and Touchstone Books, 1981.

Venzon, Anne Cipriano, editor. *The United States in the First World War: An Encyclopedia.* New York: Garland Publishing, Inc., 1995.

Villèle, Marie-Anne de, Agnès Beylot, and Alain Morgat, editors. *Du Paysage à La Carte: Trois Siècles de Cartographie Militaire de la France.* Vincennes, FR: Ministère de la Défense, Services Historiques des Armées, 2002.

Vues d'en Haut: La Photographie Aérienne Pendant la Guerre de 1914–18. Paris: Musée de l'Armée, Musée d'Histoire Contemporaine—Bibliothèque de Documentation Internationale Contemporaine, 1989.

Watkis, Nicholas C. *The Western Front from the Air.* Phoenix Mill, UK: Sutton Publishing Ltd., 1999.

Williams, George K. *Biplanes and Bombsights, British Bombing in World War I.* Maxwell Air Force Base, AL: Air University Press, 1999.

INDEX

aeroplane;

British;

Airco De Havilland (DH 4) – 83, 84, 97, 101, 118, 270, 314, 382, 410 – 412

Avro 504 – 16, 19, 28

Blériot Experimental;

BE 2 – 75, 397, 404, 406, 443

BE 2a – 15, 16, 17, 19, 397, 432

BE 2b – 397

BE 2c – 57, 75, 376, 397

BE 2d – 75, 77, 398

BE 2e – 398, 406

Bristol F.2B – 101

De Havilland or DH 4. *See* Airco De Havilland

Maurice Farman;

MF 11 – 13, 40, 43, 60, 68, 399, 418

MF 7 – 13, 399

Reconnaissance Experimental (RE 8) – 83, 99, 117, 346, 406, 438

Short 184 – 52

Sopwith 1½ Strutter – 83, 97, 112, 404, 405

French;

Blériot XI – 9, 13, 15 – 17, 26, 27, 396

Breguet 14 A2 – 101, 102, 119, 336, 344, 387, 408, 409

Caudron

G.3 – 27, 41, 400

G.4 – 27, 41, 378, 400

G.6 – 83

R.4 – 41, 83

Henri Farman;

F.20 – 15

HF 7 – 13, 68

Letord – 118

Morane-Saulnier;

L – 27, 40

T – 83, 118, 438

Nieuport 11 – 41

R.4 – 41, 83

Salmson-Moineau S.M.1 – 83

Salmson 2A2 – 101, 192, 391, 412

Sopwith 1 A2 – 83, 404, 405

SPAD;

VII – 94, 338, 339, 387

XI – 116

XIII – 338 – 340

Voisin 5 – 54, 55

German;

Albatros – 19

Fokker;

DVII – 442

Eindecker – 64, 66, 68, 71, 402

Pfalz D III – 442

Tauben – 15, 396

aeroplane recognition – 21

Aeroplex – 45, 374

Aero Squadron (U.S.). *See* U.S. Air Service

aérostat – 10, 11, 34 – 36, 40, 137, 165, 191, 192, 282, 333, 334, 345

aérostation – 13

aérostier – 40, 54, 66, 299

air-to-ground liaison – 59

Air Force. *See* Royal Air Force

air photo officer – 209, 210, 215

Airplanes. *See* Aeroplanes; Aéroplanes

Air Service Observation School – 422

Aisne, Battle of the – 24, 28 – 33, 35, 37, 45, 55, 73, 86, 117, 120, 121, 153, 162, 235

American Expeditionary Force (AEF) – 221, 422

Corps

1st Corps – 75, 115, 116, 226, 229, 248

3rd Corps – 124, 127

5th Corps – 127, 348

Divisions

2nd Division – 260, 310, 312

3rd Division – 32, 324

26th Division – 116, 162, 168, 190, 327, 360

Headquarters;

G-2 – 90, 94, 117, 121, 124, 126, 127, 129, 140, 146, 148, 151, 155, 163, 164, 173, 177, 178, 185, 186, 199, 204, 210, 223 – 227, 229, 242, 244, 248, 251, 255, 259, 261 – 263, 269, 273, 294, 329, 419, 444, 451

G-2-C Topography – 117, 124, 155, 223 – 226

Amiens – 16, 22, 110, 123, 168, 216

annotation – 144, 145, 157

antiaircraft – 17, 44, 54, 56, 57, 101, 116, 125, 204, 270, 272, 293, 310, 313, 343 – 345, 371, 395, 412, 432, 437, 438

Archie. *See* antiaircraft

Armament Experimental Station – 366

Armée;

Groupe des Armées;

Ième Armée – 13, 43, 178